MODERN GERMAN

Second Edition

MODERN GERMAN

Second Edition

Van Horn Vail

Kimberly Sparks

Thomas Huber

Middlebury College

HARCOURT BRACE JOVANOVICH, PUBLISHERS

San Diego   New York   Chicago   Austin
London   Sydney   Toronto

Acknowledgment

The authors wish to thank Luchterhand Verlag for permission to reprint Peter Bichsel, "Der Mann mit dem Gedächtnis," from: Peter Bichsel, *Kindergeschichten,* 1969, Luchterhand Verlag, Darmstadt und Neuwied.

Illustration Credits

The cover photograph is by Werner H. Müller, from Peter Arnold, Inc. All interior photographs are by Van Horn Vail and Kimberly Sparks, except the photograph on page 459, from Lufthansa. The map on page 384 was drawn by Jean Tremblay.

ISBN: 0-15-561316-2

Library of Congress Catalog Card Number: 78-56037

Printed in the United States of America

Introduction

We have prepared this new edition of *Modern German* with the goal of the First Edition in mind: to give students—all students—firm, active control of natural, contemporary German. We have, however, changed the book in three important ways. First, we have simplified and shortened some of the drill sequences, especially those in the later chapters, so that they can be mastered more quickly and with less effort. More important, we have added a set of ten readings that begin early on to present the student with connected texts, which, taken together, form an introduction to modern German life. Finally, we have illustrated these readings with pictures that are fresh images of today's German culture.

Any method that claims to address all students must of course recognize that not all students learn at the same rate—or even in the same way. Consequently, we have given considerable thought to how students learn in the classroom and how they learn outside the classroom. One central difference is immediately apparent: the pace of the class hour depends on the instructor's sense of how fast a *group* of students can learn and perform. Outside the classroom, the talents and needs of *individual* students determine how long they spend preparing for class and just how they go about it.

We have written *Modern German* to meet both the needs of the group and the needs of the individual. On one hand, we know that the class hour should run at a pace that satisfies every student and the instructor as well. If we had to choose a word to characterize our method, that word would be *tempo*. Tempo gives the necessary game-sense to the classroom; it gives a class that special quality called *esprit*. But tempo is possible only when students can achieve the desired level of performance outside the classroom; and it is here that *Modern German* has particular strength. The text is designed to maximize the self-teaching and self-pacing functions so crucial to language learning; it is a teaching instrument that enables all language students to perform on the level of their most gifted classmates.

Presentation of Grammar

The grammar presentations in *Modern German* proceed from the known to the new; they build on grammatical structures the student has already mastered, or they emphasize structural similarities between English and German. Contrastive German-English grammar is also used to illustrate divergent points in the two languages.

Nothing is presupposed: even such basic notions as "subject" and "object" are treated fully and simply, and numerous charts and diagrams make for an easy grasp of the materials. Above all, we have tried to avoid overwhelming students with long and tedious explanations. Our guiding principle has been to present a masterable amount of grammar, then to drill it immediately. Both grammar presentations and drill sequences follow the same bit-by-bit development.

Grammar is of great help to students: it lets the curious learner know what is happening and why, and it provides a constant synopsis of the material being covered. We feel that an understanding of grammar is best acquired in out-of-class time, and have therefore tried to make the grammar presentations entirely self-teaching, reserving the classroom for drill, oral practice, and on-the-spot help from the instructor.

Drills

Drills are the heart of language learning. While grammar explanations can orient students and make them aware of what is going on, the drills bring them to real mastery of linguistic structure and to fluent performance in the language.

Effective drilling is based on breaking down a body of new material into its constituent parts, or "bits," and then recombining these bits in a graduated sequence of drills. At the beginning of a sequence, drilling is done in controlled, stable environments in which students are presented with minimal grammatical choices. Once students have mastered several grammatical bits in this way, they are asked to combine these bits in a "mixed drill." The process continues until the students are in control of the entire body of new material. Most important, the patterns have become so automatic that they seem natural even when they occur in mixed grammatical surroundings.

Readings

The readings prepare students for living in a German-speaking country by focusing on the everyday situations in which students will find themselves—from finding a place to stay, eating out, shopping, and getting around a city, to going through customs, getting a taxi, using the telephone, and cashing traveler's checks. The first three readings are primarily in dialogue form; the rest are a mixture of dialogue and narrative.

Dialogues

Dialogues are used for situations in which students have to take an active part; they show what kind of language students will hear in these situations, and they provide model responses. This means that in real life students will know what to expect and how to respond. Drills on the dialogues are at the end of each reading.

Narratives

The narrative parts of the readings give students additional information they will need in order to function confidently in a German-speaking country. But the narratives present this information in connected text. These sections of the readings are drilled by questions with cued responses, a technique that provides a constant review of grammar while ensuring that new information is both used and retained.

The early readings confirm that meaningful communication in German is possible from the very start. And, beginning with the fourth reading, where a substantial narrative is included, students find that they can read whole pages of connected text with very little difficulty. Appearing in the final two readings is an unedited story by a contemporary author, Peter Bichsel. Working with such a text demonstrates that students have mastered *Modern German* and that they are well prepared for further reading.

How to Use the Readings

The readings come between the grammar lessons in the book; they presuppose only the grammar the students have had up to that point. Each reading has a unifying theme, but is not meant to be done at one sitting or as one long assignment. Rather, it should be divided and assigned along with the grammar drills of the lesson that follows. For example, the fifth reading should be assigned while the students are working on Lesson 6. To make this easier, each reading has been clearly divided into several sections, and the sections have been keyed to their corresponding questions or exercises. Instructors will want to assign part of the reading for the same day that they assign grammar drills from the following lesson. This assures variety and change of pace in each class hour, with the greater part of the hour devoted to the grammar drills of the new lesson and a portion of the hour reserved for readings that review and confirm the grammar of the preceding lesson.

Testing

In a very real sense, each class hour is a test of the students' oral performance—a test to which great significance should be attached, for it is here that students demonstrate their ability to the fullest. But we also suggest that written tests be given every two weeks or so. The purpose is twofold: tests are a guarantee of regular writing practice; they also require students to function in a more mixed grammatical environment than that of a normal class hour. A normal hour directs students' attention to a single structural problem; the test period asks them to remain in firm control while performing in several grammatical areas at once. It is important to test the readings, too, and their inclusion in each written test should reflect the proportion of class time spent on them.

Flexibility

Modern German is designed for maximum classroom flexibility. There are many ways for instructors to adapt the material to their own special classroom situations:

- Some instructors will want to do all the drill sequences in class, using the final drills ("Express in German") as a last check of the students' control of both grammatical structure and new vocabulary. Again, it should be stressed that these drills use

English sentences merely as cues to the German sentences that the student has already learned.

- Other instructors may want to concentrate in class on the initial drills of each sequence, assigning a selection of the "Express in German" exercises and some of the final mixed drills as written work. This is also a valid approach, for the initial drills establish basic control of new material. The final mixes train the student to function in less tightly controlled circumstances. The approach employed depends on the degree of active control desired by the instructor.

- Still other instructors may want to assign the initial drills of a sequence as homework, reserving the class hour for the mixed drills at the end of the sequence. This variation would seem appropriate to highly motivated classes in an accelerated program.

- The readings offer instructors further ways to vary the pace and tone of each class hour. Again, we suggest that the readings be divided into small units for study over several class hours. The interests of individual instructors and individual classes will ultimately determine the ratio of time spent on the readings to time spent on the grammatical exercises.

No matter how individual instructors may choose to use this book, we recognize their need to complement and vary the materials, to "tinker" with the textbook. The design of the book is such that the effects of any omissions or additions will be immediately apparent.

Finally, what this book offers is the security of knowing that the basic structures of modern conversational German are fully understood and completely mastered. It is this security that allows instructors to enliven their classrooms in those special ways that correspond to their own talents and to the interests and needs of their students.

Van Horn Vail
Kimberly Sparks
Thomas Huber

Contents

Reading IV   Deutsche Gaststätten und Restaurants   174

Lesson 5   182

Reading V   Deutsche Hotels   234

Lesson 6   243

Reading VIII Besuch in Mainz

Lesson 9

MODERN GERMAN

Second Edition

Phonology

I German Vowels

One of the most characteristic differences between German and English is that German has "purer" vowel sounds. Take the German **e,** for example. It is pronounced almost like the long "ay" sound in the English word "hay." But you can hear a very real difference between the English and German sounds. Pronounce the English word "hay" very slowly:

HAY ee

You can hear the "ay" sound glide off into an "ee" sound at the finish. This is called an off-glide, and it is characteristic of this English vowel.

If the same word is pronounced with a German accent, there is no off-glide at the end:

HAY

There is another important difference between English and German vowels: German vowels are more tense. If you pronounce the word "hay" with a good German accent, you will feel extreme tension in your throat.

Most of the following exercises begin with a set of English words. Use these words as cues to the German vowel sound.

More important, if you say these words with a German accent, you will immediately hear the difference between the familiar English sounds and the new sounds you are making.

A Pure Vowels

1 The German e

a. The long **e** is similar to the vowel sound in the English word "hay." But it is tenser and has no off-glide. Pronounce the following English words with a German accent:

> hay
> day
> make
> take

Now say the following German words that have long **e** sounds:

> den
> dem
> geh
> Beet
> he

b. The short **e** is similar to the "e" in "let." The real difference is in the tension.

1

Pronounce the following English words with a German accent:

bet
met
get
pep

Now say the following German words that have short **e** sounds:

denn
Bett
keck
fett
Depp

2   The German **i**

a. The long **i** (usually spelled **ie**) is similar to the vowel sound in the English word "meet." Say the following English words with a German accent:

meet
beet
feet
keep
peep

Now pronounce the following German words:

die
Kies
nie
tief
mies

b. The short **i** is like the vowel sound in the English word "pit." Again, the difference is in the tension. Say the following English words with a German accent:

pit
kit
bit
kick
tip

Now say the following German words:

mit
bin
nimm

3   The German **u**

a. The long **u** is similar to the vowel sound in the English word "boon." Round your lips and keep them rounded and tense as you say the following English words with a German accent:

toot
boot
kook
boon
noon

Now say the following German words:

buk
tut
tun
gut

b. The short **u** is like the vowel sound in the English word "book." Pronounce the following words with a German accent:

took
book
put
cook
foot

Now say the following German words:

duck
Duft
dumm
guck

4   The German **o**

a. The long **o** is like the vowel sound in the English word "boat." Remember that the German **o** is a pure, tense sound without off-glide or any other complications. First, some English words with a German accent:

tow
go
boat
known

Now say the following German words:

Ton
tot
Mohn
Boot
Not

b. The short **o** doesn't have a really close English counterpart. The closest English sound is the "aw" sound in "paw" or "caught." The German sound, however, is shorter and tenser. Pronounce the following German words that have the short **o** sound:

Gott
topp
komm
Dock

5   The German a

a. The long **a** is like the "a" in "father." But the German sound is longer than its English counterpart. Pronounce the following German words with a long **a**:

kam
Bahn
nah
nahm

b. The short **a** has the same vowel quality as the "a" in "father," but it is much shorter and tenser. The following German words all have a short **a**:

Kamm
Bann
Pack
matt
dann

B   The Final Unstressed e

When a German **e** comes at the end of a word and is *unstressed*, it is called a **schwa** and is pronounced like the "uh" sound in the English word "sofa." The following German words all end with a **schwa**:

bitte
Mitte
Gatte
Puppe
Tanne
Biene
Messe

C   Diphthongs

So far you have been practicing simple vowel sounds like **i, e, a, o,** and **u.** A *diphthong* is a compound vowel sound made up of two simple vowel sounds. Take the German diphthong **au** as an example. It starts off as an **a** and quickly shifts to a **u.** Like the simple vowel sounds, German diphthongs are tenser than their English counterparts.

1   The German au

First say the following English words with a German accent. Remember that the diphthong is made up only of **a** and **u**; there are no other sounds in it. Make the sound fast and tense.

cow
how
bow
Dow

Now say the following German words with **au:**

kauft
Bau
Haus
Dessau

2 The German ei

The diphthong **ei** is like the "y" sound in the English word "my," but it is shorter and much tenser. Try some English words with a German accent:

> my
> buy
> die
> kite

Now say some German words with **ei:**

> Bein
> dein
> mein
> kein

3 The German eu (also written äu)

The diphthong **eu (äu)** is like the "oy" in "boy." First, try some English words with a German accent.

> boy
> toy
> coin
> moist

Now say some German words with **eu** and **äu:**

> Heu
> Bäume
> deute
> neun
> Beute

II The Final -en

When an **en** comes at the end of a German word and is not stressed, it is pronounced like the "en" in "hidden." First say the following English words with a German accent:

> hidden   button
> gotten   mutton

You will notice that the "-en (-on)" is made by releasing the air through your nose (a nasal release).

The same nasal release is used to pronounce the final **-en** in German. Now practice some German words with final **-en:**

> hatten
> bitten
> baden
> Buden
> packen

When **-en** comes after an **m,** a **p,** or a **b,** it is often pronounced like an **m.** The reason for this is that **m, p,** and **b** all force you to press your lips together. (Try to make an "n" sound with your lips closed. It's impossible.) Say the following German words:

> geben   (geb'm)
> kippen   (kipp'm)
> kommen   (komm'm)

III Sibilants (s, ss, ß, sch, z, tz)

A Voiced and Voiceless s

Voiced means that the vocal chords are buzzing; voiceless means that they are not. Say the word "Buzz." The "zz" here is a voiced "s." Now say "bus." The "s" here is voiceless.

1 s is voiced before vowels

> so   Hose
> Sie   Besen
> Sinn   Nase
> Sohn   Weise
> Satan

2 s is voiceless

a. In final position:

> Haus
> das
> dies
> Kies
> Moos

b. Before consonants:

> gehst
> hast
> bist
> fast
> basta

B ss and ß

The two sibilants **ss** and **ß** are *always* pronounced like an unvoiced "s." Say the following words:

Messe	gießen
Kasse	naß
Genosse	muß
Gusse	Faß
Gasse	Biß

Compare the following:

> hassen *but* Hasen
> lassen *but* lasen

C sch

The German **sch** is a fuller sound than its English counterpart, "sh." To pronounce **sch**, round your lips and push them slightly forward:

Fisch	fesch
Tisch	Mensch
Tasche	Tusch
Masche	Busch

▶ **Note** **st** and **sp** are pronounced **scht** and **schp** when they come at the beginning of a word:

stecken	spotten
stehen	spucken
Stimme	Speck
stumm	Spuk
Stock	Spann

D z and tz

These sibilants, **z** and **tz,** are both pronounced like the "zz" in "pizza." Try the following progression:

> pizza
> izza
> za
> zu

Now say these German words with **z** and **tz:**

zu	sitzen
Zoo	fetzen
ziehen	setzen
zum	nutzen
Zahn	Katzen
zisch	spitzen

IV Final b, d, and g

b is pronounced **p** ⎤
d is pronounced **t** ⎬ before a consonant or at the end of a word
g is pronounced **k** ⎦

end of a word:
gib (gi**p**)   Bad (Ba**t**)   Tag (Ta**k**)

before a consonant:
gibt (gi**p**t)   tagt (ta**k**t)

but before a vowel:
gebe (ge**b**e)   bade (ba**d**e)   Tage (Ta**g**e)

The following exercises have **b**, **d**, and **g** in mixed surroundings:

b	d	g
habt	mied	sog
gebe	bade	Tage
Diebe	Sud	mag
Staub	Tod	biege
Abt	Bude	Stieg
habe	Eid	magisch
Stab	fand	Tag

V   The **v** and **w**

V is pronounced like the "f" in the English word "fall." Say the following German words:

von
Vieh
vom

W is pronounced like the "v" in the English word "very." Try these words:

was
wenn
wo
wohnen
Wunde
Wagen

VI   The Glottal Stop

The glottal stop is characteristic of words (or syllables) that begin with a vowel. It is made by closing off the flow of air, then releasing it immediately with a sudden rush. This sudden release always accompanies an initial vowel sound. The glottal stop can be heard in the following finger-waving admonition:

uh-uh-uh!

Try these words:

am	auf
ist	aus
ein	es
ob	und

The glottal stop is also used to separate words. English, which doesn't use the glottal stop as much, often uses the end of one word as the beginning of the next. Look at the phrase

of it

It is usually pronounced

uvvit

This kind of run-on is uncharacteristic of German, and it is the glottal stop that prevents it. Say these German phrases:

es ist
aus Essen
ein Anzug
eine andere

VII   The German **l**

The German **l** is very different from the English "l." You can hear the difference when the following words are pronounced with a German accent:

tell
hell
fill
mill
tool
coal
feel

If you have difficulty making this sound, try saying "lalala" very fast. Do this several times. Now omit the final "a":

lalal

If you're still having trouble, try imitating the stretched-out double "l" sound in this Italian word:

be*ll*a

Now practice these German words:

hell	Fall	Kohle	Gold
schnell	Schall	Mole	bald
Kiel	voll	Sohle	Geld
viel	soll		

VIII   Front and Back ch

A   The Front ch

Say the English word "cue." The initial "k" sound is followed by a rush of air against the ridge directly behind the teeth. The friction sound made by this rush of air is very similar to the German "front ch." Try to isolate this sound by exaggerating it as you say the word "cue":

cue

Now say "I.Q." a few times, still exaggerating the friction sound:

I.Q.   I.Q.   I.Q.

Now say "I.Q." again, this time leaving out the "k" sound from the "Q." What you are saying could be written in German as

ei**ch**ju

Say this several times:

eich   eich   eich

Now practice the following German words:

Teich	dich
weich	sich
euch	Pech
ich	Blech
mich	

Practice the following progressions:

ich	ech
icht	echt
nicht	echte
Nichte	

B   The Back ch

The "back ch" is produced by forcing air through a small opening in the back of the throat. The sound itself is caused by the friction of the air against the throat. This sound may in fact already be familiar to you, either from pronouncing the name of the German composer

Bach

or from having used the American expression *of disgust*

yuch

If you have trouble with this sound, follow these steps:

1. Put your head back and say

AAH

2. Now, without moving your mouth at all, keep your head back and say (very slowly)

aka   aka

As you pronounce the "k" between the two "a"'s in "aka," you will feel your throat close, then open again. To form the back ch, do the same thing again, but this time don't let your throat close completely for the "k" sound. Close your throat down until there is only a very small opening left between the back of the tongue and the soft palate. The back ch is formed by forcing air through this small opening.

3. Now make some back ch's by gliding through the "k" in "aka" without letting your throat close completely. The result will be

a**ch**a

Practice the following German words with back **ch**:

ach	doch	Buch	auch
mach	Koch	Tuch	Bauch
Bach	noch	such	Tauch

Try some more combinations:

mache	machte	macht
koche	kochte	kocht
suche	suchte	sucht
tauche	tauchte	taucht

Now contrast the front **ch** and the back **ch**:

ich	$\longrightarrow$	ach
mich		mach
euch		auch
Teich		Tuch
fecht		focht
nicht		Nacht

IX   The German r

The German **r** is completely different from the English "r." The English "r" is made by putting the tip of the tongue up toward the roof of the mouth. To guard against making this kind of an "r," lock the tip of your tongue behind your lower teeth. Now try to pronounce the English word

>   rip

As you can see, it's impossible to form a normal English "r" this way. Either you make the "r" sound in the back of your throat (like a German uvular rolled **r**) or you replace the "r" with a "w":

>   wip

The German **r** is related to the back **ch** (a**ch**). The difference is that the **r** is voiced (the vocal cords are vibrating) and the back **ch** is voiceless. To make a German **r**, follow these steps:

1. First say **acha** two or three times:

>   acha   acha   acha

2. Now say **acha** very slowly. If you put your hand on your voice box, you can feel your vocal cords turn off when you pronounce the **ch**. They turn on for the first **a**:

>   a**cha**

They turn off for the **ch**:

>   ac**ha**

and they turn back on for the final **a**:

>   ac**ha**

3. Now say **acha** again, slowly and very loudly. This time, force yourself to *keep your vocal cords buzzing* as you slide through the **ch** sound. The result is a German **r**:

>   ara

4. Practice this a few times emphasizing the **r**:

>   ara   ara   ara

5. Now do the following exercises:

a. **r** in initial position

ara	arei
arat	arein
Rat	rein
aro	areu
arot	areut
rot	reut
aru	arie
aruht	ariet
ruht	riet
arau	areh
arauf	Reh
rauf	

a series of initial **r**'s

Rat	rein
rot	reut
ruht	riet
rauf	Reh

b. consonant + **r**

frei	tritt
fromm	Braten
prima	braun
Probe	Gras
Pracht	Greis
treten	Grube

c. **r** between two vowels

This is the same **r** that you have been drilling. It's just normally less emphasized between vowels:

Bahre	Tiere
Beere	bohren
ihre	fuhren

d. **r** + consonant

R is not rolled before a consonant. It is still made in the back of the throat, but there is no friction:

hart	wert
Bart	fern
fort	

e. unstressed **-er** at the end of a word

This sound is close to the "aw" sound in the English word "paw." But the German sound is shorter and much tenser:

bitter	seiner
Butter	dieser
Vater	Bruder
Mutter	

Now contrast final unstressed **e** (the "uh" sound in sof*a*) with final unstressed **er**:

-e	**-er**
bitte	bitter
diese	dieser
seine	seiner
Pauke	Pauker

f. stressed vowel + **r**

The **r** here is pronounced like a final unstressed **e** or **schwa (ə)**, as in bitt**e**:

mir (**miə**)
dir
wir
ihr
hier
vier
wer
her

X   Umlauts

A   ü (**u**-umlaut)

1   The long **ü** (long **i (ie)** + lip-rounding)

a. Say the English word "eat" with a German accent. Say it several times:

eat
eat
eat

b. Now round your lips as though you were going to whistle. You should feel strong tension in your lips.

c. With your lips in this position, say the word "eat" again. The result is a long **u**-umlaut:

ü t

Practice this several times.

d. To hear the vowel change from **ie** (the vowel sound in "eat") to **ü**, draw out a long **ie**. While doing so, round your lips. The sound you are making will shift from

ie to **ü**

e. Now practice the following contrasts:

Without lip-rounding	With lip-rounding
sieht	Süd
miede	müde
Kien	Kühn
vier	für
liege	Lüge

2   The short ü (short i + lip-rounding)

a. Say the English word "dinner" with a German accent.

b. Now say the same word, using strong lip-rounding. The result is a short **u**-umlaut:

dünner

c. Practice the following contrasts:

Without lip-rounding	With lip-rounding
missen	müssen
Mitter	Mütter
kissen	küssen
Kiste	Küste

Now say a series of words with short **ü:**

dünner
dümmer
Mütter
müssen
fünf

B   ö (o-umlaut)

1   The short ö (short e + lip-rounding)

a. Say the English word "getter" with a German accent. Say it several times.

b. Now say the same word with lip-rounding. The result is a short **o**-umlaut:

Götter

c. Practice the following contrasts:

Without lip-rounding	With lip-rounding
kennen	können
helle	Hölle
retten	rötten
stecke	Stöcke

Now practice a series of words with short **ö:**

Götter
können
Stöcke
Töchter
Hölle

2   The long ö (drawn out short e with strong lip-rounding)

The long **o**-umlaut is the same basic sound. It is merely longer.

a. First say **Tenne,** using a short German **e.**

b. Then draw out the vowel, changing just its length, not the vowel quality:

Teenne   Teenne   Teenne

c. Now say the same thing using strong lip-rounding. The result is a long **o**-umlaut:

Töne

d. Practice the following contrasts:

Short e	Drawn out short e	Drawn out short e with lip-rounding
Tenne	Teenne	Töne
nette	neette	Nöte
helle	heelle	Höhle
Hennen	Heennen	höhnen
Sennen	Seennen	Söhnen

Now practice a series of words with long **ö:**

Töne
Söhne
Höhle
dösen
böse

C ä (a-umlaut) and äu (au-umlaut)

These are not new sounds but only different ways of spelling sounds you have already learned.

Long **ä** is pronounced like long **e**, as in:

den

Thus, **denen** is pronounced the same as **Dänen.**

Short **ä** is pronounced like short **e**, as in:

Bett

Betten rhymes with **hätten.**

äu is pronounced **oi (eu)**, as in:

heute

And **heute** rhymes with **läute.**

Practice the following:

Long ä	Short ä	äu
spät	hätte	läuft
schläft	Mäntel	Häuser
fährt	Nächte	säuft
Väter		

XI Clusters

A tsch

Tsch is pronounced like the "ch" sounds in "*church*." But it's a fuller sound and has more lip-rounding:

deutsch
lutschen
patschen
Matsch

B chs

Chs is pronounced like the English "x":

sechs
Lachs
wachsen

C ng

English has two ways of pronouncing "ng." In some words the "g" is voiced as a hard "g":

longer   stronger   anger

In other words it is not:

singer, tangy

German follows only the second pattern:

Klingel	länger
bringen	strenger
enger	Zunge

D Final -ig

Final **-ig** is pronounced **-ich:**

fleißig

But if a vowel follows the **-ig,** the final **g** is hard; that is, it is pronounced in the usual way:

fleißige

Practice the following contrasts:

fleißig	fleißige
mutig	mutige
ständig	ständige

E Contrast ie and ei

Because of the spelling, many students tend to confuse the pronunciation of **ie** and **ei.** As you remember:

> **ie** is similar to the vowel sound in "meet"
>
> **ei** is a diphthong: it is pronounced like the vowel sound in "buy"

If you have trouble remembering, you can look at it this way:

> **ie** is pronounced like English "e"
> **ei** is pronounced like English "i"

Practice the following contrasts:

ei	ie
bleiben	blieben
schreiben	schrieben
steigen	stiegen
heißen	hießen
Leid	Lied
meine	Miene
treibe	Triebe

Now pronounce them when they are mixed:

blieben	steigen
Leid	Miene
schreiben	heißen
stiegen	Lied
Triebe	deine
meine	treibe
hießen	schrieben
bleiben	fein

F Cluster Practice

Practice pronouncing the following sequences. Pronounce each syllable very slowly at first. Then build up speed.

ich	ech	ach
rich	rech	rach
sprich	sprech	sprach
spricht	sprecht	spracht
sprichst		sprachst

ich	ech	ach
rich	rech	mach
richt	recht	macht
richtig		machst

ich		ach
nich		nach
nicht		nacht

nich-zu	rech-zu	nach-zu
nich-ze	rech-ze	nach-ze
nichts	rechts	nachts

Continued Phonology Practice

Phonology practice doesn't end with this section—it has just started here. The drills in this unit (and the accompanying tapes) should be reviewed intensively during the first two lessons of this book. The first few weeks are decisive in acquiring a good pronunciation; use this phonology section as a constant aid.

Lesson 1   Level ONE

A Personal Pronouns

Look at the following table:

	SINGULAR		PLURAL	
1ST PERSON	ich	I	wir	we
2ND PERSON	**du**	*you*	**ihr**	*you*
3RD PERSON	er	he	sie	they
	sie	she		
	es	it	**Sie**	*you*

As you can see from the table, German and English pronouns follow a similar pattern. The only major difference is that German has *three ways* of saying "you." **Du** and **ihr** are the *familiar forms*. You use them to address members of the family, close friends, and children up to the age of thirteen or fourteen. **Du** is the singular form; you use it when addressing *one person:*

> Wo bist **du, Hans?**
> (Where are *you, Hans?*)

Ihr is the plural form; you use it to address two or more people:

> Wo seid **ihr, Kinder?**
> (Where are *you, children?*)

Sie is the *polite form.* Generally speaking, **Sie** is used when you address someone as **Herr** (Mr.), **Frau** (Mrs.), or **Fräulein** (Miss). It is both singular and plural.

> Wo sind **Sie, Herr Lenz?**
> (Where are *you, Mr. Lenz?*)

The same English sentence ("Where are you?") *has three possible equivalents in German.* The choice depends on who you are talking to.

DRILLS

1 Forms of address

● Supply the German pronoun suggested by the context of the English sentence.

> du   you (familiar singular)
> ihr   you (familiar plural)
> Sie   you (polite singular and plural)

EXAMPLE   Where are *you* going, *Hans?*   __du__

1. What do *you* think, *Mr. Schmidt?*   *Sie*
2. *You* look great, *Anna.*   *du*
3. What are *you* doing, *children?*   *ihr*
4. Would *you* gentlemen like a drink?   *Sie*
5. *You* guys are crazy.   *ihr*
6. *You're* right, *Inge.**   *du*
7. *You're* next, *Mr. Weber.*   *Sie*

8. *Hans, Inge!* Can *you* two help me?   *du*
9. Will *you* have time today, *Miss Meyer?*   *Sie*
10. Can *you* lend me ten dollars, *Dad?*   *du*
11. *You children* are too much.   *ihr*
12. How do *you* feel, *darling?*   *du*
13. What do *you* recommend, *Mr. Keller?*   *Sie*
14. *You* just don't understand, *Mother.*   *du*

2 First person pronouns

● Give the German pronoun suggested by the English sentence.

> ich   I
> wir   we

EXAMPLE   *I*'ll do it.   __ich__

1. *We*'ll do it later.   *wir*
2. *I*'m tired.   *ich*

3. Do *we* have time?   *wir*
4. *I*'m hungry.   *ich*

5. *We*'ll wait here.   *wir*
6. *I*'ll do it.   *ich*

3 Third person pronouns

● Give the German pronoun suggested by the English sentence.

> er   he   sie   they
> sie   she
> es   it

EXAMPLE   *He*'s coming tomorrow.   __er__

1. *She*'s very nice.   *sie*
2. *He*'s not here.   *er*
3. Where do *they* live?   *sie*
4. *It*'s too hard.   *es*
5. Where does *she* work?   *sie*
6. *He*'s coming tomorrow.   *er*

7. *It*'s late.   *es*
8. *They* always come late.   *sie*
9. *He*'s looking well.   *er*
10. *She*'s not here.   *sie*
11. *They*'re working today.   *sie*
12. Where is *it?*   *es*

---

*__Inge:__ German first name for girls.

4 Mixed drills

• Supply the German pronoun suggested by the English sentence.

a.
1. You're next, *Mr. Weber.* — Sie
2. I'm tired. — Ich
3. We'll wait here. — wir
4. You look great, *Anna.* — du
5. It's late. — es
6. *Hans, Inge!* Can you two help me? — ihr
7. *She's* very nice. — sie
8. *They* always come late. — sie
9. What do *you* think, *Mr. Schmidt?* — Sie
10. Do *we* have time? — wir

b.
1. *He's* not here. — er
2. I'll do it. — Ich
3. Can you lend me ten dollars, *Dad?* — ihr
4. Where is *it?* — es
5. *You* guys are crazy. — ihr

6. Where does *she* work? — sie
7. I'm hungry. — Ich
8. Where do *they* live? — sie
9. *He's* coming tomorrow. — er
10. Would *you gentlemen* like a drink? — Sie

c.
1. *We'll* do it later. — Wir
2. *You're* right, *Inge.* — du
3. Will *you* have time today, *Miss Meyer?* — Sie
4. *It's* too hard. — es
5. *You children* are too much. — ihr
6. *They're* working today. — sie
7. How do *you* feel, *darling?* — du
8. *He's* looking well. — er
9. What do *you* recommend, *Mr. Keller?* — Sie
10. *She's* not here. — sie

B Verbs

1 Infinitives and verb stems

The infinitive is the form of the verb found in dictionaries. Most German infinitives end in **-en.** By removing this **-en** ending, you arrive at the verb *stem*:

Infinitive	Stem	
kommen	komm-	to come
schreiben	schreib-	to write

2 Present tense endings

The present tense is formed by adding a set of *endings* to the stem:

kommen *to come*			
ich	komm **e**	wir	komm **en**
du	komm **st**	ihr	komm **t**
er / sie / es	komm **t**	sie / Sie	komm **en**

► Note The polite form **Sie,** which can be either singular or plural in meaning, always takes the 3rd person plural form of the verb. Grammatically speaking, **Sie** (*you,* singular and plural) behaves just like **sie** (*they*).

3 Usage

a. German: no emphatic or progressive forms

In addition to the simple present tense form (he writes), English has an emphatic form (he does write) and a progressive form (he is writing). German has *only one present tense form* **(er schreibt).**

$$
\left.\begin{array}{l}
\text{he writes} \\
\text{he does write} \\
\text{he is writing}
\end{array}\right\} \quad \textbf{er schreibt}
$$

b. Present tense with future meaning

English often uses a present tense form to refer to the future:

He's coming tomorrow.

"is coming" is the progressive form of the *present tense,* but "tomorrow" clearly refers to future time.

German makes much more frequent use of this convention. In fact, conversational German normally uses the present tense to express future meaning:

Er kommt morgen. (He's coming tomorrow.)

► Note   English can express future time in any of three ways:

He's *coming* tomorrow.   (is coming)
He'll *come* tomorrow.   (will come)
He's *going to come* tomorrow.   (is going to come)

German doesn't have this choice. The one present tense form in German expresses all three English variations.

$$
\text{Er } \textbf{kommt} \text{ morgen.} \quad \textbf{kommt} \left\{\begin{array}{l}
\text{is coming} \\
\text{will come} \\
\text{is going to come}
\end{array}\right.
$$

4 Basic sentence structure

A normal English sentence consists of a subject, a verb, and something else. This "something else" is called a *complement,* because it completes the meaning of the sentence.

Subject	Verb	Complement
He	is coming	tomorrow.
She	is doing	it.

a. The subject: Who is doing it?

You can identify the subject of a sentence by asking yourself the simple question, "Who is doing it?"

> He is coming tomorrow.
> She is doing it.

Who is coming tomorrow? *He* (the subject) is. *Who* is doing it? *She* is.

b. The verb: What is going on?

The verb is easy to identify; it tells you what is going on.

> He *is coming* tomorrow.
> She *is doing* it.

What is going on can range from *strong actions* (he *hit* me) to the *simple state of being* (I *am* here) or *having* (I *have* time).

c. The complement: when, where, how, what, who, who to, who for?

The subject and the verb of a normal statement can each be identified by a simple question (Who is doing it? What is going on?). The complement is what gives a sentence its color and variety—it can answer a number of questions.

> 1. *When?*   He is coming *tomorrow.*
> 2. *Where?*   He lives *here.*
> 3. *What?*   He has *time.*
> 4. *Who?*   He hit *me.*
> 5. *Who to?* He gave it *to me.*
> 6. *Who for?* He bought it *for me.*

For the present, we will restrict ourselves to simple complements that answer only one question, like the first four examples above. Later you will see sentences with complements that answer two questions (like sentences 5 and 6 above) or more. For example:

> I'll give   it   to you   later.
>   (what)   (who to)   (when)

5 Basic sentence structure in German

Simple statements in German and English follow exactly the same logic.

Subject	Verb	Complement
He	is coming	tomorrow.
Er	**kommt**	**morgen.**
I	have	time.
Ich	**habe**	**Zeit.***

---

*All German nouns are capitalized: Ich habe **Z**eit.

a. Basic word order in German: verb second

In a normal German statement the subject comes first and *the verb comes second.*

(1)   (2)   (3)

Er kommt morgen.

b. Word order after question words: verb second

wann?	when?			
was?	what?	(1)	(2)	(3)
wo?	where?	Wann	kommt	er? (When is he coming?)

In such sentences, the question word is the first element, the verb is second, *and the subject comes right after the verb*—that is, the subject is in the third position.

DRILLS

- Supply the appropriate verb form.

- **kommen:** to come

  1. Ich *komme* nicht.   (**nicht:** not)
  2. Wir *kommen* später.   (**später:** later)
  3. Wann *kommen* Sie, Herr Braun?

     (**wann:** when; **Herr:** Mr.)

  4. Er *kommt* morgen.   (**morgen:** tomorrow)
  5. Sie (*they*) *kommen* nicht.
  6. Wann *kommst* du?
  7. Sie (*she*) *kommt* heute.   (**heute:** today)

- **schreiben:** to write

  1. Ich *schreibe* es morgen.
  2. Er *schreibt* später.
  3. Wann *schreiben* Sie es?
  4. Was *schreibst* du da?   (**da:** there)
  5. Sie (*she*) *schreibt* es nicht.

- **machen:** to do, make

  1. Wir *machen* es morgen.
  2. Ich *mache* es nicht.
  3. Was *macht* sie (*she*) da?
  4. Wann *machen* Sie es, Frau Meyer?
  5. Ich *mache* es später.
  6. Was *macht* ihr, Kinder?

     (**Kinder:** children)

  7. Wann _____ du das, Hans?   (**das:** that)

- **kaufen:** to buy

  1. Er _____ es morgen.
  2. Was _____ ihr?
  3. Wir _____ es später.
  4. Wann _____ du es, Inge?
  5. Sie (*they*) _____ es nicht.
  6. Ich _____ es.

- **wohnen:** to live

  1. Wir _____ hier.   (**hier:** here)
  2. Wo _____ du jetzt, Hanno?* (**jetzt:** now)
  3. Wo _____ ihr jetzt?
  4. Wo _____ Sie jetzt, Herr Lenz?
  5. Ich _____ hier.
  6. Er _____ da.

- **gehen:** to go

  1. Ich _____ nach Hause.

     (**nach Hause:** home)

  2. Wann _____ sie (*they*) weg?

     (**gehen . . . weg:** to go . . . away)

  3. Wo _____ du hin?

     (**wo . . . hin:** where . . . [to])†

  4. Wir _____ nach Hause.
  5. Wann _____ er weg?
  6. Wo _____ Sie hin?
  7. Wann _____ du nach Hause?
  8. Er _____ weg.
  9. Wo _____ sie (*they*) hin?

---

*__Hanno:__ German first name for boys.

†German uses **wo** by itself to mean "where" when there is *no motion:* **Wo** ist er? (Where is he?)
When there is *motion,* **wo . . . hin** must be used: **Wo** gehst du **hin**? (Where are you going [to]?)

C Variation on the Normal Pattern of Verb Endings

If the verb stem ends in **-d** or **-t,** *all* of the endings begin with **e.**

finden *to find*				
ich	find **e**	wir	find **en**
du	find **est**	ihr	find **et**
er / sie / es	find **et**	sie / Sie	find **en**

The **e** in the 2nd and 3rd person singular and in the 2nd person plural makes the endings easier to say and hear.

du find<u>e</u>st   er find<u>e</u>t   ihr find<u>e</u>t

DRILLS

• Supply the appropriate verb form.

• **finden:** to find

1. Wir _____ es später.
2. Du _____ es nicht. (*You won't find it.*)
3. Ich _____ es zu schwer.
                        (**zu schwer:** too hard)
4. Er _____ das leicht.
               (**das:** that; **leicht:** easy)
5. Ihr _____ es nicht.
6. Wo _____ ich das?

• **arbeiten:** to work

1. Er _____ hier.
2. Wo _____ du?
3. Wann _____ Sie?
4. Ich _____ heute.   (**heute:** today)
5. Er _____ nicht viel. (**nicht viel:** not much)
6. Wo _____ ihr?
7. Warum _____ du nicht? (**warum:** why)
8. Sie (*she*) _____ heute.

D Haben and Sein

Haben (*to have*) and **sein** (*to be*) are unlike any other verbs, which means that their forms have to be memorized.

1 haben

haben *to have*			
ich	habe	wir	haben
du	hast	ihr	habt
er / sie / es	hat	sie / Sie	haben

DRILLS

- Supply the appropriate form of the verb **haben.**

  1. Ich _____ Zeit. (**Zeit:** time)
  2. Wann _____ du Zeit?
  3. Was _____ er da?
  4. Du _____ es.
  5. Wir _____ Hunger.
     (*We're hungry; lit.: We have hunger.*)
  6. Was _____ du da?

  7. Wann _____ Sie Zeit?
  8. Er _____ Hunger.
  9. Wann _____ ihr Zeit?
  10. Ich _____ Hunger.
  11. Sie (*they*) _____ es.
  12. Was _____ ihr da?
  13. Sie (*she*) _____ Hunger.

2 sein

	sein *to be*		
ich	bin	wir	sind
du	bist	ihr	seid
er / sie / es	ist	sie / Sie	sind

DRILLS

- Supply the appropriate form of the verb **sein.**

  1. Wo _____ ich?
  2. Das _____ zu schwer. (**das:** that)
  3. Wir _____ hier.
  4. Du _____ verrückt. (**verrückt:** crazy)
  5. Nein, sie (*they*) _____ nicht hier.
  6. Es _____ zu spät. (**zu spät:** too late)
  7. Wo _____ du, Heidi?
  8. Hans, Peter! Wo _____ ihr?

  9. Wo _____ es?
  10. Sie (*they*) _____ nett. (**nett:** nice)
  11. Wo _____ wir jetzt?
  12. Er _____ nicht hier.
  13. Sie (*she*) _____ nett.
  14. Kinder, ihr _____ verrückt.
  15. Nein, Liebling, ich _____ zu müde.
      (**Liebling:** darling; **müde:** tired)

- Supply the appropriate form of **haben** or **sein.**

  a. 1. Was _____ du da?
          (haben)
      2. Es _____ zu spät.
          (sein)
      3. Wir _____ hier.
          (sein)
      4. Ich _____ Hunger.
          (haben)
      5. Wo _____ er jetzt?
          (sein)
      6. Wann _____ Sie Zeit?
          (haben)
      7. Du _____ verrückt.
          (sein)

      8. Sie (*they*) _____ es.
          (haben)
      9. Hans, Peter! Wo _____ ihr?
          (sein)
      10. Ich _____ zu müde.
          (sein)

  b. 1. Wir _____ Hunger.
          (haben)
      2. Das _____ nett.
          (sein)
      3. Wo _____ du, Heidi?
          (sein)
      4. Ich _____ Zeit.
          (haben)

5. Was _____ Sie da?
(haben)

6. Wo _____ sie (they)?
(sein)

7. Wann _____ du Zeit?
(haben)

8. Was _____ er da?
(haben)

9. Kinder, ihr _____ verrückt.
(sein)

10. Das _____ zu schwer.
(sein)

c. 1. Was _____ ihr da?
(haben)

2. Nein, sie (they) _____ nicht hier.
(sein)   (nein: no)

3. Sie (she) _____ Hunger.
(haben)

4. Wo _____ ich?
(sein)

5. Sie (she) _____ nicht hier.
(sein)

6. Du _____ es.
(haben)

7. Sie (they) _____ nett.
(sein)

8. Er _____ Hunger.
(haben)

9. Wo _____ wir jetzt?
(sein)

10. Wann _____ ihr Zeit?
(haben)

d. 1. Wir _____ zu müde.
(sein)

2. Was _____ Sie da?
(haben)

3. Wo _____ es?
(sein)

4. Er _____ verrückt.
(sein)

MIXED DRILLS

• Supply the appropriate verb form.

a. 1. Er _____ morgen.
(kommen)

2. Wann _____ du das, Hans?
(machen)

3. Ja, ich _____ Zeit.   (ja: yes)
(haben)

4. Wir _____ es später.
(kaufen)

5. Wann _____ er weg?
(gehen)

6. Wo _____ Sie jetzt, Herr Lenz?
(wohnen)

7. Du _____ verrückt.
(sein)

8. Sie (she) _____ heute.
(arbeiten)

9. Du _____ es nicht.
(finden)

10. Ich _____ es morgen.
(schreiben)

b. 1. Es _____ zu spät.
(sein)

2. Wir _____ später.
(kommen)

3. Er _____ hier.
(arbeiten)

4. Sie (she) _____ Hunger.
(haben)

5. Ich _____ es später.
(machen)

6. Wo _____ es?
(sein)

7. Was _____ du da?
(schreiben)

8. Wir _____ nach Hause.
(gehen)

9. Ich _____ zu müde.
(sein)

10. Wann _____ Sie?
(arbeiten)

c. 1. Wann _____ du Zeit?
(haben)

2. Wir _____ hier.
(sein)

3. Ich _____ es zu schwer.
(finden)

4. Er _____ es morgen.
(kaufen)

5. Wann _____ du nach Hause?
   (gehen)

6. Sie (*they*) _____ nicht.
   (kommen)

7. Wo _____ ich das?
   (finden)

8. Wir _____ es morgen.
   (machen)

9. Wo _____ du, Heidi?
   (sein)

10. Er _____ Hunger.
    (haben)

d. 1. Wann _____ Sie es, Frau Meyer?
      (machen)

   2. Wo _____ du jetzt, Hanno?
      (wohnen)

   3. Sie (*they*) _____ nett.
      (sein)

   4. Ich _____ es nicht.
      (machen)

   5. Wir _____ Hunger.
      (haben)

   6. Kinder, ihr _____ verrückt.
      (sein)

   7. Wann _____ du?
      (kommen)

   8. Wann _____ ihr Zeit?
      (haben)

   9. Er _____ das leicht.
      (finden)

   10. Wo _____ wir jetzt?
       (sein)

e. 1. Ich _____ nach Hause.
      (gehen)

   2. Hans, Peter! Wo _____ ihr?
      (sein)

   3. Sie (*they*) _____ es nicht.
      (kaufen)

   4. Wann _____ Sie Zeit?
      (haben)

   5. Warum _____ du nicht?
      (arbeiten)

   6. Ich _____ hier.
      (wohnen)

   7. Er _____ später.
      (schreiben)

   8. Wo _____ sie (*they*)?
      (sein)

9. Was _____ ihr, Kinder?
   (machen)

10. Wir _____ zu müde.
    (sein)

f. 1. Er _____ weg.
      (gehen)

   2. Das _____ nett.
      (sein)

   3. Ich _____ es nicht.
      (machen)

   4. Wo _____ du hin?
      (gehen)

   5. Was _____ er da?
      (haben)

   6. Wann _____ Sie es?
      (schreiben)

   7. Wir _____ es später.
      (finden)

   8. Ich _____ es.
      (kaufen)

   9. Wo _____ du?
      (arbeiten)

   10. Wo _____ ich?
       (sein)

g. 1. Was _____ sie (*she*) da?
      (machen)

   2. Du _____ es.
      (haben)

   3. Wann _____ sie (*they*) weg?
      (gehen)

   4. Er _____ verrückt.
      (sein)

   5. Ich _____ heute.
      (arbeiten)

   6. Was _____ Sie da?
      (haben)

   7. Wo _____ ihr jetzt?
      (wohnen)

   8. Ich _____ Hunger.
      (haben)

   9. Er _____ da.
      (wohnen)

   10. Wo _____ ihr?
       (arbeiten)

h. 1. Was _____ du da?
      (haben)

   2. Wann _____ du es, Inge?
      (kaufen)

3. Sie (she) _____ es nicht.
   (schreiben)

4. Er _____ das leicht.
   (finden)

5. Wo _____ sie (they) hin?
   (gehen)

6. Nein, ich _____ nicht.
   (kommen)

7. Wir _____ hier.
   (wohnen)

8. Das _____ zu schwer.
   (sein)

9. Ihr _____ es nicht.
   (finden)

10. Nein, sie (they) _____ nicht hier.
    (sein)

EXPRESS IN GERMAN

● Although many of these English sentences make use of future forms, all of their German counterparts use the present tense.

a. 1. It's too late.
    2. We'll do it tomorrow.
    3. When are you (du) coming?
    4. I live here.
    5. When do you (Sie) work?
    6. He's coming tomorrow.
    7. I'm going home.
    8. Where is it?
    9. They aren't coming.
    10. When are you going to do that, Hans?

b. 1. I'll buy it.
    2. When will you (Sie) have time?
    3. You're (du) crazy.
    4. I'm too tired.
    5. Where are you living now, Hans?
    6. We're going home.
    7. What are you doing, children?
    8. She's hungry.
    9. When is he leaving? (going away)
    10. When are you (Sie) going to write it?

c. 1. I'll do it later.
    2. You (du) won't find it.
    3. That's too hard.
    4. We're coming later.
    5. I'm working today.
    6. He lives there.
    7. When are you going to buy it, Inge?
    8. When will you (ihr) have time?
    9. No, they aren't here. (not here: **nicht hier**)
    10. She's working today.

d. 1. I find it too hard.
    2. What are you (du) writing there?
    3. No, I'm not coming.
    4. He'll write later.
    5. We live here.
    6. That's nice.
    7. I'm hungry.
    8. You (ihr) won't find it.
    9. They aren't going to buy it.
    10. When are you (du) going home?

e. 1. He works here.
    2. When are you (Sie) going to do it?
    3. We're hungry.
    4. I'm not going to do it.
    5. Where are they?
    6. Kids, you're crazy.
    7. You (du) have it.
    8. We'll find it later.
    9. He's going to buy it tomorrow.
    10. When are they leaving? (going away)

f. 1. Where are you, Heidi?
    2. Where do you (ihr) work?
    3. What do you (Sie) have there?
    4. We're too tired.
    5. Where are you (du) going (to)?
       (use **wo . . . hin**)
    6. I'll write it tomorrow.
    7. We'll buy it later.
    8. Yes, I have time.
    9. He's crazy.
    10. Where do you (du) work?

g. 1. What is she doing there?
    2. Where are they going (to)?
       (use **wo . . . hin**)
    3. She isn't going to write it.
    4. Hans, Peter! Where are you?
    5. We're here.
    6. When will you (du) have time?
    7. He finds that easy.
    8. Where are you living now, Mr. Lenz?
    9. She's nice.
    10. I'm not going to do it.

VOCABULARY

antworten to answer
arbeiten to work
da there
das that
du you (*fam. sing.*)
er he
es it
finden to find
gehen to go
gehen ... weg
    to go ... away
haben to have
Herr Mr.
heute today
hier here
Hunger hunger
Hunger haben
    to be hungry
ich I

ihr you (*fam. pl.*)
ja yes
jetzt now
kaufen to buy
Kinder children
kommen to come
leicht easy
Liebling darling
machen to do, make
morgen tomorrow
müde tired
nach Hause
    home (*with motion*)
nein no
nett nice
nicht not
schreiben to write
schwer hard, difficult
sein to be

sie she
sie they
Sie you (*polite sing.
    and pl.*)
spät late
später later
verrückt crazy
viel much
wann when
warum why
was what
weg away
wir we
wo where
wo...hin where...
    (to) (*with motion*)
wohnen to live
Zeit time
zu too

Lesson **1**   Level**TWO**

A Questions

German has two basic ways of forming questions.

1 Questions introduced by question words

As you saw in Level 1, a question may be formed by using a question word.

EXAMPLE   **Wann** **kommt er?**   (*When* is he coming?)

The most common German question words are:

wer	who
was	what
wo	where
wann	when
warum	why
wie	how
wieviel	how much

2 Questions introduced by a verb

A German question can also be formed by putting the *verb* in *first position*.

STATEMENT	Er **ist** hier.	(He *is* here.)
QUESTION	**Ist** er hier?	(*Is* he here?)
STATEMENT	Er **kommt** heute.	(He *is coming* today.)
QUESTION	**Kommt** er heute?	(*Is* he *coming* today?)
STATEMENT	Sie **arbeitet** hier.	(She *works* here.)
QUESTION	**Arbeitet** sie hier?	(*Does* she *work* here?)

Both German and English can form questions by putting the verb first. But the German pattern is easier, since German has no progressive (*is* he *coming*) or emphatic (*does* she *work*) form. In German, the verb is always a one-word form, and it is immediately followed by the subject. Like English questions, German questions have falling intonation when they begin with a question word and rising intonation when they ask for a "yes" or "no" answer.

DRILLS

1 Question words

- Insert **wer** or **warum**.

1. _____ ist da?
   (Who)
2. _____ machen Sie das?
   (Why)
3. _____ sind sie?
   (Who)
4. _____ wartest du hier? (**warten**: to wait)
   (Why)

5. _____ kommt er nicht?
   (Why)
6. _____ ist es?
   (Who)
7. _____ kaufen Sie es nicht?
   (Why)

- Insert **wie** or **wieviel**.

1. _____ kostet das? (**kosten**: to cost)
   (How much)
2. _____ geht's?
   (How)
   (*How are you? Lit.: How goes it?*)
3. _____ heißen Sie?
   (How)
   (Lit.: *How are you called?* English
   equivalent: *What's your name?*)
   (**heißen**: to be called)

4. _____ brauchst du?
   (How much)
   (**brauchen**: to need)
5. _____ heißt er?
   (How)
6. _____ haben Sie?
   (How much)
7. _____ macht man das?
   (How)
   (**man**: one, as in "How does one do that?")*

- Mixed drill: Insert the correct question word.

a. 1. _____ kommt er nicht?
      (Why)
   2. _____ brauchst du?
      (How much)
   3. _____ geht er nach Deutschland?
      (When)
      (**nach Deutschland**: to Germany)
   4. _____ geht's?
      (How)
   5. _____ brauchst du?
      (What)
   6. _____ ist es?
      (Who)
   7. _____ machen Sie das?
      (Why)
   8. _____ ist es?
      (Where)

9. _____ kostet das?
   (How much)
10. _____ kommst du nach Amerika?
    (When)
    (**nach Amerika**: to America)

b. 1. _____ heißt er?
      (How)
      (*What's his name?*)
   2. _____ sind sie?
      (Who)
   3. _____ steht er? (**stehen**: to stand)
      (Where)
   4. _____ wartest du hier? (**warten**: to wait)
      (Why)
   5. _____ macht man das?
      (How)
   6. _____ brauchst du es?
      (When)

_____

* **Man** is not stuffy in German. The natural English equivalent of this sentence is, "How do *you* do that?"

7. _____ heißen Sie?
   (How)
   (*What's your name?*)

8. _____ ist da?
   (Who)

9. _____ macht er in Deutschland?
   (What)

   (**in Deutschland**: in Germany)

10. _____ kaufen Sie es nicht?
    (Why)

c. 1. _____ haben Sie?
   (How much)

- Express in German.

a. 1. Who's there?
   2. What do you (**du**) need?
   3. How much does that cost?
   4. Why don't you (**Sie**) buy it?
   5. Where is he standing?
   6. How are you? (*Lit.*: How goes it?)
   7. When is he going to Germany?
   8. Who are they?
   9. Why isn't he coming?
   10. How do you (**man**) do that?

b. 1. How much do you (**du**) need?
   2. What's his name? (*Lit.*: How is he called?)

   3. Where is it?
   4. Why are you (**du**) waiting here?
   5. When do you (**du**) need it?
   6. How much do you (**Sie**) have?
   7. Who is it?
   8. What's he doing in Germany?
   9. What's your name? (*Lit.*: How are you [**Sie**] called?)
   10. Why are you (**Sie**) doing that?

c. 1. When are you (**du**) coming to America?

2 Questions introduced by a verb

- Make questions out of the following statements by reversing the order of the subject and the verb and by using rising intonation.

1. Sie wohnen hier.
2. Er hat es.
3. Wir brauchen es.
4. Er wartet noch.   (**noch**: still)
5. Sie kommen heute.
6. Er lebt noch.   (**leben**: to live, be alive)*
7. Du machst es morgen.
8. Sie ist hier.

9. Sie kennen Berlin.   (**kennen**: to know)
10. Du brauchst es.
11. Er steht noch da.   (**noch da**: still there)
12. Du kennst Frau Meyer.
13. Sie arbeiten noch da.
14. Sie leben noch in Amerika.
15. Er geht nach Hause.

- Express in German.

1. Are they coming today?
2. Do you (**du**) need it?

3. Is he going home?
4. Do they live here?

_____

* **Leben** is used when referring to life (He's still *alive*) and *may* also be used in connection with cities or countries:

   Er **lebt** in Berlin.   (He lives in Berlin.)
   Lebt er noch in Amerika?   (Does he still live in America?)

Wohnen means "live" in the sense of "reside." "**Wohnt** er hier?" means "Does he *live* here?" ("Is this his house?") In this context, **wohnen** must be used instead of **leben. Wohnen** must also be used with addresses (He lives on Main Street).

   Wo **wohnt** er?   (Where does he live? [What is his address?])

5. Is he still waiting?
6. Do you **(Sie)** know Berlin?
7. Is she here?
8. Do they still work there?
9. Do you **(du)** know Mrs. Meyer?
10. Is he still alive? (Is he still living?)

11. Do we need it?
12. Are they still living in America?
13. Is he still standing there?
14. Does he have it?
15. Are you going to do it tomorrow?

B Verbs with Stems Ending in -s or -z

If the stem of a verb ends in any sort of "s" or "z" sound **(-s, -ss, -ß, -tz, -z),** the **du**-form ending of the verb is **-t** (not the usual **-st**).

	heißen *to be called*		
ich	heiß **e**	wir	heiß **en**
du	heiß **t**	ihr	heiß **t**
er / sie / es	heiß **t**	sie / Sie	heiß **en**

DRILLS

• Replace the subjects of the following sentences with the words in parentheses, making the necessary changes in the verb forms.

1. Wo sitzen sie? (du, ihr)   **(sitzen:** to sit)
2. Wie heißen Sie? (du, er)
3. Wir sitzen hier. (ich, du)

4. Ich heiße Meyer. (er, sie [*they*])
5. Warum sitzt er noch da? (du, Sie)

• Express in German.

1. Where are you **(du)** sitting?
2. What's his name?
3. Why is he still sitting there?
4. Her name is Anna.

5. Why are you **(du)** still sitting here?
6. Where are they sitting?
7. What's your name? **(du**-form)

C Stem-Vowel Change

A number of common verbs have **-e-** as their stem vowel:

Infinitive	**Stem**	
gehen	geh-	to go
kennen	kenn-	to know
sprechen	sprech-	to speak
sehen	seh-	to see

Some of these verbs (and you must learn which ones) change their stem vowels to -i- or -ie- in the 2nd and 3rd person singular.

NO STEM-VOWEL CHANGE	STEM-VOWEL CHANGE	
leben *to live, be alive*	**sprechen** *to speak*	**sehen** *to see*
ich lebe	ich spreche	ich sehe
du lebst	du sprichst	du siehst
er lebt	er spricht	er sieht
wir leben	wir sprechen	wir sehen
ihr lebt	ihr sprecht	ihr seht
sie leben	sie sprechen	sie sehen

If the **-e-** in the stem is short (sprechen), then the shift is to short -i-; if the **-e-** is long (sehen), the shift is to long -ie-.

DRILLS

Here are five verbs whose stems *do not* change:

gehen	to go
kennen	to know, be familiar with
leben	to live
stehen	to stand
trinken	to drink

• Replace the subjects of the following sentences, making the necessary changes in the verb forms.

1. Ich gehe nach Hause. (er)
2. Kennen Sie Frau Lenz? (du)
3. Sie leben noch in Amerika. (er)
4. Wo stehen sie? (er)
5. Wo gehen Sie hin? (du)
6. Sie trinken Bier. (er)

7. Sie kennen Berlin. (du, ihr)
8. Er steht da drüben. (wir) **(da drüben:** over there)
9. Er lebt noch. (sie [*they*])
10. Was trinken Sie? (du)

Here are three verbs whose stems *do* change:

sprechen	du sprichst, er spricht	to speak
sehen	du siehst, er sieht	to see
empfehlen	du empfiehlst, er empfiehlt	to recommend

• Replace the subjects of the following sentences, making the necessary changes in the verb forms.

1. Sprechen Sie Deutsch? (du, er, ihr)

   (Deutsch: German)

2. Ich sehe es nicht. (er, sie [*they*])
3. Empfehlen Sie das? (du, er)
4. Sie sprechen Deutsch. (er, wir, ich)
5. Warum empfehlen Sie das? (du, er)

6. Sehen Sie es? (du, er)
7. Ich empfehle das nicht. (er, wir)
8. Du sprichst zu schnell. (Sie, er) **(schnell:** fast)
9. Was siehst du da? (er, Sie)
10. Was empfiehlst du? (Sie, er, ihr)

Here are three more verbs whose stems change. But their stems also end in an "s" sound, which means that the verb ending in the *2nd person singular is* -t (not **-st**).

essen *to eat*	vergessen *to forget*	lesen *to read*
ich esse	ich vergesse	ich lese
du ißt	du vergißt	du liest
er ißt	er vergißt	er liest
wir essen	wir vergessen	wir lesen
ihr eßt	ihr vergeßt	ihr lest
sie essen	sie vergessen	sie lesen

▶ Note   Digraph (ß)

Essen and **vergessen** have a **ß** (**digraph s**) rather than an **ss** in their 2nd and 3rd person singular and their 2nd person plural forms. There is, however, no difference in pronunciation. **ss** is used when the verb ending begins with a *vowel* (**-e** or **-en**):

ich verge**ss**e, wir verge**ss**en

ß is used when the verb ending begins with a *consonant* (**-t**):

du vergi**ß**t, er vergi**ß**t, ihr verge**ß**t

● Replace the subjects of the following sentences, making the necessary changes in the verb forms.

1. Was essen Sie da? (du, er, ihr)
2. Ich lese es nicht. (er, wir)
3. Ihr eßt zu schnell. (du, er, Sie)
4. Was lesen Sie heute? (du, er, wir)
5. Sie vergessen alles. (du, er, ihr)

(**alles:** everything)

6. Er ißt zu viel. (Sie, du, ihr)
7. Warum lesen Sie das? (du, wir, er)
8. Wo ißt du heute? (Sie, er, ihr)
9. Was liest du da? (Sie, er)
10. Er vergißt es nicht. (wir, du, ich)
11. Er liest zu viel. (sie [*they*], du, ich)

MIXED DRILLS

a. 1. Sprechen Sie Deutsch? (du, ihr, sie [*she*])
2. Ihr eßt zu schnell. (du, Sie, er)
3. Ich gehe nach Hause. (er, wir)
4. Sehen Sie es? (du, er)
5. Warum lesen Sie das? (du, wir, er)
6. Kennen Sie Frau Lenz? (du)
7. Was siehst du da? (Sie, er)
8. Empfehlen Sie das? (du, er)
9. Wir stehen da drüben. (er, sie [*they*])
10. Du sprichst zu schnell. (Sie, er)

b. 1. Sie vergessen alles. (du, wir, er)
2. Wo ißt du heute? (Sie, er, ihr)
3. Ich lese es nicht. (er, wir)
4. Wo stehen Sie? (er, du)
5. Warum empfehlen Sie das? (du, er)
6. Er vergißt es nicht. (wir, du, ich)
7. Sie sprechen Deutsch. (er, ich)
8. Was lesen Sie heute? (du, wir, er)
9. Er ißt zu viel. (Sie, du, ihr)
10. Wo gehen Sie hin? (du, ihr)

c. 1. Leben sie noch? (er, du)
2. Was empfiehlst du? (Sie, er)
3. Was essen Sie da? (du, ihr, er)

4. Ich sehe es nicht. (sie [they], er)
5. Er liest zu viel. (sie [they], du, ich)

EXPRESS IN GERMAN

a. 1. Do you (Sie) speak German?
2. Do you (du) speak German?
3. He eats too much.
4. They eat too much.
5. Do you (Sie) see it?
6. Does she see it?
7. Where are they going?
8. Where are you (du) going?
9. You (du) forget everything.
10. They forget everything.

b. 1. What do you (Sie) recommend?
2. What does he recommend?
3. I'm not going to read it.
4. He's not going to read it.
5. Do you (du) know Mrs. Lenz?
6. Do you (ihr) know Mrs. Lenz?
7. He speaks too fast.
8. Where are you (du) eating today?
9. I don't recommend that.
10. What are you (du) reading today?

c. 1. He won't forget it.
2. Where is he standing?
3. Why do they recommend that?

4. What's he eating there?
5. You (du) read too much.
6. He's speaking German.
7. What are you (du) drinking?
8. What do you (du) see there?
9. Why are we reading that?
10. He's going home.

d. 1. Do you (du) recommend that?
2. We won't forget it.
3. What's he reading there?
4. I don't see it.
5. He knows Berlin.
6. Where are you (Sie) eating today?
7. You (ihr) forget everything.
8. Do you (du) see it?
9. What are you (du) eating?
10. I don't recommend that.

e. 1. He still lives in America.
2. You (du) speak too fast.
3. Does he speak German?
4. What are you (Sie) reading there?
5. You (du) eat too fast.
6. He's standing over there.

VOCABULARY

alles everything
Amerika America
brauchen to need
da there
da drüben over there
Deutsch German
Deutschland Germany
empfehlen (empfiehlt) to recommend
essen (ißt) to eat
Frau Mrs.
gehen to go

heißen to be called
in in
kennen to know, be familiar with
kosten to cost
leben to live, be alive
lesen (liest) to read
man one, "you"
nach to
noch still
schnell fast
sehen (sieht) to see

sitzen to sit
sprechen (spricht) to speak
stehen to stand
trinken to drink
vergessen (vergißt) to forget
warten to wait
warum why
wer who
wie how
wieviel how much

Lesson 1 Level THREE

A Stem-Vowel Change: a ⟶ ä, au ⟶ äu

A number of verbs having **a** or **au** as their stem vowels take an *umlaut* in the 2nd and 3rd person singular.

fahren *to drive*	schlafen *to sleep*	laufen *to run*
ich fahre	ich schlafe	ich laufe
du fährst	du schläfst	du läufst
er fährt	er schläft	er läuft

The plural forms of these verbs are regular; they do not take an umlaut.

DRILLS

• Replace the subjects of the following sentences with the words in parentheses, making the necessary changes in the verb forms.

1. Wir fahren nach Berlin. (er, ich)
2. Warum laufen Sie weg? (du, ihr, er)
3. Ich schlafe zu viel. (er, Sie, du)
4. Fahren Sie nach Mainz? (du, er)
5. Wo laufen Sie hin? (er, ihr, du)
6. Wann schlafen sie? (du, ihr, er)
7. Du fährst zu schnell. (sie [*they*], er)

• Express in German.

1. He sleeps too much.
2. We're driving to Berlin.
3. Where are you (**du**) running to?
4. When do you (**du**) sleep?
5. He drives too fast.
6. Why are they running away?
7. Are you (**du**) driving to Mainz?
8. You (**Sie**) sleep too much.
9. Why is he running away?
10. You (**du**) drive too fast.
11. When does he sleep?
12. Where are they running to?
13. I'm driving home.
14. You (**du**) sleep too much.

B Imperative Forms

The imperative is the form of the verb used to give commands or make suggestions. German has three forms of the imperative—one each for the **du-**, **ihr-**, and **Sie-**forms of the verb.

1 The basic pattern

Look at the following examples:

du-form	**Komm**	später, Albrecht!
ihr-form	**Kommt**	später, Kinder!
Sie-form	**Kommen Sie**	später, Herr Holschuh!

a. **du**-form

The *verb stem* is used for the **du**-form of the imperative.

> **Komm** später, Albrecht!   (*Come* later, Albrecht.)

b. **ihr**-form

The **ihr**-form of the imperative is identical to the **ihr**-form of the present tense.

> **Kommt** später, Kinder!   (*Come* later, children.)

c. **Sie**-form

The **Sie**-form of the imperative is the same as the present tense question form. The verb comes first and *is immediately followed by the pronoun* **Sie**. (The only difference is in the intonation.)

> **Kommen Sie** später, Herr Holschuh!   (*Come* later, Mr. Holschuh.)

▶ Note   Imperatives are commonly followed by an exclamation mark.

2 Verb stems ending in **-t** or **-d**

du-form	War**te**	hier!
ihr-form	Wartet	hier!
Sie-form	Warten Sie	hier!

The only variation from the basic pattern is that the **du**-form takes an **-e** ending. For example:

> War**te** hier!

3 Verbs with stem-vowel change: **e → i** or **ie**

	vergessen *to forget*		lesen *to read*	
du-form	Vergiß	das nicht!	Lies	langsamer!
ihr-form	Vergeßt	das nicht!	Lest	langsamer!
Sie-form	Vergessen Sie	das nicht!	Lesen Sie	langsamer!

If the stem vowel of the verb shifts from **e** to **i** or **ie**, the **du**-form of the imperative is identical to the changed stem. (Vergiß, Lies)

4 Verbs with stem-vowel change: **a → ä, au → äu**

du-form	Schlaf	gut!	Lauf	schneller!
ihr-form	Schlaft	gut!	Lauft	schneller!
Sie-form	Schlafen Sie	gut!	Laufen Sie	schneller!

(gut: well)

(schneller: faster)

▶ Note   The **du**-form of the imperative does *not* take an umlaut. The imperatives for these verbs thus follow the basic pattern. (Schlaf, Lauf)

5 **sein**: irregular imperative forms

du-form	Sei	vernünftig!
ihr-form	Seid	vernünftig!
Sie-form	Seien Sie	vernünftig!

(vernünftig: reasonable)

6 First person plural imperative: **Gehen wir!** (Let's go.)

The **wir**-form of the imperative is the same as the present tense of the question form: The verb comes first and *is immediately followed by the pronoun* **wir**. (No stem-vowel change is involved.)

Gehen wir!   (Let's go.)
Essen wir zu Hause!   (Let's eat at home.)

Imperative sentences have emphatic stress.

DRILLS

1   Basic pattern

• Supply the suggested imperative forms.

1. (machen)
   _____ es morgen, Hans!
   _____ es morgen! **(ihr-form)**
   _____ es morgen, Herr Schröder!

2. (kaufen)
   _____ es nicht, Herr Ohl!
   _____ es nicht, Konrad!

3. (stehen)

_____ still, Hannes!   (still: still)

_____ still, Kinder!

4. (gehen)

_____ weg, Georg!

_____ weg, Kinder!

5. (kommen)

_____ später, Renate!

_____ später, Kinder!

_____ später, Frau Arndt!

6. (bleiben)

_____ da, Karl!   (bleiben: to stay)

_____ da, Jungens!   (Jungens: boys, you guys)

_____ da, Herr Bischoff!

7. (kommen)

_____ mit, Jungens!

_____ mit, Eva!

_____ mit, Fräulein Markus!

8. (gehen)

_____ nach Hause, Heidi!

2   Verb stems ending in -t

• Supply the suggested imperative forms.

1. (warten)

_____ hier, Herr Heller!

_____ hier, Karl!

2. (arbeiten)

_____ schneller, Jungens!   (schneller: faster)

_____ schneller, Hans!

3   Stem-vowel change: e → i or ie

• Supply the suggested imperative forms.

1. (essen)

_____ langsamer, Kinder!   (langsamer: slower)

_____ langsamer, Hannes!

2. (vergessen)

_____ es nicht, Herr Lenz!

_____ es nicht, Franz!

_____ es nicht!   (**ihr**-form)

3. (sprechen)

_____ langsamer, Dieter!

_____ langsamer, Herr Kafitz!

4. (lesen)

_____ nicht so schnell, Herr Schröder!   (so: so)

_____ nicht so schnell, Hans!

5. (empfehlen)

_____ etwas, Herr Ober!

(**etwas**: something; **Herr Ober**: waiter)

6. (essen)

_____ das nicht, Gustav!

4   Verb stems that take umlauts

• Supply the suggested imperative forms.

1. (fahren)

_____ langsamer, Karl!

_____ langsamer!   (**Sie**-form)

2. (laufen)

_____ schneller!   (**Sie**-form)

_____ schneller, Klaus!

3. (schlafen)

_____ gut!   (**Sie**-form)   (**gut**: good, well)

_____ gut, Kinder!

_____ gut, Helga!

5   sein

• Supply the suggested imperative forms of **sein**.

1. _____ doch nett!   (**Sie**-form)

(**doch**: "aw," as in "Aw, be nice.")

_____ doch nett, Ursel!

_____ doch nett!   (**ihr**-form)

2. _____ still, Hannes!   (still: quiet)

_____ still, Kinder!

_____ still!   (**Sie**-form)

3. _____ vorsichtig! (**ihr**-form)

                       (**vorsichtig:** careful)

   _____ vorsichtig, Dieter!

   _____ vorsichtig! (**Sie**-form)

4. _____ doch nicht so dumm, Karl!

                       (**dumm:** dumb)

   _____ doch nicht so dumm! (**Sie**-form)

   _____ doch nicht so dumm! (**ihr**-form)

5. _____ vernünftig, Inge!

                       (**vernünftig:** reasonable)

6 First person plural imperatives (Let's . . .)

• Supply the suggested imperative forms.

PATTERN   _____ nach Mainz!
              (Let's drive)

            Fahren wir nach Mainz!

1. _____ es später!
   (Let's do)

2. _____ nach Hause!
   (Let's go)

3. _____ es morgen!
   (Let's write)

4. _____ zu Hause!
   (Let's stay)

       (**bleiben:** to stay; **zu Hause:** at home)

5. _____ es jetzt!
   (Let's buy)

6. _____ das nicht!
   (Let's . . . forget)

7. _____ zu Hause!
   (Let's eat)

8. _____ hier!
   (Let's wait)

MIXED DRILLS

• Use the following elements to make complete commands or suggestions.

EXAMPLE   Sprechen / langsamer // Hans!
            Sprich langsamer, Hans!

a. 1. Bleiben / da // Karl!
   2. Stehen / still // Kinder!
   3. Kommen / mit // Fräulein Markus!
   4. Sprechen / langsamer // Dieter!
   5. Essen / das / nicht // Gustav!
   6. Machen / es morgen! (**ihr**-form)
   7. Fahren / langsamer // Karl!
   8. Sein / still! (**Sie**-form)
   9. Arbeiten / schneller // Hans!
  10. Lesen / nicht so schnell // Herr Schröder!

b. 1. Gehen / weg // Kinder!
   2. Schlafen / gut // Helga!
   3. Warten / hier // Herr Heller!
   4. Sein / vorsichtig // Dieter!
   5. Essen / langsamer // Hannes!
   6. Bleiben / da // Jungens!
   7. Kaufen / es nicht // Herr Ohl!
   8. Sein / vorsichtig // Dieter!

   9. Gehen / nach Hause! (**wir**-form)
  10. Laufen / schneller // Klaus!

c. 1. Empfehlen / etwas // Herr Ober!
   2. Kommen / später // Renate!
   3. Arbeiten / schneller // Jungens!
   4. Sein / doch nett! (**Sie**-form)
   5. Vergessen / das nicht // Franz!
   6. Bleiben / zu Hause! (**wir**-form)
   7. Machen / es morgen // Hans!
   8. Sein / still // Kinder!
   9. Laufen / schneller! (**Sie**-form)
  10. Kommen / mit // Eva!

d. 1. Essen / zu Hause! (**wir**-form)
   2. Sein / doch nicht so dumm // Karl!
   3. Fahren / langsamer! (**Sie**-form)
   4. Vergessen / es nicht! (**ihr**-form)
   5. Warten / hier // Karl!

6. Machen / es morgen // Herr Schröder!
7. Schreiben / es jetzt! (**wir**-form)
8. Kommen / mit // Jungens!
9. Lesen / nicht so schnell // Hans!
10. Sein / vorsichtig! (**Sie**-form)

e. 1. Warten / hier! (**wir**-form)
2. Stehen / still // Hannes!
3. Essen / langsamer // Kinder!

4. Sein / vernünftig // Inge!
5. Machen / es später! (**wir**-form)
6. Kommen / später // Frau Arndt!
7. Gehen / weg // Georg!
8. Schlafen / gut! (**Sie**-form)
9. Sein / doch nett // Helga!
10. Sprechen / langsamer // Herr Kafitz!

f. 1. Gehen / nach Hause // Heidi!

EXPRESS IN GERMAN

a. 1. Come later, Renate.
2. Wait here, Mr. Heller.
3. Speak slower, Dieter.
4. Recommend something, waiter.
5. Come along, boys.
6. Be careful, Franz.
7. Let's do it later.
8. Eat slower, Hans.
9. Don't buy it. (**Sie**-form)
10. Work faster, Hans.

b. 1. Sleep well. (**Sie**-form)
2. Be still. (**Sie**-form)
3. Let's go home.
4. Don't eat that, Gustav.
5. Do it tomorrow. (**ihr**-form)
6. Drive slower, Karl.
7. Aw, be nice. (**Sie**-form)
8. Don't forget it, Franz.
9. Go away, children.
10. Let's stay home.

c. 1. Come along, Eva.
2. Run faster. (**Sie**-form)
3. Be reasonable, Inge.

4. Go away, George.
5. Let's eat at home.
6. Work faster, boys.
7. Don't read so fast. (**Sie**-form)
8. Do it tomorrow, Hans.
9. Be careful. (**Sie**-form)
10. Don't read so fast, Hans.

d. 1. Let's wait here.
2. Sleep well, Helga.
3. Eat slower, children.
4. Stay there, Karl.
5. Don't be so stupid. (**Sie**-form)
6. Run faster, Klaus.
7. Stand still, children.
8. Wait here, Karl.
9. Speak slower. (**Sie**-form)
10. Let's buy it now.

e. 1. Don't forget it. (**ihr**-form)
2. Aw, be nice, Ursel.
3. Drive slower. (**Sie**-form)
4. Don't be so stupid, Karl.
5. Go home, Heidi.

VOCABULARY

bleiben to stay
doch aw, come on
dumm dumb, stupid
etwas something
fahren (fährt) to drive
Fräulein Miss
gut good, well
Herr Ober waiter
  (used when addressing him)

Jungens
  boys, you guys
langsamer slower
laufen (läuft) to run
laufen . . . hin
  to run . . . to
schlafen (schläft)
  to sleep
schneller faster

so so
still still, quiet
vernünftig reasonable
vorsichtig careful
warten to wait
zu Hause at home
  (without motion)

Reading I

German Greetings

German doesn't have a one-word equivalent to the American *hello* or *hi*. Instead it uses *good morning* **(guten Morgen)**, *good day* **(guten Tag)** and *good evening* **(guten Abend)** to mean *hello*. *Good day* sounds stuffy in English, but **guten Tag** is perfectly normal in German. In more casual speech one omits the **guten** from these expressions and simply says **Tag, Morgen,** or **Abend.**

Auf Wiedersehen, or simply **Wiedersehen** means *good-bye* in German. When people know each other well they often use a more colloquial version of *good-bye:* **Tschüß.**

KLAUS:
Herr Wagner, das ist meine Freundin, Renate Berger.
HERR WAGNER:
Guten Tag,* Fräulein Berger.
RENATE:
Guten Tag, Herr Wagner.

KLAUS:
Mr. Wagner, this is my friend, Renate Berger.
MR. WAGNER:
Hello, [*lit.:* good day] Miss Berger.
RENATE:
Pleased to meet you, [*lit.:* good day] Mr. Wagner.

* * *

HERR SCHÄFER:
Guten Morgen, Frau Lutz.
FRAU LUTZ:
Guten Morgen, Herr Schäfer. Kaffee wie immer?
HERR SCHÄFER:
Ja, bitte.
FRAU LUTZ:
Gut. Kommt gleich.

MR. SCHÄFER:
Good morning, Mrs. Lutz.
MRS. LUTZ:
Good morning, Mr. Schäfer. Coffee as usual?
MR. SCHÄFER:
Yes, please.
MRS. LUTZ:
Fine. Right away. [*lit.:* coming right away]

* * *

---

* **Guten Tag** is even commonly used in introductions. One simply says **Guten Tag** to the person being introduced rather than the German equivalent of *pleased to meet you,* which is becoming increasingly old-fashioned in Germany.

A: Guten Tag.	A: Hi. [*lit.:* good day]
B: Tag. Wie geht's?	B: Hi. How are you?
A: Danke, gut.	A: Fine, thanks.

* * *

A: Abend.	A: Hi. [*lit.:* evening]
B: Abend. Ist die Arbeit schon fertig?	B: Hi. Is your [*lit.:* the] paper already done?
A: Ja. Trinken wir ein Bier?	A: Yes. Let's have [*lit.:* drink] a beer.
B: Ja. Gehen wir!	B: Sure. Let's go!

* * *

A: Ich bin müde.	A: I'm tired.
B: Ich auch. Schlaf gut.	B: Me too. Sleep well.
A: Du auch. Gute Nacht.	A: You too. Good night.

* * *

A: Gehen Sie jetzt?	A: Are you going now?
B: Ja, auf Wiedersehen.	B: Yes. Good-bye.
A: Wiedersehen.	A: Good-bye.

* * *

A: Gehst du jetzt?	A: Are you going now?
B: Ja, Tschüß.	B: Yeah, bye.
A: Tschüß, bis später.	A: Bye. See you later. [*lit.:* until later]

* * *

A: Entschuldigung. Wo ist Zimmer hundertzehn?	A: Excuse me. Where is room one ten [*lit.:* hundred ten]?
B: Gleich da drüben.	B: Right over there.
A: Ach, danke schön.	A: Oh, thanks.
B: Bitte schön.	B: You're welcome.

Stehimbiß und Straßenverkauf

(Snack Bars and Street Vending)

It's much easier to eat in the street in Germany than it is here. In fact, it's hard to find a major street where there isn't some sort of stand or shop selling food to passers-by. There are simple pretzel stands that sell nothing but pretzels. There are ice cream vendors in the summer and chestnut vendors in the winter. There are stand-up snack bars **(Stehimbisse)** where you can get various kinds of hot sausages, French fries, Coke, beer—and nowadays even hamburgers. And there are short-order restaurants with street-side windows **(Straßenverkauf)** for take-home orders. In this case, home may be no farther than the next park bench.

Ordering food at a **Stehimbiß** is much less complicated than it is in a restaurant. First of all, the menu is very simple and visible. More important, there aren't the more compli-

cated formulas you have to use with a waiter or waitress, which means that you don't have to be nervous about what to say—or about what somebody might say to you. You just name your food and say **bitte** (*please*). Best of all, there is no tipping at a **Stehimbiß**, which means you can put off rapid calculation until you are a little more at home with German numbers and prices.

The following dialogues will show you just how easy it all is. First use them to practice your pronunciation and intonation. Then cover up the German and reproduce the dialogues, using the English equivalents as cues.

A: Mensch, ich habe Hunger.   A: Man, I'm hungry.
B: Da ist ein* Stehimbiß.   B: There's a snack bar.
A: Ich esse eine* Wurst mit Brot.   A: I'm going to have [*lit.*: eat] a sausage and bread.

B: Ich trinke nur ein Bier.   B: I'll just have a beer.

*   *   *

***Ein** and **eine** both mean *a* (as in *a beer*). It's the noun that determines which form is used. You just have to memorize that it's **eine Wurst,** but **ein Bier.** The following nouns are used in this set of dialogues:

ein Stehimbiß	eine Wurst (Bratwurst)	eine Cola
ein Bier	eine Mark	eine Brezel
ein Eis		

SIE:
    Einmal Pommes frites, bitte.*
VERKÄUFER:
    So, bitte schön.*
SIE:
    Was macht das?
VERKÄUFER:
    Eine Mark, bitte.

YOU:
    An order of French fries, please.
VENDOR:
    There you are.
YOU:
    How much is that?
VENDOR:
    One mark, please.

*   *   *

A: Ißt du ein Eis?

B: Ja, gern.

A: Zweimal† Erdbeereis, bitte.
VERKÄUFER:
    Groß oder klein?
A: Einmal groß, einmal klein. Wieviel
    macht das, bitte?
VERKÄUFER:
    Zwei Mark.

A: How about some [lit.: Are you
    going to eat an] ice cream?
B: Yeah, fine.

A: Two strawberry ice creams, please.
VENDOR:
    Large or small?
A: One large, one small. How
    much is that?
VENDOR:
    Two marks.

*   *   *

A: Hast du Durst?
B: Und wie! Trinken wir eine
    Cola!

A: Zwei Cola, bitte.
VERKÄUFER:
    Bitte schön, zwei Cola. Das
    macht drei Mark zusammen.
    (And if you give him a five
    mark piece, he'll say:)
    Und zwei Mark zurück.

A: Are you thirsty?
B: And how! Let's have [lit.:
    drink] a Coke.

A: Two Cokes, please.
VENDOR:
    There you are, two Cokes.
    That's three marks together.

    And two marks back.

*   *   *

SIE:
    Eine Brezel, bitte.
VERKÄUFER:
    Ach, zehn Mark! Haben Sie
    es nicht kleiner?
SIE:
    Nein, leider nicht.

YOU:
    A pretzel please.
VENDOR:
    Oh, ten marks! Don't you have
    anything [lit.: it] smaller?
YOU:
    No, I'm sorry.

*   *   *

---

*Bitte has several meanings. It means *please* (**Einmal Pommes frites, bitte**). It means *There you are*. (**So, bitte schön**). And it means *You're welcome*. The word **schön** is often added to **bitte** when it means *There you are* or *You're welcome*.

†In this context **zweimal** means *two orders of* and **einmal** means *one order of*.

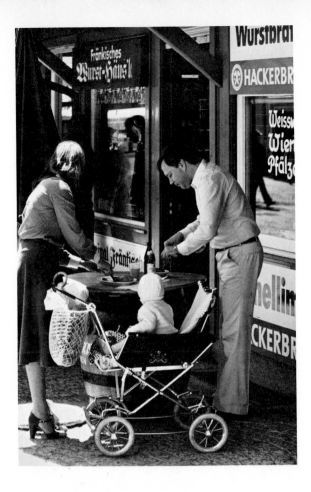

A: Ich habe Hunger. Ich esse
eine Bratwurst.

B: Ich auch.

A: Zweimal Bratwurst, bitte.

VERKÄUFER:
Mit Senf?

A: Ja, bitte. Und ein Bier dazu.

B: Ich trinke auch ein Bier.

A: Was macht das, bitte?

VERKÄUFER:
Zusammen?

A: Ja, bitte.

VERKÄUFER:
Zweimal Bratwurst macht
vier Mark, und zwei Bier
drei Mark. Also sieben
Mark zusammen.

A: I'm hungry. I'm going to have
[*lit.*: eat] a bratwurst.

B: Me too.

A: Two bratwursts, please.

VENDOR:
With mustard?

A: Yes, please. And a beer along with it.

B: I'll have [*lit.*: drink] a beer, too.

A: How much is that?

VENDOR:
Together?

A: Yes, please.

VENDOR:
Two orders of bratwurst are
four marks, and two beers are
three marks. Seven marks all
together, then.

Lesson 2   Level ONE

A Subjects and Direct Objects

1 Subject: nominative case

In Lesson 1 you practiced using the personal pronouns as the *subjects* of simple statements and questions:

Er kommt heute.   (*He* is coming today.)
Warum läufst du weg?   (Why are *you* running away?)

When you used personal pronouns as subjects, you were using special "subject forms" of the pronouns. These special forms are said to be in the *nominative case*. (Nominative case is a grammatical label for the subject forms of words.)

2 Direct object: accusative case

Personal pronouns can also be used as sentence complements. One kind of complement answers the question, "Who (what) is it being done to?" This sort of complement is called a *direct object*.

Subject	Verb	Direct Object	
I	see	*him.*	(Who is being seen? I see *him.*)
I	see	*it.*	(What is being seen? I see *it.*)

Like English, German has special forms of the personal pronoun that are used when the pronoun is a direct object. These forms are said to be in the *accusative case*.

The following table gives you the personal pronouns in their nominative (subject) and accusative (direct object) forms:

44

PERSONAL PRONOUNS									
	Singular					*Plural*			
NOM.	ich	du	er	sie	es	wir	ihr	sie / Sie	
ACC.	mich	dich	ihn	sie	es	uns	euch	sie / Sie	
NOM.	I	you	he	she	it	we	you	they / you	
ACC.	me	you	him	her	it	us	you	them / you	

DRILLS

1 Forms of address: accusative case

NOM.	du	ihr	Sie
ACC.	dich	euch	Sie

● Supply the appropriate *accusative* form of the personal pronoun.

a. 1. Ich verstehe _____, Hans.
   (you)
   (**verstehen:** to understand)

2. Ich verstehe _____, Herr Kunz.
   (you)

3. Ich verstehe _____, Inge und Peter.
   (you)

4. Ich verstehe _____, Liebling.
   (you)

b. 1. Sie suchen _____, Dieter.
   (you)
   (**suchen:** to look for, hunt for)

2. Sie suchen _____, Kinder.
   (you)

3. Sie suchen _____, Fräulein Sutter.
   (you)

4. Sie suchen _____, Monika.
   (you)

c. 1. Er fragt _____, Frau Schmidt.
   (you)
   (**fragen:** to ask)

2. Er fragt _____, Renate.
   (you)

3. Er fragt _____, Kinder.
   (you)

4. Er fragt _____, Herr Lenz.
   (you)

2 First person singular and plural: accusative case

NOM.	ich	wir
ACC.	mich	uns

● Supply the appropriate *accusative* form of the personal pronoun.

a. 1. Fragst du _____?
   (me)

   2. Fragst du _____?
   (us)

b. 1. Sucht er _____?
   (us)

   2. Sucht er _____?
   (me)

c. 1. Verstehen Sie _____?
   (us)

   2. Verstehen Sie _____?
   (me)

3 Third person singular and plural: accusative case

	Singular			Plural
NOM.	er	es	sie	sie
ACC.	ihn	es	sie	sie

● Supply the appropriate *accusative* form of the personal pronoun.

a. 1. Ich sehe _____ nicht.
   (him)

   2. Ich sehe _____ nicht.
   (her)

   3. Ich sehe _____ nicht.
   (it)

   4. Ich sehe _____ nicht.
   (them)

b. 1. Wir suchen _____.
   (her)

   2. Wir suchen _____.
   (it)

   3. Wir suchen _____.
   (them)

   4. Wir suchen _____.
   (him)

c. 1. Kennst du _____?
   (them)

   2. Kennst du _____?
   (him)

   3. Kennst du _____?
   (her)

   4. Kennst du _____?
   (it)

d. 1. Fragen Sie _____!
   (her)

   2. Fragen Sie _____!
   (him)

   3. Fragen Sie _____!
   (them)

e. 1. Ich verstehe _____ nicht.
   (it)

   2. Ich verstehe _____ nicht.
   (them)

   3. Ich verstehe _____ nicht.
   (him)

   4. Ich verstehe _____ nicht.
   (her)

4 Mixed drill: all personal pronouns

● Supply the appropriate *accusative* form of the personal pronoun.

1. Sie suchen _____, Dieter.
   (you)

   Sie suchen _____, Herr Kunz.
   (you)

   Sie suchen _____.
   (him)

   Sie suchen _____.
   (me)

2. Er sucht _____.
   (her)

   Er sucht _____, Kinder.
      (you)

   Er sucht _____.
      (us)

   Er sucht _____.
      (them)

   Er sucht _____.
      (it)

3. Ich verstehe _____, Karl.
      (you)

   Ich verstehe _____.
      (him)

   Ich verstehe _____, Herr Lenz.
      (you)

4. Verstehen Sie _____?
      (me)

   Verstehen Sie _____?
      (us)

   Verstehen Sie _____?
      (her)

5. Ich verstehe _____ nicht.
      (them)

   Ich verstehe _____ nicht.
      (it)

   Ich verstehe _____ nicht, Kinder.
      (you)

6. Er kennt _____ nicht.
      (them)

   Er kennt _____ nicht.
      (us)

7. Kennst du _____?
      (her)

   Kennst du _____?
      (it)

8. Sie kennen _____ nicht, Dieter.
      (you)

   Sie kennen _____ nicht.
      (him)

9. Er fragt _____ nicht, Paul.
      (you)

   Er fragt _____ nicht, Herr Kunz.
      (you)

10. Fragst du _____?
      (her)

   Fragst du _____?
      (me)

11. Fragen Sie _____!
      (them)

   Fragen Sie _____!
      (him)

12. Ich sehe _____ nicht.
      (her)

   Ich sehe _____ nicht.
      (them)

13. Siehst du _____?
      (us)

   Siehst du _____?
      (him)

14. Er sieht _____ nicht, Herr Braun.
      (you)

   Er sieht _____ nicht.
      (it)

MIXED DRILLS

● Supply the appropriate *accusative* form of the personal pronoun.

a. 1. Ich verstehe _____ nicht.
      (it)

  2. Sucht er _____?
     (us)

  3. Siehst du _____?
     (him)

  4. Er kennt _____ nicht.
     (me)

  5. Sie suchen _____, Dieter.
     (you)

  6. Fragen Sie _____!
     (them)

  7. Verstehen Sie _____?
     (me)

  8. Er sieht _____ nicht, Herr Lenz.
     (you)

  9. Er sucht _____, Kinder.
     (you)

  10. Kennst du _____?
     (him)

b. 1. Fragen Sie _____!
     (her)

  2. Er kennt _____ nicht.
     (us)

3. Ich verstehe _____, Liebling.
   (you)

4. Wir suchen _____.
   (it)

5. Siehst du _____?
   (her)

6. Fragen Sie _____?
   (me)

7. Er sucht _____, Fräulein Sutter.
   (you)

8. Ich sehe _____ nicht.
   (him)

9. Kennst du _____?
   (them)

10. Er versteht _____ nicht, Paul.
    (you)

c. 1. Sie sehen _____ nicht.
      (us)

2. Ich suche _____.
   (them)

● Express in German.

a. 1. Do you (du) know them?
   2. I don't understand it.
   3. They're looking for you, Dieter.
   4. Are you (Sie) asking me?
   5. They don't see us.
   6. Do you (Sie) know him?
   7. He's looking for you, Miss Sutter.
   8. Do you (du) understand me?
   9. Ask her.
   10. Do you (du) see him?

b. 1. He doesn't know us.
   2. I'm looking for them.

3. He doesn't understand you, Paul.
4. He doesn't see you, Mr. Lenz.
5. We're looking for it.
6. Ask them.
7. I don't see him.
8. He doesn't know me.
9. Is he looking for us?
10. Do you (Sie) see her?

c. 1. I understand you, darling.
   2. He's looking for you, children.

B German Nouns: Definite and Indefinite Articles

As you have seen before, all German nouns are capitalized.

> Wann hast du **Z**eit?
> Ich habe **H**unger.
> Er geht nach **H**ause.

Like English, German nouns can have a *definite article* (*the* suit; **der** Anzug) and an *indefinite article* (*a* suit; **ein** Anzug). The meaning of these terms is clear. If someone says

> "I'll take *the* suit."

he has a specific (or *definite*) suit in mind (and uses the *definite* article). On the other hand, if someone says

> "I want to buy *a* suit."

he has *not* decided on a specific suit (and uses the *indefinite* article).

1 Nominative and accusative cases

When we speak of the *case* of definite or indefinite articles, we are talking about grammatical labels that make it easier to distinguish between subjects and objects.

Look at the following examples:

Subject	Direct Object
Der **Anzug** kostet zu viel.	Ich nehme **den Anzug.**
(The suit costs too much.)	(I'll take the suit.)

As you see, German can show whether a noun is being used as a *subject* or as a *direct object* by using different forms of the definite article (**der** Anzug: subject; **den** Anzug: direct object). As with personal pronouns:

> the case used for *subjects* is called *nominative*
> the case used for *direct objects* is called *accusative*

2 Gender

Both English and German have three genders: *masculine, feminine,* and *neuter.*

a. English: natural gender

English uses natural gender. Natural gender means simply this:

1. The *masculine* and *feminine* genders are reserved for people and some animals.

the man	he
the woman	she

2. All other English nouns are *neuter* in gender. These may range from things or concrete objects (tables, cars, etc.) to theoretical abstractions or states of being (love, motherhood, etc.).

the suit	*it*
the shirt	*it*
the tie	*it*

▶ Note   In English, it is only the personal pronouns (he, she, and it) that show gender. The definite and indefinite articles (the, a) are used with all nouns, regardless of their gender.

b. German: grammatical gender

In German, even concrete objects (as well as abstractions) can be masculine and feminine, as well as neuter, in gender. Look at the following examples:

Gender	Definite Article + Noun		Pronoun
MASC.	**der**	Anzug	**er**
NEUT.	**das**	Hemd	**es**
FEM.	**die**	Krawatte	**sie**

(*Lit.:*   the suit: he
the shirt: it
the tie: she)

As you see, gender affects

1. The form of the article

Masculine	der
Neuter	das
Feminine	die

2. The personal pronoun which can replace the noun

der Anzug er

▶ Note   In German, you should learn *the gender of a noun at the same time as you learn the noun.* Otherwise the noun itself isn't particularly useful. For example, if you are given the words **Anzug** (suit) and **groß** (big), you still can't form the sentence:

The suit is too big.

To do so, you need to know the gender of **Anzug,** since this will determine the German equivalent of the English word "the." Knowing that **Anzug** is *masculine,* you can form the sentence:

Der Anzug ist zu groß.

3 Table of definite and indefinite articles

As you have seen, German has three genders (masculine, feminine, and neuter), each of which has nominative and accusative forms. Theoretically, there could be six different forms for both the definite and the indefinite article. Mercifully, there are some duplications:

DEFINITE ARTICLES					
	Masculine		*Neuter*		*Feminine*
NOM.	**der** Anzug	**(er)**	**das** Hemd **(es)**		**die** Krawatte **(sie)**
ACC.	**den** Anzug	**(ihn)**	**das** Hemd **(es)**		**die** Krawatte **(sie)**

INDEFINITE ARTICLES					
	Masculine		*Neuter*		*Feminine*
NOM.	**ein** Anzug	**(er)**	**ein** Hemd **(es)**		**eine** Krawatte **(sie)**
ACC.	**einen** Anzug	**(ihn)**	**ein** Hemd **(es)**		**eine** Krawatte **(sie)**

(**der Anzug:** suit)   (**das Hemd:** shirt)   (**die Krawatte:** tie)

If a personal pronoun is substituted for a noun, it must "agree" with the noun it replaces. That is, it will reflect the same *gender* and *case*:

MASCULINE, NOMINATIVE	Wo ist **der** Anzug?	(Where is the suit?)
	Wo ist **er**?	(Where is it?)
MASCULINE, ACCUSATIVE	Ich sehe **den** Anzug nicht.	(I don't see the suit.)
	Ich sehe **ihn** nicht.	(I don't see it.)

DRILLS

1 Definite article: nominative and accusative cases

	Masc.	Neut.	Fem.
NOM.	der	das	die
ACC.	den	das	die

• Supply the appropriate *accusative* form of the definite article.

PATTERN   Wo ist der Anzug?   Ich sehe <u>den</u> Anzug nicht.   (der Anzug: suit)

1. Wo ist der Hut?	Ich sehe _____ Hut nicht.	(der Hut: hat)
2. Wo ist die Jacke?	Ich sehe _____ Jacke nicht.	(die Jacke: sports coat)
3. Wo ist das Hemd?	Ich sehe _____ Hemd nicht.	(das Hemd: shirt)
4. Wo ist die Frau?	Ich sehe _____ Frau nicht.	(die Frau: woman)
5. Wo ist der Mann?	Ich sehe _____ Mann nicht.	(der Mann: man)
6. Wo ist das Haus?	Ich sehe _____ Haus nicht.	(das Haus: house)
7. Wo ist die Hose?	Ich sehe _____ Hose nicht.	(die Hose: pants)*
8. Wo ist der Mantel?	Ich sehe _____ Mantel nicht.	(der Mantel: coat)
9. Wo ist das Kleid?	Ich sehe _____ Kleid nicht.	(das Kleid: dress)
10. Wo ist die Krawatte?	Ich sehe _____ Krawatte nicht.	(die Krawatte: tie)

• Supply the appropriate *nominative* form of the definite article.

PATTERN   Ich sehe den Mann nicht.   Wo ist <u>der</u> Mann?

1. Ich sehe den Anzug nicht.	Wo ist _____ Anzug?
2. Ich sehe die Jacke nicht.	Wo ist _____ Jacke?
3. Ich sehe das Haus nicht.	Wo ist _____ Haus?
4. Ich sehe den Mantel nicht.	Wo ist _____ Mantel?
5. Ich sehe die Krawatte nicht.	Wo ist _____ Krawatte?
6. Ich sehe das Hemd nicht.	Wo ist _____ Hemd?
7. Ich sehe den Hut nicht.	Wo ist _____ Hut?
8. Ich sehe die Hose nicht.	Wo ist _____ Hose?
9. Ich sehe das Kleid nicht.	Wo ist _____ Kleid?
10. Ich sehe die Frau nicht.	Wo ist _____ Frau?

---

*die Hose (pants, pair of pants) is singular in German.   Contrast: GERMAN   Wo **ist** die Hose?
                                                                    ENGLISH   Where *are* the pants?

• Supply the appropriate form of the definite article. This drill will acquaint you with the environments or surroundings in which subjects and direct objects commonly occur.

Subjects: nominative case	Objects: accusative case
1. Wo ist _____ Haus?	Ich sehe _____ Haus nicht.
2. Was kostet _____ Mantel?	Ich kaufe _____ Mantel.
3. Da ist _____ Jacke.	Brauchen Sie _____ Jacke?
4. Wo ist _____ Mann?	Siehst du _____ Mann?
5. Hier ist _____ Kleid.	Suchen Sie _____ Kleid?
6. Was kostet _____ Hose?	Ich kaufe _____ Hose.
7. Wo ist _____ Hut?	Hast du _____ Hut?
8. Wo ist _____ Hemd?	Ich habe _____ Hemd.
9. _____ Krawatte ist hübsch.	Kaufen Sie _____ Krawatte?
10. _____ Haus kostet zu viel.	Kauf _____ Haus nicht!
11. _____ Anzug ist zu klein.	Ich kaufe _____ Anzug nicht.

(**hubsch:** pretty)
(**zu viel:** too much)
(**zu klein:** too small)

• Mixed drill: supply the appropriate form of the definite article.

1. Wo ist _____ Hut?
2. Kaufen Sie _____ Krawatte?
3. _____ Haus kostet zu viel.
4. Siehst du _____ Mann?
5. Wo ist _____ Haus?
6. Brauchen Sie _____ Jacke?
7. _____ Anzug ist zu klein.
8. Suchst du _____ Kleid?
9. Ich kaufe _____ Mantel.
10. Da ist _____ Jacke.
11. Wo ist _____ Hemd?
12. Hast du _____ Hut?
13. Kauf _____ Haus nicht!

14. Was kostet _____ Hose?
15. _____ Krawatte ist hübsch.
16. Ich kaufe _____ Anzug nicht.
17. Hier ist _____ Kleid.
18. Wo ist _____ Mann?
19. Ich habe _____ Hemd.
20. Ich kaufe _____ Hose.
21. Was kostet _____ Mantel?
22. Siehst du _____ Haus?

• Express in German.

1. I'm not going to buy the suit.
2. The tie is pretty.
3. Where is the house?
4. What's the coat cost?
5. The house costs too much.
6. Are you going to buy the tie?
7. Do you see the man?
8. Where is the shirt?
9. What do the pants cost? (*singular in German*)
10. The suit's too small.
11. Don't buy the house.

12. I'm going to buy the pants.
13. Do you have the hat?
14. Here's the dress.
15. I'll buy the coat.
16. There's the sports coat.
17. Do you see the house?
18. Where's the man?
19. Do you need the sports coat?

2   Indefinite article: nominative and accusative cases

	Masc.	*Neut.*	*Fem.*
NOM.	ein	ein	eine
ACC.	einen	ein	eine

• Supply the appropriate *accusative* form of the indefinite article.

PATTERN   Hier ist ein Anzug.   Ich brauche <u>einen</u> Anzug.

1. Hier ist ein Hemd.   Ich brauche _____ Hemd.
2. Hier ist eine Hose.   Ich brauche _____ Hose.
3. Hier ist ein Mantel.   Ich brauche _____ Mantel.
4. Hier ist eine Jacke.   Ich brauche _____ Jacke.
5. Hier ist ein Hut.   Ich brauche _____ Hut.
6. Hier ist ein Kleid.   Ich brauche _____ Kleid.
7. Hier ist eine Krawatte.   Ich brauche _____ Krawatte.
8. Hier ist ein Anzug.   Ich brauche _____ Anzug.
9. Da ist eine Frau.   Ich sehe _____ Frau.
10. Da ist ein Haus.   Ich sehe _____ Haus.
11. Da ist ein Mann.   Ich sehe _____ Mann.

• Supply the appropriate *nominative* form of the indefinite article.

PATTERN   Ich brauche eine Jacke.   Hier ist <u>eine</u> Jacke.

1. Ich brauche einen Hut.   Hier ist _____ Hut.
2. Ich brauche ein Hemd.   Hier ist _____ Hemd.
3. Ich brauche eine Hose.   Hier ist _____ Hose.
4. Ich brauche einen Mantel.   Hier ist _____ Mantel.
5. Ich brauche ein Kleid.   Hier ist _____ Kleid.
6. Ich brauche eine Krawatte.   Hier ist _____ Krawatte.
7. Ich brauche einen Anzug.   Hier ist _____ Anzug.
8. Ich brauche eine Jacke.   Hier ist _____ Jacke.
9. Ich sehe einen Mann.   Da ist _____ Mann.
10. Ich sehe ein Haus.   Da ist _____ Haus.
11. Ich sehe eine Frau.   Da ist _____ Frau.

• Supply the appropriate form of the indefinite article.

Subjects: nominative case

1. Hier ist _____ Kleid.
2. Da ist _____ Mantel.
3. Was kostet _____ Jacke?
4. Da ist _____ Mann.
5. Wo ist _____ Krawatte?

Objects: accusative case

Suchst du _____ Kleid?
Brauchen Sie _____ Mantel?
Ich brauche _____ Jacke.
Ich sehe _____ Mann.
Ich brauche _____ Krawatte.

Objects: accusative case

6. Suchen Sie _____ Haus?
7. Ich sehe _____ Frau.
8. Ich suche _____ Anzug.
9. Kaufst du _____ Hose?
10. Suchen Sie _____ Hut?
11. Ich brauche _____ Hemd.

Subjects: nominative case

Nein, _____ Haus kostet zu viel.
Da ist _____ Frau.
Da ist _____ Anzug.
Was kostet _____ Hose?
Da ist _____ Hut.
Wo ist _____ Hemd?

• Mixed drill: supply the appropriate form of the indefinite article.

1. Brauchen Sie _____ Mantel?
2. Da ist _____ Frau.
3. Was kostet _____ Jacke?
4. Ich suche _____ Anzug.
5. Hier ist _____ Kleid.

6. Ich brauche _____ Krawatte.
7. Da ist _____ Mantel.
8. Suchen Sie _____ Haus?
9. Ich sehe _____ Mann.
10. Da ist _____ Hut.

11. Ich brauche _____ Hemd.
12. Wo ist _____ Krawatte?
13. Suchst du _____ Kleid?
14. Suchen Sie _____ Hut?
15. Nein, _____ Haus kostet zu viel.

16. Kaufst du _____ Hose?
17. Ich sehe _____ Frau.
18. Da ist _____ Anzug.
19. Ich brauche _____ Jacke.
20. Da ist _____ Mann.

• Express in German.

1. Do you need a coat?
2. Are you looking for a dress?
3. I need a tie.
4. There's a suit.
5. Here's a dress.
6. I need a sports coat.
7. I'm looking for a suit.
8. Where's a tie?
9. No. A house costs too much.

10. Are you looking for a hat?
11. Are you going to buy a pair of pants?
    (*singular in German*)
12. There's a coat.
13. Are you looking for a house?
14. What's a sports coat cost?
15. I need a shirt.
16. There's a hat.

3 Nominative patterns

• Supply the appropriate indefinite article.

Definite Article	→	*Indefinite Article*
der	→	ein
das	→	ein
die	→	eine

PATTERN Da ist der Mann.   Da ist **ein** Mann.

1. Da ist die Frau.   Da ist _____ Frau.
2. Da ist das Kleid.   Da ist _____ Kleid.
3. Wo ist der Mantel?   Wo ist _____ Mantel?
4. Wo ist die Krawatte?   Wo ist _____ Krawatte?
5. Hier ist das Hemd.   Hier ist _____ Hemd.
6. Hier ist der Hut.   Hier ist _____ Hut.
7. Hier ist die Jacke.   Hier ist _____ Jacke.
8. Was kostet der Anzug?   Was kostet _____ Anzug?
9. Was kostet die Hose?   Was kostet _____ Hose?
10. Das Haus kostet zu viel. _____ Haus kostet zu viel.
11. Der Mantel kostet zu viel. _____ Mantel kostet zu viel.

• Supply the appropriate personal pronoun.

	Noun	→	*Pronoun*
MASC.	der Anzug	→	er
NEUT.	das Hemd	→	es
FEM.	die Krawatte	→	sie

PATTERN Da ist der Anzug.   Da ist **er**.

1. Da ist das Kleid.   Da ist _____ .
2. Da ist die Frau.   Da ist _____ .

3. Da ist der Mann.   Da ist _____.
4. Wo ist die Krawatte?   Wo ist _____?
5. Wo ist der Mantel?   Wo ist _____?
6. Hier ist das Hemd.   Hier ist _____.
7. Hier ist die Jacke.   Hier ist _____.
8. Hier ist der Hut.   Hier ist _____.
9. Was kostet die Hose?   Was kostet _____?
10. Was kostet der Anzug?   Was kostet _____?
11. Das Haus kostet zu viel.   _____ kostet zu viel.
12. Der Mantel kostet zu viel.   _____ kostet zu viel.

- Supply the appropriate definite article and personal pronoun.

	Indefinite Article →	Definite Article →	Personal Pronoun
MASC.	ein Anzug →	der Anzug →	er
NEUT.	ein Hemd →	das Hemd →	es
FEM.	eine Hose →	die Hose →	sie

PATTERN   Da ist ein Anzug.   Da ist <u>der</u> Anzug.   Da ist <u>er</u>.

1. Da ist ein Kleid.   Da ist _____ Kleid.   Da ist _____.
2. Da ist ein Mann.   Da ist _____ Mann.   Da ist _____.
3. Da ist eine Frau.   Da ist _____ Frau.   Da ist _____.
4. Wo ist ein Mantel?   Wo ist _____ Mantel?   Wo ist _____?
5. Wo ist eine Krawatte?   Wo ist _____ Krawatte?   Wo ist _____?
6. Hier ist ein Hut.   Hier ist _____ Hut.   Hier ist _____.
7. Hier ist ein Hemd.   Hier ist _____ Hemd.   Hier ist _____.
8. Hier ist eine Jacke.   Hier ist _____ Jacke.   Hier ist _____.
9. Was kostet ein Anzug?   Was kostet _____ Anzug?   Was kostet _____?
10. Was kostet eine Hose?   Was kostet _____ Hose?   Was kostet _____?
11. Ein Mantel kostet zu viel.   _____ Mantel kostet zu viel.   _____ kostet zu viel.
12. Ein Haus kostet zu viel.   _____ Haus kostet zu viel.   _____ kostet zu viel.

- Express the following nominative patterns in German.

1. There's a suit.
   There's the suit.
   There it is.
2. There's a woman.
   There's the woman.
   There she is.
3. Here's a shirt.
   Here's the shirt.
   Here it is.
4. Here's a hat.
   Here's the hat.
   Here it is.
5. Where's a tie?
   Where's the tie?
   Where is it?
6. There's a dress.
   There's the dress.
   There it is.

7. What's a suit cost?
   What's the suit cost?
   What does it cost?
8. A house costs too much.
   The house costs too much.
   It costs too much.
9. There's a man.
   There's the man.
   There he is.
10. Where's a coat?
   Where's the coat?
   Where is it?
11. Here's a sports coat.
   Here's the sports coat.
   Here it is.
12. What does a pair of pants cost?
   What do the pants cost?
   What do they (*lit.:* does it) cost?

4 Accusative patterns

• Supply the appropriate indefinite article.

	Definite Article	➔	Indefinite Article
MASC.	den	➔	einen
NEUT.	das	➔	ein
FEM.	die	➔	eine

PATTERN   Ich brauche den Anzug.   Ich brauche **einen** Anzug.

1. Ich brauche das Kleid.   Ich brauche _____ Kleid.
2. Ich brauche die Jacke.   Ich brauche _____ Jacke.
3. Kaufen Sie das Hemd?   Kaufen Sie _____ Hemd?
4. Kaufen Sie die Hose?   Kaufen Sie _____ Hose?
5. Ich suche den Mantel.   Ich suche _____ Mantel.
6. Ich suche das Haus.   Ich suche _____ Haus.
7. Hast du die Krawatte?   Hast du _____ Krawatte?
8. Hast du den Hut?   Hast du _____ Hut?
9. Ich sehe die Frau.   Ich sehe _____ Frau.
10. Ich sehe den Mann.   Ich sehe _____ Mann.

• Supply the appropriate personal pronoun.

	Noun	➔	Pronoun
MASC.	den Anzug	➔	ihn
NEUT.	das Hemd	➔	es
FEM.	die Krawatte	➔	sie

PATTERN   Ich brauche den Anzug.   Ich brauche **ihn**.

1. Ich brauche die Jacke.   Ich brauche _____.
2. Ich brauche das Kleid.   Ich brauche _____.
3. Hast du den Hut?   Hast du _____?
4. Hast du die Krawatte?   Hast du _____?
5. Ich suche das Haus.   Ich suche _____.
6. Ich suche den Mantel.   Ich suche _____.
7. Ich sehe die Frau.   Ich sehe _____.
8. Ich sehe den Mann.   Ich sehe _____.
9. Kaufen Sie das Hemd?   Kaufen Sie _____?
10. Kaufen Sie die Hose?   Kaufen Sie _____?

• Supply the appropriate definite article and personal pronoun.

	Indefinite Article	➔	Definite Article	➔	Personal Pronoun
MASC.	einen Anzug	➔	den Anzug	➔	ihn
NEUT.	ein Hemd	➔	das Hemd	➔	es
FEM.	eine Krawatte	➔	die Krawatte	➔	sie

PATTERN   Ich brauche einen Anzug.   Ich brauche <u>den</u> Anzug.   Ich brauche <u>ihn</u>.

1. Ich brauche ein Kleid.   Ich brauche _____ Kleid.   Ich brauche _____.
2. Ich brauche eine Jacke.   Ich brauche _____ Jacke.   Ich brauche _____.
3. Ich sehe einen Mann.   Ich sehe _____ Mann.   Ich sehe _____.
4. Ich sehe eine Frau.   Ich sehe _____ Frau.   Ich sehe _____.
5. Kaufen Sie ein Hemd?   Kaufen Sie _____ Hemd?   Kaufen Sie _____?
6. Kaufen Sie eine Hose?   Kaufen Sie _____ Hose?   Kaufen Sie _____?
7. Ich suche ein Haus.   Ich suche _____ Haus.   Ich suche _____.
8. Ich suche einen Mantel.   Ich suche _____ Mantel.   Ich suche _____.
9. Hast du eine Krawatte?   Hast du _____ Krawatte?   Hast du _____?
10. Hast du einen Hut?   Hast du _____ Hut?   Hast du _____?

- Express the following accusative patterns in German.

1. I need a dress.
   I need the dress.
   I need it.
2. I need a suit.
   I need the suit.
   I need it.
3. Do you have a tie?
   Do you have the tie?
   Do you have it?
4. Are you going to buy a shirt?
   Are you going to buy the shirt?
   Are you going to buy it?
5. I'm looking for a coat.
   I'm looking for the coat.
   I'm looking for it.
6. I see a woman.
   I see the woman.
   I see her.

7. Do you have a hat?
   Do you have the hat?
   Do you have it?
8. I need a sports coat.
   I need the sports coat.
   I need it.
9. I'm looking for a house.
   I'm looking for the house.
   I'm looking for it.
10. I see a man.
    I see the man.
    I see him.
11. Are you going to buy a pair of pants?
    (*singular in German*)
    Are you going to buy the pants?
    Are you going to buy them? (*Lit.: it*)

MIXED DRILLS

- Supply the German article or personal pronoun suggested by the English cues.

EXAMPLE   1. (a) Ich kaufe _____ Anzug nicht.   (b) Ich kaufe _____ nicht.
                           (the)   (it)

Ich kaufe **den** Anzug nicht.   Ich kaufe **ihn** nicht.

- When there are two sentences, (a) and (b), sentence (b) will require the personal pronoun that agrees with the noun used in sentence (a).

EXAMPLE   Ich kaufe **den** Anzug nicht.   (**den** is *masculine accusative*)
           Ich kaufe **ihn** nicht.   (**ihn** is *masculine accusative*)

a. 1. (a) _____ Anzug ist zu klein.   2. (a) Sehen Sie _____ Haus?
              (The)   (the)

   (b) _____ ist zu klein.   (b) Sehen Sie _____?
          (It)   (it)

3. Ich brauche _____ Jacke.
   (a)

4. Hier ist _____ Mantel.
   (a)

5. (a) _____ Jacke kostet zu viel.
   (The)

   (b) _____ kostet zu viel.
   (It)

6. Haben Sie _____ Hut?
   (a)

7. (a) Kaufen Sie _____ Hemd?
   (the)

   (b) Kaufen Sie _____?
   (it)

8. Hier ist _____ Krawatte.
   (a)

9. Ich brauche _____ Kleid.
   (a)

10. (a) Da ist _____ Mann.
    (the)

    (b) Da ist _____.
    (he)

b. 1. (a) Sehen Sie _____ Frau da
       (the)
       drüben?   (da drüben: over there)

    (b) Sehen Sie _____?
        (her)

   2. Hier ist _____ Hemd.
      (a)

   3. Ich brauche _____ Hose.
      (a)

   4. (a) Ich kaufe _____ Anzug nicht.
         (the)

      (b) Ich kaufe _____ nicht.
          (it)

   5. (a) _____ Haus kostet zu viel.
         (The)

      (b) _____ kostet zu viel.
          (It)

   6. Brauchen Sie _____ Mantel?
      (a)

   7. (a) Was kostet _____ Hose?
         (the)

      (b) Was kostet _____?
          (it)

   8. Da ist _____ Anzug.
      (a)

   9. (a) _____ Krawatte ist hübsch.
         (The)

      (b) _____ ist hübsch.
          (It)

10. (a) Ich kaufe _____ Mantel.
       (the)

    (b) Ich kaufe _____.
        (it)

c. 1. Wir suchen _____ Haus.
      (a)

   2. (a) Was kostet _____ Hut?
         (the)

      (b) Was kostet _____?
          (it)

   3. (a) Sehen Sie _____ Mann da drüben?
         (the)

      (b) Sehen Sie _____?
          (him)

   4. Hier ist _____ Jacke.
      (a)

   5. Ich brauche _____ Hemd.
      (a)

   6. (a) Da ist _____ Anzug.
         (the)

      (b) Da ist _____.
          (it)

   7. (a) Kaufen Sie _____ Hose?
         (the)

      (b) Kaufen Sie _____?
          (it)

   8. (a) Wo ist _____ Haus?
         (the)

      (b) Wo ist _____?
          (it)

   9. Haben Sie _____ Krawatte?
      (a)

10. Da ist _____ Hut.
    (a)

d. 1. (a) _____ Kleid kostet zu viel.
       (The)

    (b) _____ kostet zu viel.
        (It)

   2. (a) Da ist _____ Frau.
         (the)

      (b) Da ist _____.
          (she)

   3. Ich brauche _____ Anzug.
      (a)

   4. (a) Wo ist _____ Hemd?
         (the)

      (b) Wo ist _____?
          (it)

EXPRESS IN GERMAN

- When there are two sentences under one number, make the personal pronoun in the second sentence agree with the noun in the first sentence.

a.
1. I need a suit.
2. The house costs too much.
   It costs too much.
3. There's the woman.
   There she is.
4. I need a dress.
5. There's the coat.
   There it is.
6. Do you have a tie?
7. What do the pants cost?
   What do they cost? (*Lit.:* it)
8. There's a hat.
9. I'm not going to buy the suit.
   I'm not going to buy it.
10. We're looking for a house.

b.
1. Here's a sports coat.
2. The suit's too small.
   It's too small.
3. Are you going to buy the shirt?
   Are you going to buy it?
4. Here's a tie.
5. Do you need a coat?
6. The dress costs too much.
   It costs too much.
7. Do you see the man over there?
   Do you see him?
8. I need a sports coat.

9. Do you have a hat?
10. Are you going to buy the pants?
    Are you going to buy them?

c.
1. Here's a shirt.
2. Do you see the house?
   Do you see it?
3. The tie is pretty.
   It's pretty.
4. I'll buy the coat.
   I'll buy it.
5. I need a pair of pants.
6. Where's the shirt?
   Where is it?
7. There's the man.
   There he is.
8. I need a shirt.
9. Here's a coat.
10. The sports coat costs too much.
    It costs too much.

d.
1. Where's the house?
   Where is it?
2. There's a suit.
3. Do you see the woman over there?
   Do you see her?
4. What does the hat cost?
   What does it cost?

VOCABULARY

der **Anzug** suit	**hübsch** pretty	**sie** them
da drüben over there	der **Hut** hat	**Sie** you (*polite, sing.*
dich you (*sing. form*)	**ihn** him	*and pl.*)
es it	die **Jacke** sports coat	**suchen** to look for,
euch you (*fam. pl.*)	das **Kleid** dress	hunt for
fragen to ask	**klein** small	**uns** us
die **Frau** woman	die **Krawatte** tie	**verstehen** to understand
das **Haus** house	der **Mann** man	**viel** much
das **Hemd** shirt	der **Mantel** coat	
die **Hose** pants (*sing.*	**mich** me	
in German)	**sie** her	

Lesson 2 Level TWO

A Direct Objects and Indirect Objects: Personal Pronouns

1 Direct object: accusative case

In Level One of this lesson you practiced using the personal pronouns as direct objects in simple sentences:

	Direct Object
Sie suchen	**dich.**
Ich sehe	**ihn.**

2 Indirect object: dative case

Look at the following sentence:

Ich zeige es dir.   (I'll show it *to you*.)

Subject	Verb	Complement
Ich	zeige	es dir.
(I	will show	it to you.)

The complement of this sentence is no longer a simple complement because it answers *two* questions. First, "What is being shown?" The answer is **es. Es** is the **direct** object; consequently, it is in the **accusative** case. But there is a second question answered by the complement of this sentence:

Who is it being shown *to?*

The answer is **dir** (to you). This kind of complement is called an **indirect** object, and it answers the questions *who to* (and occasionally *who for*).

Ich zeige es dir. (I'll show it *to you*.)	*Who* is it being shown *to?* **dir** (to you)
Ich kaufe es dir. (I'll buy it *for you*.)	*Who's* it being bought *for?* **dir** (for you)

The special forms of the personal pronoun used for indirect objects are in the *dative case.*

60

3 Dative personal pronouns

As you can see from the following table, German has dative forms of the personal pronoun that are for the most part different from the accusative forms.

PERSONAL PRONOUNS: NOMINATIVE, ACCUSATIVE, AND DATIVE								
	Singular					*Plural*		
NOM.	ich	du	er	sie	es	wir	ihr	sie / Sie
ACC.	mich	dich	ihn	sie	es	uns	euch	sie / Sie
DAT.	mir	dir	ihm	ihr	ihm	uns	euch	ihnen / Ihnen

4 Contrastive grammar

Like German, English can also use personal pronouns as *indirect objects:*

I'll show *you* the house.   (Who is the house being shown to? *To you.*)

Unlike German, English can answer the question "who to" with a *prepositional phrase.*

		Prepositional Phrase
	I'll show it	*to you.*

But German does not replace the indirect object with a prepositional phrase.

		Prepositional Phrase
ENGLISH	I'll show it	*to you.*

		Dative Object
But GERMAN	Ich zeige es	**dir.**

DRILLS

1   Forms of address: dative case

NOM.	du	ihr	Sie
ACC.	dich	euch	Sie
DAT.	dir	euch	Ihnen

• Supply the appropriate *dative* form of the personal pronoun.

a. 1. Ich zeige es _____ später, Dieter.
   (to you)
   (**zeigen**: to show)

2. Ich zeige es _____ später,
   (to you)
   Herr Schröder.

3. Ich zeige es _____ später, Kinder.
   (to you)

4. Ich zeige es _____ später, Christa.
   (to you)

b. 1. Wir schicken es _____ morgen,
   (to you)
   Herr Wolff.   (**schicken**: to send)

2. Wir schicken es _____ morgen, Karl.
   (to you)

3. Wir schicken es _____ morgen,
   (to you)
   Frau Heller.

4. Wir schicken es _____, Jungens.
   (to you)

   (**Jungens**: boys, you guys)

c. 1. Ich bringe es _____, Renate.
   (to you)
   (**bringen**: to bring)

2. Ich bringe es _____, Kinder.
   (to you)

3. Ich bringe es _____, Herr Lenz.
   (to you)

4. Ich bringe es _____, Hans und
   (to you)
   Christa.

d. 1. Er kauft es _____, Frau Arndt.
   (for you)
   (**kaufen**: to buy)

2. Er kauft es _____, Klaus.
   (for you)

3. Er kauft es _____, Kinder.
   (for you)

4. Er kauft es _____, Lisbeth.
   (for you)

5. Er kauft es _____, Herr Schmidt.
   (for you)

2   First person singular and plural: dative case

NOM.	ich	wir
ACC.	mich	uns
DAT.	mir	uns

• Supply the appropriate *dative* form of the personal pronoun.

a. 1. Schicken Sie es _____!
   (to me)

2. Schicken Sie es _____!
   (to us)

b. 1. Zeigst du es _____?
   (to us)

2. Zeigst du es _____?
   (to me)

c. 1 Er bringt es _____ morgen.
   (to us)

2. Er bringt es _____ morgen.
   (to me)

d. 1. Kaufst du es _____?
   (for us)

2. Kaufst du es _____?
   (for me)

3   Third person singular and plural: dative case

	Singular			*Plural*
NOM.	er	es	sie	sie
ACC.	ihn	es	sie	sie
DAT.	ihm	ihm	ihr	ihnen

Supply the appropriate *dative* form of the personal pronoun.

a. 1. Er zeigt es _____.
       (to him)

  2. Er zeigt es _____.
       (to her)

  3. Er zeigt es _____.
       (to them)

b. 1. Schickst du es _____?
       (to her)

  2. Schickst du es _____?
       (to them)

  3. Schickst du es _____?
       (to him)

c. 1. Wir bringen es _____ später.
       (to them)
       (bringen: to take)*

  2. Wir bringen es _____ später.
       (to him)

  3. Wir bringen es _____ später.
       (to her)

d. 1. Ich kaufe es _____.
       (for him)

  2. Ich kaufe es _____.
       (for her)

  3. Ich kaufe es _____.
       (for them)

4 All personal pronouns

Supply the appropriate *dative* form of the personal pronoun.

1. Ich zeige es _____ später, Lisbeth.
       (to you)

  Ich zeige es _____ später.
       (to them)

  Ich zeige es _____ später.
       (to her)

  Ich zeige es _____ später, Kinder.
       (to you)

2. Er zeigt es _____.
       (to him)

  Er zeigt es _____.
       (to us)

  Er zeigt es _____, Herr Schmidt.
       (to you)

3. Zeigst du es _____?
       (to me)

  Zeigst du es _____?
       (to him)

  Zeigst du es _____?
       (to her)

4. Er bringt es _____ morgen, Willi.
       (to you)

  Er bringt es _____ morgen.
       (to us)

  Er bringt es _____ morgen.
       (to me)

5. Wir bringen es _____ später.
       (to them)

  Wir bringen es _____ später.
       (to her)

  Wir bringen es _____, Hans und Christa.
       (to you)

6. Ich bringe es _____, Frau Heller.
       (to you)

  Ich bringe es _____.
       (to him)

  Ich bringe es _____, Klaus.
       (to you)

---

*Depending on its context, **bringen** means either "to bring" or "to take."

He'll *bring* it to me.
I'll *take* it to him.

The German verb **bringen** covers *both* meanings.

Er **bringt** es mir.
Ich **bringe** es ihm.

7. Schicken Sie es _____!
   (to me)

   Schicken Sie es _____!
   (to them)

   Schicken Sie es _____!
   (to him)

8. Schickt er es _____?
   (to us)

   Schickt er es _____?
   (to her)

   Schickt er es _____, Renate?
   (to you)

9. Wir schicken es _____ morgen.
   (to him)

   Wir schicken es _____ morgen,
   (to you)
   Herr Lenz.

10. Ich kaufe es _____, Klaus.
    (for you)

    Ich kaufe es _____.
    (for her)

    Ich kaufe es _____, Kinder.
    (for you)

11. Kaufst du es _____?
    (for him)

    Kaufst du es _____?
    (for them)

    Kaufst du es _____?
    (for me)

12. Er kauft es _____.
    (for her)

    Er kauft es _____.
    (for us)

    Er kauft es _____, Frau Heller.
    (for you)

MIXED DRILLS

● Supply the appropriate *dative* form of the personal pronoun.

a. 1. Er zeigt es _____.
       (to us)

    2. Er bringt es _____ morgen.
       (to me)

    3. Schicken Sie es _____!
       (to them)

    4. Kaufst du es _____?
       (for him)

    5. Ich zeige es _____ später, Lisbeth.
       (to you)

    6. Schickt er es _____?
       (to her)

    7. Ich zeige es _____ später, Kinder.
       (to you)

    8. Er kauft es _____.
       (for us)

    9. Ich bringe es _____, Frau Heller.
       (to you)

    10. Wir schicken es _____ morgen.
        (to him)

b. 1. Zeigst du es _____?
       (to me)

    2. Wir bringen es _____ später.
       (to them)

    3. Ich kaufe es _____, Klaus.
       (for you)

4. Zeigst du es _____?
   (to her)

5. Wir bringen es _____, Kinder.
   (to you)

6. Schickt er es _____?
   (to us)

7. Er zeigt es _____.
   (to him)

8. Kaufst du es _____?
   (for me)

9. Wir bringen es _____ später.
   (to her)

10. Wir schicken es _____ morgen,
    (to you)
    Herr Lenz.

c. 1. Ich kaufe es _____, Kinder.
       (for you)

    2. Ich zeige es _____ später.
       (to them)

    3. Er bringt es _____ morgen, Willi.
       (to you)

    4. Schicken Sie es _____!
       (to me)

    5. Er kauft es _____.
       (for her)

    6. Ich bringe es _____.
       (to him)

7. Kaufst du es _____ ?
   (for them)

8. Ich zeige es _____ später.
   (to her)

9. Er bringt es _____ morgen.
   (to us)

10. Schickt er es _____ , Renate?
   (to you)

d. 1. Er kauft es _____ , Frau Heller.
   (for you)

2. Zeigst du es _____ ?
   (to him)

3. Ich kaufe es _____ .
   (for her)

4. Er schickt es _____ , Herr Schmidt.
   (to you)

5. Ich bringe es _____ , Klaus.
   (to you)

6. Schicken Sie es _____ !
   (to him)

- **Express in German.**

a. 1. I'll show it to them later.
   2. Is he going to send it to us?
   3. I'll buy it for you, Klaus.
   4. We'll take it to her later.
   5. Send it to me.
   6. He'll show it to you, Mr. Schmidt.
   7. Are you going to buy it for him?
   8. I'll bring it to you, Klaus.
   9. He'll show it to us.
   10. We'll send it to you tomorrow, Mr. Lenz.

b. 1. I'll buy it for you children.
   2. He'll bring it to me tomorrow.
   3. Are you going to show it to her?
   4. Send it to him.
   5. We'll take it to them later.

6. I'll show it to you later, Lisbeth.
   7. He'll buy it for us.
   8. Is he going to send it to her?
   9. I'll take it to him.
   10. Will you show it to me?

c. 1. I'll bring it to you, Mrs. Heller.
   2. We'll send it to him tomorrow.
   3. He's going to buy it for her.
   4. I'll show it to you later, children.
   5. He'll bring it to us tomorrow.
   6. Are you going to buy it for them?
   7. Is he going to send it to you, Renate?
   8. I'm going to buy it for her.
   9. Are you going to send it to them?
   10. He'll bring it to you tomorrow, Willi.

5 The special case of **sagen**

Look at the following example:

Ich sage **es dir** morgen.   (I'll tell *you* tomorrow.)

The English verb "to tell" does not need a direct object, although the idea of a direct object is there (obviously, I'll tell you *something* tomorrow). But its German equivalent, **sagen,** must always have a direct object:

Ich sage **es** dir morgen.   (I'll tell *it* to you tomorrow.)

sagen

- Supply the appropriate *dative* form of the personal pronoun.

1. Ich sage es _____ später, Herr Lenz.
   (you)

2. Sag es _____ !
   (him)

3. Wir sagen es _____ morgen.
   (her)

4. Sagen Sie es _____ nicht!
   (them)

5. Ich sage es _____ später, Franz.
   (you)

6. Sag es _____ !
   (me)

7. Er sagt es _____ morgen.
   (us)

• Express in German.

1. We'll tell her tomorrow.
2. I'll tell you later, Franz.
3. Don't tell them.
4. He'll tell us tomorrow.

5. I'll tell you later, Mr. Lenz.
6. Tell me.
7. Tell him.

6 geben

geben *to give*		Imperative Forms
ich gebe	wir geben	Gib!
du gibst	ihr gebt	Gebt!
er gibt	sie geben	Geben Sie!

Geben (like **sprechen**) changes its stem vowel from **-e-** to -i- in the 2nd and 3rd person singular.

geben

• Supply the appropriate *dative* form of the personal pronoun.

1. Ich gebe es _____ später, Hans.
   (to you)

2. Wann gibst du es _____ ?
   (to us)

3. Wir geben es _____ morgen.
   (to them)

4. Gib es _____ , Karl!
   (to me)

5. Geben Sie es _____ , Herr Wolff!
   (to me)

6. Er gibt es _____ morgen.
   (to her)

7. Sie gibt es _____ später, Karl.
   (to you)

• Supply the correct form of **geben**.

1. Wir _____ es ihnen morgen.
2. Sie (she) _____ es dir später, Karl.
3. Wann _____ du es uns?
4. Ich _____ es dir später, Hans.

5. _____ es mir, Dieter! (*imperative*)
6. _____ Sie es ihm! (*imperative*)
7. Er _____ es ihr morgen.
8. Ich _____ es dir später, Hans.

• Express in German.

1. She'll give it to you later, Karl.
2. We're giving it to them tomorrow.
3. When are you (**du**) going to give it to us?
4. He'll give it to her tomorrow.

5. Give it to me, Karl.
6. Give it to him, Mr. Wolff.
7. I'll give it to you later, Hans.

7 Verbs that take only dative objects

A small number of German verbs take *only dative objects*. Since there is no way to identify them, they must be memorized. Two common verbs of this type are:

helfen (to help)	Ich helfe **ihm**.	(I'll help *him*.)
antworten (to answer)	Antworten Sie **mir**!	(Answer *me*.)

helfen

helfen *to help*		*Imperative Forms*
ich helfe	wir helfen	Hilf!
du hilfst	ihr helft	Helft!
er hilft	sie helfen	Helfen Sie!

• Supply the appropriate *dative* form of the personal pronoun.

1. Ich helfe _____, Renate.
   (you)
2. Er hilft _____.
   (them)
3. Hilfst du _____?
   (him)
4. Helfen Sie _____!
   (us)
5. Hilf _____!
   (me)

6. Moment! Ich helfe _____, Herr Schmidt.
   (you)
   (**Moment!**: Just a minute!)
7. Hilfst du _____?
   (her)
8. Wir helfen _____, Willi.
   (you)

• Supply the correct form of **helfen**.

1. Moment! Ich _____ Ihnen, Herr Schmidt.
2. _____ du ihm?
3. Wir _____ dir.
4. _____ Sie uns!

5. _____ mir!
6. Ich _____ dir.
7. Er _____ ihnen.
8. _____ du ihr?

• Express in German.

1. We'll help you.
2. He's going to help them.
3. Are you (**du**) going to help him?
4. Just a minute. I'll help you, Mr. Schmidt.

5. Help me. (**du**-form)
6. Help us. (**Sie**-form)
7. Are you (**du**) going to help her?
8. I'll help you, Renate.

antworten

• Supply the correct form of the personal pronoun.

1. Warum antwortest du _____ nicht?
   (me)
2. Antworte _____!
   (her)

3. Antworten Sie _____!
   (me)
4. Warum antwortet sie _____ nicht?
   (him)

- Express in German.

1. Answer me.   (**Sie**-form)
2. Answer her.   (**du**-form)

3. Why don't you (**du**) answer me?
4. Why doesn't she answer him?

MIXED DRILLS

1   Contrast drill: dative and accusative

- Supply the appropriate *dative* or *accusative* personal pronoun.

1. Ich verstehe _____.
   (him)

   Ich helfe _____.
   (him)

2. Er bringt es _____ morgen.
   (to me)

   Er kennt _____ nicht.
   (me)

3. Zeigst du es _____?
   (to them)

   Siehst du _____?
   (them)

4. Fragen Sie _____!
   (her)

   Antworten Sie _____!
   (her)

5. Ich kaufe es _____, Inge.
   (for you)

   Ich verstehe _____ nicht, Inge.
   (you)

6. Sucht er _____?
   (us)

   Schickt er es _____?
   (us)

7. Er gibt es _____ morgen, Herr Wolff.
   (to you)

   Er kennt _____ nicht, Herr Wolff.
   (you)

8. Sie suchen _euch_, Jungens.
   (you)

   Sie sagen es _euch_ später, Jungens.
   (to you)

9. Antworte _ihm_!
   (him)

   Frag _ihn_!
   (him)

10. Ich zeige es _dir_ später, Klaus.
    (to you)

    Ich verstehe _dich_ nicht, Klaus.
    (you)

11. Fragst du _mich_?
    (me)

    Kaufst du es _mir_?
    (for me)

12. Ich gebe es _____ später.
    (to her)

    Ich kenne _____ nicht.
    (her)

2   Contrast drill: random mix

- Supply the appropriate *dative* or *accusative* personal pronoun.

a. 1. Ich bringe es _ihm_.
   (to him)

2. Gib es _mir_!
   (to me)

3. Kennst du _sie_?
   (them)

4. Sagen Sie es _ihr_ nicht!
   (to her)

5. Sie suchen _dich_, Willi.
   (you)

6. Schickt er es _____?
   (to us)

7. Ich verstehe _____ nicht.
   (it)

8. Ich zeige es _____ später, Herr Lenz.
   (to you)

9. Er kennt _____ nicht.
   (me)

10. Ich kaufe es _____, Christa.
    (for you)

68   Lesson 2

b. 1. Fragst du _____?
        (us)
    2. Hilf _____!
        (me)
    3. Ich sehe _____ nicht.
        (him)
    4. Er sucht _____, Frau Heller.
        (you)
    5. Zeigst du es _____?
        (to him)
    6. Ich verstehe _____ nicht.
        (her)
    7. Ich gebe es _____ später, Paul.
        (to you)
    8. Sie suchen _____, Jungens.
        (you)
    9. Antworten Sie _____!
        (her)
    10. Verstehen Sie _____?
        (me)

c. 1. Ich kenne _____ nicht.
        (him)
    2. Wir geben es _____ morgen.
        (to them)
    3. Sucht er _____?
        (us)
    4. Fragen Sie _____!
        (her)

    5. Kaufst du es _____?
        (for me)
    6. Er sieht _____ nicht, Renate.
        (you)
    7. Er bringt es _____ morgen,
        (to you)
       Herr Lenz.
    8. Frag _____!
        (him)
    9. Ich brauche _____ nicht.
        (it)
    10. Siehst du _____?
        (them)

d. 1. Sag es _____!
        (her)
    2. Ich helfe _____, Dieter.
        (you)

3 Express in German

a. 1. Help me.
    2. I don't know him.
    3. They're looking for you, Willi.
    4. We'll give it to them tomorrow.
    5. I don't understand it.
    6. Is he going to send it to us?
    7. Do you understand me?
    8. Ask her.
    9. Are you going to show it to him?
    10. I'll help you, Dieter.

b. 1. They're looking for you, boys.
    2. Do you see them?
    3. Give it to me.
    4. I don't see him.
    5. Is he looking for us?
    6. Tell her.
    7. I'll show it to you later, Mr. Lenz.
    8. I don't understand her.
    9. I don't need it.
    10. Answer her.

c. 1. He doesn't see you, Renate.
    2. Do you know them?
    3. I'll take it to him.
    4. Are you asking us?
    5. He doesn't know me.
    6. I'll give it to you later, Paul.
    7. He's looking for you, Mrs. Heller.
    8. Don't tell her.
    9. Ask him.
    10. Will you buy it for me?

B Nouns as Indirect Objects: Dative Case

Like personal pronouns, nouns can function as indirect objects:

> Zeig es **dem Verkäufer!**   (Show it to the salesman.)
> Zeig es **einem Verkäufer!**   (Show it to a salesman.)

As the examples show, the definite and indefinite articles have special forms for the dative case:

> **dem** Verkäufer   *to the* salesman
> **einem** Verkäufer   *to a* salesman

Note again that where English uses a *prepositional phrase:*

> *to the* salesman

German uses only a *dative object:*

> **dem** Verkäufer

1 Agreement of nouns and pronouns

If a pronoun is substituted for a dative noun phrase, it too must be in the dative case.

> NOUN PHRASE   Zeig es **dem Verkäufer!**   (Show it to the salesman.)
> PRONOUN   Zeig es **ihm** !   (Show it *to him*.)

2 Table of definite and indefinite articles

At this point we can expand our former tables to include the dative forms.

DEFINITE ARTICLES						
	Masculine		*Neuter*		*Feminine*	
NOM.	der Mann	(er)	das Kind	(es)	die Frau	(sie)
ACC.	den Mann	(ihn)	das Kind	(es)	die Frau	(sie)
DAT.	**dem** Mann	**(ihm)**	**dem** Kind	**(ihm)**	**der** Frau	**(ihr)**

INDEFINITE ARTICLES			
	Masculine	*Neutèr*	*Feminine*
NOM.	ein Mann	ein Kind	eine Frau
ACC.	einen Mann	ein Kind	eine Frau
DAT.	**einem** Mann	**einem** Kind	**einer** Frau

DRILLS

1 Pronoun substitution

● Replace the noun phrases with the appropriate personal pronouns.

EXAMPLE   Hilf dem Mann!   Zeigen Sie es der Kellnerin!   (die **Kellnerin**: waitress)
          Hilf **ihm**!   Zeigen Sie es **ihr**!

1. Ich gebe es der Sekretärin.   (die **Sekretärin**: secretary)
2. Sagen Sie es dem Anwalt!   (der **Anwalt**: lawyer)
3. Zeig es dem Verkäufer!   (der **Verkäufer**: salesman)
4. Antworten Sie der Frau!
5. Ich sage es dem Kellner.   (der **Kellner**: waiter)
6. Sag es der Mutter nicht!*   (die **Mutter**: mother)
7. Hilf dem Mann!
8. Zeigen Sie es der Verkäuferin!   (die **Verkäuferin**: saleswoman)
9. Sagen Sie es dem Chef!   (der **Chef**: boss)
10. Gib es der Kellnerin!
11. Sag es dem Vater* nicht!   (der **Vater**: father)
12. Helfen Sie dem Mädchen!†   (das **Mädchen**: girl)
13. Gib es der Katze!   (die **Katze**: cat)

2 Fill-ins: **dem** / **der**

● Supply the appropriate *dative* form of the definite article.

EXAMPLE   Hilf d___ Mann! (the man)   Zeigen Sie es d___ Kellnerin! (to the waitress)
          Hilf **dem** Mann!   Zeigen Sie es **der** Kellnerin!

1. Zeig es d___ Verkäufer! (to the salesman)   8. Sag es d___ Vater nicht! (Father)
2. Helfen Sie d___ Mädchen! (the girl)   9. Zeigen Sie es d___ Verkäuferin! (to the
3. Antworten Sie d___ Frau! (the woman)   saleswoman)
4. Sagen Sie es d___ Anwalt! (to the lawyer)   10. Sagen Sie es d___ Chef! (the boss)
5. Ich gebe es d___ Sekretärin. (to the secretary) 11. Gib es d___ Katze! (to the cat)
6. Hilf d___ Mann! (the man)   12. Ich sage es d___ Kellner. (the waiter)
7. Gib es d___ Kellnerin! (to the waitress)   13. Sag es d___ Mutter nicht! (Mother)

3 Express in German

1. Don't tell Father.   8. I'll tell the waiter.
2. Answer the woman.   9. Don't tell Mother.
3. Show it to the salesman.   10. Give it to the cat.
4. I'll give it to the secretary.   11. Help the girl.
5. Tell the boss.   12. Tell it to the lawyer.
6. Help the man.   13. Give it to the waitress.
7. Show it to the saleswoman.

---

*Sag es **der** Mutter (**dem** Vater) nicht! (Don't tell Mother [Father].) In German, one often uses the definite article when referring to one's mother or father.

†**Das Mädchen** (girl) is neuter in German. But the pronoun used is the feminine form **sie** (she), not the neuter form.

4 Fill-ins: **einem / einer   meinem / meiner**

- Supply the suggested form of **ein** or **mein**.*

    EXAMPLE   Ich gebe es **der** Sekretärin.
    Ich gebe es mein____ Sekretärin.   (mein: my)

    Ich gebe es **meiner** Sekretärin.

1. Zeig es **dem** Verkäufer!
   Zeig es ein____ Verkäufer!
2. Sag es **der** Mutter nicht!
   Sag es mein____ Mutter nicht!
3. Ich zeige es **dem** Professor.
   Ich zeige es mein____ Professor.
       (**der Professor:** professor)

4. Sagen Sie es **dem** Anwalt!
   Sagen Sie es ein____ Anwalt!
5. Ich gebe es **der** Sekretärin.
   Ich gebe es mein____ Sekretärin.

- Supply the appropriate *dative* form of **ein** or **mein**.

    EXAMPLE   Ich gebe es mein ____ Sekretärin.
    Ich gebe es **meiner** Sekretärin.

1. Ich zeige es mein____ Professor.
2. Ich helfe mein____ Bruder.
       (**der Bruder:** brother)
3. Sie gibt es ein____ Freundin.
       (**die Freundin:** girl friend)
4. Ich zeige es mein____ Mann.
       (**Mann,** *here:* husband)

5. Sagen Sie es ein____ Anwalt!
6. Ich gebe es mein____ Sekretärin.
7. Zeig es ein____ Verkäufer!
8. Ich zeige es mein____ Frau.   (**Frau,** *here:* wife)
9. Er gibt es ein____ Freund.   (**der Freund:** friend)
10. Sag es mein____ Mutter nicht!
11. Ich helfe mein____ Vater.

5   Express in German

1. I'll show it to my husband.
2. I'll give it to my secretary.
3. Show it to a salesman.
4. He's going to give it to a friend.
5. Don't tell my mother.
6. I'm going to show it to my professor.

7. I'm helping my father.
8. She's going to give it to a girl friend.
9. Tell it to a lawyer.
10. I'll show it to my wife.
11. I'm helping my brother.

6   Mixed drills

- Supply the suggested *dative* form of **der, mein,** or **ein**.

a. 1. Sagen Sie es _____ Chef!
           (to the)

    2. Ich zeige es _____ Frau.
           (to my)

    3. Antworten Sie _____ Frau!
           (the)

    4. Zeig es _____ Verkäufer!
           (to a)

    5. Gib es _____ Kellnerin!
           (to the)

    6. Ich helfe _____ Bruder.
           (my)

---

*__Mein__ (my) takes exactly the same endings as the indefinite article **ein.**

72   Lesson 2

7. Zeig es _____ Verkäufer!
   (to the)
8. Sag es _____ Mutter nicht!
   (to my)
9. Gib es _____ Katze!
   (to the)
10. Ich zeige es _____ Professor.
   (to my)

b. 1. Ich sage es _____ Kellner.
   (to the)
2. Sie gibt es _____ Freundin.
   (to a)
3. Hilf _____ Mann!
   (the)

4. Sagen Sie es _____ Anwalt!
   (to a)
5. Zeigen Sie es _____ Verkäuferin!
   (to the)
6. Ich zeige es _____ Mann.
   (to my)
7. Er gibt es _____ Freund.
   (to a)
8. Helfen Sie _____ Mädchen!
   (the)
9. Ich gebe es _____ Sekretärin.
   (to my)
10. Ich helfe _____ Vater.
   (my)

• Express in German.

a. 1. Show it to the salesman.
2. Don't tell my mother.
3. I'm helping my father.
4. I'll tell the waiter.
5. She's going to give it to a girl friend.
6. Answer the woman.
7. I'll show it to my husband.
8. Help the girl.
9. I'll give it to my secretary.
10. Show it to the saleswoman.

b. 1. Tell it to a lawyer.
2. Give it to the waitress.
3. I'm going to show it to my professor.
4. Tell it to the boss.
5. He's going to give it to a friend.
6. I'll show it to my wife.
7. Give it to the cat.
8. I'm helping my brother.
9. Show it to a salesman.
10. Help the man.

MIXED DRILLS

1 Contrast drill: dative and accusative

• Supply the appropriate *dative* or *accusative* endings.

1. Kennen Sie mein__ Frau?
   Ich zeige es mein__ Frau.
2. Frag d__ Verkäufer!
   Zeig es d__ Verkäufer!
3. Ich suche mein__ Vater.
   Ich helfe mein__ Vater.
4. Ich gebe es d__ Sekretärin.
   Fragen Sie d__ Sekretärin!
5. Helfen Sie d__ Mädchen!
   Ich verstehe d__ Mädchen nicht.

6. Kennst du mein__ Freundin?
   Ich zeige es mein__ Freundin.
7. Sagen Sie es d__ Chef!
   Ich suche d__ Chef.
8. Ich brauche ein__ Anwalt.
   Sagen Sie es ein__ Anwalt!
9. Siehst du ein__ Verkäuferin?
   Zeig es ein__ Verkäuferin!
10. Gib es d__ Kellnerin!
    Frag d__ Kellnerin!

2 Contrast drill: random mix

• Supply the appropriate *dative* or *accusative* endings.

a. 1. Ich suche d__ Chef.
2. Ich zeige es mein__ Frau.

3. Frag d__ Kellnerin!
4. Sagen Sie es ein__ Anwalt!

5. Ich verstehe d— Mädchen nicht.
6. Siehst du ein— Verkäuferin?
7. Sagen Sie es d— Chef!
8. Fragen Sie d— Sekretärin!
9. Ich suche mein— Vater.
10. Frag d— Verkäufer!

b. 1. Ich zeige es mein— Freundin.
2. Ich helfe mein— Vater.

3. Kennen Sie mein— Frau?
4. Helfen Sie d— Mädchen!
5. Ich brauche ein— Anwalt.
6. Ich gebe es d— Sekretärin.
7. Kennst du mein— Freundin?
8. Zeig es d— Verkäufer!
9. Gib es d— Kellnerin!
10. Zeig es ein— Verkäuferin!

3 Express in German

a. 1. I need a lawyer.
2. I'll show it to my girl friend.
3. Ask the salesman.
4. Tell the boss.
5. Do you know my wife?
6. Give it to the waitress.
7. I'm helping my father.
8. Do you see a saleswoman?
9. Help the girl.
10. I'll give it to the secretary.

b. 1. I'm looking for my father.
2. I'll show it to my wife.
3. I'm looking for the boss.
4. Show it to a saleswoman.
5. Ask the secretary.
6. Tell it to a lawyer.
7. Ask the waitress.
8. I don't understand the girl.
9. Show it to the salesman.
10. Do you know my girl friend?

C Word Order: Order of Objects

1 General rules

1. If the *direct object* is a *personal pronoun*, it comes **before** the indirect object. You have already seen sentences that illustrate this rule:

Direct Object	Indirect Object	
Gib	es	meiner Sekretärin!	(Give it to my secretary.)
Gib	es	ihr!	(Give it to her.)

2. If the *direct object* is a *noun*, it comes **after** the indirect object. Look at the following examples:

Indirect Object	Direct Object	
Gib	meiner Sekretärin	das Buch!	(Give my secretary the book.)
Gib	ihr	das Buch!	(Give her the book.)

2 Contrastive grammar

a. Pronouns as direct objects

English, like German, puts the direct object first if it is a pronoun:

Give *it* to her.   Gib **es** ihr!
Give *it* to my secretary. Gib **es** meiner Sekretärin!

b. Nouns as direct objects

But when the direct object is a noun, English has a choice:

Give the secretary *the book.*   *but*   Gib der Sekretärin **das Buch!**
Give *the book* to the secretary.

Give her *the book.*   *but*   Gib ihr **das Buch!**
Give *the book* to her.

As you can see, German has no choice.

3 alles, etwas, and nichts

Alles (everything), **etwas** (something), and **nichts** (nothing) are called indefinite pronouns. But as far as word order is concerned, *they behave like nouns.* This means that they always come **after** an indirect object.

	Indirect Object	Direct Object	
Ich zeige	dir	etwas	(I'll show you something.)

DRILLS

1   Fill-ins

• Supply the suggested dative object.

EXAMPLE   Gib _____ das Buch!   (das Buch: book)   Gib **meiner Sekretärin** das Buch!
            (my secretary)

            Gib _____ das Buch!   Gib **ihr** das Buch!
            (her)

a. 1. Ich kaufe _____ ein Kleid.
            (my wife)

     Ich kaufe _____ ein Kleid.
            (her)

  2. Bring _____ die Post!   (die Post: mail)
        (me)

  3. Ich zeige _____ mein Büro.
          (you **[du]**) (das Büro: office)

  4. Ich zeige _____ den Brief.
          (my lawyer)

     Ich zeige _____ den Brief.
          (him)   (der Brief: letter)

  5. Sagen Sie _____ die Adresse!
          (me) (die Adresse: address)

  6. Wir zeigen _____ das Haus.
         (you **[Sie]**)

  7. Sie sagt _____ alles.
         (her mother)

     Sie sagt _____ alles.
        (her) (alles: everything)

  8. Ich bringe _____ die Zeitung.
        (you **[du]**)
              (die Zeitung: newspaper)

  9. Gib _____ das Geld! (das Geld: money)
       (me)

10. Ich schicke _____ eine
         (my girl friend)
   Karte.   (die Karte: postcard)

     Ich schicke _____ eine Karte.
         (her)

b. 1. Gibst du _____ den Wagen? (him) (der Wagen: car)

2. Ich zeige _____ das Bild. (you [Sie]) (das Bild: picture)

3. Ich kaufe _____ eine Krawatte. (my husband)
   Ich kaufe _____ eine Krawatte. (him)

4. Schicken Sie _____ die Hose! (me)

5. Gibst du _____ ein Trinkgeld? (the waitress) (das Trinkgeld: tip)
   Gibst du _____ ein Trinkgeld? (her)

6. Ich kaufe _____ ein Bier. (you [du]) (das Bier: beer)

7. Zeigen Sie _____ das Buch! (my friend)
   Zeigen Sie _____ das Buch! (him)

8. Gib _____ den Fisch! (der Fisch: fish) (the cat)

9. Sag _____ meine Adresse! (him)

10. Ich sage _____ nichts. (them) (nichts: nothing, not . . . anything)

c. 1. Ich kaufe _____ etwas. (you [du]) (etwas: something)

2 Word order: noun direct object last

• Complete the sentences by putting the objects in their proper order.

EXAMPLE   Gib _____! den Brief / meiner Sekretärin

Gib meiner Sekretärin den Brief!

a. 1. Bring _____! die Post / mir

2. Gibst du _____? der Kellnerin / ein Trinkgeld

3. Ich kaufe _____. ein Bier / dir

4. Ich zeige _____. den Brief / meinem Anwalt

5. Sag _____! Hans / meine Adresse

6. Gibst du _____? den Wagen / ihm

7. Sie sagt _____. alles / der Mutter

8. Wir zeigen _____. Ihnen / das Haus

9. Gib _____! das Geld / Renate

10. Ich bringe _____. die Zeitung / dir

b. 1. Sagen Sie _____! mir / die Adresse

2. Ich kaufe _____. eine Krawatte / meinem Mann

3. Ich zeige _____. Ihnen / das Bild

4. Ich schicke _____. eine Karte / meiner Freundin

5. Ich kaufe _____. etwas / dir

6. Zeigen Sie _____! meinem Freund / das Buch

7. Ich sage _____. nichts / ihnen

8. Gib _____! der Katze / den Fisch

9. Ich zeige _____. mein Büro / dir

10. Ich kaufe _____. ein Kleid / meiner Frau

3 Express in German

a. 1. Bring me the mail.
   2. I'll show you (**du**-form) my office.
   3. Give Renate the money.
   4. I'm buying my husband a tie.

5. I'll show you (**Sie**-form) the picture.
6. She tells her mother everything.
7. Are you going to give him the car?
8. I won't tell them anything. (use **nichts**)
9. Tell me the address.
10. I'll buy you (**du**-form) a beer.

b. 1. I'm going to send a card to my girl friend.
2. Are you going to give the waitress a tip?

3. We'll show you (**Sie**-form) the house.
4. I'll bring you (**du**-form) the paper.
5. I'm going to show the letter to my lawyer.
6. Give the fish to the cat.
7. Tell Hans my address.
8. I'm buying a dress for my wife.
9. Show the book to my friend.
10. I'll buy you (**du**-form) something.

4 Pronoun substitution

● Replace the direct objects with the appropriate personal pronouns, making the necessary changes in word order.

EXAMPLE   Gib meiner Sekretärin den Brief!
            Gib ihn meiner Sekretärin!

1. Ich zeige dir mein Büro.
2. Bring mir die Post!
3. Gib Renate das Geld!
4. Ich zeige dir den Brief.
5. Sagen Sie mir die Adresse!
6. Gib der Katze den Fisch!
7. Ich zeige Ihnen das Bild.

8. Ich bringe dir die Zeitung.
9. Ich zeige meinem Anwalt den Brief.
10. Gib meiner Sekretärin das Buch!
11. Gibst du mir den Wagen?
12. Sag Hans meine Adresse!
13. Wir zeigen Ihnen das Haus.
14. Schicken Sie mir die Hose!

MIXED DRILLS

1 Word order

● Complete the sentences by putting the objects in their proper order.

1. Sagen Sie _____ !   die Adresse
                                mir

   Sagen Sie _____ !   sie
                                mir

2. Wir zeigen _____ . Ihnen
                                das Haus

   Wir zeigen _____ . Ihnen
                                es

3. Ich kaufe _____ .   etwas
                                dir

4. Gib _____ !   meiner Sekretärin
                                das Buch

   Gib _____ !   das Buch
                                ihr

   Gib _____ !   es
                                meiner Sekretärin

   Gib _____ !   ihr
                                es

5. Ich zeige _____ .   den Brief
                                dir

   Ich zeige _____ .   dir
                                ihn

6. Sie sagt _____ .   der Mutter
                                alles

7. Gibst du _____ ?   ein Trinkgeld
                                der Kellnerin

   Gibst du _____ ?   ihr
                                ein Trinkgeld

8. Ich zeige _____ .   den Brief
                                meinem Anwalt

   Ich zeige _____ .   den Brief
                                ihm

   Ich zeige _____ .   ihn
                                meinem Anwalt

9. Bring _____ ! mir
die Post

Bring _____ ! mir
sie

10. Ich kaufe _____ . ein Bier
dir

11. Sag _____ ! Hans
meine Adresse

Sag _____ ! meine Adresse
ihm

Sag _____ ! sie
Hans

Sag _____ ! ihm
sie

12. Ich kaufe _____ . meiner Frau
ein Kleid

Ich kaufe _____ . ein Kleid
ihr

13. Gibst du _____ ? den Wagen
mir

Gibst du _____ ? ihn
mir

14. Ich sage _____ . nichts
ihnen

15. Gib _____ ! Renate
das Geld

Gib _____ ! das Geld
ihr

Gib _____ ! Renate
es

Gib _____ ! es
ihr

16. Ich kaufe _____ eine Krawatte
meinem Mann

Ich kaufe _____ ihm
eine Krawatte

17. Ich zeige _____ . dir
mein Büro

Ich zeige _____ . dir
es

18. Bringen Sie _____ ! die Zeitung
mir

Bringen Sie _____ ! mir
sie

2   Express in German

1. I'll buy you a beer.
2. Are you going to give the waitress a tip?
   Are you going to give her a tip?
3. Tell Hans my address.
   Tell him my address.
   Tell it to him.
4. I'll show you the letter.
   I'll show it to you.
5. I'll buy you something.
6. I'm going to buy my wife a dress.
   I'm going to buy her a dress.
7. Bring me the mail.
   Bring it to me.
8. We'll show you the house.
   We'll show it to you.
9. I'm going to show the letter to my lawyer.
   I'm going to show him the letter.
   I'm going to show it to my lawyer.
   I'm going to show it to him.
10. She tells her mother everything.
11. Bring me the newspaper.
    Bring it to me.
12. Give the book to my secretary.
    Give her the book.
    Give it to my secretary.
    Give it to her.
13. I'm going to buy my husband a tie.
    I'm going to buy him a tie.
14. I'll show you my office.
    I'll show it to you.
15. Will you give me the car?
    Will you give it to me?
16. I won't tell them anything.
17. Give Renate the money.
    Give her the money.
    Give it to her.
18. Tell me the address.

VOCABULARY

die **Adresse** address
alles everything
antworten (+ *dat.*) to answer
der **Anwalt** lawyer
das **Bier** beer
das **Bild** picture
der **Brief** letter
bringen to bring; take
der **Bruder** brother
das **Buch** book
das **Büro** office
der **Chef** boss
dir (to you (*fam. sing., dat.*)
etwas something
euch (to) you (*fam. plur., dat.*)
der **Fisch** fish

die **Frau** woman; wife
der **Freund** friend
die **Freundin** girlfriend
geben (gibt) to give
das **Geld** money
helfen (hilft) (+ *dat.*) to help
ihm (to) him (*dat.*)
ihnen (to) them (*dat.*)
Ihnen (to) you (*polite, dat.*)
ihr (to) her (*dat.*)
die **Karte** postcard
die **Katze** cat
kaufen to buy
der **Kellner** waiter
die **Kellnerin** waitress
das **Mädchen** girl
der **Mann** man; husband
mein my

mir (to) me (*dat.*)
(der) **Moment!** Just a minute!
die **Mutter** mother
nichts nothing, not . . . anything
die **Post** mail
der **Professor** professor
sagen to tell, say
schicken to send
die **Sekretärin** secretary
das **Trinkgeld** tip
uns (to) us (*dat.*)
der **Vater** father
der **Verkäufer** salesman
die **Verkäuferin** saleswoman
der **Wagen** car
zeigen to show
die **Zeitung** newspaper

Lesson 2   Level THREE

A Nehmen

nehmen	to take
ich nehme	wir nehmen
du **nimmst**	ihr nehmt
er **nimmt**	sie nehmen

Nehmen is irregular in its 2nd and 3rd person singular. Not only does the stem vowel change from long **e** to short **i,** but the changed stem ends in **-mm** rather than **-hm.**

STEM **nehm-**
CHANGED STEM nimm-

IMPERATIVE FORMS **Nimm!**
Nehmt!
Nehmen Sie!

DRILLS

• Replace the subjects of the following sentences with the words in parentheses, making the necessary changes in the verb forms.*

1. Ich nehme es nicht. (er, wir)
2. Nehmen Sie es? (du, er)
3. Ich nehme den Anzug. (er)

4. Nimmt er den Wagen? (Sie, du)
5. Nehmen Sie ihn mit! (du, ihr) (*imperative*)
   (**nehmen : . . mit:** to take along)

• Express in German.

1. Are you going to take it?
   (**du-** and **Sie**-forms)
2. He's going to take the suit.
3. Are you taking the car? (**du** and **Sie**-forms)

4. I'm not going to take it.
5. Take him along. (**du-** and **Sie**-forms)
6. We're taking the car.
7. Is he going to take it?

---

*__nehmen__ or **bringen?**
The sentences in this drill all use **nehmen.** But confusion can arise when the word *take* is used later in an "Express in German" exercise. The rule is simple—**bringen** must be used when you are taking someone or something *to someplace else.*

Ich bringe dich **nach Hause.** (I'll take you *home.*)
Ich bringe es **ihm.** (I'll take it *to him.*)

B Negation

German has two basic ways of expressing negation.

1 nicht: not

The most common way of negating a sentence (and the way similar to English negation) is to use the word **nicht**.

Ich sehe ihn **nicht**.	(I don't see him.)
Er hat den Wagen **nicht**.	(He doesn't have the car.)
Kommen Sie **nicht** mit?	(Aren't you coming along?)

Position of **nicht** (word order)

At this level, **nicht** will practically always appear *at the end of the sentence*. The only words that can come after it are:

1. A complement that completes the meaning of the verb:

Er **kommt** nicht **mit**.	(He's not *coming along*.)
Er **geht** nicht **weg**.	(He's not *going away*.)

2. Place expressions:

Er ist nicht **hier**.	(He's not *here*.)

2 kein: not a, not any

Look at the following examples of the usage of kein:

Er hat **keinen** Wagen.	(He doesn't have *a* car.)
Er hat **kein** Geld.	(He doesn't have *any* money.)

In those cases where English uses

not a or *not any*

German *must* use **kein** plus the appropriate ending. The endings used with **kein** are exactly the same as those used with **ein**:

	Masculine	Neuter	Feminine
NOM.	kein Mann	kein Kind	kein**e** Frau
ACC.	kein**en** Mann	kein Kind	kein**e** Frau
DAT.	kein**em** Mann	kein**em** Kind	kein**er** Frau

▶ Caution **Nicht ein** may *not* be used!

DRILLS

1   Position of **nicht**: after all objects and before all other complements

● Use **nicht** to negate the following sentences.

a. 1. Ich verstehe dich.
   2. Er hilft ihnen.
   3. Nimmst du die Krawatte?
   4. Ich sage es dir.
   5. Sehen Sie ihn?
   6. Er kauft den Anzug.

b. 1. Ich komme mit.
   2. Bleibt ihr da?   **(bleiben:** to stay, remain)
   3. Sie geht weg.
   4. Wohnt er hier?

c. 1. Sehen Sie ihn?
   2. Ich verstehe dich.
   3. Bleibt ihr da?
   4. Ich sage es dir.
   5. Ich komme mit.
   6. Er kauft den Anzug.
   7. Nimmst du die Krawatte?
   8. Wohnt er hier?
   9. Er hilft ihnen.

● Express in German.

1. I'm not coming along.
2. Don't you see him?
3. He's not going to help them.
4. Aren't you going to stay there?
5. I don't understand you.

6. He's not going to buy the suit.
7. Doesn't he live here?
8. I'm not going to tell you.
9. Aren't you going to take the tie?

2   Drills with **kein**

● Negate by inserting **kein** with the correct ending.

1. Ich sehe _____ Wagen.
2. Ich kaufe _____ Jacke.
3. Er ist _____ Professor.
4. Er hat _____ Geld.

5. Wir haben _____ Post.
6. Ich sehe _____ Bild.
7. Das ist _____ Mädchen.

● Express in German.

1. We don't have any mail.
2. He's not a professor.
3. I don't see any car.
4. He doesn't have any money.

5. I'm not going to buy a sports coat.
6. That's not a girl.
7. I don't see any picture.

3   Mixed drills

● Use **nicht** or **kein** to negate the following sentences.

1. Ich sage es dir.
2. Er ist ein Professor.
3. Sehen Sie ihn?
4. Ich komme mit.
5. Ich kaufe eine Jacke.
6. Wohnt er hier?
7. Ich sehe einen Wagen.
8. Ich verstehe dich.

9. Er hat Geld.
10. Bleibt ihr da?
11. Ich sehe ein Bild.
12. Nimmst du die Krawatte?
13. Er hilft ihnen.
14. Wir haben Post.
15. Er kauft den Anzug.
16. Das ist ein Mädchen.

• Express in German.

1. He's not going to help them.
2. I'm not coming along.
3. We don't have any mail.
4. I'm not going to tell you.
5. I don't see any car.
6. That's not a girl.
7. Doesn't he live here?
8. Aren't you going to take the tie?

9. He doesn't have any money.
10. Don't you see him?
11. He's not a professor.
12. Aren't you going to stay there?
13. I'm not going to buy a sports coat.
14. I don't understand you.
15. I don't see any picture.

C Noun Plurals

1 English versus German plural forms

With a few common exceptions, the plural forms of English nouns are very predictable: an -s or -es ending is merely added to the singular form of the noun:

Singular	Plural
suit	suits
dress	dresses

German, on the other hand, makes use of many plural forms, involving:

| STEM-VOWEL CHANGE | analogous to English man/men |
| VARIOUS ENDINGS | analogous to English child/children |

Since German plural forms are rarely predictable, they must be memorized. A list of the plural forms of nouns used in previous lessons can be found in the vocabulary section at the end of this lesson.

Summary

If you know the English word "suit," you have everything you need to know about the noun:

1. You know its definite article: *the* suit (since English has only *one* definite article).
2. You can predict its plural form: suits.

By contrast, a German noun should be considered tripartite. It is composed of:

1. The noun itself	**Anzug**
2. A definite article showing its gender	**der Anzug** (*masc.*)
3. Its plural form	**Anzüge**

2 Dictionary conventions

For the sake of brevity, dictionaries usually list plural forms as an expansion of singular forms. The required ending is found after a dash, as in **die Krawatte, -n.**

An "umlaut" of a stem vowel (**Anzüge**) is indicated by putting the umlaut over the dash following the singular form, as in **der Anzug, ⸚e.**

EXAMPLES	das Hemd, -en	die Hemden
	die Krawatte, -n	die Krawatten
	der Mantel, ⸚	die Mäntel
	das Hotel, -s	die Hotels
	das Haus, ⸚er	die Häuser
	der Wagen, –	die Wagen (no change)

3 Plural forms of the definite article and of the **ein**-words

Look at the following table:

	DEFINITE ARTICLE		EIN-WORDS		PERSONAL PRONOUNS
NOM.	die	Anzüge Hemden Krawatten	keine	Anzüge Hemden Krawatten	sie
ACC.	die	Anzüge Hemden Krawatten	keine	Anzüge Hemden Krawatten	sie
DAT.	den	Anzügen Hemden Krawatten	keinen	Anzügen Hemden Krawatten	ihnen

As you see:

1. There is only *one* set of plural forms for the definite article and for the **ein**-words—*regardless* of the gender of the singular form of the noun.

Singular	Plural
der Anzug	die Anzüge
das Hemd	die Hemden
die Krawatte	die Krawatten

▶ Note   Although **ein** (the indefinite article) cannot logically have a plural, we nonetheless speak of **ein**-words. These include **kein** and the possessive adjectives (**meine** Anzüge, my suits).

2. The plural endings of the **ein**-words are similar to the final letters of the forms of the definite article.

NOM.	die	keine
ACC.	die	keine
DAT.	den	keinen

4 Formation of noun plurals

Although one can't usually predict the plural form of a given noun, there are a limited number of plural forms that are commonly used.

Singular	Plural	Changes from Singular
1. Bier	Bier**e**	**-e**
2. Mantel	M**ä**ntel	**¨**
3. Anzug	Anz**ü**g**e**	**¨e**
4. Bild	Bild**er**	**-er***
Buch	B**ü**ch**er**	**¨er**
5. Adresse	Adresse**n**	**-(e)n†**
Frau	Frau**en**	
6. Wagen	Wagen	**–(no change)**
7. Chef	Chef**s**	**-s**

DRILLS

1   Plural forms

- Put the nouns in boldface into the plural. (In some cases, you may also have to·change the verb form.)

EXAMPLE   **Das Buch** ist dort drüben.   **Die Bücher sind** dort drüben.

a. -e

1. Er schreibt **den Brief** morgen.
2. Siehst du **den Fisch?**
3. **Das Bier** in München is gut.
   (München: Munich; **gut:** good)
4. **Der Brief** ist dort drüben.
5. **Der Tag** ist heiß.   **(der Tag:** day; **heiß:** hot)
6. **Der Abend** ist kalt.
   (der Abend: evening; **kalt:** cold)

b. ¨

1. Ich habe **keinen Mantel.**
2. **Vater** sagt das immer.   **(immer:** always)
3. **Der Mantel** ist dort drüben.
4. **Keine Mutter** ist da.
5. **Vater** versteht nichts.

---

*⁽¨⁾**er**

Bild	Bilder	**-er**
Buch	Bücher	**¨er**

The group always takes an **-er** ending and takes an umlaut *if possible* (that is, if the stem vowel of the noun is a vowel that can take an umlaut). Only a (ä), o (ö), u (ü), and the diphthong au (äu) can be umlauted.

†**-(e)n**

Adresse	Adressen	**-n**
Frau	Frauen	**-en**

The plural forms of this group always end in **-en.** If the singular form ends in an **-e,** then only an **-n** ending is added.

c. ⸚e

1. **Die Nacht** ist sehr schön. (die Nacht: night)
2. **Der Anzug** ist dort drüben.
3. **Der Hut** ist schrecklich!

(schrecklich: horrible)

4. Ich sehe **keinen Anzug.**
5. Ich schicke Ihnen **den Hut.**

d. Mixed drills: plurals -e, ⸚, ⸚e

1. Ich schreibe **den Brief** morgen.
2. **Der Anzug** ist dort drüben.
3. Ich habe **keinen Mantel.**
4. **Das Bier** in München ist sehr gut.
5. **Vater** sagt das immer.
6. **Der Abend** ist kalt.
7. **Die Nacht** ist sehr schön.
8. Ich schicke Ihnen **den Hut.**
9. **Keine Mutter** ist da.
10. Siehst du **den Fisch?**
11. **Der Tag** ist heiß.
12. **Vater** versteht nichts.
13. **Der Hut** ist schrecklich.
14. **Der Brief** ist dort drüben.
15. Wo ist **der Mantel?**

e. ⸚ er

1. Fragen Sie **das Kind!**
2. **Das Kleid** ist da.
3. **Der Mann** ist da drüben.
4. Sehen Sie **das Haus** da drüben?
5. Schicken Sie mir **das Kleid!**
6. Was kostet **das Buch?**
7. Bringen Sie mir **das Bild!**
8. Was macht **der Mann** da?
9. Vergiß **das Buch** nicht, Hans!
10. Nimm **das Kind** mit!

(nehmen . . . mit: to take . . . along)

11. Ich schicke Ihnen **das Buch** morgen.
12. Was kostet **das Haus?**
13. Ich lese **das Buch** nicht.

f. -(e)n

1. Ich gebe Ihnen **die Adresse.**
2. Bringen Sie mir **die Zeitung!**
3. Vergiß **die Karte** nicht!
4. Gut, Sie nehmen **das Hemd.**
5. Kauf ihm **keine Krawatte!**
6. Ich nehme **die Jacke.**
7. Zeigen Sie mir **die Hose!**
8. **Die Frau** bleibt hier.
9. Ich gebe dir **die Katze.**
10. Sag mir **die Adresse!**
11. Siehst du **die Frau** da drüben?
12. **Die Krawatte** ist schrecklich.
13. Ich schicke Ihnen **die Karte** morgen.
14. Er hat **keine Jacke.**
15. **Die Hose** kostet zu viel. (zu viel: too much)
16. **Der Professor** ist nicht hier.
17. Frau Heller kauft **die Zeitung.**
18. Nehmen Sie **das Hemd?**

g. —

1. Ich sehe **kein Mädchen.**
2. **Der Wagen** kostet zu viel.
3. **Das Mädchen** ist nicht da.
4. Ich sehe **keinen Verkäufer.**
5. Wo ist **der Wagen?**

h. -s

1. Wo ist **das Büro?** (das Büro: the office)
2. **Das Hotel** ist zu teuer.

(das Hotel: hotel; teuer: expensive)

3. Ich sehe **kein Hotel.**
4. Kennst du **das Büro?**

i. Mixed drills: plurals ⸚er, -(e)n, –, -s

a. 1. Ich sehe **kein Mädchen.**
   2. Nehmen Sie **das Hemd?**
   3. **Das Hotel** ist zu teuer.
   4. Sehen Sie **das Haus** dort drüben?
   5. Nimm **das Kind** mit!
   6. **Die Krawatte** ist schrecklich.
   7. Kennst du **das Büro?**
   8. Ich nehme **die Jacke.**
   9. Vergiß **die Karte** nicht!
   10. Was kostet **das Buch?**

b. 1. **Das Mädchen** ist nicht da.
   2. Sag mir **die Adresse!**
   3. **Das Kleid** ist da.
   4. Was kostet **das Haus?**
   5. Bringen Sie mir **die Zeitung!**
   6. Was macht **der Mann** da?
   7. Ich schicke Ihnen **die Karte** morgen.

   8. Zeigen Sie mir **die Hose!**
   9. Ich sehe **keinen Verkäufer.**
   10. Fragen Sie **das Kind!**

c. 1. Wo ist **das Büro?**
   2. **Die Frau** bleibt hier.
   3. Ich gebe Ihnen **die Adresse.**
   4. **Der Mann** ist da drüben.
   5. Was kostet **das Buch?**
   6. Ich gebe dir **die Karte.**
   7. Gut, Sie nehmen **das Hemd.**
   8. Wo ist **der Wagen?**
   9. Ich sehe **kein Hotel.**
   10. Er hat **keine Jacke.**

d. 1. Ich lese **das Buch** nicht.
   2. **Der Wagen** kostet zu viel.

2 Express in German

a. 1. I'll write the letters tomorrow.
      I'll write them tomorrow.
   2. Where are the coats?
   3. Don't forget the postcards.
   4. Take the children along.
   5. Fathers don't understand anything.
      (not . . . anything, nothing: **nichts**)
   6. The nights are very beautiful.
   7. What do the books cost?
      What do they cost?
   8. Tell me the addresses.
   9. I'll take the shirts.
      I'll take them.
   10. The sports coats cost too much.

b. 1. Where are the offices?
      Where are they?
   2. Do you see the cars?
   3. The women are staying home.
      (home: **zu Hause**)*
   4. The suits are over there.
   5. The hotels are too expensive.
   6. I don't see any girls.
   7. What do the ties cost?
   8. The days are hot.

   9. What are the men doing there?
   10. Bring me the newspapers.

c. 1. I'll send you the pictures tomorrow.
   2. Do you see the fish? (*plural*)
   3. Inge, the dresses are here.
   4. Where are the salesmen?
      Where are they?
   5. The houses cost too much.
   6. The hats are horrible.
      They're horrible.

***nach Hause** is used with motion towards the house. You're on the way, but you're not there yet: Ich **gehe** nach Hause.

zu Hause means that you are already *at home*, in the house: Ich **bin** zu Hause.

5 Dative plural (-n)

The plural form of the noun adds an -n ending in the dative case.

EXAMPLES	Nominative and Accusative Plural	Dative Plural	
	die Anzüge (sie)	den Anzügen (ihnen)	(suits)
	die Mäntel	den Mänteln	(coats)
	die Kinder	den Kindern	(children)

▶ **Exceptions** If the plural form of the noun ends in

-n or -s

the dative plural **-n** ending is *not* added.

EXAMPLES	Nominative and Accusative Plural	Dative Plural	
	die Krawatten	den Krawatten	(ties)
	die Hotels	den Hotels	(hotels)

DRILLS

● Supply the correct *dative* plural forms.

EXAMPLES Zeigen wir es d— Kinder—!
Zeigen wir es ——————!
(to them)

Zeigen wir es **den** Kindern!
Zeigen wir es **ihnen**!

1. Sagen Sie es d— Männer—!
   Sagen Sie es ————!
   (to them)
2. Ich kaufe d— Mädchen etwas.
   Ich kaufe ———— etwas.
   (them)
3. Helfen Sie d— Damen! (die Dame, –n: lady)
   Helfen Sie ————!
   (them)
4. Zeigen wir es d— Kinder—!
   Zeigen wir es ————!
   (to them)

5. Was bringen wir d— Frauen?
   Was bringen wir ————?
   (them)
6. Mädchen sagen d— Mütter— alles.
   Sie sagen ———— alles.
   (them)
7. Jungen sagen d— Väter— nichts.
   (**nichts:** not . . . anything, nothing)
   Sie sagen ———— nichts.
   (them)

● Put the *dative* objects (in boldface) into the plural.

1. Ich kaufe **dem Mädchen** etwas.
2. Zeigen wir es **dem Kind**!
3. Sagen Sie es **dem Mann**!
4. Ein Mädchen sagt **der Mutter** alles.
   (Mädchen . . . .)

5. Helfen Sie **der Dame**!
6. Was bringen wir **der Frau**?
7. Ein Junge sagt **dem Vater** nichts.
   (Jungen . . . .)

• Express in German.

1. Let's show it to the kids.
   Let's show it to them.
2. What'll we take the women?
   What'll we take them?
3. Girls tell their (*lit.:* the) mothers everything.
   They tell them everything.
4. Tell the men.
   Tell them.

5. I'm going to buy the girls something.
   I'm going to buy them something.
6. Boys don't tell their (*lit.:* the) fathers anything. (not . . . anything: **nichts**)
   They don't tell them anything.
7. Help the ladies.
   Help them.

D Weak Nouns

A few German nouns take endings in the *singular* as well as the plural. Almost all of these nouns are *masculine* and have the ending **-en** in all cases except the *nominative singular:*

	Singular	Plural
NOM.	der Student	die Studenten
ACC.	den Studenten	die Studenten
DAT.	dem Studenten	den Studenten

(der Student: student)

If the nominative singular already ends in **-e** (for example, **der Junge:** the boy; **der Kunde:** the customer), all you do is add an **-n** to get the **-en** ending:

	Singular	Plural
NOM.	der Junge	die Jungen*
ACC.	den Jungen	die Jungen
DAT.	dem Jungen	den Jungen

(der Junge: boy)

▶ Exception

	Singular	Plural
NOM.	der Herr	die Herren
ACC.	den Herrn	die Herren
DAT.	dem Herrn	den Herren

(der Herr: gentleman, Mr.)

As you can see, Herr takes only **-n**, not **-en**, in the singular.

---

*The form **Jungens** (you guys) is a slang form and is used only as a form of address.

DRILLS

● Supply the correct form of the noun.

1. Ich sehe den Junge___ nicht. (*the boy*)
   Zeig es dem Junge___! (*to the boy*)
   Wo sind die Junge___? (*the boys*)
   Zeigen Sie es den Junge___! (*to the boys*)
2. Ich sehe keinen Kunde___. (*I do **not** see **a** customer.*)
   Zeigen Sie es dem Kunde___! (*to the customer*)
   Ich sehe keine Kunde___. (*I do **not** see **any** customers.*)
3. Er schickt es einem Student___. (*to a student*)
   Wo sind die Student___? (*the students*)
4. Schicken Sie es Herr___ Lenz! (*to Mr. Lenz*)
   Die Herr___ kommen später. (*the gentlemen*)

● Using the English sentence as a cue, complete the German noun phrase.

1. Where's the boy?	Wo ist d___ Junge?
2. Where are the boys?	Wo sind d___ Junge___?
3. He's sending it to a student.	Er schickt es ein___ Student___.
4. I don't see a customer.	Ich sehe kein___ Kunde___.
5. The gentlemen are coming later.	D___ Herr___ kommen später.
6. Show it to the customer.	Zeigen Sie es d___ Kunde___!
7. I don't see the boy.	Ich sehe d___ Junge___ nicht.
8. Where are the students?	Wo sind d___ Student___?
9. Show it to the boys.	Zeigen Sie es d___ Junge___!
10. Send it to Mr. Lenz.	Schicken Sie es Herr___ Lenz!
11. I don't see any customers.	Ich sehe kein___ Kunde___.
12. Show it to the boy.	Zeig es d___ Junge___!

● Express in German.

1. Show it to the customer.
2. Where are the boys?
3. Send it to Mr. Lenz.
4. I don't see a customer.
5. Show it to the boys.
6. Where are the students?
7. I don't see any customers.
8. He's sending it to a student.
9. The gentlemen are coming later.
10. Where's the boy?

Summary of noun plurals used in this lesson

Masculine	Neuter	Feminine
der Abend, -e	das Bier, -e	die Adresse, -n
der Anzug, ⁻e	das Bild, -er	die Frau, -en
der Brief, -e	das Buch, ⁻er	die Hose, -n
der Fisch, -e	das Büro, -s	die Jacke, -n
der Herr, -n, -en*	das Fräulein, -	die Karte, -n
der Hut, ⁻e	das Geld, -er	die Katze, -n
der Junge, -n -n*	das Haus, ⁻er	die Krawatte, -n
der Kunde, -n, -n*	das Hemd, -en	die Mutter, ⁻
der Mann, ⁻er	das Hotel, -s	die Nacht, ⁻e
der Mantel, ⁻	das Kind, -er	die Zeitung, -en
der Morgen, -	das Kleid, -er	
der Professor, -en	das Mädchen, -	
der Student, -en, -en*		
der Tag, -e		
der Vater, ⁻		
der Verkäufer, -		
der Wagen, -		

VOCABULARY

der **Abend, -e** evening
das **Buch, ⁻er** book
das **Büro, -s** office
    gut good
der **Herr, -n, -en** gentleman; Mr.
    heiß hot
das **Hotel, -s** hotel
    immer always
der **Junge, -n, -n** boy
    kalt cold
das **Kind, -er** child

der **Kunde, -n, -n** customer
    München Munich
die **Nacht, ⁻e** night
    nehmen (nimmst, nimmt) to take
    nehmen . . . mit take . . . along
    nichts nothing, not . . . anything
    schrecklich horrible
der **Student, -en, -en** student
der **Tag, -e** day
    teuer expensive
    zu viel too much

*The dictionary convention for weak nouns shows *both* the changed singular form *and* the plural form:

    der Herr, -n, -en (der Herr, den Herr**n**, die Herr**en**)
    der Student, -en, -en (der Student, den Student**en**, die Student**en**)

Reading II

Zählen und Zahlen
(Counting and Paying)

The dialogues and exercises in this unit present situations that involve numbers, counting and paying for things with German money. As you know, the mark is the basic unit of German currency (**eine Mark = 100 Pfennig**: *one mark = 100 pfennigs*). The abbreviation for Mark is **DM,** which stands for **Deutsche Mark** (*German mark*). Like the dollar sign, **DM** comes before the price, but it is spoken like this:

> DM 1.- = eine Mark
> DM 7.- = sieben Mark

Each of the dialogues in this unit is followed by exercises. In addition to the exercises, the dialogues themselves may be used for practice, as they were in Reading I. In fact, it is a good idea to reproduce the German dialogues from their English equivalents before going on to the exercises. Pay particular attention to pronunciation and intonation.

But first practice the basic German numbers.

German Numbers

Numbers 1 to 12

The numbers 1 to 12 are each separate and distinct words.

1	eins (ein-)	7	sieben
2	zwei	8	acht
3	drei	9	neun
4	vier	10	zehn
5	fünf	11	elf
6	sechs	12	zwölf

▶ Note   The word **eins** is only used in counting. If the word **ein** is followed by a noun, it must take the appropriate gender endings.

> Es kostet **eine** Mark.   (It costs a mark.)
> [*fem. acc.*]

92

Numbers 13 to 19

With two exceptions, these numbers are formed by adding the suffix **-zehn** to the numbers **drei** through **neun**:

13	dreizehn
14	vierzehn
15	fünfzehn
16	**sech**zehn
17	**sieb**zehn
18	achtzehn
19	neunzehn

▶ Note **Sech-** (not **sechs**) is used to form **sechzehn**.
Sieb- (not **sieben**) is used to form **siebzehn**.

Numbers 20 to 90

The suffix **-zig** is used to form these numbers:

20	**zwan**zig	60	**sech**zig
30	**dreißig**	70	**sieb**zig
40	vierzig	80	achtzig
50	fünfzig	90	neunzig

▶ Note As was the case with **sechzehn** and **siebzehn**, **sech-** (not **sechs**) is used to form **sechzig** and **sieb-** (not **sieben**) is used to form **siebzig**.
Zwan- (not **zwei**) is used to form **zwanzig**.
ßig (not **-zig**) is used to form **dreißig**.

DRILLS

Express the following numbers in German.

Numbers 1–12

a.			b.		
1	7		8	9
2	8		11	2
3	9		4	6
4	10		7	10
5	11		1	3
6	12		12	5

Numbers 13–19

a.			b.		
13	17		17	14
14	18		13	18
15	19		15	16
16			19	

Numbers 20–90

a.			b.		
20	60		70	30
30	70		20	80
40	80		50	60
50	90		90	40

Kinobesuch   (Going to the Movies)

A: Ich kenne den Film. Er ist großartig.
   Warum kommst du nicht mit?
B: Ich habe kein Geld. Gibst du mir
   zehn Mark bis morgen?
A: Sicher. Sind zehn Mark genug?
B: Ja, danke. Ich gebe sie dir morgen.

A: Also, gehen wir. Der Film fängt um
   acht an.

A: I know that movie. It's great. Why
   don't you come along?
B: I don't have any money. Will you
   give me ten marks until tomorrow?
A: Sure. Are ten marks enough?
B: Yeah. I'll give it back to you tomorrow.
A: O.K., let's go. The movie starts at
   eight.

* * *

B: Hier ist das Kino.
A: Was kosten die Karten?
B: Da ist die Preistafel.* Au! Die Plätze
   sind teuer.
A: Ja, Loge und Rang schon. Aber
   erster Platz und Sperrsitz sind
   in Ordnung.
B: Erster Platz, dann?

A: Nein, das ist zu weit vorne. Nehmen
   wir Sperrsitz. Das kostet nur
   eine Mark mehr.

B: Here's the theater.
A: How much are [lit.: cost] the tickets?
B: There's the price list.* Ouch! The
   seats are expensive.
A: **Loge** and **Rang** are, but **erster
   Platz** and **Sperrsitz** are O.K.

B: How about **erster Platz?** [lit.: **Erster
   Platz,** then?]
A: No, that's too far up front. Let's take
   Sperrsitz. It only costs a mark more.

* * *

B: Zweimal Sperrsitz, bitte.
KASSIERERIN:
   Das macht zwölf Mark, bitte.

B: Two **Sperrsitz,** please.
CASHIER:
   That'll be [lit.: makes] 12 marks,
   please.

EXERCISE

Two students perform this drill, one taking the role of the person buying the tickets and the other, the role of the person selling them. The first student orders either one or two tickets from the list shown in the photo on the next page. The second student uses the formula answer **Das macht _____ Mark, bitte,** inserting the price of the ticket(s) the first student has asked for.

---

*The photo on the following page shows a movie **Preistafel** (price list). As you can see, there are more categories of seating than there are in an American movie house. The closer you are to the screen, the less you pay. Except for **Loge,** the names for the seats don't have exact English equivalents, so we haven't translated them.

Kaufhaus   (Department Store)

(*Auf der Straße*)
A: Tag. Wo gehst du hin?
B: Ich gehe zu Hertie.*
   Ich brauche ein Hemd.
A: Ich gehe auch zu Hertie.
   Gehen wir zusammen.
B: Prima.

(*Bei Hertie*)
B: Verzeihung, wo ist die
   Herrenabteilung?
VERKÄUFERIN:
   Eine Treppe hoch. Dann links.
B: Danke schön.

(*In der Herrenabteilung*)
B: Wie findest du das Sporthemd
   hier?
A: Klasse. Was kostet es denn?†
B: Dreißig Mark. Ist das zu viel?
A: Ich glaube nicht. Nimm es doch.†

(*On the street*)
A: Hi. Where are you going?
B: I'm going to Hertie's.*
   I need a shirt.
A: I'm going to Hertie's, too.
   Let's go together.
B: Great.

(*At Hertie's*)
B: Excuse me, where's the
   men's department?
SALESWOMAN:
   One flight up, then left.
B: Thanks.

(*In the Men's Department*)
B: How do you like [*lit.*: find] this
   sportshirt?
A: Terrific. What does it cost?
B: Thirty marks. Is that too much?
A: I don't think so. Take it.

---

*__Hertie:__ a large chain of German department stores.

†__Denn__ and __doch__ are called particles, and they don't have any literal translations. They function to make a command or a question a little more emphatic.

         doch reinforces a command
         denn reinforces a question

(*An der Kasse*)

B: Ich nehme das Sporthemd, bitte.

KASSIERERIN:

Dreißig Mark, bitte. Ist das alles?

B: Ja. Hier, fünfzig Mark, bitte.

KASSIERERIN:

Und zwanzig Mark zurück, bitte.
Auf Wiedersehen.

B: Auf Wiedersehen.

(*At the cashier's*)

B: I'll take this [*lit.:* the] sportshirt,
   please.

CASHIER:

Thirty marks, please. Will that be all?

B: Yes. Here's fifty marks.

CASHIER:

And twenty marks back.
Good-bye.

B: Good-bye.

EXERCISE

Sonderangebot!°		Sonderangebot: sale
das Sporthemd	DM 30.–	
die Hose°	DM 40.–	die Hose: pants
der Hut	DM 60.–	
das Kleid	DM 80.–	
die Krawatte	DM 10.–	
die Bluse°	DM 20.–	die Bluse: blouse
der Pullover°	DM 40.–	der Pullover: sweater
der Bademantel°	DM 70.–	der Bademantel: bathrobe

Use this price list to perform the following dialogue between you and the cashier. Depending on the price of the item, give the cashier either fifty marks (**fünfzig Mark**) or a hundred marks (**hundert Mark**). The student playing the role of the cashier will have to give proper change.

SIE: Ich nehme d__ _____ , bitte.

KASSIERERIN: _____ Mark, bitte. Ist das alles?

SIE: Ja. Hier, _____ Mark, bitte.

KASSIERERIN: Und _____ Mark zurück. Auf Wiedersehen.

SIE: Auf Wiedersehen.

Wieviel macht das?   (How much is it?)

This exercise will let you get used to German coins and paper money in various denominations and combinations. The most common coins are the ten-pfennig piece, the fifty-pfennig piece, the one-mark piece, the two-mark piece, and the five-mark piece.

| zehn Pfennig | fünfzig Pfennig | eine Mark | zwei Mark | fünf Mark |

Look at the following combinations of coins and say what they add up to:

EXAMPLE

    = zwei Mark siebzig

German paper money comes most commonly as 10-mark, 20-mark, and 50-mark bills. Look at the following combinations of bills and say what they add up to:

= _____

= _____

= _____

= _____

= _____

Zeitungskiosk (Newsstand)

SIE: Geben Sie mir den *Spiegel*,* bitte.	YOU: Give me the *Spiegel*,* please.
VERKÄUFER: Zwei Mark fünfzig, bitte.	MAN AT NEWSSTAND: That's two marks fifty.
SIE: Ist der *Stern** auch da?	YOU: Is the *Stern** there, too?
VERKÄUFER: Ja. Nehmen Sie ihn auch?	MAN: Yes, do you want that, [*lit.*: Are you taking it] too?
SIE: Ja, bitte.	YOU: Yes, please.
VERKÄUFER: Also, zwei Mark fünfzig und zwei Mark achtzig—macht zusammen fünf Mark dreißig.	MAN: O.K. Two (marks) fifty and two (marks) eighty—makes five (marks) thirty all together.

*Spiegel and *Stern* are popular German magazines.

EXERCISE

Here is a price list for some popular German magazines and newspapers:

Quick	DM 1.80	*Schöner Wohnen*	DM 3.50
Hör zu	DM 2.20	*Eltern*	DM 2.70
Essen und Trinken	DM 3.30	*Photo*	DM 3.20
Autosport	DM 3.90	*Petra*	DM 2.60
Konkret	DM 2.60	der *Spiegel*	DM 2.50
Brigitte	DM 2.40	der *Stern*	DM 2.80

die *Zeit*	DM 1.90
die *Welt*	DM -.60*
die *Bildzeitung*	DM -.30
der *Münchner Merkur*	DM -.70
der *Tagesspiegel*	DM -.40

Your instructor will use this list to ask you for the prices. In answering the questions use the titles exactly as they appear on the list.

EXAMPLES   INSTRUCTOR: Was kostet der *Spiegel*?
STUDENT: Der *Spiegel* kostet zwei Mark fünfzig.

INSTRUCTOR: Was kostet *Essen und Trinken*?
STUDENT: *Essen und Trinken* kostet drei Mark dreißig.

Reinigung und Wäscherei   (Cleaning and Laundry)

FRAU HINTER DER THEKE:

Der Anzug und die Hose sind schon fertig.

SIE:

Und der Regenmantel?

FRAU:

Den Regenmantel haben wir erst morgen. Die Imprägnierung dauert etwas länger.

SIE:

Gut. Ich bezahle den Anzug und die Hose jetzt und den Regenmantel morgen. Ist das Ihnen recht?

FRAU:

Sicher. Ein Anzug, sieben Mark fünfzig, eine Hose, drei Mark vierzig. Also, zehn Mark neunzig zusammen, bitte.

WOMAN BEHIND THE COUNTER:

The suit and the pants are ready.

YOU:

And the raincoat?

WOMAN:

We won't have the raincoat until tomorrow. The waterproofing takes a little longer.

YOU:

Fine. I'll pay for the suit and the pants now and for the raincoat tomorrow. Is that all right with you?

WOMAN:

Of course. A suit—seven (marks) fifty, a pair of pants—three (marks) forty. Ten (marks) ninety all together, please.

---

*When the price is less than one mark, the word **Pfennig** follows the number. **DM-.50 = fünfzig Pfennig.**

SIE:	YOU:
So, bitte schön. (*Sie geben der Frau einen Zwanzigmarkschein.*)	There you are. (*You give the woman a 20-mark bill.*)
FRAU:	WOMAN:
Und neun Mark zehn zurück.	And nine (marks) ten back.
SIE:	YOU:
Danke schön.	Thanks.
FRAU:	WOMAN:
Ich danke auch. Auf Wiedersehen.	Thank you. Good-bye.
SIE:	YOU:
Auf Wiedersehen. Bis morgen.	Good-bye. See you [*lit.*: until] tomorrow.

EXERCISE

Now do a similar dialogue yourself, substituting items and prices from the **Dörr**-list* below. Use the first column price list, which is for regular cleaning (the other two columns are for special service). Choose only the first seven articles (that is, through **Kleid**).

Wäscherei und Reinigung **Dörr**			
Reinigung			
Pullover	2,40	2,90	3,90
Weste	2,90	3,40	4,40
Bluse	4,50	5,40	6,40
Sakko	4,50	5,40	6,40
Hose	3,40	4,50	5,50
D'Rock	4,50	5,40	6,40
Kleid, einfach	4,50	5,40	6,40
Mantel	7,90	8,90	9,90
Trenchmantel einschl. Imprägnierung			10,90
Zuschlag Falten	2,40	2,40	2,40

die Weste: cardigan

der Sakko: jacket

D'Rock = **der Damenrock**: skirt

der Trenchmantel: trenchcoat
der Zuschlag: extra charge
die Falten: pleats

DIE FRAU HINTER DER THEKE:	D_____ _____ ist fertig.
SIE:	Und der Regenmantel?
FRAU:	Den Regenmantel haben wir erst morgen. Die Imprägnierung dauert etwas länger.
SIE:	Gut. Ich bezahle d_____ _____ jetzt und den Regenmantel morgen. Ist das Ihnen recht?
FRAU:	Sicher.
	D_____ _____ macht DM _____.
SIE:	So. Zehn Mark, bitte.
FRAU:	Und _____ zurück.
SIE:	Danke schön.
FRAU:	Ich danke auch. Auf Wiedersehen.
SIE:	Auf Wiedersehen. Bis morgen.

*****Dörr** = chain of dry cleaners

Lesson 3   Level ONE

A Treffen

treffen	*to meet*
ich treffe	wir treffen
du triffst	ihr trefft
er trifft	sie treffen

Treffen changes its stem vowel from short **e** to short **i** in the 2nd and 3rd person singular.

▶ **Note**   **Treffen** means "meet" in the sense of "get together":

I'll meet you later.

It does *not* mean "to make someone's acquaintance."

DRILLS

- Replace the subjects of the following sentences with the words in parentheses, making the necessary changes in the verb forms.

1. Wann treffen Sie ihn? (du, wir, er)
2. Ich treffe dich später. (er, sie [*they*])
3. Er trifft ihn morgen. (ich, wir)
4. Wo treffe ich dich? (er, wir)

- Express in German.

1. He'll meet you later.
2. Where will we meet you?
3. When will you (**du**) meet him?
4. I'll meet him tomorrow.
5. Where will he meet you?

102

B Prepositions

1 The prepositional phrase

The meaning and function of prepositions can be most easily understood in their most common setting, the prepositional phrase. Here is a simple example in English:

> I'm going *to the post office.*

"to the post office" is a prepositional phrase. It is made up of:

1. *to:* a preposition   2. *the post office:* the object of the preposition

In this case, the *whole phrase* has the function of answering the question "where?" —that is, it functions as an adverb of place.

> Where are you going?
> I'm going *to the post office.*

Prepositional phrases may also specify the "when" (time) or "how" (manner) of an action or situation.

2 German prepositions

German prepositional phrases have the same function, but the *object* of a German preposition must be in a specific *case.*

ACCUSATIVE	für **ihn**	(for him)	für **den** Mann	(for the man)
DATIVE	mit **ihm**	(with him)	mit **dem** Mann	(with the man)

▶ **Rule**   The case of the object of a preposition is determined by the preposition, which is said to "govern" or "take" it.

For the present, we are concerned with two sets of prepositions: one taking the *dative case* and the other taking the *accusative case.*

C Prepositions That Take Dative Objects

1 nach / zu

a. **nach:** to (destination, with place names)

> Fahren Sie nach Berlin?   (Are you driving *to* Berlin?)

Nach is used for destinations when referring to towns, cities, states, countries, and continents (that is, names of towns and of larger units).

nach: after (referring to time)

Er schläft nach dem Mittagessen.   (He sleeps *after* [the] lunch.)

Idiom: Ich gehe nach Hause.   (I'm going *home*.)

b. **zu:** to (with places inside a town or city or with persons)

Er fährt zum Bahnhof.   (He's driving *to the* station.)
Er fährt zur Post.   (He's driving *to the* post office.)
Ich komme zu dir.   (I'll come *to* your place.)

▶ **Note** **zu dem** is contracted to **zum**, **zu der** is contracted to **zur**

Contrast:

with people: Ich komme zu dir.   (I'll come *to* your place.)
inside a city: Ich fahre zur Post.   (I'm driving *to the* post office.)
to a city: Ich fahre nach Berlin.   (I'm driving *to* Berlin.)

Idioms: motion: nach Hause gehen   (to go home)
               no motion: zu Hause sein   (to be at home)

2 aus / von

a. **aus:** from (with place names)

Peter kommt aus Berlin.   (Peter comes *from* Berlin.)
Der Brief kommt aus Berlin.   (The letter comes *from* Berlin.)

In such cases, **aus** indicates *origin*. Note that the first sentence means that Peter was either born in Berlin or that he has been living there for some time.

aus: out of (location)

Er kommt aus dem Haus.   (He's coming *out of* the house.)

b. **von:** from

Er fährt von Stuttgart nach Berlin.   (He's driving *from* Stuttgart to Berlin.)

Contrast:

Ich komme aus Stuttgart.   (Origin: I come *from* Stuttgart; that is, I live there.)
Ich fahre von Stuttgart nach Berlin.

Der Brief ist von Thomas. (with persons)
Der Brief ist aus Berlin. (with places)

3 bei / mit

a. **bei:** at, with (in the sense of "in someone's house or home")

Sie wohnt bei ihm.   (She lives *at* his *place*.)
Sie wohnt bei dem Vater.   (She lives *at* her father's *place*.)

b. **mit:** with

> Kommen Sie **mit** mir, Herr Lenz.   (Come *with* me, Mr. Lenz.)

DRILLS

1 Fill-ins

- **nach / zu***

1. Ich gehe _____ Post.
   (to the)   (**die Post:** post office)
2. Wir fahren _____ Berlin.
   (to)
3. Er fährt _____ Bahnhof.
   (to the)
   (**der Bahnhof:** railroad station)
4. Ich gehe _____ Hause. (*I'm going home.*)
5. Fahren Sie _____ Europa?
   (to)   (**Europa:** Europe)
6. Sie ist _____ Hause. (*She's at home.*)

7. Er fährt _____ Hamburg.
   (to)
8. Sie gehen _____ Kaufhaus.
   (to the)
   (**das Kaufhaus:** department store)
9. Sie trifft ihn _____ Mittagessen.
   (after [the])
   (**das Mittagessen:** lunch)
10. Wann gehst du _____ Hause, Hans?
11. Er kommt _____ Konzert.
    (after the) (**das Konzert:** concert)
12. Ich komme _____ dir.
    (to)

- **aus / von**

1. Ist der Brief _____ Kurt?
   (from)
2. Er kommt _____ Kaufhaus.
   (out of the)
3. Ich bin Berliner.† Ich komme _____
   Berlin.
   (from)
4. Er fährt _____ Frankfurt nach Berlin.
   (from)
5. Kommen Sie _____ Wien, Herr Lederer?
   (from)
   (**Wien:** Vienna)

6. Er kommt _____ Haus.
   (out of the)
7. Ist der Brief _____ ?
   (from him)
8. Hier ist eine Karte _____ Berlin.
   (from)
9. Kommen Sie _____ Deutschland?
   (from)

---

*Remember to contract **zu dem** to **zum** and **zu der** to **zur.**

†Where English says

> He's *a* New Yorker.   He's *an* American.

German says simply

> Er ist New Yorker.   Er ist Amerikaner.

German does not use the indefinite article (**ein**) with nouns indicating one's nationality or local origin.

• **bei / mit**

    1. Kommen Sie _____, Herr Lenz.
                (with me)

    2. Sie wohnt _____.
            (at Mrs. Heller's place.)

    3. Er wohnt _____.
          (at my place)

    4. Ich komme _____, Herr Schmidt.
           (with you)

    5. Ich wohne _____.
          (at his place)

    6. Wohnt sie _____, Hans?
          (at your place)

2 Mixed drills

a. 1. Er fährt _____ Bahnhof.
          (to the)

    2. Ich bin Berliner. Ich komme
      _____ Berlin.
      (from)

    3. Er wohnt _____.
          (at my place)

    4. Ist der Brief _____ Kurt?
          (from)

    5. Ich gehe _____ Post.
          (to the)

    6. Kommen Sie _____, Herr Lenz?
          (with me)

    7. Er fährt _____ Hamburg.
          (to)

    8. Ist der Brief _____?
          (from him)

    9. Hans, wohnt sie _____?
          (at your place)

    10. Wann gehst du _____ Hause, Hans?

    5. Hier ist eine Karte _____ Berlin.
          (from)

    6. Sie gehen _____ Kaufhaus.
          (to the)

    7. Sie wohnt _____.
          (at Mrs. Heller's place)

    8. Wir fahren _____ Berlin.
          (to)

    9. Er kommt _____ Kaufhaus.
          (out of the)

    10. Er kommt _____ Konzert.
          (after the)

c. 1. Ich gehe _____ Hause.

    2. Er wohnt _____.
          (at my place)

    3. Sie ist _____ Hause. (*at home*)

    4. Er kommt _____ Haus.
          (out of the)

    5. Sie trifft ihn _____ Mittagessen.
          (after [the])

    6. Ich komme _____,
          (with you)
    Herr Schmidt.

    7. Ich komme _____ dir.
          (to)

    8. Kommen Sie _____ Deutschland?
          (from)

b. 1. Kommen Sie _____ Wien, Herr Karl?
          (from)

    2. Fahren Sie _____ Europa?
          (to)

    3. Er fährt _____ Frankfurt _____
          (from)   (to)
    Berlin.

    4. Ich wohne _____.
          (at his place)

3 Express in German

a. 1. They're going to the department store.
    2. He's coming out of the house.
    3. Does she come from Germany?
    4. She lives at my place.
    5. We're going to the post office.
    6. Is the letter from Eva?
    7. Do you come from Vienna, Herbert?
    8. When are you going home, Mr. Lenz?
    9. We're going to your place.
    10. They're coming after the concert.

b. 1. Are you coming with us, Inge?
   2. We're driving to Frankfurt.
   3. I'll meet you after lunch.
   4. I'm going home.
   5. He's a Berliner. He comes from Berlin.
   6. We're driving to the station.
   7. I'm living at his place.
   8. Here's a card from Potsdam.
   9. Are you going to Europe?
      (use **fahren**)
  10. I'll come with you, Mr. Heller.

c. 1. They're at home.
   2. He lives at my place.
   3. Is the letter from her?
   4. I'm driving from Frankfurt to Berlin.
   5. She's living at our place.
   6. They're coming out of the department store.
   7. We're driving to Hamburg.
   8. I'm living at Mrs. Heller's place.
   9. She's at home.

D Prepositions That Take Accusative Objects

durch: through

> Wir gehen **durch** den Park.   (We're going *through* the park.)

für: for

> Hans! Ich habe einen Brief **für** dich.   (Hans, I have a letter *for* you.)

gegen: against

> Ich habe nichts **gegen** ihn.   (I don't have anything *against* him.)

ohne: without

> Wir gehen **ohne** ihn.   (We're going *without* him.)

um: around

> Sie sitzen **um** den Tisch.   (They're sitting *around* the table.)

▶ Note   A common contraction: **für das** → **fürs**

> Hast du Geld **für das** Kino?   Hast du Geld **fürs** Kino?

Colloquial German tends to contract **für das** to **fürs,** but this contraction is not mandatory.

DRILLS

1   Fill-ins

● **für / gegen**

1. Ich mache das _____ , Hans.
   (for you)

2. Ich habe nichts _____ Anzug.
   (against the)

3. Was gibst du mir _____ Wagen?
   (for the)
   (**der Wagen:** car)

4. Was hast du _____ ?
   (against him)

5. Hast du Geld _____ Kino?
   (for the)
   (**das Geld:** money; **das Kino:** the movies)

6. Er wirft den Ball _____ Haus.
   (against the)
   (**werfen [wirft]:** to throw; **der Ball:** ball)

● **durch / ohne / um**

1. Wir fahren _____ München.
   (through)   (**München:** Munich)

2. Was machen wir _____ Wagen?
   (without a)

3. Sie sitzen _____ Tisch.
   (around the)   (**der Tisch:** table)

4. Er fährt _____ Stadt.
   (through the)
   (**die Stadt:** town, city)

5. Er geht _____ Ecke.
   (around the)   (**die Ecke:** corner)

6. Wir gehen _____.
   (without him)

7. Er kommt _____ Tür.
   (through the)   (**die Tür:** door)

8. Die Jungen stehen _____ Wagen.
   (around the)
   (**stehen:** to stand)

9. Er geht _____ Park.
   (through the)   (**der Park:** the park)

10. Was mache ich _____, Ilse?
    (without you)

11. Der Zug fährt _____ Tunnel.
    (through a)
    (**der Zug:** train; **der Tunnel:** tunnel)

2   Mixed drills

1. Hast du Geld _____ Kino?
   (for the)

2. Wir fahren _____ München.
   (through)

3. Was machen wir _____ Wagen?
   (without a)

4. Er geht _____ Ecke.
   (around the)

5. Der Zug fährt _____ Tunnel.
   (through a)

6. Ich mache das _____, Hans.
   (for you)

7. Was hast du _____, Inge?
   (against him)

8. Wir gehen _____.
   (without him)

9. Sie sitzen _____ Tisch.
   (around the)

10. Er wirft den Ball _____ Haus.
    (against the)

11. Er fährt _____ Stadt.
    (through the)

12. Was gibst du mir _____ Wagen?
    (for the)

13. Was mache ich _____, Ilse?
    (without you)

14. Er kommt _____ Tür.
    (through the)

15. Ich habe nichts _____ Anzug.
    (against the)

16. Die Jungen stehen _____ Wagen.
    (around the)

17. Er geht _____ Park.
    (through the)

3   Express in German

1. We're driving through Munich.
2. He's going around the corner.
3. I'll do that for you, Hans.
4. What do you have against him, Inge?
5. What will you give me for the car?
6. They're sitting around the table.
7. She's driving through the city.
8. He's throwing the ball against the house.
9. Do you have money for the movies?
10. I don't have anything against the suit.
11. We're going without him.
12. I'll come through the park.
13. They're standing around the car.
14. The train is going through a tunnel.
    (use **fahren**)
15. What will we do without a car?

MIXED DRILLS

1 Dative and accusative prepositions

a. 1. Kommt sie _____ Deutschland?
    (from)

2. Er wohnt _____.
    (at my place)

3. Ich mache das _____, Hans.
    (for you)

4. Kommst du _____, Inge?
    (with us)

5. Ich habe nichts _____
    (against the)
    Anzug.

6. Sie gehen _____ Kaufhaus.
    (to the)

7. Ich fahre _____ Frankfurt _____
    (from)   (to)
    Berlin.

8. Wir gehen _____.
    (without him)

9. Ist der Brief _____?
    (from her)

10. Was machen wir _____ Wagen?
    (without a)

b. 1. Er kommt _____ Haus.
    (out of the)

2. Wir gehen _____ Post.
    (to the)

3. Ich komme _____ Park.
    (through the)

4. Ich treffe dich _____ Mittagessen.
    (after [the])

5. Hast du Geld _____ Kino?
    (for the)

6. Wir fahren _____ Berlin.
    (to)

7. Ich komme _____, Herr Heller.
    (with you)

8. Wir fahren _____ Bahnhof.
    (to the)

9. Sie sitzen _____ Tisch.
    (around the)

10. Wir gehen _____.
    (to your place)

c. 1. Sie fährt _____ Stadt.
    (through the)

2. Sie kommen _____ Kaufhaus.
    (out of the)

3. Ich wohne _____.
    (at his place)

4. Was hast du _____?
    (against him)

5. Sie kommen _____ Konzert.
    (after the)

6. Er geht _____ Ecke.
    (around the)

2 Express in German

a. 1. I'm driving from Frankfurt to Berlin.
    2. We're going to the post office.
    3. What do you have against him?
    4. They're going to the department store.
    5. What will we do without a car?
    6. She's driving through the city.
    7. He lives at my place.
    8. Does she come from Germany?
    9. They're coming after the concert.
    10. I'll do that for you, Hans.

b. 1. We're driving to the station.
    2. Do you have money for the movies?
    3. He's coming out of the house.
    4. We're driving to Berlin.

5. I don't have anything against the suit.
6. Are you coming with us?
7. I'm living at his place.
8. He's going around the corner.
9. I'll meet you after lunch.
10. We're going without him.

c. 1. They're coming out of the department
    store.
    2. They're sitting around the table.
    3. I'll come with you, Mr. Heller.
    4. Is the letter from her?
    5. We're going to your place.

VOCABULARY

aus from, out of
der **Bahnhof, ⸚e**
    railroad station
der **Ball, ⸚e** ball
bei at, with, at a
    person's place
durch through
die **Ecke, –n** corner
Europa Europe
für for
gegen against
das **Geld** money

das **Kaufhaus, ⸚er**
    department store
das **Kino, –s** the movies
das **Konzert, –e** concert
mit with
das **Mittagessen, –** lunch
(das) **München** Munich
nach to; after
ohne without
der **Park, –s** park
die **Post** post office
die **Stadt, ⸚e** city, town

stehen to stand
der **Tisch, –e** table
treffen (trifft) to meet
der **Tunnel, –s** tunnel
die **Tür, –en** door
um around
von from
der **Wagen, –** car
werfen (wirft) to throw
Wien Vienna
zu to
der **Zug, ⸚e** train

Lesson 3   Level TWO

A Werfen

werfen	*to throw*
ich werfe	wir werfen
du wirfst	ihr werft
er wirft	sie werfen

Werfen changes its stem vowel from short **e** to short **i** in the 2nd and 3rd person singular.

DRILLS

- Replace the subjects of the following sentences with the words in parentheses, making the necessary changes in the verb forms.

  1. Ich werfe es weg. (er, sie [*they*])   (**weg**: away)
  2. Werfen Sie es aufs* Sofa! (du- *and* ihr-*forms, imperative*)   (**aufs Sofa**: on[to] the sofa)
  3. Wirft er es weg? (Sie, du)

- Express in German.

  1. They're going to throw it away.
  2. Throw it on the sofa. (**Sie**-form)
  3. He's going to throw it away.
  4. Are you going to throw it away? (**du**-form)
  5. Throw it on the sofa. (**du**-form)
  6. I'm going to throw it away.
  7. Is he going to throw it away?

B Two-Way Prepositions

Two-way prepositions are prepositions that may take either the dative or the accusative case. The case used is determined by the meaning of the prepositional phrase; it is *not* optional.

*****aufs**: contraction of **auf das.**

Note the difference between the prepositional phrases used in the following English sentences:

> He's sitting *in* the living room.
> He just walked *into* the living room.

In the first sentence, the prepositional phrase (*in* the living room) gives the person's location—*where* he is. In the second sentence, the prepositional phrase (*into* the living room) gives the person's destination or the direction in which he was going—*where* he is going *to*. The preposition "into" expresses motion in a certain direction or toward a certain destination. Where there is no motion, however, "in" rather than "into" is used. One would not say: "He's sitting *into* the living room."

German two-way prepositions make the same kind of distinction. But instead of choosing between two prepositions (as English does with *in* and *into*), German chooses between the dative and the accusative case.

1 Dative: no motion (**wo?** = where?)

When there is *no motion,* two-way prepositions take dative objects, and the prepositional phrase answers the question **wo?** (*where?*).

> **Wo** ist er?   (*Where* is he?)
> Er ist in **der** Küche.   (He's in the kitchen.)

2 Accusative: motion (**wo . . . hin?** = where . . . to?)

When there is *motion,* two-way prepositions take accusative objects, and the prepositional phrase answers the question **wo . . . hin?** (*where . . . to?*).

> **Wo** geht er **hin?**   (*Where* is he going [*to*]?)
> Er geht in **die** Küche.   (He's going into the kitchen.)

3 List of two-way prepositions

über: over, above
unter: under, below

hinter: behind, in back of
vor: in front of

auf: on (horizontal surfaces)
an: on (vertical surfaces)

in: in, into
neben: beside, next to, alongside of
zwischen: between

a. über / unter

1. **über:** over, above

wo + DATIVE
Das Bild hängt **über dem Sofa.**
(The picture is hanging *over the sofa.*)

wohin + ACCUSATIVE
Er hängt das Bild **über das Sofa.**
(He's going to hang the picture *over the sofa.*)

2. **unter:** under, below

wo + DATIVE
Es ist **unter dem Tisch.**
(It's *under the table.*)

wohin + ACCUSATIVE
Stell es **unter den Tisch!**
(Put it *under the table.*)

b. hinter / vor

1. **hinter:** behind

wo + DATIVE
Der Wagen steht **hinter dem Haus.**
(The car is [standing] *behind the house.*)

wohin + ACCUSATIVE
Fahren Sie den Wagen **hinter das Haus!**
(Drive the car *behind the house.*)

2. **vor:** in front of (before)

wo + DATIVE
Die Flaschen stehen **vor der Tür.**
(The bottles are [standing] *in front of the door.*)

wohin + ACCUSATIVE
Stellen Sie die Flaschen **vor die Tür!**
(Put the bottles *in front of the door.*)

c. auf / an

1. **auf:** on (on top of)

Auf is used with *horizontal surfaces*—such as the floor, a chair, or a table:

wo + DATIVE
Es liegt **auf dem Tisch.**
(It's lying *on the table.*)

wohin + ACCUSATIVE
Stell es **auf den Tisch!**
(Put it *on the table.*)

2. **an:** on, onto

In contrast to **auf, an** is used with *vertical surfaces*—a wall or a blackboard.

wo + DATIVE
Es steht **an der Tafel.**
(It's *on the blackboard.*)

wohin + ACCUSATIVE
Schreib es **an die Tafel!**
(Write it *on the blackboard.*)

d. **in / neben / zwischen**

1. **in**: in, into

wo + DATIVE	Er ist **in der Küche.** (He's *in the kitchen.*)
wohin + ACCUSATIVE	Er geht **in die Küche.** (He is going *into the kitchen.*)

2. **neben**: next to, beside, alongside of

wo + DATIVE	Es ist **neben dem Haus.** (It's *alongside of the house.*)
wohin + ACCUSATIVE	Stellen Sie es **neben das Haus!** (Put it *alongside of the house.*)

3. **zwischen**: between

wo + DATIVE	Die Lampe steht **zwischen dem Sofa und dem Tisch.** (The lamp is [standing] *between the sofa and the table.*)
wohin + ACCUSATIVE	Stell die Lampe **zwischen das Sofa und den Tisch!** (Put the lamp *between the sofa and the table.*)

▶ Note   Some common mandatory contractions:

$$\begin{array}{ccl} \textbf{an dem} & \longrightarrow & \text{am} \\ \textbf{an das} & \longrightarrow & \text{ans} \\ \textbf{in dem} & \longrightarrow & \text{im} \\ \textbf{in das} & \longrightarrow & \text{ins} \end{array}$$

DRILLS

• The following pairs of sentences contrast *dative* (no motion) and *accusative* (motion).

• **über / unter**

1. Stell es _____ Schreibtisch!
   (under the)
   (**stellen**: to put; **der Schreibtisch**: desk)

   Es ist _____ Schreibtisch.
   (under the)

2. Ein Schild hängt _____ Tür.
   (over the)
   (**das Schild**: sign; **hängen**: to hang; **die Tür**: door)

   Er hängt ein Schild _____ Tür.
   (over the)

3. Wir hängen das Bild _____ Kamin.
   (over the)
   (**der Kamin**: fireplace)

   Es hängt _____ Kamin.
   (over the)

4. Schieben Sie den Brief _____ Tür!
   (under the)
   (**schieben**: to shove; **der Brief**: letter)

   Der Brief ist _____ Tür.
   (under the)

● **hinter / vor**

1. Er geht _____ Haus.
   (behind the)

   Sie sind _____ Haus.
   (behind the)

2. Die Flaschen stehen* _____ Tür.
   (in front of the)

   (**die Flasche, -n**: bottle; **stehen**: to be [standing])

   Stell sie _____ Tür!
   (in front of the)

3. Fahr den Wagen _____ Haus!
   (in front of the)

   Der Wagen steht _____ Haus.
   (in front of the)

4. Er steht _____ Tür.
   (behind the)

   Stellen Sie es _____ Tür!
   (behind the)

● **in / neben / zwischen**

1. Sie essen _____ Küche.
   (in the)   (**die Küche**: kitchen)

   Komm _____ Küche, Peter!
   (into the)

2. Stellen Sie es _____ Sofa!
   (next to the)

   (**das Sofa**: sofa)

   Es steht _____ Sofa.
   (next to the)

3. Sie gehen _____ Zimmer.
   (into the)   (**das Zimmer**: room)

   Sie sind _____ Zimmer.
   (in the)

4. Er arbeitet _____ Bibliothek.
   (in the)

   (**die Bibliothek**: library)

   Er geht _____ Bibliothek.
   (into the)

5. Stell die Lampe _____ Sofa
   (between the)

   und _____ Tisch!
   (the)

   (**die Lampe**: lamp; **der Tisch**: table)

   Die Lampe steht _____ Sofa
   (between the)

   und _____ Tisch.
   (the)

6. Er geht _____ Bahnhof.
   (into the)

   (**der Bahnhof**: station)

   Er ist _____ Bahnhof.
   (in the)

7. Die Schuhe sind _____ Bett.
   (alongside of the)

   (**der Schuh, -e**: shoe; **das Bett**: bed)

   Stell die Schuhe _____ Bett!
   (alongside of the)

8. Er geht _____ Wasser.
   (into the)   (**das Wasser**: water)

   Er ist _____ Wasser.
   (in the)

9. Ich meine den Tisch _____ Couch
   (between the)

   und _____ Sessel.
   (the)

   (**meinen**: to mean; **die Couch**: couch;
   der Sessel: easy chair)

   Stellen wir den Tisch _____ Couch
   (between the)

   und _____ Sessel!
   (the)

10. Wohnen Sie _____ Stadt?
    (in the)   (**die Stadt**: city, town)

    Ich fahre _____ Stadt.
    (into the)

_____

*German often uses **stehen** where colloquial English uses the verb "to be."

Die Flaschen **stehen** vor der Tür.   (The bottles *are* [*standing*] in front of the door.)

• **auf / an**

1. Die Schreibmaschine steht _____
   (on the)

   Tisch.
   (**die Schreibmaschine:** typewriter)

   Stellen Sie sie _____ Tisch!
   (on the)

2. Das Bild hängt _____ Wand.
   (on the)
   (**die Wand:** wall)

   Häng das Bild _____ Wand!
   (on the)

3. Schreiben Sie es _____ Tafel!
   (on the)
   (**schreiben:** to write; **die Tafel:** blackboard)

   Es steht _____ Tafel.
   (on the)

4. Der Mantel liegt _____ Sofa.
   (on the)
   (**liegen:** to lie)

   Wirf den Mantel _____ Sofa!
   (on the)

MIXED DRILLS

1. Die Schreibmaschine steht _____
   (on the)

   Tisch.

   Stell sie _____ Tisch!
   (on the)

2. Fahr den Wagen _____ Haus!
   (in front of the)

   Der Wagen steht _____ Haus.
   (in front of the)

3. Das Bild hängt _____ Wand.
   (on the)

   Häng das Bild _____ Wand!
   (on the)

4. Er arbeitet _____ Bibliothek.
   (in the)

   Er geht _____ Bibliothek.
   (into the)

5. Ein Schild hängt _____ Tür.
   (over the)

   Er hängt ein Schild _____ Tür.
   (over the)

6. Er geht _____ Haus.
   (behind the)

   Sie sind _____ Haus.
   (behind the)

7. Die Schuhe sind _____ Bett.
   (alongside of the)

   Stell die Schuhe _____ Bett!
   (alongside of the)

8. Komm _____ Küche!
   (into the)

   Wir essen _____ Küche.
   (in the)

9. Der Mantel liegt _____ Sofa.
   (on the)

   Er wirft den Mantel _____ Sofa.
   (on the)

10. Er geht _____ Bahnhof.
    (into the)

    Er ist _____ Bahnhof.
    (in the)

11. Stell die Lampe _____ Sofa
    (between the)

    und _____ Tisch!
    (the)

    Die Lampe steht _____ Sofa
    (between the)

    und _____ Tisch.
    (the)

12. Die Flaschen stehen _____ Tür.
    (in front of the)

    Stell sie _____ Tür!
    (in front of the)

13. Schreiben Sie es _____ Tafel!
    (on the)

    Es steht _____ Tafel.
    (on the)

14. Wir hängen das Bild _____ Kamin.
(over the)

Es hängt _____ Kamin.
(over the)

15. Es steht _____ Sofa.
(next to the)

Stellen Sie es _____ Sofa!
(next to the)

16. Sie gehen _____ Zimmer.
(into the)

Sie sind _____ Zimmer.
(in the)

17. Wohnen Sie _____ Stadt?
(in the)

Ich fahre _____ Stadt.
(in the)

18. Schieben Sie den Brief _____ Tür!
(under the)

Der Brief ist _____ Tür.
(under the)

19. Stellen wir den Tisch _____ Couch
(between the)

und _____ Sessel!
(the)

Ich meine den Tisch _____ Couch
(between the)

und _____ Sessel.
(the)

EXPRESS IN GERMAN

1. The typewriter is (standing) on the table.
   Put it on the table.
2. He's going into the library.
   He's working in the library.
3. The shoes are alongside of the bed.
   Put the shoes alongside of the bed.
4. The bottles are in front of the door.
   Put them in front of the door.
5. Write it on the blackboard.
   It's on the blackboard. (use **stehen**)
6. They're going into the room.
   They're in the room.
7. A sign is hanging over the door.
   He's hanging a sign over the door.
8. Drive the car in front of the house.
   The car is (standing) in front of the house.
9. He's going into the station.
   He's in the station.
10. The coat is lying on the sofa.
    Throw the coat on the sofa.
11. Put the lamp between the sofa and the table.
    The lamp is (standing) between the sofa and the table.
12. He's going behind the house.
    They're behind the house.
13. We're eating in the kitchen.
    Come into the kitchen.
14. Hang the picture on the wall.
    It's hanging on the wall.
15. It's (standing) next to the sofa.
    Put it next to the sofa.
16. Shove the letter under the door.
    The letter is under the door.
17. Do you live in the city?
    (Do you live downtown?)
    I'm driving into the city.
    (I'm driving downtown.)
18. Let's put the table between the couch and the easy chair.
    I mean the table between the couch and the easy chair.
19. The picture is hanging over the fireplace.
    We're hanging it over the fireplace.

VOCABULARY

an on (*vertical surfaces*)
auf (on (*horizontal surfaces*)
der **Bahnhof, ⸚e** railroad station
das **Bett, –en** bed
die **Bibliothek, –en** library
das **Bild, –er** picture
der **Brief, –e** letter
die **Couch, –es** couch
die **Flasche, –n** bottle
hängen to hang
hinter behind, in back of
in in, into
der **Kamin, –e** fireplace

die **Küche, –n** kitchen
die **Lampe, –n** lamp
liegen to lie
meinen to mean
neben beside, next to, alongside of
schieben to shove
das **Schild, -er** sign
schreiben to write
die **Schreibmaschine, –n** typewriter
der **Schreibtisch, –e** desk
der **Schuh, –e** shoe
der **Sessel, –** easy chair
das **Sofa, –s** sofa
die **Stadt, ⸚e** city, town

stehen to be (standing)
stellen to put
die **Tafel, –n** blackboard
der **Tisch, –e** table
die **Tür, –en** door
über over, above
unter under, below
vor in front of
die **Wand, ⸚e** wall
das **Wasser** water
weg away
werfen (wirft) to throw
wo where
wohin where . . . to
das **Zimmer, –** room
zwischen between

118   Lesson 3

Lesson 3 Level THREE

A Order of Adverbs

When a German sentence contains two or more adverbial expressions, they occur in the following order:

	TIME	MANNER	PLACE
	wann (when)	**wie** (how)	**wo** (where)
Ich fahre	immer	schnell.	
Ich fahre	sehr oft		nach Berlin.
Ich fahre		schnell	nach Hause.
Ich fahre	nach dem Konzert		zu dir.
Ich fahre		ohne ihn	nach Hause.

▶ Note   You will recognize the following as prepositional phrases:

nach Berlin (place = where)   **ohne ihn** (manner = how)
nach Hause   **nach dem Konzert** (time = when)
zu dir

Entire phrases can function as adverbs of time, manner, and place.

DRILLS

Word order with adverbial expressions

• Put the adverbial expressions into their proper order.

1. Ich fahre _____. (nach Berlin, morgen)
2. Er arbeitet _____. (zu Hause, immer)
3. Ich gehe _____. (zu Lulu, später)
4. Wir bleiben _____. (zwei Jahre, in Deutschland)
5. Ich arbeite _____. (im Büro, allein)
6. Ich gehe _____. (heute, ins Kino)
7. Man ißt _____. (in Frankreich, sehr gut)
8. Ich gehe _____. (jetzt, nach Hause)
9. Wir gehen _____. (zum Kaufhaus, morgen)
10. Ich komme _____. (zu dir, nach dem Konzert)
11. Er geht _____. (gerade, um die Ecke)

(immer: always)
(später: later)
(zwei: two; das Jahr, -e: year)
(allein: alone)
(ins Kino: to the movies)
(Frankreich: France)

(gerade: just, right now)

12. Wir sind _____. (da, bald)
13. Er fährt _____. (immer, sehr langsam)
14. Lauf _____! (nach Hause, schnell)
15. Wir fahren _____. (oft, nach Europa)
16. Er arbeitet _____. (in der Bibliothek, heute)
17. Sie essen _____. (immer, in der Küche)

(bald: soon)

(schnell: quickly)

● Express in German.

1. He always works at home.
2. I'm going to the movies today.
3. I'm going home now.
4. We'll be there soon.
5. We often go to Europe. (use **fahren**)
6. We're going to the department store tomorrow.
7. They always eat in the kitchen.
8. I'm driving to Berlin tomorrow.
9. One eats very well in France.
10. He works alone in the office.
11. I'll come to your place after the concert.
12. He's working in the library today.
13. We're staying two years in Germany.
14. He's just going around the corner.
15. Peter always drives slowly.
16. I'm going to Lulu's place later.

B Position of Nicht

In a simple sentence **nicht** comes

1. *after* the subject, verb, and all objects:

> Ich verstehe dich **nicht.**
> Ich kaufe dir den Anzug **nicht.**

2. *before* everything else:

> Er fährt **nicht schnell.**　　(*fast*; before expressions of manner)
> Ich gehe **nicht in die Stadt.**　　(*downtown*; before expressions of place)
> Ich arbeite **nicht immer** zu Hause.　　(*always*; before time expressions)

▶ **Exception**　　Specific time expressions:

> Ich gehe heute nicht ins Kino.
> Sie ist jetzt nicht zu Hause.

Nicht comes *after specific* time expressions (**heute:** today; **jetzt:** now), but *before general* time expressions:

> Ich arbeite nicht immer zu Hause.

DRILLS

- Negate the following sentences using **nicht.**

    1. Ich verstehe dich, Hans.
    2. Er arbeitet immer zu Hause.
    3. Ich gehe heute ins Kino.
    4. Wir bleiben hier.
    5. Ich kaufe dir den Anzug.
    6. Man ißt sehr gut in Deutschland.
    7. Er arbeitet heute in der Bibliothek.
    8. Wir essen immer in der Küche.

    9. Gehst du morgen zum Kaufhaus?
    10. Er arbeitet allein im Büro.
    11. Das ist sehr interessant.
        (**sehr:** very; **interessant:** interesting)
    12. Liegt das Hotel neben dem Bahnhof?
    13. Ich gehe heute in die Stadt.
    14. Er fährt immer langsam.
    15. Sind Sie müde?   (**müde:** tired)

- Express in German.

    1. I don't understand you, Hans.
    2. They don't always eat in the kitchen.
    3. He's not working in the library today.
    4. We're not staying here.
    5. He doesn't always drive slowly.
    6. Aren't you tired?
    7. That's not very interesting.
    8. I'm not going to the movies today.

    9. He doesn't always work at home.
    10. Isn't the hotel next to the station?
        (use **liegen**)
    11. One doesn't eat very well in Germany.
    12. Aren't you going to the department store tomorrow?
    13. He's not going downtown today.

C Possessive Adjectives

1 Possessive adjectives

As the name implies, these adjectives indicate possession: *my* book, *your* coat, *his* house. The following are the German possessives:

	SINGULAR	PLURAL
1ST PERSON	mein (my)	unser (our)
2ND PERSON	dein (your)	euer (your)
3RD PERSON	sein (his)	ihr (their)
	sein (its)	Ihr (your)
	ihr (her)	

2 Endings

Like **kein,** the possessive adjectives are **ein**-words; that is to say, they take the same set of endings as the word **ein.**

SINGULAR		
Masculine	*Neuter*	*Feminine*

	Masculine	*Neuter*	*Feminine*
NOM.	mein Anzug	mein Hemd	mein**e** Krawatte
ACC.	mein**en** Anzug	mein Hemd	mein**e** Krawatte
DAT.	mein**em** Anzug	mein**em** Hemd	mein**er** Krawatte

PLURAL	
All Genders	

	All Genders
NOM.	mein**e** Anzüge, Hemden, Krawatten
ACC.	mein**e** Anzüge, Hemden, Krawatten
DAT.	mein**en** Anzügen, Hemden, Krawatten

▶ Note **euer,** but eure

When an ending is added to **euer,** the **e** before the **r** is dropped: eu**re,** eu**ren,** eu**rem,** eu**rer.**

DRILLS

1 Nominative substitution

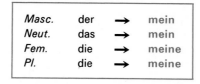

Masc.	der	→	mein
Neut.	das	→	mein
Fem.	die	→	meine
Pl.	die	→	meine

• Replace the definite article (in boldface) with the possessives in parentheses.

PATTERN   Wo ist **die** Jacke? (mein)   Wo ist meine Jacke?

1. Wo ist **das** Hemd? (mein, dein, sein)
2. Wo ist **die** Post? (unser, euer, ihr [*their*])
3. Wo ist **der** Brief? (mein, unser, euer)
4. Da ist **die** Katze. (dein, sein, euer)
5. Wo ist **das** Haus? (dein, euer, Ihr)
6. Da ist **die** Jacke. (dein, mein, Ihr)
7. Wo ist **der** Mantel? (mein, sein)
8. Da ist **die** Zeitung. (Ihr, dein, mein)
9. Wo sind **die** Bücher? (mein, unser, euer)

2 Accusative substitution

Masc.	den	→	meinen
Neut.	das	→	mein
Fem.	die	→	meine
Pl.	die	→	meine

● Replace the definite article (in boldface) with the possessives in parentheses.

PATTERN   Siehst du **die** Krawatte? (mein)   Siehst du *meine* Krawatte?

1. Ich suche **den** Brief. (mein, dein, sein)
2. Siehst du **die** Post? (mein, unser, sein)
3. Er kauft **das** Haus. (mein, unser)
4. Er hat **die** Jacke. (Ihr, dein)

5. Ich kaufe **den** Wagen. (dein, sein, euer, Ihr)
6. Siehst du das Haus? (sein, ihr)
7. Ich suche **die** Briefe. (mein, unser)

3   Dative substitution

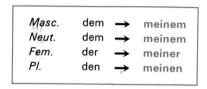

Masc.	dem	→	meinem
Neut.	dem	→	meinem
Fem.	der	→	meiner
Pl.	den	→	meinen

● Replace the definite article (in boldface) with the possessives in parentheses.

PATTERN   Ich kaufe **den** Kindern etwas. (mein)   Ich kaufe *meinen* Kindern etwas.

1. Ich gebe es **der** Frau. (mein, dein, Ihr)
2. Ich bringe **dem** Chef die Post. (mein, unser, euer)
3. Der Brief ist von **dem** Bruder. (dein, euer)   (**der Bruder**: brother)
4. Ist das Paket von **der** Schwester? (dein, euer, Ihr)   (**das Paket**: package; **die Schwester**: sister)
5. Ich kaufe **den** Kindern etwas. (mein, Ihr, euer)

4   Mixed drills

● Replace the definite article (in boldface) with the possessives in parentheses.

1. Ich gebe es **der** Frau. (mein, dein)
2. Siehst du **die** Post? (unser, mein)
3. Wo ist **der** Mantel? (Ihr, mein)
4. Ich kaufe **den** Wagen. (dein, euer)
5. Wo ist **die** Katze? (euer, Ihr)
6. Das Paket ist von **der** Schwester. (unser)
7. Ist das **das** Haus? (ihr, sein)
8. Der Brief ist von **dem** Freund. (euer)   (**der Freund**: friend)

9. Er hat **die** Jacke. (dein, Ihr)
10. Ich suche **den** Brief. (sein)
11. Wo ist **das** Hemd? (mein)
12. Da sind **die** Bücher. (dein)
13. Er bringt **dem** Chef die Post. (sein)
14. Er kauft **das** Haus. (unser)
15. Wo ist **die** Post? (mein)
16. Ich kaufe **den** Kindern etwas. (Ihr, euer)
17. Der Brief ist von **dem** Bruder. (mein)

5   Express in German

1. I'll buy your car, Hans.
2. I'm going to give it to my wife.
3. Is that his house?
4. Where's my coat?
5. He's taking the mail to his boss.
6. I'm looking for his letter.
7. Karl has your sports coat, Hans.
8. Inge, where's my shirt?
9. Do you see our car?

10. The letter is from your friend.
11. The package is from my sister.
12. They're looking for their books.
13. That's our house.
14. Here's your mail, Mr. Lenz.
15. I'm buying something for my children.
16. Is the letter from your brother? (**ihr**-form)
17. Where's your coat, Klaus?

MIXED DRILLS: GRAND MIX

- The following drills contain possessive adjectives and prepositions (dative, accusative, and two-way), as well as problems concerning the order of adverbs and the position of **nicht**.

1 Fill-ins

a.
1. Ich komme später _____, Hans.
   (to your place)
2. Deine Bücher liegen _____ Schreibtisch.
   (on my)
3. Schreiben Sie es _____ Tafel!
   (on the)
4. Kommt er _____ Deutschland?
   (from)
5. Er arbeitet heute _____
   (in the)
   Bibliothek.
6. Macht er das nicht _____?
   (for me)
7. Wir fahren morgen _____ Berlin.
   (to)
8. Er geht gerade _____ Ecke.
   (around the)
9. Wohnen Sie jetzt _____ Stadt?
   (in the)
10. Ich habe nichts _____ Anzug.
    (against his)

b.
1. Er trifft uns _____ Mittagessen.
   (after [the])
2. Ich wohne jetzt _____.
   (at his place)
3. Wirf den Ball nicht _____ Haus!
   (against the)
4. Ist das zu teuer _____, Walter?
   (for you)
5. Dein Bild hängt _____
   (above my)
   Schreibtisch.
6. Fahr mich _____ Bahnhof!
   (to the)
7. Sie fährt _____ Berlin _____
   (from)   (to)
   Stuttgart.
8. Es liegt _____ Tisch.
   (under the)
9. Die Garage ist _____ Haus.
   (behind the) **(die Garage:** garage)
10. Komm _____ Küche!
    (into the)

c.
1. Fahr deinen Wagen _____ Tür!
   (in front of the)
2. Ist der Brief _____ Bruder, Hans?
   (from your)
3. Ihr Mantel liegt _____ Sofa.
   (on the)
4. Der Zug fährt _____ Tunnel.
   (through a)
5. Gehen Sie _____ Stadt?
   (in the)
6. Er kommt gerade _____
   (out of the)
   Kaufhaus.
7. Stell die Lampe _____ Sofa
   (between the)
   und _____ Tisch!
   (the)
8. Es liegt _____ Bett.
   (alongside of the)
9. Sie fahren _____ Stadt.
   (through the)
10. Häng das Bild _____ Wand!
    (on the)

d.
1. Gehst du jetzt _____ Hause?
2. Ich habe kein Geld _____ Kino.
   (for the)
3. Ich wohne jetzt _____.
   (at Frau Heller's)
4. Ich komme _____ Konzert
   (after the)
   _____.
   (to your place)
5. Hier ist eine Karte _____ Berlin.
   (from)
6. Stell die Flaschen _____ Tür!
   (in front of the)
7. Wir gehen _____ nach Hause.
   (without him)
8. Fährst du morgen _____ Stadt?
   (into the)
9. Schieb den Brief _____ Tür!
   (under my)
10. Kommen Sie _____, Herr Lenz!
    (with me)

e. 1. Wirf deinen Mantel _____ Stuhl!
(on the)

(der Stuhl: chair)

2. Sie wohnt _____.
(at my place)

3. Sie ist jetzt nicht _____ Hause.
(at)

4. Das Bild hängt _____ Wand.
(on the)

5. Liegt es _____ Tisch?
(on the)

6. Mein Wagen steht _____ Haus.
(in front of your)

2 Express in German

a. 1. He's working in the library today.
2. I'll come to your place later.
3. Are you going home now, Hans?
4. It's lying alongside of the bed.
5. We're going home without him.
6. Does he come from Germany?
7. Your coat is lying on the sofa, Mr. Lange.
8. I'm living at Mrs. Heller's place now.
9. She's not at home now.
10. Drive your car (up) in front of the door.

b. 1. Is the letter from your brother, Hans?
2. Are you driving downtown tomorrow, Karl?
3. Your books are lying on my desk.
4. Shove the letter under my door.
5. Won't he do that for me?
6. She's living at my place.
7. He's meeting us after lunch.
8. Come into the kitchen.
9. I don't have any money for the movies.
10. The picture is hanging on the wall.

c. 1. The garage is behind the house.
2. I'll come to your place after the concert.

3. Come with me, Mr. Lange.
4. Do you live downtown now?
5. Put the lamp between the sofa and the table.
6. He's just coming out of the department store. (just: gerade)
7. We're driving to Berlin tomorrow.
8. Throw your coat on the chair, Hans.
(chair: der Stuhl)
9. He's just going around the corner.
10. Write it on the blackboard.

d. 1. It's lying under the table.
2. My car is (standing) in front of your house.
3. I live at his place now.
4. Drive me to the station, Hans.
5. Put the bottles in front of the door, Ulla.
6. Do you live downtown?
7. She's driving from Berlin to Frankfurt.
8. Is it lying on the table?
9. Hang the picture on the wall.
10. They're driving through the city.

e. 1. Here's a postcard from Berlin.
2. The train is going through a tunnel.
(use fahren)

VOCABULARY

allein alone	**heute** today	**müde** tired
bald soon	**immer** always	das **Paket, –e** package
der **Bruder, –̈** brother	**ihr** her	**schnell** quickly, fast
dein your (*fam. sing.*)	**ihr** their	die **Schwester, –n** sister
euer (eur-) your	**Ihr** your (*polite*)	**sehr** very
(*fam. plur.*)	**ins Kino** to the movies	**sein** his; its
Frankreich France	**interessant** interesting	**später** later
der **Freund, –e** friend	das **Jahr, –e** year	der **Stuhl, –̈e** chair
die **Garage, –n** garage	**jetzt** now	**unser** our
gerade just, right now	die **Katze, –n** cat	**zwei** two

Reading III

Telefonieren und Buchstabieren
(Telephoning and Spelling)

Here is the German alphabet. Practice it with your instructor, first with your books open and then with your books closed.

a	a (like f<u>a</u>ther)	**j**	jott	**s**	ess	
ä	a-umlaut	**k**	ka	**t**	te	
b	be (like <u>ba</u>ke)	**l**	ell	**u**	u	
c	tse	**m**	emm	**ü**	u-umlaut	
d	de	**n**	enn	**v**	fau	
e	e	**o**	o	**w**	ve (like <u>va</u>ne)	
f	eff	**ö**	o-umlaut	**x**	ikks (like <u>pi</u>cks)	
g	ge	**p**	pe	**y**	ypsilon (pronounce üpsilon)	
h	ha	**q**	ku	**z**	tsett	
i	i (like s<u>ee</u>k)	**r**	err	**ß**	ess-tsett	

Sometimes you'll be asked to spell a name or a word (**Wie schreibt man das?**). Pronounce the following names and then spell them, using the German alphabet.

Adam	Jonas	Pfälzer
Adler	Mahr	Quandt
Bretz	Mayer	Schorr
Emrich	Maximilian	Teiß
Gebhardt	Müller	Vater
Herlert	Oberkehr	Zeiß

(your name)

126

German telephone numbers usually look like this:

4 53 37

Normally there is a single digit followed by two groups of two digits. You would read off the number this way: **vier / fünf drei / drei sieben.**

Read the following phone numbers aloud in German:

2 47 97*	7 43 52	5 79 92	2 18 81
4 27 35	6 08 01†	7 31 08	7 03 23

---

*Zwo is often used instead of zwei in order to avoid any confusion with drei.
†Null is the German word for zero.

Telefongespräche (Telephone Conversations)

Here's what a conversation to make an appointment with a doctor sounds like:

SCHWESTER:
  Praxis Dr.* Greiner.
SIE:
  Guten Tag. Ich möchte einen Termin bei Dr. Greiner, bitte.
SCHWESTER:
  Welche Kasse,† bitte?
SIE:
  Privat.
SCHWESTER:
  Augenblick . . . Freitag um zehn. Ist das Ihnen recht?
SIE:
  Ja, gut.
SCHWESTER:
  Auf welchen Namen, bitte?

SIE: _____
  (Say your name.)
SCHWESTER:
  Wie schreibt man das, bitte?

SIE: _____
  (Spell your last name.)
SCHWESTER:
  Also, Freitag um zehn, Herr / Fräulein / Frau _____ .

NURSE:
  Dr. Greiner's office.
YOU:
  Hello. I'd like an appointment with Dr. Greiner, please.
NURSE:
  Which insurance plan, please?
YOU:
  Private.
NURSE:
  Just a minute . . . Friday at 10. Is that all right with you?
YOU:
  Yes, fine.
NURSE:
  And your name, [*lit.:* In what name] please?

YOU: _____
  (Say your name.)
NURSE:
  How do you spell [*lit.:* write] that, please?

YOU: _____
  (Spell your last name.)
NURSE:
  So, Friday at 10, Mr. / Miss / Mrs. _____ .

*   *   *

A conversation with a taxi dispatcher is much more abrupt.

TAXIZENTRALE:
  Funktaxi.
SIE:
  Ich hätte gern ein Taxi. Rheinstraße 40.

DISPATCHER:
  Radio cab.
YOU:
  I'd like a cab, Rheinstraße 40.

---

* **Dr.** = **Doktor**

† **Kasse** (short for **Krankenkasse**) refers to health insurance plans. Germany has several private plans, as well as a national one. All Germans are insured, since they must be members of the national plan (and contribute to it) unless they are privately insured. A foreigner is not covered by these plans, so you will have to answer the nurse's question „**Welche Kasse, bitte?**", with „**Privat**". This means you are not insured and will pay the bill yourself.

TAXIZENTRALE: 　Auf welchen Namen? SIE: _____ . 　　　　*(Say your name.)* 　　　_____ 　　　　*(Spell it.)*	DISPATCHER: 　What's the name? [*lit.:* In what name] YOU: _____ . 　　　　*(Say your name.)* 　　　_____ 　　　　*(Spell it.)*

*　　*　　*

Here is a conversation with a German telephone operator. You want the number for Dietrich Teiß. At first the operator can't find it.

AUSKUNFT: 　Auskunft eins.	INFORMATION: 　Operator one.
SIE: 　Ja, guten Tag, ich hätte gern 　eine Nummer in Bonn.	YOU: 　Yes, hello, I'd like to have 　a number in Bonn.
AUSKUNFT: 　Ja?	INFORMATION: 　Yes?
SIE: 　Der Name ist Dietrich Teiß. T-e-i-ß.	YOU: 　The name is Dietrich Teiß. T-e-i-ß.
AUSKUNFT: 　Moment. Und wie ist der Vorname?	INFORMATION: 　Just a moment. And what's the first 　name?
SIE: 　Dietrich.	YOU: 　Dietrich.
AUSKUNFT: 　Ich finde ihn nicht. Moment mal, 　schreibt er das mit zwei s?	INFORMATION: 　I can't find him. Just a minute, does 　he spell that with two s's?
SIE: 　Nein, mit ß.	YOU: 　No, with an ß.
AUSKUNFT: 　Ja, ich habe ihn—in der 　Winterstraße.	INFORMATION: 　Yes, I do have him—on 　[*lit.:* in the] Winterstraße.
SIE: 　Ja, richtig.	YOU: 　Yes, right.
AUSKUNFT: 　In Bad Godesberg?	INFORMATION: 　In Bad Godesberg? (*residential part 　of Bonn*)
SIE: 　Ja.	YOU: 　Yes.
AUSKUNFT: 　3 . . . 20 . . .	INFORMATION: 　3 . . . 20 . . .
SIE: 　3 . . . 20 . . .	YOU: 　3 . . . 20 . . .
AUSKUNFT: 　59.	INFORMATION: 　59.
SIE: 　59. Vielen Dank.	YOU: 　59. Thank you.

AUSKUNFT:	INFORMATION:
Bitte sehr.*	You're welcome.
SIE:	YOU:
Auf Wiederhören.†	Good-bye.
AUSKUNFT:	INFORMATION:
Auf Wiederhören.	Good-bye.

DIALOGUE

You want to call the information operator and get somebody's number. Choose a name from the directory column on the facing page, and be prepared to pronounce and spell the last name. The operator will also ask you for the first name and the street name. Then the operator will say the telephone number and give you time to repeat it. Students can play the role of the operator and of the caller.

AUSKUNFT: Auskunft eins.

    SIE: Guten Tag, ich hätte gern eine Nummer in Bonn.

AUSKUNFT: Ja?

    SIE: Der Name ist _____ .
                    (You choose a name from the directory column.)

AUSKUNFT: Moment. Wie schreibt man das?

    SIE: _____
           (You spell the name in German.)

AUSKUNFT: Und wie ist der Vorname?

    SIE: _____
           (You give the first name.)

AUSKUNFT: In welcher Straße, bitte?

    SIE: In der _____ -straße.
              (You give the street name.)

AUSKUNFT: Moment. Die Nummer ist _____
                  (Operator gives the first two groups of the number.)

    SIE: _____
           (You repeat the first two groups.)

AUSKUNFT: _____
           (Operator finishes the number.)

    SIE: _____ . Danke schön.
           (You repeat the last group.)

AUSKUNFT: Bitte schön.

    SIE: Auf Wiederhören.

AUSKUNFT: Auf Wiederhören.

---

*Variant of **bitte schön.**

†Used only on the telephone.

Directory Column for **Auskunft**	
Adam Manfred Sebastianstraße 11	4 37 23
Adler Karl Heinz Rathenaustraße 50	6 95 70
Bretz Viktoria Kaiserstraße 3	2 18 81
Emrich Luise Kölnerstraße 9	5 25 13
Gebhardt Fritz Endenicherstraße 5	2 47 97
Herlert Rainer Heerstraße 60	5 45 75
Mahr Amalia Friedrichstraße 30	7 31 08
Oberkehr Willi Schedestraße 12	2 12 98
Schorr Ilse Dr. Wittelsbacherstraße 70	4 37 23

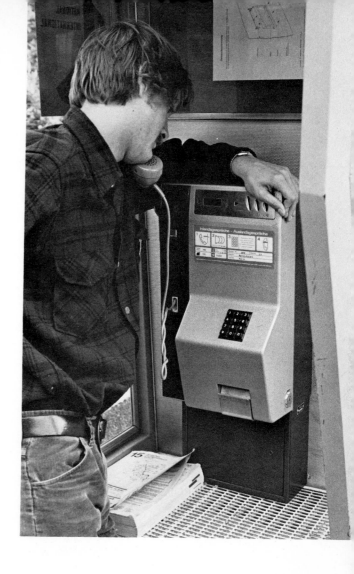

WIE SCHREIBT MAN DAS?

Sometimes you may even have to spell a common word for somebody. Practice with these:

gehen	Deutsch	Kino	ohne
Herr	heißen	Brief	viel
müde	hübsch	ja	später
nicht	Mädchen	zwei	jetzt
weg	Fisch	sehr	kaufen
Zeit	Junge	euch	Schreibmaschine

Lesson 4   Level ONE

A Modal Auxiliaries

1 The function of modal auxiliaries

Look at the following example:

He's doing it.   **Er macht es.**

This is a simple declarative statement of fact. But many situations require more information.

ability	He *can* do it.	Er **kann** es machen.
necessity	He *has to* do it.	Er **muß** es machen.
permission	He *may* (*is permitted to*) do it.	Er **darf** es machen.
volition/desire	He *wants to* do it.	Er **will** es machen.
obligation	He's *supposed to* do it.	Er **soll** es machen.

The extra information in these sentences is supplied by additional verbs (verbs like *can* [**kann**]). Such verbs show the way (*modus:* mode, modal) the subject is related to the underlying simple statement.

He *can* do it.   (shows ability)
He *has to* do it.   (shows necessity)

Since these verbs all supply additional information and since they all affect sentence structure in the same way, they are treated as a group.

2 German sentences with modal auxiliaries

Look at the following examples:

Er **kann** es **machen.**
Ich **muß** ihn morgen **sehen.**

132

As you can see, the modal sentence has two verbal parts:

A Conjugated Modal	+	A Dependent Infinitive
Er kann		es machen

1. **kann**: The conjugated form of the modal must be in second (verb) position in the sentence.

2. **machen**: The dependent infinitive must be at the end of the sentence.

3 Caution: do not use **zu**

Some English equivalents of the German modal auxiliaries require the word "to":

(He is able *to* do it.)   Er **kann** es machen.

(I have *to* see him tomorrow.)   Ich **muß** ihn morgen sehen.

Others do not:

(He can do it.)   Er **kann** es machen.

(May I help you?)   **Darf** ich Ihnen helfen?

German *never* uses **zu** (to) before the infinitives in modal expressions.

4 Conjugation of German modals

können	*to be able to, can*
ich kann	wir könn **en**
du kann **st**	ihr könn **t**
er kann	sie könn **en**

a. Stems of modals

With one exception, German modals have two stems:

one for the infinitive and the plural forms (for example, **könn-**)
one for the singular forms (for example, **kann-**)

b. Present tense endings

The present tense endings of the modals are unusual:

1. The 1st and 3rd person singular take *no endings*; that is, they use only the stem:

1ST PERSON SINGULAR   ich **kann**
3RD PERSON SINGULAR   er **kann**

2. The other four forms take the regular present tense endings (the same endings as the verb **sagen**):

2ND PERSON SINGULAR	du kann**st**
1ST PERSON PLURAL	wir könn**en**
2ND PERSON PLURAL	ihr könn**t**
3RD PERSON PLURAL	sie könn**en**

B Können (kann)

können (kann)	*to be able to, can*	
ich kann	wir könn	**en**
du kann **st**	ihr könn	**t**
er kann	sie könn	**en**

▶ Note   The singular stem is kann-; the plural stem is könn-

DRILLS

1   Fill-ins

● Supply the correct form of **können**.

1. Ich _____ heute nicht arbeiten.
2. _____ du ihn sehen?
3. Sie (*she*) _____ es nicht machen.
4. Sie (*they*) _____ uns nach dem Mittagessen treffen.
5. Ich _____ später zu dir kommen.
6. Wir _____ noch nicht nach Hause gehen.
   (**noch nicht:** not yet)
7. _____ er Deutsch sprechen?
8. _____ ihr es morgen machen?
9. _____ du mir helfen, Peter?
10. Wann _____ Sie es mir geben, Herr Lenz?
11. Wir _____ in der Küche essen.
12. Du _____ es auf meinen Schreibtisch stellen.
13. Ich _____ das für dich machen.
14. Sie (*you*) _____ den Brief unter die Tür schieben.
15. Er _____ seinen Mantel nicht finden.

2   Synthetic exercises

● Form complete sentences by (a) supplying the correct form of the modal and (b) putting the dependent infinitive at the end of the sentence.

EXAMPLES   Ich / können / **kommen** / später zu dir
            Ich **kann** später zu dir **kommen**.

            Können / du / **sehen** / ihn / ?
            Kannst du ihn **sehen**?

1. Wir / können / **essen** / in der Küche
2. Er / können / **finden** / seinen Mantel nicht
3. Ich / können / **kommen** / später zu dir
4. Können / du / **helfen** / mir / ?
5. Ich / können / **arbeiten** / heute nicht
6. Wir / können / **gehen** / noch nicht nach Hause
7. Können / er / **sprechen** / Deutsch / ?
8. Können / du / **sehen** / ihn / ?
9. Sie (*you*) / können / **schieben** / den Brief unter die Tür
10. Können / ihr / **machen** / es morgen / ?
11. Sie (*she*) / können / **machen** / es nicht
12. Sie (*they*) / können / **treffen** / uns nach dem Mittagessen
13. Du / können / **stellen** / es auf meinen Schreibtisch
14. Wann / können / Sie / **geben** / es mir / ?

3 Express in German

1. Can you see him, Hans?
2. I can't work today.
3. We can eat in the kitchen.
4. Can he speak German?
5. She can't do it.
6. You can put it on my desk, Hans.
7. We can't go home yet. (not yet: **noch nicht**)
8. I can come to your place later.
9. Can you (**ihr**) do it tomorrow?
10. Can you help me, Peter?
11. You (**Sie**) can shove the letter under the door.
12. When can you give it to me?
13. They can meet us after lunch.
14. He can't find his coat.

C Müssen (muß)

müssen (muß)	*to have to, must*
ich muß	wir müss **en**
du muß **t**	ihr müß **t**
er muß	sie müss **en**

▶ **Note**   The singular stem is **muß-**; the plural stem is **müss-** / **müß-**.

DRILLS

1   Fill-ins

• Supply the correct form of **müssen**.

1. Ich _____ ihn morgen sehen.
2. _____ du heute arbeiten, Hans?
3. Wir _____ ihn gleich finden.
4. Sie (*she*) _____ durch die Stadt fahren.
5. Sie _____ mit mir kommen, Herr Lenz.
6. _____ du zur Post gehen?
7. Dann _____ wir ihn fragen.
8. Sie (*they*) _____ hier bleiben.
9. Ich _____ jetzt in die Stadt gehen.
10. Ihr _____ das morgen machen.
11. Er _____ jetzt gehen.
12. Wir _____ es nicht vergessen.

2 Synthetic exercises

• Form complete sentences by (a) supplying the correct form of the modal and (b) putting the dependent infinitive at the end of the sentence.

1. Wir / müssen / **vergessen** / es nicht
2. Ich / müssen / **gehen** / jetzt in die Stadt
3. Ihr / müssen / **machen** / es morgen
4. Müssen / du / **arbeiten** / heute / ?
5. Wir / müssen / **finden** / ihn gleich
6. Ich / müssen / **sehen** / ihn morgen

7. Sie (*they*) / müssen / **bleiben** / hier
8. Er / müssen / **gehen** / jetzt
9. Sie (*she*) / müssen / **fahren** / durch die Stadt
10. Müssen / du / **gehen** / zur Post / ?
11. Dann / müssen / wir / **fragen** / ihn
12. Sie (*you*) / müssen / **kommen** / mit mir

3 Express in German

1. He has to go now.
2. I have to see him tomorrow.
3. We mustn't forget it.
4. I have to go downtown now.
5. They'll have to stay here.
6. You'll have to do it tomorrow, children.

7. Then we'll have to ask him.
8. Do you have to work today, Hans?
9. You'll have to come with me, Mr. Lenz.
10. She'll have to drive through the city.
11. We have to find him right away.
12. Do you (**du**) have to go to the post office?

D Dürfen (darf)

dürfen (darf)	*to be permitted to, to be allowed to, may*	
ich darf	wir dürf **en**	
du darf **st**	ihr dürf **t**	
er darf	sie dürf **en**	

▶ Note   The singular stem is darf-; the plural stem is dürf-.

DRILLS

1 Fill-ins

• Supply the correct form of **dürfen**.

1. _____ ich jetzt mit dem Chef sprechen?
2. Ihr _____ nicht aus dem Haus gehen.
3. Sie (*you*) _____ ihn jetzt sehen.
4. Du _____ heute nicht ins Kino gehen.
5. Hier _____ man nicht rauchen.

   (**rauchen**: to smoke)

6. Wann _____ wir nach Hause gehen?
7. Nein! Du _____ das nicht machen.
8. _____ ich Ihnen helfen?
9. _____ ich den Fisch empfehlen, mein Herr?   (**mein Herr**: sir)
10. _____ er das machen?

2 Synthetic exercises

● Form complete sentences by (a) supplying the correct form of the modal and (b) putting the dependent infinitive at the end of the sentence.

1. Dürfen / ich / **helfen** / Ihnen / ?
2. Dürfen / er / **machen** / das / ?
3. Du / dürfen / **gehen** / heute nicht ins Kino
4. Dürfen / ich / **sprechen** / jetzt / mit dem Chef / ?
5. Sie (you) / dürfen / **sehen** / ihn jetzt

6. Ihr / dürfen / **gehen** / nicht aus dem Haus
7. Dürfen / ich / **empfehlen** / den Fisch / ?
8. Wann / dürfen / wir / **gehen** / nach Hause / ?
9. Hier / dürfen / man / **rauchen** / nicht
10. Du / dürfen / **machen** / das nicht

3 Express in German

1. May I speak with the boss now?
2. When may we go home?
3. May he do that?
4. No. You may not go out of the house, children.
5. May I help you?

6. You **(Sie)** may see him now.
7. No. You **(du)** may not go to the movies today.
8. You **(man)** aren't allowed to smoke here. (begin the sentence with **Hier**)
9. May I recommend the fish, Sir?

E Wollen (will)

wollen (will)	*to want to*		
ich will		wir woll	**en**
du will	**st**	ihr woll	**t**
er will		sie woll	**en**

▶ Note   The singular stem is will-; the plural stem is woll-.

DRILLS

1 Fill-ins

● Supply the correct form of **wollen.**

1. Er _____ heute in der Bibliothek arbeiten.
2. Sie (*they*) _____ hier bleiben.
3. Er _____ uns nach dem Konzert treffen.
4. _____ Sie den Chef jetzt sehen?
5. Ich _____ jetzt schlafen.

6. _____ du in der Stadt bleiben?
7. Sie (*she*) _____ ihn nicht sehen.
8. Nein, wir _____ das Haus nicht kaufen.
9. _____ ihr in der Küche essen?
10. Was _____ du machen?

2 Synthetic exercises

- Form complete sentences by (a) supplying the correct form of the modal and (b) putting the dependent infinitive at the end of the sentence.

1. Er / wollen / **treffen** / uns nach dem Konzert
2. Ich / wollen / **schlafen** / jetzt
3. Wir / wollen / **kaufen** / das Haus nicht
4. Was / wollen / du / **machen** / ?
5. Er / wollen / **arbeiten** / heute in der Bibliothek
6. Wollen / ihr / **essen** / in der Küche / ?
7. Sie (*they*) / wollen / **bleiben** / hier
8. Wollen / du / **bleiben** / in der Stadt / ?
9. Sie (*she*) / wollen / **sehen** / ihn nicht
10. Wollen / Sie / **sehen** / den Chef jetzt / ?

3 Express in German

1. I want to sleep now.
2. He wants to work in the library today.
3. No. We don't want to buy the house.
4. He wants to meet us after the concert.
5. Do you (**ihr**) want to eat in the kitchen?
6. What do you (**du**) want to do?
7. They want to stay here.
8. She doesn't want to see him.
9. Do you (**Sie**) want to see the boss now?
10. Do you (**du**) want to stay downtown?

F Sollen (soll)

sollen (soll)	*to be supposed to, shall*	
ich soll	wir soll	**en**
du soll **st**	ihr soll **t**	
er soll	sie soll	**en**

▶ Note **Sollen** is the only modal that uses the same stem for both its singular and its plural forms.

DRILLS

1 Fill-ins

- Supply the correct form of **sollen**.

1. Du _____ das nicht machen.
2. _____ wir dich später treffen?
3. Er _____ jetzt in Berlin sein.
4. Sie (*they*) _____ zu mir kommen.

5. Wann _____ Grete zu Hause sein?
6. _____ ich das für dich machen?

7. Ihr _____ zu Hause bleiben, Kinder.
8. Wann _____ wir kommen?

2　Synthetic exercises

● Form complete sentences by (a) supplying the correct form of the modal and (b) putting the dependent infinitive at the end of the sentence.

1. Er / sollen / **sein** / jetzt in Berlin
2. Sollen / ich / **machen** / das für dich / ?
3. Du / sollen / **machen** / das nicht
4. Wann / sollen / Grete / **sein** / zu Hause / ?
5. Ihr / sollen / **bleiben** / zu Hause
6. Sollen / wir / **treffen** / dich später / ?
7. Sie (they) / sollen / **kommen** / zu mir

3　Express in German

1. They're supposed to come to my place.
2. You're not supposed to do that.
3. When shall we (are we supposed to) come?
4. Shall I do that for you?
5. He's supposed to be in Berlin now.
6. You're supposed to stay home, children.
7. When is she supposed to be home?
8. Shall we meet you later?

MIXED DRILLS

1　Form and structure drills

● Insert the modal auxiliaries into the following sentences.

EXAMPLE   Ich gehe jetzt nach Hause.   (müssen)
           Ich muß jetzt nach Hause gehen.

1. Gehst du jetzt zur Bank?   (wollen)
2. Ich bezahle die Rechnung.   (müssen)
3. Essen wir in einem Restaurant?   (sollen)
4. Er geht zum Friseur.   (müssen)
5. Ihr nehmt den Bus.   (können)
6. Ich trinke ein Glas Bier.*   (wollen)
7. Inge sieht den Film nicht.   (dürfen)
8. Gehen Sie heute zum Arzt?   (sollen)
9. Wir fliegen morgen nach Stuttgart.   (müssen)
10. Ich kaufe eine Fahrkarte.   (wollen)
11. Bringen Sie mir die Speisekarte.   (können)
12. Ich gehe jetzt zur Buchhandlung.   (müssen)
13. Ich rufe ihn.   (können)
14. Das ist wahr.   (müssen)

(die Bank: bank)
(bezahlen: to pay; die Rechnung: bill)

(der Friseur: barber)
(der Bus: bus)
(trinken: to drink; das Glas: glass)
(der Film: movie)
(der Arzt: doctor)
(fliegen: to fly)
(die Fahrkarte: ticket)
(die Speisekarte: menu)
(die Buchhandlung: bookstore)
(rufen: to call)
(wahr: true)

---

*ein Glas Bier: a glass of beer. German does not use a preposition in such expressions.

2 Synthetic exercises

● Form sentences using the following elements. If a verb is the first element, the sentence should be a question.

EXAMPLE   Können / du / sehen / Haus / ?
           Kannst du das Haus **sehen**?

a. 1. Sie (*they*) / können / machen / es / nicht
    2. Ich / müssen / bezahlen / Rechnung / jetzt   (**die Rechnung:** bill)
    3. Er / sollen / sein / in Berlin
    4. Ihr / können / nehmen / Bus   (**der Bus:** bus)
    5. Sie (*she*) / müssen / fahren / durch / Stadt
    6. Ich / wollen / kaufen / Fahrkarte   (**die Fahrkarte:** ticket)
    7. Sie (*they*) / dürfen / gehen / nicht / aus / Haus
    8. Wollen / du / sehen / Chef / jetzt / ?
    9. Wollen / du / gehen / jetzt / zu / Bank / ?   (**die Bank:** bank)
   10. Sollen / wir / essen / in / Restaurant / ?   (**das Restaurant:** restaurant)

b. 1. Ihr / können / machen / das / morgen
    2. Inge / dürfen / sehen / Film / nicht   (**der Film:** movie)
    3. Ich / können / rufen / ihn
    4. Wollen / Sie / bleiben / in / Stadt / ?
    5. Sollen / er / gehen / jetzt / zu / Arzt / ?   (**der Arzt:** doctor)
    6. Ich / müssen / gehen / jetzt / zu / Buchhandlung   (**die Buchhandlung:** bookstore)
    7. Er / wollen / uns / treffen / nach / Konzert
    8. Das / müssen / sein / wahr
    9. Ich / wollen / trinken / Glas Bier
   10. Wir / müssen / fliegen / nach Stuttgart

c. 1. Können / Sie / bringen / mir / Speisekarte / ?   (**die Speisekarte:** menu)
    2. Er / müssen / gehen / zu / Friseur   (**der Friseur:** barber)

3 Express in German

a. 1. You may see him now.
    2. When are we supposed to come?
    3. I have to see him tomorrow.
    4. When may we go home?
    5. We can eat in the kitchen.
    6. He wants to meet us after the concert.
    7. She can't do it.
    8. Do you have to work today?
    9. I want (to drink) a glass of beer.
   10. He's supposed to be in Berlin now.

b. 1. I have to go downtown now.
    2. Can you see him, Hans?
    3. Do you want to eat in the kitchen?
    4. She'll have to drive through the city.
    5. He has to go to the barber shop.
    6. I want to work in the library today.
    7. They're supposed to come to my place.
    8. What do you want to do today?
    9. Can he speak German?
   10. May I help you?

c. 1. We have to pay the bill.
    2. I can do that for you, Hans.
    3. Do you want to see the boss now?
    4. I want to buy a ticket.
    5. I can come to your place later.
    6. You can meet us after lunch.
    7. That must be true.
    8. We can't go home yet.
    9. Do you want to go to the bank?
   10. May we wait here?

140   Lesson 4

d. 1. You can put it on my desk.
    2. You'll have to do it tomorrow, children.
    3. When is she supposed to come?
    4. I can call him.
    5. May I speak with the boss?
    6. Can you help me, Peter?
    7. They have to stay home.
    8. You can take the bus.
    9. You aren't allowed to smoke here. (begin sentence with **Hier;** use **man**)
    10. I can't work today.

e. 1. Do you want to stay downtown?
    2. Can you bring me the menu?
    3. You're supposed to stay home, children.

    4. I have to go to the library.
    5. No. You may not go to the movies today.
    6. He has to go now.
    7. Shall we eat in a restaurant?
    8. We have to find him right away.
    9. Shall I do that for you?
    10. No. We don't want to buy the house.

f. 1. I have to fly to Stuttgart tomorrow.
    2. Are you supposed to go to the doctor?
    3. When can you give it to me, Peter?

VOCABULARY

der **Arzt, ̈e** doctor
die **Bank, –en** bank
    bezahlen to pay
die **Buchhandlung, -en** bookstore
der **Bus, –se** bus
    dürfen (darf) to be allowed to, may
die **Fahrkarte, –n** ticket
der **Film, –e** movie

fliegen to fly
der **Friseur, –e** barber
das **Glas, ̈er** glass
    mein Herr Sir
    können (kann) to be able to, can
    müssen (muß) to have to, must
noch nicht not yet
rauchen to smoke

die **Rechnung, –en** bill
das **Restaurant, –s** restaurant
    rufen to call
    sollen to be supposed to, shall
die **Speisekarte, –n** menu
    trinken to drink
    wahr true
    wollen (will) to want to

Lesson 4   Level TWO

A Strong Declension of Adjectives

1 Adjectives with strong endings

In simple adjective-noun combinations, adjectives take a set of endings called *strong endings*. These are the fullest, most explicit adjective endings in German; they show as much as the language can show about gender, case, and number. The following table illustrates these endings:

	SINGULAR		
	Masculine	*Neuter*	*Feminine*
NOM.	dies**er** Anzug	dies**es** Hemd	dies**e** Krawatte
ACC.	dies**en** Anzug	dies**es** Hemd	dies**e** Krawatte
DAT.	dies**em** Anzug	dies**em** Hemd	dies**er** Krawatte

	PLURAL		
	All Genders		
NOM.	dies**e** Anzüge, Hemden, Krawatten		
ACC.	dies**e** Anzüge, Hemden, Krawatten		
DAT.	dies**en** Anzügen, Hemden, Krawatten		

Notice how much the strong adjective endings look like the definite articles **der, das,** and **die:**

	STRONG ENDINGS				DEFINITE ARTICLE			
	Masc.	*Neut.*	*Fem.*	*Pl.*	*Masc.*	*Neut.*	*Fem.*	*Pl.*
NOM.	-er	-es	-e	-e	der	das	die	die
ACC.	-en	-es	-e	-e	den	das	die	die
DAT.	-em	-em	-er	-en	dem	dem	der	den

2 The der-words

The following adjectives *always take strong endings*. They are called **der**-words because they resemble the definite article so closely.

dieser	this
jeder	each, every, any
welcher	which? (the question word)

DRILLS

1   Masculine singular strong endings

NOM.	dieser
ACC.	diesen
DAT.	diesem

- Supply the correct *nominative* endings.

  1. Dies＿ Mantel ist zu teuer.
     (teuer: expensive)
  2. Jed＿ Student braucht Geld.
     (brauchen: to need)
  3. Was kostet dies＿ Anzug?

  4. Welch＿ Bus fährt zum Bahnhof?
  5. Ist dies＿ Platz frei?
     (der Platz: place, seat; **frei:** free)
  6. Jed＿ Bahnhof hat ein Restaurant.
     (das Restaurant: restaurant)

- Supply the correct *accusative* endings.

  1. Welch＿ Mantel meinst du?
     (meinen: to mean)
  2. Willst du dies＿ Film sehen?
     (der Film: film, movie)
  3. Ich nehme dies＿ Anzug.

  4. Welch＿ Film willst du sehen?
  5. Kennen Sie dies＿ Mann?
     (kennen: to know, be acquainted with)
  6. Welch＿ Wagen sollen wir nehmen?

- Supply the correct *dative* endings.

  1. Was machen wir mit dies＿ Tisch?
  2. Das kannst du in jed＿ Laden finden.
     (der Laden: store)

  3. Zeigen Sie dies＿ Herrn einen Anzug!
  4. Zu welch＿ Arzt gehst du?
  5. Es gibt ein Restaurant in jed＿ Bahnhof.

- Supply the correct nominative, accusative, or dative endings.

  1. Dies＿ Mantel ist zu teuer.
  2. Willst du dies＿ Film sehen?
  3. Zu welch＿ Arzt gehst du?
  4. Was kostet dies＿ Anzug?
  5. Welch＿ Mantel meinst du?
  6. Was machen wir mit dies＿ Tisch?
  7. Ich nehme dies＿ Anzug.

  8. Welch＿ Bus fährt zum Bahnhof?
  9. Welch＿ Wagen sollen wir nehmen?
  10. Jed＿ Bahnhof hat ein Restaurant.
  11. Das kannst du in jed＿ Laden finden.
  12. Welch＿ Film willst du sehen?
  13. Jed＿ Student braucht Geld.

- Express in German.

1. This coat is too expensive.
2. I'll take this suit.
3. You can find that in any store.
4. Which car shall we take?
5. Which bus goes to the station? (use **fahren**)
6. Do you want to see this movie?
7. Every railroad station has a restaurant.

8. What'll we do with this table?
9. Which doctor do you go to?
10. Every student needs money.
11. What does this suit cost?
12. Which coat do you mean?
13. Which movie (film) do you want to see?

2 Neuter singular strong endings

NOM.	dies**es**
ACC.	dies**es**
DAT.	dies**em**

- Supply the correct *nominative* endings.

1. Was kostet dies___ Hemd?
2. Welch___ Restaurant ist das?
3. Dies___ Bier ist sehr gut. (**das Bier:** beer)

4. Jed___ Kind weiß das. (**weiß:** knows)
5. Dies___ Buch ist schrecklich.
6. Dies___ Haus ist zu alt. (**zu alt:** too old)

- Supply the correct *accusative* endings.

1. Welch___ Buch lesen Sie?
2. Ich nehme dies___ Kleid.
3. Welch___ Restaurant meinst du?

4. Kennst du dies___ Mädchen?
5. Welch___ Haus kaufst du?

- Supply the correct *dative* endings.

1. Was machen wir mit dies___ Bild?
2. In welch___ Hotel bist du?
3. Zu welch___ Büro muß ich jetzt gehen?
4. In dies___ Restaurant kann man sehr gut essen.

5. Das kannst du in jed___ Kaufhaus finden.

- Supply the correct nominative, accusative, or dative endings.

1. Dies___ Buch ist schrecklich.
2. Ich nehme dies___ Kleid.
3. Was kostet dies___ Hemd?
4. In welch___ Hotel bist du?
5. Welch___ Buch lesen Sie?
6. Das kannst du in jed___ Kaufhaus finden.

7. Dies___ Haus ist zu alt.
8. Welch___ Restaurant meinst du?
9. Welch___ Haus kaufst du?
10. Jed___ Kind weiß das. (**weiß:** knows)
11. Zu welch___ Büro muß ich jetzt gehen?
12. Dies___ Bier ist sehr gut.

- Express in German.

1. Which book are you reading?
2. This house is too old.
3. What does this shirt cost?

4. You can find that in any department store.
5. Which house are you going to buy?

6. Which hotel are you in?
7. This beer is very good.
8. Which restaurant do you mean?
9. This book is horrible.

10. Which office do I have to go to now?
11. Every child knows that. (knows: **weiß**)
12. I'll take this dress.

3 Feminine singular strong endings

NOM.	dies**e**
ACC.	dies**e**
DAT.	dies**er**

● Supply the correct *nominative* endings.

1. Jed___ Stadt hat eine Bibliothek.
2. Was kostet dies___ Jacke?
3. Dies___ Krawatte ist schrecklich.

4. Jed___ Katze frißt Fisch.
   (**fressen**: to eat [use only for animals])
5. Dies___ Adresse ist nicht richtig.
   (**richtig**: correct, right)

● Supply the correct *accusative* endings.

1. Ich nehme dies___ Jacke.
2. Welch___ Krawatte wollen Sie?
3. Ich bezahle dies___ Rechnung nicht.

4. Welch___ Zeitung lesen Sie?
5. Hängen wir das Bild an dies___ Wand!
6. Welch___ Nacht meinst du?
   (**die Nacht**: night)

● Supply the correct *dative* endings.

1. In welch___ Stadt wohnt er?
2. Was machen wir mit dies___ Lampe?
   (**die Lampe**: lamp)
3. Das kannst du in jed___ Buchhandlung finden.   (**die Buchhandlung**: bookstore)
4. Die Restaurants in dies___ Stadt sind gut.

5. Bitte, gehen Sie mit dies___ Frau!
   (**bitte**: please)
6. Mit dies___ Fahrkarte können Sie den
   Schnellzug nehmen.
   (**der Schnellzug**: express train)

● Supply the correct nominative, accusative, or dative endings.

1. Welch___ Krawatte wollen Sie?
2. Was kostet dies___ Jacke?
3. Die Restaurants in dies___ Stadt sind gut.
4. Welch___ Nacht meinst du?
5. Jed___ Katze frißt Fisch.
6. In welch___ Stadt wohnt er?
7. Hängen wir das Bild an dies___ Wand!

8. Dies___ Krawatte ist schrecklich.
9. Ich bezahle dies___ Rechnung nicht.
10. Was machen wir mit dies___ Lampe?
11. Jed___ Stadt hat eine Bibliothek.
12. Welch___ Zeitung liest du?
13. Das kannst du in jed___ Buchhandlung
    finden.

● Express in German.

1. Which tie do you want?
2. What does this sports coat cost?
3. What'll we do with this lamp?
4. Which night do you mean?
5. Every cat eats fish.
6. I'm not going to pay this bill.
7. Which city does he live in?

8. Let's hang the picture on this wall.
9. You can find that in any bookstore.
10. This tie is horrible.
11. The restaurants in this city are good.
12. Every city has a library.
13. Which newspaper are you reading?

4 Plural strong endings (all genders)

NOM.	diese
ACC.	diese
DAT.	diesen

● Supply the correct *nominative* endings.

1. Was kosten dies___ Anzüge?
2. Welch___ Busse fahren zum Bahnhof?
3. Dies___ Mäntel sind zu teuer.

4. Dies___ Teller sind hübsch.
   (**der Teller:** plate; **hübsch:** pretty)
5. Dies___ Krawatten sind schrecklich.

● Supply the correct *accusative* endings.

1. Ich nehme dies___ Hemden.
2. Welch___ Bücher müssen wir lesen?
3. Ich finde dies___ Hotels zu teuer.

4. Welch___ Briefe meinst du?
5. Welch___ Koffer nimmst du?
   (**der Koffer, -:** suitcase)

● Supply the correct *dative* endings.

1. Was machen wir mit dies___ Bildern?
2. Zu welch___ Büros müssen wir jetzt gehen?
3. Mit dies___ Fahrkarten können Sie den Schnellzug nehmen.
4. Zeigen Sie dies___ Herren unsere Anzüge!

● Supply the correct nominative, accusative, or dative endings.

1. Welch___ Koffer nimmst du?
2. Was machen wir mit dies___ Bildern?
3. Was kosten dies___ Anzüge?
4. Ich nehme dies___ Hemden.
5. Welch___ Busse fahren zum Bahnhof?
6. Welch___ Briefe meinst du?
7. Dies___ Teller sind hübsch.

8. Zu welch___ Büros müssen wir jetzt gehen?
9. Welch___ Bücher müssen wir lesen?
10. Dies___ Krawatten sind schrecklich.
11. Mit dies___ Fahrkarten können Sie den Schnellzug nehmen.

● Express in German.

1. What do these suits cost?
2. Which suitcases are you taking?
3. What'll we do with these pictures?
4. These plates are pretty.
5. I'll take these shirts.
6. Which buses go to the station?
   (use **fahren**)

7. Which letters do you mean?
8. These ties are horrible.
9. Which books do we have to read?
10. With these tickets you can take the express train.
11. Which offices do we have to go to now?

MIXED DRILLS

a. 1. Welch___ Wagen (*sing.*) sollen wir nehmen?

2. Dies___ Bier ist sehr gut.
3. In welch___ Stadt wohnt er?

146   Lesson 4

4. Jed___ Student braucht Geld.
5. Was machen wir mit dies___ Lampe?
6. Ich nehme dies___ Anzug.
7. Welch___ Mantel meinst du?
8. Jed___ Stadt hat eine Bibliothek.
9. Welch___ Bus fährt zum Bahnhof?
10. Die Restaurants in dies___ Stadt sind sehr gut.

b. 1. Ich bezahle dies___ Rechnung nicht.
2. Welch___ Koffer (*pl.*) nimmst du?
3. Was kostet dies___ Hemd?
4. Welch___ Briefe meinst du?
5. Das kannst du in jed___ Laden finden.
6. Dies___ Teller sind hübsch.

7. In welch___ Hotel sind Sie?
8. Dies___ Buch ist schrecklich.
9. Welch___ Bücher müssen wir lesen?
10. Zu welch___ Arzt gehen Sie?

c. 1. Willst du dies___ Film sehen?
2. Welch___ Nacht meinen Sie?
3. Jed___ Kind weiß das.
4. Das kannst du in jed___ Buchhandlung finden.
5. Hängen wir das Bild an dies___ Wand!
6. Jed___ Bahnhof hat ein Restaurant.
7. Dies___ Mantel ist zu teuer.
8. Mit dies___ Fahrkarten kannst du den Schnellzug nehmen.

EXPRESS IN GERMAN

a. 1. What does this shirt cost?
2. Which car shall we take?
3. Every city has a library.
4. What'll we do with this lamp?
5. These plates are pretty.
6. Which coat do you mean?
7. This book is horrible.
8. You can find that in any bookstore.
9. Which letters do you mean?
10. Do you want to see this movie?

b. 1. Which city does he live in?
2. Which bus goes to the station?
3. Every student needs money.
4. Which hotel are you in?
5. Which suitcases are you taking?
6. Every railroad station has a restaurant.

7. This beer is very good.
8. Which books do we have to read?
9. Let's hang the picture on this wall.
10. Which night do you mean?

c. 1. You can find that in any store.
2. This coat is too expensive.
3. The restaurants in this city are very good.
4. I'll take this suit.
5. Every child knows that.
6. With these tickets you can take the express train.
7. I'm not going to pay this bill.
8. Which doctor do you go to?

B Summary of Irregular Verbs: Review and Expansion

1 Stem-vowel change

Certain verbs change their stem vowels in the *2nd and 3rd person singular:*

$$e \rightarrow i \text{ or } ie$$

geben *to give*		**sehen** *to see*	
ich gebe	wir geben	ich sehe	wir sehen
du **gibst**	ihr gebt	du **siehst**	ihr seht
er **gibt**	sie geben	er **sieht**	sie sehen

e → i		e → ie	
essen*	to eat	**empfehlen**	to recommend
fressen*	to eat (use only of animals)	**lesen***	to read
geben	to give	**sehen**	to see
helfen	to help		
sprechen	to speak		
treffen	to meet, hit		
vergessen*	to forget		
werfen	to throw		

▶ Exception **Nehmen** (*to take*) changes a consonant as well as the stem vowel:

ich nehme   du nimmst   er nimmt

a → ä and au → äu

fahren *to drive, travel*		**laufen** *to run*	
ich fahre	wir fahren	ich laufe	wir laufen
du **fährst**	ihr fahrt	du **läufst**	ihr lauft
er **fährt**	sie fahren	er **läuft**	sie laufen

a → ä		au → äu	
fahren	to drive, travel	**laufen**	to run
fallen	to fall	**saufen**	to drink (of animals), booze
lassen*	to let, allow		
schlafen	to sleep		
tragen	to carry		
waschen	to wash		

2 Verb stems ending in -s, -ss, -ß, -tz, -z

Verbs of this type have a -t (instead of **-st**) ending in the *2nd person singular:*

	heißen *to be called*	**lesen** *to read*	**sitzen** *to sit*
ich	heiß e	les e	sitz e
du	heiß **t**	lies **t**	sitz **t**
er	heiß **t**	lies **t**	sitz **t**

---

* See the following section, "Verb stems ending in **-s, -ss, -ß, -tz, -z**."

3 Digraph s (ß) or double s (ss)?

The rule is simple: **ss** can occur only *between vowels,* and the first vowel must be short. (Otherwise ß must be used.)* The infinitives **lassen** and **fressen** are good illustrations of **ss:** The stem vowels are short and the **ss** is followed by an **e.** Both conditions for **ss** are met.

But look at a full present tense conjugation of **lassen** (to let):

lassen	to let
ich lasse	wir lassen
du läßt	ihr laßt
er läßt	sie lassen

Notice that the **du**-form, the **er**-form, and the **ihr**-form have ß, not **ss.** True, the first vowel is still short, but the verb ending is the consonant **t,** not the vowel **e.** Thus only one of the conditions for **ss** is met, and so ß must be used.

The verbs **fressen, essen, vergessen,** and **müssen** all have short stem vowels and are conjugated like **lassen.** The verb **heißen** has a *long* stem vowel and therefore uses ß throughout.

4 Two special cases: **werden** and **wissen**

werden	to become
ich werde	wir werden
du wirst	ihr werdet
er wird	sie werden

wissen	to know
ich weiß	wir wissen
du weißt	ihr wißt
er weiß	sie wissen

5 Imperatives of verbs with stem-vowel change

$$e \longrightarrow i \text{ or } ie$$

Verbs that change their stem vowel from **e** to **i** or **ie** use the changed stem (**i** or **ie**) in the **du**-form of the imperative. The **ihr**-form and the **Sie**-form use the *unchanged infinitive stem.*

---

*ß has no upper-case form; if a word is printed all in capital letters, SS is used.

	e ⟶ i		e ⟶ ie	
	geben		**lesen**	
du-FORM	Gib	es mir!	Lies	es, Thomas!
ihr-FORM	Gebt	es mir!	Lest	es, Thomas und Ulla!
Sie-FORM	Geben Sie	es mir!	Lesen Sie	es, Herr Huber!

Verbs that take an *umlaut* in the 2nd and 3rd person singular (for example, ich schlafe, du schläfst, er schläft, and ich laufe, du läufst, er läuft) do *not* take an *umlaut* in forming the imperative:

du-FORM	**Schlaf**	gut, Hans!	**Lauf**	schneller!
ihr-FORM	**Schlaft**	gut, Freunde!	**Lauft**	schneller!
Sie-FORM	**Schlafen Sie**	gut, Herr Lange!	**Laufen Sie**	schneller!

Contrast:

Du schläfst gut, Hans.   Schlaf gut, Hans!

▶ Note   German imperatives are commonly followed by an exclamation point:

Laufen Sie schneller!

DRILLS

1   werden

● Replace the subjects of the following sentences, supplying the correct form of **werden**.

1. Ich werde müde. (er, wir, die Kinder)
2. Die Kinder werden groß. (er, du, ihr)
3. Ich werde faul. (er, du)   (**faul:** lazy)

[handwritten: wird, werde, werden / wirst, wirst, werdet / wird, werden]

● Express in German.

1. She's getting tired.
2. You're getting lazy, Hans.
3. The children are getting big.
4. He's getting fat.   (fat: **dick**)

5. You're getting tired, children.
6. They're getting boring.   (boring: **langweilig**)
7. We're getting old.   (old: **alt**)

2   wissen

● Supply the correct form of **wissen**.

1. Ich _weiß_ nicht genau.   (**genau:** exactly)
2. Wir _wissen_ nicht warum.
3. _Weißt_ du seine Telefonnummer?

   (**die Telefonnummer:** telephone number)

4. Ihr _wißt_ das schon.   (**schon:** already)
5. _Weiß_ Inge das?

● Express in German.

1. We don't know why.
2. You know that already, children.
3. Does Inge know that?
4. I don't know exactly.
5. Do you know his telephone number, Hans?

3 Mixed drill (stem-vowel change)

● Replace the subjects of the following sentences, making the necessary changes in the verb forms.

1. Wann treffen wir ihn? (du, ihr)
2. Sie fahren zu langsam. (er, ihr)
3. Lassen Sie das Kind allein? (du)
   (lassen: to leave)
4. Nehmen wir ihn mit? (du)
5. Ich wasche meinen Wagen. (er)
   (waschen: to wash)
6. Die Katze frißt Fisch. **(Alle Katzen . . .)**
7. Sie saufen zu viel. (er)
   (saufen: to drink, booze)
8. Was essen Sie da? (du)
9. Sehen Sie ihn? (du)
10. Sie lesen zu viel. (du)

11. Die Bücher fallen von dem Tisch.
    (Das Buch . . .)   **(fallen:** to fall)
12. Was empfehlen Sie? (er)
13. Wir laufen nach Hause. (er)
14. Sie vergessen alles. **(Viktor . . .)**
15. Ich gebe dir ein Beispiel. (er)
    (das Beispiel: example)
16. Ich schlafe zu viel. (du)
17. Wir helfen ihnen. (er)
18. Ich trage die Pakete nach Hause. (er)
    (tragen: to carry)
19. Sie sprechen zu leise. (er) **(leise:** softly)

MIXED DRILLS

Imperative of verbs with stem-vowel change

● Supply the suggested imperative forms.

1. treffen
   Treffen Sie uns später, Herr Lenz!
   Triff uns später, Hans!
   _____ uns später! **(ihr-form)**
2. laufen
   _____ schneller, Gerd!
   _____ schneller, Herr Weiß!
   _____ schneller, Kinder!
3. schlafen
   _____ gut, Herr Springer!
   _____ gut, Kurt!
   _____ gut, Kinder!
4. fressen
   _____ deinen Fisch, Minna!
5. helfen
   _____ mir, Albrecht!
   _____ mir, Herr Holtz!
6. saufen
   _____ nicht so viel, Franz!

7. waschen
   _____ den Wagen, Karl!
   _____ den Wagen, Kinder!
8. nehmen
   _____ mich mit, Charlotte!
9. lassen
   _____ mich in Ruhe, Herr Schmidt!
   (in Ruhe: alone; *lit.:* in peace)
   _____ mich in Ruhe, Fritz!
10. vergessen
    _____ die Adresse nicht, Rosi!
    _____ die Adresse nicht, Frau Ritter!
    _____ die Adresse nicht, Jungens!
11. tragen
    _____ die Pakete nach Hause, Hans!
    _____ die Pakete nach Hause, Kinder!
12. essen
    _____ bei uns, Christa!
    _____ bei uns, Fräulein Schmidt!

EXPRESS IN GERMAN

a. 1. She's getting tired.
   2. He's driving too slowly.
   3. Viktor forgets everything.
   4. We don't know why.
   5. Take me along, Charlotte.
   6. You're getting lazy, Günther.
   7. He's washing my car.
   8. Does Inge know that?
   9. You sleep too much, Renate.
   10. Meet us later, Dieter.

b. 1. Do you know his telephone number, Hans?
   2. He's speaking too softly.
   3. Eat your fish, Minna.
   4. Does he see her?
   5. What does he recommend?
   6. You're getting old, Gustav.
   7. Leave me alone (in peace), Inge.

   8. Don't drink so much, Willi.
   9. When are you going to meet him, Karl?
   10. All cats eat fish.

c. 1. He's running home.
   2. Sleep well, Kurt.
   3. Eat at our place, Klaus.
   4. Run faster, children.
   5. What are you eating, Erika?
   6. The children are getting big.
   7. He's carrying the packages home.
   8. Are you going to leave him alone?

VOCABULARY

alt old
das **Beispiel, -e** example
bitte please
brauchen to need
dick fat
dies- this
fallen (fällt) to fall
faul lazy
der **Film, -e** movie, film
frei free; empty (referring to seats)
fressen (frißt) to eat (of animals)
genau exactly
hübsch pretty
jed- each, every, any

kennen to know, be acquainted with
der **Koffer, -** suitcase
der **Laden, -̈** store
die **Lampe, -n** lamp
langweilig boring
lassen (läßt) to leave, let
laufen (läuft) to run
leise softly
meinen to mean
die **Nacht, -̈e** night
der **Platz, -̈e** place, seat
richtig correct, right
in Ruhe alone, lit. "in peace"

saufen to drink, booze
der **Schnellzug, -̈e** express train
schon already
die **Telefonnummer, -n** telephone number
der **Teller, -** plate
teuer expensive
tragen (trägt) to carry
waschen (wäscht) to wash
welch- which
werden (wirst, wird) to become, get
wissen (weiß) to know

Lesson 4 Level THREE

A Adjective Endings

1 The weak declension of adjectives following **der**-words

a. Introduction

So far you have seen two-word phrases consisting of a **der**-word **(dieser, jeder, welcher)** and a *noun* **(Anzug, Hemd, Krawatte).** And you have seen that the **der**-word always takes strong endings:

> dies**er** Anzug
> dies**en** Anzug
> dies**em** Anzug

Now look at *three-word* phrases consisting of a **der**-*word* plus *another adjective* plus a *noun:*

Der-Word	+	Adjective	+	Noun
dies **er**		braun **e**		Anzug
dies **en**		braun **en**		Anzug
dies **em**		braun **en**		Anzug

In the phrases above, **dieser** has *strong endings.* But the adjective **braun** has a different set of endings, called *weak endings.*

b. Forms

The following table shows the *weak adjective endings:*

	SINGULAR			PLURAL
	Masc.	*Neut.*	*Fem.*	*All Genders*
NOM.	-e	-e	-e	-en
ACC.	-en	-e	-e	-en
DAT.	-en	-en	-en	-en

► **Note**   The ending -e is required in the

MASCULINE	nominative
NEUTER	nominative and accusative
FEMININE	nominative and accusative

In all other instances the weak ending is -en.

c. Patterns

The following table shows the **der**-word **dieser** followed by an adjective and a noun:

SINGULAR		
Masculine	*Neuter*	*Feminine*
NOM. dieser braune Anzug	dieses neue Hemd	diese schöne Krawatte
ACC. diesen braunen Anzug	dieses neue Hemd	diese schöne Krawatte
DAT. diesem braunen Anzug	diesem neuen Hemd	dieser schönen Krawatte

PLURAL		
All Genders		
NOM.	diese neuen Anzüge, Hemden, Krawatten	
ACC.	diese neuen Anzüge, Hemden, Krawatten	
DAT.	diesen neuen Anzügen, Hemden, Krawatten	

As you see from the table:

1. The **der**-word (**dieser**) always takes strong endings.
2. Adjectives following the **der**-word take weak endings (**-e** and **-en**).

The same pattern holds for any number of adjectives following a **der**-word (for example, der neue braune Anzug).

DRILLS

1   Masculine singular forms with **der**-words

	Strong Ending	Weak Ending	
NOM.	dieser	braune	Anzug
ACC.	diesen	braunen	Anzug
DAT.	diesem	braunen	Anzug

- Supply the correct *nominative* endings (d ___ means that the definite article should be used).

  1. Dies*es* braun*er* Mantel ist hübsch.
  2. Jed*er* groß*er* Bahnhof hat ein Restaurant.
  3. Wer ist d*er* alt*e* Mann da drüben?
  4. Wann fährt d*er* nächst*e* Zug?
  5. Wo ist d*er* ander*e* Tisch?
  6. Was kostet d*er* braun*e* Anzug?

  (**braun:** brown; **hübsch:** pretty)
  (**groß:** large)
  (**alt:** old; **da drüben:** over there)
  (**nächst–:** next; **der Zug:** train)
  (**ander-:** other)

- Supply the correct *accusative* endings.

  1. Er will jed*en* neu*n* Film sehen.
     (**neu:** new)
  2. Ich nehme dies*en* braun*en* Mantel.
  3. Stell es auf d*en* ander*en* Tisch!

  4. Welch*en* neu*en* Film meinen Sie?
  5. Nehmen wir d*en* neu*en* Wagen!
  6. Wirf d*en* alt*en* Anzug weg! (**weg:** away)

- Supply the correct *dative* endings.

  1. Was machen wir mit dies*em* alt*en* Tisch?
  2. Hilf d*em* arm*en* Mann! (**arm:** poor)
  3. Es steht auf d*em* ander*en* Tisch.

  4. Gehst du zu d*em* neu*en* Arzt?
  5. Es gibt ein Restaurant in jed*em* deutsch*en* Bahnhof. (**deutsch:** German)

- Supply the correct nominative, accusative, or dative endings.

  1. Dies*e* braun*e* Mantel ist hübsch.
  2. Nehmen wir d*en* neu*en* Wagen!
  3. Wann fährt d*er* nächst*e* Zug?
  4. Es steht auf d*em* ander*en* Tisch.
  5. Er will jed*en* neu*en* Film sehen.
  6. Gehst du zu d*em* neu*en* Arzt?
  7. Was kostet d*er* braun*en* Anzug?
  8. Ich nehme dies*en* braun*en* Mantel.

  9. Was machen wir mit dies*em* alt*en* Tisch?
  10. Stell es auf d*em* ander*en* Tisch!
  11. Hilf d*em* arm*en* Mann!
  12. Wirf d*en* alt*en* Anzug weg!
  13. Welch*en* neu*en* Film meinen Sie?
  14. Es gibt ein Restaurant in jed*em* deutsch*en* Bahnhof.

- Express in German.

  1. What does the brown suit cost?
  2. Let's take the new car.
  3. Throw that* old suit away.
  4. Do you go to the new doctor?
  5. When does the next train leave?
     (use **fahren**)
  6. Which new movie do you mean?
  7. Help the poor man.
  8. I'll take this brown coat.
  9. It's on the other table.
  10. There's a restaurant in every German railroad station.

  11. This brown coat is pretty.
  12. He wants to see every new movie.
  13. What'll we do with this old table?
  14. Put it on the other table.

_____

*German uses the definite article to mean both "the" and "that":

  Wirf **den** alten Anzug weg! (Throw *that* old suit away.)
  (Throw *the* old suit away.)

2 Neuter singular forms with **der**-words

	Strong Ending	Weak Ending	
NOM.	dieses	blaue	Kleid
ACC.	dieses	blaue ·	Kleid'
DAT.	diesem	blauen	Kleid

- Supply the correct *nominative* endings.

  1. Wo ist d*as* neu*e* Kaufhaus?
  2. Jed*es* gut*e* Hotel hat ein Restaurant.
  3. Es ist d*as* best*e* Restaurant in München. **(best:** best)

  4. Dies*es* blau*e* Kleid ist hübsch. **(blau:** blue)
  5. Wo ist d*as* ander*e* Hemd?

- Supply the correct *accusative* endings.

  1. Ich nehme dies*es* blau*e* Kleid.
  2. Gib mir d*as* klein*e* Glas! **(klein:** small, little)
  3. Sie geht gerade in d*as* groß*e* Haus.

  4. Kennst du d*as* neu*e* Kaufhaus?
  5. Welch*es* neu*e* Restaurant meinst du?
  6. Ich kenne d*as* ander*e* Mädchen nicht.

- Supply the correct *dative* endings.

  1. Geh zu d*em* neu*en* Kaufhaus!
  2. Geben Sie es d*em* ander*en* Mädchen!
  3. Gehen Sie zu d*em* nächst*en* Büro!

  4. Es gibt ein Restaurant in jed*em* gut*en* Hotel.
  5. Das kannst du in jed*em* gut*en* Kaufhaus finden.
  6. Was machen wir mit dies*em* alt*en* Bild?

- Supply the correct nominative, accusative, or dative endings.

  1. Gib mir d*as* klein*e* Glas!
  2. Wo ist d*as* neu*e* Kaufhaus?
  3. Welch*es* neu*e* Restaurant meinst du?
  4. Was machen wir mit dies*em* alt*e* Bild?
  5. Ich kenne d*as* ander*e* Mädchen nicht.
  6. Dies___ blau___ Kleid ist hübsch.
  7. Geben Sie es d___ ander___ Mädchen!
  8. Wo ist d___ ander___ Hemd?
  9. Kennst du d___ neu___ Kaufhaus?
  10. Das kannst du in jed___ gut___ Kaufhaus finden.
  11. Es ist d___ best___ Restaurant in München.
  12. Geh zu d___ neu___ Kaufhaus!
  13. Jed___ gut___ Hotel hat ein Restaurant.
  14. Es gibt ein Restaurant in jed___ gut___ Hotel.

- Express in German.

  1. This blue dress is pretty.
  2. Go to the new department store.
  3. Where's the other shirt?
  4. Which new restaurant do you mean?
  5. What'll we do with this old picture?
  6. I don't know the other girl.
  7. It's the best restaurant in Munich.
  8. There's a restaurant in every good hotel.

  9. Where is the new department store?
  10. Give it to the other girl.
  11. Every good hotel has a restaurant.
  12. Do you know the new department store?
  13. Give me the small glass.
  14. You can find that in any good department store.

3 Feminine singular forms with **der**-words

	Strong Ending	*Weak Ending*	
NOM.	dies**e**	braun**e**	Jacke
ACC.	dies**e**	braun**e**	Jacke
DAT.	dies**er**	braun**en**	Jacke

• Supply the correct *nominative* endings.

1. Dies*e* braun*e* Jacke ist hübsch.
2. D*ie* neu*e* Buchhandlung soll sehr gut sein.
3. Jed*e* deutsch*e* Stadt hat ein Rathaus.
4. Dies*e* neu*e* Adresse ist nicht richtig.
5. Jed*e* gesund*e* Katze frißt Fisch.
6. D*ie* neu*e* Sekretärin ist hier.

(das Rathaus: city hall)

(gesund: healthy)

• Supply the correct *accusative* endings.

1. Ich nehme dies*e* grün*e* Krawatte.

   (grün: green)
2. Kennst du d*ie* neu*e* Buchhandlung?
3. Ich nehme d*ie* ander*e* Jacke.
4. Ich kann dies*e* klein*e* Rechnung bezahlen.
5. Kennst du d*ie* neu*e* Sekretärin?
6. Ich nehme dies*e* braun*e* Jacke.

• Supply the correct *dative* endings.

1. Was machen wir mit dies*er* schrecklich*e* Lampe?
2. Ich gehe zu d*er* ander*en* Buchhandlung.
3. Er arbeitet in d*er* alt*en* Bibliothek.
4. Gib es d*er* ander*en* Sekretärin!
5. Gehen wir zu d*er* ander*en* Bank!
6. Hilf d*er* arm*e* Frau!

• Supply the correct nominative, accusative, or dative endings.

1. Kennst du d__ neu__ Buchhandlung?
2. D__ neu__ Sekretärin ist hier.
3. Dies__ braun__ Jacke ist hübsch.
4. Gehen wir zu d__ ander__ Bank!
5. D__ neu__ Buchhandlung soll sehr gut sein.
6. Ich gehe zu d__ ander__ Buchhandlung.
7. Ich nehme dies__ braun__ Jacke.
8. Jed__ gesund__ Katze frißt Fisch.
9. Hilf d__ arm__ Frau!
10. Ich nehme d__ ander__ Jacke.
11. Gib es d__ ander__ Sekretärin!
12. Dies__ neu__ Adresse ist nicht richtig.
13. Kennst du d__ neu__ Sekretärin?
14. Was machen wir mit dies__ schrecklich__ Lampe?

• Express in German.

1. The new secretary is here.
2. The new bookstore is supposed to be very good.
3. What will we do with this horrible lamp?
4. Every healthy cat eats fish.
5. I'm going to the other bookstore.
6. I'll take this brown sports coat.
7. Do you know the new secretary?
8. Help the poor woman.
9. I'll take the other sports coat.
10. Let's go to the other bank.
11. Do you know the new bookstore?
12. This new address isn't correct.
13. Give it to the other secretary.
14. This brown sportscoat is pretty.

4 Plural forms with der-words

	Strong Ending	Weak Ending	
NOM.	diese	alten	Bilder
ACC.	diese	alten	Bilder
DAT.	diesen	alten	Bildern

- Supply the correct *nominative* endings.

1. Diese neuen Anzüge sind hübsch.
2. Was kosten die anderen Mäntel?
3. Diese alten Adressen sind nicht richtig.

4. Die neuen Lampen sind hier.
5. Wo sind die anderen Hemden?

- Supply the correct *accusative* endings.

1. Gib mir die kleinen Gläser!
2. Ich kenne die anderen Mädchen nicht.
3. Welche alten Bilder meinst du?

4. Ich kann diese kleinen Rechnungen bezahlen.
5. Was gibst du mir für diese alten Bücher?

- Supply the correct *dative* endings.

1. Was machen wir mit diesen alten Bildern?
2. Ich gehe mit den anderen Studenten.

3. Das findet man nur in den besten Restaurants.
4. Gib es den anderen Jungen!

- Supply the correct nominative, accusative, or dative endings.

1. Wo sind d___ ander___ Hemden?
2. Was gibst du mir für dies___ alt___ Bücher?
3. Ich gehe mit d___ ander___ Studenten.
4. Was kosten d___ ander___ Mäntel?
5. Dies___ alt___ Adressen sind nicht richtig.
6. Was machen wir mit dies___ alt___ Bildern?

7. Welch___ alt___ Bilder meinst du?
8. Gib mir d___ neu___ Gläser!
9. Gib es d___ ander___ Jungen!
   (der Junge, –n, –n: boy, guy)
10. D___ neu___ Lampen sind hier.
11. Das findet man nur in d___ best___ Restaurants.
12. Ich kenne d___ ander___ Mädchen nicht.

- Express in German.

1. What'll you give me for these old books?
2. These old addresses aren't correct.
3. Give it to the other guys.
4. What'll we do with these old pictures?
5. Which old pictures do you mean?
6. I don't know the other girls.

7. Where are the other shirts?
8. I'm going with the other students.
9. Give me the new glasses.
10. One only finds that in the best restaurants.
11. The new lamps are here.
12. What do the other coats cost?

MIXED DRILLS

• Gender, number, and case are mixed.

a.
1. Ich nehme dies_e_ braun_e_ Jacke.
2. Es gibt ein Restaurant in jed___ gut___ Hotel.
3. Jed___ gesund___ Katze frißt Fisch.
4. Wirf d___ alt___ Anzug weg!
5. D___ neu___ Lampen sind hier.
6. Gehen wir zu d___ ander___ Bank!
7. Wo sind d___ ander___ Hemden?
8. Ich kenne d___ ander___ Mädchen nicht. (sing.)
9. Geh zu d___ neu___ Kaufhaus!
10. Stell es auf d___ ander___ Tisch!

b.
1. Was kosten d___ ander___ Mäntel?
2. Gehen Sie zu d___ neu___ Arzt?
3. Ich nehme d___ ander___ Jacke.
4. Dies___ blau___ Kleid ist hübsch.
5. Was machen wir mit dies___ schrecklich___ Lampe?
6. Was kostet d___ braun___ Anzug?
7. Gib mir d___ neu___ Gläser!
8. Hilf d___ arm___ Mann!
9. Kennst du d___ neu___ Sekretärin?
10. Es ist d___ best___ Restaurant in München.

c.
1. Er will jed___ neu___ Film sehen.
2. Es steht auf d___ ander___ Tisch.
3. Ich gehe mit d___ ander___ Studenten. (pl.)
4. Welch___ neu___ Restaurant meinst du?
5. Es gibt ein Restaurant in jed___ deutsch___ Bahnhof.
6. D___ neu___ Buchhandlung soll sehr gut sein.
7. Wann fährt d___ nächst___ Zug?
8. Gib es d___ ander___ Sekretärin!
9. Nehmen wir d___ neu___ Wagen!
10. Das findet man nur in d___ best___ Restaurants.

d.
1. Jed___ gut___ Hotel hat ein Restaurant.
2. Dies___ alt___ Adressen sind nicht richtig.
3. Geben Sie es d___ ander___ Mädchen! (sing.)
4. Was gibst du mir für dies___ alt___ Bücher?

EXPRESS IN GERMAN

a.
1. What does the brown suit cost?
2. These old addresses aren't correct.
3. What'll we do with this horrible lamp?
4. It's on the other table.
5. I'll take this brown sports coat.
6. This blue dress is pretty.
7. Give it to the other girl.
8. Give me the new glasses.
9. There's a restaurant in every good hotel.
10. When does the next train leave? (use **fahren**)

b.
1. I'll take the other sports coat.
2. Help the poor man.
3. What'll you give me for these old books?
4. Every healthy cat eats fish.
5. I don't know the other girl.
6. One only finds that in the best restaurants.
7. Do you know the new secretary?

8. Every good hotel has a restaurant.
9. Let's go to the other bank.
10. Let's take the new car.

c.
1. Where are the other shirts?
2. Go to the new department store.
3. The new bookstore is supposed to be very good.
4. There's a restaurant in every German railroad station.
5. Give it to the other secretary.
6. It's the best restaurant in Munich.
7. Throw that (the) old suit away.
8. The new lamps are here.
9. He wants to see every new movie.
10. What do the other coats cost?

d.
1. Do you go to the new doctor?
2. I'm going with the other students.
3. Which new restaurant do you mean?
4. Put it on the other table.

B Ein-Words

1 Introduction

The **ein**-words are a group of words that take the *same endings* as the indefinite article **ein.** They should actually be called **kein**-words, since **ein** does not have a plural form and **kein** does.

The **ein**-words are:

ein	a, an
kein	not a, no, not any

and *the possessive adjectives:*

mein	my	unser	our
dein	your	euer	your
sein	his	ihr	their
ihr	her	Ihr	your (polite form)
sein	its		

▶ Note   The **er** at the end of **unser** and **euer** is not an ending. It is part of the adjective itself. **Euer** becomes **eur–** when it takes an ending.

2 Comparison of **dieser** and **kein**

There is an important difference between **der**-words and **ein**-words. Compare the endings of **dieser** (a **der**-word) with those of **kein** (an **ein**-word):

	SINGULAR					
	Masculine		*Neuter*		*Feminine*	
NOM.	dies**er**	kein☐	dies**es**	kein☐	dies**e**	kein**e**
ACC.	dies**en**	kein**en**	dies**es**	kein☐	dies**e**	kein**e**
DAT.	dies**em**	kein**em**	dies**em**	kein**em**	dies**er**	kein**er**

	PLURAL	
	All Genders	
NOM.	dies**e**	kein**e**
ACC.	dies**e**	kein**e**
DAT.	dies**en**	kein**en**

The table shows that

1. **Der**-words *always* take *strong* endings.
2. With three exceptions, the **ein**-words also take strong endings. These three exceptions are *masculine nominative* and *neuter nominative* and *accusative.*

Look at the following comparison of **dieser** and **kein:**

	Masculine		Neuter	
NOM.	dies**er**	kein ☐	dies**es**	kein ☐
ACC.			dies**es**	kein ☐

3 Endings on adjectives that follow **ein**-words

The same general rule applies to **ein**-words and **der**-words:

1. Whenever an **ein**-word takes a strong ending, the adjectives that follow it must take weak endings.
2. However, there are three instances where **ein**-words take no endings at all: *masculine nominative* and *neuter nominative* and *accusative.*

A specific rule applies to this situation: *In those three instances where an **ein**-word has no ending, the adjectives that follow it must have strong endings:*

	Masculine	Neuter
NOM.	ein neu**er** Wagen sein neu**er** Wagen unser neu**er** Wagen	ein neu**es** Haus sein neu**es** Haus unser neu**es** Haus
ACC.		ein neu**es** Haus sein neu**es** Haus unser neu**es** Haus

DRILLS

1 Masculine singular forms with **ein**-words

NOM.	ein	gut**er** Mantel
ACC.	ein**en**	gut**en** Mantel
DAT.	ein**em**	gut**en** Mantel

- Supply the correct *nominative* endings.

1. Dein neu*er* Wagen ist sehr hübsch.
2. Ihr braun*er* Mantel ist da drüben.
3. Das ist kein neu*er* Film.
4. Er ist mein best*er* Freund.

(**der Freund**: friend)

5. Das ist ein lang*er* Zug.

(**lang**: long; **der Zug**: train)

6. Ein gut*er* Platz ist teuer.   (**der Platz**: seat)

- Supply the correct *accusative* endings.

1. Wir können ein*en* ander*en* Bus nehmen.
2. Ich kann sein*en* letzt*en* Brief nicht finden.
3. Ich brauche kein*en* neu*en* Mantel.
4. Können Sie mir ein*en* gut*en* Arzt empfehlen?
5. Ich nehme mein*en* klein*en* Bruder mit.
6. Wollen Sie Ihr*en* alt*en* Wagen verkaufen?

(**letzt**: last)

(**verkaufen**: to sell)

- Supply the correct *dative* endings.

1. Was soll ich mit dein*em* alt*en* Mantel machen?
2. Er geht zu ein*em* gut*en* Arzt.
3. Der Brief ist von ein*em* alt*en* Freund.
4. Ich gebe es mein*em* klein*en* Bruder.
5. Es steckt in mein*em* ander*en* Anzug.

(**stecken**: to be, in the sense of be hidden)

- Supply the correct nominative, accusative, or dative endings.

1. Wir können ein*en* ander*en* Bus nehmen.
2. Ich nehme mein*en* klein*en* Bruder mit.
3. Ihr braun*er* Mantel ist da drüben.
4. Der Brief ist von ein*em* alt*en* Freund.
5. Können Sie mir ein*en* gut*en* Arzt empfehlen?
6. Er ist mein best*er* Freund.
7. Wollen Sie Ihr*en* alt*en* Wagen verkaufen?
8. Es steckt in mein*em* ander*en* Anzug.
9. Das ist kein neu*er* Film.
10. Was soll ich mit dein*em* alt*en* Mantel machen?
11. Ich kann sein*en* letzt*en* Brief nicht finden.
12. Ein gut*er* Platz ist teuer.
13. Ich brauche kein*en* neu*en* Mantel.
14. Er geht zu ein*em* gut*en* Arzt.

- Express in German.

1. Do you want to sell your old car?
2. That's not a new movie.
3. He goes to a good doctor.
4. Your brown coat is over there.
5. I'm taking my little brother along.
6. He's my best friend.
7. We can take another bus.
8. A good seat is expensive.
9. It's in my other suit.   (use **stecken**)
10. I don't need a new coat.
11. Can you recommend a good doctor?
12. I can't find his last letter.
13. The letter is from an old friend.
14. What shall I do with your old coat?

2   Neuter singular forms with **ein**-words

NOM.	ein	gut**es** Restaurant
ACC.	ein	gut**es** Restaurant
DAT.	ein**em**	gut**en** Restaurant

- Supply the correct *nominative* endings.

1. Ihr neu*es* Haus ist sehr schön.
2. Das ist sein best*es* Buch.
3. Unser alt*es* Haus ist zu klein.
4. Das ist kein schlecht*es* Bier.
5. Inge, dein neu*es* Kleid ist einfach schrecklich.
6. Wo ist euer neu*es* Büro?

(schlecht: bad)
(einfach: simply; schrecklich: horrible)

- Supply the correct *accusative* endings.

1. Sie hat ein groß*es* Zimmer.
2. Willst du unser neu*es* Haus sehen?
3. Kannst du mir ein gut*es* Hotel empfehlen?
4. Ich brauche ein ander*es* Buch.
5. Kennst du ein gut*es* Restaurant?
6. Verkaufen Sie Ihr alt*es* Haus?

(ander–: other, different)

- Supply the correct *dative* endings.

1. Was machen wir mit dein*em* alt*en* Hemd?
2. Wir wollen in ein*em* gut*en* Restaurant essen.
3. Wir können in ein*em* billig*en* Hotel bleiben.
4. Sie müssen zu ein*em* ander*en* Büro gehen.
5. Er geht mit ein*em* sehr hübsch*en* Mädchen.

(billig: cheap, inexpensive)

- Supply the correct nominative, accusative, or dative endings.

1. Sie hat ein groß*es* Zimmer.
2. Wollen Sie unser neu*es* Haus sehen?
3. Ich brauche ein ander*es* Buch.
4. Wo ist euer neu*es* Büro?
5. Wir wollen in ein*em* gut*en* Restaurant essen.
6. Unser alt*es* Haus ist zu klein.
7. Das ist kein schlecht*es* Bier.
8. Verkaufen Sie Ihr alt*es* Haus?
9. Können Sie mir ein gut*es* Hotel empfehlen?
10. Sie müssen zu ein*em* ander*en* Büro gehen.
11. Das ist sein best*es* Buch.
12. Ihr neu*es* Haus ist sehr schön, Herr Lenz.
13. Er geht mit ein*em* sehr hübsch*en* Mädchen.
14. Inge, dein neu*es* Kleid ist einfach schrecklich.

- Express in German.

1. Your new house is very pretty, Mr. Lenz.
2. She has a large room.
3. We want to eat in a good restaurant.
4. That's not a bad beer.
5. Can you recommend a good hotel?
6. Are you selling your old house?
7. You'll have to go to another office.
8. Inge, your new dress is simply horrible.
9. Do you want to see our new house?
10. He goes with a very pretty girl.
11. That's his best book.
12. Our old house is too small.
13. Where's your new office?
    (2nd person plural, familiar)
14. I need a different book.

3 Feminine singular forms with **ein**-words

NOM.	eine	andere	Bank
ACC.	eine	andere	Bank
DAT.	einer	anderen	Bank

- Supply the correct *nominative* endings.

    1. Das ist kein___ schlecht___ Idee.
    2. Es ist ein___ schön___ Nacht.
    3. Das ist ein___ gut___ Frage.
    4. Sein___ neu___ Krawatte ist schrecklich.
    5. Das ist ein___ hübsch___ Jacke.
    6. Berlin ist ein___ interessant___ Stadt.

    (die Idee: idea)

    (die Frage: question)

- Supply the correct *accusative* endings.

    1. Weißt du ihr___ neu___ Adresse?
    2. Ich brauche ein___ gut___ Jacke.
    3. Hast du kein___ ander___ Krawatte?
    4. Kennst du sein___ erst___ Frau?
    5. Ich nehme mein___ klein___ Schwester mit.
    6. Wir haben ein___ neu___ Sekretärin.

    (erst: first)

- Supply the correct *dative* endings.

    1. Ich gehe zu ein___ ander___ Bank.
    2. Ich gebe es mein___ klein___ Schwester.
    3. Er wohnt in ein___ klein___ Stadt.
    4. Ich gehe zu ein___ ander___ Buchhandlung.
    5. Was machst du mit dein___ alt___ Jacke?
    6. Er wohnt bei ein___ sehr nett___ Familie.

    (die Familie: family)

- Supply the correct nominative, accusative, or dative endings.

    1. Weißt du ihr___ neu___ Adresse?
    2. Das ist ein___ hübsch___ Jacke.
    3. Ich gehe zu ein___ ander___ Buchhandlung.
    4. Hast du kein___ ander___ Krawatte?
    5. Das ist kein___ schlecht___ Idee.
    6. Ich gebe es mein___ klein___ Schwester.
    7. Wir haben ein___ neu___ Sekretärin.
    8. Ich gehe zu ein___ ander___ Bank.
    9. Es ist ein___ schön___ Nacht.
    10. Er wohnt in ein___ klein___ Stadt in Bayern. (Bayern: Bavaria)
    11. Kennst du sein___ erst___ Frau?
    12. Sein___ neu___ Krawatte ist schrecklich.
    13. Das ist ein___ gut___ Frage.
    14. Was machst du mit dein___ alt___ Jacke?

- Express in German.

    1. We have a new secretary.
    2. Don't you have a different tie?
    3. I'm going to another bank.
    4. What are you going to do with your old sports coat?
    5. That's not a bad idea.
    6. Do you know her new address?
    7. It's a beautiful night.
    8. I'm going to give it to my little sister.
    9. Do you know his first wife?

10. That's a good question.
11. His new tie is horrible.
12. I'm going to another bookstore.

13. That's a pretty sports coat.
14. He lives in a small town in Bavaria.

4   Plural forms with **ein**-words

NOM.	unsere	besten	Studenten
ACC.	unsere	besten	Studenten
DAT.	unseren	besten	Studenten

● Supply the correct *nominative* endings.

1. Wo sind unser___ neu___ Gläser?
2. Mein___ klein___ Brüder wohnen noch zu Hause.
3. Ihr___ alt___ Briefe sind sehr interessant.
4. Mein___ best___ Ideen kommen nach dem Abendessen.

5. Dein___ neu___ Kleider sind hübsch.

(**das Glas,** ⸗er: glass)
(**der Bruder,** ⸗: brother)

(**die Idee,-n**: idea; **das Abendessen**: supper, dinner)

● Supply the correct *accusative* endings.

1. Ich sehe kein___ frei___ Plätze.
2. Er kauft unser___ alt___ Bücher.
3. Sie will ihr___ alt___ Briefe haben.
4. Ich habe ihr___ neu___ Adressen nicht.
5. Er hat kein___ gut___ Ideen.

(**frei**: free, empty; **der Platz,**⸗e: seat)

● Supply the correct *dative* endings.

1. Was machst du mit dein___ alt___ Krawatten?
2. Wir helfen unser___ best___ Studenten.
3. Was machst du mit ihr___ alt___ Briefen?

● Supply the correct nominative, accusative, or dative endings.

1. Wo sind unser___ neu___ Gläser?
2. Er hat kein___ gut___ Ideen.
3. Ich sehe kein___ frei___ Plätze.
4. Ihr___ alt___ Briefe sind sehr interessant.
5. Was machst du mit dein___ alt___ Krawatten?
6. Mein___ best___ Ideen kommen nach dem Abendessen.
7. Was machst du mit ihr___ alt___ Briefen?
8. Er kauft unser___ alt___ Bücher.
9. Ich habe ihr___ neu___ Adressen nicht.
10. Dein___ neu___ Kleider sind sehr hübsch.
11. Sie will ihr___ alt___ Briefe haben.

● Express in German.

1. Her old letters are very interesting.
2. I don't have their new addresses.
3. What are you going to do with your old ties?
4. Where are our new glasses?
5. He doesn't have any good ideas.
6. What are you going to do with her old letters?

7. My best ideas come after dinner.
8. I don't see any empty (frei) seats.
9. He's going to buy our old books.

10. Your new dresses are very pretty.
11. She wants to have her old letters.

MIXED DRILLS

• Gender, number, and case are mixed.

a. 1. Das ist ein___ gut___ Frage.
2. Er geht zu ein___ gut___ Arzt.
3. Ihr neu___ Haus ist sehr schön.
4. Ich brauche kein___ neu___ Mantel.
5. Mein___ best___ Ideen kommen nach dem Abendessen.
6. Er wohnt in ein___ klein___ Stadt in Bayern.
7. Kennen Sie sein___ erst___ Frau?
8. Können Sie mir ein___ gut___ Arzt empfehlen?
9. Wo sind unser___ neu___ Gläser?
10. Verkaufen Sie Ihr alt___ Haus?

b. 1. Es ist ein___ schön___ Nacht.
2. Das ist sein best___ Buch.
3. Es steckt in mein___ ander___ Anzug.
4. Ihr___ alt___ Briefe sind sehr interessant.
5. Das ist kein___ schlecht___ Idee.
6. Wir können ein___ ander___ Bus nehmen.
7. Was soll ich mit dein___ alt___ Mantel machen?
8. Ich gehe zu ein___ ander___ Bank.
9. Können Sie mir ein gut___ Hotel empfehlen?
10. Er ist mein best___ Freund.

c. 1. Das ist kein schlecht___ Bier.
2. Was machst du mit ihr___ alt___ Briefen?
3. Sein___ neu___ Krawatte ist schrecklich.
4. Unser alt___ Haus ist zu klein.
5. Das ist kein neu___ Film.
6. Sie will ihr___ alt___ Briefe haben.
7. Inge, dein neu___ Kleid ist einfach schrecklich.
8. Weißt du ihr___ neu___ Adresse?
9. Wir haben ein___ neu___ Sekretärin.
10. Wollen Sie unser neu___ Haus sehen?

d. 1. Wir wollen in ein___ gut___ Restaurant essen.
2. Er hat kein___ gut___ Ideen.
3. Hast du kein___ ander___ Krawatte?
4. Wollen Sie Ihr___ alt___ Wagen verkaufen?
5. Was machst du mit dein___ alt___ Jacke?
6. Der Brief ist von ein___ alt___ Freund.
7. Wo ist euer neu___ Büro?
8. Dein___ neu___ Kleider sind sehr hübsch.
9. Er geht mit ein___ sehr hübsch___ Mädchen.

EXPRESS IN GERMAN

a. 1. Are you selling your old house?
2. We have a new secretary.
3. I don't need a new coat.
4. Where are our new glasses?
5. We want to eat in a good restaurant.
6. That's a good question.
7. We can take another bus.
8. His new tie is horrible.
9. Do you want to sell your old car?
10. My best ideas come after dinner.

b. 1. What are you going to do with your old sports coat?
2. Don't you have a different tie?
3. Her old letters are very interesting.
4. That's his best book.
5. He goes to a good doctor.
6. Your new dresses are very pretty.
7. That's not a bad beer.
8. He lives in a small city in Bavaria.

9. Do you know his first wife?
10. The letter's from an old friend.

c. 1. It's a beautiful night.
  2. Inge, your new dress is simply horrible.
  3. Do you want to see our new house?
  4. Can you recommend a good doctor?
  5. What are you doing with her old letters?
  6. He goes with a very pretty girl.
  7. What shall I do with your old coat?

8. Your new house is very pretty.
9. He's my best friend.
10. Do you know her new address?

d. 1. I'm going to another bank.
  2. Our old house is too small.
  3. That's not a bad idea.
  4. Where's your new office?
  5. That's not a new movie.
  6. He doesn't have any good ideas.
  7. Can you recommend a good hotel?
  8. It's in my other suit. (use **stecken**)
  9. She wants to have her old letters.

C Adjective-Noun Phrases Without Der-Words or Ein-Words

Although most adjective-noun phrases begin with a **der**-word or an **ein**-word, some do not. For example:

Das ist **gutes** Bier.   (That's good beer.)
Armer Herr Schneider!   (Poor Mr. Schneider.)

When there is no **der**-word or **ein**-word present, *all adjectives* preceding a noun take *strong endings.*

Armer, **alter** Hans!   (Poor old Hans!)

D Viele, Wenige, Andere, Einige, Mehrere

Viele (many), **wenige** (few), **andere** (other), **einige** (some), and **mehrere** (several) are all plural adjectives suggesting indefinite quantities. They normally introduce adjective-noun phrases, and, like other adjectives not preceded by a **der**-word or an **ein**-word, they take *strong* endings. All adjectives that follow them take the same strong endings:

Er hat **viele gute** Ideen.   (He has a lot of good ideas.)
Er hat **mehrere gute** Bilder.   (He has several good pictures.)

DRILLS

• Supply the correct *nominative* endings.

1. Arm___ Frau Heller!
2. Viel___ amerikanisch___ Studenten fahren nach Deutschland. (**viele**: many; **amerikanisch**: American)
3. Was machst du da, jung___ Mann? (**jung**: young)
4. Einig___ interessant___ Leute kommen morgen. (**einige**: some; **die Leute**: people; **morgen**: tomorrow)
5. Lieb___ Fritz! (**lieb-** : dear)
6. Das ist gut___ Bier.

- Supply the correct *accusative* endings.

    1. Er hat viel___ gut___ Ideen.
    2. Wollen Sie kalt___ Milch?
    3. Er hat schrecklich___ Krawatten.
    4. Haben Sie frisch___ Brot?
    5. Inge kauft schrecklich___ Kleider.
    6. Er hat mehrer___ gut___ Bilder.
    7. Sie schreibt interessant___ Briefe.

(die **Milch**: milk)

(**frisch**: fresh; **das Brot**: bread)

(**mehrere**: several)

- Supply the correct *dative* endings.

    1. Sie schreibt mit rot___ Tinte.
    2. Pfadfinder helfen alt___ Damen.
    3. Das schmeckt gut mit kalt ___ Bier.

(**rot**: red; **die Tinte**: ink)
(**Pfadfinder**: Boy Scouts)
(**schmecken**: to taste)

- Supply the correct nominative, accusative, or dative endings.

    1. Lieb___ Fritz!
    2. Er hat viel___ gut___ Ideen.
    3. Sie schreibt interessant___ Briefe.
    4. Das ist gut___ Bier.
    5. Wollen Sie kalt___ Milch?
    6. Viel___ amerikanisch___ Studenten fahren nach Deutschland.
    7. Er hat schrecklich___ Krawatten.
    8. Sie haben mehrer___ gut___ Bilder.
    9. Sie schreibt mit rot___ Tinte.
    10. Arm_e_ Frau Heller!
    11. Einig___ interessant_e_ Leute kommen morgen.
    12. Pfadfinder helfen alt_en_ Damen.
    13. Was machst du da, jung___ Mann?
    14. Haben Sie frisch_es_ Brot?
    15. Das schmeckt gut mit kalt_em_ Bier.

- Express in German.

    1. Do you want cold milk?
    2. They have several good pictures.
    3. Poor Mrs. Heller.
    4. He has a lot of (*lit.*: many) good ideas.
    5. Some interesting people are coming tomorrow.
    6. Boy Scouts help old ladies.
    7. What are you doing there, young man?
    8. Dear Fritz.
    9. A lot of (*lit.*: many) American students go to Germany.
    10. Do you have fresh bread?
    11. He has horrible ties.
    12. She writes with red ink.
    13. That's good beer.
    14. She writes interesting letters.
    15. That tastes good with cold beer.

E Summary

1 Der-words and ein-words

Der-*Words*	Ein-*Words*
der	ein
dieser	kein
jeder	*all possessive adjectives*
welcher	

2 Strong endings

Der-words always take strong endings. **Ein**-words take strong endings, with three exceptions:

MASCULINE NOMINATIVE	**ein**☐ **Anzug**
NEUTER NOMINATIVE	**ein**☐ **Hemd**
NEUTER ACCUSATIVE	**ein**☐ **Hemd**

3 Weak endings

Adjectives that follow **der**-words or **ein**-words take the following weak endings:

		SINGULAR		PLURAL
	Masc.	*Neut.*	*Fem.*	*All Genders*
NOM.	-e	-e	-e	-en
ACC.	-en	-e	-e	-en
DAT.	-en	-en	-en	-en

▶ **Three Exceptions**   When an **ein**-word has no ending, the adjective that follows it *must* take a strong ending:

ein☐ **alter** Anzug	(masc. nom.)
ein☐ **altes** Hemd	(neut. nom.)
ein☐ **altes** Hemd	(neut. acc.)

4 Adjective-noun phrases without **der**-words or **ein**-words

When a noun phrase begins with an adjective (and *not* with a **der**-word or an **ein**-word), the adjective must take strong endings, and any adjectives following it will take the same strong endings:

Das ist gut**es** Bier.   Er hat viel**e** gut**e** Ideen.

5 Summary tables for various adjective-noun combinations

	MASCULINE		
	*With **Der**-Words*	*With **Ein**-Words*	*Without **Der** or **Ein***
NOM.	dies**er** junge Mann	ein jung**er** Mann	jung**er** Mann
ACC.	dies**en** jungen Mann	ein**en** jungen Mann	jung**en** Mann
DAT.	dies**em** jungen Mann	ein**em** jungen Mann	jung**em** Mann

NEUTER			
	With **Der**-*Words*	With **Ein**-*Words*	*Without* **Der** *or* **Ein**
NOM.	dies**es** jung**e** Mädchen	ein jung**es** Mädchen	jung**es** Mädchen
ACC.	dies**es** jung**e** Mädchen	ein jung**es** Mädchen	jung**es** Mädchen
DAT.	dies**em** jung**en** Mädchen	ein**em** jung**en** Mädchen	jung**em** Mädchen

FEMININE			
	With **Der**-*Words*	With **Ein**-*Words*	*Without* **Der** *or* **Ein**
NOM.	dies**e** jung**e** Frau	ein**e** jung**e** Frau	jung**e** Frau
ACC.	dies**e** jung**e** Frau	ein**e** jung**e** Frau	jung**e** Frau
DAT.	dies**er** jung**en** Frau	ein**er** jung**en** Frau	jung**er** Frau

PLURAL			
	With **Der**-*Words*	With **Ein**-*Words*	*Without* **Der** *or* **Ein**
NOM.	dies**e** jung**en** Leute	kein**e** jung**en** Leute	jung**e** Leute
ACC.	dies**e** jung**en** Leute	kein**e** jung**en** Leute	jung**e** Leute
DAT.	dies**en** jung**en** Leuten	kein**en** jung**en** Leuten	jung**en** Leuten

After **viele, wenige, andere, einige,** *or* **mehrere**		
NOM.	viel**e** jung**e** Leute	
ACC.	viel**e** jung**e** Leute	
DAT.	viel**en** jung**en** Leuten	

MIXED DRILLS

● Supply the correct nominative, accusative, or dative endings.

a.
1. Das schmeckt gut mit kalt ___ Bier.
2. Ich nehme dies ___ braun ___ Jacke.
3. Gehen Sie zu d ___ neu ___ Arzt?
4. Ich gehe mit d ___ ander ___ Studenten. (*pl.*)
5. Ich kenne d ___ ander ___ Mädchen nicht. (*sing.*)
6. Wirf d ___ alt ___ Anzug weg!
7. Geh zu d ___ neu ___ Kaufhaus!
8. Er hat schrecklich ___ Krawatten.
9. Dies ___ alt ___ Adressen sind nicht richtig.
10. Er ist mein best ___ Freund.

b.
1. Wann fährt d ___ nächst ___ Zug?
2. Jed ___ gesund ___ Katze frißt Fisch.
3. Nehmen wir d ___ neu ___ Wagen! (*sing.*)
4. Was kosten d ___ ander ___ Mäntel?

5. Das ist sein best___ Buch.
6. Wo ist dein neu___ Büro?
7. Lieb___ Fritz!
8. Was machen wir mit dies___ schrecklich___ Lampe?
9. Es ist auf d___ ander___ Tisch.
10. Haben Sie frisch___ Brot?

c. 1. Er hat viel___ gut___ Ideen.
2. Pfadfinder helfen alt___ Damen.
3. Das ist gut___ Bier.
4. Er will jed___ neu___ Film sehen.
5. Das ist ein___ gut___ Frage.
6. Ich brauche kein___ neu___ Mantel.
7. Es ist ein___ schön___ Nacht.
8. Sie schreibt interessant___ Briefe.
9. Es steckt in mein___ ander___ Anzug.
10. Hilf d___ arm___ Mann!

d. 1. Dein___ neu___ Kleider sind hübsch.
2. Was machst du da, jung___ Mann?
3. Wo sind unser___ neu___ Gläser?
4. Geben Sie es d___ ander___ Mädchen!
5. Er hat kein___ gut___ Ideen.
6. Es gibt ein Restaurant in jed___ deutsch___ Bahnhof.
7. Weißt du ihr___ neu___ Adresse?
8. Sie schreibt mit rot___ Tinte.
9. Es ist d___ best___ Restaurant in München.
10. Ihr___ alt___ Briefe sind sehr interessant.

e. 1. Arm___ Frau Heller!
2. Ich gehe zu ein___ ander___ Bank.
3. D___ neu___ Lampen sind hier.
4. Der Brief ist von ein___ alt___ Freund.
5. Sie haben mehrer___ gut___ Bilder.
6. Er geht mit ein___ sehr hübsch___ Mädchen.
7. Kennst du d___ neu___ Sekretärin?
8. D___ neu___ Buchhandlung soll sehr gut sein.
9. Was soll ich mit dein___ alt___ Mantel machen?
10. Jed___ gut___ Hotel hat ein Restaurant.

f. 1. Sein___ neu___ Krawatte ist schrecklich.
2. Viel___ amerikanisch___ Studenten fahren nach Deutschland.
3. Er wohnt in ein___ klein___ Stadt in Bayern.
4. Wollen Sie kalt___ Milch?
5. Willst du unser neu___ Haus sehen?
6. Mein___ best___ Ideen kommen nach dem Abendessen.
7. Gib sie d___ ander___ Sekretärin!
8. Das ist kein___ schlecht___ Idee.
9. Kennst du sein___ erst___ Frau?
10. Können Sie mir ein___ gut___ Arzt empfehlen?

g. 1. Stell es auf d___ ander___ Tisch!
2. Können Sie mir ein gut___ Hotel empfehlen?

EXPRESS IN GERMAN

a. 1. That's his best book.
2. He has a lot of good ideas.
3. When does the next train leave?
4. She writes interesting letters.
5. Do you know her new address?
6. I don't know the other girl.
7. Can you recommend a good doctor?
8. Help the poor man.
9. They have several good pictures.
10. He doesn't have any good ideas.

b. 1. Throw that old suit away.
2. Do you know his first wife?

3. Poor Mrs. Heller.
4. He wants to see every new movie.
5. Where's your new office?
6. It's on the other table.
7. She writes with red ink.
8. I don't need a new coat.
9. Go to the new department store.
10. What are you doing there, young man?

c. 1. That's a good question.
2. The new bookstore is supposed to be very good.
3. It's in my other suit. (use **stecken**)
4. Dear Fritz.

5. Your new dresses are pretty.
6. Every healthy cat eats fish.
7. What shall I do with your old coat?
8. Can you recommend a good hotel?
9. Do you know the new secretary?
10. I'm going with the other students.

d. 1. What'll we do with this horrible lamp?
2. My best ideas come after dinner.
3. Give them to the other secretary.
4. The letter's from an old friend.
5. Let's take the new car.
6. Do you want to see our new house?
7. That tastes good with cold beer.
8. That's not a bad idea.
9. He has horrible ties.
10. He lives in a small city in Bavaria (Bayern).

e. 1. There's a restaurant in every German railroad station.
2. Where are our new glasses?

3. Do you want cold milk?
4. It's a beautiful night.
5. Put it on the other table.
6. Her old letters are very interesting.
7. Do you go to the new doctor?
8. These old addresses aren't correct.
9. Boy Scouts help old ladies.
10. Every good hotel has a restaurant.

f. 1. I'm going to another bank.
2. The new lamps are here.
3. Do you have fresh bread?
4. He goes with a very pretty girl.
5. His new tie is horrible.
6. What do the other coats cost?
7. A lot of American students go to Germany.
8. He's my best friend.
9. It's the best restaurant in Munich.
10. That's good beer.

g. 1. Give it to the other girl.

VOCABULARY

das **Abendessen, –** dinner, supper
alt old
amerikanisch American
ander– other, different
arm poor
Bayern Bavaria
best– best
billig cheap, inexpensive
blau blue
braun brown
das **Brot, –e** bread
der **Bruder, ⸚** brother
deutsch German
einfach simply
einige some

erst– first
die **Familie, –n** family
die **Frage, –n** question
frei free, empty
der **Freund, –e** friend
frisch fresh
gesund healthy
das **Glas, ⸚er** glass
groß large
grün green
hübsch pretty
die **Idee, –n** idea
jung young
der **Junge, –n, –n** boy
klein small, little
lang long
letzt– last
die **Leute** (*pl. only*) people
lieb dear

mehrere several
die **Milch** milk
morgen tomorrow
nächst– next
neu new
das **Rathaus, ⸚er** city hall
rot red
schlecht bad
schmecken to taste
schrecklich horrible
stecken to be (in the sense of be hidden)
verkaufen to sell
viel much
viele many
weg away
wenige few
der **Zug, ⸚e** train

Wenn and daß

Wenn (*if*) and **daß** are called conjunctions: they join parts of sentences together. They work essentially like the English words *if* and *that*.

> **Wenn** kein Tisch ganz frei **ist,** dürfen Sie ruhig zu einem Tisch mit einem freien Platz gehen.
> (*If* no table is completely free, you can just go to a table with an empty seat.)

These sentences are made up of two clauses, each with its own verb. The **wenn-** or *if*-clause is called a subordinate clause, and the other clause is called a main clause. The only difference between German and English usage is that the subordinate clause (the **wenn**-clause) has the verb at the end of the clause. This is called subordinate word order, and the conjunction that makes this happen is called a subordinating conjunction. If a sentence starts with a subordinate clause—and **wenn**-clauses are often found at the beginning of sentences—then the main clause starts with a verb:

> **Wenn** kein Tisch ganz frei ist, **dürfen** Sie ruhig zu einem Tisch mit einem freien Platz gehen.

But a subordinate clause will often come after the main clause. This is usually the case with the subordinating conjunction **daß,** which means *that:*

> Sie werden vielleicht erwarten, **daß** Sie Ihnen ein Glas Wasser bringt.
> (Maybe you think *that* she'll bring you a glass of water.)

Like the **wenn**-clause, the **daß**–clause has its verb at the end.

> . . . **daß** Sie Ihnen ein Glas Wasser **bringt.**

But here the main clause is at the beginning of the sentence and its verb comes in the usual position. In Lesson 9 you will have extended practice on subordinate clauses. But **daß** and **wenn** are so useful that we are introducing them here, and we will use them throughout the rest of the readings in this book.

Und and aber

Und and **aber** mean *and* and *but*. German and English will frequently begin sentences with these words to make a paragraph run on more smoothly.

> **Aber** die meisten Gaststätten haben eine besondere Mittagskarte für Tagesspezialitäten.*

or

> **Und** in Deutschland essen die meisten Leute ihre Hauptmahlzeit mittags.*

As you can see, **aber** and **und** *don't have any effect on the word order of the sentence they introduce;* that is, the sentences will read exactly the same way if you eliminate the **aber** or the **und.**

> Und in Deutschland essen die meisten Leute ihre Hauptmahlzeit mittags.

or simply

> In Deutschland essen die meisten Leute ihre Hauptmahlzeit mittags.

---

*See p. 175 (last line) and p. 176 (top).

Reading IV

Deutsche Gaststätten° und Restaurants

die Gaststätte, –n: German restaurant (*defined in text*)

Eine Gaststätte ist ein einfaches,° deutsches Restaurant. In einer Gaststätte finden Sie meistens° nur° deutsche Gerichte° und Sie sehen dort° häufig° Kellnerinnen° statt° Kellner.°

einfach: simple

meistens: mostly **nur:** only
das Gericht, –e: dish, meal **dort:** there
  häufig: frequently
die Kellnerin, –nen: waitress **statt:** instead of
  der Kellner, –: waiter

Vor jeder Gaststätte hängt eine Speisekarte.° Sie können also° von Gaststätte zu Gaststätte gehen; Sie sehen die verschiedenen° Speisekarten an° und wählen° dann° ein Lokal.° Sie können also Ihr Essen° im voraus° wählen.

die Speisekarte, –n: menu

also: therefore, so

verschieden: different **sehen . . . an:** look at
wählen: to choose **dann:** then
  das Lokal, –e: (*here*) place to eat
das Essen: food, meal **im voraus:** in advance

Man geht hinein,° und man sagt normalerweise°
„Guten Tag" oder° „Guten Abend". Dieser Gruß° ist
an alle Leute° im Lokal gerichtet.° Einige Leute
sagen dann auch° „Guten Tag". Jetzt finden Sie
einen Tisch. Wenn° kein Tisch ganz frei° ist, dürfen
Sie ruhig° zu einem Tisch mit einem freien Platz°
gehen. Sie fragen einfach:° „Ist dieser Platz frei?"
Wenn er frei ist, nehmen Sie da Platz.

gehen . . . hinein: to go in, enter	
normalerweise: normally	
oder: or **der Gruß,** ⁼**e:** greeting	
die Leute [*pl. only*]: people	
gerichtet an (+ *acc.*): directed to, addressed to	
auch: also, too	
wenn: when, if **ganz frei:** completely empty	
ruhig: just, without any worry	
der Platz, ⁼**e:** (*here*) seat	
einfach: simply	

Oft° liegen° Speisekarten auf den Tischen. Nach
einer Weile° kommt eine Kellnerin zu Ihrem Tisch.
Sie erwarten° vielleicht,° daß sie ein Glas Wasser
bringt. Keineswegs.° In einer Gaststätte bekommen°
Sie kein Glas Wasser. Und wenn Sie Wasser bestellen,° bekommen Sie Sprudel.° In deutschen Lokalen
bekommt man kein Leitungswasser.°

oft: often **liegen:** to lie

die Weile: a while

erwarten: to expect **vielleicht:** maybe

keineswegs: by no means **bekommen:** to get

bestellen: to order **der Sprudel:** soda water

das Leitungswasser: tap water

Die meisten° Gaststätten sind durchgehend°
geöffnet.° Das heißt,° normalerweise von elf Uhr°
morgens° bis zwölf oder ein Uhr nachts.° Mittagessen gibt es° aber° nur° von etwa° zwölf bis zwei
Uhr und Abendessen zwischen sechs und neun
Uhr. Zwischen zwei und sechs Uhr nachmittags°
und nach neun Uhr abends° haben viele Gaststätten
nur kalte° Küche,° zum Beispiel,° Schinkenbrot°
oder Käsebrot.° Andere haben auch einfache
warme° Gerichte, wie° Gulaschsuppe,° heiße°
Würstchen° oder Spiegeleier.° Getränke° wie Bier,
Wein° oder Apfelsaft° können Sie immer bekommen.
Gaststätten haben auch einen Ruhetag.° Der Tag ist
verschieden bei verschiedenen Lokalen. Normalerweise haben sie aber nicht sonntags° geschlossen:°
sonntags haben sie immer viele Kunden und ver-
dienen° sehr gut.

die meist–: most **durchgehend:** throughout the day

geöffnet: open **heißen:** (*here*) to mean

Uhr: o'clock

morgens: in the morning **nachts:** at night

es gibt: there is **aber:** but, however

nur: only **etwa:** about, approximately

nachmittags: in the afternoon

abends: in the evening

kalt: cold **die Küche:** (*here*) food

zum Beispiel: for example

das Schinkenbrot, –e: ham sandwich (open-face)

das Käsebrot, –e: cheese sandwich (open-face)

warm: warm **wie:** like, such as

die Gulaschsuppe, –n: goulash soup **heiß:** hot

das Würstchen, –: hot dog, sausage **das Spiegelei,**

–er: fried egg **das Getränk, –e:** beverage

der Wein, –e: wine **der Apfelsaft:** apple juice

der Ruhetag, –e: day off

sonntags: on Sundays **haben . . . geschlossen:** to be closed

verdienen: to earn

Eine Gaststätte hat dieselbe° Speisekarte für das
Mittagessen und für das Abendessen. Aber die

dieselbe: the same

meisten Gaststätten haben auch eine besondere° Mittagskarte° mit Tagesspezialitäten.° Man bekommt normalerweise eine ganze° Mahlzeit,° genau° wie ein amerikanisches° Abendessen. Und in Deutschland essen die meisten Leute ihre Hauptmahlzeit° mittags.°

Fragen I, 6–10, p. 180

besonder–: special
die Mittagskarte, –n: luncheon menu
  die Tagesspezialität, –en: daily special
ganz: whole die Mahlzeit, –en: meal

genau: just, exactly amerikanisch: American

die Hauptmahlzeit, –en: main meal
  mittags: around noon

WIE MAN BESTELLT

(Sagen wir, Sie sitzen mit einem Freund in einer Gaststätte und wollen bestellen. Die Kellnerin kommt zu ihrem Tisch.)

KELLNERIN: Guten Tag. Was darf's sein?°

KURT: Ich nehme einen Apfelsaft.

KELLNERIN: Und Sie, bitte?

SIE: Ein Bier, bitte.

KELLNERIN: Ein großes oder ein kleines Bier?

SIE: Ein großes, bitte.

KELLNERIN: Wollen Sie jetzt bestellen?

KURT: Danke, wir studieren° noch die Karte.°

KELLNERIN: Gut, ich komme in ein paar° Minuten° wieder.°

(Jetzt lesen Sie die Speisekarte und wählen Ihr Essen. Die Kellnerin kommt mit den Getränken und Sie können bestellen.)

KELLNERIN: So, bitte schön.° *(Sie stellt die Getränke auf den Tisch.)*

SIE: Danke schön.

KELLNERIN: Und was darf ich Ihnen noch° bringen?

KURT: Rumpsteak,° bitte. Mit Bratkartoffeln° und Salat.° Und das Rumpsteak englisch,° bitte.

SIE: Und ich hätte gern° ein Kalbsschnitzel° mit Pommes frites.°

Was darf's sein?: What would you like?
  [*lit.*: "What may it be?"]

studieren: to study, read
  die Karte, –n: die Speisekarte

ein paar: a few, a couple of

die Minute, –n: minute kommen . . . wieder:
  to come back

So, bitte schön.: There you are.

Was . . . noch: What else . . .
das Rumpsteak, –s: rumpsteak die Bratkartoffel, –
  hash brown potatoes
der Salat, –e: salad
  englisch: English, (*here*) rare (*of meat*)
ich hätte gern: I'd like
  das Kalbsschnitzel, –: veal cutlet
die Pommes frites (*pl.*): French fried potatoes

KELLNERIN: Kalbsschnitzel mit Pommes frites.
Danke schön.

WIE MAN BEZAHLT

(*In einer Gaststätte gibt es keine Kasse.° Wenn Sie bezahlen wollen, rufen Sie die Kellnerin zu ihrem Tisch.*)

die Kasse, –n: (*here*) cashier

SIE: Fräulein! Zahlen° bitte.

KELLNERIN: Ja, ich komme gleich.°

Zahlen bitte.: (*here*) I'd like to pay.

gleich: right away

* * *

(*Nach einer Weile° kommt die Kellnerin.*)

die Weile: while

KELLNERIN: So, hat's geschmeckt?°
SIE: Ja, danke.
KELLNERIN: Sie wollen zahlen. Getrennt° oder zusammen,° bitte?
SIE: Zusammen, bitte.
KELLNERIN: Ein Apfelsaft, ein großes Bier, ein Rumpsteak mit Bratkartoffeln und Salat und ein Kalbsschnitzel mit Pommes frites.
SIE: Jawohl.°
KELLNERIN: Zweiundzwanzig Mark, bitte.
SIE: Dreiundzwanzig, bitte.
KELLNERIN: Danke schön.
SIE: Wir danken° auch.

So, hat's geschmeckt?: How was it? [*lit.* "Did it taste good?"]

getrennt: separately
zusammen: together

jawohl: yes (*stronger than* "ja")

danken: to thank

(*Sie geben der Kellnerin dreißig Mark. Sie greift° in ihren Geldbeutel° und sucht das Wechselgeld.° Dann legt° sie sieben Mark auf den Tisch.*)

greifen: to reach
der Geldbeutel, –: special wallet used by waitresses   das Wechselgeld: change
legen: to put, lay

KELLNERIN: Und sieben zurück,° danke sehr.

zurück: back

(*Sie und Ihr Freund trinken aus° und stehen auf.°*)

trinken . . . aus: to empty one's glass
stehen . . . auf: to stand up

KELLNERIN: Auf Wiedersehen.
SIE: Auf Wiedersehen.

TRINKGELD IN DEUTSCHLAND

Deutsche Lokale haben Endpreise.° In diesen
Preisen ist schon zehn bis fünfzehn Prozent° Trink-
geld eingeschlossen.° Man gibt aber meistens ein
wenig° dazu.° Sagen wir, Ihre Rechnung ist sechs
Mark fünfzig. Die meisten Leute sagen dann: sieben
Mark. Oder die Kellnerin sagt zweiundzwanzig
Mark und Sie sagen: dreiundzwanzig.

der Endpreis, –e: all-inclusive price

das Prozent: percent

eingeschlossen: included

ein wenig: a little   **dazu:** in addition, extra

RESTAURANTS

Das Wort° Restaurant gebraucht° man meistens für
teure° und vornehmere° Lokale. Die Küche ist oft
international° und die Bedienung° ist formell.° Im
Gegensatz zu° einer Gaststätte findet man in einem
Restaurant meistens Kellner statt Kellnerinnen. In
einem Restaurant begleitet° der Ober° Sie zum
Tisch; in einer Gaststätte findet man selber° einen
Platz. Und in einem Restaurant finden Sie keine
Speisekarte auf dem Tisch. Aber der Ober bringt
Ihnen eine sofort° und auch eine Weinkarte,° wenn
Sie wollen.

das Wort, ̈er: word   **gebrauchen:** to use
teuer: expensive (*takes endings like* **euer,** *see
p. 122*)   **vornehmer:** higher class
international: international   **die Bedienung:**
service   **formell:** formal
im Gegensatz zu: in contrast to

begleiten: to escort   **der Ober, –:** head waiter
selber: oneself

sofort: right away   **die Weinkarte, –n:** wine list

**Fragen II,
1–6,
p. 181**

Restaurants sind selten° durchgehend° geöffnet. Sie sind wirklich° nur für das Mittagessen und das Abendessen da. Also bestellt man kein kleines Essen in einem richtigen° Restaurant. Bahnhofsrestaurants sind Ausnahmen.° Sie sind fast° den ganzen Tag° geöffnet, auch morgens.

Man spricht auch anders° in einem Restaurant. Man sagt, zum Beispiel, nicht „Fräulein! Zahlen bitte.“ Man sagt „Herr Ober, die Rechnung bitte.“ Die meisten Leute essen in Gaststätten. Das Essen ist preiswerter° und die Atmosphäre° ist gar nicht° steif.° Deswegen° gibt es in einer deutschen Stadt viel mehr° Gaststätten als° Restaurants. Und in einer Kleinstadt° gibt es normalerweise *nur* Gaststätten.

Restaurants mit ausländischen° Spezialitäten° findet man mehr und mehr.° Besonders° beliebt° sind italienische,° jugoslawische° und chinesische° Restaurants. Sie können teurer° und vornehmer sein, oder billiger° und einfacher, aber sie heißen *alle* „Restaurants“. Die deutschen Gaststätten bleiben° aber für die meisten Leute die beliebtesten° Lokale.

selten: rarely **durchgehend**: throughout the day

wirklich: really

richtig: real

die Ausnahme, –n: exception **fast**: almost
    den ganzen Tag: all day [*lit.*: "the whole day"]

anders: differently

preiswerter: more reasonable **die Atmosphäre, –n**:
    atmosphere **gar nicht**: not at all
steif: stiff, formal **deswegen**: therefore

viel mehr: many more **als**: than

die Kleinstadt, ⸚e: small town

ausländisch: foreign **die Spezialität, –en**:
    speciality
mehr und mehr: more and more
    besonders: especially **beliebt**: popular
italienisch: Italian **jugoslawisch**: Yugoslavian
    chinesisch: Chinese
teurer: more expensive

billiger: less expensive

bleiben: to remain

beliebtest–: most popular

ragen II,
7–12,
p. 181

FRAGEN I

1. Was ist eine Gaststätte?
   (Gaststätte / sein / einfach / deutsch / Restaurant)
2. Was findet man in einer Gaststätte?
   (Man / finden / meistens / deutsch / Gerichte)
3. Warum können Sie Ihr Essen im voraus wählen?
   (Vor / jed– / deutsch / Gaststätte / hängen / Speisekarte)
   (Sie / können / gehen / also / [*from*] / Gaststätte / [*to*] / Gaststätte)
   (Sie / sehen / verschieden / Speisekarten / an)
   (Dann / Sie / wählen / Lokal)
4. Was machen Sie, wenn kein Tisch ganz frei ist?
   (Dann / Sie / gehen / zu / ein / Tisch / mit / ein / frei / Platz)
5. Was bekommen Sie nicht in einer Gaststätte?
   (In / ein / deutsch / Gaststätte / Sie / bekommen / kein / Glas Wasser)

6. Wann sind die meisten Gaststätten geöffnet?
(Sie / sein / durchgehend geöffnet)
(Das / heißen / [from] / elf Uhr morgens / [until] / zwölf Uhr nachts)

7. Wann gibt es Mittagessen und Abendessen?
(Es / geben / Mittagessen / [from] / zwölf / [until] / zwei)
(Abendessen / geben / es / [between] / sechs und neun)

8. Was können Sie zwischen zwei und sechs Uhr nachmittags bestellen?
(Man / können / bestellen / oft / nur / kalt / Küche / dann)
(Einig- / Gaststätten / haben / auch / einfach / warm / Gerichte)

9. Sind Gaststätten sieben Tage in der Woche geöffnet?   **(die Woche**: week)
(Nein // Gaststätten / haben / ein / Ruhetag)

10. Was ist ein deutsches Mittagessen?
(Ein / deutsch / Mittagessen / sein / ein / ganz / Mahlzeit)
(Es / sein / genau / wie / ein / amerikanisch / Abendessen)

WIE MAN BESTELLT

KELLNERIN: Guten Tag. Was darf's sein?
KURT: (Ich / nehmen / ein / Apfelsaft)
KELLNERIN: Und Sie, bitte?
SIE: (Bier // bitte)
KELLNERIN: Ein großes oder ein kleines Bier?
SIE: (Ein / groß // bitte)
KELLNERIN: Wollen Sie jetzt bestellen?
KURT: (Danke // wir / studieren / noch / Karte)
KELLNERIN: Gut, ich komme in ein paar Minuten wieder.

* * *

KELLNERIN: So, bitte schön.   (*Sie stellt die Getränke auf den Tisch.*)
SIE: (Danke schön)
KELLNERIN: Und was darf ich Ihnen noch bringen?
KURT: (Rumpsteak // bitte // [with] / Bratkartoffeln / Salat)
SIE: (Und / ich / hätten / gern / Kalbsschnitzel / [with] / Pommes frites)
KELLNERIN: Kalbsschnitzel mit Pommes frites. Danke schön.

* * *

KELLNERIN: (Gut- / Tag // Was / dürfen / es / sein / ?)
KURT: Ich nehme einen Apfelsaft.
KELLNERIN: (Und Sie, bitte?)
SIE: Ein Bier, bitte.
KELLNERIN: (Ein / groß / oder / ein / klein / Bier / ?)
SIE: Ein großes, bitte.
KELLNERIN: (Wollen / Sie / bestellen / jetzt / ?)
KURT: Danke, wir studieren noch die Karte.
KELLNERIN: (Gut // ich / kommen / in / paar Minuten / wieder)

* * *

KELLNERIN: (So, bitte schön)   [*Sie stellt die Getränke auf den Tisch.*]
SIE: Danke schön.
KELLNERIN: (Und / was / dürfen / ich / bringen / [to you] / noch / ?)
KURT: Rumpsteak, bitte. Mit Bratkartoffeln und Salat. Und das Rumpsteak englisch, bitte.
SIE: Und ich hätte gern ein Kalbsschnitzel mit Pommes frites.
KELLNERIN: Kalbsschnitzel mit Pommes frites. Danke schön.

WIE MAN BEZAHLT

SIE:	Fräulein! Zahlen bitte.
KELLNERIN:	(Ja // ich / kommen / gleich)

* * *

KELLNERIN:	(So // haben / es / geschmeckt / ?)
SIE:	Ja, danke.
KELLNERIN:	(Sie / wollen / zahlen)
	([separately] / oder / [together] // bitte / ?)
SIE:	Zusammen, bitte.
KELLNERIN:	(Apfelsaft // ein / groß / Bier // Rumpsteak / [with] / Bratkartoffeln / und Salat // und / Kalbsschnitzel / Pommes frites)
SIE:	Jawohl.
KELLNERIN:	(DM 22 // bitte)
SIE:	Dreiundzwanzig, bitte.
KELLNERIN:	(Danke schön.)
SIE:	Wir danken auch.
KELLNERIN:	(Und / 7 / zurück) (Auf Wiedersehen)
SIE:	Auf Wiedersehen.

FRAGEN II

1. Was sind Endpreise?
   (In / dies- / Preise / sein / 10-15 / Prozent Trinkgeld / eingeschlossen)
2. Was machen die meisten Leute?
   (meist- / Leute / geben / ein wenig dazu)
3. Die Rechnung ist sechs Mark fünfzig. Was sagt man der Kellnerin?
   (Man / sagen / [her] / DM 7)
4. Was sind Restaurants in Deutschland?
   (Restaurants / sein / meistens / teuer / vornehmer / Lokale)
   (Küche / sein / oft / international // und / Bedienung / sein / formell)
5. Wie finden Sie hier einen Tisch?
   (Ober / begleiten / Sie / zu / Tisch)
6. Wie bekommen Sie eine Speisekarte?
   (Ober / bringen / [to you] / Speisekarte / sofort)
7. Wann sind Restaurants geöffnet?
   (Sie / sein / nur / für / Mittagessen / und / Abendessen / da)
8. Was sind hier Ausnahmen?
   (Bahnhofsrestaurants / sein / Ausnahmen)
   (Sie / sein / fast / [the] / ganz / Tag / geöffnet)
9. Warum essen die meisten Leute in Gaststätten?
   (Essen / sein / preiswerter // und / Atmosphäre / sein / gar nicht steif)
10. Wo gibt es normalerweise nur Gaststätten?
    (In / ein / Kleinstadt / es / geben / nur / Gaststätten)
11. Gibt es Restaurants mit ausländischen Spezialitäten in Deutschland?
    (Ja // italienisch / jugoslawisch / und / chinesisch / Restaurants / sein / besonders / beliebt)
12. Sind sie alle teuer und vornehm?
    (Nein // sie / können / sein / auch / billiger und einfacher)

Lesson 5 Level ONE

A Past Tense and Present Perfect Tense of Weak Verbs

1 Introduction

Many English and German verbs have only *one* stem, and they use this one stem to form their present, past, and perfect tenses. These verbs are called *regular* or *weak* verbs. Look at the following English examples:

STEM FORM	*ask*	*wait*
PRESENT TENSE	he *asks*	he *waits*
PAST TENSE	he *asked*	he *waited*
PERFECT TENSE	he has *asked*	he has *waited*

As you can see, the same stem is used in all three tenses. Weak verbs in German behave the same way:

STEM FORM	**frag-**
PRESENT TENSE	er **frag**t
PAST TENSE	er **frag**te
PERFECT TENSE	er hat ge**frag**t

2 Past tense

To form the past tense, you simply add the following past tense endings to the verb stem:

fragen *to ask*			
Stem	*Endings*	*Stem*	*Endings*
ich frag	**te**	wir frag	**ten**
du frag	**test**	ihr frag	**tet**
er frag	**te**	sie frag	**ten**

If the stem ends in **-d** or **-t,** an e comes before the ending to make it pronounceable:

	warten	*to wait*		
	Stem	*Endings*	*Stem*	*Endings*
ich	wart	**ete**	wir wart	**eten**
du	wart	**etest**	ihr wart	**etet**
er	wart	**ete**	sie wart	**eten**

DRILLS

Past tense

- Replace the subjects of the following sentences, making the necessary changes in the verb forms.

1. Ich sagte es dir gestern. (er, wir, sie [*they*])   **(gestern:** yesterday)
2. Was schickte er ihm? (sie [*they*], du)
3. Wir kauften einen neuen Wagen. (ich, sie [*they*], er)
4. Sie rauchten zu viel. (er, du)
5. Ich reservierte dir ein Zimmer. (sie [*they*], er) **(reservieren:** to reserve)
6. Sie spielte Tennis. (wir, ich, sie [*they*])   **(spielen:** to play)

- Verbs with stems ending in **-t** or **-d.**

1. Ich arbeitete in der Bibliothek. (er, du, wir)
2. Sie warteten hier. (er, wir, ich)
3. Er antwortete ihm nicht. (sie [*they*], ich)

3 Present perfect tense

a. Compound forms

The present tense and the past tense—in both English and German—are called *simple* tenses because they are one-word forms. A tense that is formed with more than one word is called a *compound* tense. In both English and German the present perfect is a compound tense consisting of an *auxiliary verb* and a *past participle.*

	Auxiliary Verb	Past Participle
he	has	asked
er	hat	gefragt

The auxiliary verb here is **haben** (to have).

b. Past participles of weak verbs

The past participle of a weak verb is formed by adding the prefix ge- and the ending -t to the verb stem. The ending is -et if the stem ends in **-d** or **-t.**

Infinitive	Stem	Past Participle
fragen	frag-	ge**frag**t
warten	wart-	ge**wart**et

All verbs with infinitives ending in **-ieren** are weak verbs. But they don't add the **ge-** prefix in forming their past participles:

Infinitive	Stem	Past Participle
reservieren	reservier-	**reservier**t

c. Tense formation

In a compound tense, it is the *auxiliary verb* that changes according to person and number. The past participle remains constant.

ich **habe** . . . gefragt	wir **haben** . . . gefragt
du **hast** . . . gefragt	ihr **habt** . . . gefragt
er **hat** . . . gefragt	sie **haben** . . . gefragt

d. Word order

The *auxiliary verb* is the *second* element in the sentence. It is in the normal verb position.

Ich habe ihn gestern gefragt.   (I asked him yesterday.)

The *past participle* is the *last* element in the sentence.

Ich habe ihn gestern gefragt.

4 Use of the simple past and the present perfect tenses

The present perfect tense is used much more in conversational German than it is in English. It is used where English uses the present perfect:

I've already asked him.   **Ich habe ihn schon gefragt.**

as well as in situations where the present perfect would be impossible in English:

I asked him yesterday.   **Ich fragte ihn gestern.**
Ich habe ihn gestern gefragt.

("I have asked him yesterday" is not an English sentence.)

Because it is the most common past tense form in normal conversation, the present perfect in German is sometimes called the "conversational past." The simple past tense is sometimes called the "narrative past," because it is commonly used in narration.

1   Present perfect tense

● Supply the correct form of the auxiliary verb **haben**.

1. Er _____ ein neues Haus gekauft.
2. _____ du da gewohnt?
3. Sie (*they*) _____ Tennis gespielt.
4. Ich _____ es nicht geglaubt.

5. Was _____ du ihm geschickt?
6. Er _____ mir alles gesagt.
7. Was _____ ihr ihm geschickt?

(**glauben**: to believe)

● Supply the correct form of **haben** with these verbs with stems ending in **-t** or **-d**.

1. Wir _____ ihm nicht geantwortet.
2. Ich _____ in der Bibliothek gearbeitet.
3. Sie (*they*) _____ hier gewartet.

● Supply the correct form of **haben** with these verbs with stems ending in **-ier**.

1. Er _____ dir ein Zimmer reserviert.*
2. _____ du an der Universität Berlin studiert?*
3. _____ ihr an der Universität Berlin studiert?

(**studieren an** + *dat.:* to study at)
(**die Universität**: university)

2   Past and present perfect tenses

● Put the verb forms into the past and present perfect tenses, unless otherwise indicated.

EXAMPLE   Er kauft es.   Er **kaufte** es.   Er **hat** es **gekauft**.

1. Ich suche es.
2. Sie wohnen hier.
3. Er macht es.
4. Wir brauchen es.

5. Wo wohnst du? (*present perfect only*)
6. Sie glauben es nicht.
7. Was schickst du ihm?
(*present perfect only*)

● Verbs with stems ending in **-t** or **-d**.

1. Ich warte hier.
2. Wo arbeitest du? (*present perfect only*)
3. Was kostet es?

● Verbs with stems ending in **-ier**.

1. Er studiert* in Berlin.
2. Wir reservieren ein Zimmer.

───────────

*No **ge-** prefix. See the opposite page, "Past participles of weak verbs."

3 Mixed drills

• Put the following sentences into the past and present perfect tenses, unless otherwise indicated.

a. 1. Er wohnt bei Frau Heller.
2. Was kosten die Gläser?
3. Er kauft einen neuen Wagen.
4. Was schickst du ihm?
   (*present perfect only*)
   Was schickt ihr ihm?
   (*present perfect only*)
5. Glauben Sie das?
6. Er raucht zu viel.
7. Wir arbeiten heute in der Bibliothek.
8. Was machst du mit deinem alten Wagen?
   (*present perfect only*)
9. Er stellt es auf deinen Schreibtisch.
10. Sie antwortet ihm nicht.

b. 1. Ich brauche einen neuen Mantel.
2. Er studiert an der Universität Berlin.
3. Ich glaube es nicht.
4. Sie leben in Frankreich.
   (**Frankreich:** France)
5. Ich reserviere dir ein Zimmer.
6. Wir sagen ihm alles.
7. Wir kaufen einen neuen Fernseher.
   (**der Fernseher:** TV set)
8. Ich warte hier.
9. Wohnt er da?
10. Ich höre ihn nicht. (**hören:** to hear)

c. 1. Wir zeigen ihnen unsere neue Wohnung. (**die Wohnung:** apartment)
2. Er arbeitet immer zu Hause.
3. Ich frage ihn.

4. Was machst du da?
   (*present perfect only*)
   Was macht ihr da?
   (*present perfect only*)
5. Ich suche eine neue Wohnung.
6. Was meinst du? (*present perfect only*)
   Was meint ihr? (*present perfect only*)
7. Sie spielen Tennis.
8. Was kostet das Hemd?
9. Ich hole ein Glas.
   (**holen:** to get [go get])
10. Brauchst du mehr Zeit? (**mehr:** more)
    (*present perfect only*)
    Braucht ihr mehr Zeit?
    (*present perfect only*)

d. 1. Wir schicken es ihnen.
2. Er zeigt uns ein anderes Zimmer.
3. Sie suchen ihre Bücher.
4. Er sagt es uns.
5. Sie lernen Deutsch. (**lernen:** to learn, study)

4 Express in German

• Put each sentence in the past tense and the present perfect tense, unless otherwise indicated.

a. 1. He bought a new car.
2. He worked in the library today.
3. What did you (**du**) do there?
   (*present perfect only*)
4. I reserved a room.
5. We sent it to you.
6. I didn't believe it.
7. What did the shirt cost?
8. We bought a new TV.
9. We told him everything.
10. Did he live there?

b. 1. What did the glasses cost?
2. What did you (**du**) mean?
   (*present perfect only*)
3. I needed a new coat.
4. We showed them our apartment.
5. I asked him yesterday.
6. He lived at Mrs. Heller's place.
7. They were looking for their books.
8. He told us.
9. They studied at the University of Berlin.
10. He always worked at home.

c. 1. What did you **(du)** send him?
     (*present perfect only*)
  2. She didn't answer him.
  3. He smoked too much.
  4. They lived in France.
  5. Did you **(du)** need more time?
     (*present perfect only*)
  6. He showed us another room.
  7. They played tennis.
  8. Did you **(Sie)** believe that?
  9. He put it on your desk.
  10. I was looking for a new apartment.

d. 1. What did you **(du)** do with your
     old car?   (*present perfect only*)
  2. I didn't hear him.
  3. They learned German.

B Past Tense and Present Perfect Tense of Strong (Irregular) Verbs

1 Introduction

Both English and German have a number of verbs whose past tense and past participle are formed by changing the verb stem itself:

	English	**German**
INFINITIVE	to *sing*	**sing**en
PAST	he *sang*	er **sang**
PRESENT PERFECT	he has *sung*	er hat ge**sung**en

Since there is no way to predict what the stem changes will be, these verbs are called *irregular* or *strong verbs*. In order to form the past tense and present perfect tense of a strong verb, you have to learn its *principal parts*. The principal parts are:

1. The infinitive: **gehen** (to go) **kommen** (to come)
2. The past tense stem: **ging** **kam**
3. The past participle: **gegangen** **gekommen**

These principal parts show exactly what the stem changes are. In some cases, the change involves more than just the stem vowel. **Gehen** and "to go" both have past tense forms that are very different from the infinitive:

to go   *went*
gehen   ging

▶ Note You have already seen (Lesson 1) that some verbs have stem-vowel change in the present tense (ich laufe, er läuft). By convention, this information is given in parentheses right after the first principal part. For example, the principal parts of **laufen** are:

laufen (läuft)   **lief**   **gelaufen**

2 Past tense

Strong verbs have their own set of past tense endings that are different from those used with weak verbs:

gehen		to go	
ich ging	-	wir ging	en
du ging	st	ihr ging	t
er ging	-	sie ging	en

▶ **Note** These endings are identical to those used with the present tense of the modals. The 1st and 3rd person singular forms have no ending.

Exceptions

1. If the past tense stem ends in an "s" sound **(-s, -ss, -ß, -z),** the past tense ending of the 2nd person singular is -est (for example, du las**est**).

2. If the past tense stem ends in **-t** or **-d,** the past tense ending of the 2nd person singular is -est (for example, du bat**est**) and of the 2nd person plural is **-et** (for example, ihr bat**et**).

	gehen (normal)			**lesen** (1) **bitten** (2)		
ich	ging	—	wir	ging	en
	las	—		las	en
	bat	—		bat	en
du	ging	st	ihr	ging	t
	las	est		las	t
	bat	est		bat	et
er	ging	—	sie	ging	en
	las	—		las	en
	bat	—		bat	en

The **e** is inserted before these endings to make the verb forms pronounceable.

▶ **Note** You will rarely hear the **du-** and **ihr-**forms of verbs in the simple past tense. The reason is clear: **du** and **ihr** are forms of address used in informal conversation. If you are using **du,** you will also use the *conversational past,* that is, the present perfect. The simple past is, generally, a more formal tense and consequently sounds odd—even stilted—when used with the more informal **du-** and **ihr-**forms.

3 Present perfect tense

a. Compound forms

Like the present perfect tense of weak verbs, the present perfect of strong verbs is a compound form consisting of an *auxiliary verb* and a *past participle.*

	Auxiliary Verb (sein or haben)	Past Participle
Er	ist . . .	gegangen.
Er	hat . . .	gesungen.

As you can see from the examples, some strong verbs have **sein** as their auxiliary rather than **haben.**

b. Past participles of strong verbs

Like the past participles of weak verbs, the past participles of strong verbs begin with a **ge-** prefix: **ge**sungen, **ge**gangen. But unlike the weak verbs, the strong verbs have

1. a changed verb stem: ge**sung**en (the infinitive stem is **sing-**)
   ge**gang**en (the infinitive stem is **geh-**)
2. the ending -en: gesung**en**
   gegang**en**

c. Word order

The same rules apply to both strong and weak verbs.

1. The auxiliary verb is the second element in the sentence.

> Er **hat** zu laut gesungen.   (He sang too loud.)
> Er **ist** nach Hause gegangen.   (He went home. [He's gone home.])

2. The past participle is the last element in the sentence.

> Er ist nach Hause **gegangen**.   (He went home. [He's gone home.])

C Haben and Sein as Auxiliary Verbs

Verbs have either **haben** or **sein** as their auxiliary in the present perfect tense. But the choice between the two auxiliaries is not free. **Sein** is used as the auxiliary when:

1. The verb is *intransitive* (*cannot* take a direct object).
2. The verb expresses *motion* or *change of condition.*

Both of these conditions must be satisfied for the verb to take **sein** as its auxiliary; if only one (or neither) is satisfied, the auxiliary is **haben.** Look at the following examples of verbs taking **sein** as their auxiliary (that is, verbs satisfying both conditions of the rule):

Er **ist** nach Hause **gegangen.**
(He went home.)

1. **Gehen** is intransitive; it cannot take a direct object.
2. **Gehen** expresses motion.

Ich **bin** später **gekommen.**
(I came later.)

1. **Kommen** is intransitive.
2. **Kommen** expresses motion.

Sie **sind** nach Salzburg **gefahren**.
(They've gone to Salzburg.)

1. **Fahren** is intransitive.
2. **Fahren** expresses motion.

Es **ist** kalt **geworden**.
(It's gotten cold.)

1. **Werden** is intransitive.
2. **Werden** expresses change of condition.

Now look at some verbs that taken **haben**:

Ich **habe** es ihm **gegeben**.
(I've given it to him.)

Geben is transitive; it has a direct object **(es).**

Er **hat** nicht genug **geschlafen**.
(He hasn't slept enough.)

Schlafen is intransitive, but there is no motion or change of condition involved.

Er **hat** den Brief nicht **geschrieben**.
(He didn't write the letter.)

Schreiben is transitive; it has a direct object **(den Brief).**

Er **hat** nicht sehr oft **geschrieben**.
(He didn't write very often.)

Schreiben is still transitive; it *can* take an object, even though it doesn't in this sentence. An object is nevertheless implied; he must have been writing something.

▶ Exceptions The following two verbs take **sein** as their auxiliary even though the general rule does not apply to them.

sein (to be) Wo **sind** Sie **gewesen**? (Where have you been?)
bleiben (to stay) Er **ist** nicht da **geblieben**. (He didn't stay there.)

Now look at the verbs in this unit that require **sein**:

Intransitive Verbs of Motion	**fahren**	(to drive, go)	ist gefahren
	fallen	(to fall)	ist gefallen
	fliegen	(to fly)	ist geflogen
	gehen	(to go)	ist gegangen
	kommen	(to come)	ist gekommen
	laufen	(to run)	ist gelaufen
	steigen	(to climb)	ist gestiegen
Change of Condition	**werden**	(to become)	ist geworden
Other	**bleiben**	(to stay)	ist geblieben
	sein	(to be)	ist gewesen

▶ Note In the few instances where **fahren** and **fliegen** take explicit direct objects, they will use **haben** (rather than **sein**) as their auxiliary.

NO DIRECT OBJECT Er **ist** nach Berlin **gefahren**.
(He drove to Berlin.)

DIRECT OBJECT Er **hat** den Wagen nach Berlin **gefahren**.
(He drove *the car* to Berlin.)

Er **hat** mich zum Bahnhof **gefahren**.
(He drove *me* to the station.)

DRILLS

Past tense and present perfect tense of strong verbs

Although the stem changes of strong verbs are *not* predictable, certain recurring patterns should be noted.

1   geben, lesen, sehen, essen, fressen

	Infinitive	(3rd Person)	Past	Past Participle
	e	**(i or ie)**	a	e
to give	geben	(gibt)	gab	gegeben
to read	lesen	(liest)	las	gelesen
to see	sehen	(sieht)	sah	gesehen
to eat	essen	(ißt)	aß	**gegessen***
to eat (animals)	fressen	(frißt)	fraß	gefressen

● Past tense: Replace the subjects of the following sentences making the necessary changes in the verb forms.

1. Er gab es mir. (sie [*they*], du)
2. Ich gab es ihm. (er, du, wir, sie [*they*])
3. Wir sahen ihn heute. (ich, sie [*they*], er)
4. Er las es gestern. (ich, wir)   (**gestern:** yesterday)
5. Ich aß es nicht. (wir, er)

● Present perfect tense: Supply the correct form of the auxiliary verb **haben.**

1. Er _____ dir die Adresse gegeben.
2. Ich _____ ihn heute nicht gesehen.
3. Was _____ du ihm gegeben?
4. Wir _____ es gestern gelesen.
5. Sie (*they*) _____ es nicht gegessen.

● Put the following sentences into the past and present perfect tenses, unless otherwise indicated.

e (i or ie) ⟶ a ⟶ e

1. Er gibt es mir.
2. Wir sehen ihn heute.
3. Ich esse immer zu Hause.
4. Was gibst du ihm? (*present perfect only*)
5. Er liest zu viel.
6. Sie sehen es nicht.
7. Wir essen in einem Restaurant.
8. Minna frißt den Goldfisch.
9. Er liest es nicht.
10. Ich gebe dir die Adresse.
11. Was ißt du heute? (*present perfect only*)
12. Siehst du den neuen Film?
    (*present perfect only*)

---

*When more than the stem vowel is changed, the whole form will be in color in the tables.

2 helfen, sprechen, treffen, werfen, nehmen

	Infinitive	(3rd Person)	Past	Past Participle
	e	(i)	a	o
to help	helfen	(hilft)	half	geholfen
to speak	sprechen	(spricht)	sprach	gesprochen
to meet	treffen	(trifft)	traf	getroffen
to throw	werfen	(wirft)	warf	geworfen
to take	nehmen	(nimmt)	nahm	genommen

- Past tense: Replace the subjects in the following sentences making the necessary changes in the verb forms.

  1. Er sprach zu schnell. (Sie, ich)
  2. Wir nahmen den anderen Wagen. (ich, sie [they], er)
  3. Ich traf ihn nach dem Abendessen. (sie [they], er)
  4. Er half ihnen. (sie [they], ich, wir)
  5. Er warf es aufs Sofa. (ich, sie [they])

- Present perfect tense: Supply the correct form of the auxiliary verb **haben.**

  1. Er _____ zu schnell gesprochen.
  2. Ich _____ ein Bad genommen.
  3. Sie (they) _____ uns in der Bar getroffen.   (das Bad: bath)
  4. Du _____ mir geholfen.   (die Bar: bar)
  5. Ich _____ es aufs Sofa geworfen.
  6. Wir _____ den anderen Wagen genommen.

- Put the following sentences into past and present perfect tenses, unless otherwise indicated.

  1. Er spricht zu leise.   (leise: softly)
  2. Wir helfen ihnen.
  3. Ich treffe ihn nach dem Abendessen.
  4. Wir nehmen den anderen Wagen.
  5. Sie spricht zu schnell.

  6. Sie treffen uns in der Bar.
  7. Er hilft mir.
  8. Ich nehme ein Bad.
  9. Er wirft seinen Mantel aufs Sofa.
  10. Nimmst du es? (*present perfect only*)

3 Mixed drills

- Put the following sentences into the past and present perfect tenses, unless otherwise indicated.

  a. 1. Sie sehen es nicht.
     2. Er spricht zu schnell.
     3. Ich esse immer zu Hause.
     4. Er gibt es mir.
     5. Wir helfen ihnen.
     6. Ich nehme ein Bad.
     7. Er liest es nicht.
     8. Sie treffen uns in der Bar.

     9. Ich gebe dir die Adresse.
     10. Er wirft seinen Mantel aufs Sofa.

  b. 1. Wir sehen ihn heute.
     2. Wo ißt du heute? (*present perfect only*)
     3. Sie spricht zu leise.
     4. Siehst du den neuen Film? (*present perfect only*)

5. Ich treffe ihn nach dem Abendessen.
6. Er hilft mir.
7. Er liest zu viel.
8. Nimmst du es? *(present perfect only)*

9. Wir essen in einem Restaurant.
10. Ich nehme den anderen Wagen.

c. 1. Was gibst du ihm? *(present perfect only)*

● Express in German (past and present perfect tenses, unless otherwise indicated).

a. 1. He gave it to me.
2. We ate in a restaurant.
3. I took the other car.
4. He spoke too fast.
5. They didn't see it.
6. Where did you **(du)** eat today?
   (present perfect only)
7. He didn't read it.
8. He helped me.
9. I met him after dinner.
10. What did you give him?
    (present perfect only)

b. 1. He threw his coat on the sofa.
2. We saw him today.
3. She spoke too softly.
4. He read too much.
5. They met us in the bar.
6. I gave you the address.
7. Did you **(du)** take it? *(present perfect only)*
8. We helped them.
9. We always ate at home.
10. Did you **(du)** see the new movie?
    (present perfect only)

c. 1. I took a bath.

4   bleiben, schreiben, steigen, heißen

	Infinitive	Past	Past Participle
	ei	ie	ie
to stay	bleiben	blieb	ist geblieben
to write	schreiben	schrieb	geschrieben
to climb	steigen	stieg	ist gestiegen
to be called	heißen	hieß	geheißen*

● Past tense: Replace the subjects of the following sentences making the necessary changes in the verb forms.

1. Sie schrieb nicht sehr oft. (sie [*they*], er)
2. Sie blieben nicht da. (er, wir, ich)
3. Er stieg aus dem Wagen. (sie [*they*], ich)
4. Wie hießen sie? (er)

● Present perfect tense: Supply the correct auxiliary verb. Both **haben** and **sein** are involved in these drills.

1. Er _____ es an die Tafel geschrieben.
2. Ich _____ zwei Jahre in Deutschland geblieben.
3. Sie (they) _____ aus dem Wagen gestiegen.
4. Wie _____ er geheißen?
5. Er _____ nicht da geblieben.

(steigen . . . aus: to get out of)

---

*The past participle of **heißen** is **geheißen**. Its past participle does not conform to the pattern.

• Put the following sentences into the past and present perfect tenses, unless otherwise indicated.

1. Er schreibt es an die Tafel.
2. Sie bleiben nicht da.
3. Er steigt aus dem Wagen.
4. Wie heißt er?

5. Sie schreibt nicht sehr oft.
6. Ich bleibe zwei Jahre in Deutschland.
7. Er heißt Brandt.
8. Schreibst du ihm? *(present perfect only)*

5   fliegen, schieben, ziehen, schließen

	Infinitive	Past	Past Participle
	ie	o	o
to fly	fliegen	flog	ist geflogen
to shove, push	schieben	schob	geschoben
to pull	ziehen	zog	gezogen
to close	schließen	schloß	geschlossen

• Past tense: Replace the subjects of the following sentences making the necessary changes in the verb forms.

1. Ich schloß die Tür. (er, sie [they])
2. Er schob den Brief unter die Tür. (sie [they], ich)
3. Wir flogen nach Berlin. (er, sie [they], ich)
4. Er zog den Korken. (wir, ich)

(schließen: to close)

(**ziehen:** to pull; **der Korken:** cork)

• Present perfect tense: Supply the correct auxiliary verb. Both **haben** and **sein** are involved in these drills.

1. Ich _____ die Tür geschlossen.
2. Er _____ den Korken gezogen.
3. Sie *(they)* _____ immer mit Lufthansa geflogen.
4. Er _____ den Stuhl in die Ecke geschoben.
5. Wir _____ nach Berlin geflogen.

• Put the following sentences into the past and present perfect tenses, unless otherwise indicated.

1. Er schiebt den Brief unter die Tür.
2. Sie fliegen nach Berlin.
3. Ich schließe die Tür.
4. Er zieht den Korken.

5. Schließt du das Fenster? (**das Fenster:** window)
   (present perfect only)
6. Er schiebt den Stuhl in die Ecke.
7. Sie fliegen immer mit Lufthansa.

6   finden, singen, trinken

	Infinitive	Past	Past Participle
	i	a	u
to find	finden	fand	gefunden
to sing	singen	sang	gesungen
to drink	trinken	trank	getrunken

- Past tense: Replace the subjects of the following sentences making the necessary changes in the verb forms.

1. Ich fand es langweilig. (wir, er, sie [they]) (*I found it [thought it was] boring.*)
2. Ulla trank zu viel. (wir, ich, sie [they])
3. Sie sangen zu laut. (sie [she])

(**laut:** loud)

- Present perfect tense: Supply the correct form of the auxiliary verb **haben**.

1. Wo _____ du das gefunden?
2. Sie (*she*) _____ zu laut gesungen.
3. Sie (*they*) _____ zu viel getrunken.

- Put the following sentences into the past and present perfect tenses, unless otherwise indicated.

1. Wo findet er das? (*present perfect only*)
2. Thomas trinkt zu viel.
3. Sie singt zu laut.
4. Ich finde es langweilig. (*past tense only*)
5. Wir trinken Wein.

7   Mixed drills

- Put the following sentences into the past and present perfect tenses, unless otherwise indicated.

a.
1. Sie bleiben nicht da.
2. Sie fliegen immer mit Lufthansa.
3. Wie heißt er?
4. Ich finde es langweilig.
   (*past tense only*)
5. Er schiebt den Brief unter die Tür.
6. Schreibst du ihm?
   (*present perfect only*)
7. Thomas trinkt zu viel.
8. Ich bleibe zwei Jahre da.
9. Er steigt aus dem Wagen.
10. Wir trinken Wein.

b.
1. Er zieht den Korken.
2. Sie schreibt nicht sehr oft.
3. Ich schließe die Tür.
4. Wo findet er das? (*present perfect only*)
5. Er heißt Brandt.
6. Schließt du das Fenster?
   (*present perfect only*)
7. Sie singt zu laut.
8. Er schiebt den Stuhl in die Ecke.
9. Sie fliegen nach Berlin.
10. Er schreibt es an die Tafel.

- Express in German (past and present perfect tenses, unless otherwise indicated).

a.
1. She didn't write very often.
2. They didn't stay there.
3. Where did he find that?
   (*present perfect only*)
4. He shoved it under the door.
5. They flew to Berlin.
6. He drank too much.
7. I shut the door.
8. What was his name? (How was he called?)
9. He pulled the cork.
10. I stayed there for two years.

b.
1. Did you (**du**) shut the window?
   (*present perfect only*)
2. He got out of the car. (use **steigen**)
3. I thought it was (found it) boring.
4. His name was Brandt. (He was called . . . .)
5. She sang too loud.
6. We drank wine.
7. He wrote it on the board.
8. They always flew with Lufthansa.
9. Did you (**du**) write him?
   (*present perfect only*)
10. He pushed the chair into the corner.

8 fahren, tragen

	Infinitive	(3rd Person)	Past	Past Participle
	a	(ä)	u	a
to drive	fahren	(fährt)	fuhr	ist (hat) gefahren
to carry; wear	tragen	(trägt)	trug	getragen

● Past tense: Replace the subjects of the following sentences making the necessary changes in the verb forms.

1. Sie fuhr nach Salzburg. (wir, ich)
2. Er trug es zur Post. (sie [they], ich)
3. Er trug einen braunen Anzug. (ich)

● Present perfect tense: Supply the correct auxiliary verb (**sein** or **haben**).

1. Sie (*they*) _____ nach Salzburg gefahren.
2. Er _____ seinen Freund nach Hause getragen.
3. Sie (*she*) _____ mich zum Bahnhof gefahren.
4. Er _____ einen braunen Anzug getragen.

● Put the following sentences into the past and present perfect tenses.

1. Sie fahren nach Salzburg.
2. Er trägt es zur Post.
3. Sie fährt mich zum Bahnhof.
4. Er trägt seinen Freund nach Hause.
5. Er trägt einen braunen Anzug.

9 fallen, halten, lassen, schlafen, laufen

	Infinitive	(3rd Person)	Past	Past Participle
	a	(ä)	ie	a
to fall	fallen	(fällt)	fiel	ist gefallen
to stop	halten	(hält)	hielt	gehalten
to leave	lassen	(läßt)	ließ	gelassen
to sleep	schlafen	(schläft)	schlief	geschlafen
	au	äu	ie	au
to run	laufen	(läuft)	lief	ist gelaufen

- Past tense: Replace the subjects of the following sentences making the necessary changes in the verb forms.

1. Er lief nach Hause. (sie [they]), ich)
2. Ich schlief nicht genug. (wir, er)
   (**genug:** enough)
3. Wir ließen ihn allein. (er, sie [they])

4. Der Wagen hielt vor dem Haus.
   (sie [they], ich)
5. Es fiel vom* Tisch. (Die Bücher . . .)

- Present perfect tense: Supply the correct auxiliary verb (**sein** or **haben**).

1. Er _____ zu lange geschlafen.
2. Sie (she) _____ aus dem Bett gefallen.
3. Wo _____ der Zug gehalten?

4. Sie (they) _____ nach Hause gelaufen.
5. Sie (she) _____ es zu Hause gelassen.

- Put the following sentences into the past and present perfect tenses.

1. Er schläft nicht genug.
2. Der Wagen hält vor dem Haus.
3. Ich lasse es zu Hause.
4. Er fällt unter den Tisch.
5. Sie laufen nach Hause.

6. Ich schlafe zu lange.
7. Wo hält der Zug?
8. Wir lassen ihn allein.
9. Sie fällt aus dem Bett.

10   Mixed drills

- Put the following sentences into the past and present perfect tenses.

1. Ich schlafe zu lange.
2. Wir lassen ihn allein.
3. Sie fährt mich zum Bahnhof.
4. Wo hält der Zug?
5. Ich lasse es zu Hause.
6. Er trägt es zum Bahnhof.
7. Sie fällt aus dem Bett.

8. Sie fahren nach Salzburg.
9. Er schläft nicht genug.
10. Der Wagen hält vor dem Haus.
11. Sie laufen nach Hause.
12. Er fällt unter den Tisch.
13. Er trägt seinen Freund nach Hause.
14. Er trägt einen braunen Anzug.

- Express in German (past and present perfect tenses).

1. I left it at home.
2. She drove me to the station.
3. The car stopped in front of the house.
4. They drove to Salzburg.
5. He didn't sleep enough.
6. We left him alone.
7. She ran home.

8. Where did the train stop?
9. She fell out of bed.
10. He carried it to the station.
11. I slept too long.
12. He fell under the table.
13. He carried his friend home.
14. He was wearing a brown suit.

▶ Note   Before going on to the Grand Mix, you should review the drills on pages 186–87 of this level.

---

*__Vom__ is the contraction of **von dem.**

GRAND MIX

(See p. 209 for a summary of strong verbs.)

- Put the following sentences into the past and present perfect tenses, unless otherwise indicated. Both weak and strong verbs are included in these drills.

a. 1. Was kosten die Gläser?
    2. Sie fahren nach Salzburg.
    3. Thomas trinkt zu viel.
    4. Er zeigt uns ein anderes Zimmer.
    5. Sie sehen es nicht.
    6. Der Wagen hält vor dem Haus.
    7. Wohnt er da?
    8. Sie fliegen immer mit Lufthansa.
    9. Er stellt es auf deinen Schreibtisch.
    10. Ich lasse es zu Hause.

b. 1. Ich frage ihn.
    2. Er schläft nicht genug.
    3. Er studiert an der Universität Berlin.
    4. Sie bleiben nicht da.
    5. Sie fällt aus dem Bett.
    6. Ich esse immer zu Hause.
    7. Sie reservieren dir ein Zimmer.
    8. Ich nehme den anderen Wagen.
    9. Er gibt es mir.
    10. Wir kaufen einen neuen Fernseher.

c. 1. Sie singt zu laut.
    2. Ich schließe die Tür.
    3. Er trägt seinen Freund nach Hause.
    4. Wir schicken es ihnen.
    5. Wir trinken Wein.
    6. Was kostet das Hemd?
    7. Sie fliegen nach Berlin.
    8. Wo hält der Zug?
    9. Ich glaube es nicht.
    10. Wir sehen ihn heute.

d. 1. Sie schreibt nicht sehr oft.
    2. Sie laufen nach Hause.
    3. Ich schlafe zu lange.
    4. Was gibst du ihm?
       (*present perfect only*)
    5. Sie leben in Frankreich.
    6. Wie heißt er?
    7. Er liest es nicht.
    8. Nimmst du es? (*present perfect only*)
    9. Er kauft einen neuen Wagen.
    10. Wir helfen ihnen.

e. 1. Wo findet er das? (*present perfect only*)
    2. Er spricht zu schnell.
    3. Ich brauche einen neuen Mantel.
    4. Er steigt aus dem Wagen.
    5. Sie treffen uns in der Bar.
    6. Sie fährt mich zum Bahnhof.
    7. Wir zeigen ihnen unsere neue Wohnung.
    8. Wo ißt du heute?
       (*present perfect only*)
    9. Wir lassen ihn allein.
    10. Was schickt ihr ihm?
       (*present perfect only*)

f. 1. Er hilft mir.
    2. Wir essen in einem Restaurant.
    3. Schreibst du ihm?
       (*present perfect only*)
    4. Er schiebt den Brief unter die Tür.
    5. Er arbeitet immer zu Hause.
    6. Nimmst du es? (*present perfect only*)
    7. Er heißt Brandt.
    8. Er liest zu viel.
    9. Er sagt es uns.
    10. Er zieht den Korken.

g. 1. Brauchst du mehr Zeit?
       (*present perfect only*)
    2. Ich finde es langweilig.
    3. Er schreibt es an die Tafel.
    4. Sie spricht zu leise.
    5. Wir arbeiten heute in der Bibliothek.
    6. Ich treffe ihn nach dem Abendessen.
    7. Wir bleiben zwei Jahre da.
    8. Er wirft den Mantel aufs Sofa.
    9. Sie suchen ihre Bücher.

EXPRESS IN GERMAN

(See p. 209 for a summary of strong verbs.)

- Put each sentence into the past and present perfect tenses, unless otherwise indicated. Both weak and strong verbs are included in these drills.

a.
1. I asked him.
2. They didn't stay there.
3. He spoke too fast.
4. I slept too long.
5. We ate in a restaurant.
6. They reserved you a room.
7. The car stopped in front of the house.
8. He bought a new car.
9. We saw him today.
10. He asked for the bill.

b.
1. Where did you (du) eat today?
(present perfect only)
2. Where did he find it?
(present perfect only)
3. He always worked at home.
4. Dieter drank too much.
5. I carried him home.
6. He told us yesterday.
7. She fell out of bed.
8. They met us in the bar.
9. He studied at the University of Berlin.
10. His name was Brandt. (was called)

c.
1. They didn't see it.
2. He helped me.
3. I left it at home.
4. He wrote it on the board.
5. They flew to Frankfurt.
6. He showed us another room.
7. What did you (du) give him?
(present perfect only)
8. He read too much.
9. They were looking for their books.
10. Did you (du) take it?
(present perfect only)

d.
1. We drank wine.
2. He gave it to me.
3. They ran home.
4. I met him after dinner.
5. We were working in the library.

6. What was his name? (was he called)
7. Did you (du) need more time?
(present perfect only)
8. I took the other car.
9. Did he live there?
10. They drove to Salzburg.

e.
1. We stayed there two years.
2. He put it on your desk.
3. I closed the door.
4. We always ate at home.
5. I didn't believe it.
6. She didn't write very often.
7. She drove me to the station.
8. They always flew with Lufthansa.
9. We bought a new TV set.
10. Did you (du) take him home?
(present perfect only)

f.
1. He got out of the car.
2. We helped them.
3. He didn't read it.
4. Did you (du) write him?
(present perfect only)
5. What did you (ihr) send them.
6. We left it there.
7. He shoved the letter under the door.
8. I found it boring.
9. What did the glasses cost?
10. We sent it to them.

VOCABULARY

das **Bad, ⁼er** bath
die **Bar, -s** bar
das **Fenster, -** window
(das) **Frankreich** France
der **Fernseher, -** TV set
genug enough
gestern yesterday
glauben to believe
holen to get (go get)
hören to hear
der **Korken, -** cork
laut loud

leise softly
lernen to learn, study
mehr more
reservieren to reserve
schließen to close
schloß, geschlossen
spielen to play
steigen . . . aus to get
out of
steig . . . aus
ist ausgestiegen
studieren (an + *dat.*)
to study at

die **Universität, -en**
university
die **Wohnung, -en**
apartment
ziehen to pull
zog, gezogen

For a summary of strong verbs used in this lesson, as well as their principal parts, see Lesson 5, Level 2, p. 209.

Lesson 5   Level TWO

A Past Tense and Present Perfect Tense of Strong (Irregular) Verbs, Continued

1 Exceptions: **stehen, bitten, sitzen, kommen, gehen**

- Put the following sentences into the past and present perfect tenses.

	Infinitive	Past	Past Participle
to stand	e stehen	a stand	a gestanden

1. Wo steht er?
2. Es steht in der Zeitung.

- Put the following sentences into the past and present perfect tenses.

	Infinitive	Past	Past Participle
to request to sit	i bitten sitzen	a bat saß	e gebeten gesessen

1. Wo sitzen Sie?
2. Er bittet um die Rechnung.
   (**bitten um**: to ask for)

3. Sie sitzen auf der anderen Seite.
   (**die Seite**: side)
4. Sie bitten um Hilfe.
   (**die Hilfe**: help)

- Mixed drill: Put the following sentences into the past and present perfect tenses.

1. Sie sitzen auf der anderen Seite.
2. Es steht in der Zeitung.
3. Er bittet um die Rechnung.
4. Wo sitzen Sie?
5. Wo steht er?
6. Sie bitten um Hilfe.

- Put the following sentences into the past and present perfect tenses.

	Infinitive	Past	Past Participle
to come	o kommen	a kam	o ist gekommen

1. Ich komme später.
2. Sie kommen nicht.
3. Er kommt allein.

- Put the following sentences into the past and present perfect tenses.

	Infinitive	Past	Past Participle
to go	e gehen	i ging	a ist gegangen

1. Wir gehen nach Hause.
2. Ich gehe heute in die Stadt.
3. Er geht zum Arzt.

- Mixed drill: Put the following sentences into the past and present perfect tenses.

1. Sie kommen nicht.
2. Er geht zum Arzt.
3. Ich komme später.
4. Wir gehen nach Hause.
5. Er kommt allein.
6. Ich gehe heute in die Stadt.

- Put the following sentences into the past and present perfect tenses.

1. Wo sitzen Sie?
2. Er kommt allein.
3. Es steht in der Zeitung.
4. Wir gehen nach Hause.
5. Ich komme später.
6. Er bittet um die Rechnung.
7. Ich gehe heute in die Stadt.
8. Sie sitzen auf der anderen Seite.
9. Wo steht er?
10. Sie kommen nicht.
11. Er geht zum Arzt.
12. Sie bitten um Hilfe.

- Express in German (past and present perfect tenses).

1. I came later.
2. He went to the doctor's.
3. Where were you (Sie) sitting?
4. He asked for the bill.
5. She came alone.
6. It was in the newspaper. (use stehen)
7. We went home.
8. They were sitting on the other side.
9. She didn't come.
10. They asked for help.
11. Where was he standing?
12. I went downtown today.

2 Mixed verbs: a subgroup of weak verbs

There is a small group of verbs that follow a pattern of their own. *They change their stems* (as do strong verbs), but *they take the endings used with weak verbs:*

	bringen	*to bring*	
PAST TENSE	ich brach**te**	wir brach**ten**	
	du brach**test**	ihr brach**tet**	
	er brach**te**	sie brach**ten**	

The past participles of these verbs, like those of other weak verbs, begin with a **ge-** prefix and take the ending **-t:**

> Ich habe es gebracht.

The three most common verbs that behave this way are:

Infinitive		Past Tense	Past Participle
bringen	(to bring)	brachte	gebracht
denken	(to think)	dachte	gedacht
kennen	(to be acquainted with, to know)	kannte	gekannt

3 haben, sein, and werden

The past tense of **haben** is formed by adding the endings used with weak verbs to a new past tense stem (**hat-**).

	haben	*to have*	
PAST TENSE	ich hat **te**	wir hat **ten**	
	du hat **test**	ihr hat **tet**	
	er hat **te**	sie hat **ten**	

Gehabt is the past participle of **haben;** its auxiliary verb is **haben.**

PRESENT PERFECT	Ich habe **gehabt**, etc.

The past tense of sein is formed by adding the endings used with strong verbs to a new past tense stem (war-).

	sein *to be*		
PAST TENSE	ich war	wir war	**en**
	du war **st**	ihr war	**t**
	er war	sie war	**en**

Gewesen is the past participle of **sein;** its auxiliary verb is **sein.**

PRESENT PERFECT	Ich bin **gewesen,** etc.

The past tense of werden is unique.

	werden *to become*	
PAST TENSE	ich wurde	wir wurden
	du wurdest	ihr wurdet
	er wurde	sie wurden

Geworden is the past participle of **werden;** its auxiliary verb is **sein.**

PRESENT PERFECT	Ich bin **geworden,** etc.

DRILLS

1 bringen, denken, kennen

	Infinitive	Past	Past Participle
	e / i	a	a
to bring	bringen	brachte	gebracht
to think	denken	dachte	gedacht
to know	kennen	kannte	gekannt

In addition to stem-vowel change, this group has the following peculiarities in the past and perfect tenses:

1. They all take weak endings.

brach**te** / ge**bracht**

2. **Bringen** and **denken** change the consonants **ng** and **nk** to **ch** to form the past tense and the past participle.

bri**ng**en   bra**ch**te, ge**bracht**
de**nk**en   da**ch**te, ge**dacht**

- Past tense: Replace the subjects of the following sentences making the necessary changes in the verb forms.

  1. Er kannte ihn nicht.   (wir, ich, sie [*they*])
  2. Ich brachte die Briefe zur Post.   (sie [*they*], er)
  3. Sie dachten an etwas anderes.   (ich, wir, er)

      (denken an + *acc.*: to think of; **etwas anderes**: something else)

  4. Er kannte den Weg nicht.   (sie [*they*], ich, wir)

      (der Weg: way, road)

  5. Ich dachte an ein anderes Mädchen.   (sie [*they*], er)
  6. Wir brachten ihn nach Hause.   (ich, sie [*they*])

- Present perfect tense: Supply the correct form of the auxiliary verb **haben.**

  1. Sie (*they*) _____ den Weg nicht gekannt.
  2. Ich _____ an etwas anderes gedacht.
  3. _____ du ihn nach Hause gebracht?

- Put the following sentences into the past and present perfect tenses, unless otherwise indicated.

  1. Er kennt ihn nicht.
  2. Ich denke an ein anderes Mädchen.
  3. Bringst du ihn nach Hause?
     (*present perfect only*)
  4. Sie kennen den Weg nicht.
  5. Ich denke an etwas anderes.
  6. Sie bringt die Briefe zur Post.

- Express in German (past and present perfect tenses, unless otherwise indicated).

  1. They didn't know the way.
  2. I was thinking of something else.
  3. Did you (**du**) take him home?
     (*present perfect only*)
  4. I was thinking of another girl.
  5. He didn't know him.
  6. She took the letters to the post office.

2   **werden**

	Infinitive	Past	Past Participle
to become	werden	wurde	ist geworden

• Past tense: Replace the subjects of the following sentences making the necessary changes in the verb.

  1. Er wurde alt. (sie [they], ich)
  2. Sie wurden böse. (er, wir)

(**böse:** mad, angry)

• Present perfect tense: Supply the correct form of the auxiliary verb **sein.**

  1. Er _____ dick geworden.
  2. _____ du müde geworden?
  3. Sie (they) _____ böse geworden.

• Put the following sentences into the past and present perfect tenses, unless otherwise indicated.

  1. Es wird langweilig.
  2. Sie werden alt.
  3. Wirst du müde? (present perfect only)
  4. Sie wird böse.
  5. Sie werden dick.
  6. Es wird kalt.

3   haben

	Infinitive	Past	Past Participle
to have	haben	hatte	gehabt

• Past tense: Replace the subjects of the following sentences making the necessary changes in the verb.

  1. Er hatte keine Zeit. (wir, ich)
  2. Wir hatten keine Chance. (du, sie [they], er)
  3. Sie hatte es nicht. (wir, ich)

(**die Chance:** chance)

• Present perfect tense: Supply the correct form of the auxiliary verb **haben.**

  1. _____ Sie es gehabt?
  2. Ich _____ keine Zeit gehabt.
  3. _____ du genug Geld gehabt?

(**genug:** enough)

• Put the following sentences into the past and present perfect tenses, unless otherwise indicated.

  1. Ich habe keine Zeit.
  2. Hast du genug Geld? (present perfect only)
  3. Wir haben keine Chance.
  4. Sie hat es nicht.
  5. Haben Sie Zeit? (present perfect only)

4   sein

	Infinitive	Past	Past Participle
to be	sein	war	ist gewesen

- Past tense: Replace the subjects of the following sentences making the necessary changes in the verb.

    1. Sie war nicht zu Hause. (sie [they])
    2. Wir waren zu müde. (er, sie [they], ich)

- Present perfect tense: Supply the correct form of the auxiliary verb **sein**.

    1. Wo _____ du gewesen?
    2. Wir _____ zu müde gewesen.

    3. Sie (she) _____ sehr nett gewesen.
    4. _____ Sie da gewesen?

- Put the following sentences into the past and present perfect tenses, unless otherwise indicated.

    1. Wir sind zu müde.
    2. Er ist nicht zu Hause.
    3. Wo bist du? (present perfect only)

    4. Sie ist sehr nett.
    5. Sie sind verrückt.

MIXED DRILLS (werden, haben, sein)

- Put the following sentences into the past and present perfect tenses, unless otherwise indicated.

    1. Es wird langweilig.
    2. Er ist nicht zu Hause.
    3. Sie werden dick.
    4. Ich habe keine Zeit.
    5. Sie ist sehr nett.
    6. Hast du genug Geld?
       (present perfect only)
    7. Es wird kalt.
    8. Wo bist du? (present perfect only)

    9. Haben Sie keine Zeit?
       (present perfect only)
    10. Sie wird böse.
    11. Wir sind zu müde.
    12. Sie werden alt.
    13. Sie hat es nicht.
    14. Wirst du müde? (present perfect only)
    15. Sie sind verrückt.
    16. Wir haben keine Chance.

EXPRESS IN GERMAN

- Put each sentence into the past and present perfect tenses, unless otherwise indicated.

    1. I didn't have any time.
    2. He wasn't home.
    3. It got boring.
    4. We didn't have a chance.
    5. She got mad.
    6. We were too tired.
    7. She didn't have it.
    8. It's gotten cold. (present perfect only)
    9. Where were you (du)?
       (present perfect only)
    10. Didn't you (Sie) have any time?
        (present perfect only)
    11. He's gotten old. (present perfect only)
    12. She was very nice.

    13. Didn't you (du) get tired?
        (present perfect only)
    14. They were crazy.
    15. Did you (du) have enough money?
        (present perfect only)

GRAND MIX

• Put the following sentences into the past and present perfect tenses, unless otherwise indicated.

a.
1. Sie hat es nicht.
2. Wir gehen nach Hause.
3. Es wird kalt.
4. Sie kommen nicht.
5. Ich denke an etwas anderes.
6. Sie wird böse.
7. Wo steht er?
8. Wir sind zu müde.
9. Sie kennen den Weg nicht.
10. Wo sitzen Sie? (*present perfect only*)

b.
1. Sie ist sehr nett.
2. Wir haben keine Chance.
3. Bringst du ihn nach Hause?
4. Er bittet um die Rechnung.
5. Wirst du nicht müde?
6. Ich gehe heute in die Stadt.

7. Sie ist nicht zu Hause.
8. Ich bringe ihn nach Hause.
9. Er kommt allein.
10. Haben Sie keine Zeit?

c.
1. Es wird langweilig.
2. Sie sitzen auf der anderen Seite.
3. Wo bist du?
4. Er kennt ihn nicht.
5. Es steht in der Zeitung.
6. Ich habe keine Zeit.
7. Sie bitten um Hilfe.
8. Ich denke an ein anderes Mädchen.
9. Er geht zum Arzt.
10. Hast du genug Geld?

d.
1. Ich komme später.

EXPRESS IN GERMAN

• Put each sentence into the past and present perfect tenses, unless otherwise indicated.

a.
1. She didn't have it.
2. He went to the doctor.
3. She was very nice.
4. Where were you (**Sie**) sitting?
5. It got boring.
6. I took him home. (use **bringen**)
7. He asked for the bill.
8. I didn't have any time.
9. They didn't know the way.
10. I came later.

b.
1. Where have you (**du**) been?
2. I was thinking of another girl.
3. They didn't come.
4. She wasn't there.
5. We didn't have a chance.
6. I went downtown today.

7. She got mad.
8. It was in the newspaper.
9. We were too tired.
10. They were sitting on the other side.

c.
1. I was thinking of something else.
2. Didn't you (**du**) get tired?
3. We went home.
4. He didn't know him.
5. Did you (**du**) have enough?
6. Where was he standing?
7. Didn't you (**Sie**) have any time?
8. He came alone.
9. Did you take him home?
10. Didn't you get tired?

d.
1. They asked for help.

Summary of strong verbs

INFINITIVE	(3RD PERSON)	PAST	PRESENT PERFECT†	
bitten*		bat	gebeten	(to ask, request)
bleiben		blieb	ist geblieben	(to stay)
bringen*		brachte	gebracht	(to bring)
denken*		dachte	gedacht	(to think)
essen	(ißt)	aß	gegessen	(to eat)
fahren	(fährt)	fuhr	ist (hat) gefahren	(to drive, go)
fallen*	(fällt)	fiel	ist gefallen	(to fall)
finden		fand	gefunden	(to find)
fliegen		flog	ist (hat) geflogen	(to fly)
fressen	(frißt)	fraß	gefressen	(to eat, [only for animals])
geben	(gibt)	gab	gegeben	(to give)
gehen*		ging	ist gegangen	(to go)
haben*	(hat)	hatte	gehabt	(to have)
halten	(hält)	hielt	gehalten	(to hold)
heißen		hieß	geheißen	(to be called)
helfen	(hilft)	half	geholfen	(to help)
kennen		kannte	gekannt	(to be acquainted with, know)
kommen*		kam	ist gekommen	(to come)
lassen	(läßt)	ließ	gelassen	(to leave)
laufen	(läuft)	lief	ist gelaufen	(to run)
lesen	(liest)	las	gelesen	(to read)
nehmen*	(nimmt)	nahm	genommen	(to take)
schieben		schob	geschoben	(to push)
schlafen	(schläft)	schlief	geschlafen	(to sleep)
schließen		schloß††	geschlossen	(to close)
schreiben		schrieb	geschrieben	(to write)
sehen	(sieht)	sah	gesehen	(to see)
sein*	(ist)	war	ist gewesen	(to be)
singen		sang	gesungen	(to sing)
sitzen*		saß	gesessen	(to sit)
sprechen	(spricht)	sprach	gesprochen	(to speak)
stehen*		stand	gestanden	(to stand)
steigen		stieg	ist gestiegen	(to climb)
tragen	(trägt)	trug	getragen	(to carry)
treffen*	(trifft)	traf	getroffen	(to meet)
trinken		trank	getrunken	(to drink)
werden*	(wird)	wurde	ist geworden	(to become)
werfen*	(wirft)	warf	geworfen	(to throw)
ziehen*		zog	gezogen	(to pull)

---

*These verbs involve more than stem-vowel change; that is, the consonants are affected.

†All verbs take **haben** as their auxiliary unless otherwise indicated.

††See page 149. If **schloß** has an ending that begins with a vowel, then the ß is replaced by **ss (wir schlossen).**

B Past Perfect Tense of Weak and Strong Verbs

1 Tense formation

Like the present perfect, the past perfect is a compound form consisting of an *auxiliary verb* plus a *past participle*. The only difference is that in the past perfect the auxiliary (**sein** or **haben**) is in the past tense.

| PRESENT PERFECT | Ich **habe** es schon **gemacht.** | (I've already done it.) |
| PAST PERFECT | Ich **hatte** es schon **gemacht** | (I'd already done it.) |

| PRESENT PERFECT | Er **ist** schon nach Hause **gegangen.** | (He's already gone home.) |
| PAST PERFECT | Er **war** schon nach Hause **gegangen** | (He'd already gone home.) |

2 Word order

The past participle is the last element in a simple sentence:

Ich hatte es schon **gemacht**

3 Usage

As a tense, the past perfect has a special function. It is used when you want to show that something happened *before a point in past time.*

PAST	Ich wollte gestern ins Kino gehen.	(I wanted to go to the movies yesterday.)
PAST PERFECT	Aber ich **hatte** den Film schon **gesehen.**	(But I *had* already *seen* the picture; that is, I found out then that I had seen the picture *before*.)
PAST	Ich ging zu seinem Büro.	(I went to his office.)
PAST PERFECT	Aber er **war** schon nach Hause **gegangen.**	(But he *had* already *gone* home; that is, When I got there, he had already gone . . . *before my arrival.*)

The past perfect is used to put past events in their proper sequence. "I wanted to go to the movies yesterday" refers to a past time. The sentence that follows it ("But I had already seen the picture") refers to something *before* this past time—to a second period of past time or a *past* past time. The past perfect is the tense used for this purpose.

DRILLS

• Put the following sentences into the past perfect tense.

1. Er hat die Tür geschlossen.

2. Haben Sie den Film schon gesehen?

3. Es ist dunkel geworden.   (dunkel: dark)
4. Ich habe ihn nie vorher gesehen.

(nie: never; **vorher:** before)

5. Wir sind ins Theater gegangen.

(das Theater: theater)

6. Er hat es schon gemacht.
7. Sie ist nie so krank gewesen.   **(krank:** sick)
8. Wir sind schon nach Hause gegangen.

(schon: already)

9. Ich habe an etwas anderes gedacht.
10. Sie haben mir ein Zimmer reserviert.
11. Er hat nicht genug geschlafen.
12. Ich bin nie vorher da gewesen.
13. Er hat es schon im Radio gehört.

(das Radio: radio; **im Radio:** on the radio)

14. Hast du es schon gelesen?

● Synthetic exercises: Use the following elements to construct sentences in the past perfect tense.

1. Er / schlafen / nicht genug
2. Ich / denken / an etwas anderes
3. Wir / gehen / schon nach Hause
4. Er / hören / es schon / im Radio
5. Es / werden / dunkel
6. Lesen / du / es schon / ?
7. Ich / sehen / ihn nie vorher

8. Sie (they) / reservieren / mir / Zimmer
9. Er / machen / es schon
10. Ich / sein / nie vorher da
11. Er / schließen / Tür
12. Sehen / Sie / Film / schon / ?
13. Sie (she) / sein / nie so krank
14. Wir / gehen / Theater

● Express in German.

1. We'd already gone home.
2. They'd reserved me a room.
3. He'd already heard it on the radio.
4. It had gotten dark.
5. Had you **(du)** already read it?
6. I'd never been there before.
.7. We'd gone to the theater.

8. He'd closed the door.
9. He hadn't slept enough.
10. Had you **(Sie)** already seen the picture?
11. She'd never been so sick.
12. I'd never seen him before.
13. He'd already done it.
14. I'd thought of something else.

C Future Tense: Werden + Infinitive

1 Forms

The future tense is a compound form that consists of the auxiliary verb **werden** plus an *infinitive*.

werden			Infinitive	
Werde	ich	Zeit	haben**?**	(Will I have time?)
Wirst	du	Zeit	haben**?**	(Will you have time?)
Wird	er	Zeit	haben**?**	(Will he have time?)
Werden	wir	Zeit	haben**?**	(Will we have time?)
Werdet	ihr	Zeit	haben**?**	(Will you have time?)
Werden	sie	Zeit	haben**?**	(Will they have time?)

The auxiliary **werden** changes according to person and number; the infinitive stays constant.

2 Word order

The infinitive is the last element in the sentence.

Werden Sie Zeit haben?

3 Usage

As you already know, conversational German normally uses the present tense to express future time:

Er macht es später.   (He'll do it later. He's going to do it later.)

The presence of a *time expression* **(später)** makes it clear that the person is referring to some future time, even though he is using the present tense.
 Or take another example. If somebody is telling you about his plans for the summer, he might say:

Zuerst **besuchen** wir Freunde in Stuttgart und dann **fahren** wir nach München.
(First we're going to visit friends in Stuttgart, then we're going to drive to Munich.)

There can be no confusion as to whether he is referring to the present or to the future; at present he is standing there talking to you. When he says, "Wir fahren nach München," he has to be referring to the future.
 But look at the following example:

Ist er zu Hause?   (Is he at home?)

Without a specific context indicating that future time is meant, this sentence will be understood as referring to present time:

Is he at home (right now)?

In such cases, the future tense must be used to make it clear that one is referring to future time:

Wird er zu Hause **sein?**   (*Will* he *be* at home?)

4 wohl

Wohl means "probably" and is often used with the future tense:

Er **wird** wohl morgen **kommen.**   (He'll *probably* come tomorrow.)

Word order: comes after pronoun *objects* and before everything else.

DRILLS

- Supply the correct form of **werden**.

  1. Sie (*they*) _____ es nicht glauben.
  2. Er _____ bei mir wohnen.
  3. Wann _____ wir da sein?
  4. _____ er Zeit haben?
  5. _____ du ihn fragen?
  6. _____ Sie es nicht brauchen?
  7. Wir _____ es ihm geben.
  8. Wann _____ ihr zu Hause sein?
  9. _____ du ihn sehen?
  10. _____ du das für mich machen?
  11. _____ er zu Hause sein?

- Supply the correct form of **werden**.

  1. Er _____ wohl morgen kommen.
  2. Sie (*they*) _____ wohl mit Lufthansa fliegen.
  3. Du _____ es wohl brauchen.
  4. Sie (*they*) _____ wohl zu Hause bleiben.
  5. Ich _____ es wohl finden.
  6. Er _____ es Ihnen wohl bringen.
  7. Sie (*they*) _____ wohl Bier trinken.
  8. Er _____ es wohl vergessen.

- Put the following sentences into the future tense.

  1. Siehst du ihn?
  2. Ist er zu Hause?
  3. Wir geben es ihm.
  4. Machst du das für mich?
  5. Er wohnt bei mir.
  6. Wann sind wir da?
  7. Sie glauben es nicht.
  8. Wann seid ihr zu Hause?
  9. Fragst du ihn?
  10. Hat er Zeit?
  11. Brauchen Sie es nicht?
  12. Sie bleiben wohl zu Hause.
  13. Er kommt wohl morgen.
  14. Ich finde es wohl.
  15. Sie fliegen wohl mit Lufthansa.
  16. Er vergißt es wohl.
  17. Du brauchst es wohl.
  18. Er bringt es Ihnen wohl.
  19. Sie trinken wohl Bier.

- Express in German.

  1. Will he be at home?
  2. He'll probably come tomorrow.
  3. You (**du**) will probably need it.
  4. When will we be there?
  5. They'll probably fly with Lufthansa.
  6. They won't believe it.
  7. He'll probably forget it.
  8. Will you see him?
  9. He'll be living at my place.
  10. They'll probably stay home.
  11. We'll give it to him.
  12. Will he have time?
  13. I'll probably find it.
  14. When will you (**ihr**) be home?
  15. Won't you (**Sie**) need it?
  16. They'll probably drink beer.
  17. Will you (**du**) do that for me?
  18. Will you (**du**) ask him?
  19. He'll probably bring it to you.

D Verbs and Adjectives with Prepositions

1 Introduction

Verbs and prepositions can be combined to form new, idiomatic expressions. As idioms, they are often "unpredictable" in that the German combinations do not always correspond to the English choice of preposition.

> EXAMPLE   Ich **dachte an** einen anderen Mann.   (I *was thinking of* another man.)

a. Choice of preposition

In the example, **denken** combines with the preposition **an** to form an idiom that corresponds to the English expression "to think of." However, there is no way for the English speaker to predict that **an** will be used in the German idiom.

b. Choice of case

> Ich dachte an **einen anderen Mann.**

When a two-way preposition is used, there is no way to predict what the case will be. The usual test (accusative with motion, dative when there is no motion) does not apply. **Auf,** for example, is a two-way preposition. But the expression **warten auf** (wait for) takes an accusative object even though no motion is involved.

> ▶ Note   Prepositions that take only one case take that same case when they combine with verbs:
>
> > EXAMPLE   **sprechen mit:** to speak with
> >
> > Ich spreche mit **ihm.**   (I'll speak with him.)
>
> **Mit** can take only the dative, hence **mit ihm.**

2 Verb-preposition combinations

erinnern an (+ *acc.*): to remind of

> Er **erinnert** mich **an** meinen Bruder.   (He reminds me of my brother.)

sprechen mit: to talk to, speak with

> Haben Sie **mit** ihm **gesprochen?**   (Have you talked to him?)

warten auf (+ *acc.*): to wait for

> Er **wartet auf** dich.   (He's waiting for you.)

a. Contrastive usage: **fragen nach / bitten um**

fragen nach: to ask about, inquire about

> Er fragte nach deiner Schwester.   (He asked about your sister.)

bitten um: to ask for, request

> Er bat mich um Geld.   (He asked me for money.)

Fragen nach is used for *inquiries*. The person asking the question wants *information* as an answer.

Bitten um is used to make a *request*. The person asking the question doesn't want information; he wants a *favor* or a *tangible object* (in our example, "money").

b. Contrastive usage: **denken an / halten von**

denken an (+ *acc.*): to think of or about (not used for opinions)

> Ich dachte an einen anderen Mann.   (I was thinking of another man.)

halten von: to think of (used to ask for an opinion)

> Was hältst du von dem neuen Arzt?   (What do you think of the new doctor?)
> Was hältst du von ihm?   (What's your opinion of him?)

Was is the key to this idiom. **Halten von** is normally found in questions.

▶ Note   The present tense forms of **halten** are unusual in the second and third person singular. Although the stem of the verb ends in **-t,** the forms are:

> du hältst
> er hält

3 Adjectives with prepositions

Adjectives may combine with certain prepositions in a similar way:

böse auf (+ *acc.*): mad at

> Er ist böse auf mich.   (He's mad at me.)

fertig mit: finished with, done with

> Ich bin fertig mit der Zeitung.   (I'm finished with the newspaper.)

freundlich zu: friendly to

> Er war sehr freundlich zu mir.   (He was very friendly to me.)

zufrieden mit: satisfied with

> Ich bin zufrieden mit ihnen.   (I'm satisfied with them.)

DRILLS

1 **fragen nach:** ask about / **bitten um:** ask for

- Supply the correct prepositions.

    1. Sie fragten _____ dir.
       (about)
    2. Er bat mich _____ den Wagen.
       (for)

    3. Er fragte mich _____ meiner Schwester.
       (about)
    4. Ich bat den Ober _____ die Rechnung.
       (for)   **(der Ober:** waiter)

- Synthetic exercises: Construct sentences in the past tense.

    1. Er / bitten / mich / um / Wagen
    2. Sie (*they*) / fragen / nach / (*you*)
    3. Ich / bitten / Ober / um / Rechnung

    4. Er / fragen / mich / nach / mein / Schwester

- Express in German.

    1. They asked about you.
    2. I asked the waiter for the bill.

    3. He asked me about my sister.
    4. She asked me for the car.

2 **denken an** (+ *acc.*): think of / **halten von:** think of (opinion)

- Supply the correct prepositions.

    1. Ich dachte _____ ein anderes Buch.
       (of)
    2. Was hältst du _____ dem neuen Arzt?
       (of)

    3. Ich dachte _____ etwas anderes.
       (of)
    4. Was halten Sie _____ dem Film?
       (of)

- Synthetic exercises: Construct sentences in the tense indicated.

    1. Ich / denken / an / etwas ander-
       (*past*)
    2. Was / halten / du / von / neu / Arzt / ?
       (*present*)

    3. Ich / denken / an / ander- / Buch
       (*past*)
    4. Was / halten / du / von / Film / ?
       (*present*)

- Express in German.

    1. I was thinking of another book.
    2. What do you think of the movie?

    3. I was thinking of something else.
    4. What do you think of the new doctor?

- Express in German.

    1. I asked the waiter for the bill.
    2. I was thinking of something else.
    3. He asked me about my sister.
    4. What do you **(du)** think of the movie?

    5. She asked me for the car.
    6. I was thinking of another book.
    7. They asked about you.
    8. What do you **(du)** think of the new doctor?

3 **erinnern* an** (+ *acc.*): remind of / **sprechen mit**: talk to, speak with /
warten auf (+ *acc.*): wait for

- Supply the correct prepositions.

1. Er wartet _____ dich.
   (for)
2. Ich will _____ dem Chef sprechen.
   (with)
3. Wir warten _____ den nächsten Zug.
   (for)
4. Er erinnert mich _____ meinen Bruder.
   (of)

5. Hast du _____ ihm gesprochen?
   (with)
6. Sie erinnerte mich _____ die Party.
   (of)   (**die Party:** party)
7. Ich warte _____ einen Brief von ihm.
   (for)

- Synthetic exercises: Construct sentences in the tense indicated.

1. Er / warten / auf / (you) (*present*)
2. Sie / erinnern / mich / an / Party
   (*past*)
3. Ich / warten / auf / Brief / von /
   (him) (*present*)
4. Ich / wollen / sprechen / mit / Chef
   (*present*)

5. Er / erinnern / mich / an / mein /
   Bruder (*past*)
6. Sprechen / du / mit / (him) / ?
   (*present perfect*)
7. Wir / warten / auf / nächst- / Zug
   (*present*)

- Express in German.

1. Did you talk to (speak with) him?
   (*present perfect*)
2. He's waiting for you.
3. He reminds me of my brother.

4. I'm waiting for a letter from him.
5. I want to talk to the boss.
6. She reminded me of the party.
7. We're waiting for the next train.

4 **böse auf** (+ *acc.*): mad at / **freundlich zu**: friendly to /
fertig mit: finished with / **zufrieden mit**: satisfied with

- Supply the correct prepositions.

1. Sind Sie fertig _____ der Zeitung?
   (with)
2. Wir sind sehr zufrieden _____
   (with)
   unserem Volkswagen.

3. Sie ist böse _____ mich.
   (at)
4. Sie waren sehr freundlich _____ uns.
   (to)

***erinnern:** a few infinitives end in **-n** rather than **-en.** The stem here is **erinner-** and the present tense is as
follows:

ich erinnere	wir erinnern
du erinnerst	ihr erinnert
er erinnert	sie erinnern

The past tense uses the normal weak past tense endings.

5. Er ist fertig _____ seiner Arbeit.
    (with)

    (die Arbeit: work; term paper)

6. Sie ist böse _____ ihren Mann.
    (at)

7. Ich bin sehr zufrieden _____ ihm.
    (with)

- Synthetic exercises: Construct sentences in the present tense.

    1. Wir / sein / sehr zufrieden / mit / unser / Volkswagen
    2. Sie (*she*) / sein / böse / auf / (*me*)
    3. Sein / Sie / fertig / mit / Zeitung / ?

    4. Sie (*they*) / sein / sehr freundlich / zu / (*us*)
    5. Ich / sein / sehr zufrieden / mit / (*him*)
    6. Sie (*she*) / sein / böse / auf / ihr / Mann
    7. Er / sein / fertig / mit / sein / Arbeit

- Express in German.

    1. Are you finished with the newspaper?
    2. She's mad at me.
    3. They were very friendly to us.
    4. I'm very satisfied with him.

    5. He's finished with his paper. (use **Arbeit**)
    6. We're very satisfied with our Volkswagen.
    7. She's mad at her husband.

MIXED DRILLS

1   Fill-ins

a. 1. Ich will _____ Chef sprechen.
        (with the)

    2. Er wartet _____.
        (for you)

    3. Sie bat mich _____ Wagen.
        (for the)

    4. Ich dachte _____ Buch.
        (of another)

    5. Sind Sie fertig _____ Zeitung?
        (with the)

    6. Sie ist böse _____ Mann.
        (at her)

    7. Er fragte mich _____ Schwester.
        (about my)

    8. Was hältst du _____ neuen Arzt?
        (of the)

    9. Er erinnert mich _____ Bruder.
        (of my)

    10. Wir warten _____ nächsten Zug.
        (for the)

b. 1. Ich bin sehr zufrieden _____.
        (with him)

    2. Sie waren sehr freundlich _____.
        (to us)

    3. Ich bat den Ober _____ Rechnung.
        (for the)

    4. Hast du _____ gesprochen?
        (with him)

    5. Sie ist böse _____.
        (at me)

    6. Ich warte _____ Brief von ihm.
        (for a)

    7. Was hältst du _____ Film?
        (of the)

    8. Sie fragten _____.
        (about you)

    9. Ich dachte _____ etwas _____.
        (of)   (else)

    10. Wir sind sehr zufrieden _____
        (with our)
        Volkswagen.

c. 1. Er ist fertig _____ Arbeit.
        (with his)

    2. Sie erinnerte mich _____ Party.
        (of the)

a. 1. He's waiting for you.
    2. Are you finished with the newspaper?
    3. They asked about you.
    4. I was thinking of something else.
    5. She's mad at me.
    6. He reminds me of my brother.
    7. We're very satisfied with our Volkswagen.
    8. I asked the waiter for the bill.
    9. What do you think of the movie?
   10. They were very friendly to us.

b. 1. I want to talk to the boss.
    2. We're waiting for the next train.
    3. He's finished with his paper. (use **Arbeit**)
    4. He asked me about my sister.
    5. I was thinking of another book.
    6. She's mad at her husband.
    7. Did you **(du)** talk to him? (*present perfect*)

    8. I'm waiting for a letter from him.
    9. She asked me for the car.
   10. I'm very satisfied with him.

c. 1. What do you **(du)** think of the new doctor?
    2. She reminded me of the party.

E Da(r)-Compounds

1 Prepositions with persons

Look at the following examples:

> Er erinnert mich **an meinen Bruder**. (He reminds me *of my brother*.)
> Er erinnert mich **an ihn**. (He reminds me *of him*.)

When the object of a preposition is a person, this object may be either a noun (an meinen **Bruder**) or a pronoun (an **ihn**).

2 Prepositions with things: **da(r)**-compounds

Now look at these examples:

> Sie erinnerte mich **an die Party**. (She reminded me *of the party*.)
> Sie erinnerte mich **daran**. (She reminded me *of it*.)

When the object of a preposition is a *thing* (not a person), the object may be a noun (an die **Party**) or it can be a **da(r)**-compound **(daran)**.

a. What is a **da(r)**-compound?

A **da(r)**-compound is a short form of a prepositional phrase. **Da-** or **dar-** is prefixed to a preposition, and this prefix takes the place of a pronoun object. This substitution can only be made if the object of the preposition is a thing, not a person. Thus:

Noun Object	Da(r)-Compound
an die **Party**	**dar**an
von dem **Film**	**da**von

b. When to use **da(r)**-compounds

When the object of a preposition is a thing, a **da(r)**-compound will almost always replace a preposition plus pronoun.

3 **da-** or **dar-**

The choice between using **da-** or **dar-** is very simple. If the preposition begins with a *vowel,* **dar-** is used:

darauf   daran   darum

If the preposition begins with a *consonant,* **da-** is used:

damit   danach   davon

DRILLS

• Replace the prepositional phrases with the appropriate **da(r)**-compounds.

1. Sind Sie fertig mit der Zeitung?
2. Sie erinnerte mich an die Party.
3. Was hältst du von dem neuen Film?
4. Ich warte auf seine Antwort.   **(die Antwort:** answer)
5. Wir sind sehr zufrieden mit unserem Volkswagen.
6. Ich bin gegen diesen Plan.   **(der Plan:** plan)
7. Er hat über den Krieg geschrieben.   **(der Krieg:** war; **schreiben über** + *acc.:* to write about)
8. Er ist fertig mit seiner Arbeit.
9. Ich warte auf mein Geld.

• Replace the objects of the prepositions with the appropriate personal pronouns.

EXAMPLE   Was hältst du von dem Mann?
             Was hältst du von **ihm?**

1. Haben Sie mit seiner Frau gesprochen?
2. Du erinnerst mich an meinen Bruder.
3. Ich will mit dem Chef sprechen.
4. Er fragte mich nach meiner Schwester.
5. Was hältst du von dem neuen Arzt?
6. Ich warte auf meine Freundin.
           (die Freundin: girl friend)
7. Sie ist böse auf ihren Mann.

Replace the noun objects with the appropriate pronoun objects or **da(r)**-compounds.

1. Ich warte auf seine Antwort.
2. Sind Sie fertig mit der Zeitung?
3. Sie ist böse auf ihren Mann.
4. Ich bin gegen diesen Plan.
5. Haben Sie mit seiner Frau gesprochen?
6. Sie erinnerte mich an die Party.
7. Ich warte auf meine Freundin.
8. Was hältst du von dem neuen Arzt?
9. Wir sind sehr zufrieden mit unserem Volkswagen.

10. Er hat über den Krieg geschrieben.
11. Du erinnerst mich an meinen Bruder.
12. Ich warte auf mein Geld.
13. Er fragte nach meiner Schwester.
14. Was hältst du von dem neuen Film?
15. Er ist fertig mit seiner Arbeit.
16. Ich will mit dem Chef sprechen.

Express in German.

1. I'm against it.
2. He's finished with it.
3. I want to talk to him.
4. He asked about her.
5. She reminded me of it.
6. I'm waiting for her.
7. We're satisfied with it.
8. What do you think of him?

9. He wrote about it.
10. I'm waiting for it.
11. Have you spoken with her?
12. Are you finished with it?
13. She's mad at him.
14. What do you think of it?
15. You remind me of him.

VOCABULARY

die **Antwort, –en** answer
die **Arbeit, –en** work; term paper
   bitten (um + *acc.*) to ask for
      bat, gebeten
   böse (auf + *acc.*) mad, angry (at)
die **Chance, –n** chance
   denken **(an** + *acc.*) to think (of)
      dachte, gedacht
   dunkel dark
   erinnern (an + *acc.*) to remind of
   etwas anderes something else
   fertig (mit + *dat.*) to be finished (with)
   fragen (nach + *dat.*) to ask for (information)

die **Freundin, –nen** girl friend
   freundlich (zu + *dat.*) friendly (to)
   halten **(von** + *dat.*) to think of (opinion)
      (hält), hielt, gehalten
die **Hilfe** help
   krank sick
der **Krieg, –e** war
   nie never
der **Ober, –** waiter
die **Party, Parties** party
der **Plan, –̈e** plan
das **Radio** radio
   im Radio on the radio
   schon already

   schreiben **(über** + *acc.*) to write (about)
      schrieb, geschrieben
die **Seite, –n** side
   sprechen **(mit** + *dat.*) to talk to, speak (with)
      (spricht), sprach, gesprochen
das **Theater, –** theater
   vorher before
   warten (auf + *acc.*) to wait (for)
der **Weg, –e** way, road
   wohl probably
   zufrieden (mit + *dat.*) satisfied (with)

Lesson 5 Level THREE

A Verbs with Inseparable Prefixes

1 Introduction

A verb prefix is a syllable or a word that changes the meaning of the verb it is attached to. Look at the following examples:

stehen	to stand	**ver**stehen	to understand
kommen	to come	be**kommen**	to get, receive
stellen	to put	be**stellen**	to order

The addition of a prefix can alter the meaning of a verb considerably.

2 Inseparable prefixes

The prefixes you have just seen are called *inseparable prefixes* because they remain permanently attached to the basic verb. Look at the following examples:

a. A weak verb: **bezahlen** (to pay)

PRESENT	Ich bezahle die Rechnung.	(I'll pay the bill.)
PAST	Ich bezahlte die Rechnung.	(I paid the bill.)
PRES. PERF.	Ich habe die Rechnung bezahlt.	(I've paid the bill.)

b. A strong verb: **verstehen** (to understand)

PRESENT	Ich verstehe es nicht.	(I don't understand it.)
PAST	Ich verstand es nicht.	(I didn't understand it.)
PRES. PERF.	Ich habe es nicht verstanden.	(I haven't understood it.)

You should notice two things:

1. Adding an inseparable prefix to a verb doesn't affect the basic conjugation of the verb. If the basic verb is strong, the prefixed verb is also strong; if the basic verb is weak, the prefixed verb is also weak.

2. Verbs with inseparable prefixes do not take a **ge-** prefix in forming their past participles:

Ich habe die Rechnung bezahlt.
Er hat es nicht verstanden.

222

3 sein or haben

To take the auxiliary **sein,** a verb must satisfy two conditions.

1. It must be intransitive (that is, not take a direct object).
2. It must express motion or change of condition.

Otherwise the verb uses the auxiliary **haben.** (See pp. 189–90.)

The addition of a prefix gives the basic verb a new meaning that determines whether the prefixed verb takes **sein** or **haben.** For example, the verb **kommen** is *intransitive* (does not take a direct object) and expresses *motion*. **Kommen** therefore satisfies both conditions for the auxiliary verb **sein.**

On the other hand, the prefixed verb **bekommen** (to get, receive) is *transitive* (it takes a direct object). Therefore, the auxiliary verb is **haben.**

Er **ist** gestern **gekommen.**   (He came yesterday.)

but   Er **hat** das Paket gestern **bekommen.**   (He got [received] the package yesterday.)

One must decide in each individual case whether a given verb (with or without prefix) takes **sein** or **haben.**

4 Stress

Inseparable prefixes are *not* stressed: **bezáhlen, verstéhen.**

DRILLS

• Put the following sentences into the simple past tense.

1. Er verkauft sein Haus.
2. Ich verstehe ihn nicht.
3. Er vergißt* alles.
4. Sie besprechen das Problem.
   (besprechen: to discuss; **das Problem:** problem)

5. Ich bezahle die Rechnung.   (*weak verb*)
   (bezahlen: to pay)
6. Er empfiehlt† das Schnitzel.
7. Ich erkenne ihn nicht.
   (erkennen: to recognize)

• Put the following sentences into the present perfect tense.

1. Er vergißt alles.
2. Ich bezahle die Rechnung.   (*weak verb*)
3. Erkennen Sie ihn?
4. Er verkauft sein Haus.

5. Sie besprechen das Problem.
6. Ich verstehe ihn nicht.
7. Er empfiehlt das Schnitzel.

---

*Principal parts: **vergessen (vergißt), vergaß, vergessen.**

†Principal parts: **empfehlen (empfiehlt), empfahl, empfohlen.**

• Put the following sentences into the past and present perfect tenses, unless otherwise indicated.

a. 1. Er verkauft sein Haus.
    2. Ich bestelle den Wein.
       (**bestellen:** to order)
    3. Sie besprechen das Problem.
    4. Er übersetzt es für mich. (*weak verb*)
       (**übersetzen:** to translate)
    5. Ich empfehle das andere Restaurant.
    6. Erkennen Sie ihn?
       (*present perfect only*)
    7. Unterschreibt er den Brief?
       (**unterschreiben:** to sign)
    8. Ich bezahle die Rechnung.
    9. Wir behalten* unsere alte Wohnung.
       (**behalten:** to keep)
   10. Er vergißt alles.

b. 1. Ich bekomme es von einem Freund.
       (**bekommen:** to get, receive)
    2. Übersetzt er das Buch?

    3. Er empfiehlt das Schnitzel.
    4. Ich verstehe ihn nicht.
    5. Wir vergessen die Adresse.
    6. Behalten sie das Geld?
    7. Ich bespreche es mit ihm.
    8. Er verkauft seine alten Bücher.
    9. Wo bekommen Sie das?
       (*present perfect only*)
   10. Ich unterschreibe den Scheck nicht.
       (**der Scheck:** check)

c. 1. Ich erkenne ihn nicht.
    2. Verstehen Sie das?
       (*present perfect only*)
    3. Wir bestellen das Buch für Sie.

B Verbs with Separable Prefixes

1 Introduction

You have already seen examples of *separable prefixes*. They were introduced before as verbal complements:

Er kommt **mit**.	(He's coming *along*.)
Wann geht er **weg**?	(When's he going *away*?)

Separable prefixes are normally prepositions or adverbs. That is, they are complete words in their own right.

mit·kommen	(come *along*)
weg·gehen	(go *away*)

2 Word order

Look at the following examples:

a. A weak verb: **aufmachen** (to open)

PRESENT	Sie **macht** die Tür **auf**.	(She's opening the door.)
PAST	Sie **machte** die Tür **auf**.	(She opened the door.)
PRES. PERF.	Sie **hat** die Tür **aufgemacht**.	(She has opened the door.)

---

*Principal parts: **behalten (behält), behielt, behalten.**

b. A strong verb: **mitkommen** (to come along)

PRESENT	Er **kommt** nicht **mit**.	(He's not coming along.)
PAST	Er **kam** nicht **mit**.	(He didn't come along.)
PRES. PERF.	Er **ist** nicht **mitgekommen**.	(He hasn't come along.)

You should notice two things:

1. The separable prefix always comes at the end of the sentence.

2. Unlike inseparable prefixes, separable prefixes *do* use the normal **ge-** prefix in forming their past participles. Compare these two sentences:

Er ist nicht **gekommen**.   (He didn't come [hasn't come].)
Er ist nicht **mitgekommen**.   (He didn't come along [hasn't come along].)

In both examples, the past participle is formed in essentially the same way: **gekommen**, mit**gekommen**. When a separable prefix is present, it immediately precedes the basic past participle. The two parts are written as one word:

mitgekommen

3 The infinitive: **mitkommen**

Er will nicht **mitkommen**.   (He doesn't want *to come along*.)

The infinitive form of a verb with a separable prefix is written as one word: **mitkommen.**

▶ Note   When they are glossed in this book, verbs with separable prefixes will be shown with a dot (·) between the separable prefix and the basic verb (for example, **mit·kommen**) so that you can easily identify them.

4 **sein** or **haben**

As with inseparable prefixes, the meaning of the *prefixed verb* determines whether the auxiliary will be **sein** or **haben**. For example, **stehen** (to stand) is intransitive (meeting one condition for **sein**), but it clearly doesn't express motion. Therefore, it takes **haben**. But **aufstehen** (to stand up, get up) fulfills both conditions—it is intransitive *and* it expresses motion—so it takes **sein** as its auxiliary verb.

Wir **sind** sehr früh **aufgestanden**.   (We got up very early.)

5 Stress

Separable prefixes—rather than the stem vowel of the verb—receive the primary stress: **ánkommen, aúfmachen.**

6 Verbs as separable prefixes

kennen **lernen**   to meet (someone), make someone's acquaintance
stehen **bleiben**   to stop

Even verbs may function as separable prefixes. When they do, they remain *constant;* (that is, they always appear in their *infinitive* forms). In the examples below, **kennen** and **stehen** are functioning as separable prefixes; they remain unchanged.

Er **bleibt** stehen.   Ich **lerne** ihn kennen.
Er **blieb** stehen.   Ich **lernte** ihn kennen.
Er **ist**   stehen geblieben.   Ich **habe** ihn kennen gelernt.

The second verb of each compound (**bleiben** and **lernen**) is conjugated and shows tense.

DRILLS

• Put the following sentences into the simple past tense.

1. Er kommt nicht mit.
2. Ich bringe die Bücher zurück.
3. Wann gehen sie weg?
4. Ich mache das Fenster zu.
5. Sie macht die Tür auf.
6. Ich rufe ihn später an.
7. Sie kommen nach dem Abendessen vorbei.
8. Wir stehen sehr früh auf.
9. Ich lerne ihn heute kennen. (*weak verb*)

10. Er hört dir nicht zu. (*weak verb*)

(**zurück·bringen:** to bring back, take back)
(**weg·gehen:** to leave, go away)
(**zu·machen:** to close)
(**auf·machen:** to open)
(**an·rufen:*** to call up, telephone)
(**vorbei·kommen:** to come by, drop by)
(**auf·stehen:** to get up; **früh:** early)
(**kennen·lernen:** to meet, make one's acquaintance
[**lernen:** to learn])
(**zu·hören:**† to listen [**hören:** to hear])

• Put the following sentences into the present perfect tense. **(s)** indicates verbs that use **sein** as their auxiliary.

EXAMPLE   Er geht weg.
            Er **ist weggegangen.**

(**weg·gehen [s]:** to leave)

1. Sie macht die Tür auf.
2. Ich mache das Fenster zu.
3. Wann gehen sie weg?
4. Er hört dir nicht zu.
5. Er kommt nicht mit.
6. Wir stehen sehr früh auf.

(**mit·kommen [s]:** to come along)
(**auf·stehen [s]:** to get up)

---

*Principal parts: **ruft ... an, rief ... an, angerufen.**

†**zu·hören** requires a dative object:

Er hört **dir** nicht zu.   (He's not listening to you.)

7. Wann lernst du ihn kennen?
8. Ich bringe die Bücher zurück.
9. Sie kommen nach dem Abendessen vorbei.
10. Ich rufe ihn später an.

(vorbei·kommen [s]: to come by)
(an·rufen: to call up)

● Put the following sentences into the past and present perfect tenses, unless otherwise indicated.

a. 1. Er kommt nicht mit.
    2. Wann gehen sie weg?
    3. Ich mache das Radio an.
    4. Er macht das Licht aus.
    5. Sie kommen nach dem Abendessen vorbei.
    6. Wir holen ihn zu Hause ab. (*weak verb*)
    7. Ich bringe die Bücher zurück.
    8. Er kommt heute zurück.
    9. Sie hören ihm nicht zu.
   10. Er zieht seinen Mantel aus.

(an·machen: to turn on)
(aus·machen: to turn off; das Licht: light)

(ab·holen: to pick up)

(zurück·kommen [s]: to come back)

(aus·ziehen: to take off [of clothes])

b. 1. Ich ziehe meine Jacke an.
    2. Wir stehen sehr früh auf.
    3. Ich stelle die Bücher zurück.
    4. Wann lernst du ihn kennen? (*present perfect only*)
    5. Er bleibt plötzlich stehen.
    6. Ich mache das Fenster zu.
    7. Sie macht die Tür auf.
    8. Wir gehen nicht oft aus.
    9. Er nimmt seine Frau mit.
   10. Ich bringe den Wagen zurück.

(an·ziehen: to put on [clothes])

(zurück·stellen: to put back)

stehen·bleiben [s]: to stop; plötzlich: suddenly)

(aus·gehen [s]: to go out)
(mit·nehmen: to take along)

c. 1. Machst du das Licht aus? (*present perfect only*)
    2. Ich mache den Fernseher an.
    3. Wann kommt der Zug an?
    4. Wann holen Sie ihn ab?
    5. Ich rufe ihn später an.
    6. Sie geben zu viel Geld aus.
    7. Er hört dir nicht zu.
    8. Nimmst du ihn mit? (*present perfect only*)
    9. Warum gehen sie weg?
   10. Er sieht sehr müde aus.

(an·kommen [s]: to arrive)

(aus·geben: to spend [of money])

(aus·sehen: to look, appear)

d. 1. Wann kommen sie zurück?
    2. Das Licht geht aus.
    3. Sie (*she*) bleibt vor meinem Haus stehen.
    4. Rufen Sie ihn an? (*present perfect only*)
    5. Sie sieht deprimiert aus.
    6. Wann stehen sie gewöhnlich auf?
    7. Ich ziehe ein anderes Hemd an.
    8. Sie zieht ihre Schuhe aus.
    9. Er kommt heute an.

(deprimiert: depressed)
(gewöhnlich: usually)

MIXED DRILLS

1   Inseparable prefixes

● Supply the correct form of the prefixed verb. Put each sentence in the present, past, and present perfect tenses, unless otherwise indicated.

EXAMPLE   Er _____ sein Haus.   Er **verkauft** sein Haus.
            (verkaufen)   Er **verkaufte** sein Haus.
                                              Er **hat** sein Haus **verkauft**.

a.   1. Ich _____ die Rechnung.
          (bezahlen)

    2. Er _____ es für mich.
          (übersetzen)

    3. Wir _____ die Adresse.
          (vergessen)
      (past and present perfect)

    4. Ich _____ ihn nicht.
          (erkennen)

    5. _____ er den Brief?
          (Unterschreiben)

    6. Wir _____ das Buch für Sie.
          (bestellen)
      (past and present perfect)

    7. Ich _____ das andere Buch.
          (empfehlen)

    8. Er _____ seine alten Bücher.
          (verkaufen)

    9. Sie (they) _____ das Problem.
          (besprechen)
      (past and present perfect)

   10. Ich _____ es von einem Freund.
          (bekommen)

b.   1. _____ Sie das?
          (Verstehen)
      (present perfect only)

    2. Wir _____ unsere alte Wohnung.
          (behalten)
      (past and present perfect)

    3. _____ er das Buch?
          (Übersetzen)

    4. Ich _____ den Wein.
          (bestellen)

    5. Er _____ alles.
          (vergessen)

    6. _____ Sie ihn?
          (Erkennen)
      (present perfect only)

    7. Er _____ das Schnitzel.
          (empfehlen)

    8. Ich _____ den Scheck nicht.
          (unterschreiben)

    9. Er _____ sein Haus.
          (verkaufen)

   10. _____ sie (they) das Geld?
          (Behalten)
      (past and present perfect)

c.   1. Wo _____ Sie das?
          (bekommen)
      (present perfect only)

    2. Ich _____ es mit ihm.
          (besprechen)

    3. _____ Sie das?
          (Verstehen)
      (present perfect only)

2 Separable prefixes

● Supply the correct form of the prefixed verb. Put each sentence in the present, past, and present perfect tenses, unless otherwise indicated.

EXAMPLE   Er _____ nicht.   Er **kommt** nicht **mit**.
             (mitkommen)   Er **kam** nicht **mit**.
                                     Er **ist** nicht **mitgekommen**.

a.
1. Ich _____ den Fernseher.
(anmachen)
2. Er _____ das Licht.
(ausmachen)
3. Sie (they) _____ nach dem
(vorbeikommen)
Abendessen.
4. Wir _____ sehr früh.
(aufstehen)
5. Er _____ seine Frau.
(mitnehmen)
6. Sie (she) _____ deprimiert.
(aussehen)
7. Ich _____ ihn später.
(anrufen)
8. Warum _____ sie (they)?
(weggehen)
9. Ich _____ das Fenster.
(zumachen)
10. Er _____ heute.
(zurückkommen)

b.
1. Wir _____ ihn zu Hause.
(abholen)
2. Er _____ seinen Mantel.
(ausziehen)
3. Ich _____ meine Jacke.
(anziehen)
4. Sie (they) _____ ihm nicht.
(zuhören)
5. Er _____ plötzlich.
(stehenbleiben)
6. Ich _____ den Wagen.
(zurückbringen)
7. Wann _____ der Zug?
(ankommen)
8. Er _____ nicht.
(mitkommen)
9. Ich _____ die Bücher.
(zurückstellen)
10. Sie (she) _____ die Tür.
(aufmachen)

c.
1. Wann _____ sie (they)?
(aufstehen)
2. Er _____ dir nicht.
(zuhören)
3. Wann _____ du ihn?
(kennenlernen)
(present perfect only)
4. Ich _____ das Radio.
(anmachen)
5. Wann _____ Sie ihn?
(abholen)
6. Sie (she) _____ ihre Schuhe.
(ausziehen)
7. Ich _____ ein anderes Hemd.
(anziehen)
8. Sie (they) _____ zu viel Geld.
(ausgeben)
9. Er _____ heute.
(ankommen)
10. Sie (she) _____ vor
(stehenbleiben)
meinem Haus.

d.
1. Ich _____ die Bücher.
(zurückbringen)
2. Wann _____ sie (they)?
(weggehen)
3. _____ du das Licht?
(Ausmachen)
(present and present perfect)
4. Wir _____ nicht sehr oft.
(ausgehen)
5. Wann _____ sie (they)?
(zurückkommen)
6. _____ du ihn?
(Mitnehmen)
(present and present perfect)
7. Er _____ sehr müde.
(aussehen)
8. _____ Sie ihn?
(Anrufen)
(present and present perfect)
9. Das Licht _____.
(ausgehen)

3 Separable and inseparable prefixes

- Put the sentences in the present, past, and present perfect tenses, unless otherwise indicated.

a. 1. Ich _____ die Rechnung.
      (bezahlen)

   2. Er _____ nicht.
      (mitkommen)

   3. Sie (they) _____ zu viel Geld.
      (ausgeben)

   4. Wir _____ das Buch für Sie.
      (bestellen)

   5. Er _____ seine Frau.
      (mitnehmen)

   6. Wir _____ ihn zu Hause.
      (abholen)

   7. Er _____ seine Bücher.
      (verkaufen)

   8. Ich _____ das Buch.
      (zurückstellen)

   9. Das Licht _____.
      (ausgehen)

  10. Er _____ sein Haus.
      (verkaufen)

b. 1. Ich _____ das Fenster.
      (zumachen)

   2. Sie (they) _____ nach dem
      (vorbeikommen)
      Abendessen.

   3. Wir _____ unsere alte Wohnung.
      (behalten)

   4. Sie (she) _____ die Tür.
      (aufmachen)

   5. Er _____ das Schnitzel.
      (empfehlen)

   6. Wann _____ der Zug?
      (ankommen)

   7. Er _____ heute.
      (zurückkommen)

   8. Wir _____ sehr früh.
      (aufstehen)

   9. Er _____ es für mich.
      (übersetzen)

  10. Sie (they) _____ das Problem.
      (besprechen)

c. 1. Er _____ das Licht.
      (ausmachen)

   2. _____ du ihn?
      (Erkennen)
      (present and present perfect)

3. Ich _____ den Fernseher.
   (anmachen)

4. Er _____ alles.
   (vergessen)

5. Wir _____ nicht sehr oft.
   (ausgehen)

6. Sie (she) _____ deprimiert.
   (aussehen)

7. Ich _____ meine Jacke.
   (anziehen)

8. Wann _____ du gewöhnlich?
   (aufstehen)
   (present and present perfect)

9. Sie (she) _____ vor
   (stehenbleiben)
   meinem Haus.

10. _____ er den Brief?
    (Unterschreiben)

d. 1. Ich _____ ihn nicht.
      (erkennen)

   2. Er _____ seinen Mantel.
      (ausziehen)

   3. Ich _____ das andere
      (empfehlen)
      Restaurant.

   4. _____ du das?
      (Verstehen)
      (present perfect only)

   5. Wann _____ Sie ihn?
      (kennenlernen)
      (present and present perfect)

   6. Ich _____ den Wagen.
      (zurückbringen)

   7. Wir _____ die Adresse.
      (vergessen)
      (past and present perfect)

   8. Wann _____ sie (they)?
      (weggehen)

   9. _____ du das Licht?
      (Ausmachen)
      (present perfect only)

  10. Ich _____ ein anderes Hemd.
      (anziehen)

e. 1. _____ sie (they) das Geld?
      (Behalten)
      (past and present perfect)

2. Wann _____ Sie ihn?
   (abholen)

3. Ich _____ den Scheck nicht.
   (unterschreiben)

4. Er _____ sehr müde.
   (aussehen)

5. Ich _____ es mit ihm.
   (besprechen)

6. Er _____ plötzlich.
   (stehenbleiben)

7. Ich _____ es von einem Freund.
   (bekommen)

8. _____ du ihn?
   (Mitnehmen)
   (present and present perfect)

9. Sie (*she*) _____ ihre Schuhe.
   (ausziehen)

10. Ich _____ den Wein.
    (bestellen)

f. 1. Wann _____ sie (*they*)?
       (zurückkommen)

    2. Er _____ dir nicht.
       (zuhören)

    3. Ich _____ ihn später.
       (anrufen)

    4. _____ er das Buch?
       (Übersetzen)

    5. Ich _____ das Radio.
       (anmachen)

6. _____ du ihn?
   (Anrufen)
   (present perfect only)

7. Warum _____ sie (*they*)?
   (weggehen)

8. Ich _____ die Bücher.
   (zurückbringen)

9. Er _____ heute.
   (ankommen)

10. Wo _____ du das?
    (bekommen)
    (present perfect only)

g. 1. Ich _____ ihn nicht.
       (verstehen)

    2. Sie (*they*) _____ ihm nicht.
       (zuhören)

4   Express in German

a. 1. I closed the window. *(past and present perfect)*
    2. When do you usually get up?
    3. I paid the bill. *(past and present perfect)*
    4. She opened the door. *(past and present perfect)*
    5. He's not coming along.
    6. I didn't recognize him. *(past and present perfect)*
    7. The light went out. *(past and present perfect)*
    8. He's translating it for me.
    9. I took the books back. *(past and present perfect)*
    10. Did you turn out the light? *(present perfect only)*

b. 1. I'll discuss it with him.
    2. He arrived today. *(past and present perfect)*
    3. They came by after dinner. *(past and present perfect)*
    4. We forgot the address. *(past and present perfect)*
    5. He's not listening to you.

6. He took his wife along. (*past and present perfect*)
7. I didn't understand him. (*past and present perfect*)
8. When are they coming back?
9. He took off his coat. (*past and present perfect*)
10. They spent too much money. (*past and present perfect*)

c. 1. We'll order the book for you.
2. I put on my sportscoat. (*past and present perfect*)
3. He stopped suddenly. (*past and present perfect*)
4. When did they leave? (*present perfect only*)
5. We're keeping our old apartment.
6. He sold his house. (*past and present perfect*)
7. I put the book back. (*past and present perfect*)
8. He looks very tired.
9. I got it from a friend. (*past and present perfect*)
10. When did you meet him? (*present perfect only*)

d. 1. We picked him up at home. (*past and present perfect*)
2. I turned on the radio. (*past and present perfect*)
3. We don't go out very often.
4. I ordered the wine. (*past and present perfect*)
5. He recommended the "Schnitzel." (*past and present perfect*)
6. Why did they leave? (*past and present perfect*)
7. He's coming back today.
8. I called him up later. (*past and present perfect*)
9. Did he sign the letter? (*past and present perfect*)
10. They didn't listen to him. (*past and present perfect*)

e. 1. She looked depressed. (*past and present perfect*)
2. When are you going to pick him up?
3. They discussed the problem. (*past and present perfect*)
4. She took off her shoes. (*past and present perfect*)
5. When does the train arrive?
6. He sold his old books. (*past and present perfect*)
7. She stopped in front of my house. (*past and present perfect*)
8. I didn't sign the check. (*past and present perfect*)
9. I'll take the car back.
10. We got up very early. (*past and present perfect*)

f. 1. He turned off the light. (*past and present perfect*)
2. I recommend the other restaurant.
3. Did you call him up? (*present perfect only*)
4. Did he translate the book? (*past and present perfect*)
5. I turned on the TV. (*past and present perfect*)
6. Where did you get that? (*present perfect only*)
7. I'll put on another shirt.
8. Did they keep the money? (*past and present perfect*)
9. Do you recognize him?
10. He forgot everything. (*past and present perfect*)

g. 1. Did you take him along? (*present perfect only*)
2. Did you understand that? (*present perfect only*)

VOCABULARY

ab·holen to pick up
an·kommen to arrive
  kam . . . an,
  ist angekommen
an·machen to turn on
an·rufen to call up,
  telephone
  rief . . . an, angerufen
an·ziehen to put on (clothes)
  zog . . . an, angezogen
auf·machen to open
auf·stehen to get up
  stand . . . auf,
  ist aufgestanden
aus·geben to spend
  (of money)
  (gibt . . . aus), gab . . . aus,
  ausgegeben
aus·gehen to go out
  ging . . . aus,
  ist ausgegangen
aus·machen to turn off
aus·sehen to look, appear
  (sieht . . . aus), sah . . . aus,
  ausgesehen
aus·ziehen to take off
  (clothes)
  zog . . . aus, ausgezogen
behalten to keep
  (behält), behielt, behalten
bekommen to get, receive
  bekam, bekommen
besprechen to discuss
  (bespricht), besprach,
  besprochen

bestellen to order
bezahlen to pay
deprimiert depressed
empfehlen to
  recommend
  (empfiehlt), empfahl,
  empfohlen
erkennen to recognize
  erkannte, erkannt
früh early
gewöhnlich usually
hören to hear
kennen·lernen to meet,
  make someone's
  acquaintance
lernen to learn
das Licht, -er light
mit·kommen to come
  along
  kam . . . mit, ist
  mitgekommen
mit·nehmen to take
  along
  (nimmt . . . mit), nahm
  . . . mit, mitgenommen
plötzlich suddenly
das Problem problem
der Scheck, -s check
stehen·bleiben to stop
  blieb . . . stehen,
  ist stehengeblieben
übersetzen to translate

unterschreiben to sign
  unterschrieb,
  unterschrieben
vergessen to forget
  (vergißt), vergaß,
  vergessen
verstehen to understand
  verstand, verstanden
vorbei·kommen to come
  by, drop in
  kam . . . vorbei,
  ist vorbeigekommen
weg·gehen to leave, go
  away
  ging . . . weg, ist
  weggegangen
zu·hören to listen
zu·machen to close
zurück·bringen to bring
  back, take back
  brachte . . . zurück,
  zurückgebracht
zurück·kommen to
  come back
  kam . . . zurück,
  ist zurückgekommen
zurück·stellen to put back

Reading V

Deutsche Hotels

Er saß da. Er saß einfach° da neben seinem Koffer und wußte° nicht wohin.° Niemand° sprach mit ihm, niemand kannte ihn, die Leute gingen einfach an ihm vorbei.° Auch° hatte er keine Freunde in dieser Stadt. Gestern war er noch in Ohio gewesen

einfach: simply
wußte: knew, *past tense of* **wissen**
  wohin: (*here*) where to go   **niemand:** no one

vorbei · gehen an(+*dat.*): to walk past
  auch: also, besides that

und jetzt saß er in einem großen, lauten,° deutschen Bahnhof. Er hatte wenig° geschlafen und sah betäubt° und ein wenig deprimiert aus. Er dachte eigentlich° an nichts, aber Durst° hatte er, und er wußte schon, daß jeder deutsche Bahnhof ein Restaurant hat. Er stand langsam auf und trug seinen Koffer ins Bahnhofsrestaurant. Da fand er einen freien° Tisch und bestellte ein großes Bier. Nach einer Weile° brachte der Kellner das Bier, und der junge Mann trank ein wenig davon.° Jetzt sah die Welt° schon° etwas° besser° aus. Mindestens° war sein Durst weg;° auch war er weniger betäubt als vorher.° Er sah in sein Bierglas, und trank noch einmal° daraus.° Dann° sah er seinen Tisch eine Weile an,° dann den Tisch nebenan,° und endlich° das ganze Bahnhofsrestaurant. Langsam, sehr langsam, dachte er an etwas ganz anderes. Sein erstes Gefühl° war Angst°—Panik.° Etwas stieg in seinem Kopf° hinauf:° ein Gedanke!° Dieser Gedanke war die ganze Zeit° mit ihm gewesen, nur hatte er es nicht gewußt.° Man muß irgendwo° hingehen. Man muß irgendwo schlafen. Man muß ein Zimmer

laut: loud, noisy

wenig: little

betäubt: benumbed

eigentlich: actually   **der Durst**: thirst

frei: (*here*) empty

die Weile: while

davon: of it
die Welt: world   **schon**: already   **etwas**: a little, somewhat   **besser**: better   **mindestens**: at least
weg: (*here*) gone

vorher: before

noch einmal: again   **daraus**: out of it   **dann**: then
an·sehen: to look at   **nebenan**: next to it
endlich: finally

das Gefühl, –e: feeling   **die Angst, ⸚e**: fear
die Panik: panic
der Kopf, ⸚e: head   **hinauf·steigen**: (*here*) to rise   **der Gedanke, –n**: thought
die Zeit, -en: time

gewußt: *past participle of* **wissen**
irgendwo: somewhere

haben! Wie bekommt man—in einer fremden° Stadt, in einem fremden Land°—ein Hotelzimmer? Wo geht man hin? Wen° fragt man? Es kann ein furchtbares° Gefühl sein, wenn man auf° diese Fragen keine Antworten° hat.

Fragen I, p. 241

fremd: (*here*) strange, foreign

das Land, ⸚er: (*here*) country

wen: who (*acc. of* **wer**)

furchtbar: frightful, frightening   **auf**: (*here*) to

die Antwort, –en: answer

WIE BEKOMMT MAN EIN HOTELZIMMER?

(*Es gibt ein paar° Möglichkeiten.° Einmal,° Sie gehen direkt° zu einem Hotel und fragen am Empfang;° dann° sieht Ihr Gespräch° etwa so° aus:*)

ein paar: a couple of   **die Möglichkeit, –en**: possibility   **einmal**: (*here*) first of all
direkt: directly
am Empfang: at the reception desk   **dann**: then   **das Gespräch, –e**: conversation   **etwa so**: something like this

SIE:

Guten Tag.

EMPFANG:°

Guten Tag. Bitte sehr?°

der Empfang: (*here*) desk clerk

Bitte sehr?: (*here*) What would you like?

SIE:

Haben Sie ein Zimmer frei?°

frei·haben: to have available

EMPFANG:

Brauchen Sie ein Einzelzimmer° oder ein Doppelzimmer?°

das Einzelzimmer, –: single room

das Doppelzimmer, –: double room

SIE:

Ein Einzelzimmer, bitte.

EMPFANG:

Und für wie lange° soll das sein?

wie lange: how long

236

SIE:

Für zwei Nächte, also bis Montag.°

EMPFANG:

Augenblick° bitte, ich muß nachsehen.°

* * *

Ja, wir haben ein Einzelzimmer frei, ohne Bad°
allerdings;° 35 Mark mit Frühstück.°

SIE:

Gut, das ist mir recht.°

EMPFANG:

Also,° Sie haben Zimmer 40, das ist im zweiten°
Stock.° Hier ist das Anmeldeformular,° bitte.

(*Die Dame am Empfang gibt Ihnen ein Anmeldeformular, und Sie füllen es aus.° Sie schreiben Ihren
Namen,° Geburtstag,° Geburtsort,° Ihre Nationa-
lität° und Paßnummer° und dann geben Sie der
Dame das ausgefüllte° Formular zurück.*)

SIE:

Bitte sehr, und wann kann ich frühstücken?°

EMPFANG:

Unser Frühstückszimmer° ist von 7 bis 10 geöffnet.°
Es ist hier im Erdgeschoß,° gleich° da drüben. Hier
ist Ihr Schlüssel.° Haben Sie viel Gepäck?°

SIE:

Nein danke, nur die zwei Koffer° hier und die° kann
ich selber° hochtragen.°

EMPFANG:

Also, der Aufzug° ist da links° um die Ecke. Tele-
fon° haben Sie im Zimmer; Sie können anrufen,
wenn Sie etwas wollen.

SIE:

Ist recht, danke schön.

(*Eine andere Möglichkeit ist, Sie gehen zum Zimmernachweis.°*)

---

der Montag: Monday

der Augenblick, -e: moment
　　nach · sehen: to take a look, check

das Bad, ⁻er: bath
allerdings: however, but
　　das Frühstück: breakfast

einem recht sein: to be all right (with
　　someone)

also: (*here*) O.K.　zweit-: second
der Stock: floor
　　das Anmeldeformular, -e: registration form

aus · füllen: to fill out
der Name, -n, -n: name (*weak noun*)
　　der Geburtstag, -e: birthday
　　der Geburtsort, -e: birthplace
die Nationalität, -en: nationality
　　die Paßnummer, -n: passport number
ausgefüllt: filled out, completed

frühstücken: to have breakfast

das Frühstückszimmer, -: breakfast room
　　(normally a separate room for breakfast only)
　　geöffnet: open
das Erdgeschoß: main floor, (*here*) lobby
　　gleich: right, immediately
der Schlüssel, -: key　das Gepäck: luggage

der Koffer, -: suitcase　die: (*here*) them (**sie**)

selber: myself　hoch · tragen: to carry up

der Aufzug, ⁻e: elevator　links: to the left
das Telefon, -e: telephone

der Zimmernachweis, -e: list of available
　　hotel rooms

ercise,
p. 241

ZIMMERNACHWEIS

In den meisten Städten gibt es einen Zimmernachweis (Zimmervermittlung°). Den findet man meistens beim° Hauptbahnhof,° oder sogar° im Hauptbahnhof selber.° Der Zimmernachweis kann einfach
eine Leuchttafel° sein. An dieser Tafel finden Sie die
Namen von den meisten Hotels in der Stadt. Ein
grünes° Licht neben dem Namen zeigt Ihnen, daß
Zimmer frei sind. Ein rotes° Licht bedeutet,° daß das
Hotel keine freien Zimmer hat. In den Großstädten°
steht neben den Namen von den Hotels auch die
Zahl° von den freien Einzelzimmern und Doppel-
zimmern. Manchmal° ist auch ein Stadtplan°
dabei.° Dort können Sie sehen, wo das Hotel liegt:°
wie weit° vom Hauptbahnhof, vom Stadtzentrum,°
und so weiter.° Wenn Sie sicher° sein wollen,
können Sie das Hotel anrufen und nach dem Zim-
merpreis° fragen:

die Zimmervermittlung, –en: room agency
 (explained in text)
bei: *(here)* near, in the vicinity of
 der Hauptbahnhof, ⁼e: main railroad
 station **sogar:** even
selber: itself

die Leuchttafel, –n: illuminated sign

grün: green

rot: red **bedeuten:** to mean

die Großstadt, ⁼e: large city

die Zahl, -en: number

manchmal: sometimes
 der Stadtplan, ⁼e: map of the city
dabei: nearby **liegen:** to be located
wie weit: how far
 das Stadtzentrum: center of town
und so weiter: and so on
 sicher: sure, certain

der Zimmerpreis, –e: price of the room

**Fragen II,
pp. 241–42**

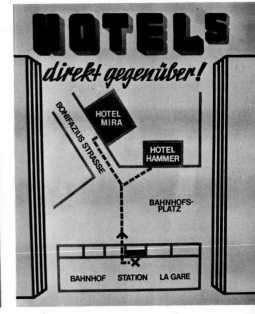

WENN MAN IM VORAUS TELEFONIERT

EMPFANG:

Hotel Hammer. Bitte schön?°

SIE:

Ich sehe am Zimmernachweis, Sie haben noch° Zimmer frei. Was kostet ein Einzelzimmer?

EMPFANG:

Ohne Bad 35 Mark, mit Bad 45 Mark.

SIE:

Geben Sie mir ein Zimmer ohne Bad. Ich bin in 20 Minuten° dort. Können Sie mir das Zimmer so lange° freihalten?°

EMPFANG:

Sicher.° Auf welchen Namen,° bitte?

SIE:

Lehmann, Klaus Lehmann.

EMPFANG:

Gut. Geht in Ordnung,° Herr Lehmann. Auf Wiederhören.

SIE:

Wiederhören.

Ein Zimmernachweis kann auch ein Büro sein. Dann nennt° man ihn auch eine „Zimmervermittlung". Dieses Büro hat eine Liste° von den verschiedenen° Hotels mit freien Zimmern. Hier können Sie auch nach den Hotels fragen, wo sie liegen, was sie kosten, usw.°

In so einer° Zimmervermittlung muß man ein paar Mark bezahlen. Der Mann hinter der Theke° ruft an und reserviert° ein Zimmer für Sie. Sie bekommen eine Quittung° und diese Quittung zeigen Sie dem Empfang im Hotel.

Bitte schön?: May I help you?

noch: still

die Minute, —n: minute
so lange: that long   **frei·halten**: to hold

sicher: certainly
Auf welchen Namen?: In what name?

Geht in Ordnung: That's fine.

nennen: to call

die Liste, -n: list   **verschieden**: different

usw. = und so weiter

so ein: such a

die Theke, —n: counter

reservieren: to reserve

die Quittung, —en: receipt

ercise, p. 242

gen III, p. 242

ABREISE° VOM HOTEL

Am Nachmittag° vor Ihrer Abreise sagen Sie dem Empfang, daß Sie morgen abreisen° und nach dem Frühstück Ihre Rechnung bezahlen wollen. Am nächsten Morgen ist alles fertig.° Oder Sie können die Rechnung im voraus bezahlen, wenn Sie wollen, etwa° am Abend vorher°:

SIE:

Ich reise morgen ab. Können Sie bitte meine Rechnung fertigmachen?°

EMPFANG:

Gern.° Wann wollen Sie sie haben?

SIE:

Ich möchte° heute bezahlen. Kann ich meine Rechnung in einer Stunde° haben?

EMPFANG:

Sicher, mein Herr. Zimmer 40, ja?

SIE:

Ja. Ich komme dann später° herunter.°

die Abreise, –n: departure

der Nachmittag, -e: afternoon
ab·reisen: to depart

fertig: ready

etwa: (here) let's say, perhaps
   am Abend vorher: the evening before

fertig·machen: to get ready

gern: gladly

ich möchte: I would like to
die Stunde, –n: hour

später: later   herunter: down

Exercise, p. 242

FRAGEN I

1. Warum sah der junge Mann deprimiert aus?
(Er / wissen / nicht / wohin)
(Niemand / sprechen / mit / [him])
(Er / haben / kein / Freunde / in / dies– / Stadt)
(Auch / er / schlafen / wenig) [past perf.]

2. Was machte er dann endlich?
(Er / auf·stehen // und / gehen / in / Bahnhofsrestaurant)
(Da / er / finden / frei / Tisch // und / bestellen / Bier)

3. Wie wurde sein Horizont weiter?   (der Horizont: horizon   weiter: broader)
(Zuerst / er / sehen / nur / in / Bierglas)
(Dann / er / an·sehen / Tisch)
(Und / endlich / er / an·sehen / ganz / Restaurant)

4. Welche Gedanken hat er die ganze Zeit gehabt?
(Man / müssen / hin·gehen / irgendwo)
(Man / müssen / schlafen / irgendwo)

5. Was muß man finden?
(Man / müssen / finden / Hotelzimmer)

WIE BEKOMMT MAN EIN HOTELZIMMER?

SIE: (Gut / Tag)
EMPFANG: Guten Tag. Bitte sehr?
SIE: (frei·haben / Sie / Zimmer / ?)
EMPFANG: Brauchen Sie ein Einzelzimmer oder ein Doppelzimmer?
SIE: (Einzelzimmer)
EMPFANG: Und für wie lange soll das sein?
SIE: (2 / Nächte // also / Montag)
EMPFANG: Augenblick bitte, ich muß nachsehen. Ja, wir haben ein Einzelzimmer frei, ohne Bad allerdings, 35 Mark mit Frühstück.
SIE: (Das / recht·sein / [to me])
EMPFANG: Also, Sie haben Zimmer 40, das ist im zweiten Stock. Hier ist das Anmeldeformular, bitte.

* * *

SIE: (Wann / ich / können / frühstücken / ?)
EMPFANG: Unser Frühstückszimmer ist von 7 bis 10 geöffnet. Es ist hier im Erdgeschoß, gleich da drüben. Hier ist Ihr Schlüssel. Haben Sie viel Gepäck?
SIE: (Nein // nur / 2 Koffer // und / ich / können / hoch·tragen / die / selber)
EMPFANG: Der Aufzug ist da links um die Ecke. Telefon haben Sie im Zimmer; Sie können anrufen, wenn Sie etwas wollen.
SIE: (recht·sein // danke)

FRAGEN II

1. Wo findet man meistens einen Zimmernachweis?
(Man / finden / Zimmernachweis / bei / Bahnhof / oder / in / Bahnhof selber)

2. Was findet man an der Leuchttafel?
(Man / finden / Namen / von / meist- / Hotels / in / Stadt)

3. Was bedeutet ein grünes Licht an der Leuchttafel?
   (grün / Licht / bedeuten // daß / Zimmer / sein / frei)

4. Ein rotes Licht?
   (rot / Licht / bedeuten // daß / kein / Zimmer / sein / frei)

5. Was kann man auf dem Stadtplan sehen?
   (Man / können / sehen // wo / Hotels / liegen)

6. Was können Sie machen, wenn Sie sicher sein wollen?
   (Sie / können / an·rufen / Hotel)
   (Und / Sie / können / fragen / nach / Zimmerpreis)

WENN MAN IM VORAUS TELEFONIERT

EMPFANG: Hotel Hammer. Bitte schön?
SIE: (Ich / sehen / an / Zimmernachweis // Sie / frei·haben / Zimmer)
(Was / kosten / Einzelzimmer / ?)
EMPFANG: Ohne Bad 35 Mark, mit Bad 45 Mark.
SIE: (Geben / Sie / [to me] / Zimmer / ohne . . .)
EMPFANG: Sicher. Auf welchen Namen bitte?
SIE: (Student gives last name.)
EMPFANG: Wie schreibt man das, bitte?
SIE: (Student spells last name.)
EMPFANG: Gut. Geht in Ordnung, (insert student's name). Auf Wiederhören.
SIE: Wiederhören.

FRAGEN III

1. Wie nennt man einen Zimmernachweis oft, wenn er ein Büro ist?
   (Man / nennen / [it] / Zimmervermittlung)

2. Was findet man in einer Zimmervermittlung?
   (Da / man / finden / Liste / von / Hotels / mit / frei / Zimmer)

3. Was macht die Zimmervermittlung für Sie?
   (Zimmervermittlung / an·rufen // und / reservieren / Zimmer)

4. Die Zimmervermittlung gibt Ihnen eine Quittung. Was machen Sie damit?
   (Sie / zeigen / [it] / Empfang / in / Hotel)

ABREISE VOM HOTEL

SIE: (Ich / ab·reisen / morgen)
(Können / Sie / fertig·machen / mein / Rechnung / ?)
EMPFANG: Gern. Wann wollen Sie sie haben?
SIE: (Ich / möchten / bezahlen / heute)
(Können / ich / haben / mein / Rechnung / in / ein / Stunde / ?)
EMPFANG: Sicher, (insert student's name). Zimmer 40, ja?
SIE: (Ja // ich / herunter·kommen / dann / später)

Lesson 6   Level ONE

A Adjectives and Adverbs

The same German adjective can function in three different ways. Let's take the adjective **schnell** as an example.

1. *Attributive adjective:* It stands directly in front of the noun it modifies and takes the usual adjective endings:

   > Das ist ein **schneller** Wagen.   (That's a fast car.)

2. *Predicate adjective:* It is separated from the noun it modifies and takes no endings:

   > Dieser Wagen ist **schnell.**   (This car is fast.)

3. *Adverb:* It modifies a verb:

   > Peter fährt **schnell.**   (Peter drives fast.)

   Here **schnell** refers to *how* Peter *drives,* not to *what* Peter *is.* In this case, the distinction between a predicate adjective and adverb is one of function, not of form.

B Comparison of Predicate Adjectives and Adverbs

German adverbs and predicate adjectives have three basic forms: a positive, a comparative, and a superlative.

POSITIVE	schnell	fast
COMPARATIVE	schneller	faster
SUPERLATIVE	schnellst-	fastest

1. The *positive* is the form you find in dictionaries or word lists: it is the basic form of the adjective:

   > schnell

2. The *comparative* is formed by adding the suffix -er to the positive form:

schneller

3. The *superlative stem* is formed by adding the suffix -st to the positive form:

schnellst-

But the result is a stem that *cannot stand by itself.* When used as a *predicate adjective* or an *adverb,* the superlative stem always occurs in the following matrix:

am ————en

am schnellsten

Summary

When **schnell** is used as a *predicate adjective* or an *adverb,* it occurs in these three forms:

POSITIVE	schnell
COMPARATIVE	schneller
SUPERLATIVE	**am** schnellst**en**

C Variations in the Formation of the Comparative and Superlative

1. If the positive form ends in **-d, -t,** or an "s" sound, the superlative is formed by adding -est (rather than just **-st**):

interessant	heiß (hot)	hübsch
interessanter	heißer	hübscher
am interessantesten	am heißesten	am hübschesten

2. If the positive form ends in **-e,** the comparative is formed by adding **-r** (rather than **-er**):

leise

leiser

am leisesten

3. If the positive form ends in **-el,** the e is dropped in forming the comparative

dunkel (dark)

dunkler (*not* dunkeler)

am dunkelsten

4. If the positive form ends in **-euer,** the second **e** is dropped in forming the comparative:

teuer

teurer (*not* teuerer)

am teuersten

This is analogous to the forms of **euer** (**euer** but **eure**).

DRILLS

1   Comparative

● Put the adjectives and adverbs into the comparative.

1. Sein Zimmer ist **klein.**
2. Er ist **dick** geworden.
3. Dieses Brot ist **frisch.**
4. Ich finde das **interessant.**
5. Sprechen Sie **laut,** bitte!
6. Es ist **dunkel** geworden.   (**dunkel:** dark)
7. Fahren Sie **langsam!**
8. Er war **freundlich** heute.
9. Sie ist **hübsch** geworden.
10. Diese Anzüge sind **billig.**   (**billig:** cheap)
11. Fahr **schnell,** Hans!
12. Das finde ich **leicht.**
13. Seine erste Frau war **interessant.**
14. Das Essen hier ist **schlecht** geworden.
                         (**das Essen:** food)
15. Kannst du nicht **leise** spielen?
16. Es wird **heiß.**
17. Benzin ist **teuer** geworden.
                     (**das Benzin:** gasoline)
18. Das ist **einfach.**
19. Sprechen Sie **leise!**
20. Dieser Wagen kostet **wenig.**

● Supply the appropriate comparative form.

1. Fahren Sie _____ !
        (slower)
2. Das ist _____ .
        (simpler)
3. Sie ist _____ geworden.
        (prettier)
4. Ich finde das _____ .
        (more interesting)
5. Sprechen Sie _____ , bitte!
        (louder)
6. Das Essen hier ist _____
  geworden.   (worse)
7. Sein Zimmer ist _____ .
        (smaller)
8. Fahr _____ , Hans!
        (faster)
9. Er ist _____ geworden.
        (fatter)
10. Dieser Wagen kostet _____ .
        (less)
  (*comparative form of* **wenig**)

11. Das finde ich _____ .
        (easier)
12. Benzin ist _____ geworden.
        (more expensive)
13. Er war _____ heute.
        (friendlier)
14. Sprechen Sie _____ !
        (more softly)
15. Dieses Brot ist _____ .
        (fresher)
16. Seine erste Frau war _____ .
        (more interesting)
17. Es wird _____ .
        (hotter)
18. Diese Anzüge sind _____ .
        (cheaper)
19. Es ist _____ geworden.
        (darker)
20. Kannst du nicht _____ spielen?
        (more softly)

2   Superlative

The superlative stem is formed by adding **-st** or **-est** to the positive form:

              POSITIVE   klein
              SUPERLATIVE STEM   **kleinst-**

When a superlative is used as a *predicate adjective* or an *adverb,* it takes an **-en** ending and is preceded by the word **am:**

          am kleinsten

• In this exercise, the superlative stems are given. Complete the following sentences by supplying the missing elements of the superlative expression.

EXAMPLE   Sein Zimmer ist ___ kleinst___.
                Sein Zimmer ist **am** kleinst**en**.

1. Dieser Wagen ist ___ schnellst___.
2. Das ist ___ einfachst___.
3. Welcher Fernseher kostet ___ wenigst___?
4. Dieses Kleid ist ___ hübschest___.
5. Spanisch ist ___ leichtest___.

6. Das Hilton ist ___ teuerst___.
7. Diese Mäntel sind ___ billigst___.
8. Hier ist es ___ dunkelst___.
9. Er war ___ schlechtest___.
10. Das finde ich ___ leichtest___.

• Put the adjectives and adverbs into the superlative.

EXAMPLE   Sein Zimmer ist **klein**.
                Sein Zimmer ist **am kleinsten**.

1. Dieses Kleid ist **hübsch.**
2. Das ist **einfach.**
3. Das finde ich **leicht.**
4. Dieser Wagen ist **schnell.**
5. Das Hilton ist **teuer.**

6. Diese Mäntel sind **billig.**
7. Er war **schlecht.**
8. Dieser Fernseher kostet **wenig.**
9. Hier ist es **dunkel.**
10. Spanisch ist **leicht.**

• Supply the appropriate superlative form.

1. Welcher Fernseher kostet _____?
                      (the least)
2. Das Hilton ist _____.
               (the most expensive)
3. Das finde ich _____.
               (easiest)
4. Dieser Wagen ist _____.
               (fastest)
5. Spanisch ist _____.
               (easiest)

6. Er war _____.
               (the worst)
7. Dieses Kleid ist _____.
               (prettiest)
8. Das ist _____.
               (simplest)
9. Hier ist es _____.
               (darkest)
10. Diese Mäntel sind _____.
               (cheapest)

3   Mixed drills

• Supply the appropriate comparative or superlative form.

a.   1. Das ist _____.
               (simpler)
     2. Es wird _____.
               (hotter)
     3. Dieses Kleid ist _____.
               (prettiest)
     4. Er ist _____ geworden.
               (fatter)
     5. Seine erste Frau war _____.
               (more interesting)
     6. Diese Mäntel sind _____.
               (cheapest)

7. Er war _____ heute.
               (more friendly)
8. Es ist _____ geworden.
               (darker)
9. Das Hilton ist _____.
               (the most expensive)
10. Dieser Wagen kostet _____.
               (less)

b.   1. Fahr _____, Hans!
               (faster)

2. Kannst du nicht _____ spielen?
(more softly)

3. Sie ist _____ geworden.
(prettier)

4. Diese Anzüge sind _____.
(cheaper)

5. Das Essen hier ist _____ geworden.
(worse)

6. Das finde ich _____.
(easiest)

7. Welcher Fernseher kostet _____?
(the least)

8. Sein Zimmer ist _____.
(smaller)

9. Sprechen Sie _____!
(more softly)

10. Ich finde das _____.
(more interesting)

c. 1. Dieser Wagen ist _____.
(fastest)

2. Sprechen Sie _____, bitte!
(louder)

3. Spanisch ist _____.
(easiest)

4. Benzin ist _____ geworden.
(more expensive)

5. Fahren Sie _____!
(slower)

6. Er war _____.
(the worst)

7. Dieses Brot ist _____.
(fresher)

8. Hier ist es _____.
(darkest)

9. Das finde ich _____.
(easier)

10. Das ist _____.
(simplest)

● Express in German.

a. 1. Drive slower.
   2. It's getting hotter.
   3. These coats are cheapest.
   4. He's gotten fatter.
   5. She was friendlier today.
   6. Which TV costs the least?
   7. That's simpler.
   8. His first wife was more interesting.
   9. This bread is freshest.
   10. His room is smaller.

b. 1. Can't you play more softly?
   2. The Hilton is the most expensive.
   3. The food here has gotten worse.
   4. This dress is prettiest.

   5. It's gotten darker.
   6. Drive faster, Hans.
   7. Spanish is the easiest.
   8. Speak louder, please.
   9. This car costs less.
   10. He was the worst.

c. 1. Gas has gotten more expensive.
   2. I find that more interesting.
   3. That's simplest.
   4. These suits are cheaper.
   5. Speak more softly.
   6. This car is fastest.
   7. She's gotten prettier.
   8. I find that easier.

D Umlaut

Most one-syllable adjectives with the stem vowels **a** and **u** have an umlaut in their comparative and superlative forms.

alt	(old)	jung	(young)
älter	(older)	jünger	(younger)
am ältesten	(oldest)	am jüngsten	(youngest)

Here is a list of common adjectives that have an umlaut in the comparative and superlative:

alt	kalt	lang*	stark
jung	warm	kurz	schwach

_____
*The adverb form is **lange**.

1 Comparative

● First read each sentence as it is printed with the adjective or adverb in the positive form. Then reread each sentence, putting the adjective or adverb into the comparative.

1. Es ist **kalt** geworden.
2. Es ist **warm** heute.
3. Der Patient ist **schwach** geworden.
4. Dieser Schnaps ist **stark.**
5. Er sah **alt** aus.
6. Ihre Schwester ist **jung.**
7. Sein neues Buch ist **lang.**
8. Die Schlange ist **kurz** geworden.
9. Der andere Mantel war **warm.**
10. Dieser Motor ist **stark.**

(**kalt:** cold)
(**warm:** warm)
(**der Patient:** patient; **schwach:** weak)
(**der Schnaps:** schnapps; **stark:** strong)

(**jung:** young)
(**lang:** long)
(**die Schlange,** *here:* line)

(**der Motor:** motor; **stark:** strong, powerful)

2 Superlative

● In this exercise the superlative stems are given. Complete the sentences by supplying the missing elements.

EXAMPLE　　Georg ist ___ jüngst ___ .
　　　　　　Georg ist am jüngsten .

1. Dieser Schnaps ist ___ stärkst ___ .
2. Er ist ___ schwächst ___ .
3. Mein Lodenmantel ist ___ wärmst ___ .
4. Im Januar ist es ___ kältest ___ .
5. Dieser Rock ist ___ kürzest ___ .
6. Wir sind ___ längst ___ hier gewesen.
7. Georg ist ___ jüngst ___ . Aber er sieht ___ ältest ___ aus.

(**der Lodenmantel:** loden coat)
(**im Januar:** in January)
(**der Rock:** skirt)

● Put the adjectives and adverbs into the superlative.

1. Wir sind **lange** hier gewesen.
2. Im Januar ist es **kalt.**
3. Dieser Schnaps ist **stark.**
4. Mein Lodenmantel ist **warm.**
5. Georg ist **jung.** Aber er sieht **alt** aus.

6. Dieser Rock ist **kurz.**
7. Er ist **schwach.**

3 Mixed drills

● Put the adjectives and adverbs into the comparative and superlative.

1. Dieser Rock ist **kurz.**
2. Mein Lodenmantel ist **warm.**
3. Im Januar ist es **kalt.**
4. Wir sind **lange** hier gewesen.
5. Dieser Schnaps ist **stark.**

6. Er ist **jung.**
7. Er ist **schwach.**

- Supply the appropriate comparative or superlative forms.

1. Er sah _____ aus.
   (older)
2. Die Schlange ist _____ geworden.
   (shorter)
3. Dieser Schnaps ist _____.
   (strongest)
4. Der Patient ist _____ geworden.
   (weaker)
5. Georg ist _____. Aber
   (the youngest)
   er sieht _____ aus.
   (the oldest)
6. Sein neues Buch ist _____.
   (longer)
7. Mein Lodenmantel ist _____.
   (the warmest)
8. Es ist _____ geworden.
   (colder)

9. Wir sind _____ hier gewesen.
   (the longest)
10. Es ist _____ heute.
    (warmer)
11. Im Januar ist es _____.
    (coldest)
12. Dieser Schnaps ist _____.
    (stronger)
13. Er ist _____.
    (the weakest)
14. Der andere Mantel war _____.
    (warmer)
15. Ihre Schwester ist _____.
    (younger)
16. Dieser Rock ist _____.
    (shortest)
17. Dieser Motor ist _____.
    (stronger)

- Express in German.

1. It's gotten colder.
2. The other coat was warmer.
3. This schnapps is strongest.
4. His new book is longer.
5. It's coldest in January.
   (Im Januar . . . .)
6. This motor is stronger.
7. Georg is the youngest.
   But he looks the oldest.
8. The patient's gotten weaker.

9. We've been here the longest.
10. It's warmer today.
11. Her sister's younger.
12. This skirt is the shortest.
13. He looked older.
14. He's the weakest.
15. This schnapps is stronger.
16. My loden coat is the warmest.
17. The line has gotten shorter.

E Irregular Forms

Positive		Comparative	Superlative
groß	(big, large)	größer	am größten
gut	(good)	besser	am besten
hoch	(high, tall)	höher	am höchsten
viel	(much)	mehr	am meisten
gern	(like to)	lieber	am liebsten

▶ Note   **Gut** means both "good" and "well."

Dieser Fisch ist gut.   (This fish is *good*.)
Das macht er sehr gut.   (He does that very *well*.)

The adverb **gern** adds the meaning of "to like to" to the verb:

Ich spiele Tennis.   (I play tennis.)
Ich spiele gern Tennis.   (I *like to* play tennis.)

Lieber adds the meaning of "to prefer" or "I'd rather" to the verb:

Ich spiele Golf. (I play golf.)
Ich spiele **lieber** Golf. (I *prefer* to play golf; *I'd rather* play golf.)

Am liebsten means "to like best of all."

Ich spiele Fußball. (I play soccer.)
Ich spiele **am liebsten** Fußball. (I *like* to play soccer *best of all.*)

DRILLS

1 Comparative

● First read each sentence as it is printed with the adjective or adverb in the positive form. Then reread each sentence, putting the adjective or adverb into the comparative.

● **groß** / **größer** **hoch** / **höher** **gut** / **besser**

1. Dieser Wein ist **gut.**
2. Er ist **groß** geworden.
3. Das ist **gut.**
4. Ihre Preise sind **hoch.**

(**der Preis, -e:** price; **hoch:** high)

5. Das Wohnzimmer ist **groß.**
6. Die Miete ist **hoch** geworden.

(**die Miete:** rent)

● **viel** / **mehr** **gern** / **lieber**

1. Er hat **viel** gegessen.
2. Ich trinke **gern** Kaffee. (**der Kaffee:** coffee)
3. Kostet es **viel?**

4. Ich bleibe **gern** hier.
5. Was trinkst du **gern?**

● Mixed drills

1. Das ist **gut.**
2. Ich trinke **gern** Kaffee.
3. Er ist **groß** geworden.
4. Kostet es **viel?**
5. Ihre Preise sind **hoch.**
6. Ich bleibe **gern** hier.

7. Dieser Wein ist **gut.**
8. Er hat **viel** gegessen.
9. Das Wohnzimmer ist **groß.**
10. Die Miete ist **hoch** geworden.
11. Was trinkst du **gern?**

2 Superlative

● Complete the following sentences by supplying the missing elements.

EXAMPLE   Er ist ___ größt___.
          Er ist **am** größt**en**.

1. Dieser Wein ist ___ best___.
2. Das Wohnzimmer ist ___ größt___.
3. Ihre Preise sind ___ höchst___.
4. Er ist ___ größt___ und er trinkt ___ meist___.
5. Sie trinkt ___ liebst___ Wein.

6. Ich kenne ihn ___ best___.
7. Das kostet ___ meist___.
8. Was machst du ___ liebst___?
9. Dieses Gebäude ist ___ höchst___.

(**das Gebäude:** building)

10. Was trinken Sie ___ liebst___?

● Put the adjectives and adverbs into the superlative.

1. Ihre Preise sind **hoch.**
2. Ich kenne ihn **gut.**
3. Das kostet **viel.**
4. Was trinken Sie **gern?**
5. Das Wohnzimmer ist **groß.**

6. Sie trinkt **gern** Wein.
7. Dieser Wein ist **gut.**
8. Dieses Gebäude ist **hoch.**
9. Er ist **groß** und er trinkt **viel.**
10. Was machst du **gern?**

3 Mixed drills

● Put the adjectives and adverbs into the comparative and superlative.

1. Das kostet **viel.**
2. Was trinkst du **gern?**
3. Ihre Preise sind **hoch.**
4. Ich kenne ihn **gut.**
5. Das Wohnzimmer ist **groß.**

6. Sie trinkt **gern** Wein.
7. Dieser Wein ist **gut.**
8. Was machst du **gern?**
9. Dieses Gebäude ist **hoch.**
10. Er ist **groß** und er trinkt **viel.**

● Supply the appropriate comparative or superlative forms.

1. Er ist _____ geworden.
   (bigger)

2. Dieser Wein ist _____.
   (best)

3. Kostet es _____?
   (more)

4. Ihre Preise sind _____.
   (highest)

5. Ich trinke _____ Wein.
   (would rather [drink])

6. Das Wohnzimmer ist _____.
   (larger)

7. Das kostet _____.
   (most)

8. Ich kenne ihn _____.
   (better)

9. Was trinken Sie _____?
   (like [to drink] best)

10. Die Miete ist _____ geworden.
    (higher)

11. Er ist _____ und er trinkt
    (the biggest)
    _____.
    (the most)

12. Ich bleibe _____ hier.
    (would rather [stay])

13. Das ist _____.
    (better)

14. Dieses Gebäude ist _____.
    (highest)

15. Sie trinkt _____ Wein.
    (likes [to drink] best)

16. Er hat _____ gegessen.
    (more)

17. Ich kenne ihn _____.
    (best)

18. Was machst du _____?
    (do you like [to do] best)

19. Ihre Preise sind _____.
    (higher)

20. Ich trinke _____ Kaffee.
    (like [to drink])

● Express in German.

1. That's better.
2. That costs the most.
3. He's gotten bigger.
4. I know him best.

5. I like to drink coffee.
6. I'd rather drink wine.
7. Does it cost more?
8. Their prices are highest.

9. She likes to drink wine best.
10. I know him better.
11. He's the biggest and he drinks the most.
12. I'd rather stay here.
13. The rent has gotten higher.
14. What do you like to do best?
15. He ate more.
16. This building is highest.
17. What do you like to drink best?
18. The living room is larger.
19. Their prices are higher.
20. This wine is best.

F Two Common Formulas

1 Comparative with als

schneller **als**: faster *than*

Er fährt **schneller als** du.   (He drives *faster than* you.)

2 Positive with so . . . wie

so schnell **wie**: *as* fast *as*

Er fährt nicht **so schnell wie** du.   (He doesn't drive *as fast as* you.)

The **so . . . wie** formula is commonly introduced by either **genau** (just) or **nicht** (not):

genau so schnell wie: *just as fast as*
nicht so schnell wie: *not as fast as*

DRILLS

1   als + comparative

Supply the appropriate comparative form.

1. Frankfurt ist _____ als Berlin.
   (smaller)

2. Sie ist viel _____ als ihre Schwester.
   (younger)

3. Er liest _____ als ich.
   (faster)

4. Und es kostet _____ als fünf Mark.
   (less)

5. Es ist _____ als gestern.
   (warmer)

6. Nichts ist _____ als das!
   (easier)

7. Ich zahle _____ Miete als du.
   (more)   (**zahlen**: to pay)

8. Es ist _____ als ich dachte.
   (more expensive)

9. Dieser Wein ist _____ als der andere.
   (better)

10. Er ist viel _____ als seine Frau.
    (older)

2   so . . . wie + positive

Supply the appropriate positive form.

1. Es ist nicht so _____ wie gestern.
   (cold)

2. Sie ist genau so _____ wie ihre
   Mutter.
   (pretty)
   (**genau**: just, exactly)

3. Er spielt nicht so _____ wie du.
   (well)

4. Er ist genau so _____ wie ich dachte.
   (stupid)

5. Deutsch ist nicht so _____ wie Spanisch.
(easy)

6. Er ißt nicht so _____ wie ich.
(much)

3 Mixed drills

1. Er liest _____ ich.
(faster than)

2. Dieser Wein ist _____ der andere.
(better than)

3. Es ist nicht _____ gestern.
(as cold as)

4. Frankfurt ist _____ Berlin.
(smaller than)

5. Es ist _____ ich dachte.
(more expensive than)

6. Er spielt nicht _____ du.
(as well as)

7. Er ist viel _____ seine Frau.
(older than)

8. Deutsch ist nicht _____ Spanisch.
(as easy as)

9. Und es kostet _____ fünf Mark.
(less than)

10. Sie ist genau _____ ihre Mutter.
(as pretty as)

11. Ich zahle _____ Miete _____ du.
(more)   (than)

12. Er ist genau _____ ich dachte.
(as stupid as)

13. Es ist _____ gestern.
(warmer than)

14. Sie ist viel _____ ihre Schwester.
(younger than)

15. Er ißt nicht _____ ich.
(as much as)

16. Nichts ist _____ das!
(easier than)

G Two More Common Formulas

1 Comparative with **immer**

immer besser: better *and better* (better *all the time*)

Es wird **immer besser.**   (It's getting *better all the time.*)

2 Comparative with **je . . . desto . . .**

je mehr, **desto** besser: *the* more, *the* better

DRILLS

1 **immer** or **je . . . desto . . .** + comparative

1. Die Preise werden _____.
(higher and higher)

2. Sie wird _____.
(prettier and prettier)

3. Je _____, desto _____.
(more)   (better)

4. Je _____ er ißt, desto _____ wird er.
(more)   (fatter)

5. Der Patient wurde _____.
(weaker and weaker)

6. Er wird _____.
(bigger and bigger)

7. Wie singt man das? Je _____, desto
(softer)

_____.
(better)

8. Je _____ er arbeitet, desto
(more)

_____ wird er.
(more tired)

9. Es wird _____.
(better all the time)

2 Express in German (all four formulas)

a. 1. Frankfurt is smaller than Berlin.
2. It's warmer than yesterday.
3. She's just as pretty as her mother.
4. Prices are getting higher and higher.
5. He's much older than his wife.
6. It's not as cold as yesterday.
7. She's getting prettier and prettier.
8. The more, the better.
9. It's more expensive than I thought.
10. German isn't as easy as Spanish.

b. 1. The more he works, the more tired he gets.
2. The patient got weaker and weaker.

3. He reads faster than I.
4. This wine is better than the other (one).
5. He's getting bigger and bigger.
6. She's much younger than her sister.
7. He doesn't play as well as you.
8. It's getting better all the time.
9. And it costs less than five marks.
10. He doesn't eat as much as I (do).

c. 1. I pay more rent than you.
2. The more he eats, the fatter he gets.
3. He's just as stupid as I thought.
4. Nothing is easier than that.

H Positive, Comparative, and Superlative Forms with Adjective Endings

Adjectives that immediately precede the nouns they modify are called *attributive adjectives*. They take the usual adjective endings.

1 Stem form of attributive adjectives

billig (cheap, inexpensive)
billiger
billigst-

Billig, billiger, and **billigst-** are all basic forms; they take normal adjective endings when they precede a noun.

POSITIVE   The stem **billig-** plus endings:

Das ist ein **billiger** Anzug.
Zeigen Sie mir einen **billigen** Anzug!
Haben Sie **billige** Anzüge?

COMPARATIVE   The stem **billiger-** plus endings:

Das ist ein **billigerer** Anzug.
Zeigen Sie mir einen **billigeren** Anzug!
Haben Sie **billigere** Anzüge?

SUPERLATIVE   The stem **billigst-** plus endings:

Das ist der **billigste** Anzug.
Zeigen Sie mir den **billigsten** Anzug!
Wo sind die **billigsten** Anzüge?

► **Note** Attributive adjectives use only the superlative stem (for example, **billigst-**) plus the adjective endings. The **am . . . -en** matrix (for example, **am billigsten**) is used only with predicate adjectives and adverbs.

2 Irregular forms

The following adjectives have irregular forms:

Positive	Comparative	Superlative
groß	größer	größt-
gut	besser	best-
hoch (hoh-)	höher	höchst-
viel	mehr	meist-*

► **Note** As a predicate adjective, **hoch** is regular: Die Preise sind **hoch.** As an attributive adjective, it is irregular, dropping the **c** from the stem when it takes endings:

Das† sind **hohe** Preise.
(Those† are *high* prices.)

DRILLS

1 Comparatives with adjective endings

● Supply the appropriate adjective endings.

1. Er sucht ein___ größer___ Wohnung.
2. Er braucht ein___ dunkler___ Anzug.
3. Haben Sie kein___ billiger___ Mäntel?
4. Kennst du kein besser___ Restaurant?
5. Das ist mein älter___ Bruder.
6. Ich wohne jetzt in ein___ kleiner___ Zimmer.
7. Älter___ Herren schicken Blumen.
   (die Blume, -n: flower)

8. Das ist ihr___ jünger___ Schwester.
9. Ich kaufe ein___ besser___ Wagen.
10. Die Kinder brauchen wärmer___ Kleider.
11. Das findest du in ein___ größer___ Buchhandlung.
12. Ich kenne kein netter___ Mädchen.
13. Ich habe nie ein___ kürzer___ Rock gesehen.

2 Superlatives with adjective endings

● Supply the appropriate adjective endings.

1. Es ist d___ ältest___ Haus in der Stadt.
2. Er trug sein___ best___ Anzug.
3. Er hat d___ interessantest___ Arbeit geschrieben. **(die Arbeit:** term paper)
4. D___ meist___ Studenten trinken Bier.

5. Er kauft nur d___ best___ Wein.
6. Sie trägt nur d___ einfachst___ Kleider.
7. Er ist mein best___ Freund.
8. D___ teuerst___ Weine kommen aus Frankreich.

** **die meisten Leute** (most people); **die meisten Kinder** (most children). Unlike English, German uses the definite article in such expressions.*

*†**Das** can mean either "that" or "those." If it means "that," it is followed by a singular verb—Das **ist** ein hoher Preis. If it means "those," it is followed by a plural verb—Das **sind** hohe Preise.*

3   Mixed drills

1. Ich kenne kein netter___ Mädchen.
2. Er sucht ein___ größer___ Wohnung.
3. Er ist mein best___ Freund.
4. Haben Sie kein___ billiger___ Mäntel?
5. Es ist d___ ältest___ Haus in der Stadt.
6. Ich kaufe ein___ besser___ Wagen.
7. Älter___ Herren schicken Blumen.
8. Er kauft nur d___ best___ Wein.
9. Das ist ihr___ jünger___ Schwester.
10. D___ meist___ Studenten trinken Bier.
11. Ich wohne jetzt in ein___ kleiner___ Zimmer.
12. Er trug sein___ best___ Anzug.
13. Kennst du kein besser___ Restaurant?
14. Sie trägt nur d___ einfachst___ Kleider.
15. Das ist mein älter___ Bruder.
16. Die Kinder brauchen wärmer___ Kleider.
17. Er hat d___ interessantest___ Arbeit geschrieben.
18. Das findest du in ein___ größer___ Buchhandlung.
19. Er braucht ein___ dunkler___ Anzug.
20. D___ teuerst___ Weine kommen aus Frankreich.
21. Ich habe nie ein___ kürzer___ Rock gesehen.

4   Express in German

1. He's my best friend.
2. He's looking for a larger apartment.
3. That's my older brother.
4. It's the oldest house in the city.
5. The children need warmer clothes.
6. Don't you know a better restaurant?
7. Most students drink beer.
8. That's her younger sister.
9. He wore his best suit.
10. I don't know a nicer girl.
11. You'll find that in a larger bookstore.
12. Older gentlemen send flowers.
13. He only buys the best wine.
14. I'm going to buy a better car.
15. I'm living in a smaller room now.
16. He wrote the most interesting paper.
17. He needs a darker suit.
18. Don't you have any cheaper coats?
19. I've never seen a shorter skirt.

GRAND MIX

1   Fill-ins

a. 1. Sein Zimmer ist _____.
         (smaller)

    2. Es wird _____.
         (hotter)

    3. Sein neues Buch ist _____.
         (longer)

    4. Es ist _____ gestern.
         (warmer than)

    5. Er ist _____ Freund.
         (my best)

    6. Frankfurt ist _____ Berlin.
         (smaller than)

    7. Sie ist genau _____ ihre Mutter.
         (as pretty as)

    8. Seine erste Frau war _____.
         (more interesting)

    9. Das ist _____.
         (better)

    10. Dieser Wagen ist _____.
         (fastest)

b. 1. Der Patient ist _____ geworden.
         (weaker)

    2. Sie wird _____.
         (prettier and prettier)

    3. Er kauft nur _____ Wein.
         (the best)

    4. Es ist nicht _____ gestern.
         (as cold as)

    5. Benzin ist _____ geworden.
         (more expensive)

    6. Er braucht _____ Anzug.
         (a darker)

7. Und es kostet _____ fünf Mark.
(less than)

8. Diese Mäntel sind _____.
(cheapest)

9. Ihre Preise sind _____.
(higher)

10. Er sah _____ aus.
(older)

c. 1. Im Januar ist es _____.
(coldest)

2. Es ist _____ geworden.
(darker)

3. Das ist _____.
(simpler)

4. Ich bleibe _____ hier.
(would rather [stay])

5. Er liest _____ ich.
(faster than)

6. Kostet es _____?
(more)

7. Das Hilton ist _____.
(the most expensive)

8. Es ist _____ Haus in der Stadt.
(the oldest)

9. Das Wohnzimmer ist _____.
(larger)

10. Dieser Schnaps ist _____.
(strongest)

d. 1. Je _____, desto _____!
(more)   (better)

2. Was trinken Sie _____?
(like to [drink] best)

3. Das ist _____ Schwester.
(her younger)

4. Die Miete ist _____ geworden.
(higher)

5. Wir sind _____ hier gewesen.
(the longest)

6. Er spielt nicht _____ du.
(as well as)

7. Sprechen Sie _____, bitte!
(louder)

8. Er trug _____ Anzug.
(his best)

9. Der Patient wurde _____.
(weaker and weaker)

10. Ich kaufe _____ Wagen.
(a better)

e. 1. Er ist _____ geworden.
(bigger)

2. Spanisch ist _____.
(the easiest)

3. Dieser Schnaps ist _____.
(stronger)

4. Er sucht _____ Wohnung.
(a larger)

5. Ich kenne ihn _____.
(best)

6. Der andere Mantel war _____.
(warmer)

7. Die Preise werden _____.
(higher and higher)

8. _____ Studenten trinken Bier.
(Most)

9. Kennst du _____ Restaurant?
(a better)

10. Sie ist viel _____ ihre
(younger than)
Schwester.

f. 1. Er ist _____ und er trinkt
(the biggest)
_____.
(the most)

2. Kannst du nicht _____
(more softly)
spielen?

3. Ich wohne jetzt in _____
(a smaller)
Zimmer.

4. Ich trinke _____ Wein.
(would rather [drink])

5. Er sieht _____ aus.
(the oldest)

6. Ich zahle _____ Miete als du.
(more)

7. Es ist _____ geworden.
(colder)

8. Es ist _____ ich dachte.
(more expensive than)

9. Dieser Wein ist _____ der
(better than)
andere.

10. Sie trinkt _____ Wein.
(likes to [drink] best)

g. 1. Die Schlange ist _____ geworden.
        (shorter)

    2. Dieses Kleid ist _____.
        (prettiest)

    3. Je _____ er arbeitet, desto
        (more)

        _____ wird er.
        (more tired)

    4. Das ist _____ Bruder.
        (my older)

    5. Es ist _____ heute.
        (warmer)

    6. Nichts ist _____ das!
        (easier than)

    7. _____ Herren schicken Blumen.
        (Older)

    8. Ich kenne ihn _____.
        (better)

    9. Er wird _____.
        (bigger and bigger)

    10. Ihre Preise sind _____.
        (highest)

h. 1. Er ist viel _____ seine Frau.
        (older than)

    2. Dieser Wein ist _____.
        (best)

    3. Das findest du in _____
        (a larger)
        Buchhandlung.

    4. Ich trinke _____ Kaffee.
        (like to [drink])

    5. Je _____ er ißt, desto _____
        (more)   (fatter)
        wird er.

    6. Das Essen hier ist _____
        (worse)
        geworden.

    7. Er ist genau _____ ich dachte.
        (as stupid as)

    8. Fahren Sie _____!
        (slower)

    9. Ich habe nie _____ Rock gesehen.
        (a shorter)

    10. Es wird _____.
        (better all the time)

2 Express in German

a. 1. Drive slower.
    2. His room is smaller.
    3. That's better.
    4. This dress is prettiest.
    5. It's gotten colder.
    6. He's my best friend.
    7. Frankfurt is smaller than Berlin.
    8. He looked older.
    9. And it costs less than five marks.
    10. He wore his best suit.

b. 1. Their prices are higher.
    2. This car is fastest.
    3. His new book is longer.
    4. It's not as cold as yesterday.
    5. She's just as pretty as her mother.
    6. He's gotten bigger.
    7. This wine is best.
    8. It's getting hotter.
    9. She's much younger than her sister.
    10. It's the oldest house in the city.

c. 1. Speak louder, please.
    2. It's warmer today.

    3. The rent has gotten higher.
    4. Most students drink beer.
    5. This schnapps is strongest.
    6. He reads faster than I (do).
    7. Prices are getting higher and higher.
    8. I'd rather stay here.
    9. Older gentlemen send flowers.
    10. It's more expensive than I thought.

d. 1. Does it cost more?
    2. He needs a darker suit.
    3. The more, the better.
    4. Can't you play more softly?
    5. I know him better.
    6. He's looking for a larger apartment.
    7. He's much older than his wife.
    8. The patient has gotten weaker.
    9. Their prices are highest.
    10. The other coat was warmer.

e. 1. It's gotten darker.
    2. I'm living in a smaller room now.
    3. I like to drink coffee.
    4. The Hilton is the most expensive.

5. The food here has gotten worse.
6. This schnapps is stronger.
7. The patient got weaker and weaker.
8. I'd rather drink wine.
9. Nothing is easier than that.
10. Do you know a better restaurant?

f.
1. I pay more rent than you (do).
2. These coats are cheapest.
3. His first wife was more interesting.
4. The living room is larger.
5. The line has gotten shorter.
6. That's her younger sister.
7. This wine is better than the other one.
8. He's the biggest and he drinks the most.
9. That's simpler.
10. That's my older brother.

g.
1. What do you like to drink best?
2. He's just as stupid as I thought.
3. Gas has gotten more expensive.
4. The more he works, the more tired he gets.
5. He's getting bigger and bigger.
6. It's coldest in January.
7. I'm going to buy a better car.
8. He doesn't play as well as you.
9. Spanish is the easiest.
10. She's getting prettier and prettier.

h.
1. He looks the oldest.
2. He only buys the best wine.
3. I've never seen a shorter skirt.
4. It's getting better all the time.

VOCABULARY

als than
alt old
älter older
ältest– oldest
die **Arbeit, –en** term paper; work
das **Benzin** gas
billig cheap
die **Blume, –n** flower
dunkel dark
dunkler darker
dunkelst– darkest
das **Essen, –** food
das **Gebäude, –** building
genau just, exactly
gern (lieber, liebst–) like to, prefer to, like to best of all
groß big
größer bigger
größt– biggest
gut (besser, best–) good, better, best
hoch (hoh–) high
höher higher

höchst– highest
immer (+ comp. adj.) . . . and . . .
  e.g. **immer besser** better and better
der **Januar** January
  im Januar in January
je . . . desto the . . . the
  e.g. **je mehr, desto besser** the more the better
jung young
jünger younger
jüngst– youngest
der **Kaffee** coffee
kalt cold
kälter colder
kältest– coldest
kurz short
kürzer shorter
kürzest– shortest
lang long
länger longer
längst– longest
lange for a long time (adv.)

der **Lodenmantel, –̈** loden coat (heavy winter coat)
die **Mark, –** mark (currency)
die **Miete, –n** rent
der **Motor, –en** motor
der **Patient, –en, –en** patient
der **Preis, –e** price
der **Rock, –̈e** skirt
die **Schlange, –n** here: line
der **Schnaps, –̈e** schnapps
schwach weak
schwächer weaker
schwächst– weakest
so . . . wie as . . . as
stark strong, powerful
stärker stronger
stärkst– strongest
viel (mehr, meist–) much, more, most
warm warm
wärmer warmer
wärmst– warmest
zahlen to pay

Lesson 6 Level TWO

A Cardinal Numbers: Review and Expansion

Cardinal numbers are the numbers used in counting, in indicating quantity, and in answering the question "How many?"

Er hat **drei** Kinder.　　(He has *three* children.)
Wir blieben **vier** Tage.　(We stayed *four* days.)

Cardinal numbers *do not take adjective endings.* (See note below.)

1 Number formation

English uses the numbers 1 to 9 as the basis for forming most of its other numbers (from 13 to 99). For example:

seven　　*seventeen*　　*seventy*　　*seventy-seven*

Exceptions, however, are quite common:

five　　*fifteen*　　*fifty*

German behaves in a very similar manner and has far fewer exceptions than English.

a. Numbers 1 to 12

The numbers 1 to 12 are each separate and distinct words.

1	eins (ein-)	5	fünf	9	neun
2	zwei	6	sechs	10	zehn
3	drei	7	sieben	11	elf
4	vier	8	acht	12	zwölf

▶ **Note**　The word **eins** is only used in counting. If the number **ein** is followed by a noun, it must take the appropriate adjective endings.

Er hat nur **einen** Wagen.　　(He only has one car.)

As you can see, written German cannot distinguish between "He only has *a* car" and "He has only *one* car." The distinction is made in spoken German by stressing the word **einen.** When *stressed*, **ein** means "one." When *unstressed*, it means "a."

b. Numbers 13 to 19

Basically, these numbers are formed by adding the suffix **-zehn** to the numbers **drei** through **neun:**

13	dreizehn	17	siebzehn
14	vierzehn	18	achtzehn
15	fünfzehn	19	neunzehn
16	sechzehn		

▶ **Note**   **Sech-** (not **sechs**) is used to form **sechzehn.**
Sieb- (not **sieben**) is used to form **siebzehn.**

c. Numbers 20 to 90

The suffix **-zig** is used to form these numbers:

20	zwanzig	60	sechzig
30	dreißig	70	siebzig
40	vierzig	80	achtzig
50	fünfzig	90	neunzig

▶ **Note**   As was the case with **sechzehn** and **siebzehn**, **sech-** (not **sechs**) is used to form **sechzig** and **sieb-** (not **sieben**) is used to form **siebzig.**

Zwan- (not **zwei**) is used to form **zwanzig.**

-ßig is the ending for **dreißig.**

d. Numbers 21 to 29, and so on

The German pattern is like the phrase: "four and twenty blackbirds":

21	einundzwanzig	24	vierundzwanzig	27	siebenundzwanzig
22	zweiundzwanzig	25	fünfundzwanzig	28	achtundzwanzig
23	dreiundzwanzig	26	sechsundzwanzig	29	neunundzwanzig

These numbers are always written as *one word.*

▶ **Note**   **Ein** (not **eins**) is used in these cases.

e. 100s and 1000s

Look at the following examples:

100	hundert (or einhundert)	1000	tausend (or eintausend)
103	hundertdrei	1003	tausenddrei
154	hundertvierundfünfzig	2354	zweitausenddreihundertvierundfünfzig
200	zweihundert		

Compound numbers such as these are all written as *one word.*

▶ Note English often puts the word "and" between 100 (or 1000) and numbers under 99. For example:

103	one hundred *and* three
154	one hundred *and* fifty-four
1003	one thousand *and* three

German *never* uses the word **und** in such cases:

hundertdrei

1. As a date, 1978 is read:

neunzehnhundertachtundsiebzig   (*nineteen hundred seventy-eight*)

2. **Einhundert** must be used for 100 if it is preceded by an expression using **tausend**:

zweitausend**ein**hundertfünfzig   (2150)

2 Summary table

eins	elf	(zehn)	hundert
zwei	zwölf	**zwan**zig	tausend
drei	dreizehn	drei**ß**ig	
vier	vierzehn	vierzig	
fünf	fünfzehn	fünfzig	
sechs	**sech**zehn	**sech**zig	
sieben	**sieb**zehn	**sieb**zig	
acht	achtzehn	achtzig	
neun	neunzehn	neunzig	
zehn	(zwanzig)	(hundert)	

DRILLS

Cardinal numbers: express in German

● Numbers 1–12

a.	1	7	b.	3	5
	2	8		7	12
	3	9		11	4
	4	10		2	10
	5	11		9	6
	6	12		1	8

● Numbers 13–19

a.	13	17	b.	16	18
	14	18		13	14
	15	19		19	17
	16			15	

● Numbers 20–90

a.	20	60	b.	50	30
	30	70		80	90
	40	80		20	40
	50	90		60	70

● Numbers 21–29, and so on

a.	21	26	b.	27	23
	22	27		22	26
	23	28		25	24
	24	29		29	28
	25			21	

c. 32	69	d. 73	23
36	71	25	52
38	73	98	69
43	78	44	41
45	82	61	87
49	86	39	26
51	87	86	94
54	93	57	35
57	96	92	73
62	99	35	28
65		78	

- Mixed numbers

17	85	21
93	6	650
5	16	58
46	1	125
12	7500	35
2	4	3
109	210	69
18	11	10
327	115	975

- Numbers in the 100s and 1000s

100	428	1590
108	560	4750
115	735	7265
175	1000	
193	1007	
210	1050	
385	1085	

- Express as dates.

1492	1933
1749	1978
1776	1984
1812	2001

B Ordinal Numbers

Ordinal numbers refer to a specific number in a series; in other words, they answer the question "Which one?" (rather than "How many?").

CARDINAL	**zwei** Kinder	(*two* children)	(*How many* children?)
ORDINAL	sein **zweites** Kind	(his *second* child)	(*Which* child?)

Unlike cardinal numbers, ordinal numbers *always take adjective endings:*

sein **zweit**es Kind, seine **erst**e Frau

a. Numbers 1 to 19

With a few exceptions (printed in color), these ordinal numbers are formed by adding -t + *the appropriate adjective ending* to the cardinal number:

the first	der **erste**	(new stem)
second	zweite	
third	**dritte**	(new stem)
fourth	vierte	
fifth	fünfte	
sixth	sechste	
seventh	**siebte**	(**sieb-** not **sieben-**)
eighth	**achte**	(**ach-** not **acht-**)
ninth	neunte	
tenth	zehnte	
and so on		

b. From number 20 on

Beginning with the number 20 **(zwanzig),** ordinal numbers are formed by adding
-st + *the appropriate adjective ending* to the cardinal number:

the 20th	der zwanzig**ste**	the 30th	der dreißig**ste**
21st	einundzwanzig**ste**	100th	hundert**ste**
22nd	zweiundzwanzig**ste**	1000th	tausend**ste**

DRILLS

Ordinal numbers: express in German

- **Numbers 1–19**

  PATTERN   der . . . -te

a. the 1st	8th	b. the 18th	2nd
2nd	9th	5th	8th
3rd	10th	1st	16th
4th	12th	9th	7th
5th	15th	13th	17th
6th	19th	3rd	4th
7th		10th	

- **From number 20 on**

  PATTERN   der . . . -ste

a. the 20th	72nd	b. the 51st	34th
26th	74th	27th	65th
37th	81st	83rd	29th
39th	86th	48th	150th
42nd	93rd	92nd	76th
45th	97th	100th	1000th
51st	100th		
58th	120th		
66th	500th		
69th	1000th		

- **Mixed numbers**

the 4th	the 75th	the 500th
20th	1st	12th
15th	17th	3rd
41st	90th	59th
8th	6th	30th

- **Dates**

  a. Heute ist _____ Januar.
     (the 1st)

     _____ Februar.
     (the 5th)

     _____ März.
     (the 15th)

     _____ April.
     (the 20th)

     _____ Mai.
     (the 28th)

     _____ Juni.
     (the 3rd)

     _____ Juli.
     (the 14th)

     _____ August.
     (the 25th)

     _____ September.
     (the 2nd)

     _____ Oktober.
     (the 13th)

     _____ November.
     (the 28th)

     _____ Dezember.
     (the 7th)

  b. Today is the 1st of April.*

23rd of December.	4th of July.
12th of October.	15th of March.
3rd of May.	30th of September.
29th of February.	3rd of June.
7th of January.	20th of August.
28th of November.	

---

*German has no word corresponding to the word "of" in "the 1st *of* April."

264   Lesson 6

Lesson 6   Level THREE

A Telling Time

1 Asking the time

There are two ways of asking for the time of day in German:

Wie spät ist es?   (How late is it?)
Wieviel Uhr ist es?   (How much "o'clock" is it?)

Both correspond to the English question, "What time is it?"

2 Telling the time

a. Full hours

Es ist drei Uhr.   (It's three o'clock.)

In time expressions, the word **Uhr** is the equivalent of the English word "o'clock."
Like the word "o'clock," the word **Uhr** may be omitted. But when **Uhr** is omitted
from the German equivalent of "one o'clock," the number **ein** has to be changed
to **eins:**

Es ist **ein** Uhr.   *but*   Es ist eins.

b. Half hours

When giving the time in half hours, English refers back to the full hour just completed, and so the English expression is

half *past* seven   (7:30)

But German thinks of the full hour that's coming up:

halb acht (7:30)   (*Lit.:* half eight, meaning halfway to eight)

c. Quarter hours

The most common way of giving the time in quarter hours is to use the expressions
viertel nach (quarter after) and **viertel vor** (quarter to, quarter of).

Es ist viertel nach drei. (3:15)   (It's *quarter after* three.)
Es ist viertel vor drei.   (2:45)   (It's *quarter to* three.)

d. Minutes

Expressions that give the time in minutes use the same prepositions: **nach** and **vor.**

Es ist zehn (Minuten) **nach** drei.	(3:10)	(It's ten [minutes] *after* three.)
Es ist zehn (Minuten) **vor** vier.	(3:50)	(It's ten [minutes] *to* four.)

Like the word "minutes," the word **Minuten** is often omitted.

3 um

Where English uses the preposition "at" (at five o'clock), German uses the preposition **um (um fünf Uhr).**

Er kommt **um** fünf Uhr. Er kommt **um** fünf.
(He's coming *at* five o'clock. He's coming *at* five.)

Again, the words **Uhr** and "o'clock" are often omitted from these expressions.

DRILLS

1 Fill-ins

1. Es ist _____. (three o'clock)
   _____. (seven o'clock)
   _____. (eleven o'clock)
   _____. (one o'clock)
   _____. (ten o'clock)
   _____. (five o'clock)
2. Es ist _____. (5:30)
   _____. (2:30)
   _____. (11:30)
   _____. (7:30)
   _____. (1:30)
   _____. (3:30)
   _____. (12:30)

3. Es ist _____. (quarter after three)
   _____. (quarter after eight)
   _____. (ten after six)
   _____. (twenty after eleven)
   _____. (quarter after seven)
   _____. (five after one)
4. Es ist _____. (quarter to twelve)
   _____. (quarter to two)
   _____. (ten to eight)
   _____. (twenty-five to one)
   _____. (quarter to five)
   _____. (eighteen to ten)

2 Mixed drills

1. Es ist _____. (three o'clock)
   _____. (seven-thirty)
   _____. (quarter after six)
   _____. (ten to eight)
   _____. (twenty after two)
   _____. (twelve-thirty)
   _____. (quarter to one)
   Es ist _____. (four-thirty)
   _____. (five to eleven)
   _____. (quarter after two)
   _____. (three-thirty)
   _____. (ten to seven)
   _____. (nine o'clock)
   _____. (six-thirty)

2. Er kam _____. (at five o'clock)
   _____. (at two-thirty)
   _____. (at quarter after nine)
   _____. (at ten to four)
   _____. (at seven-thirty)
   _____. (at quarter after six)
   _____. (at eleven o'clock)
   Er kam _____. (at twenty-five to ten)
   _____. (at one-thirty)
   _____. (at quarter to twelve)
   _____. (at five after two)
   _____. (at quarter to seven)
   _____. (at six-thirty)

B Days and Parts of Days

1 Gender

The parts of the day are *all masculine* in German, with the exception of **die Nacht.**

der Morgen (morning)	*but* die Nacht (night)
der Nachmittag (afternoon)	
der Abend (evening)	

All expressions referring to whole days are masculine:

1. The word for "day": **der Tag**

2. The days of the week:

der Sonntag	(Sunday)
der Montag	(Monday)
der Dienstag	(Tuesday)
der Mittwoch	(Wednesday)
der Donnerstag	(Thursday)
der Freitag	(Friday)
der Samstag	(Saturday)

3. Dates: **der erste Mai** (the first of May)

2 am

Am (the contraction of **an dem**) is used with whole days, and dates:

am **Dienstag**	(on Tuesday)
am **ersten Mai**	(on the first of May)

The usual English equivalent of **am** is "on" or "on the" (*on* Tuesday, *on the* first).

3 Adverbs of time

The days of the week and the parts of the day can be used as one-word adverbs. These adverbs are formed by adding the ending **-s** to the noun. Like all other German adverbs, they are not capitalized:

Nouns	**Adverbs**	
der Dienstag	**dienstags**	(Tuesdays, on Tuesday)
der Morgen	**morgens**	(mornings)
die Nacht	**nachts**	(nights)

These adverbs have a special function: They are used to express regular repetition.

Ich gehe **samstags** immer ins Kino.   (I always go the movies *on Saturday*.)

▶ **Exception**   **tagsüber** (during the day). **Tagsüber** is a unique, idiomatic form:

Tagsüber ist es sehr heiß.   (It's very hot *during the day*.)

DRILLS

1   Days of the week: **am Montag** (*on* Monday)

● Synthetic exercises: Form complete sentences in the tense indicated.

EXAMPLE   Er / zurückbringen / Wagen / Donnerstag   (*present perfect*)
Er hat den Wagen **am** Donnerstag zurückgebracht.

1. Er / kommen / Montag   (*present*)
2. Wir / sehen / Hans / Dienstag   (*present*)
3. Sie (*she*) / gehen / Mittwoch / ins Kino   (*present*)
4. Er / zurückbringen / Wagen / Donnerstag   (*present perfect*)
5. Sie (*they*) / vorbeikommen / Freitag   (*present perfect*)
6. Ich / anrufen / ihn / Samstag   (*present*)
7. Wir / gehen / Sonntag / ins Theater   (*present*)

● Supply **am** + the appropriate day of the week.

1. Sie geht _____ ins Kino.
   (on Wednesday)

2. Ich rufe ihn _____ an.
   (on Saturday)

3. Er kommt _____.
   (on Monday)

4. Sie sind _____ vorbeigekommen.
   (on Friday)

5. Wir gehen _____ ins Theater.
   (on Sunday)

6. Wir sehen Hans _____.
   (on Tuesday)

7. Er hat den Wagen _____ zurückgebracht.
   (on Thursday)

● Express in German.

1. They came by on Friday.
2. We'll see Hans on Tuesday.
3. We're going to the theater on Sunday.
4. He brought the car back on Thursday.
5. He's coming on Monday.
6. I'll call him on Saturday.
7. She's going to the movies on Wednesday.

2 Dates: **am** with ordinal number + adjective ending **-en (am zwanzigsten)**

- Supply the correct dates.

    1. Er kommt _____ März.
       (on the 5th)
    2. Ich sehe ihn _____.
       (on the 20th)

    3. Sie demonstrieren _____ Mai.
       (on the 1st)
    4. Ich komme _____ zurück.
       (on the 15th)

- Synthetic exercises: Form complete sentences in the present tense.

    1. Ich / sehen / ihn / 20.
    2. Sie / demonstrieren / 1. / Mai

    3. Ich / zurückkommen / 15.
    4. Er / kommen / 5. / März

- Express in German.

    1. I'll see him on the 20th.
    2. He's coming on the 5th of March.
    3. I'm coming back on the 15th.
    4. They're going to demonstrate on the first of May.

3 Adverbs of time: days (**montags:** Mondays) and parts of days (**nachts:** nights)

- Supply the correct adverb of time.

    1. Ich gehe _____ immer ins Kino.
       (Saturdays)
    2. Inge arbeitet _____.
       (nights)
    3. _____ bin ich immer im Büro.
       (Afternoons)

    4. _____ bleiben wir immer zu Hause.
       (Evenings)
    5. _____ stehen wir später auf.
       (Sundays)
    6. _____ ist es sehr heiß.
       (During the day)

- Express in German. If the time expression is <u>underlined</u>, make it the first element in the German sentence.

    EXAMPLE   It's very hot <u>during the day</u>.
                 Tagsüber ist es sehr heiß.

    1. We always stay home <u>evenings</u>.
    2. <u>Saturdays</u> I always go to the movies.
    3. Inge works nights.

    4. It's very hot <u>during the day</u>.
    5. <u>Sundays</u> we get up later.

C Months and Seasons

1 Gender

The months and the seasons are all masculine:

MONTHS	
der Januar	(January)
der Februar	(February)
der März	(March)
der April	(April)
der Mai	(May)
der Juni	(June)
der Juli	(July)
der August	(August)
der September	(September)
der Oktober	(October)
der November	(November)
der Dezember	(December)

SEASONS	
der Frühling	(spring)
der Sommer	(summer)
der Herbst	(autumn, fall)
der Winter	(winter)

2 im

Im (the contraction of **in dem**) is used with months and seasons:

Er kommt **im** Juni.	(He's coming in June.)
Er ist **im** Winter hier gewesen.	(He was here in winter.)

D Years

There are two ways of saying "in 1978" in German. You can either use the phrase **im Jahre 1978** or you can simply say **1978 (neunzehnhundertachtundsiebzig).** But it is a false carryover from English to say **in 1978.**

Both of the following sentences are correct German sentences and they mean exactly the same thing, but the latter is more commonly used.

Er ist **im Jahre 1970** nach Amerika gekommen. (He came to America *in 1970*.)
Er ist **1970** nach Amerika gekommen. (He came to America *in 1970*.)

DRILLS

1   Months, seasons, years (**im:** in)

- Supply **im** and the correct month.

1. _____ ist es viel kälter.
   (In January)
2. Das Semester beginnt _____.
                         (in September)   (**das Semester:** semester)
3. _____ werde ich mehr Zeit haben.
   (In July)
4. Er ist _____ zurückgekommen.
            (in August)
5. _____ fliegt er nach Deutschland.
   (In February)
6. Besuchst du uns _____?
                    (in June)
7. _____ kaufen wir einen neuen Wagen.
   (In May)
8. _____ fahren wir nach Berlin.
   (In December)

- Synthetic exercises: Form complete sentences in the tense indicated.

1. Frühling / sein / es / sehr schön hier   (*present*)
2. Sommer / arbeiten / er / weniger   (*present*)
3. Herbst / sein / wir / in Berlin   (*past*)
4. Winter / fahren / wir / nach Italien   (*present*)   (**Italien:** Italy)

- Supply the correct phrase for the following years.

1. _____ war ich in Wien.   3. _____ wohnte er bei uns.
   (In 1977)   (In 1973)
              (**Wien:** Vienna)
2. Er ist _____ geboren.
            (in 1954)
         (**ist . . . geboren:** was born)

2   Mixed drills

- Supply the correct phrase.

1. Das Semester beginnt _____.   2. _____ fahren wir nach Berlin.
                        (in September)   (In December)

3. _____ ist es sehr schön hier.
   (In the spring)

4. Er ist _____ zurückgekommen.
   (in August)

5. Er ist _____ geboren.
   (in 1954)

6. _____ arbeitet er weniger.
   (In the summer)

7. _____ kaufen wir einen neuen
   (In May)
   Wagen.

8. Besuchst du uns _____?
   (in June)

9. _____ war er in Wien.
   (In 1974)

10. _____ ist es viel kälter.
    (In January)

11. _____ gehen wir sehr oft aus.
    (In the winter)

12. _____ werde ich mehr Zeit haben.
    (In July)

13. _____ trage ich nur eine Jacke.
    (In the fall)

14. _____ fliegt er nach Deutschland.
    (In February)

15. _____ wohnte sie bei uns.
    (In 1973)

● Express in German. If the time expression is <u>underlined</u>, make it the first element in the German sentence.

1. He came back in August.
2. He was born in 1954.
3. Are you going to visit us in June?
4. The semester begins in September.
5. He's flying to Germany in February.
6. He works less in the summer.
7. It's much colder in January.
8. It's very pretty here in the spring.
9. He lived at our place in 1973.
10. I'll have more time in July.
11. We're going to Berlin in December.
12. We're going to buy a new car in May.
13. He was in Vienna in 1974.

E Definite Time

1 Accusative with definite time

The time phrases you have seen until now have all been prepositional phrases:

um fünf Uhr	(at five o'clock)
am Montag	(on Monday)
im Mai	(in May)

But many time phrases consist simply of an adjective plus a noun. When such phrases indicate a definite or specific time (for example, *next Sunday*), they are in the *accusative case*:

Waren Sie **letzten Montag** im Büro?	(Were you in the office *last Monday?*)
Ich besuche dich **nächstes Jahr**.	(I'll visit you next year.)

2 gestern, heute, morgen + parts of days

English combines words like "yesterday" and "tomorrow" with parts of the day to form a set of more precise time expressions:

yesterday afternoon   tomorrow morning

German does the same sort of thing. In fact, German goes even farther: Where English says "*this* morning" or "*this* evening," German makes combinations with the word **heute.**

heute morgen (*this morning*)   **heute** abend (*this evening*)

To form these combinations, simply choose one word from column *A* and one from column *B*:

A	B
gestern	morgen
heute	nachmittag
morgen	abend

▶ **Exception**   The German expression for "tomorrow morning" is **morgen früh** (not **morgen morgen**).

These expressions are *adverbs*, which means that the parts of the day are not capitalized: gestern **a**bend, heute **n**achmittag.

DRILLS

1   Accusative with definite time

● Supply the correct adjective endings.

1. Er fährt jed___ Sommer nach Deutschland.
2. Waren Sie letzt___ Montag im Büro?
3. Sie kommen nächst___ Monat.
4. Wo bist du letzt___ Woche gewesen?
5. Wir gehen jed___ Winter skilaufen.
6. Er blieb d___ ganz___ Tag zu Hause.
7. Ich besuche dich nächst___ Jahr.
8. Und so geht es jed___ Frühling.

(**der Monat:** month)
(**die Woche:** week)
(**gehen . . . skilaufen:** to go skiing)
(**ganz:** whole, all; **der Tag:** day)
(**das Jahr:** year)

● Supply the time expressions.

1. Er fährt _____ nach
     (every summer)
   Deutschland.
2. Wo bist du _____ gewesen?
     (last week)
3. Ich besuche dich _____.
     (next year)
4. Wir gehen _____ skilaufen.
     (every winter)

5. Waren Sie _____ im Büro?
     (last Monday)
6. Er blieb _____
     (all day; *lit.*: the whole day)
   zu Hause.
7. Sie kommen _____.
     (next month)
8. Und so geht es _____.
     (every spring)

● Express in German.

1. They are coming next month.
2. He goes to Germany every summer.
3. I'll visit you next year.
4. Were you in the office last Monday?
5. Where were you last week, Inge?

6. And so it goes every spring.
7. He stayed home all day.
     (*lit.*: the whole day)
8. We go skiing every winter.

2 Combinations with **gestern, heute,** and **morgen**

- Complete the combinations by supplying the correct parts of the day.

1. Wir bringen es morgen _____ (evening) zurück.

2. Ich bin heute _____ früh (morning) aufgestanden.

3. Wo waren Sie gestern _____? (afternoon)

4. Ich hole sie heute _____ ab. (evening)

5. Ich rufe ihn morgen _____ an. (afternoon)

6. Er hat mich heute _____ angerufen. (morning)

7. Ich bin gestern _____ vorbeigekommen. (evening)

8. Sie geht heute _____ in die Stadt. (afternoon)

9. Er kommt morgen _____. (morning)

- Supply the correct combinations.

1. Wo waren Sie _____? (yesterday afternoon)

2. Ich hole sie _____ ab. (this evening)

3. Er hat mich _____ (this morning) angerufen.

4. Wir bringen es _____ (tomorrow evening) zurück.

5. Er kommt _____. (tomorrow morning)

6. Ich bin _____ vorbeigekommen. (yesterday evening)

7. Sie geht _____ in die Stadt. (this afternoon)

8. Ich bin _____ früh aufgestanden. (this morning)

9. Ich rufe ihn _____ an. (tomorrow afternoon)

- Express in German.

1. I'll pick him up this evening.
2. Where were you yesterday afternoon?
3. We'll bring it back tomorrow evening.
4. I got up early this morning.
5. I'll call him up tomorrow afternoon.

6. He's coming tomorrow morning.
7. She's going downtown this afternoon.
8. I came by yesterday evening.
9. He called me up this morning.

F Other Common Time Expressions

1 Other time expressions with prepositions

a. **seit**: a dative preposition

Seit, like any other dative preposition, takes only dative objects:

Er wohnt **seit einer Woche** bei uns. (He's been living with us *for a week.*)

Present tense with **seit**: If **seit** refers to something that began in the past and that is still going on, the verb is in the *present tense*. This is in contrast with equivalent English expressions, which normally use the present perfect:

GERMAN PRESENT | Er **wohnt** seit einer Woche bei uns.
ENGLISH PRESENT PERFECT | He *has been living* with us for a week.

b. Two-way prepositions with time expressions

When two-way prepositions are used in time expressions there is an easy way to tell whether the expression is dative or accusative:

1. vor and in (when? / **wann?**): dative case

If the prepositional phrase answers the question "When?" (at what point in time?), the two-way preposition takes the dative:

Sie gingen **vor einer Stunde** weg. (They left an hour ago.)
Wir kommen **in einer Woche** zurück. (We're coming back in a week.)

When did they leave? (At what point in time?) Answer: **vor einer Stunde** (dative).

When are we coming back? (At what point in time?) Answer: **in einer Woche** (dative).

2. über and auf (how long? / **wie lange?**): accusative case

If the prepositional phrase answers the question "How long?" (for what period of time?), the two-way preposition takes the accusative:

Er ist **über eine Woche** da geblieben. (He stayed there over a week.)
Ich fahre **auf ein Jahr** nach Deutschland. (I'm going to Germany for a year.)

How long did he stay there? (For what period of time?) Answer: **über eine Woche** (accusative).

How long am I going for? (For what period of time?) Answer: **auf ein Jahr** (accusative).

c. seit and auf: a comparison

seit: *for* a period of past time
auf: *for* a period of future time

Both **seit** and **auf** mean "for" in time expressions, and they both suggest periods of time. Furthermore, they are both most commonly used with the present tense. The difference between them is this:

seit einem Jahr: the reference is to a year *already past*
auf ein Jahr: the reference is to a year *yet to come*

Ich wohne **seit einem Jahr** in Deutschland.   (The year is behind me.)
Ich fahre **auf ein Jahr** nach Deutschland.   (The year is still ahead of me.)

2 Expressions using -mal or Mal

a. **einmal** once, one time (**-mal**)

once, one time	**einmal**
twice, two times	**zweimal**
ten times	**zehnmal**
a hundred times	**hundertmal**

Expressions indicating a number of times (how many times?) are formed by adding **-mal** to the cardinal number. The cardinal number **eins** drops its **s** in forming **einmal.**

▶ Note 1   In expressions such as *a* hundred times, *a* thousand times, German does not have an equivalent to the English "a."

a hundred times: **hundertmal**

▶ Note 2   German never uses the word **Zeit** in such expressions.

b. **das erste Mal** the first time (**Mal**)

das dritte (achte, nächste) Mal: the third (eighth, next) time

Here English and German behave similarly. In the examples below, **Mal** is a noun and is therefore capitalized. Again, German never uses **Zeit** in this context.

c. **zum ersten Mal:** *for the* first time **(Mal)**

zum dritten (letzten) Mal: *for the* third (last) time

Contrast:

Ich habe es **das** letzte Mal gemacht.   (I did it *the* last time.)
Ich sage dir das **zum** letzten Mal.   (I'm telling you that *for the* last time.)

DRILLS

1 Time and prepositions

seit + dative (present tense)

• Supply the correct endings.

1. Sie wohnen seit ein___ Jahr in
   dieser Stadt.

2. Er wohnt seit ein___ Woche bei uns.
3. Sie arbeiten seit drei Jahre___ hier.

• Supply the full time expression.

1. Er wohnt _____ bei uns.
   (for a week)

2. Sie arbeiten _____ hier.
   (for three years)

3. Sie wohnen _____ in dieser
   (for a year)
   Stadt.

2 Two-way prepositions

vor or in + dative case (referring to a point in time: Wann?)

vor einer Woche	a week *ago*	
in einer Woche	*in* a week (a week from now)	

• Supply the correct form of **ein.**

1. Sie sind vor _____ Woche gekommen.
   (a)

2. In _____ Monat wissen wir das.
   (a)

3. Wir kommen in _____ Woche zurück.
   (a)

4. Er ist vor _____ Monat nach Berlin geflogen.
   (a)

5. Sie gingen vor _____ Stunde weg.
   (a)

(der Monat: month)

(die Stunde: hour)

• Supply the full time expression.

1. Wir kommen _____ zurück.
   (in a week)

2. Sie gingen _____ weg.
   (an hour ago)

3. _____ wissen wir das.
   (In a month)

4. Sie sind _____ gekommen.
   (a week ago)

5. Er ist _____ nach Berlin
   (a month ago)
   geflogen.

über or auf + accusative case (referring to a period of time: **Wie lange?**)

über eine Woche	*over* a week
auf eine Woche	*for* a week

- Supply the correct form of **ein**.

    1. Er blieb über _____ Jahr in Mainz.
       (a)
    2. Ich fahre auf _____ Monat nach Wien.
       (a)

    3. Er ist über _____ Woche da geblieben.
       (a)
    4. Ich fahre auf _____ Jahr nach Deutschland.
       (a)

- Supply the full time expression.

    1. Er ist _____ da geblieben.
       (over a week)
    2. Ich fahre _____ nach Deutschland.
       (for a year)

    3. Ich fahre _____ nach Wien.
       (for a month)
    4. Er blieb _____ in Mainz.
       (over a year)

3 Mixed drills: time expressions with dative or accusative

- Supply the correct form of **ein**.

    1. Er blieb über _____ Jahr in Mainz.
       (a)
    2. Sie sind vor _____ Woche gekommen.
       (a)
    3. Ich fahre auf _____ Monat nach Wien.
       (a)
    4. Sie wohnen seit _____ Jahr in dieser Stadt.
       (a)
    5. Wir kommen in _____ Woche zurück.
       (a)
    6. Er ist vor _____ Monat nach Berlin geflogen.
       (a)

    7. Er ist über _____ Woche da geblieben.
       (a)
    8. In _____ Monat wissen wir das.
       (a)
    9. Er wohnt seit _____ Woche bei uns.
       (a)
    10. Ich fahre auf _____ Jahr nach Deutschland.
        (a)

- Supply the full time expression.

    1. Sie sind _____ gekommen.
       (a week ago)
    2. Sie wohnen _____ in dieser Stadt.
       (for a year)
       (*They have been living in this city for a year.*)

    3. Wir kommen _____ zurück.
       (in a week)
    4. Ich fahre _____ nach Wien.
       (for a month)

5. Er ist _____ da geblieben.
   (over a year)
6. Er wohnt _____ bei uns.
   (for a week)
   (*He has been living at our place for a week.*)
7. _____ wissen wir das.
   (In a month)

8. Er blieb _____ in Mainz.
   (over a month)
9. Er ist _____ nach Berlin geflogen.
   (a week ago)
10. Ich fahre _____ nach Deutschland.
    (for a year)

- Express in German.

1. He stayed over a year in Mainz.
2. We're coming back in a week.
3. They've been living in this town for a year.
4. He flew to Berlin a month ago.
5. I'm going to Germany for a year.

6. We'll know that in a month.
7. He stayed there over a week.
8. They came a week ago.
9. I'm going to Vienna for a month.
10. He's been living at our place for a week.

4 Expressions using -mal or Mal

- Supply the correct cardinal number + -mal.

1. Ich habe es ihm _____ gesagt.
   (ten times)
2. Er hat den Film _____ gesehen.
   (twice)
3. Ich habe ihn nur _____ gesehen.
   (once)

4. Du mußt es _____ sagen.
   (three times)
5. Nein! Nein! _____ nein!
   ([A] thousand times)

- Supply the correct endings for these phrases with **Mal**.

1. D__ zweit__ Mal war es leichter.
2. D__ nächst__ Mal bleibst du zu Hause.

3. Ich habe es d__ letzt__ Mal gemacht.
4. Ich sage dir das zum letzt__ Mal.
   (*for the last time*)

- Supply the correct -mal or **Mal** expressions.

1. Ich habe es ihm _____ gesagt.
   (ten times)
2. _____ bleibst du zu Hause.
   (The next time)
3. Ich habe ihn nur _____ gesehen.
   (once)
4. Ich habe es _____ gemacht.
   (the last time)

5. Er hat den Film _____ gesehen.
   (three times)
6. Ich sage dir das _____.
   (for the last time)
7. _____ war es leichter.
   (The second time)

- Express in German.

1. I've only seen him once.
2. I told him ten times.
3. I did it the last time.
4. The next time you're staying home.

5. He's seen the movie three times.
6. The second time it was easier.
7. I'm telling you that for the last time.

MIXED DRILLS

a. 1. Sie kommen _____.
(at 9:15)

2. _____ fahren wir nach
(In December)
Berlin.

3. Sie sind _____ gekommen.
(a week ago)

4. Wir gehen _____ skilaufen.
(every winter)

5. Er hat den Film _____
(three times)
gesehen.

6. Er ist _____ zurückgekommen.
(in August)

7. Ich sehe ihn _____.
(on the 20th)

8. Ich hole sie _____ ab.
(this evening)

9. Er kommt _____.
(on Monday)

10. _____ wissen wir das.
(In a month)

b. 1. _____ war ich in Frankfurt.
(In 1972)

2. Es ist _____.
(1:20)

3. Das Semester beginnt
_____.
(in September)

4. _____ war es leichter.
(The second time)

5. Wir sehen Hans _____.
(on Tuesday)

6. _____ werde ich mehr Zeit
(In July)
haben.

7. Sie wohnen (*have been living*)
_____ in dieser Stadt.
(for a year)

8. Wo waren Sie _____?
(yesterday afternoon)

9. Er fährt _____ nach
(every summer)
Deutschland.

10. Er kommt _____.
(at 12:30)

c. 1. _____ bleiben wir zu Hause.
(Evenings)

2. Ich rufe ihn _____ an.
(on Saturday)

3. Er ist _____ nach Berlin
(a week ago)
geflogen.

4. _____ bleibst du zu Hause.
(The next time)

5. Sie demonstrieren _____ Mai.
(on the first [of])

6. Er ist _____ geboren.
(in 1954)

7. Ich habe es ihm _____ gesagt.
(ten times)

8. Besuchst du uns _____?
(in June)

9. Sie ist _____ vorbeigekommen.
(on Friday)

10. Er blieb _____ in Mainz.
(over a year)

d. 1. Wir sind _____ da.
(at 8:45)

2. _____ wohnte sie bei uns.
(In 1973)

3. Inge arbeitet _____.
(nights)

4. Er kommt _____.
(on the 5th [of] March)

5. Ich rufe ihn _____ an.
(tomorrow afternoon)

6. Ich fahre _____ nach Wien.
(for a month)

7. _____ ist es sehr schön hier.
(In the spring)

8. Waren Sie _____ im Büro?
(last Monday)

9. Er kommt _____.
(tomorrow morning)

10. Es ist _____.
(3:20)

e. 1. _____ bin ich immer im Büro.
(Afternoons)

2. _____ arbeitet er weniger.
(In the summer)

3. Ich habe ihn nur _____ gesehen.
   (once)
4. Ich fahre _____ nach
   (for a year)
   Deutschland.
5. Wir gehen _____ ins Theater.
   (on Sunday)
6. _____ ist es viel kälter.
   (In January)
7. Sie kommen _____.
   (at seven o'clock)
8. Ich sage dir das _____.
   (for the last time)
9. Er hat mich _____
   (this morning)
   angerufen.
10. Wo bist du _____ gewesen?
    (last week)

f. 1. Wir kommen _____ zurück.
      (in a week)
   2. _____ ist es sehr heiß.
      (During the day)
   3. Ich besuche dich _____.
      (next year)
   4. Ich bin _____
      (yesterday evening)
      vorbeigekommen.
   5. Es ist _____.
      (9:45)
   6. Er wohnt (*has been living*)
      _____ bei uns.
      (for a week)

7. Ich bin _____ früh
   (this morning)
   aufgestanden.
8. Er brachte den Wagen _____
   (on Thursday)
   zurück.
9. Und so geht es _____.
   (every spring)
10. Ich komme _____ zurück.
    (on the 15th)

g. 1. Sie kommen _____.
      (next month)
   2. Sie sind _____ gekommen.
      (at 4:30)
   3. Er blieb _____ zu Hause.
      (all day)
   4. Ich sehe ihn _____.
      (this afternoon)
   5. Wir bringen es _____
      (tomorrow evening)
      zurück.
   6. Ich habe es _____ gemacht.
      (the last time)
   7. _____ stehen wir später auf.
      (Sundays)

EXPRESS IN GERMAN

a. 1. He came back in August.
   2. She's coming on the 5th of March.
   3. He works less in the summer.
   4. It's quarter to ten.
   5. Afternoons I'm always in the office.
   6. Are you going to visit us in June?
   7. Where were you yesterday afternoon?
   8. He's coming on Monday.
   9. I'm driving to Vienna for a week.
   10. Where were you last week, Inge?

b. 1. He's coming at twelve thirty.
   2. And so it goes every spring.
   3. They came a week ago.

   4. We'll see Hans on Tuesday.
   5. He goes to Germany every summer.
   6. I'm going to pick her up this evening.
   7. I'll see him on the 20th.
   8. They're coming next month.
   9. He stayed home all day.
   10. In the spring it's very pretty here.

c. 1. We're going to the theater on Sunday.
   2. In January it's much colder.
   3. They're coming at seven o'clock.
   4. In 1972 I was in Frankfurt.
   5. They're going to demonstrate on the
      first of May.

6. They're coming at quarter after nine.
7. In 1973 she was living at our place.
8. We'll bring it back tomorrow morning.
9. We're going to Berlin in December.
10. He's seen the movie three times.

d. 1. The semester begins in September.
2. Were you in your office last Monday?
3. They're coming back in a week.
4. I got up early this morning.
5. He's coming tomorrow morning.
6. I did it the last time.
7. He flew to Berlin a week ago.
8. They have been living in this city for a year.
9. It's twenty after three.
10. He was born in 1954.

e. 1. We stay home evenings.
2. I'll call him Saturday.
3. They stayed over a year in Mainz.

4. We'll be there at quarter to ten.
5. Inge works nights.
6. During the day it's very hot.
7. I'm coming back on the 15th.
8. He came by yesterday evening.
9. We'll know that in a month.
10. They go skiing every winter.

f. 1. I'll call him tomorrow afternoon.
2. He's going to Germany for a year.
3. The next time you'll stay home.
4. He's been living at our place for a week.
5. It's twenty after one.
6. He called me up this morning.
7. She came by on Friday.
8. The second time it was easier.
9. I'll visit you next year.

VOCABULARY

der **Abend, -e** evening
abends evenings
auf (+ *acc.*) for
(*period of future time*)
der **Dienstag** Tuesday
dienstags Tuesdays
der **Donnerstag** Thursday
dreimal three times
einmal once
der **Freitag** Friday
der **Frühling** spring
ganz whole
geboren (ist) was born
gehen . . . skilaufen
go skiing
gestern yesterday
halb (*telling time*)
half way to the next
hour
der **Herbst** fall, autumn
heute today
in (*with time*) in
(from now)

Italien Italy
das **Jahr, -e** year
das **Mal** time
das **(___te) Mal**
the (___th) time
die **Minute, -n** minute
der **Mittwoch** Wednesday
der **Monat, -e** month
der **Montag** Monday
morgen tomorrow
der **Morgen, -** morning
morgens mornings
nach after
der **Nachmittag, -e**
afternoon
nachmittags afternoons
die **Nacht, ~** night
nachts nights
der **Samstag** Saturday
samstags Saturdays
seit (*with time expr.*)
for (period of
past time)

das **Semester, -** semester
der **Sommer** summer
der **Sonntag** Sunday
sonntags Sundays
die **Stunde, -n** hour
der **Tag, -e** day
tagsüber during
the day
tausendmal a thousand
times
über (*with time*) over
(longer than)
Uhr o'clock
die **Uhr, -en** clock
um (*with time*) at
vor before; to; ago
(*with time expr.*)
Wien Vienna
der **Winter, -** winter
die **Woche, -n** week
zehnmal ten times
zweimal twice

Reading VI

Mit der Eisenbahn° fahren

die Eisenbahn, –en: railroad

In Deutschland fährt man viel häufiger° mit der Eisenbahn als in den Vereinigten Staaten.° Die Bahnverbindungen° sind meistens° sehr gut, und die Züge° sind zuverlässig° und nicht allzu° teuer.

häufiger: more frequently
die Vereinigten Staaten: the United States
die Bahnverbindung, –en: train connection
meistens: usually
der Zug, ⁼e: train **zuverlässig**: reliable
allzu: all too

Wenn Sie in Deutschland sind, ist es ziemlich° sicher, daß Sie mehrmals° mit dem Zug fahren werden. Aber vorher° muß man verschiedenes° wissen. Zum Beispiel:° Was für Züge gibt es? Wie liest man einen Fahrplan?° Und wie kauft man Fahrkarten?

Die normalen Züge sind die Eilzüge° und die Schnellzüge (auch D-Züge genannt°). Der Unterschied° zwischen den beiden° ist, daß ein Schnellzug nicht so oft° hält,° wie ein Eilzug. Wenn Sie also zwischen größeren Städten reisen,° nehmen Sie am besten einen Schnellzug. Sie sparen° viel Zeit.° Wenn Sie in° eine kleinere Stadt fahren, müssen Sie normalerweise° einen Eilzug nehmen. Das dauert° etwas° länger. Eilzüge und Schnellzüge haben beide eine erste und eine zweite Klasse.° Die erste Klasse kostet allerdings° ungefähr° 60 Prozent° mehr als die zweite, ist aber auch viel bequemer° und weniger besetzt.°

Beide Arten° von Zügen sehen innen° anders° als amerikanische Züge aus. In einem deutschen Zug haben die Wagen° Abteile.° Jedes Abteil hat Sitzplätze° für 6 Personen,° ein eigenes° Fenster, Platz° für Gepäck° und eine Schiebetür.° Die Schiebetür geht auf° einen Korridor;° dieser Korridor geht den ganzen Wagen entlang° und führt° zum Übergang° in den nächsten Wagen. So können Sie von Ihrem

ziemlich: rather

mehrmals: several times

vorher: before that, in advance
   verschiedenes: several different things
zum Beispiel: for instance, for example

der Fahrplan, ⸚e: timetable

der Eilzug, ⸚e: *lit.:* "fast train"

genannt: called (*past participle of* **nennen**)
der Unterschied, -e: difference
   beide: (*here*) the two of them
oft: often   **halten:** (*here*) to stop

reisen: to travel

sparen: to save   **die Zeit:** time
in: in (*used here because you're travelling right into town*)

normalerweise: normally   **dauern:** to take (*of time*)

etwas: (*here*) somewhat

die Klasse, -n: class
allerdings: to be sure   **ungefähr:** about
   Prozent: percent

bequem: comfortable

besetzt: (*here*) crowded, occupied

die Art, -en: kind, sort   **innen:** inside
   anders: different
der Wagen, -: (*here*) railroad car
   das Abteil, -e: compartment
der Sitzplatz, ⸚e: seat   **die Person, -en:** person
   eigen: of its own   **der Platz:** (*here*) space
das Gepäck: luggage   **die Schiebetür, -en:** sliding door
gehen auf (+ *acc.*): (*here*) to lead to
der Korridor, -e: corridor
entlang·gehen (+ *acc.*): (*here*) to go through, along   **führen:** to lead   **der Übergang, ⸚e:** passage

gen I,
1–5,
p. 290

Abteil zum Speisewagen° gehen. Aber vorsichtig!° Nur D-Züge haben einen Speisewagen, Eilzüge haben keinen.

der Speisewagen, –: dining car
Aber vorsichtig!: But watch out!

Für längere Reisen° gibt es auch die TEE (Trans Europa Express)-Züge zwischen Großstädten. Diese sind die schnellsten Züge und sie halten nur sehr selten.° Sie sind eigentlich° da für Strecken° über 300 Kilometer,° z.B.° zwischen Frankfurt und München, oder Hamburg und Köln.° Touristen° benutzen° die TEE-Züge auch für Auslandsreisen.° Sie können von Stuttgart nach Amsterdam fahren, oder von München nach Mailand,° wenn Sie wollen. TEE-Züge haben nur erste Klasse, und man soll im voraus einen Platz reservieren.

die Reise, –n: trip

selten: rarely, seldom   **eigentlich**: actually
   die Strecke, –n: (*here*) distance
der Kilometer, –: kilometer   **z.B.** = **zum Beispiel**

Köln: Cologne   **der Tourist, –en**: tourist

benutzen: to use   **die Auslandsreise, –n**:
   trips abroad; **das Ausland**: foreign countries

Mailand: Milan (Italy)

Auch gibt es die IC (Intercity)-Züge. Sie sind wie die TEE-Züge, nur daß sie nicht ins Ausland fahren. Für beide Arten von Zügen muß man einen Zuschlag° von 10 Mark bezahlen. Für kurze Strecken ist der Zuschlag einfach° zu teuer, und die meisten Leute nehmen einen anderen Zug. Und das ist genau,° was die Deutsche Bundesbahn° will. Denn, wie gesagt,° diese Züge sind für längere Strecken da.

Für kurze Strecken gibt es Nahverkehrszüge.° Diese haben oft nur zweite Klasse und haben keine Abteile in den Wagen. Sie halten auch an den kleinsten Bahnhöfen,° und eine kurze Reise kann deshalb° lange dauern.°

Fragen I, 6–10, pp. 290–91

FAHRPLÄNE°

Jetzt kennen Sie die verschiedenen° Arten von Zügen. Sehen Sie den folgenden° kleinen Fahrplan an. Sagen wir, Sie wollen von Mainz (1) nach München (12) fahren. Den ersten Zug, D 203, können Sie nicht nehmen, er fährt nämlich° nur bis Mannheim. Mit dem Intercity 115, dem TEE 25 und mit

---

Glossary (right margin):

der Zuschlag, ⸚e: surcharge

einfach: simply

genau: exactly

die Deutsche Bundesbahn: German Federal Railroad   wie gesagt: as said

der Nahverkehrszug, ⸚e: local train

der Bahnhof, ⸚e: train station   deshalb: for that reason   lange dauern: to take a long time

der Fahrplan, ⸚e: timetable

verschieden: different

folgend: following

nämlich: in fact

---

ab = **Ab**fahrt: departure
an = **An**kunft: arrival
Hbf = **H**aupt**b**ahn**h**of: main station

		ZUGNUMMER				
		D 203	IC 115	E 2027	TEE 25	D 411
1	MAINZ Hbf ab	13:42	14:45		14:50	15:15
2	WORMS Hbf					
3	LUDWIGSHAFEN					
4	MANNHEIM Hbf	14:26	15:29			16:04
5	HEIDELBERG Hbf		15:40			
6	BRUCHSAL					
7	STUTTGART Hbf		16:57	17:05		17:46
8	GÖPPINGEN			17:33		
9	GEISLINGEN			17:47		
10	ULM Hbf		17:54	18:15		18:49
11	AUGSBURG Hbf		18:38	19:08	18:42	19:46
12	MÜNCHEN Hbf an		19:11	19:46	19:15	20:34

dem D 411 können Sie direkt zwischen den beiden Städten fahren, aber nur der D-Zug hat zweite Klasse, und Sie bezahlen auch die 10 Mark Zuschlag nicht.

Sagen wir dagegen,° Sie wollen von Mannheim (4) nach Geislingen (9) fahren. Hier gibt es nur eine Möglichkeit.° Sie müssen über° Stuttgart (7) fahren und dieses Mal müssen Sie umsteigen.° Zuerst nehmen Sie den Intercity 115. Sie steigen in Mannheim (4) um* 15 Uhr 29 ein° und in Stuttgart (7) 16 Uhr 57 aus.° Jetzt steigen Sie um und nehmen den Eilzug 2027. Sie steigen 17 Uhr 5 ein und kommen 17 Uhr 47 in Geislingen an.

dagegen: on the other hand

die Möglichkeit, –en: possibility
  über: (*here*) via, by way of
um · steigen: to change trains

ein · steigen: to board a train

aus · steigen: to get off a train

Wie Sie sehen, benutzt° die Eisenbahn die 24-Stunden Uhr.° Nach Mittag° zählen Sie zu der „normalen" Zeit einfach 12 hinzu:° 4 Uhr nachmittags ist also 16 Uhr, 9 Uhr abends ist also 21 Uhr. Die Minuten zählt man einfach von 1 bis 59, zum Beispiel:

benutzen: to use
die 24-Stunden Uhr: 24-hour clock
  der Mittag: noon
hinzu · zählen: to add

Drills, p. 291

$$4.30 \text{ nachmittags} = 16 \text{ Uhr } 30$$
$$9.47 \text{ abends} = 21 \text{ Uhr } 47$$

WIE MAN FAHRKARTEN KAUFT

Sie können Ihre Fahrkarten im voraus in einem Reisebüro° kaufen, wenn Sie wollen. Gewöhnlich° aber gehen Sie zu einem Fahrkartenschalter° im Bahnhof. Für die Strecke Mannheim—Geislingen kann das Gespräch° so aussehen:

das Reisebüro, –s: travel agency
  gewöhnlich: usually
der Fahrkartenschalter, –: ticket window

das Gespräch, –e: conversation

SIE:

Einmal zweiter Klasse° nach Geislingen. Das geht über Stuttgart, nicht?

einmal zweiter Klasse: one second class ticket

---

*With exact train-times, **um** may be omitted.

MANN AM SCHALTER:

Moment mal.° (*Er schlägt es nach.*°) Ja, wollen Sie gleich fahren?

SIE:

Ja, so bald wie möglich.

ER:

In 20 Minuten fährt der Intercity 115. Er hat aber nur erste Klasse und Sie müssen auch Zuschlag zahlen.

SIE:

Also, ist recht. Habe ich gleich Anschluß° in Stutt-gart?

ER:

Ja, ein Eilzug fährt 17 Uhr 5 von Stuttgart ab. Da sind Sie 17 Uhr 47 in Geislingen. Soll das jetzt auch erste Klasse sein?

SIE:

Bitte.

Moment mal.: Just a moment.
nach·schlagen: to look (something) up

der Anschluß, ¨sse: connecting train

ER:

Einfach° oder hin und zurück?°

   einfach: (*here*) one way ticket
      hin und zurück: (*here*) return ticket

SIE:

Einfach, bitte.

ER:

Gut, das macht dann 49 Mark mit Zuschlag.

SIE:

Bitte schön. Welches Gleis,° bitte?

   das Gleis, –e: track

ER:

Gleis 5.

(*Sie geben ihm einen Fünfziger,° der Mann gibt Ihnen Ihre Fahrkarte, die Zuschlagskarte° und eine Mark zurück.*)

   der Fünfziger, –: 50-mark bill
   die Zuschlagskarte, –n: surcharge ticket

* * *

Für die Strecke Mainz—München wird alles viel einfacher aussehen, besonders° wenn Sie den D–Zug nehmen:

   besonders: especially

SIE:

Einmal zweiter° nach München, hin und zurück.

   einmal zweiter: one second class (ticket)

ER:

Moment. Das macht 112 Mark.

NAHVERKEHR°

   der Nahverkehr: local trains

Für den Nahverkehr (unter 100 Kilometer) gibt es Fahrkartenautomaten° und Selbstbedienung.° Am Automat ist ein Netzplan° und verschiedene Farben° zeigen an,° wie weit weg Ihr Ziel° ist. Sagen wir, Ihr Ziel ist in dem grünen Gebiet.° Sie drücken° also die Taste° für das grüne Gebiet. Dann zeigt Ihnen eine kleine Leuchttafel° den Fahrpreis.° Jetzt können Sie Münzen° einwerfen.° Sie bekommen dann Ihre Fahrkarte und Ihr Wechselgeld.° Vergessen Sie aber nicht, daß Automaten meistens nur Münzen annehmen,° von 10 Pfennig bis 5 Mark, aber keine Geldscheine.°

   der Fahrkartenautomat, –en: ticket machine
      die Selbstbedienung: self service
   der Netzplan, ⁼e: (*here*) map of the area
      serviced by the local trains
   die Farbe, –n: color an·zeigen: to show,
      indicate das Ziel: destination
   das Gebiet, –e: area drücken: to push
   die Taste, –n: button, key
   die Leuchttafel, –n: illuminated sign
      der Fahrpreis, –e: price of the ticket
   die Münze, –n: coin ein·werfen: (*here*) to insert

   das Wechselgeld: change

   ᴀn·nehmen: (*here*) to take

   der Geldschein, –e: bill

rcises,
pp.
91–92

ABFAHRTS-° UND ANKUNFTSTAFELN°

die Abfahrtstafel, –n: departure board
die Ankunftstafel, –n: arrival board

Jeder Bahnhof hat Abfahrts- und Ankunftstafeln. Da können Sie sehen, wann und wohin° die Züge fahren, sie erfahren° auch, was für° Züge es sind, die Gleisnummern° und fast alle anderen wichtigen° Auskünfte.° Nehmen wir an,° Sie sind in Mainz und wollen am Nachmittag nach München fahren. Sie gehen im Mainzer Bahnhof zur Abfahrtstafel und sehen nach,° wann die Züge fahren. Wenn die Verbindungen° komplizierter° sind, zum Beispiel, wenn Sie umsteigen müssen, können Sie um Auskunft bitten, oder im Fahrplan nachsehen.

wohin: where . . . to

erfahren: to find out   was für: what kind of

die Gleisnummer, –n: track number
   wichtig: important
die Auskunft, ⁀e: information
   an·nehmen: (here) to assume

nach·sehen: to take a look
die Verbindung, –en: (here) train connection
   kompliziert: complicated

KURSWAGEN°

der Kurswagen, –: passenger car with special destination

Viele Züge haben Kurswagen. Diese Wagen fahren nicht nach dem Hauptziel° von Ihrem Zug. Sie werden unterwegs° in einen anderen Zug eingestellt° und fahren dann nach einem anderen Ziel. Aber Sie können diese Wagen gleich erkennen. Innen° und außen° sehen Sie Schilder mit ihrem Zielbahnhof.° Zum Beispiel, wenn Sie von Frankfurt nach Hamburg fahren, passen Sie auf,° daß sie nicht in einen Kurswagen nach Bremen einsteigen.

das Hauptziel, –e: main destination

unterwegs: on the way

ein·stellen in (+ acc.): to transfer to

innen: inside   außen: outside

der Zielbahnhof, ⁀e: station where the car is going

auf·passen: to watch out, be careful

Fragen II, p. 292

FRAGEN I

1. Was ist der Unterschied zwischen einem D–Zug und einem Eilzug?
   (D–Zug / halten / nicht so oft / wie / Eilzug)
2. Warum soll man einen D–Zug nehmen, wenn man zwischen größeren Städten reist?
   (Man / sparen / Zeit // wenn / man / nehmen / D–Zug)
3. Was ist der Unterschied zwischen der ersten und der zweiten Klasse?
   (erst- / Klasse / sein / bequemer // aber / sie / kosten / 60% / mehr)
4. Beschreiben Sie ein Abteil in einem deutschen Zug.
   (Abteil / haben / Sitzplätze / 6 Personen)
   (Es / haben / auch / Platz / Gepäck / und / Schiebetür)
5. Wohin führt der Korridor?
   (Korridor / führen / zu / Übergang / in / nächst- / Wagen)
6. Was sind TEE–Züge?
   (Sie / sein / schnellst- / Züge // und / halten / selten)
   (Sie / sein / Züge / für / länger- / Strecken // z.B. / Stuttgart—Amsterdam)

7. Was sind andere wichtige Unterschiede zwischen TEE- und D-Zügen?
(TEE / haben / nur / 1. Klasse // und / man / sollen / reservieren / Platz)

8. Was ist der Unterschied zwischen TEE-Zügen und Intercity-Zügen?
(Intercity-Züge / fahren / nicht / in / Ausland)

9. Was ist eine Ähnlichkeit zwischen Intercity- und TEE-Zügen?   (**Ähnlichkeit:** similarity)
(Man / müssen / bezahlen / Zuschlag / 10 Mark)

10. Beschreiben Sie einen Nahverkehrszug.
(Nahverkehrszug / haben / kein / Abteile // und / halten / an / kleinst- / Bahnhöfe)

DRILLS

Practice saying the following train numbers. Before reading, first note that

E is pronounced E
D is pronounced D
TEE is pronounced T-E-E
IC is pronounced "Intercity," with a German accent. (The abbreviation is not used in conversation.)

Note also that the train numbers are read like regular numbers. For example "D-vierhundertelf."

1.			2.	
D 379	E 3456	TEE 72	TEE 72	E 2027
D 411	E 2074	IC 115	D 411	TEE 25
D 453	E 3122	IC 129	IC 129	D 588
D 247	E 3156	IC 174	E 3456	E 3122
D 588	TEE 25	IC 184	IC 115	IC 184
D 774	TEE 66			

Practice railroad time by saying the following departure and arrival times aloud.

ab 7.53	ab 11.27	ab 8.19	ab 14.30	ab 20.47
an 14.13	an 12.26	an 14.01	an 22.11	an 22.26
ab 14.22	ab 12.11	ab 14.21	ab 18.43	ab 0.13*
an 15.47	an 13.36	an 17.28	an 19.48	an 0.52

WIE MAN FAHRKARTEN KAUFT

SIE: (Einmal / zweit- / Klasse / Geislingen)
(Gehen / das / über / Stuttgart / ?)

ER: Moment mal. Ja, wollen Sie gleich fahren?

SIE: (bald / möglich)

ER: In 20 Minuten fährt der Intercity 115. Er hat aber nur erste Klasse und Sie müssen auch Zuschlag zahlen.

SIE: (Sein / recht)
(Haben / ich / Anschluß in Stuttgart / ?)

ER: Ja, ein Eilzug fährt von Stuttgart um 17 Uhr 5 ab. Da sind Sie 17 Uhr 47 in Geislingen. Soll das jetzt auch erste Klasse sein?

SIE: (Bitte)

ER: Einfach oder hin und zurück?

SIE: (Einfach)

ER: Gut, das macht dann 49 Mark mit Zuschlag.

SIE: (Bitte // welch- / Gleis / ?)

ER: Gleis 5.

* * *

_____
* *Here read:* null Uhr dreizehn

SIE: Einmal zweiter Klasse nach Geislingen. Das geht über Stuttgart, nicht?
ER: (Wollen / Sie / fahren / gleich / ?)
SIE: Ja, so bald wie möglich.
ER: (20 Minuten / fahren / Intercity 115)
    (Er / haben / nur / erst- / Klasse // und / Sie / müssen / zahlen / Zuschlag)
SIE: Also, ist recht. Habe ich gleich Anschluß in Stuttgart?
ER: (Eilzug / ab · fahren / 17.05 / Stuttgart)
    (Sie / sein / 17.47 / Geislingen)
    (Sollen / das / sein / erst- / Klasse / ?)
SIE: Bitte.
ER: (Einfach / oder / . . . / ?)
SIE: Einfach, bitte.
ER: (Das / machen / 49 Mark)
SIE: Bitte schön. Welches Gleis, bitte?
ER: (5)

FRAGEN II

1. Was zeigt Ihnen der Netzplan am Fahrkartenautomat?
   (Netzplan / zeigen // wie weit weg / Ziel / sein)

2. Sagen wir, Ihr Ziel ist in dem grünen Gebiet. Was machen Sie?
   (Man / drücken / Taste / für / grün / Gebiet)
   (Leuchttafel / zeigen / Fahrpreis)
   (Man / ein · werfen / Münzen)
   (Dann / man / bekommen / Fahrkarte / und / Wechselgeld)

3. Sie wollen nach München fahren. Was lesen Sie an der Abfahrtstafel?
   (Man / lesen // wann / Züge / fahren)

4. Was erfahren Sie noch?   (noch: else)
   (Man / erfahren / auch / Gleisnummer)

5. Was machen Sie, wenn die Verbindungen komplizierter sind?
   (Man / können / bitten / Auskunft // oder man / können / nach · sehen / in / Fahrplan)
   (Oder / man / können / sitzen / einfach / da)

6. Wo fahren Kurswagen hin?
   (Kurswagen / fahren / nicht / nach / Hauptziel / von / Zug)
   (Sie / fahren / nach / ander- / Ziel)

7. Wie kann man sie erkennen?
   (Innen / außen / sehen / man / Schilder / mit / Zielbahnhof)

ÜBUNGEN

Benutzen Sie den folgenden Fahrplan für diese Übungen:

1. Welche Züge fahren von Frankfurt (3) nach Fulda (5)? Wann fahren sie ab und wann kommen sie an?
   a. (TEE 72 / ab · fahren / 11.27 / Frankfurt // und / an · kommen / 12.26 / Fulda)
   b. (E 3456 / ab · fahren / 12.11 / Frankfurt // und / an · kommen / 13.36 / Fulda)
   c. (Intercity 174 / ab · fahren / 15.28 / Frankfurt // und / an · kommen / 16.26 / Fulda)

2. a. Sie sind in München (1) und wollen früh am Morgen nach Hamburg (15) fahren. Freunde holen Sie ungefähr um 4 Uhr nachmittags in Hamburg ab. Welchen Zug nehmen Sie? Um wieviel Uhr fahren Sie ab? Wann kommen Sie in Hamburg an?
   (nehmen / D 588 // und / ab · fahren / 7.55)
   (an · kommen / 15.54 / Hamburg)

b. Sie nehmen denselben Zug wie in 2a, aber Sie wollen nicht nach Hamburg, sondern nach Bremen (16) fahren. Wo steigen Sie ein? Wo und um wieviel Uhr steigen Sie um? Wann steigen Sie in Bremen aus?

(ein · steigen / 7.55 / München // und / um · steigen / 14.13 / Hannover)
(ab · fahren / 14.22 / Hannover // und / aus · steigen / 15.47 / Bremen)

3. a. Sie wollen am späten Nachmittag von Frankfurt (3) nach Hamburg (15). Welche direkten Verbindungen haben Sie? Wann fahren die Züge von Frankfurt ab, und wann kommen sie in Hamburg an?

(IC 174 und D 370 / fahren / direkt / Frankfurt / Hamburg)
(IC 174 / ab · fahren / 15.28 / Frankfurt // und / an · kommen / 20.15 / Hamburg)
(D 370 / ab · fahren / 16.34 / Frankfurt // und an · kommen / 22.19 / Hamburg)

b. Sie wollen am späten Nachmittag von Frankfurt (3) nach Bremen (16) fahren. In diesem Fall müssen Sie umsteigen. Beschreiben Sie Ihre Reise, die Züge, die Sie nehmen, wo und wann Sie einsteigen, umsteigen und aussteigen.

(Sie / nehmen / D 370 / und / E 3156)
(Sie / ein · steigen / 16.34 / Frankfurt // und / aus · steigen / 20.42 / Hannover)
(Hier / Sie / um · steigen // Sie / ab · fahren / 20.47 // und / an · kommen / 22.26 / Bremen)

4. Jetzt fahren Sie von Kassel (10) nach Berlin (13). Welche Züge nehmen Sie? Wann fahren Sie ab? Wann und wo steigen Sie um? Wann kommen Sie in Berlin an?

(Sie / nehmen / D 774 / und / D 247)
(Sie / ab · fahren / 14.21 / Kassel // und / an · kommen / 16.17 / Hannover)
(Hier / Sie / müssen / um · steigen)
(Sie / ab · fahren / 18.00 / Hannover // und / an · kommen / 22.11 / Berlin)

				D 588	E 3122	TEE 72	E 3456	D 774	D 247	IC 174	D 370	E 3156
								ZUGNUMMER				
1	MÜNCHEN	Hbf	ab	7.55								
2	WÜRZBURG	Hbf	ab	10.33								
3	FRANKFURT	Hbf	ab			11.27	12.11	12.14		15.28	16.34	
4	GELNHAUSEN						12.46					
5	FULDA					12.26	13.36			16.26		
6	GIESSEN							12.56			17.16	
7	MARBURG (LAHN)							13.17			17.36	
8	KÖLN	Hbf	ab						14.30			
9	DORTMUND	Hbf	ab									
10	KASSEL	Hbf						14.21			18.40	
11	GÖTTINGEN			13.12		13.53		15.17		17.52		
12	HANNOVER	Hbf		14.13	14.22	14.53		16.17	18.00	18.48	20.42	20.47
13	BERLIN								22.11			
14	LÜNEBURG							17.28				
15	HAMBURG	Hbf		15.54		16.19				20.15	22.19	
16	BREMEN	Hbf	an		15.47							22.26

Lesson 7 Level ONE

A The Genitive Case

1 Introduction to usage

a. Contrast: possessives and genitive phrases

Pauls Wagen   Paul's car
der Wagen des Direktors   the director's car

These two German phrases are grammatically very different. **Pauls** (like the English "Paul's") is a *possessive,* and it *precedes the noun it refers to.* **Des Direktors** is a *genitive phrase,* and it *follows the noun it refers to.*

b. Possessive forms in German: proper names only

Peters Wagen   Peter's car
Inges Hut   Inge's hat

A German name forms its possessive by adding an **s,** without an apostrophe.

c. Genitive phrases

Der Direktor is not a proper name. If you want to say "the director's car" in German, you must use a genitive phrase:

der Wagen **des Direktors**   the director's car

Genitive phrases in German correspond not only to English possessives but also to a wide range of English phrases that use the preposition "of":

der Wagen **des Direktors**   *the director's* car
das Ende **des Filmes**   the end *of the movie*
der Anfang **des Semesters**   the beginning *of the semester*

Where English uses the preposition "of," German gets the same idea across grammatically by using the *genitive case.*

2 Forms of the genitive case

a. Genitive of the definite article

The definite article has the following special forms for the genitive case:

Masculine	Neuter	Feminine	Plural
des Mannes	**des** Kindes	**der** Frau	**der** Männer Kinder Frauen

As you can see, there are two different genitive patterns:

1. A masculine-and-neuter pattern

The genitive form of the definite article is

$$des$$

The nouns themselves end in

$$-(e)s$$

des Mannes (the man's, of the man)
des Kindes (the child's, of the child)
des Wagens (the car's, of the car)

2. Feminine-and-plural pattern

For both feminine and plural nouns the genitive form of the definite article is

$$der$$

The nouns themselves *do not add endings:*

der Frau   (the woman's, of the woman)
der Männer (the men's, of the men)
der Kinder (the children's, of the children)
der Frauen (the women's, of the women)

b. Noun endings

As you have seen, only masculine and neuter nouns take genitive endings.

1. -es ending

The general rule is that the ending **-es** is used:

With the nouns of one syllable:

des Mann**es**, des Kind**es**

With all nouns ending in an "s" sound:

des Kaufhaus**es**, des Schreibtisch**es**

2. -s ending

All other nouns of more than one syllable end in **-s**:

des Wagen**s**, des Monat**s**

3. Weak nouns

Weak nouns, which take **-(e)n** endings in the accusative and the dative, take the same -(e)n ending in the genitive case:

	Weak Nouns	
NOM.	der Student	der Kunde
ACC.	den Studenten	den Kunden
DAT.	dem Studenten	dem Kunden
GEN.	des Student**en**	des Kund**en**

c. Genitive forms of other **der**-words

All of the **der**-words take genitive endings that are exactly the same as the last two letters of the definite article (**des** and **der**):

Masculine	Neuter	Feminine	Plural
dies**es** Mannes	dies**es** Kindes	dies**er** Frau	dies**er** Männer
d**es** Mannes	d**es** Kindes	d**er** Frau	d**er** Männer

DRILLS

Genitive endings

● Supply the correct *masculine* and *neuter* endings.

1. Wer war der Fahrer d___ Wagen___?
2. Das Ende d___ Film___ war langweilig.
3. Am Ende d___ Monat___ sind wir immer pleite.
4. Der Anfang dies___ Roman___ ist schwach.
5. Er saß am anderen Ende d___ Tisch___.
6. Am Anfang d___ Monat___ bekomme ich meinen Scheck.
7. Sein Zimmer liegt am Ende d___ Korridor___.
8. Der Anfang d___ Semester___ ist immer schwer.

(**der Fahrer**: driver)
(**das Ende**: end)
(**am Ende**: at the end; **pleite**: broke)
(**der Anfang**: beginning; **der Roman**: novel)

(**der Korridor**: hall)
(**das Semester**: semester)

● Supply the correct *feminine* and *plural* endings.

1. Er kommt am Ende d___ Woche.
2. Hast du eine Liste d___ Adressen?

(**die Liste**: list)

3. Es stand auf der ersten Seite d____ Zeitung. (die Seite, *here:* page; die Zeitung: newspaper)
4. Sein Haus liegt am Ende d____ Straße.
5. Die Resultate d____ Experimente sind gut. (das Resultat, -e: result; das Experiment, -e: experiment)
6. Das ist ein Zeichen d____ Zeit.* (das Zeichen: sign)
7. Er wohnt auf der anderen Seite d____ Straße. (die Seite, *here:* side)

- Mixed drill. Supply the correct endings.

1. Das Ende d____ Film____ war langweilig.
2. Hast du eine Liste d____ Adressen?
3. Er saß am anderen Ende d____ Tisch____.
4. Wer war der Fahrer d____ Wagen____?
5. Es stand auf der ersten Seite d____ Zeitung.
6. Sein Zimmer ist am Ende d____ Korridor____.
7. Das ist ein Zeichen d____ Zeit.
8. Sein Haus liegt am Ende d____ Straße.
9. Der Anfang d____ Semester____ ist immer schwer.
10. Er kommt am Ende d____ Woche.
11. Am Anfang d____ Monat____ bekomme ich meinen Scheck.
12. Er wohnt auf der anderen Seite d____ Straße.
13. Am Ende d____ Monat____ sind wir immer pleite.
14. Die Resultate d____ Experimente sind gut.
15. Der Anfang dies____ Roman____ ist schwach.

- Express in German.

1. The end of the film was boring.
2. Who was the driver of the car?
3. He's coming at the end of the week.
4. Do you have a list of the addresses?
5. At the end of the month we're always broke.
6. His room is at the end of the hall.
7. It's a sign of the times.
8. It was on the first page of the newspaper. (use **stehen**)
9. The beginning of the semester is always hard.
10. He lives on the other side of the street.
11. I get my check at the beginning of the month.
12. His house is at the end of the street.
13. He was sitting at the other end of the table.
14. The results of the experiments are good.
15. The beginning of this novel is weak.

3 The **ein**-words

There is nothing new here: The **ein**-words take exactly the same genitive endings as do the **der**-words.

Masculine	Neuter	Feminine	Plural
mein**es** Mann**es**	mein**es** Kind**es**	mein**er** Frau	mein**er** Kinder
(dies**es** Mann**es**)	(dies**es** Kind**es**)	(dies**er** Frau)	(dies**er** Kinder)
(des Mann**es**)	(des Kind**es**)	(**der** Frau)	(**der** Kinder)

---

*English: a sign of the *times* (plural); German: ein Zeichen **der Zeit** (singular).

4 The weak endings of the genitive case

The weak ending -en is used with all adjectives following genitive **der-** and **ein-** words.

MASCULINE	des ander**en** Wagens	(of the other car)
NEUTER	seines neu**en** Stückes	(of his new play)
FEMININE	seiner erst**en** Frau	(of his first wife)
PLURAL	dieser neu**en** Experimente	(of these new experiments)

5 Summary tables

At this point we can make complete tables of the definite and indefinite articles as well as the weak adjective endings:

THE DEFINITE ARTICLE			
	Masculine	*Neuter*	*Feminine*	*Plural*
NOM.	der Mann	das Kind	die Frau	die Männer
ACC.	den Mann	das Kind	die Frau	die Männer
DAT.	dem Mann	dem Kind	der Frau	den Männern
GEN.	des Mannes	des Kindes	der Frau	der Männer

THE INDEFINITE ARTICLE			
	Masculine	*Neuter*	*Feminine*	*Plural*
NOM.	ein Mann	ein Kind	eine Frau	keine Männer
ACC.	einen Mann	ein Kind	eine Frau	keine Männer
DAT.	einem Mann	einem Kind	einer Frau	keinen Männern
GEN.	eines Mannes	eines Kindes	einer Frau	keiner Männer

WEAK ADJECTIVE ENDINGS			
	Masculine	*Neuter*	*Feminine*	*Plural*
NOM.	-e	-e	-e	-en
ACC.	-en	-e	-e	-en
DAT.	-en	-en	-en	-en
GEN.	**-en**	**-en**	**-en**	**-en**

As you can see, all genitive weak endings are **–en**.

DRILLS

1 Genitive endings with **ein**-words

• Supply the correct *masculine* and *neuter* endings.

1. Er hat die Augen sein___ Vater___.
2. Er kommt am Anfang d___ Semester___. ,
3. Die Farbe ein___ Wein___ ist auch wichtig.
4. Die Mutter mein___ Mann___ wohnt noch bei uns.
5. Das Leben ein___ Student___ ist schwer.
6. Das Leben ein___ Hund___ ist nicht viel besser.

(das Auge, -n: eye)

(die Farbe: color; **wichtig**: important)
(**noch**: still)
(das Leben: life)
(der Hund: dog)

• Supply the correct *feminine* and *plural* endings.

1. Die Titel sein___ Filme sind immer interessant.
2. Das ist die Schwäche sein___ Arbeit.
3. Die Resultate mein___ Experimente waren gut.
4. Ich habe das Ende dein___ Arbeit nicht verstanden.
5. Was ist die Farbe ihr___ Augen?
6. Es ist das Ende ein___ Epoche.

(der Titel, -: title)
(die Schwäche: weakness)

(die Epoche: era)

• Supply the correct endings (all genders and the plural).

1. Die Farbe ein___ Wein___ ist auch wichtig.
2. Das ist die Schwäche sein___ Arbeit.
3. Was ist die Farbe ihr___ Augen?
4. Die Mutter mein___ Mann___ wohnt noch bei uns.
5. Es ist das Ende ein___ Epoche.
6. Die Resultate mein___ Experimente waren gut.
7. Er hat die Augen sein___ Vater___.
8. Die Titel sein___ Filme sind sehr interessant.
9. Ich habe das Ende sein___ Arbeit nicht verstanden.
10. Das Leben ein___ Student___ ist schwer.

• Express in German.

1. What's the color of her eyes?
2. I didn't understand the end of your paper.
3. The results of my experiments were good.
4. He has his father's eyes.
5. That's the weakness of his paper.
6. The color of a wine is important, too.
7. The titles of his films are always interesting.
8. My husband's mother is still living at our place.
9. A student's life is hard.
10. It's the end of an era.

2 Weak endings

• Supply the correct *masculine* and *neuter* endings.

1. Wer war der Fahrer d___ ander___ Wagen___? *(sing.)*
2. Er ging am Ende d___ erst___ Semester___ weg.
3. Die Farbe ein___ gut___ Wein___ ist wichtig.
4. Der Anfang ein___ neu___ Semester___ ist immer schwer.

- Supply the correct *feminine* and *plural* endings.

1. Er ist Direktor* ein___ groß___ Firma.   **(der Direktor:** director; **die Firma:** [business] firm)
2. Hast du eine Liste d___ neu___ Adressen?
3. Wie war der Name sein___ erst___ Frau?†   **(der Name:** name)
4. Heißt das Stück „Der Besuch ein___ alt___ Dame" oder „Der Besuch d___ alt___ Dame"?
                                         (das Stück: play; **der Besuch:** visit)
5. Die Resultate sein___ neu___ Experimente sind gut.

- Supply the correct endings (all genders and the plural).

1. Wie war der Name sein___ erst___ Frau?
2. Er ging am Ende d___ erst___ Semester___ weg.
3. Hast du eine Liste d___ neu___ Adressen?
4. Der Anfang ein___ neu___ Semester___ ist immer schwer.
5. Er ist Direktor ein___ groß___ Firma.
6. Heißt das Stück „Der Besuch ein___ alt___ Dame" oder „Der Besuch d___ alt___ Dame"?
7. Wer war der Fahrer d___ ander___ Wagen___?
8. Die Resultate sein___ neu___ Experimente sind gut.

- Express in German.

1. Do you have a list of the new addresses?
2. Who was the driver of the other car?
3. The results of his new experiments are good.
4. He left at the end of the first semester.
5. He's the director of a large firm.
6. The beginning of a new semester is always hard.
7. Is the play called "The Visit of an Old Lady" or "The Visit of the Old Lady"?
8. What was his first wife's name?

6 Other uses of the genitive case

a. Prepositions that take the genitive case

The following prepositions take genitive objects:

trotz: in spite of

> Er will trotz seiner Erkältung mitkommen.
> (He wants to come along *in spite of his cold.*)

während: during

> Während des Semesters muß er viel arbeiten.
> (*During the semester* he has to work a lot.)

---

*When indicating nationality or profession, the article is usually omitted.

    NATIONALITY   Er ist Deutscher.   (He's a German.)
    PROFESSION   Er ist Direktor einer großen Firma.   (He's the director of a large firm.)

†**Wie** war der Name? When asking about names, German uses **wie** where English uses "what."

                          Wie war sein Name?
                          (*What* was his name?)

wegen: because of, due to, on account of

> Er ist nur **wegen seiner Eltern** zur Uni gegangen.
> (He only went to college *because of his parents*.)

b. The genitive of indefinite time

These expressions all begin with a genitive form of **ein:**

> **Eines Morgens** ist er vorbeigekommen. (He came by *one morning*.)
> **Eines Tages** sage ich ihr alles. (*One day* I'll tell her everything.)

DRILLS

1 Genitive of indefinite time

• Supply the correct endings.

1. Ein___ Tag___ sage ich ihr alles.
2. Ein___ Morgen___ wurde er krank.
3. Er ist ein___ Abend___ vorbeigekommen.
4. Ein___ schön___ Tag___ ging sie einfach weg.   (**schön,** *here:* fine; **einfach:** simply)

2 Prepositions that take the genitive case

• **während:** during

1. Während d___ Semester___ muß er viel arbeiten.
2. Das mache ich während d___ Ferien.   (**die Ferien** [*plural only*]: vacation)
3. Während d___ Krieg___ war ich in England.   (**der Krieg:** war)

• **wegen:** because of, on account of

1. Wegen sein___ Arbeit muß er viel reisen.   (**reisen:** to travel)
2. Sie sind wegen d___ Kinder zusammengeblieben.   (**zusammen·bleiben** [s]: to stay together)
3. Sie ist nur wegen ihr___ Eltern zur Uni gegangen.
     (**die Eltern:** parents; **die Uni** [*slightly slangy*]: university, college)

• **trotz:** in spite of

1. Er will trotz sein___ Erkältung mitkommen.   (**die Erkältung:** cold)
2. Trotz ihr___ Familie hat sie den Jungen geheiratet.   (**heiraten:** to marry)

• Supply the correct genitive endings.

1. Das mache ich während d___ Ferien.
2. Er ist ein___ Abend___ vorbeigekommen.
3. Er will trotz sein___ Erkältung mitkommen.
4. Ein___ schön___ Tag___ ging sie einfach weg.
5. Wegen sein___ Arbeit muß er viel reisen.
6. Während d___ Semester___ muß er viel arbeiten.
7. Trotz ihr___ Familie hat sie den Jungen geheiratet.
8. Ein___ Morgen___ wurde er krank.
9. Sie ist nur wegen ihr___ Eltern zur Uni gegangen.
10. Während d___ Krieg___ war ich in England.
11. Sie sind wegen d___ Kinder zusammengeblieben.
12. Ein___ Tag___ sage ich ihr alles.

3 Mixed drills

• Supply the correct genitive phrases.

1. _____ wurde er krank.
   (One morning)

2. _____ muß er viel reisen.
   (Because of his work)

3. _____ war ich in England.
   (During the war)

4. _____ sage ich ihr alles.
   (One day)

5. Sie sind nur _____
   (because of the children)
   zusammengeblieben.

6. Das mache ich _____ .
   (during the vacation)

7. Er ist _____ vorbeigekommen.
   (one evening)

8. _____ hat sie den
   (In spite of her family)
   Jungen geheiratet.

9. _____ muß er viel arbeiten.
   (During the semester)

10. Sie ist nur _____ zur
    (because of her parents)
    Uni gegangen.

11. _____ ging sie einfach weg.
    (One fine day)

12. Er will _____ mitkommen.
    (in spite of his cold)

• Express in German.

1. One morning he got sick.
2. During the semester he has to work a lot.
3. He wants to come along in spite of his cold.
4. They stayed together because of the children.
5. Someday I'll tell her everything. (*Lit.*: one day)

6. During the war I was in England.
7. Because of his work he has to travel a lot.
8. She married the boy in spite of her family.
9. He came by one evening.
10. I'll do that during the vacation.
11. She only went to college because of her parents.
12. One fine day she simply went away.

MIXED DRILLS

a. 1. Sein Haus ist am Ende d__ Straße.
   2. Er ist ein__ Abend__ vorbeigekommen.
   3. Am Anfang d__ Monat__ bekomme ich meinen Scheck.
   4. Es stand auf der ersten Seite d__ Zeitung.
   5. Sein Zimmer ist am Ende d__ Korridor__.
   6. Er will trotz sein__ Erkältung mitkommen.
   7. Das ist die Schwäche sein__ Arbeit.
   8. Der Anfang ein__ neu__ Semester__ ist immer schwer.
   9. Wegen sein__ Arbeit muß er viel reisen.
   10. Er kommt am Ende d__ Woche.

   2. Während d__ Semester__ muß er viel arbeiten.
   3. Die Resultate sein__ neu__Experimente sind gut.
   4. Das Ende d__ Film__ war langweilig.
   5. Ein__ Morgen__ wurde er krank.
   6. Es ist das Ende ein__ Epoche.
   7. Heißt das Stück „Der Besuch ein__ alt __ Dame" oder „Der Besuch d__ alt __ Dame"?
   8. Trotz ihr__ Familie hat sie den Jungen geheiratet.
   9. Das Leben ein__ Student__ ist schwer.
   10. Das Leben ein__ Hund__ ist nicht viel besser.

b. 1. Sie sind wegen d__ Kinder zusammengeblieben.

c.
1. Wer war der Fahrer d___ ander___ Wagen___?
2. Was ist die Farbe ihr___ Augen?
3. Er saß am anderen Ende d___ Tisch___.
4. Ein___ Tag___ sage ich ihr alles.
5. Ich habe das Ende dein___ Arbeit nicht verstanden.
6. Die Mutter mein___ Mann___ wohnt noch bei uns.
7. Sie ist nur wegen ihr___ Eltern zur Uni gegangen.
8. Er ging am Ende d___ erst___ Semester___ weg.
9. Das mache ich während d___ Ferien.
10. Er wohnt auf der anderen Seite d___ Straße.

d.
1. Er ist Direktor ein___ groß___ Firma.
2. Am Ende d___ Monat___ sind wir immer pleite.
3. Die Farbe ein___ Wein___ ist auch wichtig.
4. Wie war der Name sein___ erst___ Frau?
5. Ein___ Tag___ ging sie einfach weg.
6. Es ist ein Zeichen d___ Zeit.
7. Er hat die Augen sein___ Vater___.
8. Hast du eine Liste d___ neu___Adressen.

EXPRESS IN GERMAN

a.
1. His room is at the end of the hall.
2. What's the color of her eyes?
3. He came by one evening.
4. The end of the film was boring.
5. They stayed together because of the children.
6. One fine day she simply went away.
7. It's a sign of the times.
8. Who was the driver of the other car?
9. That's the weakness of his paper.
10. Do you have a list of the new addresses?

b.
1. He has his father's eyes.
2. He's the director of a large firm.
3. His house is at the end of the street.
4. I'll do that during the vacation.
5. I get my check at the beginning of the month.
6. What was his first wife's name?
7. He's coming at the end of the week.
8. He wants to come along in spite of his cold.
9. The beginning of a new semester is always hard.
10. It was on the first page of the paper.

c.
1. The color of a wine is important, too.
2. I didn't understand the end of your paper.
3. One morning he got sick.
4. He left at the end of the first semester.
5. At the end of the month we're always broke.
6. She only went to college because of her parents.
7. The results of his new experiments are good.
8. Because of his work he has to travel a lot.
9. He lives on the other side of the street.
10. She married the boy in spite of her family.

d.
1. Is the play called "The Visit of an Old Lady" or "The Visit of the Old Lady"?
2. He was sitting at the other end of the table.
3. My husband's mother is still living at our place.
4. A student's life is hard.
5. A dog's life isn't much better.
6. During the semester he has to work a lot.
7. Someday I'll tell her everything.
8. It's the end of an era.

B Adjectival Nouns

1 Introduction

Look at the following English sentences:

Do you see *that blonde woman* over there?
Do you see *that blonde* over there?

In the first example, "blonde" is an adjective modifying the noun "woman." In the second example, "blonde" is an adjective being used as a noun (an adjectival noun).

2 Adjectival nouns in German

Adjectival nouns are more common in German than they are in English. Look at the following examples:

ADJECTIVE	bekannt	known (from **kennen**: to know)
ADJECTIVAL NOUN	ein Bekannter	a friend, acquaintance; someone *known* to you
	eine Bekannte	a (female) friend, acquaintance

As the examples show, adjectives functioning as nouns are *capitalized:*

ein **Bekannter**

German adjectives take the same endings when they function as nouns as they do when they function as normal adjectives. The following tables show **bekannt** used as an adjectival noun in various surroundings:

WITH DER-WORDS		
Masculine	*Feminine*	*Plural*
NOM. der Bekannte	die Bekannte	die Bekannten
ACC. den Bekannten	die Bekannte	die Bekannten
DAT. dem Bekannten	der Bekannten	den Bekannten
GEN. des Bekannten	der Bekannten	der Bekannten

WITH EIN-WORDS		
Masculine	*Feminine*	*Plural*
NOM. ein Bekannter	eine Bekannte	keine Bekannten
ACC. einen Bekannten	eine Bekannte	keine Bekannten
DAT. einem Bekannten	einer Bekannten	keinen Bekannten
GEN. eines Bekannten	einer Bekannten	keiner Bekannten

With **viele, mehrere, wenige, einige, andere**	
NOM.	viele Bekann**te**
ACC.	viele Bekann**te**
DAT.	vielen Bekann**ten**
GEN.	vieler Bekann**ter**

Common adjectival nouns:

der Bekannte	acquaintance, friend
der Verwandte	relative
der Alte	old man
der Arme	poor man
der Deutsche	German
der Fremde	stranger, tourist
der Kleine	little man, boy
der Lange	tall man
der Tote	dead man
die Blonde	blonde girl or woman

3 Gender of adjectival nouns

1. *Masculine* and *feminine* adjectival nouns usually refer to people:

der Alte	the old man
die Alte	the old woman

2. *Neuter* adjectival nouns refer to things, qualities, or characteristics:

Das ist das Gute (Schlechte, Dumme) daran.
(That's *the good thing* (*bad thing, stupid thing*) about it.)

Neuter adjectival nouns are commonly found after **etwas, nichts, viel, wenig,** and **alles:**

Wir haben nichts Neues gehört.	(We haven't heard anything new.)
Ich brauche etwas Größeres.	(I need something bigger.)

Adjectives following **etwas, nichts, viel,** and **wenig** take *strong* endings:

etwas anderes*	(something else)
nichts Besonderes	(nothing special)
viel Gutes	(much that is good)

Adjectives following **alles** take *weak* endings:

alles mögliche*	(everything possible)

---

* **andere(s)** and **mögliche(s)** are *not* capitalized.

NEUTER FORMS		
	With a **Der**-*Word*	Without a **Der**-*Word* or **Ein**-*Word*
NOM.	das Gute	etwas Gutes
ACC.	das Gute	etwas Gutes
DAT.	dem Guten	etwas Gutem

DRILLS

1 Masculine and feminine adjectival nouns

● Supply the correct *masculine* endings.

1. Er ist ein Fremd___.
2. Er ist ein alt___ Bekannt___ von mir. (. . . *of mine*)
3. Hat die Polizei d___ Tot___ identifiziert?

(**die Polizei** [*singular*]: police; **tot**: dead; **identifizieren**: to identify)

4. Na, Klein___, suchst du etwas?

(**na**: well)

5. Er wohnt bei ein___ Verwandt___.
6. Ach, Hans, du Arm___!
7. Nein, mein Lieb___, das können wir nicht machen. (*my friend*)
8. Ich gab es ein___ Bekannt___.
9. Mein Alt___ hat den Scheck nicht geschickt. (*my old man*)

● Supply the correct *feminine* endings.

1. D___ Blond___ da drüben ist sehr interessant.
2. Er hat sein___ Alt___ zu Hause gelassen. (*his old lady*)
3. Ich habe es von ein___ Verwandt___ bekommen.
4. Kennst du d___ Klein___ da?
5. Sie ist ein___ alt___ Bekannt___ von mir.
6. Na, Klein___, kann ich dir helfen?

● Supply the correct *plural* endings.

1. Er kennt viel___ Deutsch___.
2. Er hat viel___ Bekannt___ in dieser Stadt.
3. Ich gehe zu mein___ Verwandt___.
4. D___ Arm___ haben viele Kinder.
5. Er muß sein___ Verwandt___ besuchen.
6. Mein___ Bekannt___ waren alle da.

● Supply the correct endings (masculine and feminine, singular and plural).

1. Er kennt viel___ Deutsch___.
2. Er wohnt bei ein___ Verwandt___. (*masc.*)
3. Sie ist ein___ alt___ Bekannt___ von mir.
4. Ach, Hans, du Arm___!
5. Hat die Polizei d___ Tot___ (*masc.*) identifiziert?
6. Ich gab es ein___ Bekannt___. (*masc.*)
7. Er hat sein___ Alt___ (*fem.*) zu Hause gelassen.

8. Sie hat viel___ Verwandt___ in Deutschland.
9. Er ist ein Fremd___.
10. D___ Blond___ da drüben ist sehr interessant.
11. Er hat viel___ Bekannt___ in dieser Stadt.
12. Na, Klein___ (*fem.*), kann ich dir helfen?
13. Ich habe es von ein___ Verwandt___ (*fem.*) bekommen.

14. Mein Alt___ (*masc.*) hat den Scheck nicht geschickt.
15. Ich gehe zu mein___ Verwandt___. (*pl.*)
16. Er ist ein alt___ Bekannt___ von mir.
17. Er muß sein___ Verwandt___ (*pl.*) besuchen.
18. Na, Klein___ (*masc.*), suchst du etwas?
19. Nein, mein Lieb___ (*masc.*), das können wir nicht machen.
20. Mein___ Bekannt___ waren alle da.

2   Neuter adjectival nouns

● Supply the correct endings.

1. Ich will etwas Einfach___ kaufen.
2. Wir haben nichts Neu___ gehört.
3. Ich möchte etwas Kalt___ trinken.
    (**Ich möchte:** I'd like to)
4. Das war das Interessant___ daran.
    (**daran:** about it)
5. Haben Sie nichts ander___?
6. „Hat er etwas Interessant___ gesagt?"
    „Nichts Besonder___." (*nothing special*)
7. Wir versuchen alles möglich___.
    (*everything possible*)   (**versuchen:** try)
8. Haben Sie nichts Besser___?

9. Ich möchte etwas Gut___ kaufen.
10. Das war das Nett___ daran.
11. Das ist nichts Wichtig___.
    (**wichtig:** important)
12. Ich möchte eine Jacke, bitte. Etwas Dunkl___.
13. Alles Gut___! (Lit.: *All the best [to you]!*)
14. Ich brauche etwas Größer___.
15. Das war das Gut___ daran.

MIXED DRILLS

a. 1. Na, Klein___ (*masc.*), suchst du etwas?
    2. Ich brauche etwas Größer___.
    3. Ich gab es ein___ Bekannt___. (*masc.*)
    4. Haben Sie nichts ander___?
    5. Das war das Gut___ daran.
    6. Ich habe viel___ Bekannt___ in dieser Stadt.
    7. Haben Sie nichts Besser___?
    8. Er wohnt bei ein___ Verwandt___. (*masc.*)
    9. Ich will etwas Einfach___ kaufen.
    10. Wir haben nichts Neu___ gehört.

b. 1. Ich habe es von ein___ Verwandt___ (*fem.*) bekommen.
    2. Er ist ein Fremd___.
    3. Ich möchte etwas Kalt___ trinken.
    4. Mein Alt___ (*masc.*) hat den Scheck nicht geschickt.

    5. Ich gehe zu mein___ Verwandt___. (*pl.*)
    6. Das war das Nett___ daran.
    7. Sie ist ein___ alt___ Bekannt___ von mir.
    8. Das ist nichts Wichtig___.
    9. Er kennt viel___ Deutsch___.
    10. Hat die Polizei d___ Tot___ (*masc.*) identifiziert?

c. 1. Wir versuchen alles möglich___.
    2. Sie hat viel___ Verwandt___ in Deutschland.
    3. Ich möchte eine Jacke, bitte. Etwas Dunkl___.
    4. Er hat sein___ Alt___ (*fem.*) zu Hause gelassen.
    5. Na, Klein___ (*fem.*), kann ich dir helfen?

6. Er ist ein alt___ Bekannt___ (*masc.*) von mir.
7. Alles Gut___!
8. Mein___ Bekannt___ waren alle da.
9. „Hat er etwas Interessant___ gesagt?" „Nichts Besonder___."
10. Das war das Interessant___ daran.

d. 1. Die Blond___ da drüben ist sehr interessant.
2. Ich möchte etwas Gut___ kaufen.
3. Ach, Hans, du Arm___!
4. Er muß sein___ Verwandt___ (*pl.*) besuchen.
5. Nein, mein___ Lieb___ (*fem.*), das können wir nicht machen.

EXPRESS IN GERMAN

a. 1. He's a stranger.
2. That was the nice thing about it.
3. He lives at a relative's place.
4. The blond over there is very interesting.
5. Oh, Hans, you poor guy!
6. I'd like a sportscoat, please. Something dark.
7. She's an old friend (acquaintance) of mine.
8. He left his old lady at home.
9. We haven't heard anything new.
10. I need something bigger.

b. 1. My friends (acquaintances) were all there.
2. That was the good thing about it.
3. He knows a lot of Germans.
4. Well, little man, are you looking for something?
5. „Did he say anything interesting?" „Nothing special."

6. All the best!
7. My old man didn't send the check.
8. I'd like to buy something good.
9. He has to visit his relatives.
10. He's an old friend (acquaintance) of mine.

c. 1. I'd like to drink something cold.
2. That was the interesting thing about it.
3. She has a lot of relatives in Germany.
4. We're trying everything possible.
5. I gave it to a friend (acquaintance).
6. Don't you have anything better?
7. I want to buy something simple.
8. That's nothing important.
9. Don't you have anything else?
10. I'm going to my relatives'.

VOCABULARY

der, die **Alte** old man, old woman
  der **Anfang, -̈e** beginning
    am Anfang at the beginning
der, die **Arme** (*adj. noun*) poor man, poor
      guy, poor woman
  das **Auge, -n** eye
der, die **Bekannte** (*adj. noun*) acquaintance,
     friend
  besonder- special
  der **Besuch, -e** visit
der, die **Blonde** (*adj. noun*) blond
  daran about it
der, die **Deutsche** (*adj. noun*) German
  der **Direktor, -en** director
  einfach simply
  die **Eltern** (*pl. only*) parents
  das **Ende, -n** end
    am Ende at the end
  die **Epoche, -n** era
  die **Erkältung, -en** cold
  das **Experiment, -e** experiment
  der **Fahrer, -** driver
  die **Farbe, -n** color
  die **Ferien** (*pl. only*) vacation
  die **Firma, Firmen** firm
der, die **Fremde** (*adj. noun*) stranger
  heiraten to marry
  der **Hund, -e** dog
  identifizieren to identify
  der **Kleine** (*adj. noun*) little man, boy
  die **Kleine** (*adj. noun*) short woman; girl
  der **Korridor, -e** corridor, hall
  der **Krieg, -e** war
  der **Kunde, -n, -n** customer
der, die **Lange** tall man, tall women
  das **Leben, -** life

meine Liebe (*adj. noun*) my friend
  (*fem.*)
mein Lieber (*adj. noun*) my friend
  (*masc.*)
die **Liste, -n** list
möchten to like to
möglich possible
na well
der **Name** name
noch still
pleite broke
die **Polizei** (*sing.*) police
reisen (*with* **sein**) to travel
das **Resultat, -e** result
der **Roman, -e** novel
die **Schwäche, -en** weakness
die **Seite, -n** page; side
das **Semester, -** semester
das **Stück, -e** piece, play
der **Student, -en, -en** student
schön fine, beautiful
der **Titel** title
der, die **Tote** (*adj. noun*) dead man or woman
trotz in spite of
die **Uni** (*slightly slangy*) university, college
versuchen to try
der, die **Verwandte** (*adj. noun*) relative
während during
wegen because of, on account of
wichtig important
das **Zeichen, -** sign (indication)
die **Zeitung, -en** newspaper
zusammen · bleiben to stay together
blieb . . . zusammen
ist zusammengeblieben

Lesson 7 Level TWO

A Review and Expansion of Prepositions Taking the Dative Case

The following prepositions take dative objects:

nach	aus	bei	außer	seit
zu	von	mit	gegenüber	

1 nach / zu

a. nach: to (destination, with place names)

Nächsten Sommer fahre ich nach Berlin.   (I'm going *to* Berlin next summer.)

nach: after (time expressions)

Ich treffe dich nach der Party.   (I'll meet you *after* the party.)
Es ist zwanzig nach drei.   (It's twenty *after* three.)

b. zu: to (with people or with destinations within the limits of a city or town)

Er geht zu einem Freund.   (He's going *to* a friend's place.)

▶ Note   German uses only a dative object with **zu (zu einem Freund),** while English uses a possessive (to a friend's place, or to a friend's).

See also: pp. 103–4

DRILLS   nach / zu

• Supply the correct dative expressions.

1. Er fährt mich _____ Kaufhaus.
   (to the)

2. Ich treffe dich _____ Party.
   (after the)
   (**die Party:** party)

3. Nächsten Sommer fahre ich _____ Berlin.
   (to)

4. Er ist _____ Arbeit vorbeigekommen.
   (after [the])

5. Ich muß jetzt _____ Arzt gehen.
   (to the)

6. Es ist 8.25.

7. Er geht _____ Freund.
   (to a [friend's place])

8. Wie kommt man _____ Bahnhof?
   (to the)

9. Gehst du heute morgen _____ Friseur?
   (to the)

310

2 aus / von

a. **aus**: from (with place names)

> Hier ist ein Paket aus Deutschland.   (Here's a package *from* Germany.)

aus: out of

> Er kommt gerade aus dem Haus.   (He's just coming *out of* the house.)

b. **von**: from

> Ich habe ein Telegramm von ihm bekommen.   (I got a telegram *from* him.)

von: by

> Wir werden drei Erzählungen von Kafka lesen.
> (We're going to read three stories *by* Kafka.)

von: of (showing possession)

> Er ist ein guter Freund von mir.   (He's a good friend *of* mine.)

▶ Note   In English, a possessive follows the preposition: of *mine*. In German, **von** is followed by a simple dative object: von **mir**.

See also: p. 104

DRILLS   aus / von

• Supply the correct dative expressions.

1. Sie wollen _____ Stuttgart nach Heidelberg fahren.
   (from)

2. Er kommt gerade _____ Kneipe.   (die Kneipe: bar)
   (out of the)

3. Es ist ein Geschenk _____ Freundin.   (das Geschenk: gift; die Freundin: girl friend)
   (from his)

4. Er ist ein guter Freund _____ mir.
   (of)

5. Hier ist ein Paket _____ Deutschland.
   (from)

6. Wir werden drei Erzählungen _____ Kafka lesen.   (die Erzählung, -en: story)
   (by)

7. Wie kommt man _____ Gebäude?   (das Gebäude: building)
   (out of this)

8. Ich habe ein Telegramm _____ bekommen.   (das Telegramm: telegram)
   (from him)

3 bei / mit

a. **bei**: at (at somebody's house)

> Er wohnt bei mir.   (He lives *at* my house.)

bei: at (with business or professional establishments)

Er ist jetzt beim* Friseur.   (He's *at* the barber's now.)

▶ Note   English uses a possessive (at the barber's), but German does not.

bei: with (in the sense of "on one's person")

Ich habe kein Geld bei mir.   (I don't have any money *with* me [*on* me].)

b. **mit: with**

Ich fahre mit meinem Bruder nach Wien.   (I'm going to Vienna *with* my brother.)

mit: by (means of travel)

Fliegt er, oder kommt er mit dem Zug?   (Is he flying or is he coming *by* train.)

▶ Note   German uses the definite article (mit **dem** Zug), but English does not.

DRILLS   bei / mit

• Supply the correct dative expressions.

1. Sie wohnt _____.
   (at my place)

2. Ich fahre _____ Bruder nach Wien.
   (with my)

3. Er ist jetzt _____ Friseur.
   (at the)

4. Fliegt er, oder kommt er _____ Zug?
   (by [the])

5. Ich habe kein Geld _____.
   (on me)

6. Inge wohnt noch _____ Eltern.
   (at her)   (noch: still)

4 außer / gegenüber / seit

a. **außer: except (for), besides, aside from**

Außer ihr war niemand da.   (There was nobody there *except* her.)

b. **gegenüber: opposite, across from**

Er saß mir gegenüber.   (He sat *across from* me.)

▶ Note   **Gegenüber** *follows* its object.

c. **seit: for** (with periods of time)

Ich kenne ihn seit vielen Jahren.   (I've known him *for* many years.)

seit: since (with a point in time)

Wir warten seit ein Uhr hier.   (We've been waiting here *since* one o'clock.)

_____

*beim is the contraction of bei dem.

▶ **Note**   When **seit** refers to an action that began in the past and is still going on, German uses the present tense. English uses the present perfect in equivalent expressions.

DRILLS   außer / gegenüber / seit

• Supply the correct dative expressions.

1. Er wohnt _____ Jahr hier.
   (for a)

2. _____ war niemand da.
   (Aside from her)   (**niemand**: no one)

3. _____ Haus _____ ist ein gutes
   (Across from our [house])
   Restaurant.

4. Wir warten _____ ein Uhr* hier.
   (since)

5. Er saß _____.
   (across from me)

6. Ich kenne ihn _____ Jahren.
   (for many)

7. _____ Mutter war niemand
   (Except for her)
   dagegen.   (**dagegen**: against it)

MIXED DRILLS

a. 1. Nächsten Sommer fahre ich _____
       (to)
       Berlin.

    2. Hier ist ein Paket _____ Deutschland.
       (from)

    3. Ich fahre _____ Bruder _____
       (with my)   (to)
       Wien.

    4. Inge wohnt noch _____ Eltern.
       (at her)

    5. Wir warten _____ ein Uhr hier.
       (since)

    6. _____ Mutter war niemand
       (Except for her)
       dagegen.

    7. Gehst du heute morgen _____
       (to the)
       Friseur?

    8. Er ist jetzt _____ Friseur.
       (at the)

    9. Er fährt mich _____ Kaufhaus.
       (to the)

    10. Es ist 8.25.

b. 1. Es ist ein Geschenk _____
       (from his)
       Freundin.

    2. Er saß _____.
       (across from me)

    3. Ich kenne ihn _____ Jahren.
       (for many)

    4. Er ist _____ Arbeit vorbeige-
       (after [the])
       kommen.

    5. Sie wollen _____ Stuttgart _____
       (from)   (to)
       Heidelberg fahren.

    6. Fliegt er, oder kommt er _____ Zug?
       (by [the])

    7. _____ war niemand da.
       (Aside from her)

    8. Er kommt gerade _____ Kneipe.
       (out of the)

    9. Ich muß jetzt _____ Arzt gehen.
       (to the)

    10. Ich habe ein Telegramm _____
        (from him)
        bekommen.

c. 1. Ich treffe dich _____ Party.
       (after the)

    2. Er ist ein guter Freund _____ mir.
       (of)

    3. Er geht _____ Freund.
       (to a)

    4. _____ Haus _____ ist ein
       (Across from our [house])
       gutes Restaurant.

    5. Wie kommt man _____ Bahnhof?
       (to the)

_____
*Ein Uhr is a frozen expression: it never takes endings.

6. Sie wohnt _____.
   (at my place)

7. Wir werden drei Erzählungen _____ Kafka lesen.
   (by)

8. Er wohnt _____ Jahr hier.
   (for a)

9. Wie kommt man _____ Gebäude?
   (out of this)

EXPRESS IN GERMAN

a.
1. It's twenty-five after eight.
2. Here is a package from Germany.
3. I have to go to the doctor's now.
4. I got a telegram from him.
5. He's been living here for a year.
6. I'll meet you after the party.
7. He's just coming out of the bar.
8. He's a good friend of mine.
9. She lives at my place.
10. He sat across from me.

b.
1. I'm going to Berlin next summer.
2. We're going to read three stories by Kafka.
3. Are you going to the barber's this morning?
4. He's at the barber's now.
5. How does one get out of this building?
6. Is he flying or is he coming by train?

7. Except for her mother no one was against it.
8. He's driving me to the department store.
9. He's going to a friend's place.
10. I've known him for many years.

c.
1. I'm driving to Vienna with my brother.
2. Aside from her no one was there.
3. It's a present from his girl friend.
4. How does one get to the railroad station?
5. There's a good restaurant across from our house.
6. We've been waiting here since one o'clock.
7. They want to drive from Stuttgart to Heidelberg.
8. He came by after work.
9. Inge still lives at her parent's place.

B Prepositions Taking the Accusative Case

The following prepositions take accusative objects:

bis   durch   für   gegen   ohne   um

1 bis / durch / für

a. **bis:** until (with time expressions)

Ich habe bis sechs Uhr gewartet.   (I waited *until* six o'clock.)

bis: as far as (with places)

Wir fahren nur bis Mainz.   (We're only going *as far as* Mainz.)

b. **durch:** through

Sind sie durch die Stadt gefahren?   (Did you drive *through* [the] town?)

c. **für:** for

Er hat das Buch für mich bestellt.   (He ordered the book *for* me.)

DRILLS   bis / durch / für

- Supply the correct accusative expressions.

1. Ich wartete _____ sechs Uhr.
   (until)
2. Sie sind _____ Park gegangen.
   (through the)
   (der Park: park)
3. Er hat das Buch _____ bestellt.
   (for me)
4. Ich fahre nur _____ Mainz.
   (as far as)

5. In der Mensa kann man _____ eine
   (for)
   Mark achtzig essen.
   (die Mensa: student dining hall;
   eine Mark achtzig: a mark eighty)
6. Was hast du _____ neuen Wagen
   (for your)
   bezahlt?
7. Sind Sie _____ Stadt gefahren?
   (through the)

2 gegen / ohne / um

a. **gegen**: against

Was haben Sie gegen seine Freundin?   (What do you have *against* his girl friend?)

gegen: into, up against

Ich bin gegen einen Baum gefahren.   ' (I ran *into* a tree.)

b. **ohne**: without

Er ist ohne seinen Mantel weggegangen.   (He left *without* his coat.)

c. **um**: around

Er kommt gerade um die Ecke.   (He's just coming *around* the corner.)

um: at (in time expressions)

Sie ist um 10.30 aufgestanden.   (She got up *at* ten thirty.)

DRILLS   gegen / ohne / um

- Supply the correct accusative expressions.

1. Ich bin _____ Baum gefahren.
   (into a)   (der Baum: tree)
2. Sie saßen _____ großen Tisch.
   (around a)
3. Ich habe nichts _____ .
   (against him)
4. Er geht nie _____ Frau aus.
   (without his)
5. Sie ist _____ 10.30 aufgestanden.
   (at)

6. Er kommt gerade _____ Ecke.
   (around the)
   (gerade: just; die Ecke: corner)
7. Er ist _____ Mantel weggegangen.
   (without his)
8. Was haben Sie _____ Freundin?
   (against his)

MIXED DRILLS

1. Sie ist _____ 10.30 aufgestanden.
   (at)

2. Sie saßen _____ großen Tisch.
   (around a)

3. Sie sind _____ Park gegangen.
   (through the)

4. Ich fahre nur _____ Mainz.
   (as far as)

5. Was haben Sie _____ Freundin?
   (against his)

6. Er geht nie _____ Frau aus.
   (without his)

7. Was hast du _____ neuen Wagen
   bezahlt?   (for your)

8. Ich bin _____ Baum gefahren.
   (into a)

9. Er ist _____ Mantel weggegangen.
   (without his)

10. In der Mensa kann man _____ eine
    Mark achtzig essen.   (for)

11. Ich wartete _____ sechs Uhr.
    (until)

12. Sind Sie _____ Stadt gefahren?
    (through the)

13. Er kommt gerade _____ Ecke.
    (around the)

14. Er hat das Buch _____ bestellt.
    (for me)

15. Ich habe nichts _____ .
    (against him)

EXPRESS IN GERMAN

1. He's just coming around the corner.
2. She got up at ten thirty.
3. I don't have anything against him.
4. He left without his coat.
5. They went through the park.
6. I waited until six o'clock.
7. What did you pay for your new car?
8. They were sitting around a large table.

9. He ordered the book for me.
10. He never goes out without his wife.
11. I ran into a tree.
12. What do you have against his girl friend?
13. I'm only driving as far as Mainz.
14. Did you drive through the city?
15. In the "Mensa" you can eat for a mark eighty. (use **man**)

GRAND MIX: DATIVE AND ACCUSATIVE

1 Fill-ins

a. 1. Es ist ein Geschenk _____
      Freundin.   (from his)

   2. Nächsten Sommer fahre ich _____
      Berlin.   (to)

   3. Er kommt gerade _____ Ecke.
      (around the)

   4. Ich treffe dich _____ Party.
      (after the)

   5. Er ist jetzt _____ Friseur.
      (at the)

   6. Fliegt er, oder kommt er _____
      Zug?   (by [the])

   7. Ich wartete _____ sechs Uhr.
      (until)

   8. Es ist 8.25.

   9. Er kommt gerade _____ Kneipe.
      (out of the)

   10. _____ Mutter war niemand
       (Except for her)
       dagegen.

b. 1. Sie sind _____ Park gegangen.
      (through the)

   2. Er fährt mich _____ Kaufhaus.
      (to the)

   3. Er wohnt _____ Jahr hier.
      (for a)

4. Hier ist ein Paket _____
   (from)
   Deutschland.

5. Er hat das Buch _____ bestellt.
   (for me)

6. Ich habe ein Telegramm _____
   (from him)
   bekommen.

7. Ich fahre _____ Bruder _____
   (with my)   (to)
   Wien.

8. Er ist _____ Mantel
   (without his)
   weggegangen.

9. Er saß _____.
   (across from me)

10. Wie kommt man _____ Bahnhof?
    (to the)

c. 1. Er ist ein guter Freund _____.
      (of mine)

   2. Sind Sie _____ Stadt
                 (through the)
      gefahren?

   3. Sie wohnt _____.
      (at my place)

   4. Wie kommt man _____
                      (out of this)
      Gebäude?

   5. Was hast du _____ Freundin?
      (against his)

   6. Ich muß jetzt _____ Arzt gehen.
      (to the)

7. In der Mensa kann man _____
   (for a)
   Mark achtzig essen.

8. _____ Haus _____ ist ein gutes
   (Across from our [house])
   Restaurant.

9. Sie ist _____ 10.30 aufgestanden.
   (at)

10. Er ist _____ Arbeit
    (after [the])
    vorbeigekommen.

d. 1. Gehst du heute morgen _____
      (to the)
      Friseur?

   2. Ich fahre nur _____ Mainz.
      (as far as)

   3. Wir werden drei Erzählungen _____
      (by)
      Kafka lesen.

   4. Er geht nie _____ Frau aus.
      (without his)

   5. Wir warten _____ ein Uhr hier.
      (since)

   6. Ich bin _____ Baum gefahren.
      (into a)

   7. Was hast du _____ neuen Wagen
      (for your)
      bezahlt?

   8. Sie geht _____ Freund.
      (to a)

   9. _____ war niemand da.
      (Aside from her)

2 Express in German

a. 1. I got a telegram from him.
   2. It's twenty-five after eight.
   3. I waited until six o'clock.
   4. He's driving me to the department
      store.
   5. He left without his coat.
   6. I'll meet you after the party.
   7. He sat across from me.
   8. She got up at 10:30.
   9. He's a good friend of mine.
   10. Is he flying or is he coming by train?

b. 1. I'm only driving as far as Mainz.
   2. We've been waiting here since one
      o'clock.
   3. He came by after work.
   4. I have to go to the doctor's now.

   5. He's just coming out of the bar.
   6. What did you pay for your new car?
   7. It's a present from his girl friend.
   8. He never goes out without his wife.
   9. Aside from her no one was there.
   10. Are you going to the barber's this
       morning?

c. 1. He ordered the book for me.
   2. I'm going to Berlin next summer.
   3. He's just coming around the corner.
   4. There's a good restaurant across
      from our house.
   5. She lives at my place.
   6. We're going to read three stories by Kafka.
   7. They went through the park.
   8. Here's a package from Germany.

9. He's been living here for a year.
10. He's at the barber's now.

d. 1. I ran into a tree.
   2. How do you get out of this building? (use **man**)
   3. Except for her mother no one was against it.
   4. He's going to a friend's place.
   5. In the "Mensa" you can eat for a mark eighty.
   6. I'm driving to Vienna with my brother.
   7. How do you get to the railroad station? (use **man**)
   8. Did you drive through the city?

C Two-way Prepositions

Choice of case

1. Dative: no motion (wo?)

When there is no motion, two-way prepositions take the dative case:

Dein Koffer ist **unter dem Bett.**   (Your suitcase is *under the bed.*)

2. Accusative: motion (wo . . . hin?)

When there is motion in a definite direction, two-way prepositions take the accusative case:

Schieb deinen Koffer **unter das Bett!**   (Push your suitcase *under the bed.*)

1 auf / an

a. auf: on (on top of)

Auf is used with horizontal surfaces: a floor, a chair, a table top.

| DATIVE (wo?) | Es liegt **auf dem Stuhl.*** | (It's lying *on the chair.*) |

| ACCUSATIVE (wohin?) | Leg es **auf den Stuhl!** | (Lay it *on the chair.*) |

Auf also means "on" in more figurative expressions:

DATIVE (wo?)   Sie sind jetzt **auf einer Reise.**
(They're *on a trip* now.)

ACCUSATIVE (wohin?)   Sie gehen nächsten Sommer **auf eine Reise.**
(They're going *on a trip* next summer.)

auf: in (with languages)

auf deutsch, auf französisch   in German, in French

Die Vorlesung war auf deutsch.   (The lecture was *in German.*)

▶ Note   Since **auf deutsch** is an adverbial expression in German, **deutsch** is not capitalized.

---

*See Note 1, opposite page.

b. **an**: on, onto

In contrast to **auf, an** is normally used with vertical surfaces: a wall, a blackboard.

DATIVE **(wo?)**	Das Bild hing **an der Wand.*** (The picture was hanging *on the wall.*)
ACCUSATIVE **(wohin?)**	Ich hängte es **an die Wand.** (I hung it *on the wall.*)

an: at, over to

DATIVE **(wo?)**	Er stand **am Fenster.**	(He stood *at the window.*)
ACCUSATIVE **(wohin?)**	Er ging **ans Fenster.**	(He went [over] *to the window.*)

Like a wall, a window is a vertical surface.

▶ **Note 1** liegen / lag / gelegen: to lie (intransitive; takes no direct object)

The strong verb **liegen** is used when there is no motion:

> Es **liegt auf dem Tisch.**   (It *is lying on the table.*)

This whole sentence answers the question **wo?** The two-way preposition **auf** takes the dative case.

legen / legte / gelegt: to lay (transitive: takes a direct object)

The weak verb **legen** is used when there is motion:

> **Leg** es **auf den Tisch!**   (*Lay* it *on the table.*)

The prepositional phrase **auf den Tisch** answers the question **wohin?**

▶ **Note 2** hängen / hing / gehangen: to hang (intransitive: takes no direct object)

The strong verb **hängen** is used when there is no motion:

> Das Bild **hing an der Wand.**   (The picture *was hanging on the wall.*)

There is no motion here. The prepositional phrase **an der Wand** answers the question **wo?**

hängen / hängte / gehängt: to hang (transitive: takes a direct object)

The weak verb **hängen** is used when there is motion:

> Ich **hängte** es **an die Wand.**   (I *hung* it *on the wall.*)

The prepositional phrase **an die Wand** answers the question **wohin?**

---

*See Note 2.

• Supply the correct dative or accusative expressions.

1. Es liegt _____ Stuhl.
   (on the)
   (liegen, lag, gelegen: to lie)

   Leg es _____ Stuhl!
   (on the)

2. Hängen wir das Bild _____ Wand!
   (on this)
   (hängen, hing, gehangen: to hang)

   Das Bild hing _____ Wand da drüben.
   (on the)

3. Die Bücher sind _____ Schreibtisch.
   (on your)

   Leg die Bücher _____ Schreibtisch!
   (on my)

4. Er schrieb es _____ Tafel.
   (on the)

   Es stand _____ Tafel.
   (on the)

5. Sie ging _____ Fenster.
   (to the)
   (das Fenster: window)

   Er stand _____ Fenster.
   (at the)

6. Deine Mappe liegt _____ Sofa.
   (on the)
   (die Mappe: briefcase)

   Wirf deine Mappe _____ Sofa!
   (on the)

7. Sie gehen nächsten Sommer _____ Reise.
   (on a)
   (die Reise: trip)

   Sie sind jetzt _____ Reise.
   (on a)

8. Die Vorlesung war _____ deutsch.
   (in)
   (die Vorlesung: lecture)

9. Stell die Kerzen _____ Sarg!
   (on the)
   (die Kerze, -n: candle; der Sarg: coffin)

10. Sie saß _____ Schoß.
    (on his)
    (der Schoß: lap)

2 über / unter

a. über: over

DATIVE (wo?)	Dein Mantel liegt über meinem. (Your coat's lying over mine.)
ACCUSATIVE (wohin?)	Leg deinen Mantel über meinen! (Lay your coat over mine.)

über: across

ACCUSATIVE (wohin?)	Er ist gerade über die Straße gegangen. (He just went across the street.)

b. unter: under

DATIVE (wo?)	Dein Koffer ist unter dem Bett. (Your suitcase is under the bed.)
ACCUSATIVE (wohin?)	Schieb deinen Koffer unter das Bett! (Push your suitcase under the bed.)

DRILLS über / unter

● Supply the correct dative or accusative expressions.

1. Ich hängte das Bild _____ Kamin.
   (over my)   (**hängen, hängte, gehängt:** to hang [motion]; **der Kamin:** fireplace)

   Ihr Bild hing _____ Schreibtisch.
   (over his)   (**hängen, hing, gehangen:** to hang [no motion])

2. Deine Schreibmaschine ist _____ Tisch.
   (under the)   (**die Schreibmaschine:** typewriter)

   Stell die Schreibmaschine _____ Tisch!
   (under the)

3. Legen Sie Ihren Mantel _____!
   (over mine)*   (**legen:** to lay)

   Ihr Mantel liegt _____.
   (over mine)

4. Dein Koffer ist _____ Bett.
   (under the)   (**der Koffer:** suitcase)

   Schieb deinen Koffer _____ Bett!
   (under the)

5. Er ist gerade _____ Straße gegangen.
   (across the)

3 vor / hinter

a. vor: in front of, (up) in front of

DATIVE (**wo?**)   Sein Wagen stand **vor dem Haus.**
(His car was standing *in front of the house.*)

ACCUSATIVE (**wohin?**)   Er fuhr den Wagen **vor das Haus.**
(He drove the car [up] *in front of the house.*)

b. hinter: behind, in back of

DATIVE (**wo?**)   Er arbeitete **hinter der Garage.**
(He was working *behind the garage.*)

ACCUSATIVE (**wohin?**)   Er ist gerade **hinter die Garage** gegangen.
(He just went *behind the garage.*)

DRILLS vor / hinter

● Supply the correct dative or accusative expressions.

1. Er fuhr den Wagen _____ Haus.
   (in front of the)

   Mein Wagen stand _____ Haus.
   (in front of the)

---

*Use the possessive adjective **mein** plus correct ending.

2. Ich habe es _____ Tür gefunden.
(behind the)

Stell es _____ Tür!
(behind the)

3. Stell das Sofa _____ Kamin!
(in front of the)

Das Sofa steht _____ Kamin.
(in front of the)

4. Er ging _____ Garage.
(behind the)

Er arbeitet _____ Garage.
(behind the)

5. Wir stehen _____ Katastrophe.   (die Katastrophe: catastrophe)
([standing] in front of a;
that is, facing a)

6. Er saß _____ .
(behind me)

7. Er ist gerade _____ Haus gegangen.
(behind the)

4 in / neben / zwischen

a. in: in, into

DATIVE **(wo?)**	Wohnt er **in diesem Haus?** (Does he live *in this house?*)
ACCUSATIVE **(wohin?)**	Komm sofort **ins Haus!** (Come *into the house* right away.)

The following idioms use **in:**

im Theater	*at* the theater
ins Theater	*to* the theater
in die Schweiz*	*to* Switzerland
in der Schweiz	*in* Switzerland
im 3. Stock† (im dritten Stock)	*on* the 4th (!) floor

---

*The definite article is used in all expressions referring to Switzerland (**die Schweiz**).

†**im 3. Stock:** on the 4th floor. In German, the ground floor (our first floor) is called **das Erdgeschoß.**
Our second floor is called **der erste Stock,** our third floor is **der zweite Stock,** and so on. Remember,
when climbing stairs in Germany, you always have one more flight than you thought you did.

b. **neben**: next to, alongside of, beside

DATIVE **(wo?)**	Dein Koffer steht **neben dem Bett.**
	(Your suitcase is [standing] *next to the bed.*)
ACCUSATIVE **(wohin?)**	Stell den Koffer **neben das Bett!**
	(Put the suitcase *next to the bed.*)

c. **zwischen**: between

DATIVE **(wo?)**

Ich meine die Lampe **zwischen dem Sofa und dem Schreibtisch.**
(I mean the lamp *between the sofa and the desk.*)

ACCUSATIVE **(wohin?)**

Stell die Lampe **zwischen das Sofa und den Schreibtisch!**
(Put the lamp *between the sofa and the desk.*)

DRILLS   in / neben / zwischen

● Supply the correct dative or accusative expressions.

1. Wir gehen heute abend _____ Kino.
   (to the)

   Wir waren gestern nachmittag _____ Theater.
   (at the)

2. Dein Koffer ist _____ Bett.
   (alongside [of] the)

   Stell den Koffer _____ Bett.
   (alongside [of] the)

3. Wir fahren nächste Woche _____ Schweiz.
   (to)

   Sie wohnen seit Jahren _____ Schweiz.
   (in)

4. Stell den kleinen Tisch _____ Fenster.
   (next to the)

   Ich meine den Tisch _____ Fenster.   (meinen: to mean)
   (next to the)

5. Stell die Lampe _____ Sofa und _____ Klavier!   (das Klavier: piano)
   (between the)   (the)

6. Er wohnt _____ dritten Stock.   (der Stock: floor)
   (on the)

7. Sie saß _____.
   (next to me)

8. Nein, Gregor, nicht _____ Haus!
   (in my)

MIXED DRILLS

a. 1. Wir gehen heute abend _____ (to the) Kino.

2. Die Vorlesung war _____ (in) deutsch.

3. Er ist gerade _____ (behind the) Haus gegangen.

4. Es liegt _____ (on the) Stuhl.

5. Hängen wir das Bild _____ (on this) Wand!

6. Ich meine den Tisch _____ (next to the) Fenster.

7. Nein, Gregor, nicht _____ (in my) Haus!

8. Stell die Schreibmaschine _____ (under the) Tisch!

9. Sie saß _____ (next to me).

10. Stell die Lampe _____ (between the) Sofa und _____ (the) Klavier!

b. 1. Ich habe es _____ (behind the) Tür gefunden.

2. Er schrieb es _____ (on the) Tafel.

3. Stell das Sofa _____ (in front of the) Kamin!

4. Wir fahren nächste Woche _____ (to) Schweiz.

5. Er stand _____ (at the) Fenster.

6. Dein Koffer ist _____ (next to the) Bett.

7. Ihr Bild hing _____ (over his) Schreibtisch.

8. Sie gehen nächsten Sommer _____ (on a) Reise.

9. Er saß _____ (behind me).

10. Die Bücher sind _____ (on your) Schreibtisch.

c. 1. Das Bild hing _____ (on the) Wand da drüben.

2. Stell die Kerzen _____ (on the) Sarg!

3. Legen Sie Ihren Mantel _____ (over mine)!

4. Leg die Bücher _____ (on my) Schreibtisch!

5. Er arbeitet _____ (behind the) Garage.

6. Ich hängte das Bild _____ (over my) Kamin.

7. Wir waren gestern nachmittag _____ (at the) Theater.

8. Leg es _____ (on the) Stuhl!

9. Er fuhr den Wagen _____ (in front of the) Haus.

10. Sie ging _____ (to the) Fenster.

d. 1. Sie saß _____ (on his) Schoß.

2. Er wohnt _____ (on the) 3. Stock.

3. Dein Koffer ist _____ (under the) Bett.

4. Stell es _____ (behind the) Tür!

5. Wir stehen _____ (in front of a) Katastrophe.

6. Sie wohnen seit Jahren _____ (in) Schweiz.

7. Sein Wagen stand _____ (in front of the) Haus.

8. Stell deinen Koffer _____ Bett!
(next to the)

9. Ihr Mantel liegt _____.
(over mine)

10. Es stand _____ Tafel.
(on the)

e. 1. Er ging _____ Garage.
(behind the)

2. Stell den kleinen Tisch _____
(next to the)
Fenster!

3. Er ist gerade _____ Straße
(across the)
gegangen.

4. Das Sofa steht _____
(in front of the)
Kamin.

5. Schieb deinen Koffer _____
(under the)
Bett!

6. Sie sind jetzt _____ Reise.
(on a)

7. Deine Schreibmaschine ist
_____ Tisch.
(under the)

8. Wirf deine Mappe _____ Sofa!
(on the)

EXPRESS IN GERMAN

a. 1. His car was standing in front of the house.
2. She went (over) to the window.
3. Your coat's lying over mine.
4. She sat on his lap.
5. Push your suitcase under the bed.
6. The sofa is in front of the fireplace. (use **stehen**)
7. He wrote it on the blackboard.
8. We're going to the movies this evening.
9. He just went across the street.
10. The books are on your desk.

b. 1. Put it on the chair. (use **legen**)
2. We're driving to Switzerland next week.
3. Your typewriter is under the table.
4. Put the little table next to the window.
5. Her picture was hanging over his desk.
6. He's working behind the garage.
7. It's lying on the chair.
8. Put it behind the door.
9. We're facing a catastrophe.
10. Your suitcase is under the bed.

c. 1. I mean the table next to the window.
2. No, Gregor, not in my house.
3. He sat behind me.
4. The lecture was in German.

5. Put the lamp between the sofa and the piano.
6. They've been living in Switzerland for years.
7. The picture was hanging on the wall over there.
8. Put the books on my desk. (use **legen**)
9. It was on the blackboard. (use **stehen**)
10. He drove the car (up) in front of the house.

d. 1. She sat next to me.
2. Put the sofa in front of the fireplace.
3. Put your suitcase next to the bed.
4. They're on a trip now.
5. We were at the theater yesterday afternoon.
6. Lay your coat over mine.
7. He was standing at the window.
8. Put the typewriter under the table.
9. I hung the picture over my fireplace.
10. He lives on the fourth floor.

e. 1. Your suitcase is alongside of the bed.
2. Throw your briefcase on the sofa.
3. Let's hang the picture on this wall.
4. He just went behind the house.
5. They're going on a trip next summer.
6. Put the candles on the coffin.

VOCABULARY

an (+ *dat.* or acc.)
on, onto (*vertical surfaces*)

auf (+ *dat.* or acc.) on, onto (*horizontal surfaces*)

aus (+ *dat.*) from; out of

außer (+ *dat.*) except (for), besides

außerdem in addition to

der Baum, ⸚e tree

bei (+ *dat.*) at, with

bis (+ acc.) until, as far as

dagegen against it

durch (+ acc.) through

die Ecke, -n corner

die Erzählung, -en story

das Fenster, - window

die Freundin, -nen girl friend

für (+ acc.) for

das Gebäude, - building

gegen (+ acc.) against; into

gegenüber (+ *dat.*) across from, opposite

gerade just, right now

das Geschenk, -e present

hängen to hang (*no motion*)
hing, gehangen

hängen to hang (*motion*)

hinter (+ *dat.* or acc.) behind

in (+ *dat.* or acc.) in, into; at; on

der Kamin, -e fireplace

die Katastrophe, -n castastrophe

die Kerze, -n candle

das Klavier, -e piano

die Kneipe, -n bar

der Koffer,- suitcase

legen to lay (*motion*)
liegen to lie (*no motion*)
lag, gelegen

die Mappe, -n briefcase

meinen to mean

die Mensa student dining hall

mit (+ *dat.*) with; by

nach (+ *dat.*) to; after

neben (+ *dat.* or acc.) next to, beside, alongside of

niemand no one

noch still

ohne (+ acc.) without

der Park, -s park

die Party, Parties party

die Reise, -n trip

der Sarg, ⸚e coffin

der Schoß, ⸚e lap

die Schreibmaschine, -n typewriter

seit (+ *dat.*) for; since

der Stock floor

der Stuhl, ⸚e chair

das Telegramm, -e telegram

über (+ *dat.* or acc.) over, across

um (+ acc.) around, at

unter (+ *dat.* or acc.) under

von (+ *dat.*) from; by; of

vor (+ *dat.* or acc.) in front of

die Vorlesung, -en lecture

zu (+ *dat*) to

zwischen (+ *dat.* or acc.) between

Lesson 7 Level THREE

A Modal Auxiliaries: Past Tense and Review of Present Tense

1 General rules

a. Word order

(1)   **(2)**

Ich kann es morgen machen.   (I can do it tomorrow.)

1. The *modal auxiliary* **(kann)** is the conjugated verb and is in the *second* position in the sentence.
2. The *dependent infinitive* **(machen)** is the *last* element in the sentence.

b. Caution: Do not use **zu!**

Some English equivalents of the German modal auxiliaries require the word "to."

I want *to* do it.

German, on the other hand, *never* uses **zu** before infinitives in modal expressions.

Ich **muß** nach Hause **gehen.**   (I have *to* go home.)
Ich **will** es **machen.**   (I want *to* do it.)

2 Forms and meanings of German modals

The *past tense* of modals is formed by adding *weak* verb *endings* to a past tense stem.

ich	—te	wir	—ten
du	—test	ihr	—tet
er	—te	sie	—ten

a. **müssen**

	Present Tense		Past Tense	
	ich muß wir müssen		ich mußte wir mußten	
	du mußt ihr müßt		du mußtest ihr mußtet	
	er muß sie müssen		er mußte sie mußten	
STEMS	**muß-** **müss-**		**muß-**	

327

must, have to (necessity)

PRESENT Ich muß ihn gleich finden. (I *have to* find him right away.)
PAST Sie mußte in die Stadt gehen. (She *had to* go downtown.)

DRILLS

- Supply present tense forms.

  1. Er _____ heute zu Hause bleiben.
  2. Wir _____ sehr früh aufstehen.
  3. Du _____ mit dem Chef sprechen.
  4. _____ ihr das heute machen?

  5. Ich _____ jetzt zur Bank gehen.
  6. Sie (*you*) _____ mit dem Zug fahren.
  7. Er _____ im Februar nach Mainz fliegen.

- Supply past tense forms.

  1. Er _____ zum Friseur gehen.
  2. Wir _____ durch die Stadt fahren.
  3. _____ du gestern arbeiten?
  4. Ich _____ heute in die Stadt gehen.

  5. _____ Sie die Rechnung bezahlen?
  6. Wir _____ zu einer anderen Bank gehen.
  7. Inge _____ vor zehn Uhr dà sein.

  (**vor**: before)

- Express in German.

  1. I have to go to the bank.
  2. We have to get up very early.
  3. Inge had to be there before 10 o'clock.
  4. We had to drive through the city.
  5. He has to stay home today.
  6. We had to go to another bank.
  7. Did you have to work yesterday? (**du**-form)

  8. He has to fly to Mainz in February.
  9. Did you have to pay the bill?
  10. Do you have to do that today? (**Sie**-form)
  11. He had to go to the barber's.
  12. You have to take the train. (**Sie**-form)
  13. I had to go downtown.

b. **können**

	Present Tense		Past Tense	
	ich kann	wir können	ich konnte	wir konnten
	du kannst	ihr könnt	du konntest	ihr konntet
	er kann	sie können	er konnte	sie konnten
STEMS	**kann-**	**könn-**	**konn-**	

can, be able to (ability)

PRESENT Ich kann es machen. (I *can* do it.)
PAST Sie konnte ihn nicht finden. (She *couldn't* find him.)

can (possibility)

PRESENT Das kann nicht wahr sein. (That *can't* be true.)

DRILLS

● Supply present tense forms.

1. Das _____ du nicht machen.
2. _____ Sie mir ein gutes Restaurant empfehlen?
3. Das _____ nicht wahr sein.　(**wahr:** true)

4. Wir _____ Ihnen nicht helfen.
5. Ich _____ meinen Mantel nicht finden.
6. Sie (*they*) _____ später kommen.

● Supply past tense forms.

1. Sie (*they*) _____ gestern abend nicht kommen.
2. Ich _____ ihn kaum verstehen.
　　　(**kaum:** scarcely, hardly)
3. _____ sie Deutsch sprechen?

4. Er _____ den Brief nicht übersetzen.
5. Wir _____ ihn nicht erkennen.
6. _____ du ihn sehen?
7. Sie (*she*) _____ ihn nicht finden.

● Express in German.

1. I can't find my coat.
2. We couldn't recognize him.
3. They can come later.
4. I could hardly understand him.
5. That can't be true.
6. Can you recommend a good restaurant (to me)?　(**Sie**-form)
7. Were you able to see him?　(**du**-form)

8. They couldn't come yesterday evening.
9. You can't do that.
10. He couldn't translate the letter.
11. Could they speak German?
12. We can't help you.
13. She couldn't find him.

c. dürfen

	Present Tense		Past Tense	
	ich darf	wir dürfen	ich durfte	wir durften
	du darfst	ihr dürft	du durftest	ihr durftet
	er darf	sie dürfen	er durfte	sie durften
STEMS	darf-	dürf-	durf-	

may, be permitted to, be allowed to (permission)

PRESENT	Dürfen wir jetzt gehen?	(*May* we go now?)
PAST	Er durfte nicht mitkommen.	(He *wasn't allowed to* come along.)
		(He *didn't get to* come along.)

DRILLS

● Supply present tense forms.

1. _____ wir etwas später kommen?
　　　(**etwas später:** a little later)
2. _____ ich Ihnen helfen?

3. _____ sie (*they*) mitkommen?
4. Nein, ihr _____ heute abend nicht ins Kino gehen.

5. Die Arme! Sie (*she*) _____ nie ausgehen.
6. _____ ich Ihre Frage beantworten?
   (**die Frage:** question; **beantworten:** to
   answer a question, not a person)

7. Du _____ nächstes Mal mitkommen.
8. Sie (*you*) _____ ihn jetzt sehen.

● Supply past tense forms.

1. Er _____ es nicht machen.
2. Wir _____ ein wenig später aufstehen.
3. _____ du den neuen Wagen nehmen?
4. _____ Sie später zurückkommen?

5. Sie _____ ihn nicht sehen.
6. _____ Sie mit dem Chef sprechen?
7. _____ du da bleiben?

● Express in German.

1. May I help you?
2. You may see him now. (**Sie**-form)
3. We got to (were allowed to) get up a
   little later.
4. The poor girl. She never gets to go out.
5. Did you get to take the new car?
   (**du**-form)
6. May we come a little later?

7. He didn't get to do it.
8. May they come along?
9. She didn't get to see him.
10. Did you get to stay there? (**du**-form)
11. May I answer your question?
12. Did you get to talk with the boss?

d. **mögen**

	Present Tense		Past Tense	
	ich mag	wir mög**en**	ich moch**te**	wir moch**ten**
	du mag**st**	ihr mög**t**	du moch**test**	ihr moch**tet**
	er mag	sie mög**en**	er moch**te**	sie moch**ten**
STEMS	**mag-**	**mög-**	**moch-**	

like (liking, fondness)

PRESENT Ich mag ihn nicht. (I *don't like* him.)
PAST Sie mochte die Suppe nicht. (She *didn't like* the soup.)

The simple past tense of **mögen** is not commonly used in colloquial German.

DRILLS

● Supply present tense forms.

1. Nein, ich _____ diese Suppe nicht.
2. Wir _____ den neuen Chef nicht.

3. _____ du seine Frau?
4. _____ Sie diesen Anzug?

● Supply past tense forms.

1. Wir _____ es nicht.
2. Sie (*they*) _____ das Essen nicht.
   (**das Essen:** food)

3. Er _____ das Stück nicht.
4. Ich _____ seine Stimme nicht.
   (**die Stimme:** voice)

- Express in German.

1. No, I don't like this soup.
2. We didn't like it.
3. He didn't like the play.
4. We don't like the new boss.
5. Do you like his wife? (**du**-form)
6. They didn't like the food.
7. I didn't like his voice.
8. Do you like this suit? (**Sie**-form)

e. **wollen**

	Present Tense		Past Tense	
	ich will	wir woll**en**	ich woll**te**	wir woll**ten**
	du will**st**	ihr woll**t**	du woll**test**	ihr woll**tet**
	er will	sie woll**en**	er woll**te**	sie woll**ten**
STEMS	**will-**	**woll-**	**woll-**	

want to (volition)

PRESENT   Sie will zu Hause bleiben.   (She *wants to* stay home.)
PAST   Er wollte den Chef sehen.   (He *wanted to* see the boss.)

claim to, consider oneself (assertion, opinion)

PRESENT   Er will ein Freund von dir sein.   (He *claims to* be a friend of yours.)

DRILLS

- Supply present tense forms.

1. _____ Sie Ihren Mantel ausziehen?
2. Sie (she) _____ heute abend vorbeikommen.
3. Wir _____ in der Stadt wohnen.
4. Er _____ ein Freund von dir sein.

5. Ich _____ ihr etwas Nettes schenken.
   (schenken: to give [of presents])
6. Was _____ du machen?
7. _____ Sie mitkommen?

- Supply past tense forms.

1. Sie (they) _____ einen neuen Wagen kaufen.
2. Ich _____ ihn gestern besuchen.
3. Wir _____ nur ein Glas Bier trinken.

4. Er _____ heute im Büro arbeiten.
5. _____ Sie ihm einen Brief schreiben?
6. _____ du nicht zu Hause bleiben?
7. Er _____ nicht da bleiben.

- Express in German.

1. I want to give her something nice.
2. We want to live downtown.
3. I wanted to visit him yesterday.

4. Did you want to write him a letter? (**Sie**-form)
5. He says (claims) he is a friend of yours.

6. They wanted to buy a new car.
7. He didn't want to stay there.
8. Do you want to take off your coat? (**Sie**-form)
9. He wanted to work in the office.
10. What do you want to do? (**du**-form)
11. We just wanted to drink a glass of beer.
12. She wants to come by this evening.
13. Didn't you want to stay home? (**du**-form)
14. Do you want to come along? (**Sie**-form)

f. sollen

	Present Tense		Past Tense	
	ich soll	wir soll**en**	ich soll**te**	wir soll**ten**
	du soll**st**	ihr soll**t**	du soll**test**	ihr soll**tet**
	er soll	sie soll**en**	er soll**te**	sie soll**ten**
STEMS	**soll-**	**soll-**	**soll-**	

be supposed to (obligation)

PRESENT   Du **sollst** später kommen.   (You're *supposed to* come later.)
PAST   Wann **sollten** sie ankommen?   (When *were* they *supposed to* arrive.)

be said to, be supposed to (supposition)

PRESENT   Sein neues Buch **soll** sehr interessant sein.
(His new book *is supposed to* be [*said to* be] very interesting.)

shall (suggestion)

PRESENT   **Sollen** wir hier bleiben?   (*Shall* we stay here?)

DRILLS

- Supply present tense forms.

  1. _____ ich die Fahrkarten kaufen?
  2. Was _____ wir jetzt machen?
  3. Er _____ völlig verrückt sein.
     (**völlig:** completely; **verrückt:** crazy, mad)
  4. _____ wir ihnen helfen?
  5. Du _____ später kommen.
  6. Sie (*they*) _____ sehr nett sein.
  7. Sie (*she*) _____ sehr hübsch sein.

- Supply past tense forms.

  1. Er _____ gestern zurückkommen.
  2. Wir _____ bis sechs Uhr arbeiten.
  3. Ich _____ ihm das Geld geben.
  4. Wann _____ sie (*they*) ankommen?
  5. Ich _____ ihn gestern anrufen.

- Express in German.

  1. He was supposed to come back yesterday.
  2. Shall we help them?
  3. Shall I buy the tickets?

4. They're supposed to be very nice.
5. I was supposed to call him yesterday.
6. What shall we do now?
7. I was supposed to give him the money.
8. She's supposed to be very pretty.

9. We were supposed to work until six o'clock.
10. You're supposed to come later. (**du**-form)
11. When were they supposed to arrive?
12. He's supposed to be completely mad.

3 Summary

a. Present tense

1. Present tense stems

Five of the German modals have *two stems*: one for the *infinitive* and the *plural* forms, and a different stem for the *singular* forms.

Infinitive and Plural Stem	Singular Stem
müss-	muß-
könn-	kann-
dürf-	darf-
mög-	mag-
woll-	will-

The one remaining modal has only *one* stem:

Infinitive and Plural Stem	Singular Stem
soll-	soll-

2. Present tense endings

The present tense forms of the modals are unusual; the 1st and 3rd person singular take no endings:

ich kann	-	wir könn	en
du kann	st	ihr könn	t
er kann	-	sie könn	en

b. Past tense

1. Past tense stems

The past tense forms have only *one stem*. As a group the past tense stems are similar to the infinitive stems *without an umlaut:*

Infinitive Stem	Past Tense Stem
müss-	muß-
könn-	konn-
dürf-	durf-
mög-	mo**ch**-
woll-	woll-
soll-	soll-

Only **mögen** changes more than its stem vowel.

2. Past tense endings

German modals use the *weak* (or *regular*) *endings* to form their past tense:

ich	konn	**te**	wir	konn	**ten**
du	konn	**test**	ihr	konn	**tet**
er	konn	**te**	sie	konn	**ten**

DRILLS

• Insert the modal auxiliaries into the following sentences. The tense required is indicated by the tense of the verb in the original sentence. For example, when the verb is in the past tense, the modal must also be in the past tense.

EXAMPLES   Ich gehe jetzt zur Bank. (müssen)
Ich **muß** jetzt zur Bank **gehen**.

Er blieb zu Hause. (wollen)
Er **wollte** zu Hause **bleiben**.

1. Sie ißt nicht viel. (können)
2. Ich kaufte ein Geschenk für meinen Onkel. (müssen)   (**das Geschenk**: gift; **der Onkel**: uncle)
3. Wir holen ihn später ab. (können)
4. Übernachten Sie in Frankfurt? (wollen)   (**übernachten**: to spend the night)
5. Er fuhr mich zum Flughafen. (sollen)   (**der Flughafen**: airport)
6. Sie operieren heute nachmittag. (müssen)   (**operieren**: to operate on someone)
7. Sie blieben bis Mitternacht. (dürfen)   (**Mitternacht**: midnight)
8. Er fährt nach England. (wollen)
9. Wir erledigen es sofort. (sollen)   (**erledigen**: to take care of something; **sofort**: immediately)
10. Nimmt er deinen Wagen? (dürfen)
11. Er blieb nicht da. (wollen)
12. Der Kühlschrank ist kaputt. (müssen)   (**der Kühlschrank**: refrigerator; **kaputt**: broken)
13. Stellten Sie eine Frage? (wollen)   (**eine Frage stellen**: to ask a question)
14. Ich ging nach Hause. (müssen)
15. Laden wir Willi ein? (sollen)   (**ein·laden, lädt . . . ein, lud . . . ein, eingeladen**: to invite)
16. Er fand das Haus nicht. (können)
17. Wir kauften einen neuen Plattenspieler. (wollen)   (**der Plattenspieler**: record player)
18. Reparieren Sie den Wagen? (können)   (**reparieren**: to repair)
19. Sie nimmt den Zug. (wollen)   (**der Zug**: train)
20. Wir besprechen es mit ihm. (sollen)

• Synthetic exercises: Form sentences using the following elements.

1. Ich / müssen / gehen / nach Hause (*past*)
2. Sie / können / essen / nicht viel (*past*)
3. Wir / sollen / erledigen / es / sofort (*present*)
4. Sie (*she*) / wollen / nehmen / Zug (*present*)
5. Er / sollen / fahren / mich / zu / Flughafen (*past*)
6. Sie / müssen / operieren / gestern (*past*)
7. Können / Sie / reparieren / Wagen / ? (*present*)
8. Sollen / wir / einladen / Willi / ? (*present*)

9. Wir / sollen / besprechen / es mit ihm   (*past*)
10. Kühlschrank / müssen / sein / kaputt   (*present*)
11. Ich / müssen / kaufen / Geschenk / für / mein / Onkel   (*past*)
12. Wollen / du / stellen / Frage / ?   (*past*)
13. Wir / können / abholen / ihn / später   (*present*)
14. Er / können / finden / Haus / nicht   (*past*)
15. Wollen / Sie / übernachten / hier / ?   (*present*)
16. Sie (*she*) / dürfen / bleiben / bis Mitternacht   (*past*)
17. Er / wollen / bleiben / nicht / da   (*past*)
18. Dürfen / er / nehmen / dein / Wagen / ?   (*present*)
19. Wir / wollen / kaufen / neu / Plattenspieler   (*past*)
20. Er / wollen / fahren / nach England   (*present*)

● Express in German.

a. 1. May they come along?
   2. He had to go to the barber's.
   3. No, I don't like this soup.
   4. I was supposed to give him the money.
   5. What do you want to do?   (**du**-form)
   6. I could hardly understand him.
   7. Do you want to spend the night here?   (**Sie**-form)
   8. I have to go to the bank.
   9. He didn't want to stay there.
   10. He didn't like the play.

b. 1. We can't help you.
   2. Shall I buy the tickets?
   3. She couldn't eat much.
   4. The poor girl! She never gets to go out.
   5. He wanted to work in his office today.
   6. That can't be true.
   7. We had to go to another bank.
   8. They're supposed to be very nice.
   9. I wanted to visit him yesterday.
   10. We can pick him up later.

c. 1. May I answer your question?
   2. We had to drive through the city.
   3. He was supposed to come back yesterday.
   4. I had to go home.
   5. They couldn't come yesterday evening.
   6. You can come along next time. (**du**-form)
   7. Did you have to pay the bill? (**du**-form)
   8. I want to give her something nice.
   9. They had to operate yesterday.
   10. I can't find my coat.

d. 1. We were supposed to work until six o'clock.
   2. He wants to go to England.
   3. You have to take the train. (**Sie**-form)
   4. Do you want to take off your coat? (**Sie**-form)
   5. What shall we do now?
   6. Do you want to come along? (**Sie**-form)
   7. He wanted to stay here.
   8. We have to get up very early.
   9. May he take your car?
   10. We're supposed to take care of it immediately.

e. 1. We couldn't recognize him.
   2. He wants to live downtown.
   3. Shall we help them?
   4. He couldn't find the house.
   5. Do you have to do that today? (**Sie**-form)
   6. He was supposed to drive me to the airport.
   7. We got to get up a little later.
   8. He claims to be a friend of yours.
   9. Shall we invite Willi?
   10. The refrigerator must be broken.

f. 1. He couldn't translate the letter.
   2. May I help you?
   3. Did you have to work yesterday? (**du**-form)
   4. Did you want to ask a question? (**Sie**-form)
   5. I was supposed to call him yesterday.
   6. He has to fly to Mainz in February.
   7. Can you repair the car? (**Sie**-form)
   8. He didn't get to do it.

9. You're supposed to come later.
   (**du**-form)
10. We wanted to buy a new record
    player.

g. 1. Could they speak German?
   2. We just wanted to drink a glass
      of beer.
   3. I don't like the new boss.
   4. I have to buy a present for
      my uncle.
   5. He has to stay home today.

6. May we come a little later?
7. She got to stay until midnight.
8. Do you like his wife?
9. She's supposed to be very pretty.
10. She wants to come by this evening.

h. 1. She had to be there before ten
      o'clock.
   2. She wants to take the train.
   3. You may see him now. (**Sie**-form)

B Compound Tenses of Modal Auxiliaries

1 Present perfect tense: without dependent infinitives

a. Usage

Occasionally modals are used *without* dependent infinitives. Look at the following
examples:

> Er **wollte** meinen Wagen **nehmen.**   (He *wanted to take* my car.)
> Er **wollte** meinen Wagen.   (He *wanted* my car.)

As you can see, a dependent infinitive can sometimes be omitted without really
affecting the meaning of the sentence.

In other cases the context of a conversation might make the use of a dependent
infinitive repetitious:

> **Muß** er heute **arbeiten?**   (*Does* he *have to work* today?)
> Ja, er **muß.**   (Yes. He *has to.*)

b. Forms

When there is no dependent infinitive involved, the formation of the present perfect
tense is completely regular. It consists of:

An Auxiliary Verb (the present tense of **haben**)	+	Past Participle
Er **hat** deinen Wagen		**gewollt.**

Look at the following forms:

Past Tense	Present Perfect Tense
Er **muß**te . . .	Er hat . . . ge**muß**t
Er **konn**te . . .	Er hat . . . ge**konn**t
Er **durf**te . . .	Er hat . . . ge**durf**t
Er **moch**te . . .	Er hat . . . ge**moch**t
Er **woll**te . . .	Er hat . . . ge**woll**t
Er **soll**te . . .	Er hat . . . ge**soll**t

1. All modal auxiliaries use **haben** (rather than **sein**) to form their perfect tenses:

Er hat meinen Wagen **gewollt.**

2. The stems of the past participles are identical to the past tense stems:

gemußt   mußte

DRILLS

- Put the following sentences into the present perfect tense. All the sentences require the *past participle* of the modal.

EXAMPLE   Ich wollte nur ein Buch.
Ich **habe** nur ein Buch **gewollt.**

1. Er wollte meinen Wagen.
2. Er konnte nicht.
3. Ich mochte seine Stimme nicht.
4. Er wollte es nicht.

5. Wir durften nicht.
6. Wir mochten das Essen nicht.
7. Er wollte nur ein Bier.

- Synthetic exercises: Use the following elements to construct sentences in the past tense and the present perfect tense.

EXAMPLE   Ich / wollen / nur ein Buch

Ich **wollte** nur ein Buch.
Ich **habe** nur ein Buch **gewollt.**

1. Er / wollen / es nicht
2. Wir / mögen / Essen / nicht
3. Er / wollen / mein- / Wagen
4. Er / können / nicht
5. Ich / mögen / sein- / Stimme / nicht

6. Er / wollen / nur ein Bier
7. Wir / dürfen / nicht

- Express in German (past tense and present perfect tense).

1. He just wanted a beer.
2. I didn't like his voice.
3. He didn't want it.
4. He wasn't able to.

5. We didn't like the food.
6. He wanted my car.
7. We didn't get to.

2 Future tense: **werden** + infinitive

As usual, the future tense is composed of **werden** + an *infinitive.*

PRESENT TENSE   Er **muß** nach Hause gehen.   (*has to go*)
FUTURE TENSE   Er **wird** nach Hause gehen **müssen.**   (*will have to go*)

The only difference between these two sentences is that the modal has changed tenses. The present tense form **muß** has been replaced by **wird . . . müssen.**

▶ **Note** When a dependent infinitive is involved, there will be *two* infinitives at the end of the sentence:

1. the dependent infinitive, *and*
2. the infinitival form of the modal

$$\text{Er wird nach Hause } \overset{\textbf{(1)}}{\text{gehen}} \ \overset{\textbf{(2)}}{\text{müssen.}}$$

The infinitival form of the modal (**müssen**) will always be the *last* element in the sentence.

DRILLS

● Supply the correct form of **werden**.

1. _____ du ihm helfen können?
2. Er _____ wohl mitkommen dürfen.
3. Du _____ ihn nicht erkennen können.
4. Wir _____ ihn nicht sehen können.
5. Ich _____ es wohl machen müssen.
6. Sie (*they*) _____ lange warten müssen.
7. Sie (*she*) _____ nicht viel essen können.
8. _____ Sie die Rechnung bezahlen können?
9. Ich _____ durch die Stadt fahren müssen.
10. Wir _____ wohl operieren müssen.
11. Du _____ es nicht finden können.
12. Ihr _____ früh aufstehen müssen.
13. _____ er den Wagen reparieren können?
14. Wir _____ es sofort erledigen müssen.

● Put the following sentences into the future tense by using the auxiliary **werden**.

EXAMPLE Können Sie es machen?
  Werden Sie es machen **können?**

1. Ich muß es wohl machen.
2. Können Sie die Rechnung bezahlen?
3. Wir müssen wohl operieren.
4. Du kannst es nicht finden.
5. Er darf wohl mitkommen.
6. Wir müssen es sofort erledigen.
7. Sie kann nicht viel essen.
8. Wir können ihn nicht sehen.
9. Kannst du ihm helfen?
10. Ich muß durch die Stadt fahren.
11. Kann er den Wagen reparieren?
12. Sie müssen lange warten.
13. Du kannst ihn nicht erkennen.
14. Ihr müßt früh aufstehen.

● Supply the missing infinitives.

EXAMPLE Er wird wohl nach Hause _____.
              (have to go)
  Er wird wohl nach Hause **gehen müssen.**

1. Ich werde es wohl _____.
              (have to do)
2. Sie werden lange _____.
              (have to wait)
3. Du wirst es nicht _____.
              (be able to find)

4. Werden Sie die Rechnung _____?
   (be able to pay)

5. Wir werden wohl _____.
   (have to operate)

6. Sie wird nicht viel _____.
   (be able to eat)

7. Wird er den Wagen _____?
   (be able to repair)

8. Ich werde durch die Stadt _____.
   (have to drive)

9. Wir werden ihn nicht _____.
   (be able to see)

10. Er wird wohl _____.
    (get to come along)

11. Du wirst ihn nicht _____.
    (be able to recognize)

12. Ihr werdet früh _____.
    (have to get up)

13. Wirst du ihm _____?
    (be able to help)

14. Wir werden es sofort _____.
    (have to take care of)

• Express in German.

1. We'll probably have to operate.
2. Will you be able to pay the bill? (**Sie**-form)
3. I'll probably have to do it.
4. You won't be able to recognize him. (**du**-form)
5. They'll have to wait a long time.
6. She won't be able to eat much.
7. You'll have to get up early. (**ihr**-form)

8. He'll probably get to come along.
9. We'll have to take care of it immediately.
10. Will he be able to repair the car?
11. You won't be able to find it. (**du**-form)
12. We won't be able to see him.
13. I'll have to drive through the city.
14. Will you be able to help him? (**du**-form)

3 Present perfect tense with dependent infinitives: *the double infinitive construction*

a. Usage

Although modal auxiliaries are occasionally used alone, it is far more common for them to be used in conjunction with a dependent infinitive.

b. Forms

When a sentence contains a dependent infinitive, the present perfect tense differs from the normal pattern. Look at the following examples:

PRESENT   Ich **muß** nach Hause gehen.
PRESENT PERFECT   Ich **habe** nach Hause gehen **müssen**.

The present tense form **muß** has been replaced by **habe . . . müssen.** The actual past participle of **müssen** is **gemußt,** which means that the perfect tense of **Ich muß** is **Ich habe . . . gemußt.** But when the sentence contains a dependent infinitive:

Ich muß nach Hause **gehen.**

the modal forms its present perfect with its *infinitive* **(müssen)** instead of with its past participle **(gemußt):**

Ich habe nach Hause gehen müssen.

The result is called a *double-infinitive construction.* Note that the infinitive of the *modal* **(müssen)** is the last element in the sentence.

Without Dependent Infinitive	With Dependent Infinitive
Ich habe . . . **gemußt**	Ich habe . . . gehen **müssen**
Ich habe . . . **gekonnt**	Ich habe . . . gehen **können**
Ich habe . . . **gedurft**	Ich habe . . . gehen **dürfen**
Ich habe . . . **gewollt**	Ich habe . . . gehen **wollen**
Ich habe . . . **gesollt**	Ich habe . . . gehen **sollen**
Ich habe . . . **gemocht**	Ich habe . . . gehen **mögen**

DRILLS

● Supply the correct form of the auxiliary **haben.**

1. Er _____ den Kurs nicht nehmen wollen.
2. Wir _____ es nicht machen dürfen.
3. Ich _____ keinen Unterschied sehen können.
4. Was _____ du da machen wollen?
5. Sie (*they*) _____ bis Mitternacht bleiben dürfen.
6. Er _____ einen Scheck einlösen wollen.
7. _____ Sie die Rechnung bezahlen müssen?
8. Ich _____ ihn nicht erreichen können.
9. Er _____ es nicht erklären können.
10. Wir _____ es sofort erledigen müssen.

(der Kurs: course)

(der Unterschied: difference)

(ein·lösen: to cash [a check])

(erreichen: to reach, get hold of)
(erklären: to explain)

● Put the following sentences into the present perfect tense. All the sentences require a double-infinitive construction.

EXAMPLE   Ich mußte zur Bank gehen.
           Ich **habe** zur Bank gehen **müssen.**

1. Sie konnte nicht viel essen.
2. Mußten Sie die Rechnung bezahlen?
3. Wir durften es nicht machen.
4. Was wolltest du da machen?
5. Wir konnten das Haus nicht finden.
6. Er konnte es nicht erklären.
7. Wir wollten einen neuen Plattenspieler kaufen.
8. Ich konnte meinen Stift nicht finden.
   (der Stift: pen or pencil [any writing implement])
9. Sie durften bis Mitternacht bleiben.
10. Er wollte den Kurs nicht nehmen.
11. Konnten sie den Wagen reparieren?
12. Er wollte eine Pause machen.
    (eine Pause machen: to take a break)

13. Wir mußten es sofort erledigen.
14. Ich konnte ihn nicht erreichen.
15. Sie wollte eine Frage stellen.
16. Er mußte einen Scheck einlösen.
17. Sie konnten die Miete nicht bezahlen.

                    (die Miete: rent)

18. Durfte er den Wagen nehmen?
19. Ich konnte keinen Unterschied sehen.

20. Sie wollte den Tisch decken.

        (den Tisch decken: to set the table)

21. Du lieber Gott, Inge! Ich wollte nur
helfen.   **(Du lieber Gott!:** Good God!)
22. Wir mußten ihn einladen.
23. Er wollte nach England fahren.
24. Sie konnten nicht viel Geld sparen.

                 (sparen: to save)

● Synthetic exercises: Use the following elements to construct sentences in the past tense and the present perfect tense.

EXAMPLE   Er / müssen / einlösen / Scheck

        Er **mußte** einen Scheck **einlösen.**
        Er **hat** einen Scheck **einlösen müssen.**

1. Wir / müssen / einladen / ihn
2. Sie (she) / können / essen / nicht viel
3. Ich / können / erreichen / ihn nicht
4. Wir / können / finden / Haus / nicht
5. Sie (she) / wollen / decken / Tisch
6. Wir / müssen / erledigen / es / sofort
7. Ich / können / finden / mein- / Stift / nicht
8. Dürfen / er / nehmen / Wagen / ?
9. Sie (they) / können / sparen / nicht viel Geld
10. Was / wollen / du / machen / da / ?
11. Wir / dürfen / machen / es / nicht
12. Sie (they) / können / bezahlen / Miete / nicht
13. Er / wollen / fahren / nach England
14. Müssen / Sie / bezahlen / Rechnung?
15. Ich / können / sehen / kein- / Unterschied
16. Wir / wollen / kaufen / neu- / Plattenspieler
17. Er / wollen / nehmen / Kurs / nicht
18. Er / müssen / einlösen / Scheck
19. Du / lieb- / Gott / ! / Ich / wollen / helfen / nur
20. Er / wollen / machen / Pause
21. Sie (she) / wollen / stellen / Frage
22. Können / sie (they) / reparieren / Wagen / ?
23. Er / können / erklären / es nicht
24. Sie (they) / dürfen / bleiben / bis Mitternacht

● Express each of the following sentences in German in the past tense and the present perfect tense.

1. We couldn't find the house.
2. She couldn't eat much.
3. He didn't want to take the course.
4. We had to invite him.
5. Did you have to pay the bill? **(Sie**-form)
6. He wanted to go to England.
7. I couldn't reach him.
8. She wanted to set the table.
9. We didn't get to do it.
10. They couldn't save much money.
11. Good God, Inge! I only wanted to help.
12. He had to cash a check.
13. Did he get to take the car?
14. They couldn't pay the rent.

15. We wanted to buy a new record player.
16. He couldn't explain it.
17. We had to take care of it immediately.
18. I couldn't find my pencil.
19. She wanted to ask a question.
20. I couldn't see any difference.
21. What did you want to do there? (**du**-form)
22. Were they able to repair the car?
23. He wanted to take a break.

4 Summary

PRINCIPAL PARTS OF THE MODAL AUXILIARIES			
Infinitive	*3rd Person Singular*	*Past*	*Past Participle*
müssen	muß	mußte	gemußt
können	kann	konnte	gekonnt
dürfen	darf	durfte	gedurft
mögen	mag	mochte	gemocht
wollen	will	wollte	gewollt
sollen	soll	sollte	gesollt

TENSES OF MODAL AUXILIARIES			
Without Dependent Infinitive		*With Dependent Infinitive*	
Ich **muß** . . .	(have to . . .)	Ich **muß** . . . gehen	
Ich **mußte** . . .	(had to . . .)	Ich **mußte** . . . gehen	
Ich **werde** . . . **müssen**	(will have to . . .)	Ich **werde** . . . gehen **müssen**	
Ich **habe** . . . **gemußt**	(have had to . . .)	Ich **habe** . . . gehen **müssen**	
Ich **hatte** . . . **gemußt**	(had had to . . .)	Ich **hatte** . . . gehen **müssen**	

Tense change

The only elements that change in the sentences above are the forms of the modal: **muß, mußte, werde . . . müssen.**

PERFECT TENSES		
	Without Dependent Infinitive	*With Dependent Infinitive*
PRESENT PERFECT	Ich habe . . . **gemußt**	Ich habe . . . **gehen müssen**
PAST PERFECT	Ich hatte . . . **gemußt**	Ich hatte . . . **gehen müssen**
	(Past Participle)	(Double-Infinitive Construction)

GRAND MIX: EXPRESS IN GERMAN

- Express the following sentences in the tense or tenses indicated.

a. 1. We had to invite him. (*past and perfect*)
    2. We'll probably have to operate. (*future*)
    3. She couldn't eat much. (*past and perfect*)
    4. He wanted to go to England. (*past and perfect*)
    5. I'll probably have to do it. (*future*)
    6. He had to cash a check. (*past and perfect*)
    7. You **(du)** won't be able to find it. (*future*)
    8. He just wanted a beer. (*past and perfect*)
    9. They couldn't pay the rent. (*past and perfect*)
   10. We didn't get to do it. (*past and perfect*)

b. 1. Will you **(du)** be able to help him? (*future*)
    2. We wanted to buy a new record player. (*past and perfect*)
    3. I couldn't see any difference. (*past and perfect*)
    4. He wanted my car. (*past and perfect*)
    5. We'll have to take care of it immediately. (*future*)
    6. Did he get to take the car? (*past and perfect*)
    7. I couldn't reach him. (*past and perfect*)
    8. They'll have to wait a long time. (*future*)
    9. We didn't get to. (*past and perfect*)
   10. He wanted to take a break. (*past and perfect*)

c. 1. She won't be able to eat much. (*future*)
    2. We didn't like the food. (*past and perfect*)
    3. He couldn't explain it. (*past and perfect*)
    4. Good God, Inge! I only wanted to help. (*past and perfect*)
    5. You **(du)** won't be able to recognize him. (*future*)
    6. He didn't want it. (*past and perfect*)
    7. She wanted to ask a question. (*past and perfect*)
    8. We won't be able to see him. (*future*)
    9. I didn't like his voice. (*past and perfect*)
   10. They couldn't save much money. (*past and perfect*)

d. 1. You'll **(ihr)** have to get up early. (*future*)
    2. I couldn't find my pencil. (*past and perfect*)
    3. He didn't want to take the course. (*past and perfect*)
    4. I'll have to drive through the city. (*future*)
    5. Were they able to repair the car? (*past and perfect*)
    6. What did you **(du)** want to do there? (*past and perfect*)
    7. He'll probably get to come along. (*future*)
    8. She wanted to set the table. (*past and perfect*)
    9. We couldn't find the house. (*past and perfect*)

beantworten to answer (*a question, not a person*)

decken to set (*a table*)

dürfen (darf) may, get to, be permitted to, to be allowed to
    durfte, gedurft

ein·laden (lädt ... ein) to invite
    lud ... ein, eingeladen

ein·lösen to cash (*a check*)

erklären to explain

erledigen to take care of something

erreichen to reach, get hold of

das **Essen** food

etwas (später) a little (later)

der **Flughafen, ꞉** airport

die **Frage, –n** question
    eine Frage stellen to ask a question

Gott God
    Du lieber Gott! Good God!

kaputt broken

kaum scarcely, hardly

können (kann) can, to be able to (ability); can (possibility)
    konnte, gekonnt

der **Kühlschrank, ꞉e** refrigerator

der **Kurs, –e** course

die **Miete, –n** rent

die **Mitternacht** midnight

mögen (mag) to like (liking, fondness)
    mochte, gemocht

müssen (muß) must, have to
    mußte, gemußt

der **Onkel, –** uncle

operieren to operate on someone

die **Pause, –n** break
    eine Pause machen to take a break

der **Plattenspieler, –** record player

reparieren to repair

schenken to give (*of presents*)

sofort immediately

sollen (soll) to be supposed to (obligation); to be said to, supposed to (supposition); shall (suggestion)
    sollte, gesollt

sparen to save

der **Stift, –e** pen or pencil (*any writing implement*)

die **Stimme, –n** voice

übernachten to spend the night

der **Unterschied, –e** difference

verrückt mad, crazy

völlig completely

vor (+ *dat.*) before (*with time expr.*)

wahr true

wollen (will) to want to (volition); claim to, consider oneself (assertion, opinion)
    wollte, gewollt

der **Zug, ꞉e** train

Reading **VII**

Einkaufen° in Deutschland

das **Einkaufen**: buying, shopping

Ein Supermarkt° im Keller° eines Kaufhauses?°
Jawohl,° nur daß man es „Lebensmittelabteilung"°
nennt.° Sogar° die meisten Kaufhäuser in Deutschland haben in ihrem Untergeschoß° (das Wort°
„Untergeschoß" klingt° einfach besser als das Wort

der **Supermarkt, ⁻e**: supermarket
  der **Keller, –**: cellar das **Kaufhaus, ⁻er**:
  department store
jawohl: yes, indeed die **Lebensmittelabteilung,
  –en**: grocery department
nennen: to call **sogar**: (*here*) in fact
das **Untergeschoß, –sse**: lower level
  das **Wort, ⁻er**: word
klingen: to sound

„Keller") eine Lebensmittelabteilung. Nichts Kleines, nein, sie sind so groß wie die amerikanischen Supermärkte und haben eine genau so reiche° Auswahl,° ja manchmal° sogar° eine bessere. Als Mitglied° der EWG (**E**uropäische **W**irtschafts-**g**emeinschaft°) bekommen die Deutschen die Waren° ihrer Partner° billiger als etwa° wir. Besonders° in den letzten 15 Jahren ist die Auswahl Jahr für Jahr größer und internationaler geworden. Dreißig Sorten° französischer° Käse,° Fisch aus Holland, Scotch aus England. Wie?° Scotch in einer Lebensmittelabteilung? Ja, warum nicht? Und Bourbon aus den Vereinigten Staaten auch. Aber Bourbon ist viel teurer als Scotch. Warum? Die USA° sind nicht in der EWG. Wie Sie sehen, deutsche Lebensmittelabteilungen haben außer Lebensmitteln° auch allerlei° Getränke.°

Fragen 1–6, p. 355

reich: (*here*) varied   **die Auswahl**: selection   **manchmal**: sometimes   **sogar**: even   **das Mitglied, –er**: member

die EWG: European Common Market   **die Ware, –n**: merchandise   **der Partner, –**: partner, (*here*) member of the EWG   **etwa**: (*here*) for instance   **besonders**: especially

die Sorte, –n: kind   **französisch**: French   **der Käse, –**: cheese   **wie**: (*here*) what?

die USA: USA [*note:* in German it is a plural form]

das Lebensmittel, –: grocery item   **allerlei**: all kinds of   **das Getränk, –e**: beverage

Das Einkaufen in einer deutschen Lebensmittelabteilung hat viele Ähnlichkeiten° mit dem Einkaufen in einem amerikanischen Supermarkt, aber Sie werden auch Unterschiede° finden. Als erstes° gehen Sie durch ein Drehkreuz,° nehmen einen Einkaufswagen,° normalerweise viel kleiner als in den Vereinigten Staaten, und ziehen los.° In Deutschland kauft man meistens nur für zwei Tage ein,° denn ein deutscher Kühlschrank° ist ungefähr° nur halb so groß wie ein amerikanischer. Deshalb° sind die Einkaufswagen so klein.

die Ähnlichkeit, –en: similarity

der Unterschied, –e: difference   **als erstes**: the first thing (you do)

das Drehkreuz, –e: turnstile

der Einkaufswagen, –: shopping cart

los·ziehen (*colloq.*): to start, to set off

ein·kaufen: to shop, buy   **der Kühlschrank, ⁼e**: refrigerator   **ungefähr**: approximately, about   **deshalb**: that's why

Wie in den Vereinigten Staaten kann man hier fast° alles kaufen, was man braucht. Man geht durch die Gänge° zwischen den Regalen° und nimmt, was man will. Es gibt also auch hier Selbstbedienung. Aber wie in den USA gibt es Spezialabteilungen° für Fleisch,° Gemüse° und Feinkost.° Außerdem° gibt es in Deutschland spezielle° Abteilungen für Back-

fast: almost

der Gang, ⁼e: aisle   **das Regal, –e**: shelf

die Spezialabteilung, –en: special department   **das Fleisch**: meat   **das Gemüse**: vegetables   **die Feinkost**: delicatessen   **außerdem**: besides that   **speziell**: special

waren,° Käse, Fisch und Wein. Der Verkäufer° in der Weinabteilung gibt Ihnen manchmal° sogar Kostproben,° besonders wenn er Sonderangebote° hat. Wenn Sie alles haben, was Sie brauchen, gehen Sie mit Ihrem Einkaufswagen zu einer der Kassen.° Sie legen Ihre Einkäufe° auf das Transportband,° und die Kassiererin° addiert° die Beträge° auf der Kasse.° Dann sagt sie Ihnen schnell, was alles kostet, und Sie zahlen. Ihre Einkäufe sind nun° schon vorne° und aus dem Weg° der Kassiererin. Jetzt geht es etwas anders zu,° als° Sie erwarten.° Sie bedient° schon den nächsten Kunden,° und Sie müssen Ihre Sachen° schnell selber° einpacken.° Wenn Sie keine Einkaufstasche° mitgebracht° haben, können Sie von der Kassiererin einen Plastikbeutel° bekommen.

die **Backwaren** (*pl. only*): baked goods
   der **Verkäufer**, –: salesman
manchmal: sometimes
die **Kostprobe**, –n: sample   das **Sonderangebot**, –e: special, sale-priced item

die **Kasse**, –n: (*here*) checkout
der **Einkauf**, ⁼e: purchase   das **Transportband**, ⁼er: conveyor belt
die **Kassiererin**, –nen: checkout clerk   **addieren**: to add up, total   der **Betrag**, ⁼e: amount
die **Kasse**, –n: (*here*) cash register

nun: now
vorne: up front   **aus dem Weg sein**: to be out of the way

es geht anders zu: things go differently   **als**: than   **erwarten**: to expect   **bedienen**: to wait on
der **Kunde**, –n, –n (*weak noun*) customer
die **Sache**, –n: thing   **selber**: (*here*) yourself
   ein·packen: to pack
die **Einkaufstasche**, –n: shopping bag, a satchel for carrying groceries
   mit·bringen: to bring along
der **Plastikbeutel**, –: sturdy plastic bag

Fragen
7–12, pp.
355–56

Den Einkaufswagen lassen Sie da stehen—in der Lebensmittelabteilung. Von da an° müssen Sie Ihre Sachen selber tragen, und wenn Sie Flaschen° haben, kann das mit der Zeit° ziemlich° schwer° werden.

von da an: from that point on

die Flasche, –n: bottle

mit der Zeit: in time **ziemlich:** rather **schwer:** heavy

Sonst° ist ein deutsches Kaufhaus fast° wie ein amerikanisches, mit seinen verschiedenen Abteilungen° in 4 bis 6 Stockwerken.° Man nimmt eine Rolltreppe° zwischen den Stockwerken. Aufzüge gibt es auch, aber die Leute benutzen° sie nur selten. Auch finden Sie eine Orientierungstafel° in jedem Stockwerk. Wollen Sie Glühbirnen° kaufen? Sie sehen die Tafel an° und finden Elektroartikel° im 4. Stock.

sonst: otherwise **fast:** almost

die Abteilung, –en: department

das Stockwerk, –e: story

die Rolltreppe, –n: escalator

benutzen: to use

die Orientierungstafel, –n: directory

die Glühbirne, –n: lightbulb

an · sehen: to look at

die Elektroartikel (pl.): electrical supplies

Die bekanntesten° Kaufhausgruppen° heißen *Quelle, Hertie* und *Kaufhof,* und Sie finden sie in fast jeder Großstadt, aber außerdem° gibt es verschiedene Fachgeschäfte.° Viele sind wie die Fachgeschäfte in den USA, zum Beispiel: Geschäfte° für Damen–und Herrenbekleidung,° Schuhgeschäfte,° Buchhandlungen° und Fotogeschäfte.° Auch die Wäschereien° sind in den letzten Jahren wie die° in den Vereinigten Staaten geworden, sie nehmen Stückwäsche° an°— von Taschentüchern° bis Bettlaken.° Und Sachen für die chemische Reinigung° nehmen sie auch an, zum Beispiel, Anzüge und Pullover. Andere Fachgeschäfte, wie z.B. Bäckereien,° Metzgereien° und Gemüseläden,° findet man viel häufiger° in Deutschland als in den USA. Natürlich° kann man die Waren dieser Geschäfte auch in der Lebensmittelabteilung in einem Kaufhaus bekommen, aber viele Deutsche kaufen lieber in kleinen Geschäften. Einige deutsche Fachgeschäfte gibt es in den USA gar nicht,° oder in anderer Form.° Eine Drogerie ist nicht identisch mit° einem „drugstore". In einer deutschen Drogerie finden Sie z.B. Toilettenartikel,° Wasch-

bekannt: known **die Kaufhausgruppe, –n:** department store chain

außerdem: besides that

das Fachgeschäft, –e: specialized store

das Geschäft, –e: store

die Bekleidung: clothing

das Schuhgeschäft, –e: shoestore

die Buchhandlung, –en: bookstore

das Fotogeschäft, –e: photography shop

die Wäscherei, –en: laundry

die: those

die Stückwäsche: things to be washed and ironed **an · nehmen:** to take, accept

das Taschentuch, ¨er: handkerchief

das Bettlaken, –: sheet

chemische Reinigung: dry cleaning

die Bäckerei, –en: bakery

die Metzgerei, –en: butcher shop

der Gemüseladen, ¨: vegetable shop

häufig: frequently

natürlich: naturally

gar nicht: not at all **die Form:** form

identisch mit: identical to

die Toilettenartikel (*pl*): toiletries

mittel° und rezeptfreie° Medikamente,° aber keine Zeitschriften,° Schreibwaren,° Tabakwaren,° oder Haushaltsartikel.° Eine Apotheke° dagegen° hat rezeptpflichtige° und rezeptfreie Medikamente, aber keine Toilettenartikel oder Waschmittel.

Schreibwarengeschäfte° gibt es auch häufig in Deutschland, und da kann man nur Schreibwaren kaufen, z.B. Briefpapier,° Ringbuchpapier,° Bleistifte° und Kugelschreiber.° In einem Elektrogeschäft° finden Sie nur elektrische Artikel,° wie z.B. Lampen, Glühbirnen, Sicherungen° und Verlängerungsschnüre.° Das Tabakwarengeschäft ist eine typisch° deutsche Einrichtung.° Dort kaufen die meisten Deutschen ihre Zigaretten,° Zigarren,° Streichhölzer° und Feuerzeuge,° aber auch ihre Zeitungen und Zeitschriften.

agen
–19, 356

Wann sind die Geschäfte geöffnet?° Das ist auch ein wenig anders als in den Vereinigten Staaten. Die Kaufhäuser und die meisten anderen Geschäfte machen von Montag bis Freitag um 9 Uhr auf und

das Waschmittel, –: laundry supplies
rezeptfrei: nonprescription (drug)
das Medikament, –e: medication, drug
die Zeitschrift, –en: magazine
die Schreibwaren (*pl. only*): writing supplies **die Tabakwaren** (*pl. only*): various kinds of tobacco products
die Haushaltsartikel (*pl*): household goods
die Apotheke, –n: pharmacy
dagegen: on the other hand
rezeptpflichtig: prescription (drug)
das Schreibwarengeschäft, –e: stationery store
das Briefpapier: stationery
das Ringbuchpapier: paper for ring binders
der Bleistift, –e: pencil **der Kugelschreiber, –:** ball-point pen **das Elektrogeschäft, –e:** special store for electrical supplies
der Artikel, –: item, thing
die Sicherung, –en: fuse
die Verlängerungsschnur, ¨e: extension cord
typisch: typically **die Einrichtung:** (*here*) institution
die Zigarette, –n: cigarette **die Zigarre, –n:** cigar
das Streichholz, ¨er: match
das Feuerzeug, –e: lighter

geöffnet: open

um halb sieben zu. Ein paar Geschäfte, wie Bäckereien und Gemüseläden, machen früher° auf. Aber jetzt eine Überraschung:° am Samstag sind alle Geschäfte normalerweise nur bis 2 Uhr nachmittags geöffnet. Ihre Wochenendeinkäufe° müssen also vor 2 Uhr am Samstag erledigt° sein. Nur am ersten Samstag im Monat ist es anders. Das ist der sogenannte° „lange Samstag", und die Geschäfte machen dann erst° um 6 Uhr zu. Am Sonntag und an den vielen deutschen Feiertagen° ist fast alles zu.° Nur eine Apotheke in jedem Stadtteil° bleibt geöffnet. Sie werden also große Schwierigkeiten° haben, wenn Sie am Sonntag etwas außer Medikamenten haben wollen. Bestenfalls° finden Sie Imbißautomaten° mit „Erfrischungen",° wie Getränke, Brötchen° und kleine Fisch- und Fleischdosen.° Aber die Auswahl ist nicht besonders groß und auch nicht sehr appetitlich.° In dem Fall° gehen Sie besser in eine Gaststätte und essen und trinken Sie etwas Anständiges.°

früher: earlier

die Überraschung, –en: surprise

die Wochenendeinkäufe (*pl. only*): what you buy for the weekend
erledigt: taken care of

sogenannt: so-called

erst: (*here*) not until

der Feiertag, –e: holiday

zu·sein: to be closed **der Stadtteil, –e**: part of town
die Schwierigkeit, –en: difficulty

bestenfalls: at best
der Imbißautomat, –en: snack vending machine **die Erfrischung, –en**: refreshment
das Brötchen, –: hard roll

die Dose, –n: can

appetitlich: appetizing **der Fall**: case

anständig: decent

Am Anfang hat man immer Schwellenangst° in einem fremden Land. Aber hier hilft Ihnen eine einfache° Formel° aus:°

die Schwellenangst: fear of entering a place

einfach: simple **die Formel, –n**: formula
aus·helfen: to help out

> „Ich sehe mich nur um, danke."
> (*I'm just looking [around], thanks.*)

Fragen 20–25, p. 356

Wenn sie diese Formel hören, lassen die Verkäufer° und Verkäuferinnen° Sie in Ruhe. Aber es kann Ihnen nur helfen, wenn Sie ein paar° Einkaufssituationen° üben°:

der Verkäufer, –: salesman

die Verkäuferin, –nen: saleswoman

ein paar: a few
die Einkaufssituation, –en: shopping situation **üben**: to practice

BUCHHANDLUNG

BUCHHÄNDLER:°
Guten Tag, bitte schön?

der Buchhändler, –: salesman in a bookstore

SIE:

Guten Tag. Haben Sie die Taschenbuchausgabe° von Bölls° *Billiard*° *um halb zehn*?

BUCHHÄNDLER:

Ja, Augenblick,° ich hole° es Ihnen. Haben Sie noch einen Wunsch?°

SIE:

Haben Sie auch sein *Gruppenbild*° *mit Dame*?

BUCHHÄNDLER:

Nein, das muß ich für Sie bestellen. Aber wir haben es in zwei Tagen. Kommen Sie am Donnerstag nachmittag wieder vorbei.

SIE:

Gut, mache ich.° Und was kostet *Billiard um halb zehn*?

BUCHHÄNDLER:

Vier Mark achtzig, bitte. Soll ich es Ihnen einpacken?°

SIE:

Nein, danke. Ich stecke° es in die Tasche.° Hier, zehn Mark, bitte.

BUCHHÄNDLER:

Und fünf Mark zwanzig zurück. Danke schön.

SIE:

Ich danke auch. Auf Wiedersehen.

die Taschenbuchausgabe, –n: paperback edition
Böll: Heinrich Böll, German author, Nobel Prize for Literature 1972 **das Billiard**: billiards
Augenblick: (*here*) just a moment **holen**: to get
der Wunsch, ⸚e: wish

das Gruppenbild, –er: group portrait

mache ich.: (*here*) I'll do that.

ein·packen: to wrap

stecken: to put **die Tasche, –n**: pocket

xercise, p. 356

DROGERIE

VERKÄUFERIN:

Guten Tag. Was darf's sein?°

SIE:

Eine kleine Tube° *Colgate*° mit Fluor,° bitte.

VERKÄUFERIN:

Und sonst° noch etwas?

SIE:

Ja bitte, ich brauche auch ein Shampoo° gegen Schuppen.° Können Sie mir etwas empfehlen?

Was darf's sein?: What'll it be? What would you like?

die Tube, –n: tube *Colgate*: brand of toothpaste; pronounced *Col-ga-te* in German **das Fluor**: (stannous) fluoride
sonst: besides that

das Shampoo: shampoo

die Schuppen (*pl.*): dandruff

VERKÄUFERIN:

Ja, da nehmen Sie am besten *Sulfrin.*° Das soll sehr gut sein.

Sulfrin: common dandruff shampoo

SIE:

Und ich hätte gern° auch eine kleine Packung° *Persil.*°

ich hätte gern: I'd like   **die Packung, –en:** (*here*) box
Persil: common laundry detergent

VERKÄUFERIN:

Ist das dann° alles?

dann: then

SIE:

Ja, ich glaube schon.

Exercise, p. 357

VERKÄUFERIN:

Dann zahlen Sie bitte an der Kasse da drüben.

LEBENSMITTELABTEILUNG
(Spezialabteilung° für Fleisch)

die Spezialabteilung, –en: special department

VERKÄUFERIN:

Bitte schön, der Herr?°

der Herr: (*here*) sir

SIE:

Geben Sie mir ein Pfund° Hackfleisch,° bitte.

das Pfund: pound (*metric*)
   das Hackfleisch: ground meat

VERKÄUFERIN:

Sonst noch etwas?

SIE:

Ja. Ein Kalbsschnitzel,° ungefähr° ein halbes Pfund, und vier von den Bratwürsten° da.

das Kalbsschnitzel, –: veal cutlet
ungefähr: about
die Bratwurst, ⸚e: sausage

VERKÄUFERIN:

So, bitte.

Exercise, p. 357

(*Sie packt die Sachen ein und gibt Ihnen eine Papiertüte° mit dem Kassenbon° darauf.*)

die Papiertüte, –n: paper bag   der Kassenbon,
–s: chit, receipt   (**Bon**: pronounced "bong")

TABAKWARENGESCHÄFT

SIE:

Eine Packung *Milde Sorte,*° bitte. Und eine Schachtel° Streichhölzer.

Milde Sorte: brand of cigarettes
die Schachtel, –n: pack
das Streichholz, ⸚er: match

VERKÄUFER:

Noch 'was?°

'was = etwas

SIE:

Ach ja, haben Sie den neuen *Spiegel?*°

Der Spiegel: German news magazine

VERKÄUFER:

Der neue *Spiegel* kommt erst am Montag. Der° im Regal° ist der alte.

Der: (*here*) that one

das Regal, –e: (*here*) rack

SIE:

Ach, den° habe ich schon.

den: (*here*) that one (masc. acc.)

VERKÄUFER:

Exercise, p. 357 Das macht dann drei Mark für die Zigaretten und 20 Pfennig für die Streichhölzer.

SCHREIBWARENGESCHÄFT

SIE:

Guten Morgen.

VERKÄUFERIN:

Guten Morgen. Kann ich Ihnen helfen?

SIE:

Ja, bitte. Ich möchte Briefpapier, eine kleine Packung.

VERKÄUFERIN:

Mit Umschlägen° in derselben° Packung?

der Umschlag, ⸚e: envelope
derselb–: the same

SIE:

Ja, und einen Kugelschreiber° brauche ich auch.

der Kugelschreiber, –: ball point pen

VERKÄUFERIN:

In welcher Preislage,° bitte?

die Preislage, –n: price, price range

SIE:

Ach, etwas Billiges.

VERKÄUFERIN:

Hier haben wir welche° zu einer Mark fünfzig.

welche: some

SIE:

Ich nehme den schwarzen° da.

schwarz: black

VERKÄUFERIN:

Sonst noch etwas, bitte?

SIE:

Nein, danke, das war's.°

Das war's.: That's all.

VERKÄUFERIN:

Schön. Das Briefpapier kostet vier Mark zwanzig und eine Mark fünfzig macht zusammen fünf Mark siebzig.

* * *

(Sie sind in einer Fachabteilung in einem Kaufhaus. Eine junge hilfsbereite° Dame kommt auf Sie zu° und trotz der Übung° haben Sie Angst.)

hilfsbereit: eager, wanting to be helpful
auf einen zu·kommen: to come towards a person
die Übung, –en: exercise

VERKÄUFERIN:

Suchen Sie etwas Bestimmtes?°

etwas **Bestimmtes**: something in particular

SIE:

Nein, danke, ich sehe mich nur um.

FRAGEN

1. Wo findet man eine Lebensmittelabteilung?
   (Man / finden / Lebensmittelabteilung / in / Keller / Kaufhaus [gen.])
2. Was ist der Unterschied zwischen einem Untergeschoß und einem Keller?
   (Wort / Untergeschoß / klingen / besser / als / Wort / Keller)
3. Warum bekommen die Deutschen französische Waren billiger als wir?
   (Deutschland / sein / Mitglied / EWG)
4. Wie ist die Auswahl in einer deutschen Lebensmittelabteilung?
   (Auswahl / werden / größer und internationaler) [present perfect]
5. Warum sind amerikanische Waren teurer als z.B. holländische?   (holländisch: Dutch)
   (USA / sein / nicht / in / EWG)
6. Was gibt es außer Lebensmitteln in einer deutschen Lebensmittelabteilung?
   (Außer / Lebensmittel / es / geben / allerlei / Getränke)
7. Was macht man als erstes in einer deutschen Lebensmittelabteilung?   (als erstes: first)
   (Man / gehen / durch / Drehkreuz // und / nehmen / Einkaufswagen)
8. Warum ist ein deutscher Einkaufswagen viel kleiner als ein amerikanischer?
   (In / Deutschland / man / ein·kaufen / meistens / für / zwei Tage)
9. Was bedeutet Selbstbedienung in einer Lebensmittelabteilung?
   (Man / gehen / durch / Gänge / und / nehmen // was / man / wollen)
10. Was geschieht an der Kasse?   (geschehen [geschieht]: to happen)
    (Man / legen / Einkäufe / auf / Transportband)
    (Kassiererin / addieren / Beträge // und / man / zahlen)

11. Wie geht es jetzt anders zu, als Sie erwarten?
(Kassiererin / bedienen / schon / nächst- / Kunde // und / man / müssen / ein · packen Sachen / selber)

12. Was macht man mit dem Einkaufswagen?
(Man / lassen / Einkaufswagen / in / Lebensmittelabteilung)
(Man / müssen / tragen / Sachen / selber)

13. Wie kommt man von einem Stockwerk zum anderen?
(Man / nehmen / Rolltreppe / zwischen / Stockwerke)

14. Sie wollen etwas Bestimmtes kaufen und Sie wissen nicht, wo es ist. Was machen Sie?
(Sie / an · sehen / Orientierungstafel)

15. Was nehmen Wäschereien an?
(Sie / an · nehmen / Stückwäsche / und / Sachen / für / chemisch / Reinigung)

16. Warum gibt es in Deutschland so viele Bäckereien und Metzgereien?
(Viel / Deutsch- / kaufen / lieber / in / klein / Geschäfte)

17. Wo findet man rezeptpflichtige Medikamente?
(Rezeptpflichtig / Medikamente / man / finden / nur / in / Apotheke)

18. Wo findet man Briefpapier?
(Man / finden / Briefpapier / in / Schreibwarengeschäft)

19. Was findet man außer Tabak in einem Tabakwarengeschäft?
(Dort / man / finden / Zeitungen und Zeitschriften)

20. Wann sind die meisten Geschäfte geöffnet?
(meist- / Geschäfte / auf · machen / 9 // und / zu · machen / 6.30)

21. Wann sind die Geschäfte am Samstag normalerweise geöffnet?
(An / Samstag / Geschäfte / sein / normalerweise / nur / [until] / 2 / geöffnet)

22. Was ist der „lange Samstag"?
(lang / Samstag / sein / erst- / Samstag / in / Monat)

23. Wann machen die Geschäfte dann zu?
(Geschäfte / zu · machen / dann / 6)

24. Welche Geschäfte sind am Sonntag geöffnet?
(Nur / ein / Apotheke / in / jed- / Stadtteil / sein / geöffnet)

25. Was hilft Ihnen aus, wenn Sie Schwellenangst haben?
(Man / sagen // „ich / um · sehen / mich / nur")

BUCHHANDLUNG

BUCHHÄNDLER: Guten Tag, bitte schön?
SIE: (Tag // haben / Taschenbuchausgabe / Bölls *Billiard um halb zehn* / ?)
BUCHHÄNDLER: Ja, Augenblick, ich hole es Ihnen. Haben Sie noch einen Wunsch?
SIE: (Haben / auch / *Gruppenbild mit Dame* / ?)
BUCHHÄNDLER: Nein, das muß ich für Sie bestellen. Aber wir haben es in zwei Tagen. Kommen Sie am Donnerstag nachmittag wieder vorbei.
SIE: (Gut // machen / ich)
(Was / kosten / *Billiard um halb zehn* / ?)
BUCHHÄNDLER: DM 4.80, bitte. Soll ich es Ihnen einpacken?
SIE: (Nein // ich / stecken / es / in / Tasche)
(Hier / DM 10 / bitte)
BUCHHÄNDLER: Und DM 5.20 zurück. Danke schön.
SIE: (Ich / danken / auch // Wiedersehen)

DROGERIE

VERKÄUFERIN: Guten Tag. Was darf's sein?
SIE: (klein / Tube / *Colgate* / Fluor)
VERKÄUFERIN: Und sonst noch etwas?
SIE: (Ja // ich / brauchen / Shampoo / gegen Schuppen)
(Können / Sie / empfehlen / [to me] / etwas / ?)
VERKÄUFERIN: Ja, da nehmen Sie am besten *Sulfrin*. Das soll sehr gut sein.
SIE: (Und / ich / hätten / gern / klein / Packung *Persil*)
VERKÄUFERIN: Ist das dann alles?
SIE: (Ich / glauben / schon)
VERKÄUFERIN: Dann zahlen Sie bitte an der Kasse da drüben.

LEBENSMITTELABTEILUNG (Spezialabteilung für Fleisch)

VERKÄUFERIN: Bitte schön, der Herr?
SIE: (Geben / Sie / [me] / Pfund Hackfleisch)
VERKÄUFERIN: Sonst noch etwas?
SIE: (Ja // Kalbsschnitzel // halb / Pfund // und / 4 / von / Bratwürste)
VERKÄUFERIN: So, bitte.

TABAKWARENGESCHÄFT

SIE: (Packung / *Milde Sorte* // Schachtel / Streichhölzer)
VERKÄUFER: Noch 'was?
SIE: (Haben / neu / *Spiegel* / ?)
VERKÄUFER: Der neue *Spiegel* kommt erst am Montag. Der im Regal ist der alte.
SIE: (haben / schon)
VERKÄUFER: Das macht dann 3 Mark für die Zigaretten und 20 Pfennig für die Streichhölzer.

SCHREIBWARENGESCHÄFT

SIE: (Morgen)
VERKÄUFERIN: Guten Morgen. Kann ich Ihnen helfen?
SIE: (Ja // ich / möchten / Briefpapier // klein / Packung)
VERKÄUFERIN: Mit Umschlägen in derselben Packung?
SIE: (Ja // und / ich / brauchen / Kugelschreiber)
VERKÄUFERIN: In welcher Preislage, bitte?
SIE: (Etwas / Billig-)
VERKÄUFERIN: Hier haben wir welche zu 1 Mark 50.
SIE: (Ich / nehmen / schwarz-)
VERKÄUFERIN: Sonst noch etwas, bitte?
SIE: (Nein // das / sein / es) [*past tense*]
VERKÄUFERIN: Schön. Das Briefpapier kostet DM 4.20 und DM 1.50 macht zusammen DM 5.70.

KAUFHAUS

(*Sie sind in einer Fachabteilung in einem Kaufhaus. Eine junge hilfsbereite Dame kommt auf Sie zu und trotz der Übung haben Sie immer noch Angst.*)

VERKÄUFERIN: Suchen Sie etwas Bestimmtes?
SIE: (Nein // ich / um · sehen / mich / nur)

Lesson 8   Level ONE

A Reflexive Pronouns and Verbs

1 Reflexive pronouns

Look at the following example:

> I cut *myself.*

"I" (the *subject*) and "myself" (the pronoun *object*) obviously refer to the same person, or: *The pronoun object refers back to the subject of the sentence.* Such pronoun objects are called *reflexive.*

Forms

English uses the suffixes "-self" or "-selves" (for example: myself, yourself, himself, ourselves) in forming reflexive pronouns. Instead of using the regular personal pronouns, such as:

> I cut *me.*

English requires:

> I cut *myself.*

But German doesn't use suffixes. It has a set of reflexive pronouns that are *identical to the personal pronouns in all but the 3rd person* (singular and plural), *where the reflexive pronoun is* **sich**

	SINGULAR		PLURAL	
	Accusative	*Dative*	*Accusative*	*Dative*
1ST PERSON	mich	mir	uns	uns
2ND PERSON	dich	dir	euch	euch
3RD PERSON	**sich**	**sich**	**sich**	**sich**

358

► Note   The polite form of the reflexive pronoun is *not* capitalized:

> Wollen **S**ie **s**ich waschen?
> (Do you want to wash? [*Lit.*: wash yourself])

2 Reflexive verbs

A verb is reflexive when its subject and object refer to the same person:

Reflexive	Nonreflexive
I cut *myself.*	I cut the bread.
	I cut it.

As you can see, some verbs can be used either reflexively or nonreflexively. For example, the verb "cut" is called a reflexive verb only when it uses a reflexive pronoun to complete its meaning (for example: I cut *myself*). When the subject and the object do not refer to the same person, the verb is not reflexive and nouns or *personal* pronouns are used (I cut *the bread;* I cut *it*).

3 German usage

Reflexive pronouns must be used when an *object* refers back to the subject of a sentence. This means that a reflexive pronoun can be:

a. A direct object

Reflexive	Nonreflexive
Er hat **sich** geschnitten.	**Er** hat das Brot geschnitten.
(*He* cut *himself.*)	(He cut the bread.)

b. An indirect object

Reflexive	Nonreflexive
Er bestellte **sich** ein Steak.	**Er** bestellte ihr ein Steak.
(He ordered *himself* a steak.)	(He ordered her a steak.)

B Reflexive Verbs with Direct Objects: Accusative Case

1 Verbs that are both reflexive and nonreflexive

Many verbs may be used either reflexively or nonreflexively:

Reflexive	Nonreflexive
Er machte **sich** fertig.	**Er** machte es fertig.
(He got [himself] ready.)	(He got it ready.)

English often omits the reflexive pronoun. Instead of saying

He got himself ready.

one normally says

He got ready.

But in the German equivalent (Er machte **sich** fertig), the reflexive pronoun cannot be omitted. In this, German reflexive verbs behave like the English verb "to cut." The statements

He cut the bread.
and He cut himself.

are *complete* sentences. But the words "He cut" do *not* form a complete sentence. If you mean "He cut *himself*" you must use the reflexive pronoun (himself) to complete the meaning of the sentence.

The following examples contrast common English and German usage:

He's shaving.	Er rasiert sich.	(*Lit.:* He's shaving himself.)
I'm washing.	Ich wasche mich.	(*Lit.:* I'm washing myself.)

▶ Note 2   Look at the following examples:

Reflexive	**Nonreflexive**
Er zog sich an.	Er zog seinen Mantel an.
(He *got dressed; lit.:* He dressed himself.)	(He *put on* his coat.)

As you can see, there may be a difference in meaning and translation, depending on whether a verb is used reflexively or nonreflexively:

	an·ziehen	means	*to put on* (an article of clothing)
but	sich an·ziehen	means	*to dress,* or *get dressed*

Study the following examples:

	Nonreflexive	**Reflexive**
an·ziehen	Er zog seinen Mantel an. (He put on his coat.)	Er zog sich an. (He got dressed.)
aus·ziehen	Er zog seine Jacke aus. (He took off his sports coat.)	Er zog sich aus. (He got undressed.)
entschuldigen	Er hat ihn entschuldigt. (He excused him.)	Er hat sich entschuldigt. (He excused himself.)
erinnern	Er erinnerte mich daran. (He reminded me of it.)	Er erinnerte sich daran. (He remembered it.)
fertig·machen	Er machte es fertig. (He got it ready.)	Er machte sich fertig. (He got ready.)
hin·legen	Er legte das Messer hin. (He put the knife down.)	Er legte sich hin. (He lay down.)

	Nonreflexive	**Reflexive**

rasieren	Er rasiert einen Kunden. (He's shaving a customer.)	Er rasiert sich. (He's shaving.)
schneiden	Er hat das Brot geschnitten. (He cut the bread.)	Er hat sich geschnitten. (He cut himself.)
setzen	Er setzte das Kind aufs Bett. (He put [set] the child on the bed.)	Er setzte sich aufs Bett. (He sat down on the bed.)
waschen	Sie wäscht meine Hemden. (She's washing my shirts.)	Sie wäscht sich. (She's washing.)
interessieren	Politik interessiert ihn. (Politics interests him.)	Er interessiert sich für Politik. (He is interested in politics.)
wundern	Das wunderte ihn. (That surprised him.)	Er wunderte sich. (He was surprised.)

2 Verbs that are only reflexive

The following verbs never occur without a reflexive pronoun:

sich beeilen
(to hurry)

Er muß **sich** beeilen.
(He has to hurry.)

sich entschließen
(to decide)

Hast **du dich** schon entschlossen?
(Have you decided yet?)

sich erkälten
(to catch cold)

Sie hat **sich** erkältet.
(She caught cold.)

sich freuen auf + *acc.*
(to look forward to)

Er freut **sich** auf das Wochenende.
(He's looking forward to the weekend.)

sich gewöhnen an + *acc.*
(to get used to)

Wir können **uns** an den Lärm nicht gewöhnen.
(We can't get used to the noise.)

DRILLS

Reflexive verbs with accusative objects

1 Fill-ins

● Supply the correct reflexive pronouns.

1. Er hat _____ geschnitten.
   Hast du _____ geschnitten?
   Haben Sie _____ geschnitten?

   (**sich schneiden, schneiden, schnitt,
   geschnitten:** to cut oneself)

2. Hast du _____ entschuldigt?
   Nein, ich werde _____ nicht
   entschuldigen.

   (**sich entschuldigen:** to apologize)

3. Er hat _____ schon vorgestellt.
Darf ich _____ vorstellen?

      (**sich vor·stellen:** to introduce oneself)

4. Ihr müßt _____ fertigmachen.
Machen Sie _____ fertig!
Mach _____ fertig! (**du**-form)
Macht _____ fertig! (**ihr**-form)

      (**sich fertig·machen:** to get ready)

5. Wir waschen _____ später.
Wollen Sie _____ waschen?

      (**sich waschen:** to wash [up])

6. Hast du _____ rasiert?
Er muß _____ rasieren.

      (**sich rasieren:** to shave)

7. Setzen Sie _____ auf die Couch!
Setz _____ auf die Couch! (**du**-form)
Er setzte _____ an den Tisch.

      (**sich setzen:** to sit down)

8. Ich will _____ für eine Weile hinlegen.
Er hat _____ für eine Weile hingelegt.

      (**sich hin·legen:** to lie down; **die Weile:** while)

9. Wir müssen _____ beeilen.
Ihr müßt _____ beeilen.
Beeilen Sie _____!

      (**sich beeilen:** to hurry, hurry up)

10. Erinnerst du _____ an den Film?
Erinnern Sie _____ an ihn?

      (**sich erinnern an** + *acc.:* to remember)

11. Wir müssen _____ warm anziehen.
Ich muß _____ anziehen.
Hat sie _____ noch nicht angezogen?

      (**sich an·ziehen:** to dress, get dressed;
      noch nicht: not yet)

12. Er zog _____ aus und ging ins Bett.

      (**sich aus·ziehen:** to undress, get undressed;
      ins Bett: *to* bed)

13. Interessierst du _____ für den Kurs?
Er interessiert _____ nicht für Mädchen.

      (**sich interessieren für:** to be interested in)

14. Du wirst _____ wundern.
Ihr werdet _____ wundern.
Sie werden _____ wundern.

      (**sich wundern:** to be surprised)

15. Ich habe _____ erkältet.
Er wird _____ erkälten.

      (**sich erkälten:** to catch cold)

16. Ich kann _____ nicht entschließen.
Hat er _____ schon entschlossen?

      (**sich entschließen, entschließen, entschloß,**
      entschlossen: to decide)

17. Wir haben _____ an den Lärm gewöhnt.
Er konnte _____ nicht daran gewöhnen.
Ihr werdet _____ daran gewöhnen.

      (**sich gewöhnen an** + *acc.:* to get used to;
      der Lärm: noise)

18. Wir freuen _____ auf die Ferien.
Freust du _____ darauf?

      (**sich freuen auf** + *acc.:* to look forward to;
      darauf: to it)

2   Replacement drills

● Restate the following sentences using the suggested subjects. Remember to make the necessary changes in both the *verb* and the *reflexive pronoun*.

EXAMPLE   Wir müssen uns anziehen. (er)
                Er muß **sich** anziehen.

When the imperative is used, remember that only the **Sie**-form has a subject.

EXAMPLE   Setzen **Sie sich** auf die Couch! (**du**-form, **ihr**-form)

              Setz **dich** auf die Couch!
              Setzt **euch** auf die Couch!

a. 1. Ich will mich für eine Weile hinlegen.
     (er, wir)
  2. Haben Sie sich entschuldigt? (du, er)
  3. Wir waschen uns später. (ich, er)

  4. Er muß sich rasieren. (ich, du)
  5. Du mußt dich beeilen. (wir, ihr)
  6. Erinnern Sie sich an den Film?
     (du, er)

7. Ich muß mich fertigmachen.
(wir, er, ihr)
8. Setzen Sie sich auf die Couch!
(**du**-form, **ihr**-form)
9. Hat er sich schon entschlossen?
(Sie, du)
10. Hast du dich geschnitten? (er, Sie)

b. 1. Du mußt dich warm anziehen.
(ich, wir)
2. Wir haben uns an den Lärm gewöhnt.
(ich, er)
3. Er wird sich erkälten. (du, Sie)
4. Ich zog mich aus und ging ins Bett.
(er)
5. Du wirst dich wundern. (Sie, ihr)
6. Ich konnte mich nicht daran gewöhnen.
(er)
7. Wir freuen uns auf die Ferien. (ich, er)
8. Er hat sich schon vorgestellt. (ich, wir)

9. Interessieren Sie sich für den Kurs?
(du, ihr)
10. Erinnerst du dich an ihn? (Sie)

c. 1. Haben Sie sich rasiert? (du)
2. Ich setzte mich an den Tisch. (er)
3. Er kann sich nicht entschließen. (ich)
4. Wir haben uns für eine Weile
hingelegt. (er)
5. Willst du dich waschen? (Sie)
6. Machen Sie sich fertig!
(**du**-form, **ihr**-form)
7. Hast du dich noch nicht angezogen?
(sie [*she*])
8. Ich habe mich geschnitten. (er)
9. Beeile dich! (**Sie**-form, **ihr**-form)
10. Wir interessieren uns nicht für
Mädchen. (er)

d. 1. Er hat sich erkältet. (ich)
2. Freuen Sie sich darauf? (du)

3 Express in German (cued)

1. He cut himself. (**sich schneiden, schnitt, geschnitten**)
Did you (**Sie**) cut yourself?
2. I'll wash later. (**sich waschen**)
Do you (**Sie**) want to wash?
3. I have to shave. (**sich rasieren**)
Have you (**du**) shaved?
4. We have to hurry. (**sich beeilen**)
Hurry up. (**Sie**-form)
5. I can't decide. (**sich entschließen, entschloß, entschlossen**)
Has he decided yet?
6. He lay down for a while. (**sich hin·legen**)
I want to lie down for a while.
7. Did you (**du**) apologize? (**sich entschuldigen**)
8. He sat down at the table. (**sich setzen**)
Sit down. (**Sie**-form)
Sit down. (**ihr**-form)
Sit down on the couch. (**du**-form)
9. We'll have to dress warmly. (**sich an·ziehen**)
Hasn't she gotten dressed yet?
10. He got undressed and went to bed. (**sich aus·ziehen**)
11. Do you (**Sie**) remember the film? (**sich erinnern an** + *acc.*)
Do you (**du**) remember him?
12. He's already introduced himself. (**sich vor·stellen**)
13. Are you (**du**) interested in the course? (**sich interessieren für**)
He's not interested in girls.
14. I caught cold. (**sich erkälten**)
He'll catch cold.
15. You (**Sie**) have to get ready. (**sich fertig·machen**)
Get ready. (**Sie**-form)
Get ready. (**du**-form)
Get ready. (**ihr**-form)

16. We've gotten used to the noise. **(sich gewöhnen an** + *acc.*)
    He couldn't get used to it.
17. You'll **(du)** be surprised. **(sich wundern)**
    You'll **(Sie)** be surprised.
18. We're looking forward to the vacation. **(sich freuen auf** + *acc.*)
    Are you **(du)** looking forward to it?

4 Express in German

a. 1. I'll wash later.
   2. We have to hurry.
   3. Sit down. **(Sie**-form)
   4. He'll catch cold.
   5. I want to lie down for a while.
   6. You'll **(du)** be surprised.
   7. He cut himself.
   8. We'll have to dress warmly.
   9. He got undressed and went to bed.
   10. Have you **(du)** shaved?

b. 1. I can't decide.
   2. We're looking forward to the vacation.
   3. Did you **(Sie)** cut yourself?
   4. He sat down at the table.
   5. Did you **(du)** apologize?
   6. You **(Sie)** have to get ready.
   7. I have to shave.
   8. Do you **(Sie)** remember the film?
   9. Sit down on the couch. **(du**-form)
   10. I caught cold.

c. 1. Are you **(du)** looking forward to it?
   2. He lay down for a while.
   3. We've gotten used to the noise.
   4. Get ready. **(du**-form)
   5. Hurry up. **(Sie**-form)
   6. Have you **(Sie)** decided yet?
   7. Do you **(Sie)** want to wash?
   8. Are you **(du)** interested in the course?
   9. Sit down. **(ihr**-form)
   10. He couldn't get used to it.

d. 1. He's already introduced himself.
   2. You'll **(Sie)** be surprised.
   3. Hasn't she gotten dressed yet?
   4. Get ready. **(ihr**-form)
   5. Do you **(du)** remember him?

C Verbs with Reflexive Indirect Objects

There are three kinds of reflexive indirect objects.

1 Normal dative usage

Look at the following examples:

Nonreflexive	**Reflexive**
Er bestellte **ihr** ein Steak.	Er bestellte **sich** ein Steak.
(He ordered *her* a steak.)	(He ordered *himself* a steak.)

The only difference between these two sentences is in the choice of the indirect object. In the first sentence, "He ordered a steak *for her*," **ihr** is a normal indirect object. In the second sentence, "He ordered a steak *for himself*," the subject and the indirect object refer to the same person, so that a reflexive pronoun must be used: **sich.** This kind of reflexive object doesn't change the basic meaning of the verb. In fact, the reflexive object can even be omitted without changing the meaning of the verb at all.

Er bestellte ein Steak.   (He ordered a steak.)

2 The reflexive with parts of the body

Compare the following German sentences with their English counterparts:

Ich habe mir den Arm gebrochen.   (I broke *my arm.*)
Er will sich die Haare waschen.   (He wants to wash *his hair.*)

Unlike English, German does not use possessive pronouns (*my arm*) when referring to actions that affect parts of the body. Instead, it uses a definite article (**den** Arm) preceded by a dative reflexive pronoun (**mir** den Arm).

mir den Arm   (*my arm*)
sich die Haare   (*his hair*)

3 Purely reflexive indirect objects

Compare the meanings of the verbs in the following pairs:

an·sehen   Ich sah ihn lange an.
(to look at)   (I looked at him for a long time.)

sich etwas an·sehen   **Ich** will **mir** die Bücher ansehen.
(to take a look at, look over, inspect)   (I want to take a look at the books
                                      [look them over].)

vor·stellen   Stellen Sie mich vor!
(to introduce)   (Introduce me.)

sich etwas vor·stellen   Das kann **ich mir** vorstellen.
(to imagine, picture to oneself)   (I can imagine that.)

In these cases, the addition of a reflexive indirect object has a profound effect on the basic meaning of the verbs.

▶ Note   As a general guideline, remember that a verb can only have *one direct (accusative) object.* If the direct object "slot" is filled with a noun or a personal pronoun, the reflexive pronoun will have to be an indirect object (that is, in the dative case).

	Indirect Object	**Direct Object**	
Ich will	**mir**	**die Bücher**	ansehen.

DRILLS

Verbs with reflexive indirect objects

● Supply the correct dative indirect objects.

    1. Du mußt _____ eine größere Wohnung suchen.
    2. Wir wollen _____ einen neuen Plattenspieler kaufen.
    3. Ich will _____ einen Fernseher kaufen.
    4. Er bestellte _____ ein Glas Wein.   **(ein Glas Wein:** a glass of wine)
    5. Ich bestellte _____ ein Steak.

● Supply the correct indirect objects with the parts of the body.

    1. Ich muß _____ die Zähne putzen.   **(der Zahn, ∹e:** tooth; **putzen:** to brush, clean)
    2. Er will _____ die Haare waschen.   **(das Haar, -e:** hair [normally used in plural in German])
    3. Ich habe _____ den Arm gebrochen.   **(der Arm:** arm; **brechen, bricht, brach, gebrochen:** to break)
    4. Willst du _____ die Hände waschen?   **(die Hand, ∹e:** hand)

● Supply the correct purely reflexive indirect objects.

    1. Ich will _____ die Bücher ansehen.   **(sich etwas ansehen:** to have a look at something)
    2. Das kann ich _____ vorstellen.   **(sich etwas vorstellen:** to imagine something)
    3. Darf ich _____ das Haus ansehen?
    4. Stell _____ das mal vor! **(du**-form)   **(mal,** *here:* just, as in "Just imagine that!")

● Mixed drill: Supply the correct form of the reflexive pronoun.

    1. Willst du _____ die Hände waschen?
    2. Er bestellte _____ ein Glas Wein.
    3. Ich muß _____ die Zähne putzen.
    4. Er will _____ die Bücher ansehen.
    5. Ich will _____ einen Fernseher kaufen.
    6. Er will _____ die Haare waschen.
    7. Das kann ich _____ vorstellen.
    8. Wir wollen _____ einen neuen Plattenspieler kaufen.
    9. Ich habe _____ den Arm gebrochen.
  10. Du mußt _____ eine größere Wohnung suchen.
  11. Darf ich _____ das Haus ansehen?
  12. Ich bestellte _____ ein Steak.   **(das Steak:** steak)
  13. Stell _____ das mal vor!

2   Replacement drills

● Restate the following sentences using the suggested subjects.

    1. Darf ich mir das Haus ansehen? (er, wir)
    2. Ich habe mir den Arm gebrochen. (sie [*she*])
    3. Sie will sich einen Fernseher kaufen. (ich, wir)
    4. Willst du dir die Hände waschen? (Sie)
    5. Er will sich die Haare waschen. (ich)
    6. Das kann ich mir vorstellen. (du, Sie)
    7. Ihr müßt euch eine größere Wohnung suchen. (ich, wir)

8. Ich muß mir die Zähne putzen.   (er, ihr)
9. Wir wollen uns einen neuen Plattenspieler kaufen.   (ich, er)
10. Stell dir das mal vor!   (**Sie**-form)
11. Er bestellte sich ein Glas Wein.   (ich)
12. Ich will mir die Bücher ansehen.   (er, wir)
13. Er bestellte sich ein Steak.   (ich)

3   Synthetic exercises

• Form complete sentences using reflexive pronouns. Use the present tense unless otherwise indicated.

EXAMPLE   Wollen / du / waschen / Hände / ?
           Willst du **dir** die Hände waschen?

1. Er / wollen / waschen / Haare
2. Du / müssen / suchen / größer / Wohnung
3. Ich / wollen / kaufen / Fernseher
4. Ich / müssen / putzen / Zähne
5. Er / wollen / ansehen / Bücher
6. Ich / bestellen / Steak   (*past tense*)
7. Das / können / ich / vorstellen
8. Wollen / du / waschen / Hände / ?
9. Er / bestellen / Glas Wein   (*past tense*)
10. Dürfen / ich / ansehen / Haus / ?
11. Ich / brechen / Arm   (*present perfect*)
12. Wir / wollen / kaufen / neu / Plattenspieler
13. Vorstellen / das mal / !   (**du**-form)

4   Express in German

1. I want to buy myself a TV.
2. He wants to wash his hair.
3. I ordered myself a steak.
4. I have to brush my teeth.
5. May I take a look at the house?
6. He ordered himself a glass of wine.
7. I can imagine that.   (**Das . . . .**)
8. Do you want to wash your hands?
9. We want to buy ourselves a new record player.
10. I broke my arm.
11. Just imagine that!   (use **mal**)
12. I want to take a look at the books.

MIXED DRILLS: DATIVE AND ACCUSATIVE

• Supply the correct reflexive pronouns.

a. 1. Er hat _____ geschnitten.
    2. Wir müssen _____ beeilen.
    3. Ich will _____ die Zähne putzen.
    4. Er setzte _____ an den Tisch.
    5. Freust du _____ darauf?
    6. Setzen Sie _____!
    7. Ich habe _____ erkältet.
    8. Ich bestellte _____ ein Steak.
    9. Hast du _____ entschuldigt?
    10. Er zog _____ aus und ging ins Bett.

b. 1. Ich habe _____ den Arm gebrochen.
    2. Wollen Sie _____ waschen?
    3. Er legte _____ für eine Weile hin.
    4. Mach _____ fertig!

5. Wir wollen _____ einen neuen Plattenspieler kaufen.
6. Erinnerst du _____ an ihn?
7. Ich muß _____ rasieren.
8. Wir müssen _____ warm anziehen.
9. Du wirst _____ wundern.
10. Beeilen Sie _____!

c. 1. Ich will _____ einen Fernseher kaufen.
    2. Haben Sie _____ schon entschlossen?
    3. Macht _____ fertig!
    4. Ich will _____ die Bücher ansehen.
    5. Er wird _____ erkälten.

6. Interessierst du _____ für den Kurs?
7. Er konnte _____ nicht daran gewöhnen.
8. Er bestellte _____ ein Glas Wein.
9. Wir freuen _____ auf die Ferien.
10. Haben Sie _____ geschnitten?

d. 1. Setzt _____ auf die Couch!
2. Darf ich _____ das Haus ansehen?
3. Das kann ich _____ vorstellen.
4. Wir haben _____ an den Lärm gewöhnt.
5. Ich wasche _____ später.
6. Setz _____ auf die Couch!
7. Er will _____ die Haare waschen.
8. Hast du _____ rasiert?
9. Hat sie _____ noch nicht angezogen?
10. Stell _____ das mal vor!

e. 1. Sie werden _____ wundern.
2. Ich will _____ für eine Weile hinlegen.
3. Erinnern Sie _____ an den Film?
4. Er hat _____ schon vorgestellt.
5. Willst du _____ die Hände waschen?
6. Sie müssen _____ fertigmachen.
7. Ich kann _____ nicht entschließen.

● Express in German.

a. 1. I caught cold.
2. We have to hurry.
3. He lay down for a while.
4. I broke my arm.
5. He cut himself.
6. You'll **(du)** be surprised.
7. Hurry up. **(Sie**-form)
8. I ordered myself a steak.
9. You **(Sie)** have to get ready.
10. We'll have to dress warmly.

b. 1. Have you **(du)** shaved?
2. Sit down. **(Sie**-form)
3. He ordered himself a glass of wine.
4. I can't decide.
5. We've gotten used to the noise.
6. He got undressed and went to bed.
7. I have to brush my teeth.
8. Get ready. **(du**-form)
9. He sat down at the table.
10. You'll **(Sie)** be surprised.

c. 1. I'll wash later.
2. Sit down on the couch. **(du**-form)
3. He's already introduced himself.
4. I want to buy myself a TV.
5. Are you **(du)** interested in the course?

6. Did you **(Sie)** cut yourself?
7. Are you **(du)** looking forward to it?
8. Sit down. **(ihr**-form)
9. May I take a look at the house?
10. Do you **(Sie)** remember the film?

d. 1. He'll catch cold.
2. Get ready. **(ihr**-form)
3. Do you **(du)** want to wash your hands?
4. I have to shave.
5. We're looking forward to the vacation.
6. Hasn't she gotten dressed yet?
7. Just imagine that!
8. Do you **(du)** remember him?
9. I want to lie down for a while.
10. Have you **(Sie)** decided already?

e. 1. We want to buy ourselves a new record player.
2. Do you **(Sie)** want to wash?
3. He couldn't get used to it.
4. I can imagine that.
5. Did you **(du)** apologize?
6. I want to take a look at the books.

VOCABULARY

an·sehen (sieht . . . an)
    to look at
sah . . . an, angesehen
sich etwas an·sehen
    to take a look at,
    look over, inspect
an·ziehen to put on
    (clothing)
zog . . . an, angezogen
sich an·ziehen
    to get dressed
der Arm, –e arm
aus·ziehen to take off
    (clothing)
zog . . . aus, ausgezogen
sich aus·ziehen
    to get undressed
sich beeilen to hurry
Bett: ins Bett to bed
brechen (bricht)
    to break
brach, gebrochen
darauf to it
sich entschließen to decide,
    make up one's
    mind
entschloß sich,
sich entschlossen
entschuldigen to excuse

sich entschuldigen
    to excuse oneself,
    apologize
erinnern (an + acc.)
    to remind (of)
sich erinnern (an + acc.)
    to remember
sich erkälten to catch cold
fertig·machen to get
    (something) ready
sich fertig·machen
    to get (oneself)
    ready
sich freuen auf (+ acc.)
    to look forward to
sich gewöhnen an (+ acc.)
    to get used to
das Glas, ⸚er glass
das Haar, –e hair
die Hand, ⸚e hand
hin·legen to put down
sich hin·legen
    to lie down
interessieren to interest
sich interessieren
    (für + acc.) to be
    interested (in)
der Lärm noise
mal just

noch nicht not yet
putzen to brush, clean
rasieren to shave
    (someone)
sich rasieren
    to shave (oneself)
schneiden to cut
schnitt, geschnitten
sich schneiden to cut
    oneself
setzen to put, set
sich setzen to sit down
das Steak, –s Steak
vor·stellen to introduce
sich vor·stellen
    to introduce oneself
sich etwas vor·stellen
    to imagine, picture
    to oneself
waschen (wäscht) to wash
wusch, gewaschen
sich waschen
    to wash (oneself)
die Weile, –n while
der Wein, –e wine
wundern to surprise
sich wundern to
    be surprised
der Zahn, ⸚e tooth

Lesson 8   Level TWO

A Active Voice and Passive Voice

Up to this point, all of the sentences you have seen have been in what is called the *active* voice. Look at the following examples of sentences in the active:

ACTIVE (subject acting)

Subject	Verb	Other
I	am buying	a tie.
Ich	**kaufe**	**eine Krawatte.**
He	is going	downtown.
Er	**geht**	**in die Stadt.**

The subjects of these sentences are *doing* something: They are performing an *action.* In short, they are *active,* and the verbs are in the *active* voice.

Now look at the following sentences in the *passive* voice:

PASSIVE (subject not acting)

Subject	Verb	Other
The program	is being changed	this year.
He	was run over	by a truck.

In *passive* sentences, the subjects do *not* perform an action; on the contrary, something is *being done to* the subjects. In short, they are *passive,* and the verbs are in the *passive* voice.

In English, the passive consists of a form of "to be" plus a *past participle:*

to be	+ Past Participle
is being	changed
was	run over

B The German Passive

1 Formation

German passive sentences are formed in essentially the same way as English ones. But where English uses a form of "to be" with the past participle, German uses a form of werden with the past participle:

werden	+ Past Participle
wird (is being)	**geändert** (changed)

370

2 Position of past participle

In German the past participle appears at the end of the sentence:

| **werden** | **Past Participle** |

Das Programm **wird** dieses Jahr **geändert**.
(The program *is being changed* this year.)

DRILLS

1 Present tense

• Supply the correct form of **werden**.

1. Ich _____ von einem Freund nach Hause gebracht.
2. Der Fernseher _____ heute geliefert.
3. Das Paket _____ heute abgeschickt.
4. Sie (*they*) _____ nicht eingeladen.
5. Alles _____ gut vorbereitet.
6. Dieses Zimmer _____ nicht viel benutzt.
7. Ich _____ später abgeholt.
8. Die Rechnungen _____ am Anfang des Monats bezahlt.
9. Das _____ geändert.
10. Das _____ von vielen Ärzten empfohlen.
11. Er _____ immer von der Presse kritisiert.
12. Sie (*you*) _____ erwartet, mein Herr.
13. Wir _____ von Freunden abgeholt.

(**liefern**: to deliver)
(**ab·schicken**: to send off)

(**vor·bereiten**: to prepare)
(**benutzen**: to use)

(**ändern**: to change)
(**der Arzt**, ⸚e: doctor)
(**die Presse**: press; **kritisieren**: to criticize)
(**erwarten**: to expect)

2 Synthetic exercises

• Form complete sentences in the passive.

EXAMPLE   Programm / **geändert** / dies- / Jahr
            Das Programm **wird** dieses Jahr **geändert**.

1. Paket / **abgeschickt** / heute
2. Ich / **abgeholt** / später
3. Fernseher / **geliefert** / heute
4. Wir / **abgeholt** / von Freunden
5. Er / **kritisiert** / immer / von / Presse
6. Dies- / Zimmer / **benutzt** / nicht viel
7. Sie (*you*) / **erwartet** // mein Herr

8. Alles / **vorbereitet** / gut
9. Ich / **gebracht** / von / Freund / nach Hause
10. Das / **geändert**
11. Sie (*they*) / **eingeladen** / nicht
12. Rechnungen / **bezahlt** / Anfang / Monat
13. Das / **empfohlen** / von / viel- / Ärzte

3 The constant factor: the past participle

• Supply the missing past participle.

1. Die Rechnungen werden am Anfang des Monats _____.

(paid)

2. Dieses Zimmer wird nicht viel _____ .
   (used)

3. Wir werden von Freunden _____ .
   (picked up)

4. Er wird immer von der Presse _____ .
   (criticized)

5. Ich werde von einem Freund
   nach Hause _____ .
   (taken; *lit.:* brought)

6. Das wird von vielen Ärzten _____ .
   (recommended)

7. Sie werden nicht _____ .
   (invited)

8. Das Paket wird heute _____ .
   (sent off)

9. Sie werden _____ , mein Herr.
   (expected)

10. Der Fernseher wird heute _____ .
    (delivered)

11. Ich werde später _____ .
    (picked up)

12. Alles wird gut _____ .
    (prepared)

13. Das wird _____ .
    (changed)

4   Express in German

1. I'm being picked up later.
2. That's being changed.
3. The TV's being delivered today.
4. Everything is being well prepared.
5. We're being picked up by friends.
6. This room isn't used much.
7. He's always criticized by the press.
8. You're expected, Sir.

9. The package is being sent off today.
10. I'm being taken home by a friend.
    (use **bringen**)
11. That's recommended by a lot of doctors.
12. the bills are paid at the beginning of
    the month.
13. They aren't being invited.

C Other Tenses of the Passive

Our model sentence for the present tense of the passive was:

Das Programm wird dieses Jahr geändert.

Now we will take this same sentence and put it into the past, future, and perfect tenses.

1 Past tense

PRESENT	Das Programm **wird**	dieses Jahr geändert.
PAST	Das Programm **wurde**	dieses Jahr geändert.

The present tense form of **werden (wird)** has been replaced by the past form: **wurde.**

2 Future tense

PRESENT	Das Programm **wird** dieses Jahr geändert.
FUTURE	Das Programm **wird** dieses Jahr geändert **werden.**

The present tense form of **werden (wird)** has been replaced by the future form: **wird ... werden.**

3 Present perfect

PRESENT	Das Programm **wird** dieses Jahr geändert.
PRESENT PERFECT	Das Programm ist dieses Jahr geändert worden.

The principle is the same: The present tense form of **werden (wird)** is replaced by the present perfect form: **ist ... worden.**

▶ Note   The normal past participle of **werden** is geworden. This participle is used when **werden** has the meaning of "get" or "become" (Er ist dick **geworden.** [He has *gotten* fat.]) But when **werden** is used in passive constructions, its past participle is contracted to worden. The **ge-** prefix is missing. Thus

ist ... geändert worden

4 Past perfect

PRESENT PERFECT	Das Programm **ist** dieses Jahr geändert **worden.**
PAST PERFECT	Das Programm war dieses Jahr geändert worden.

D A Summary of Passive Forms

Look at our model sentence in the tenses we have used:

Present	Das Programm wird	dieses Jahr	geändert.
Past		wurde	geändert.
Future		wird	geändert werden.
Present Perfect		ist	geändert worden.
Past Perfect		war	geändert worden.

Comparison of the English and German passive forms:

is (being) changed	**wird**	... geändert
was (being) changed	**wurde**	... geändert
will be changed	**wird**	... geändert **werden**
has been changed	**ist**	... geändert **worden**
had been changed	**war**	... geändert **worden**

You will notice:

1. Where English uses a form of "to be" and the past participle to form the passive, German uses a form of:

	werden +	Past Participle	
Present	wird	geändert	
Past	wurde	geändert	
Future	wird	geändert	werden
Present Perfect	ist	geändert	worden
Past Perfect	war	geändert	worden

All changes of tense in the passive affect only the form of **werden** (in German) and the form "to be" (in English).

2. **Werden** uses sein as its auxiliary. The passive uses a contracted form of **geworden** in which the **ge-** prefix is missing:

ist geändert **worden**	*has been* changed
war geändert **worden**	*had been* changed

DRILLS

1 Tense formation

• Put the following sentences into the simple past and present perfect tenses.

EXAMPLE   Das Programm wird dieses Jahr geändert.

Das Programm wurde dieses Jahr geändert.
Das Programm ist dieses Jahr geändert worden

1. Alles wird gut vorbereitet.
2. Dieses Zimmer wird nicht viel benutzt.
3. Sie werden nicht eingeladen.
4. Die Bar wird von der Polizei geschlossen.
   (**die Bar**: bar; **die Polizei**: police; schließen, schloß, **geschlossen**: to close)
5. Wird es übersetzt?
6. Er wird immer von der Presse kritisiert.
7. Ich werde später abgeholt.
8. Er wird ans Telefon gerufen.
   (**ans Telefon**: to the telephone)
9. Das Haus wird verkauft.
10. Das Paket wird heute abgeschickt.
11. Das Programm wird dieses Jahr geändert.
12. Sie wird ins Krankenhaus gebracht.
    (**ins Krankenhaus**: to the hospital)
13. Der Fernseher wird heute geliefert.
14. Das Abendessen wird später serviert.
    (**servieren**: to serve)
15. Das wird am Montag erledigt.
    (**erledigen**: to take care of)
16. Ich werde von einem Freund nach Hause gebracht.
17. Er wird nicht erkannt.
18. Das wird von vielen Ärzten empfohlen.
19. Die Rechnungen werden am Anfang des Monats bezahlt.
20. Wir werden von Freunden abgeholt.
21. Sie wird aus dem Zimmer geschickt.
22. Sie werden erwartet.

● Put the following sentences into the past perfect tense.

    EXAMPLE   Das Programm ist schon geändert worden.
                Das Programm **war** schon geändert **worden**.

    1. Alles ist gut vorbereitet worden.
    2. Die Rechnungen sind schon bezahlt worden.
    3. Sie sind schon abgeholt worden.
    4. Das Programm ist schon geändert worden.
    5. Das Paket ist schon abgeschickt worden.

● Put the following present tense sentences into the future tense with **werden**.

    1. Alles wird gut vorbereitet.
    2. Das wird geändert.
    3. Wird es übersetzt?
    4. Wir werden von Freunden abgeholt.
    5. Das wird am Montag erledigt.
    6. Du wirst nicht erkannt.

● Put the following present tense sentences into the tenses indicated in parentheses.

    1. Er wird ans Telefon gerufen. (*past*)
    2. Das Haus wird verkauft. (*present perfect*)
    3. Das wird geändert. (*present perfect*)
    4. Der Fernseher wird heute geliefert. (*past*)
    5. Sie wird ins Krankenhaus gebracht. (*present perfect*)
    6. Ich werde von einem Freund nach Hause gebracht. (*past*)
    7. Er wird nicht erkannt. (*future*)
    8. Ich werde später abgeholt. (*past*)
    9. Alles wird gut vorbereitet. (*past perfect*)
    10. Wird es übersetzt? (*future*)
    11. Wir werden von Freunden abgeholt. (*present perfect*)
    12. Die Rechnungen werden bezahlt. (*past perfect*)
    13. Das Paket wird abgeschickt. (*present perfect*)
    14. Er wird immer von der Presse kritisiert. (*past*)
    15. Das wird später erledigt. (*future*)
    16. Die Bar wird von der Polizei geschlossen. (*present perfect*)

2   The variable factor: the form of **werden**

● Supply the form of **werden** suggested by the English words in parentheses.

  a. 1. (is being)   Das _____ geändert.
       2. (was)   Der Fernseher _____ heute geliefert.
       3. (was)   Ich _____ von einem Freund nach Hause gebracht.
       4. (has been)   Das Haus _____ verkauft _____.
       5. (has been)   Sie _____ ins Krankenhaus gebracht _____.
       6. (is being)   Das Abendessen _____ später serviert.
       7. (will be)   Das _____ später erledigt _____.
       8. (was)   Er _____ ans Telefon gerufen.
       9. (has been)   Das Paket _____ schon abgeschickt _____.
      10. (had been)   Alles _____ gut vorbereitet _____.

b. 1. (am being)   Ich _____ später abgeholt.
   2. (will be)   _____ es übersetzt _____?
   3. (has been)   Der Fernseher _____ noch nicht repariert _____.   (noch nicht: not yet)
   4. (has been)   Es _____ noch nicht gefunden _____.
   5. (will be)   Er _____ nicht erkannt _____.
   6. (was)   Er _____ immer von der Presse kritisiert.
   7. (has been)   Die Bar _____ von der Polizei geschlossen _____.
   8. (are being)   Wir _____ von Freunden abgeholt.
   9. (has been)   Er _____ noch nicht identifiziert _____.
  10. (was)   Sie (she) _____ nie wieder gesehen.   (nie wieder: never again)

c. 1. (are)   Sie _____ erwartet, mein Herr.
   2. (has been)   Dieser Scheck _____ nicht unterschrieben _____.
                      (unterschreiben, unterschrieb, unterschrieben: to sign)
   3. (is)   Dieses Zimmer _____ nicht viel benutzt.
   4. (had been)   Die Rechnungen _____ schon bezahlt _____.
   5. (is)   Das _____ von vielen Ärzten empfohlen.
   6. (has been)   Unser Wagen _____ gestohlen _____.
                      (stehlen, stiehlt, stahl, gestohlen: to steal)

   7. (was)   Er _____ von einem Lastwagen überfahren.
         (der Lastwagen: truck; überfahren, überfährt, überfuhr, überfahren: to run over)

3   Synthetic exercises

• Use the following elements to form passive sentences in the tense indicated.

1. Abendessen / serviert / später   (present)
2. Fernseher / repariert / noch nicht   (present perfect)
3. Bar / geschlossen / von / Polizei   (present perfect)
4. Er / gerufen / an / Telefon   (past)
5. Er / erkannt / nicht   (future)
6. Sie (you) / erwartet // mein Herr   (present)
7. Es / gefunden / noch nicht   (present perfect)
8. Rechnungen / bezahlt / schon   (past perfect)
9. Er / kritisiert / von / Presse   (past)
10. Alles / vorbereitet / gut   (past perfect)
11. Fernseher / geliefert / heute   (present)
12. Sie (she) / gesehen / nie wieder   (past)
13. Dies- / Scheck / unterschrieben / noch nicht   (present perfect)
14. Unser Wagen / gestohlen   (present perfect)
15. Er / überfahren / von / Lastwagen   (past)
16. Er / identifiziert / noch nicht   (present perfect)

4   Express in German

a. 1. That's being changed.
   2. He was called to the telephone.
   3. The house has been sold.
   4. This room isn't used much.
   5. The TV hasn't been repaired yet.

   6. The bills had already been paid.
   7. I was taken home by a friend.
   8. He won't be recognized.
   9. She was never seen again.
  10. Dinner is being served later.

b.
1. Is it going to be translated?
2. The bar's been closed by the police.
3. The TV was delivered today.
4. The package has already been sent off.
5. We're being picked up by friends.
6. This check hasn't been signed.
7. You're expected, sir.
8. It hasn't been found yet.
9. I'm being picked up later.
10. Our car's been stolen.

c.
1. He was always criticized by the press.
2. That'll be taken care of later.
3. That's recommended by a lot of doctors.
4. Everything had been well prepared.
5. She has been taken to the hospital.
6. He was run over by a truck.
7. He hasn't been identified yet.

VOCABULARY

ab·schicken to send off
ändern to change
der **Arzt, ⁼e** doctor
die **Bar, –s** bar
benutzen to use
erledigen to take care of (something)
erwarten to expect
das **Krankenhaus, ⁼er** hospital
ins Krankenhaus to the hospital

kritisieren to criticize
der **Lastwagen, –** truck
liefern to deliver
nie wieder never again
die **Polizei** (sing.) police
die **Presse** press
das **Programm, –e** program
schließen to close
schloß, geschlossen
servieren to serve
stehlen (stiehlt) to steal

stahl, gestohlen
das **Telefon, –e** telephone
ans Telefon to the telephone
überfahren, (überfährt) to run over
überfuhr, überfahren
unterschreiben to sign
unterschrieb, unterschrieben
vor·bereiten to prepare

Lesson 8 Level THREE

A The False or Apparent Passive

1 Passive (action performed on subject)

Look at the following examples of true passive sentences:

> Das Haus **wird** verkauft.   (The house *is being* sold.)
> Der Fernseher **wird** repariert.   (The TV *is being* repaired.)

Something is happening to the subjects: The TV *is being* repaired. In other words, the passive voice focuses attention on an *action*.

2 False passive (condition)

Now look at the following examples of "false passive":

> Das Haus **ist** verkauft.   (The house *is* sold.)
> Der Fernseher **ist** repariert.   (The TV *is* repaired.)

Nothing is happening to the subjects (the TV *is* repaired and you can turn it on and watch it). In other words, the "false passive" focuses on the *result* of an action, that is, on a *condition*.

To recapitulate:

1. **Der Fernseher** wird **repariert** means that the TV is in the process of being repaired.

2. **Der Fernseher** ist **repariert** means that it is already repaired (a *state* or *condition* rather than an action).

The difference in meaning is clear. If a man says, "Der Fernseher **wird** repariert," he means that it's in the shop and that you can't watch it. If he says, "Der Fernseher **ist** repariert," he means that it's fixed and that you can watch it.

Grammatically, the false passive is the same as **sein** + *an adjective*. The past participle functions exactly like an adjective:

> Der Fernseher **ist** teuer.   (The TV is *expensive*.)
> Der Fernseher **ist** repariert.   (The TV is *repaired*.)

378

This makes forming the past tense quite simple:

Der Fernseher **war** teuer.   (The TV was expensive.)
Der Fernseher **war** repariert.   (The TV was repaired.)

▶ Note The distinction between passive (action) and false passive (condition) also holds for past situations:

ACTION Der Laden **wurde** um sechs Uhr geschlossen.
(The store was closed at six o'clock.)

CONDITION Der Laden **war** den ganzen Tag geschlossen.
(The store was closed all day.)

DRILLS

1 Synthetic exercises

● Form "false passive" sentences in the tenses indicated.

EXAMPLE Alles / sein / gut vorbereitet (*present and past*)

Alles **ist** gut **vorbereitet**.
Alles **war** gut **vorbereitet**.

1. Dies- / Haus / sein / schon verkauft (*present*)
2. Zimmer / sein / schon reserviert (*present and past*)
3. Bar / sein / geschlossen (*present and past*)   (**geschlossen**: closed)
4. Scheck / sein / nicht unterschrieben (*present and past*)
5. Bücher / sein / schon bestellt (*present*)
6. Das / sein / schon erledigt (*present*)
7. Alles / sein / verloren (*present and past*)   (**verloren**: lost)
8. Rechnung / sein / schon bezahlt (*present*)
9. Laden / sein / ganz- / Tag / geschlossen (*present and past*)
10. Halt! // Sie / sein / verhaftet (*present*)   (**Halt!**: halt stop; **verhaftet**: arrested, [under arrest])
11. Alles / sein / gut vorbereitet (*present and past*)
12. Er / sein / geschieden (*present*)   (**geschieden**: divorced)
13. Fernseher / sein / repariert (*present*)

2 Express in German

1. The room is already reserved.
2. This house is already sold.
3. The bar is closed.
4. The store was closed all day.
5. That's already taken care of.
6. The books are already ordered.
7. Everything was well prepared.
8. He is divorced.
9. The check wasn't signed. (had no signature)
10. The TV is repaired.
11. The bills are already paid.
12. Stop! You're under arrest.
13. All is lost.

3 Mixed drills

● This exercise contains both passive and false passive sentences.

1. The house is being sold.
   The house is already sold.
2. Everything is well prepared.
   Everything is being well prepared.
3. The check wasn't signed.
   (had no signature)
   The check was signed yesterday.
4. That's being taken care of today.
   That's already taken care of.

5. The bill is already paid.
   The bill is being paid.
6. The store was closed all day.
   The store was closed at six o'clock.
7. The TV is being repaired.
   The TV is repaired.

B Passive with Indefinite Subjects: Passive Idioms

Most German passive sentences have definite (clearly identifiable) subjects.

Subject

Das Haus wird verkauft.
Das Programm wird dieses Jahr geändert.

But German passive sentences may have an *indefinite subject,* or even no apparent subject at all. This results in German sentences that have no grammatical equivalents in English. Look at the following example:

Es wird heute abend getanzt.
(There's a dance this evening. *Lit.: It* is being danced this evening.)

1 Indefinite subject: **es** (it)

The indefinite subject is always es (it) and it is quite literally indefinite; it does not refer to anything concrete. In fact, it does not refer to anything at all.

In the example above, the subject **es** is not referring to a specific dance (waltz, fox-trot, polka) that is being performed. In other words, it has no real meaning. There is only one reason why it couldn't be omitted from the sentence entirely:

☐ wird heute abend getanzt.

If the indefinite subject **es** were left out, the sentence would begin with a verb, making it a question rather than a statement. The only function of the subject **es** is to insure that the verb is in the second position in the sentence (the position the verb must be in if one is making a statement).

2 Sentences without subjects (absentee subjects)

As you have seen, the only reason for using the indefinite subject **es** is to insure proper word order. If another element of the passive sentence (such as a time expression, like **heute abend**) can sensibly be put in the first position of the sentence, the word **es** may be omitted. Its only function has been taken over by the element that is now in the first position.

(1)   (2)

Heute abend **wird** getanzt.

(There is a dance this evening.

Lit.: This evening is being danced.)

The result is a *sentence without an apparent subject.*

▶ Note   But even when it is not expressed, the *subject* of such sentences is an implied **es;** for this reason, the verb *always* remains in the *3rd person singular:* **wird** (or **wurde**).

DRILLS

1   Familiarization drill

● Supply the correct form of **werden** and take careful note of the English equivalents. Use the present tense unless otherwise indicated.

1. Heute abend _____ getanzt.
   (There is a dance this evening. *Lit.:* This evening is being danced.)

2. Sonntags _____ nicht gearbeitet.
   (There is no work on Sunday. *Lit.:* On Sunday is not being worked.)

3. Es _____ laut gelacht. (*past*)
   (There was loud laughter. *Lit.:* It was loudly laughed.)

4. Hier _____ nicht geraucht.
   (There is no smoking here. *Lit.:* Here is not being smoked.)

5. Samstags _____ nicht geliefert.
   (There are no deliveries on Saturday. *Lit.:* On Saturday is not being delivered.)

6. Vor Frankfurt _____ nicht gehalten. (*past*)
   (There were no stops before Frankfurt. *Lit.:* Before Frankfurt was not being stopped.)

7. Für Gepäck _____ nicht gehaftet.
   (Not responsible for luggage. *Lit.:* For luggage is not being guaranteed.)

2 Synthetic exercises

• Form passive sentences in the present tense, unless otherwise indicated.

EXAMPLE   Hier / geraucht / nicht
           Hier **wird** nicht **geraucht.**

1. Sonntags / gearbeitet / nicht
2. Hier / geraucht / nicht
3. Heute abend / getanzt
4. Vor Frankfurt / gehalten / nicht (*past*)

5. Für Gepäck / gehaftet / nicht
6. Es / gelacht / laut (*past*)
7. Samstags / geliefert / nicht

3 Fill-ins

• Supply the suggested past participles.

1. Sonntags wird nicht _____ .
                        (worked)
2. Heute abend wird _____ .
                     (danced)
3. Samstags wird nicht _____ .
                        (delivered)
4. Vor Frankfurt wurde nicht _____ .
                             (stopped)

5. Hier wird nicht _____ .
                   (smoked)
6. Es wurde laut _____ .
                 (laughed)
7. Für Gepäck wird nicht _____ .
                         (guaranteed)

4 Express in German

• Begin the German sentences with the words in parentheses.

1. There's a dance tonight. **(Heute abend . . .)**
2. There were no stops before Frankfurt. **(Vor Frankfurt . . .)**
3. There's no work on Sunday. **(Sonntags . . .)**
4. There's no smoking here. **(Hier . . .)**
5. There was loud laughter **(Es . . .)**
6. Not responsible for luggage. **(Für Gepäck . . .)**
7. There are no deliveries on Saturday. **(Samstags . . .)**

VOCABULARY

gehaftet guaranteed
geschieden (*adj.*) divorced
geschlossen (*adj.*) closed

Halt! Stop!
halten (hält) to stop
  hielt, gehalten

liefern to deliver
verhaftet (*adj.*) arrested
verloren (*adj.*) lost

Reading **VIII**

Besuch in Mainz

Wann soll man in einer Stadt ankommen? Diese Frage wird allzu° selten° gestellt.° Man kann es sich schwer machen° und spät am Abend ankommen. Dann ist die Zimmervermittlung zu° und es gibt vielleicht° keine freien Zimmer mehr. Machen Sie es sich lieber einfach° und kommen Sie morgens oder am frühen Nachmittag an, und am besten nicht an einem Sonntag.

allzu: all too **selten:** seldom **eine Frage stellen:** to ask a question
es sich (*dat.*) **schwer machen:** to make life difficult for oneself
zu·sein: to be closed

vielleicht: perhaps

es sich (*dat.*) **einfach machen:** to make things easy for oneself

Als erstes° sollen Sie Ihr Gepäck loswerden.° In den meisten Bahnhöfen gibt es Schließfächer.° Für ein paar° Mark können Sie Ihre Sachen° für den ganzen Tag da lassen. Jetzt fühlen Sie sich° schon besser. Sie brauchen° Ihre schweren Koffer nicht durch die ganze Stadt zu schleppen.° Dann gehen Sie zu dem Kiosk° im Bahnhof und kaufen sich einen Stadtplan° und vielleicht auch eine Zeitung. Nun gehen Sie ins Bahnhofsrestaurant und suchen sich einen freien Tisch aus.° Sie brauchen kein großes Essen zu bestellen. Bestellen Sie sich bloß° eine Tasse° Kaffee° oder ein Bier und Sie können so lange da sitzen, wie sie wollen. Jetzt können Sie auch den Stadtplan in aller Ruhe ansehen und sich über die Stadt orientieren.°

als erstes: first, the first thing you should do
los·werden: to get rid of
das Schließfach, ⸚er: locker
ein paar: a couple of, a few
die Sache, −n: thing
sich fühlen: to feel

brauchen: to need

schleppen: to drag

der Kiosk: newsstand

der Stadtplan: map of the city

sich etwas aus·suchen: to look for something

bloß: just **die Tasse:** cup

der Kaffee: coffee

sich orientieren über: to acquaint oneself with, to get to know

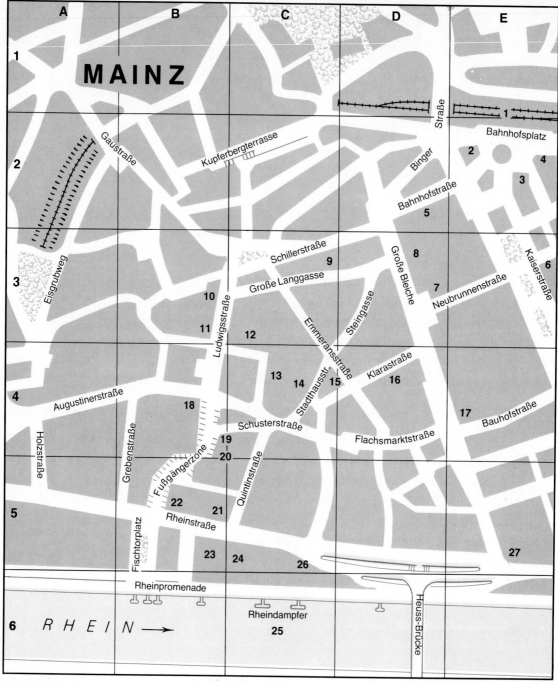

MAINZ

A B C D E

Gaustraße
Kupferbergterrasse
Straße
Bahnhofsplatz
Binger
Bahnhofstraße
Eisgrubweg
Schillerstraße
Große Langgasse
Neubrunnenstraße
Kaiserstraße
Ludwigstraße
Große Bleiche
Steingasse
Emmeransstraße
Augustinerstraße
Klarastraße
Stadthausstr.
Schusterstraße
Flachsmarktstraße
Bauhofstraße
Holzstraße
Grebenstraße
Fußgängerzone
Quintinstraße
Fischtorplatz
Rheinstraße
Rheinpromenade
Rheindampfer
Heuss-Brücke

R H E I N →

1. Hauptbahnhof
2. Zimmervermittlung
3. Hotel Hammer
4. Eden Hotel
5. Hauptpost
6. Europahotel
7. Regina-Kino
8. Dresdner Bank
9. Residenz-Kino
10. Deutsche Bank
11. Kaufhaus Hertie
12. Haus des Deutschen Weines
13. Stadttheater
14. Brauhaus zur Sonne
15. Kaufhaus Kaufhof
16. Polizeipräsidium
17. Landesmuseum
18. Dom
19. Marktschänke
20. Gutenberg-Museum
21. Lipizzaner Restaurant
22. Gaststätte Goldne Schipp
23. Rathaus
24. Rheingoldhalle
25. Rheindampfer
26. Hilton Hotel
27. Kurfürstliches Schloß

Fragen Sie entweder° den Kellner oder die Frau im Kiosk nach der Zimmervermittlung (2),* und Sie erfahren,° daß sie gleich gegenüber vom° Bahnhof ist. In der Zimmervermittlung bekommen Sie dann einen kleinen Plan° vom Stadtzentrum,° wie der auf Seite 384. Und, wie Sie wissen, hier können Sie auch ein Hotelzimmer reservieren:

Fragen I, 1–8, pp. 393–94

entweder . . . oder: either . . . or

erfahren: to find out gleich gegenüber von: right across from

der Plan: (here) Stadtplan
  das Stadtzentrum: center of town

IN DER ZIMMERVERMITTLUNG

DIE DAME HINTER DER THEKE:

Guten Tag, bitte sehr?

SIE:

Guten Tag. Ich brauche ein Einzelzimmer für zwei Nächte.

DAME:

Und in welcher Preislage, bitte?

SIE:

Mittlere° Preislage,° nicht zu teuer.

DAME:

mittel: (here) medium
  die Preislage: price range

Da haben wir das Hotel Hammer (3) hier am Bahnhofsplatz,° 35 Mark mit Frühstück. Das liegt sehr zentral,° und es ist zwei Minuten zu Fuß von hier.

SIE:

Und das Hotel da, auf der anderen Seite vom Bahnhofsplatz?

DAME:

Das ist das Eden Hotel, das ist schon etwas teurer.

SIE:

Schön. Dann nehme ich das Hotel Hammer.

DAME:

Augenblick, ich rufe an. Auf welchen Namen, bitte?

SIE:

[Give your last name and spell it.]

(Pause. Die Dame telefoniert und wendet sich wieder zu° Ihnen.)

der Platz: square

liegt . . . zentral: is centrally located

sich wenden zu: to turn to

---

*All numbers in parentheses refer to the map on p. 384.

DAME:

Ja, das Hotel Hammer hält ein Zimmer für Sie frei. Das macht dann zwei Mark, bitte. Hier ist Ihre Quittung.

Exercise, p. 394

SIE:

Danke schön.

Wenn Sie vormittags° ankommen, ist es möglich, daß Ihr Zimmer erst später° frei wird, etwa° um ein Uhr. Dann haben Sie Zeit und können sich die Stadt ein wenig ansehen. Aber normalerweise° wird das Hotel ein Zimmer für Sie bereit° haben. Sie gehen dann zum Hauptbahnhof zurück und holen° sich Ihr Gepäck aus dem Schließfach.

vormittags: before noon

erst später: not until later **etwa:** let's say, about

normalerweise: normally
bereit: ready
holen: to get (go get)

Wenn Ihr Hotel aber weiter weg liegt, nehmen Sie ein Taxi.° Es lohnt sich,° wenn Sie Gepäck haben. Vor jedem Bahnhof stehen Taxis. Sie steigen ein und sagen dem Taxifahrer z.B.: „Europahotel bitte." Er fährt Sie zum Hotel und sagt Ihnen, was es kostet. Sie geben ihm das Geld und ungefähr° zehn Prozent Trinkgeld. Dann steigen Sie aus und melden sich im Hotel an.°

das Taxi, –s: taxi **sich lohnen:** to be worth while

ungefähr: about

sich an · melden: to check in

Jetzt haben Sie den ganzen Nachmittag frei und können sich die Stadt ansehen. Sie können einfach mit Ihrem Stadtplan losziehen° (Sehenswürdigkeiten° sind auf fast° allen Stadtplänen eingezeichnet°) oder Sie können am Empfang um Auskunft° bitten. Sagen Sie nur: „Verzeihung,° wie komme ich zum Rathaus?"° Dieses Mal sind wir aber Ihre Fremdenführer.°

los · ziehen: to take off (on your own)

die Sehenswürdigkeit, –en: sight, place of interest **fast:** almost
eingezeichnet: indicated
die Auskunft: information
Verzeihung: Pardon me
das Rathaus: city hall

der Fremdenführer,–: tour guide

Fragen II, 1–5, p. 395

Geben Sie Ihren Schlüssel° am Empfang ab.° Jetzt gehen Sie von Ihrem Hotel (3) links° über den Bahnhofsplatz. Sie gehen die Bahnhofstraße hinunter° bis zur° Großen Bleiche, einer der größten, lebhaftesten° Straßen in Mainz. (Wie Sie sehen, nicht

der Schlüssel: key **ab · geben:** to turn in, leave
links: left, to the left

hinunter: down **biz zu:** as far as, up to
lebhaft: busy

Das neue Rathaus

alle Straßen heißen „Straße".) Da gehen Sie links bis zum Landesmuseum° (17) an der Ecke von der Bauhofstraße. Dann gehen Sie die Große Bleiche weiter hinunter° bis zum Kurfürstlichen Schloß° (27). Ein Teil° davon ist jetzt das Römisch–Germanische Zentralmuseum.° Von hier gehen Sie über die Rheinstraße zur Rheinpromenade. Sie gehen nach rechts° den Rhein entlang° und Sie sehen das Hilton Hotel (26), die Rheingoldhalle° (24) und das neue Rathaus (23). Hinter der Rheingoldhalle sind die Rheindampfer° (25). Von hier aus° erreicht° man das schönste Gebiet° am Rhein in nur einer Stunde. Am Fischtorplatz gehen Sie nach rechts und geradeaus° über die Rheinstraße zur Fußgänger-zone.° Da liegt rechts das Gutenberg-Museum° (20) und links der mittelalterliche° Dom° (18). Die Fußgängerzone endet° vor der Ludwigsstraße.

das Landesmuseum: state museum

weiter hinunter: farther down
das Kurfürstliche Schloß: (former) residence of the Prince-Elector of Mainz
der Teil, –e: part

das Römisch–Germanische Zentralmuseum: museum housing Roman and Germanic artifacts
rechts: to the right **entlang·gehen** (+*acc.*): to walk along
die Rheingoldhalle: major convention and concert hall

der Rheindampfer, –: Rhine river steamer
von hier aus: from here **erreichen**: to get to, reach
das Gebiet: area

geradeaus: straight ahead
die Fußgängerzone: pedestrian mall
das Gutenberg-Museum: museum of the history of printing
mittelalterlich: medieval **der Dom**: cathedral
enden: to end, stop

Gegenüber auf der rechten Seite ist das Stadttheater° (13).

das Stadttheater: civic theater

Jetzt ist es fast Abend und Sie haben einen vollen° Tag hinter sich. Glücklicherweise° stehen Sie gleich neben dem Haus des Deutschen Weines (12). Es ist ein Restaurant und eine Weinstube° zugleich.° Hier gibt es ungefähr dreißig offene Weine° und Sie können aus allen deutschen Weingebieten° wählen.° Hier können Sie auch essen, aber Sie müssen nicht. Wenn Sie billiger essen wollen, können Sie zur Marktschänke (19) in der Fußgängerzone zurückgehen, oder Sie können im Brauhaus zur Sonne (14) in der Stadthausstraße essen.

voll: full

glücklicherweise: fortunately

die Weinstube: establishment specializing in wine   **zugleich**: at the same time
offene Weine: wines served by the glass
das Weingebiet, –e: area where wine is grown
   wählen: to choose

Fragen II, 6–10, pp. 395–96

Nach dem Abendessen können Sie ins Kino gehen. Ein paar Straßen weiter,° die Ludwigsstraße hinauf,° ist die Schillerstraße. Da finden Sie das Residenz-Kino (9). Sie sind auch vorher° an dem Regina-Kino (7) in der Neubrunnenstraße (Ecke° Große Bleiche) vorbeigegangen.° Vielleicht° haben Sie sich die Plakate° dort angesehen und etwas Interessantes gefunden. Sie gehen zur Kasse, und Sie sehen, daß es Eintrittskarten° zu° verschiedenen° Preisen° gibt. Die besseren, teureren Plätze sind in der Mitte° und weiter hinten.° Die billigsten Plätze sind ganz vorne.° An der Kasse ist eine Tafel mit den verschiedenen Preisen und mit den Anfangszeiten.° In Deutschland gilt° eine Eintrittskarte nur für eine Vorstellung.° Wenn Sie nach Beginn° des Hauptfilms° hineingehen, werden Sie den Anfang *nie* sehen. Oder Sie müssen zurück zur Kasse und eine zweite Karte kaufen, denn das Kino wird nach jeder Vorstellung geräumt.° Noch ein Unterschied° zwischen deutschen und amerikanischen Kinos ist, daß vor dem Hauptfilm Werbung° gezeigt° wird. Es können entweder Farbdias° mit Kommentar,° oder

weiter: further

hinauf: up

vorher: earlier

Ecke: (*here*) on the corner of
an etwas (*dat.*) **vorbeigehen**: to go by something   **vielleicht**: perhaps, maybe

das Plakat, –e: poster

die Eintrittskarte, –n: ticket (for admission)
zu: (*here*) for   **verschieden**: different
der Preis, –e: price

die Mitte: middle   **hinten**: in the back

vorne: in the front

die Anfangszeit, –en: time the film starts

gelten (gilt) für: to be valid for

die Vorstellung: showing
   der Beginn: beginning
   der Hauptfilm: feature film

räumen: to clear, empty   **der Unterschied, –e**: difference

die Werbung: advertising   **zeigen**: to show

das Farbdia, –s: color slide
   der Kommentar: commentary

richtige, kurze Werbefilme° sein. Nach dem Kino können Sie zurück ins Hotel gehen. Sie bitten den Empfang um Ihren Schlüssel und gehen in Ihr Zimmer hinauf.°

der Werbefilm, —e: filmed commercial

hinauf·gehen: to go upstairs

Am nächsten Tag frühstücken° Sie im Hotel. Wie Sie wissen, es ist schon bezahlt. Gehen Sie dann zum Empfang und stellen Sie ein paar Fragen:°

frühstücken: to have breakfast

Fragen stellen: to ask questions

AM EMPFANG IM HOTEL

SIE:

Guten Morgen. Ich möchte heute einkaufen° gehen. Wo geht man am besten hin?

ein·kaufen gehen: to go shopping

EMPFANG:

Da gehen Sie am besten in die Ludwigsstraße. Wissen Sie, wo das ist?

SIE:

Ja, da war ich gestern, das ist in der Nähe° vom Stadttheater, nicht?

die Nähe: vicinity

EMPFANG:

Ja, dort sind die meisten Geschäfte.

SIE:

Ist auch eine Bank° da? Ich muß ein paar Reiseschecks° wechseln.°

die Bank: bank

der Reisescheck, —s: traveler's check
wechseln: to cash (of traveler's checks)

EMPFANG:

Sicher.° Die Deutsche Bank (10) ist gleich neben Hertie (11).

sicher: certainly, sure

SIE:

Und können Sie ein gutes Restaurant empfehlen?

EMPFANG:

Gern. Neben dem Stadttheater ist das Haus des Deutschen Weines.

SIE:

Das habe ich gestern selber gefunden. Es war wirklich sehr gut.

EMPFANG:

Ach, Sie kennen sich schon ein wenig aus.° Wollen Sie heute abend vielleicht jugoslawisch essen?° In der Rheinstraße ist ein gutes jugoslawisches Restaurant. „Lipizzaner" (21) heißt es. Hier, gegenüber vom Rathaus, in **B–5**.* Ich kreuze es auf Ihrem Stadtplan an.°

SIE:

Und wie komme ich am schnellsten zur Ludwigsstraße? Gestern bin ich zu Fuß° gegangen.

EMPFANG:

Gleich vor der Zimmervermittlung hier am Bahnhofsplatz ist eine Bushaltestelle.° Nehmen Sie entweder die Linie° 7 oder die Linie 19 und steigen Sie in der Ludwigsstraße aus. Die Haltestelle heißt „Höfchen."

SIE:

Danke schön.

Vor dem Bahnhof finden Sie einen Automat für Busfahrkarten. Sie werfen drei Mark ein und bekommen vier Fahrkarten. Jetzt gehen Sie zur Haltestelle. Da ist ein Schild mit einem großen H (für „Haltestelle") darauf.° Wenn Sie in den Bus° einsteigen, werden Sie noch einen Automat sehen. Dieser Automat hat einen Schlitz° und Sie schieben Ihre Fahrkarte hinein,° bis es klingelt.° Dann ziehen Sie Ihre Fahrkarte wieder heraus.° Auf der Karte stehen jetzt Buslinie, Datum° und Uhrzeit.° Jetzt fahren Sie die Bahnhofstraße hinunter, durch die Schillerstraße bis zur Ludwigsstraße. Hier biegt° der Bus um die Ecke und Sie steigen an° der nächsten Haltestelle aus.

Jetzt können Sie zur Deutschen Bank (10) gehen. Reiseschecks werden in der Auslandsabteilung° ge-

*Refers to quadrant on the map, p. 384.

sich aus · kennen: to know one's way around
jugoslawisch essen: to eat in a Yugoslavian restaurant

an · kreuzen: to mark, check

zu Fuß gehen: to walk

die Bushaltestelle: bus stop
die Linie: number of bus

der Automat, –en: machine

darauf: on it **der Bus:** bus

der Schlitz: slot

hinein · schieben: to insert **bis es klingelt:** until a bell rings
heraus · ziehen: to withdraw, pull out
das Datum: date **die Uhrzeit:** time of day

biegen: to turn

an: (*here*) at

die Auslandsabteilung: foreign exchange department

wechselt. An der Kurstafel° sehen Sie den Wechselkurs,° nämlich° wieviel Mark pro Dollar Sie bekommen. Vergessen Sie Ihren Reisepaß° nicht! Sie müssen
ihn vorzeigen,° wenn Sie Reiseschecks wechseln. Sie
unterschreiben die Schecks und geben sie, zusammen
mit Ihrem Reisepaß, der Angestellten° hinter der
Theke. Die Angestellte füllt ein Formular aus und gibt
Ihnen Ihren Paß° zurück. Sie bekommen auch eine
Kopie° von dem Formular. Diese Kopie geben Sie der
Kassiererin nebenan,° und von ihr bekommen Sie
dann Ihr Geld.

Jetzt können Sie einkaufen gehen. Hertie **(11)** ist
gleich nebenan, der Kaufhof **(15)** ist ein paar Straßen
weiter (oben rechts in **C–4**) und dazwischen° sind
viele andere Geschäfte. Und nach dem Einkaufen
können Sie im Brauhaus zur Sonne **(14)** etwas zu
trinken bestellen und ein paar Briefe oder Post-
karten° schreiben. Auf dem Weg zurück zum Hotel
können Sie zur Hauptpost° **(5)** gehen (rechts unten°

Die Fußgängerzone

en III,
-6, pp.
97-98

die Kurstafel: sign showing exchange rates
der Wechselkurs: rate of exchange
  nämlich: namely
der Reisepaß: passport

vor · zeigen: to show, present

die Angestellte [*adj. noun*]: employee (*fem.*)

der Paß: *short for* **Reisepaß**
die Kopie: copy
nebenan: (*here*) at the next window

dazwischen: in between

die Postkarte, –n: postcard
die Hauptpost: main post office
  unten: below, down

Am Rhein

in **D–2**). Sie gehen zu einem Schalter° mit dem Schild „Wertzeichen"° (Briefmarken)° und legen Ihre Briefe oder Karten einfach auf die Theke. Der Mann hinter der Theke gibt Ihnen die richtigen Briefmarken für jeden Brief und jede Karte. Aber vergessen Sie nicht, sie müssen „Luftpost"° darauf schreiben, sonst° sind *Sie* wahrscheinlich° vor Ihren Karten zu Hause.

der Schalter, –: window

das Wertzeichen, –: officialese for "stamp"
die Briefmarke, –n: stamp

die Luftpost: air mail
sonst: otherwise   **wahrscheinlich:** probably

Wenn Sie in Deutschland reisen, werden Sie sicher einige Sachen kaufen. Aber Übergewicht° im Flugzeug° kostet eine Menge Geld.° Auch da kann Ihnen die Post helfen. In vielen Geschäften können Sie Kartons° bekommen. Packen° Sie Ihre Einkäufe° in Kartons und schicken Sie sie mit der Post. Sie gehen einfach zum Schalter mit dem Schild „Paketannahme".° Sie werden sich viel Geld sparen.

das Übergewicht: excess baggage

das Flugzeug: airplane   **eine Menge Geld:** a lot of money

der Karton, –s: carton, box   **packen:** to pack
der Einkauf, ⸚e: purchase

die Paketannahme: counter for mailing packages

Jetzt kennen Sie sich ziemlich° gut aus. Jede Stadt ist etwas anders,° aber in jeder Stadt begegnen° Sie denselben° Problemen. Genießen° Sie ein gutes Abendessen und verbringen° Sie den Abend, wie Sie wollen. Morgen reisen Sie mit dem Zug ab. Aber das können Sie jetzt selber erledigen.

III, -13, 398

ziemlich: rather

etwas anders: somewhat different
  begegnen (+ *dat.*): to run into
denselben: the same (*dat. pl. of* derselbe)
  genießen: to enjoy
verbringen: to spend (of time)

FRAGEN I

1a. Wann soll man in einer Stadt ankommen?
 (Man / sollen / an · kommen / morgens / oder / an / früh / Nachmittag)
 b. Wann soll man nicht in einer Stadt ankommen?
 (Man / sollen / an · kommen / nicht / an / Abend / oder / an / Sonntag)
 c. Warum nicht?
 (Zimmervermittlung / sein / zu // und / es / geben / vielleicht / kein / frei / Zimmer)

2a. Was soll man als erstes tun?
 (Man / sollen / los · werden / sein– / Gepäck)
 b. Wo kann man sein Gepäck lassen?
 (Man / können / lassen / Gepäck / in / ein / Schließfach)

3. Wo geht man dann hin?
 (Man / gehen / zu / Kiosk / und / kaufen / Stadtplan // dann / man / gehen / in / Bahnhofsrestaurant)

4. Braucht man im Bahnhofsrestaurant ein ganzes Essen zu bestellen?
(Nein // man / brauchen / bestellen / bloß / Tasse Kaffee / oder / Bier)

5. Was macht man jetzt am besten?
(Man / an · sehen / Stadtplan // und / orientieren [*refl.*] / über / Stadt)

6. Wen kann man fragen, wo die Zimmervermittlung ist?   (**Wen**: who [*acc.* of **wer**])
(Man / können / fragen / entweder / Kellner / oder / Frau / in / Kiosk)

7. Was erfährt man hier in Mainz?
(Man / erfahren // daß / Zimmervermittlung / sein / gegenüber / von / Bahnhof)

8. Was bekommt man in der Zimmervermittlung?
(Man / bekommen / klein / Plan / von / Stadtzentrum)

IN DER ZIMMERVERMITTLUNG

DIE DAME HINTER
DER THEKE: Guten Tag, bitte sehr?
SIE: (Gut- / Tag // ich / brauchen / Einzelzimmer / zwei / Nächte)
DAME: Und in welcher Preislage, bitte?
SIE: (Mittler- / Preislage)
DAME: Da haben wir das Hotel Hammer **(3)**, hier am Bahnhofsplatz, 35 Mark mit Frühstück. Das liegt sehr zentral und es ist nur zwei Minuten zu Fuß von hier.
SIE: (Und / Hotel / da // auf / ander- / Seite / von / Bahnhofsplatz / ?)
DAME: Das ist das Eden Hotel, das ist schon etwas teurer.
SIE: (Schön // dann / ich / nehmen / Hotel Hammer)
DAME: Augenblick, ich rufe an. Auf welchen Namen, bitte?
SIE: [*Give your last name and spell it.*]
(*Pause. Die Dame telefoniert und wendet sich wieder zu Ihnen.*)
DAME: Ja, das Hotel Hammer hält ein Zimmer für Sie frei. Das macht dann zwei Mark, bitte. Hier ist Ihre Quittung.
SIE: Danke schön.

DIE DAME HINTER
DER THEKE: (Gut- / Tag // bitte / ?)
SIE: Guten Tag. Ich brauche ein Einzelzimmer für zwei Nächte.
DAME: (Und / in / welch- / Preislage // bitte / ?)
SIE: Mittlere Preislage, nicht zu teuer.
DAME: (Da / wir / haben / Hotel Hammer / hier / an / Bahnhofsplatz // 35 Mark / Frühstück)
(Das / liegen / sehr zentral)
SIE: Und das Hotel da, auf der anderen Seite vom Bahnhofsplatz?
DAME: (Das / sein / Eden Hotel // das / sein / teurer)
SIE: Schön. Dann nehme ich das Hotel Hammer.
DAME: (Augenblick // ich / an · rufen / auf / welch- / Name // bitte / ?)
SIE: [*Give your last name and spell it.*]
(*Pause. Die Dame telefoniert und wendet sich wieder zu Ihnen.*)
DAME: (Ja // Hotel Hammer / frei · halten / Zimmer)
(Das / machen / DM 2)
(Hier / sein / Quittung)
SIE: Danke schön.

FUNK-TAXI
Göttingen

☎ 0551 **5 78 88**
☎ 0551 **4 60 66**

FRAGEN II

1a. Was ist möglich, wenn Sie vormittags ankommen?
  (Es / sein / möglich // daß / Zimmer / werden / später / frei)

  b. Was wird normalerweise der Fall sein?   (**der Fall**: case)
  (Normalerweise / Hotel / haben / Zimmer / bereit) [*future*]

2a. Was macht man jetzt?
  (Man / holen / Gepäck / aus / Schließfach)

  b. Was macht man, wenn das Hotel weiter weg liegt?
  (Man / nehmen / Taxi / zu / Hotel)

3. Wo finden Sie ein Taxi?
  (Taxis / stehen / vor / jed– / Bahnhof)

4a. Was sagt der Taxifahrer, wenn er vor dem Hotel hält?
  (Er / sagen // was / es / kosten)

  b. Was macht man dann?
  (Man / geben / [*to him*] / Geld // und / 10% / Trinkgeld)

5. Wo kann man um Auskunft bitten?
  (Man / können / fragen / an / Empfang / in / Hotel)

6. Sie stehen vor dem Hotel Hammer (3). Wie kommt man zum Landesmuseum (17)?
  (Man / gehen / über / Bahnhofsplatz / zu / Bahnhofstraße)
  (Man / gehen / Bahnhofstraße / hinunter / bis zu / Große Bleiche [*fem.*])
  (Da / man / gehen / links / bis zu / Landesmuseum / an / Ecke / von / Bauhofstraße)

7. Wo sind die Rheindampfer (25)?
  (Sie / sein / hinter / Rheingoldhalle)

8. Wie kommt man vom Rathaus (23) zur Fußgängerzone?
  (Man / gehen / zu / Fischtorplatz)
  (An / Fischtorplatz / man / gehen / rechts)
  (Dann / man / gehen / geradeaus / über / Rheinstraße / zu / Fußgängerzone)

9a. Was ist das Haus des Deutschen Weines?
  (Es / sein / Restaurant / und / Weinstube / zugleich)

  b. Wo liegt es?
  (Es / liegen / gleich neben / Stadttheater)

10. Wo kann man billiger essen?
    (Man / können / essen / in / Marktschänke / in / Fußgängerzone)
    (Oder / man / können / essen / in / Brauhaus zur Sonne / in / Stadthausstraße)

11. Sie sind vor dem Stadttheater (13). Wie kommt man zum Residenz-Kino (9)?
    (Man / hinauf · gehen / Ludwigsstraße / bis / zu / Schillerstraße)
    (Da / man / finden / Residenz-Kino)

12. Was findet man an der Kinokasse?
    (An / Kasse / sein / Tafel / mit / verschieden / Preise / und / mit / Anfangszeiten)

13. Warum soll man nicht nach Beginn eines Hauptfilmes hereinkommen?
    (Eintrittskarte / gelten / nur / für / ein- / Vorstellung)

14. Was geschieht nach jeder Vorstellung?   (geschehen [geschieht]: to happen)
    (Kino / geräumt [*passive*] / nach / jed- / Vorstellung)

15. Was ist noch ein Unterschied zwischen deutschen und amerikanischen Kinos?
    (Vor / Hauptfilm / Werbung / gezeigt [*passive*])

AM EMPFANG IM HOTEL

SIE: (Gut- / Morgen // ich / möchten / gehen / ein · kaufen / heute)
          (Wo / man / hin · gehen / am / best- / ?)
EMPFANG: Da gehen Sie am besten in die Ludwigsstraße.
          Wissen Sie, wo das ist?
SIE: (Ja // da / ich / sein / gestern) [*past tense*]
          (Das / sein / in / Nähe / von / Stadttheater // nicht / ?)
EMPFANG: Ja, dort sind die meisten Geschäfte.
SIE: (Sein / auch / ein / Bank / da / ?)
          (Ich / müssen / wechseln / paar / Reiseschecks)
EMPFANG: Sicher. Die Deutsche Bank (10) ist gleich neben Hertie (11).
SIE: (Und / können / Sie / empfehlen / ein / gut / Restaurant / ?)
EMPFANG: Gern. Neben dem Stadttheater ist das Haus des Deutchen Weines.
SIE: (Das / ich / finden / gestern / selber) [*present perfect*]
          (Es / sein / wirklich / sehr gut) [*past*]
EMPFANG: Ach, Sie kennen sich schon ein wenig aus. Wollen Sie heute abend vielleicht
          jugoslawisch essen? In der Rheinstraße ist ein gutes, jugoslawisches Restaurant.
          „Lipizzaner" (21) heißt es. Hier, gegenüber vom Rathaus, in B–5. Ich kreuze es auf
          Ihrem Stadtplan an.
SIE: (Und / wie / ich / kommen / am / schnellst- / zu / Ludwigsstraße ?)
          (Gestern / ich / gehen / zu Fuß) [*present perfect*]
EMPFANG: Gleich vor der Zimmervermittlung ist eine Bushaltestelle. Nehmen Sie entweder die
          Linie 7 oder die Linie 19 und steigen Sie in der Ludwigsstraße aus. Die Haltestelle heißt
          „Höfchen".
SIE: Danke schön.

SIE: Guten Morgen. Ich möchte heute einkaufen gehen. Wo geht man am besten hin?
EMPFANG: (Da / Sie / gehen / am best- / in / Ludwigsstraße)
          (Wissen / Sie // wo / das / sein / ?)
SIE: Ja, da war ich gestern, das ist in der Nähe vom Stadttheater, nicht?
EMPFANG: (Ja // dort / sein / meist- / Geschäfte)
SIE: Ist auch eine Bank da? Ich muß ein paar Reiseschecks wechseln.
EMPFANG: (Sicher // Deutsch / Bank / sein / gleich neben Hertie)
SIE: Und können Sie ein gutes Restaurant empfehlen?
EMPFANG: (Gern // neben / Stadttheater / sein / Haus / Deutsch / Wein [*gen.*])

SIE: Das habe ich gestern selber gefunden. Es war wirklich sehr gut.

EMPFANG: (Ach // Sie / aus·kennen [*refl.*] / schon / ein / wenig)

(Wollen / Sie / essen / heute abend / jugoslawisch / ?)

(In / Rheinstraße / sein / ein / gut / jugoslawisch / Restaurant)

(Es / heißen / „Lipizzaner")

(Hier // gegenüber / von / Rathaus)

SIE: Und wie komme ich am schnellsten zur Ludwigsstraße? Gestern bin ich zu Fuß gegangen.

EMPFANG: (Geich / vor / Zimmervermittlung / sein / Bushaltestelle)

(Nehmen / Sie / entweder / Linie 7 / oder / Linie 19)

(Aus·steigen / Sie / in / Ludwigsstraße)

(Haltestelle / heißen / „Höfchen")

SIE: Danke schön.

FRAGEN III

1. Wie kauft man Busfahrkarten vom Automat?
(Man / ein·werfen / DM 3 // und / bekommen / vier / Fahrkarten)

2. Was macht man mit der Fahrkarte, wenn man in den Bus einsteigt?
(Man / schieben / Karte / in / Automat // bis / es / klingeln)

3. Beschreiben Sie die Busfahrt vom Bahnhofsplatz bis zur Ludwigsstraße.

(**beschreiben**: to describe)
(**die Busfahrt**: bus ride)

(Bus / hinunter·fahren / Bahnhofstraße)
(Dann / Bus / fahren / durch / Schillerstraße // und / biegen / links / um / Ecke / in [*acc.*] / Ludwigsstraße)

4. Wo kann man Reiseschecks wechseln?
(Reiseschecks / gewechselt [*passive*] / in / Auslandsabteilung)

5. Warum muß man seinen Reisepaß mitbringen?
   (Man / müssen / vor·zeigen / Reisepaß // wenn / man/wechseln / Reiseschecks)

6. Von wem bekommt man sein Geld?
   (Man / bekommen / Geld / von / Kassiererin)

7. Wo kann man hier in der Gegend einkaufen?   **(die Gegend**: [*here*] part of towr
   (Es / geben / Hertie und Kaufhof / und / viel- / ander- / Geschäfte)

8. Zu welchem Schalter in der Hauptpost geht man mit seinen Briefen und Postkarten?
   (Man / gehen / zu / Schalter / mit / Schild / „Wertzeichen")

9. Was bekommt man dort?
   (Man / bekommen / richtig / Briefmarken / für / jed- / Brief / und / jed- / Karte)

10. Was muß man auf seine Briefe schreiben, wenn sie schnell ankommen sollen?
    (Man / müssen / schreiben / „Luftpost" / auf / Briefe)

11. Was macht man am besten, wenn man Übergewicht hat?
    (Man / packen / sein- / Einkäufe / in Kartons // und / schicken / sie / mit / Post)

12. Wo bekommt man Kartons?
    (Man / können / bekommen / Kartons / in / viel- / Geschäfte)

13. Wo geht man mit seinen Kartons hin?
    (Man / gehen / zu / Schalter / mit / Schild / „Paketannahme")

ÜBUNGEN

Use the map on p. 384 to give the directions needed in the following exercises:

1. Sie stehen vor dem Hotel Hammer **(3)**. Wie kommen Sie zur Deutschen Bank **(10)**?
2. Heute ist ein Konzert im Kurfürstlichen Schloß **(27)**. Ich bin mit dem Zug gekommen. Wie komme ich zum Schloß?
3. Ich bin mit dem Rheindampfer **(25)** in Mainz angekommen und ich will zum Haus des Deutschen Weines **(12)**. Wie komme ich hin?
4. Wir stehen vor dem Kaufhaus Hertie **(11)** und wollen zum Kaufhof **(15)**. Wie kommt man hin?
5. Sie haben ein paar Karten im Brauhaus zur Sonne **(14)** geschrieben und wollen sie zur Post **(5)** bringen. Wie kommen Sie hin?
6a. Ich habe in der Goldnen Schipp **(22)** gegessen und will zum Regina-Kino **(7)** in der Neubrunnenstraße. Wie komme ich hin?
  b. Nach dem Kino will ich ein Glas Bier trinken. Wo kann ich hingehen und wie komme ich dahin?

Useful expressions in giving directions:

links: left, to the left, on the left
rechts: right, to the right, on the right
geradeaus: straight ahead

hinauf (+*acc.*): up a street
hinunter (+*acc.*): down a street
   (The distinction is clear when a street is on a hill, but one also takes a street as *down* towards a river. Thus, in Mainz if you are taking the Große Bleiche in the direction of the Rhein, you are going „die Große Bleiche hinunter".

entlang (+*acc.*): along (in Mainz, for streets running parallel to the Rhein)
über (+*acc.*): across
bis zu (zur, zum): to, as far as
in die (Ludwigs)straße gehen (NOTE: *acc.*): turn into (Ludwigs)straße
auf der (linken/rechten) Seite (NOTE: *dat.*): on the (left/right) side

Lesson 9   Level ONE

A Conjunctions

Conjunctions join units of language together. Look at the following example:

SIMPLE SENTENCE	He went home.
	He was sick.
COMPOUND SENTENCE	He went home *because* he was sick.

This illustrates the most common use of conjunctions: a conjunction is being used to *join simple sentences together* in order to form a compound sentence. The parts of the newly formed compound sentence are referred to as clauses:

1st Clause	2nd Clause
He went home	because he was sick.

1 Meaning

The choice of a conjunction clearly affects the meaning of the compound sentence. In both English and German, it is necessary to select the right conjunction to define the right relationship between the clauses.

2 Word order

Some German conjunctions affect the word order, some do not. Look at the following examples:

Ich suchte ihn.   Ich **konnte** ihn nicht finden.
Ich suchte ihn, aber ich **konnte** ihn nicht finden.   (aber: but)

Er ging nach Hause.   Er **war** krank.
Er ging nach Hause, weil er krank **war**.   (weil: because)

As you see, the conjunction **aber** has not affected word order in any way, whereas the conjunction **weil** has a profound effect on the word order of the clause it introduces.

B General Rules

1 Coordinating conjunctions

Some German conjunctions *do not* affect word order:

> Ich suchte ihn.   Ich konnte ihn nicht finden.
> Ich suchte ihn, **aber** ich konnte ihn nicht finden.

These are called *coordinating* conjunctions.

▶ **Note**   The verb of the second clause appears to be in the *third position* rather than the second. The word order of the clause is thus behaving as if the *coordinating* conjunctions were not there. Coordinating conjunctions are not counted as clause elements as far as word order is concerned.

2 Subordinating conjunctions

Other German conjunctions *do* affect word order:

> Er ging nach Hause.   Er war krank.
> Er ging nach Hause, **weil** er krank **war.**

These are called *subordinating* conjunctions. When a clause is introduced by a subordinating conjunction, the conjugated verb form (in this case, **war**) is at the end of the clause.

> . . . , **weil** er krank **war.**

The other elements of the clause remain in their original order.

▶ **Note**   Commas are normally found between joined clauses. (See section **D**, p. 401.)

C Coordinating Conjunctions

The coordinating conjunctions **aber, oder,** and **und** *do not* affect word order.

aber: but, however

> Ich suchte ihn, **aber** ich konnte ihn nicht finden.
> (I looked for him *but* I couldn't find him.)

oder: or

> Ich kann ihn abholen, **oder** willst du es machen?
> (I can pick him up *or* do you want to do it?)

▶ **Note**   . . . , **oder willst** du es machen?
A coordinating conjunction does not affect the word order of a question. As far as word order is concerned, **oder** is inert and **willst** is the first element of the clause.

und: and

> Ich gehe zur Apotheke, **und** dann gehe ich nach Hause.
> (I'm going to the drugstore *and* then I'm going home.)

D Omission of Repeated Elements

Look at the following examples:

> **Sie** stand auf, und **sie** ging in die Küche. (*She* got up and *she* went into the kitchen.)
> **Sie** stand auf und ging in die Küche. (*She* got up and went into the kitchen.)

When the conjunction is **und**, elements common to both clauses of a compound sentence are often dropped from the second clause.

▶ **Note 1** Punctuation

If an element is omitted from the second clause, the comma is also omitted from the sentence.

> Sie stand auf und ging in die Küche.

▶ **Note 2** Common elements can only be omitted when both clauses use normal declarative word order (subject, verb, other).

> Er kaufte etwas, und **dann ging er** nach Hause.

The second clause *does not* use normal declarative word order (the subject **er** is in the third position rather than in the first position), so the word **er** cannot be omitted from the second clause.

DRILLS

1 Sentence combination

● Combine the following pairs of sentences using the German conjunctions suggested by the English word in parentheses. Omit repeated elements if possible.

EXAMPLE   Ich suchte es. (*but*) Ich konnte es nicht finden.
             Ich suchte es **aber** konnte es nicht finden.

1. Er wollte. (*but*) Er konnte nicht.
2. Sie machte das Licht aus. (*and*) Sie ging ins Bett.
3. Hände hoch! (*or*) Ich schieße. (**Hände hoch!**: hands up; **schießen, schoß, geschossen**: to shoot)
4. Ich habe ihn gesucht. (*but*) Ich habe ihn nicht finden können.
5. Sie verließ die Stadt. (*and*) Sie wurde nie wieder gesehen.
   (**verlassen, verläßt, verließ, verlassen**: to leave)
6. Soll ich es ihm sagen? (*or*) Wollen Sie es machen?

7. Es ist gut. (*but*) Es kostet zu viel.
8. Ich gehe zur Apotheke. (*and*) Dann gehe ich nach Hause.

(**die Apotheke**: "drugstore," pharmacy)

  9. Er wollte heute abend vorbeikommen. (*but*) Er hatte keine Zeit.
10. Soll ich ein Taxi anrufen? (*or*) Willst du zu Fuß gehen?

(**zu Fuß gehen**: to walk; *lit.:* to go on foot)

2 Synthetic exercises

• Put the second clause in the tense indicated.

EXAMPLE   Ich suchte es, aber / ich / können / finden / es nicht (*past*)
               Ich suchte es, aber ich **konnte** es nicht **finden.**

  1. Es ist gut, aber / es / kosten / zu viel (*present*)
  2. Sie machte das Licht aus und / gehen / ins Bett (*past*)
  3. Hände hoch, oder / ich / schießen / ! (*present*)
  4. Er wollte heute abend vorbeikommen, aber / er / haben / keine Zeit (*past*)
  5. Sie verließ die Stadt und / gesehen (*passive*) / nie wieder (*past*)
  6. Er wollte, aber / er / können / nicht (*past*)
  7. Soll ich es ihm sagen, oder / wollen / Sie / machen / es / ? (*present*)
  8. Ich gehe zur Apotheke, und / dann / gehen / ich / nach Hause (*present*)
  9. Ich habe ihn gesucht, aber / ich / können / finden / ihn nicht (*present perfect*)
10. Soll ich ein Taxi anrufen, oder / wollen / du / gehen / zu Fuß / ? (*present*)

• Use the following elements to make complete compound sentences. The symbol // indicates the beginning of a new clause.

EXAMPLE   Ich / suchen / es // aber / ich / können / finden / es nicht (*past*)
               Ich suchte es, aber ich **konnte** es nicht **finden.**

  1. Sie (*she*) / ausmachen / Licht // und / gehen / in / Bett (*past*)
  2. Es / sein / gut // aber / es / kosten / zu viel (*present*)
  3. Sollen / ich / sagen / es ihm // oder / wollen / Sie / machen / es / ? (*present*)
  4. Er / wollen // aber / er / können / nicht (*past*)
  5. Ich / gehen / zu / Apotheke // und / dann / gehen / ich / nach Hause (*present*)
  6. Hände hoch // oder / ich / schießen / ! (*present*)
  7. Er / wollen / vorbeikommen / heute abend // aber / er / haben / kein- / Zeit (*past*)
  8. Sie (*she*) / verlassen / Stadt // und / gesehen (*passive*) / nie wieder (*past*)
  9. Sollen / ich / anrufen / Taxi // oder / wollen / du / gehen / zu Fuß / ? (*present*)
10. Ich / suchen / ihn // aber / ich / können / finden / ihn nicht (*past and present perfect*)

3 Express in German

  1. He wanted to but he couldn't.
  2. I'm going to the drugstore and then I'm going home.
  3. Shall I call a taxi or do you want to walk?
  4. It's good but it costs too much.
  5. She turned out the light and went to bed.

6. Hands up or I'll shoot!
7. He wanted to come by this evening but he didn't have (any) time.
8. She left (the) town and was never seen again.
9. Shall I tell him or do you want to do it?
10. I looked for him but I couldn't find him.

E Subordinating Conjunctions

Subordinating conjunctions *do* affect word order. Look at the following examples:

1. If a clause is introduced by a subordinating conjunction, the conjugated verb is at *the end of the clause.*

Main Clause   **Subordinate Clause**

Er wohnte in Stuttgart, **als** er jung **war.**
(He lived in Stuttgart *when* he was young.)

2. A sentence may begin with a subordinate clause. If it does, *the main clause begins with a conjugated verb.*

Subordinate Clause   **Main Clause**

Als er jung war,   **wohnte** er in Stuttgart.

▶ **Note** This is in keeping with the *normal word order* of the German declarative sentence, which requires the conjugated *verb* to be the *second element of the sentence.*

   (1)   **(2)**
Letztes Jahr   **wohnte** er in Stuttgart.   (He lived in Stuttgart last year.)
Als er jung war, wohnte er in Stuttgart.   (When he was young, he lived in Stuttgart.)

As you can see, an entire subordinate clause (**Als er jung war**) can be used in place of the time expression **letztes Jahr.** The entire subordinate clause is functioning as a single (although extended) element as far as the word order of the main clause is concerned. A conjugated verb that comes right after a subordinate clause is actually in the second (or verb) position.

1 daß / weil

daß: that

Er sagte, **daß** sie sehr nett **war.**
(He said *that* she was very nice.)

weil: because

Sie ging nach Hause, **weil** sie krank **war.**
(She went home *because* she was sick.)

DRILLS

daß / weil

● Supply the German conjunctions suggested by the English equivalents.

1. Er sagte, _____ sie sehr nett war.

(that)

2. Sie ging nach Hause, _____ sie müde war.

(because)

3. Glaubst du, _____ es zu schwer ist?

(that)

4. Sie sagte es nur, _____ sie böse war.   (nur: only)

(because)

5. Ich merkte nicht, _____ er im Zimmer war.   (merken: to notice)

(that)

6. Wir konnten es nicht machen, _____ wir keine Zeit hatten.

(because)

7. Er sagte, _____ er nach Hause gehen wollte.

(that)

● Combine the following pairs of sentences using the German conjunctions suggested by the English equivalents. Omit items in parentheses from the compound sentences.

EXAMPLE   Sie sagte (es). *(that)* Sie wollte nach Hause gehen.

            Sie sagte, **daß** sie nach Hause gehen **wollte** .

1. Ich merkte (es) nicht. *(that)* Er war im Zimmer.
2. Sie ging nach Hause. *(because)* Sie war müde.
3. Er sagte (es). *(that)* Er wollte nach Hause gehen.
4. Wir konnten es nicht machen. *(because)* Wir hatten keine Zeit.
5. Er sagte (es). *(that)* Sie war sehr nett.
6. Sie sagte es. *(because)* Sie war böse.
7. Glaubst du (es)? *(that)* Es ist zu schwer.

● Synthetic exercises (subordinate clause): Use the following elements to form complete compound sentences.

1. Er sagte, daß / sie *(she)* / sein / sehr nett *(past)*
2. Wir konnten es nicht machen, weil / wir / haben / keine Zeit *(past)*
3. Glaubst du, daß / es / sein / zu schwer / ? *(present)*
4. Sie sagte es nur, weil / sie *(she)* / sein / böse *(past)*
5. Er sagte, daß / er / wollen / gehen / nach Hause *(past)*
6. Sie ging nach Hause, weil / sie / sein / müde *(past)*
7. Ich merkte nicht, daß / er / sein / im Zimmer *(past)*

● Express in German.

1. She went home because she was tired.
2. I didn't notice that he was in the room.
3. He said that he wanted to go home.
4. She only said it because she was mad.
5. Do you think that it's too hard?
6. We couldn't do it because we didn't have (any) time.
7. He said that she was very nice.

404   Lesson 9

2 bevor / nachdem / seitdem / bis

The following conjunctions have to do with *time* (before, after, since, and until). Since these conjunctions tend to juxtapose different *times* (past, present, and future), the two clauses may require different *tenses*.

bevor: before

> Entschließen Sie sich, **bevor** es zu spät **ist.**
> (Decide *before* it's too late.)

nachdem: after

> Ich rufe dich an, **nachdem** ich mit ihm gesprochen **habe.**
> (I'll call you up *after* I've talked with him.)

seitdem: since, ever since

> Haben Sie ihn gesehen, **seitdem** er zurückgekommen **ist?**
> (Have you seen him *since* he returned?)

bis: until

> Ich habe gelesen, **bis** ich eingeschlafen **bin.**
> (I read *until* I went to sleep.)

bevor / nachdem / seitdem / bis

● Supply the German conjunctions suggested by the English equivalents.

a. 1. Machen Sie das Licht aus, _____ Sie weggehen.
    (before)

 2. Ich rufe dich an, _____ ich mit ihm gesprochen habe.
    (after)

 3. Entschließen Sie sich, _____ es zu spät ist.
    (before)

 4. Kommen Sie zurück, _____ Sie es erledigt haben.
    (after)

b. 1. Ich habe gelesen, _____ ich eingeschlafen bin.   (ein·schlafen [s]: to go to sleep)
    (until)

 2. Hast du ihn gesehen, _____ er zurückgekommen ist?
    (since)

 3. Ich warte hier, _____ du zurückkommst.
    (until)

 4. Er hat sich verändert, _____ ich ihn das letzte Mal gesehen habe.
    (since)   (sich verändern: to change [of people])

 5. Sie müssen warten, _____ er zurückkommt.
    (until)

c. 1. Ich warte hier, _____ du zurückkommst.
    (until)

 2. Entschließen Sie sich, _____ es zu spät ist!
    (before)

3. Kommen Sie zurück, _____ Sie es erledigt haben!
        (after)

4. Ich habe gelesen, _____ ich eingeschlafen bin.
        (until)

5. Hast du ihn gesehen, _____ er zurückgekommen ist?
        (since)

6. Machen Sie das Licht aus, _____ Sie weggehen!
        (before)

7. Sie müssen warten, _____ er zurückkommt.
        (until)

8. Er hat sich verändert, _____ ich ihn das letzte Mal gesehen habe.
        (since)

9. Ich rufe dich an, _____ ich mit ihm gesprochen habe.
        (after)

- Combine the following pairs of sentences using the German conjunctions suggested by the English equivalents.

    1. Ich warte hier. (*until*) Du kommst zurück.
    2. Ich rufe dich an. (*after*) Ich habe mit ihm gesprochen.
    3. Machen Sie das Licht aus! (*before*) Sie gehen weg.
    4. Hast du ihn gesehen? (*since*) Er ist zurückgekommen.
    5. Ich habe gelesen. (*until*) Ich bin eingeschlafen.
    6. Entschließen Sie sich! (*before*) Es ist zu spät!
    7. Kommen Sie zurück! (*after*) Sie haben es erledigt.
    8. Er hat sich verändert. (*since*) Ich habe ihn das letzte Mal gesehen.
    9. Sie müssen warten. (*until*) Er kommt zurück.

- Synthetic exercises (subordinate clause): Use the following elements to form complete compound sentences.

    1. Entschließen Sie sich, bevor / es / sein / zu spät / ! (*present*)
    2. Ich warte hier, bis / du / zurückkommen (*present*)
    3. Ich rufe dich an, nachdem / ich / sprechen / mit ihm (*present perfect*)
    4. Hast du ihn gesehen, seitdem / er / zurückkommen / ? (*present perfect*)
    5. Ich habe gelesen, bis / ich / einschlafen (*present perfect*)
    6. Machen Sie das Licht aus, bevor / Sie / weggehen / ! (*present*)
    7. Kommen Sie zurück, nachdem / Sie / erledigen / es / ! (*present perfect*)
    8. Er hat sich verändert, seitdem / ich / sehen / ihn / letzt- / Mal (*present perfect*)
    9. Sie müssen hier warten, bis / er / zurückkommen (*present*)

- Express in German.

    1. Turn out the light before you leave.
    2. You'll have to wait until he comes back.
    3. I'll call you up after I've talked to him.
    4. I read until I went to sleep.
    5. Have you seen him since he came back?
    6. Decide before it's too late.
    7. Come back after you have taken care of it.
    8. He's changed since I saw him the last time.
    9. I'll wait here until you come back.

3 als / wenn / ob

These three conjunctions pose lexical problems. Their meanings and usage should be contrasted with each other and with their English equivalents.

a. Two ways of saying "when"

als: when (past time only)

> Als er jung **war,** wohnte er in Stuttgart.
> (*When* he was young, he lived in Stuttgart.)

wenn: when (present and future)

> Ich rufe dich an, **wenn** er **ankommt.**
> (I'll call you up *when* he arrives.)

The choice between **als** and **wenn** depends entirely on the *tense of the verb.*

b. Two ways of saying "if"

wenn: if

> **Wenn** das Wetter schön **ist,** gehen wir spazieren.
> (*If* the weather is nice, we'll take a walk.)

ob: if, whether

> Ich weiß nicht, **ob** sie zu Hause **ist.**
> (I don't know *if* (*whether*) she is home.)

Here the choice depends on what you want to say (not on the tense of the verb). **Ob** must be used if you can sensibly substitute "whether" for "if."

> I don't know *whether* she's coming (*or not*).

als / wenn / ob

● Combine the following pairs of sentences. (The subordinate clause is the second clause.)

EXAMPLE   Ich sage es dir. **wenn** Ich finde es.
Ich sage es dir, **wenn** ich es **finde.**

1. Ich helfe dir. **wenn** Ich kann.
2. Ich sage es dir. **wenn** Ich finde es.
3. Ist es dir recht? (*Is it all right with you?*) **wenn** Wir kommen später.

Once again, remember that a compound sentence may also begin with a subordinate clause. When this is the case, the *main clause begins with a conjugated verb.* (See page 403.)

Subordinate Clause	Main Clause
Wenn ich es finde,	**sage** ich es dir.

• Put the verb in boldface at the end of its clause.

EXAMPLE   Wenn (ich **finde** es), sage ich es dir.
           Wenn ich es **finde**, sage ich es dir.

1. Wenn (ich **finde** es), gebe ich es dir.
2. Wenn (ich **habe** Zeit), werde ich es machen.
3. Wenn (du **beeilst** dich nicht), wirst du den Zug verpassen.
4. Wenn (das Wetter **ist** schön), gehen wir spazieren.

• Combine the following pairs of sentences. The subordinate clause comes first.

EXAMPLE   **wenn** Ich finde es. Ich gebe es dir.
           Wenn ich es **finde, gebe** ich es dir.

1. **wenn** Ich habe Zeit. Ich werde es machen.
2. **wenn** Das Wetter ist schön. Wir gehen spazieren.   (spazieren·gehen: to take a walk)
3. **wenn** Ich finde es. Ich gebe es dir.
4. **wenn** Du beeilst dich nicht. Du wirst den Zug verpassen.   (verpassen: to miss [a train])

• Combine the following pairs of sentences.

1. **wenn** Ich finde es. Ich gebe es dir.
2. Ich helfe dir. **wenn** Ich kann.
3. **wenn** Das Wetter ist schön. Wir gehen spazieren.
4. Ich sage es dir. **wenn** Ich finde es.
5. **wenn** Du beeilst dich nicht. Du wirst den Zug verpassen.
6. Ist es dir recht? **wenn** Wir kommen später.
7. **wenn** Ich habe Zeit. Ich werde es machen.

• Combine the following pairs of sentences with **wenn** or **ob** (used as "if" in the sense of "whether").

1. Ist es dir recht? **wenn** Wir kommen später.
2. Ich helfe dir. **wenn** Ich kann.
3. Ich weiß nicht. **ob** Sie sind zu Hause.
4. **wenn** Das Wetter ist schön. Wir gehen spazieren.
5. Ich sage es dir. **wenn** Ich finde es.
6. Weißt du (es)? **ob** Sie kommt heute abend.
7. **wenn** Ich habe Zeit. Ich werde es machen.
8. **wenn** Du beeilst dich nicht. Du wirst den Zug verpassen.
9. Frag ihn! **ob** Er will mitkommen.
10. **wenn** Ich finde es. Ich gebe es dir.

• Supply the conjunctions **wenn** or **ob**.

1. Ich sage es dir, _____ ich es finde.
                      (if)

2. _____ ich Zeit habe, werde ich es machen.
   (If)

3. Frag ihn, _____ er mitkommen will!
             (if)

4. Ich helfe dir, _____ ich kann.
                   (if)

5. _____ du dich nicht beeilst, wirst du den Zug verpassen.
   (If)

6. Ich weiß nicht, _____ sie zu Hause ist.
   (if)

7. Ist es dir recht, _____ wir später kommen?
   (if)

8. Weißt du, _____ sie heute abend kommt?
   (if)

9. _____ ich es finde, gebe ich es dir.
   (If)

10. _____ das Wetter schön ist, gehen wir spazieren.
    (If)

• Synthetic exercises: Use the following elements to form compound sentences in the present tense.

1. Ich helfe dir, wenn / ich / können
2. Wenn / ich / haben / Zeit, werde ich es machen
3. Ich weiß nicht, ob / sie (she) / sein / zu Hause
4. Ist es dir recht, wenn / wir / kommen / später / ?
5. Wenn / ich / finden / es, gebe ich es dir
6. Frag ihn, ob / er / wollen / mitkommen / !
7. Wenn / Wetter / sein / schön, gehen wir spazieren
8. Ich sage es dir, wenn / ich / finden / es
9. Weißt du, ob / sie (she) / kommen / heute abend / ?
10. Wenn / du / beeilen / nicht, wirst du den Zug verpassen

• Express in German.

1. I'll help you if I can.
2. If I find it, I'll give it to you.
3. Do you know if she's coming this evening?
4. Is it all right with you if we come later?
5. If I have time, I'll do it.
6. Ask him if he wants to come along.
7. I'll tell you if I find it.
8. If you don't hurry, you'll miss the train.
9. I don't know if she's home.
10. If the weather is nice, we'll take a walk.

• Combine the following pairs of sentences, using **wenn** with the present and future and **als** with the past.

1. Ich rufe ihn an. **wenn** Er kommt an.
2. Wir kauften es. **als** Wir waren in Deutschland.
3. Sie wird es machen. **wenn** Sie kommt zurück.
4. Ich lernte ihn kennen. **als** Ich wohnte in München.
5. Ich sage es ihm. **wenn** Ich sehe ihn.
6. **als** Er kam endlich. Es war zu spät.

(endlich: finally)

● Supply the conjunctions **wenn** or **als**.

   1. Wir kauften es, _____ wir in Deutschland waren.
                (when)

   2. Ich sage es ihm, _____ ich ihn sehe.
               (when)

   3. Ich lernte ihn kennen, _____ ich in München wohnte.
                   (when)

   4. _____ er endlich kam, war es zu spät.
     (When)

   5. Ich rufe ihn an, _____ er ankommt.
             (when)

   6. Sie wird es machen, _____ sie zurückkommt.
              (when)

● Synthetic exercises: Use the following elements to form complete compound sentences.

   1. Ich lernte ihn kennen, als / ich / wohnen / München (*past*)
   2. Ich rufe ihn an, wenn / er / ankommen (*present*)
   3. Wir kauften es, als / wir / sein / Deutschland (*past*)
   4. Sie wird es machen, wenn / sie (*she*) / zurückkommen (*present*)
   5. Ich sage es ihm, wenn / ich / sehen / ihn (*present*)
   6. Als / er / kommen / endlich, war es zu spät (*past*)

● Express in German.

   1. We bought it when we were in Germany.
   2. I'll tell him when I see him.
   3. When he finally came, it was too late.
   4. She'll do it when she comes back.
   5. I met him when I lived in Munich.
   6. I'll call him when he arrives.

F Question Words Functioning as Subordinating Conjunctions

Subordinate clauses can also be introduced by question words **(wo, wie, wann, warum, etc.)**. When this is the case, *the question word behaves exactly like a subordinating conjunction:*

SIMPLE SENTENCES	Können Sie (es) mir sagen? **Wo** kann ich ihn finden?
COMPOUND SENTENCE	Können Sie mir sagen, wo ich ihn finden kann?
SIMPLE SENTENCES	Ich weiß (es) nicht. **Wann** werden wir ihn sehen?
COMPOUND SENTENCE	Ich weiß nicht, wann wir ihn sehen werden.

DRILLS

- Combine the following pairs of sentences. Omit items in parentheses from the compound sentences.

EXAMPLE   Ich weiß (es) nicht.
           Wann kann er kommen?

           Ich weiß nicht, **wann** er kommen **kann.**

1. Ich weiß (es) nicht.
   Wann kommt er zurück?
2. Können Sie (es) mir sagen?
   Wo kann ich ihn finden?
3. Ich weiß (es) nicht.
   Wieviel verdient er?   (**verdienen:** to earn)
4. Wissen Sie (es)?
   Warum sind sie nicht hier?
5. Können Sie (es) mir sagen?
   Wie spät ist es?
   (*What time is it?* Lit.: *How late is it?*)

6. Weißt du (es)?
   Wo wohnt sie jetzt?
7. Können Sie (es) mir sagen?
   Wieviel kostet es?
8. Ich bin nicht sicher.   (**sicher:** sure)
   Wohin ist er gegangen?
   (*Where's he gone [to]?*)
9. Können Sie (es) mir sagen?
   Wie kommt man zum Bahnhof?
10. Ich weiß (es) nicht.
    Wann sehe ich ihn?

- Supply the German conjunctions suggested by the English equivalents.

1. Weißt du, _____ sie jetzt wohnt?
               (where)
2. Ich bin nicht sicher, _____ er zurückkommt.
                          (when)
3. Können Sie mir sagen, _____ es kostet?
                          (how much)
4. Wissen Sie, _____ sie nicht hier sind?
               (why)
5. Können Sie mir sagen, _____ ich ihn finden kann?
                          (where)
6. Ich bin nicht sicher, _____ er gegangen ist.
                          (where . . . to)
7. Können Sie mir sagen, _____ man zum Bahnhof kommt?
                          (how)
8. Ich weiß nicht, _____ ich ihn sehe.
                    (when)
9. Können Sie mir sagen, _____ spät es ist?   (Lit.: *what time it is*)
                          (how)
10. Ich weiß nicht, _____ er verdient.
                     (how much)

- Synthetic exercises (subordinate clause): Use the following elements to form complete compound sentences. Use the present tense unless otherwise indicated.

1. Können Sie mir sagen, wieviel / es / kosten / ?
2. Ich bin nicht sicher, wann / er / zurückkommen
3. Können Sie mir sagen, wie / man / kommen / zu / Bahnhof / ?
4. Weißt du, wo / sie (*she*) / wohnen / jetzt / ?
5. Ich bin nicht sicher, wohin / er / gehen   (*present perfect*)
6. Wissen Sie, warum / sie (*they*) / sein / nicht hier / ?

7. Können Sie mir sagen, wie / spät / es / sein / ?
8. Ich weiß nicht, wann / ich / sehen / ihn
9. Können Sie mir sagen, wo / ich / können / finden / ihn / ?
10. Ich weiß nicht, wieviel / er / verdienen

● Express in German.

1. Do you know where she lives now?
2. I don't know when he's coming back.
3. Can you tell me what time it is?
   (*Lit.:* how late it is)
4. Do you know why they aren't here?
5. Can you tell me where I can find him?

6. I don't know how much he earns.
7. Can you tell me how to get to the
   railroad station?   (*Lit.:* how one gets)
8. I don't know when I'll see him.
9. Can you tell me how much it costs?
10. I'm not sure where he went (to).

G wenn / als / wann

Wenn, als, and **wann** are all translated as "when." As you have seen before, **wenn** is used when referring to *present* or *future* time:

> Ich rufe dich an, **wenn** er **ankommt.**   (. . . *when* he *arrives*)

Als is used when referring to *past* time:

> Wir kauften es, **als** wir in Deutschland **waren.**   (. . . *when* we *were* in Germany)

But as you have seen, the question word **wann** may also function as a subordinating conjunction, and it too must be translated by the word "when." **Wann** must be used when the compound sentence contains an *underlying question*:

QUESTION	**Wann** kommt er zurück?
UNDERLYING QUESTION	Ich weiß nicht, **wann** er zurückkommt.
	Wissen Sie, **wann** er zurückkommt?
	Ich bin nicht sicher, **wann** er zurückkommt.
	Können Sie mir sagen, **wann** er zurückkommt?

The underlying question (When is he coming back?) is present in every case. The introductory clause (I don't know . . . ; Do you know . . . ?) merely puts the underlying question in a broader context. The result may be either *a question:*

> Wissen Sie, wann er zurückkommt?

or *an answer to the underlying question:*

QUESTION	Wann kommt er zurück?	(When's he coming back?)
ANSWER	Ich weiß nicht.	(I don't know.)
COMPOUND ANSWER	Ich weiß nicht, wann er zurückkommt.	

Underlying questions may also be found in other tenses:

QUESTION	Wann ist er zurückgekommen?	(When did he come back?)
ANSWER	Ich weiß nicht.	(I don't know.)
COMPOUND ANSWER	Ich weiß nicht, wann er zurückgekommen ist.	

DRILLS

- Synthetic exercises: Use the following elements to form compound sentences in the tenses indicated.

  1. Ich weiß nicht, wann / er / zurückkommen (*present*)
  2. Wir kauften es, als / wir / sein / in Deutschland (*past*)
  3. Sie wird es machen, wenn / sie (*she*) / zurückkommen (*present*)
  4. Ich weiß nicht, wann / ich / sehen / ihn (*present*)
  5. Als / er / kommen / endlich, war es zu spät (*past*)
  6. Ich rufe ihn an, wenn / er / ankommen (*present*)
  7. Wissen Sie, wann / er / zurückkommen / ? (*present perfect*)
  8. Ich lernte ihn kennen, als / ich / wohnen / in München (*past*)
  9. Ich sage es ihm, wenn / ich / sehen / ihn (*present*)

- Supply the German conjunctions **wenn, als,** or **wann,** as suggested by the English equivalents.

  1. Ich lernte ihn kennen, _____ ich in München wohnte.
     (when)
  2. Sie wird es machen, _____ sie zurückkommt.
     (when)
  3. Ich weiß nicht, _____ ich ihn sehe.
     (when)
  4. _____ er endlich kam, war es zu spät.
     (When)
  5. Wissen Sie, _____ er zurückgekommen ist?
     (when)
  6. Ich sage es ihm, _____ ich ihn sehe.
     (when)
  7. Wir kauften es, _____ wir in Deutschland waren.
     (when)
  8. Ich rufe ihn an, _____ er ankommt.
     (when)
  9. Ich weiß nicht, _____ er zurückkommt.
     (when)

- Express in German.

  1. I'll tell him when I see him.
  2. We bought it when we were in Germany.
  3. I don't know when he's coming back.
  4. I'll call him up when he arrives.
  5. Do you know when he came back?
  6. I met him when I lived in Munich.
  7. She'll do it when she comes back.
  8. I don't know when I'll see him.
  9. When he finally came it was too late.

MIXED DRILLS

1 Fill-ins

- Supply the German conjunctions suggested by the English equivalents.

  a. 1. Wir machten es nicht, _____ wir keine Zeit hatten.
        (because)
     2. Machen Sie das Licht aus, _____ Sie nach Hause gehen!
        (before)

3. Es ist gut, _____ es kostet zu viel.
(but)

4. Wissen Sie, _____ sie jetzt wohnt?
(where)

5. Er sagte, _____ er nach Hause gehen wollte.
(that)

6. Wir kauften es, _____ wir in Deutschland waren.
(when)

7. Ich warte hier, _____ du zurückkommst.
(until)

8. Sie machte das Licht aus _____ ging ins Bett.
(and)

9. Können Sie mir sagen, _____ es kostet?
(how much)

10. _____ ich Zeit habe, werde ich es machen.
(If)

b. 1. Kommen Sie zurück, _____ Sie es erledigt haben!
(after)

2. Weißt du, _____ sie heute abend kommt?
(if)

3. Soll ich ein Taxi anrufen, _____ willst du zu Fuß gehen?
(or)

4. Ich sage es ihm, _____ ich ihn sehe.
(when)

5. Wissen Sie, _____ sie nicht hier sind?
(why)

6. _____ das Wetter schön ist, gehen wir spazieren.
(If)

7. Er sagte, _____ sie sehr nett war.
(that)

8. Ich suchte ihn, _____ ich konnte ihn nicht finden.
(but)

9. Frag ihn, _____ er mitkommen will!
(if)

10. Ich lernte ihn kennen, _____ er in München wohnte.
(when)

c. 1. Können Sie mir sagen, _____ man zum Bahnhof kommt?
(how)

2. Haben Sie ihn gesehen, _____ er zurückgekommen ist?
(since)

3. _____ ich Zeit habe, werde ich es machen.
(If)

4. Sie verließ die Stadt _____ wurde nie wieder gesehen.
(and)

5. Ich weiß nicht, _____ er zurückkommt.
(when)

6. Sie sagte es nur, _____ sie böse war.
(because)

7. Ich helfe dir, _____ ich kann.
(if)

8. Soll ich es ihm sagen, _____ wollen Sie es machen?
     (or)

9. Können Sie mir sagen, _____ ich ihn finden kann?
     (where)

10. Ich habe gelesen, _____ ich eingeschlafen bin.
     (until)

d. 1. Sie wird es machen, _____ sie zurückkommt.
     (when)

2. Ich gehe zur Apotheke, _____ dann gehe ich nach Hause.
     (and)

3. Er hat sich verändert, _____ ich ihn das letzte Mal gesehen habe.
     (since)

4. Können Sie mir sagen, _____ spät es ist?
     (how)

5. Ich merkte nicht, _____ er im Zimmer war.
     (that)

6. Ist es dir recht, _____ wir später kommen?
     (if)

7. Er wollte, _____ er konnte nicht.
     (but)

8. Ich bin nicht sicher, _____ er gegangen ist.
     (where . . . [to])

9. Ich rufe ihn an, _____ er ankommt.
     (when)

10. Sie war groß und blond, _____ sie trug Lederstiefel.
     (and)

(**groß:** tall; **blond:** blonde; **tragen:** to wear; **Lederstiefel:** leather boots)

e. 1. _____ du dich nicht beeilst, wirst du den Zug verpassen.
     (If)

2. Sie ging nach Hause, _____ sie müde war.
     (because)

3. Ich weiß nicht, _____ er verdient.
     (how much)

4. Entschließen Sie sich, _____ es zu spät ist.
     (before)

5. Hände hoch, _____ ich schieße!
     (or)

6. Ich weiß nicht, _____ sie zu Hause ist.
     (if)

7. Sie müssen warten, _____ er zurückkommt.
     (until)

8. _____ er endlich kam, war es zu spät.
     (When)

9. Ich sage es dir, _____ ich es finde.
     (if)

10. Er wollte heute abend vorbeikommen, _____ er hatte keine Zeit.
     (but)

f. 1. Ich rufe dich an, _____ ich mit ihm gesprochen habe.
          (after)

    2. Glaubst du, _____ es zu schwer ist?
          (that)

    3. Ich weiß nicht, _____ ich ihn sehe.
          (when)

2   Sentence combination

● Combine the following sentences using the German conjunctions suggested by the English equivalents; omit items in parentheses. Note that both *coordinating* and *subordinating* conjunctions are involved. Be sure to use the correct word order.

EXAMPLES   Ich suchte ihn. *(but)* Ich konnte ihn nicht finden.
           Ich suchte ihn, **aber** ich konnte ihn nicht finden.

           Ich lernte ihn kennen. *(when)* Ich wohnte in München.
           Ich lernte ihn kennen, **als** ich in München **wohnte**

           Weißt du (es). **Wo** wohnt sie jetzt?
           Weißt du, **wo** sie jetzt **wohn?**

a. 1. Er sagte (es). *(that)* Sie war sehr nett.
    2. Ich warte hier. *(until)* Du kommst zurück.
    3. Wir kauften es. *(when)* Wir waren in Deutschland.
    4. Er wollte. *(but)* Er konnte nicht.
    5. Sie ging nach Hause. *(because)* Sie war müde.
    6. Ich helfe dir. *(if)* Ich kann.
    7. Entschließen Sie sich! *(before)* Es ist zu spät.
    8. Weißt du (es)? **Wo** wohnt sie jetzt?
    9. Sie machte das Licht aus. *(and)* Sie ging ins Bett.
   10. Ich rufe ihn an. *(when)* Er kommt an.

b. 1. Er sagte (es). *(that)* Er wollte nach Hause gehen.
    2. Ich rufe dich an. *(after)* Ich habe mit ihm gesprochen.
    3. Können Sie (es) mir sagen? **Wieviel** kostet es?
    4. Soll ich ein Taxi anrufen? *(or)* Willst du zu Fuß gehen?
    5. Ich weiß (es) nicht. *(if)* Sie ist zu Hause.
    6. Haben Sie ihn gesehen? *(since)* Er ist zurückgekommen.
    7. Ich weiß (es) nicht. **Wann** kommt er zurück?
    8. Wir machten es nicht. *(because)* Wir hatten keine Zeit.
    9. Es ist gut. *(but)* Es kostet zu viel.
   10. Ich bin nicht sicher. **Wohin** ist er gegangen?

c. 1. *(If)* Ich finde es. Ich gebe es dir.
    2. Machen Sie das Licht aus! *(before)* Sie gehen weg.
    3. Ich lernte ihn kennen. *(when)* Ich wohnte in München.
    4. *(If)* Ich habe Zeit. Ich werde es machen.
    5. Sie müssen warten. *(until)* Er kommt zurück.
    6. Können Sie (es) mir sagen? **Wie** kommt man zum Bahnhof?
    7. Sie verließ die Stadt. *(and)* Sie wurde nie wieder gesehen.
    8. Ich merkte (es) nicht. *(that)* Er war im Zimmer.
    9. Ich sage es ihm. *(when)* Ich sehe ihn.
   10. Kommen Sie zurück! *(after)* Sie haben es erledigt.

d. 1. (*If*) Das Wetter ist schön. Wir gehen spazieren.
2. Können Sie (es) mir sagen? **Wo** kann ich ihn finden?
3. Soll ich es ihm sagen? (*or*) Wollen Sie es machen?
4. Ist es dir recht? (*if*) Wir kommen später.
5. (*When*) Er kam endlich. Es war zu spät.
6. Ich weiß (es) nicht. **Wieviel** verdient er?
7. Fragen Sie ihn! (*if*) Er will mitkommen.
8. Ich gehe zur Apotheke. (*and*) Dann gehe ich nach Hause.
9. Sie sagte es nur. (*because*) Sie war böse.
10. Hände hoch! (*or*) Ich schieße.

e. 1. (*If*) Du beeilst dich nicht. Du wirst den Zug verpassen.
2. Können Sie (es) mir sagen? **Wie** spät ist es?
3. Sie wird es machen. (*when*) Sie kommt zurück.
4. Ich suchte ihn. (*but*) Ich konnte ihn nicht finden.
5. Wissen Sie (es)? **Warum** sind sie nicht hier?
6. Glaubst du (es)? (*that*) Es ist zu schwer.
7. Ich sage es dir. (*if*) Ich finde es.
8. Er hat sich verändert. (*since*) Ich habe ihn das letzte Mal gesehen.
9. Ich weiß (es) nicht. **Wann** sehe ich ihn?
10. Er wollte heute abend vorbeikommen. (*but*) Er hatte keine Zeit.

f. 1. Ich habe gelesen. (*until*) Ich bin eingeschlafen.
2. Weißt du (es)? (*if*) Sie kommt heute abend.
3. Sie war groß und blond. (*and*) Sie trug Lederstiefel.

3 Synthetic exercises

● Use the following elements to form complete compound sentences. Put the subordinate clauses in the tenses indicated.

a. 1. Er sagte, daß / er / wollen / gehen / nach Hause (*past*)
2. Machen Sie das Licht aus, bevor / Sie / weggehen / ! (*present*)
3. Ich weiß nicht, wieviel / er / verdienen (*present*)
4. Es ist gut, aber / es / kosten / zu viel (*present*)
5. Ich sage es dir, wenn / ich / finden / es (*present*)
6. Wir kauften es, als / wir / sein / in Deutschland (*past*)
7. Weißt du, wo / sie (*she*) / wohnen / jetzt / ? (*present*)
8. Ich warte hier, bis / du / zurückkommen (*present*)
9. Sie verließ die Stadt und / gesehen (*passive*) / nie wieder (*past*)
10. Ich helfe dir, wenn / ich / können (*present*)

b. 1. Ich rufe dich an, nachdem / ich / sprechen / mit ihm (*present perfect*)
2. Sie ging nach Hause, weil / sie (*she*) / sein / müde (*past*)
3. Ich rufe ihn an, wenn / er / ankommen (*present*)
4. Können Sie mir sagen, wie spät / es / sein / ? (*present*)
5. Er sagte, daß / sie (*she*) / sein / sehr nett (*past*)
6. Haben Sie ihn gesehen, seitdem / er / zurückkommen / ? (*present perfect*)
7. Wenn / ich / haben / Zeit, werde ich es machen (*present*)
8. Ich suchte ihn, aber / ich / können / finden / ihn nicht (*past*)
9. Können Sie mir sagen, wie / man / kommen / zu / Bahnhof / ? (*present*)
10. Wenn / Wetter / sein / schön, gehen wir spazieren (*present*)

c. 1. Ich lernte ihn kennen, als / ich / wohnen / in München (*past*)
   2. Ich bin nicht sicher, wohin / er / gehen (*present perfect*)
   3. Sie machte das Licht aus und / gehen / in / Bett (*past*)
   4. Ich weiß nicht, ob / sie (*she*) / sein / zu Hause (*present*)
   5. Wir konnten es nicht machen, weil / wir / haben / kein- / Zeit (*past*)
   6. Wenn / ich / finden / es, gebe ich es dir (*present*)
   7. Soll ich es ihm sagen, oder / wollen / Sie / machen / es / ? (*present*)
   8. Sie müssen warten, bis / er / zurückkommen (*present*)
   9. Ich weiß nicht, wann / ich / sehen / ihn (*present*)
  10. Kommen Sie zurück, nachdem / Sie / erledigen / es / ! (*present perfect*)

d. 1. Wenn / du / beeilen / nicht, wirst du den Zug verpassen (*present*)
   2. Er wollte, aber / er / können / nicht (*past*)
   3. Können Sie mir sagen, wo / ich / können / finden / ihn / ? (*present*)
   4. Ich habe gelesen, bis / ich / einschlafen (*present perfect*)
   5. Ich merkte nicht, daß / er / sein / in / Zimmer (*past*)
   6. Sie wird es machen, wenn / sie (*she*) / zurückkommen (*present*)
   7. Ich gehe zur Apotheke, und / dann / ich / gehen / nach Hause (*present*)
   8. Weißt du, ob / sie (*she*) / kommen / heute abend / ? (*present*)
   9. Können Sie mir sagen, wieviel / es / kosten / ? (*present*)
  10. Soll ich ein Taxi anrufen, oder / wollen / du / gehen / zu Fuß / ? (*present*)

e. 1. Ist es dir recht, wenn / wir / kommen / später / ? (*present*)
   2. Sie sagte es nur, weil / sie / sein / böse (*past*)
   3. Er wollte heute abend vorbeikommen, aber / er / haben / kein- / Zeit (*past*)
   4. Als / er / kommen / endlich, war es zu spät (*past*)
   5. Wissen Sie, warum / sie (*they*) / sein / nicht hier / ? (*present*)
   6. Ich sage es ihm, wenn / ich / sehen / ihn (*present*)
   7. Entschließen Sie sich, bevor / es / sein / zu spät / ! (*present*)
   8. Hände hoch, oder / ich / schießen / ! (*present*)
   9. Er hat sich verändert, seitdem / ich / sehen / ihn / letzt- / Mal (*present perfect*)
  10. Ich weiß nicht, wann / er / zurückkommen (*present*)

f. 1. Frag ihn, ob / er / wollen / mitkommen / ! (*present*)
   2. Glaubst du, daß / es / sein / zu schwer / ? (*present*)

4   Express in German

a. 1. He said that he wanted to go home.
   2. Do you know where she lives now?
   3. We bought it when we were in Germany.
   4. He wanted to but he couldn't.
   5. She went home because she was tired.
   6. I'll help you if I can.
   7. Do you know why they aren't here?
   8. I'll wait here until you come back.
   9. Turn out the light before you leave.
  10. I'll tell him when I see him.

b. 1. Have you seen him since he came back?
   2. I'm going to the drugstore and then I'm going home.
   3. Ask him if he wants to come along.
   4. Can you tell me how much it costs?
   5. I'll call you up after I've talked with him.
   6. He said that she was very nice.
   7. Shall I tell him or do you want to do it?

8. If the weather is nice, we'll take a walk.
9. When he finally came it was too late.
10. I don't know how much he earns.

c. 1. I'll tell you if I find it.
2. You'll have to wait until he comes back.
3. It's good but it costs too much.
4. If I find it, I'll give it to you.
5. She only said it because she was mad.
6. I don't know when I'll see him.
7. Shall I call a taxi or do you want to walk?
8. Is it all right with you if we come later?
9. Come back after you've taken care of it.
10. Can you tell me where I can find him?

d. 1. I didn't notice that he was in the room.
2. I'll call him when he arrives.
3. He wanted to come by this evening but he didn't have (any) time.
4. Can you tell me what time it is? (*Lit.*: how late it is)

5. I don't know if she's home.
6. Decide before it's too late.
7. She left (the) town and was never seen again.
8. If I have time, I'll do it.
9. I met him when I lived in Munich.
10. Do you think that it's too hard?

e. 1. I looked for him but I couldn't find him.
2. I don't know when he's coming back.
3. He's changed since I saw him the last time.
4. Can you tell me how to get to the railroad station? (*Lit.*: how one gets)
5. Hands up or I'll shoot!
6. I read until I went to sleep.
7. If you don't hurry, you'll miss the train.
8. She turned out the light and went to bed.
9. I'm not sure where he went (to).
10. Do you know if she's coming this evening?

f. 1. We couldn't do it because we didn't have (any) time.
2. She'll do it when she comes back.

H Word Order in Subordinate Clauses: Double-Infinitive Construction

Look at the following example:

> Er sagte, **daß** er den Wagen nicht reparieren konnte.

In a subordinate clause, the conjugated verb form is normally in the *final position*. However, when a double-infinitive construction is present, the conjugated form immediately precedes the two infinitives:

SIMPLE SENTENCES	Er sagte es.
	Er **hat** den Wagen nicht reparieren können.
COMPOUND SENTENCE	Er sagte, **daß** er den Wagen nicht **hat** reparieren können.

The same rule also applies to the future tense:

SIMPLE SENTENCES	Ich glaube es.
	Ich **werde** es machen müssen.
COMPOUND SENTENCE	Ich glaube, **daß** ich es **werde** machen müssen.

DRILLS

1 Fill-ins

● Present perfect tense: Supply the correct form of the auxiliary **haben**.

    1. Er sagte, daß er ihn nicht _____ erreichen können.
    2. Sie sagten, daß sie (*they*) das Büro nicht _____ finden können.
    3. Er sagte, daß er den Wagen nicht _____ reparieren können.
    4. Ich wußte nicht, daß er _____ mitkommen wollen.   (**wissen, weiß, wußte, gewußt:** to know)

● Future tense: Supply the correct form of the auxiliary **werden**.

    1. Ich glaube, daß ich es _____ machen müssen.
    2. Ich glaube, daß ich die Rechnung _____ bezahlen müssen.

2 Sentence combination

● Combine the following pairs of sentences. Omit items in parentheses from the compound sentences.

    1. Er sagte (es). **daß** Er hat ihn nicht erreichen können.
    2. Ich wußte (es) nicht. **daß** Er hat mitkommen wollen.
    3. Er sagte (es). **daß** Er hat den Wagen nicht reparieren können.
    4. Ich glaube (es). **daß** Ich werde die Rechnung bezahlen müssen.
    5. Sie sagten (es). **daß** Sie haben das Büro nicht finden können.
    6. Ich glaube (es). **daß** Ich werde es machen müssen.

3 Synthetic exercises (subordinate clause)

● Form complete compound sentences using the tenses indicated.

    1. Er sagte, daß / er / können / reparieren / Wagen / nicht (*present perfect*)
    2. Sie sagten, daß / sie (*they*) / können / finden / Büro / nicht (*present perfect*)
    3. Ich wußte nicht, daß / er / wollen / mitkommen (*present perfect*)
    4. Ich glaube, daß / ich / müssen / machen / es (*future*)
    5. Er sagte, daß / er / können / erreichen / ihn nicht (*present perfect*)
    6. Ich glaube, daß / ich / müssen / bezahlen / Rechnung (*future*)

4 Express in German

● Put the verbs in italics in the tenses indicated in parentheses.

    1. I didn't know that he *wanted to* come along. (*present perfect*)
    2. He said that he *couldn't* repair the car. (*present perfect*)
    3. They said that they *couldn't* find the office. (*present perfect*)
    4. I think that I'*ll have to* pay the bill. (*future*)
    5. He said that he *couldn't* reach him. (*present perfect*)
    6. I think that I'*ll have to* do it. (*future*)

VOCABULARY

COORDINATING
CONJUNCTIONS
aber but, however
oder but
und and

SUBORDINATING
CONJUNCTIONS
als when (past time only)
bevor before
bis until
daß that
nachdem after
ob if, whether
seitdem since, ever since
weil because
wenn when (*present* or *future* only); if

die **Apotheke, –n** drugstore, pharmacy
blond blond
ein · schlafen to go to sleep
(schläft . . . ein)
schlief . . . ein, ist eingeschlafen
der **Fuß, ⸚e** foot
zu Fuß gehen to walk (lit. "to go on foot")
groß tall
Hände hoch! Hands up!
der **Lederstiefel, –** leather boot
merken to notice
nur only

schießen to shoot
schoß, geschossen
sicher sure
spazieren · gehen to take a walk
ging . . . spazieren
ist spazierengegangen
tragen (trägt) to wear
trug, getragen
sich **verändern** to change (*of people*)
verdienen to earn
verlassen (verläßt) to leave
verließ, verlassen
verpassen to miss (*a train*)
wissen (weiß) to know
wußte, gewußt

Lesson 9 Level TWO

A Conditional Sentences

1 The "if . . . then" formula

Look at two simple statements of fact:

> He has the money.   He will buy it.

Now look at the same two sentences joined together in an "if . . . then" sentence:

> If he has the money,   (then)   he'll buy it.

The use of the "if . . . then" formula has changed the simple sentences in two ways:

a. The word "if" has removed the two underlying sentences from the realm of simple fact. By using the word "if" the speaker is showing that he doesn't know whether the person has the money or not.

b. The "if . . . then" formula establishes a *conditional* relationship between the two underlying sentences:

Condition	Conclusion
If X	*then* Y
If he has the money	he will buy it.

2 Mood

A speaker can have different attitudes toward an "if . . . then" situation. By choosing either the indicative or the subjunctive mood, he can show what his attitude is.

a. Indicative in conditional sentences

Up to this point, the sentences you have seen have been in what is called the *indicative mood.*

> If he *has* the money, he *will buy* it.

Here the speaker is making the most open kind of if-then statement. In using the indicative, he is taking no stand at all (the person may have the money, or he may not).

422

b. Subjunctive in conditional sentences (contrary-to-fact conditional)

By using the subjunctive the speaker shows a different attitude: He is saying that the if-clause is *not true* (in other words, it is contrary to fact). Look at the following example:

> If he had the money, he'd buy it.

The speaker is implying that the person in question *does not have the money*. The example above is in the present tense of the subjunctive:

> If he had the money (*right now*), he'd buy it.

The subjunctive also has past tense forms:

> If he *had had* the money (*back then*), he *would have bought* it.

B The English Subjunctive in Conditional Sentences

1 Present tense

The present tense forms of the English subjunctive are the same as the past tense forms of the indicative:

PAST INDICATIVE	He had the money.
PRESENT SUBJUNCTIVE	If he had the money . . . .

The forms are identical, but there is clearly a difference in time, and therefore in meaning, between the past tense of the indicative and the present tense of the subjunctive:

PAST INDICATIVE	He *had* the money (yesterday).
	(*past time* using a *past tense form*)
PRESENT SUBJUNCTIVE	If he *had* the money (now) . . . .
	(*present time* using a *past tense form*)

The present tense of the subjunctive is easy to recognize in English: *past tense forms* are used in *present tense situations*.

▶ Note   The verb "to be" is the only verb whose present tense subjunctive forms are different from the past tense indicative forms:

PAST INDICATIVE	He *was* here.
PRESENT SUBJUNCTIVE	If he *were* here . . . .

2 Past tense

The *past tense forms of the subjunctive* are the same as the *past perfect tense forms of the indicative*:

PAST PERFECT INDICATIVE	He *had had* the money.
PAST SUBJUNCTIVE	If he *had had* the money . . . .
PAST PERFECT INDICATIVE	He *had needed* it.
PAST SUBJUNCTIVE	If he *had needed* it . . . .

Summary

The English subjunctive has only two tenses:

1. the *present tense*, the forms of which are usually identical with those of the *past indicative*, and

2. the *past tense*, the forms of which are always identical with those of the *past perfect indicative*.

C The German Subjunctive: Subjunctive II

German and English follow basically the same pattern in using the indicative and subjunctive moods in conditional sentences. Look at the following examples:

PRESENT INDICATIVE	If he *needs* it . . . .
	Wenn er es **braucht** . . . .
PRESENT SUBJUNCTIVE	If he *needed* it . . . .
	Wenn er es **brauchte** . . . .
PAST SUBJUNCTIVE	If he *had needed* it . . . .
	Wenn er es **gebraucht hätte** . . . .

The form of the German subjunctive used in these **wenn**-clauses is called subjunctive II. (Subjunctive I is a less common mood which will be introduced later.)

1 Word order

Wenn (if) is a subordinating conjunction, and so the *conjugated verb form appears at the end of the clause:*

Wenn er es *brauchte* . . . .
Wenn er es gebraucht hätte . . . .

2 Present tense forms of subjunctive II

The present tense of subjunctive II is derived from *the past tense of the indicative*.

1. Weak (regular) verbs

In the case of weak verbs, the present tense of subjunctive II is exactly the same as the past tense of the indicative.

ich brauchte	wir brauchten
du brauchtest	ihr brauchtet
er brauchte	sie brauchten

EXAMPLES   Wenn er es **brauchte** . . . .   (If he *needed* it . . . .)
Wenn sie näher **wohnten** . . . .   (If they *lived* closer . . . .)

2. Strong (irregular) verbs

The present tense of subjunctive II of strong verbs is formed in the following way. Take the past stem of the indicative:

war
ging
kam
flog

Add an umlaut where possible (**a, o,** and **u**):

wär-
ging-
käm-
flög-

Add the subjunctive endings:

ich wär **e**	wir wär **en**
du wär **est**	ihr wär **et**
er wär **e**	sie wär **en**

EXAMPLES   Wenn er hier **wäre** . . . .   (If he *were* here . . . .)
Wenn wir jetzt **gingen** . . . .   (If we *went* now . . . .)

3. Exceptions

A few verbs form the present tense of subjunctive II by simply adding an umlaut to the past tense indicative.

Past Indicative	Present Subjunctive II
hatte	**hä**tte
konnte	**kö**nnte

The commonly used verbs of this class are:

(a) **haben** and **werden**

Infinitive	Past Indicative	Present Subjunctive II
haben	hatte	hätte
werden	wurde	würde

(b) four of the modals and **wissen**

	Infinitive	Past Indicative	Present Subjunctive II
	wissen	wußte	wüßte
	dürfen	durfte	dürfte
	können	konnte	könnte
	mögen	mochte	möchte
	müssen	mußte	müßte
but	sollen	sollte	**sollte**
	wollen	wollte	**wollte**

▶ Note   **Sollte** und **wollte** do *not* take an umlaut in the subjunctive II. The past tense indicative and the subjunctive II present of these two verbs are identical.

EXAMPLES   Wenn ich einen Wagen **hätte** . . . .   (If I *had* a car . . . .)
Wenn sie es tun **könnten** . . . .   (If they *could* do it . . . .)

DRILLS

1   Present tense subjunctive II of weak verbs

● Pattern drills: Use the following sentences to practice the conjugation of weak verbs in the present tense of subjunctive II.

1. Wenn ich näher **wohnte** . . . .   (näher: closer)
   Wenn du näher _____ . . . .
   Wenn er näher _____ . . . .
   Wenn wir näher _____ . . . .
   Wenn ihr näher _____ . . . .
   Wenn Sie näher _____ . . . .
2. Wenn ich es **machte** . . . .
   Wenn du es _____ . . . .
   Wenn er es _____ . . . .
   Wenn wir es _____ . . . .
   Wenn ihr es _____ . . . .
   Wenn Sie es _____ . . . .
3. Wenn ich es **brauchte** . . . .
   Wenn du es _____ . . . .
   Wenn er es _____ . . . .
   Wenn wir es _____ . . . .
   Wenn ihr es _____ . . . .
   Wenn Sie es _____ . . . .

● Put the following **wenn**-clauses into the present tense of subjunctive II.

EXAMPLE   Wenn er es kauft . . . .
Wenn er es **kaufte** . . . .

1. Wenn er mehr arbeitet . . . .
2. Wenn es nicht so viel kostet . . . .
3. Wenn sie näher wohnen . . . .
4. Wenn Sie mehr verdienen . . . .

(verdienen: to earn)

5. Wenn ich es brauche . . . .

6. Wenn wir ihnen eine Karte schicken . . . .
7. Wenn er es glaubt . . . .
8. Wenn er weniger raucht . . . .
9. Wenn ich es mache . . . .
10. Wenn du ihn fragst . . . .

- Synthetic exercises: Use the following elements to construct subjunctive II clauses in the present tense.

EXAMPLE   Wenn / er / kaufen / es . . . .
              Wenn er es **kaufte** . . . .

1. Wenn / er / rauchen / weniger . . . .
2. Wenn / sie (they) / wohnen / näher . . . .
3. Wenn / ich / brauchen / es . . . .
4. Wenn / er / arbeiten / mehr . . . .
5. Wenn / wir / schicken / ihnen eine Karte . . . .

6. Wenn / du / fragen / ihn . . . .
7. Wenn / es / kosten / nicht so viel . . . .
8. Wenn / ich / machen / es . . . .
9. Wenn / er / glauben / es . . . .
10. Wenn / Sie / verdienen / mehr . . . .

- Express in German.

1. If you asked him . . . .   **(du**-form)
2. If he worked more . . . .
3. If I needed it . . . .
4. If we sent them a card . . . .
5. If they lived closer . . . .

6. If it didn't cost so much . . . .
7. If I did it . . . .
8. If you earned more . . . .   **(Sie**-form)
9. If he smoked less . . . .
10. If he believed it . . . .

2   Present subjunctive II of strong verbs

- Pattern drills: Use the following clauses to practice the conjugation of strong verbs in the present tense of subjunctive II.

1. Wenn ich sicher **wäre** . . . .
   Wenn du sicher _____ . . . .
   Wenn er sicher _____ . . . .
   Wenn wir sicher _____ . . . .
   Wenn ihr sicher _____ . . . .
   Wenn sie sicher _____ . . . .
2. Wenn ich früher ins Bett **ginge** . . . .
   Wenn du früher ins Bett _____ . . . .
   Wenn er früher ins Bett _____ . . . .
   Wenn wir früher ins Bett _____ . . . .
   Wenn ihr früher ins Bett _____ . . . .
   Wenn sie früher ins Bett _____ . . . .

3. Wenn ich später **käme** . . . .
   Wenn du später _____ . . . .
   Wenn er später _____ . . . .
   Wenn wir später _____ . . . .
   Wenn ihr später _____ . . . .
   Wenn sie später _____ . . . .

- Put the following past tense indicative verbs into the present tense of subjunctive II. (Remember: Umlaut where possible and be sure to use proper endings.)

EXAMPLE   du kamst
               du **käm**est

1. er war
2. ich ging

3. wir gaben
4. du riefst ihn an

5. sie kamen
6. er flog
7. ich blieb
8. wir fuhren

9. er fiel
10. ich sah
11. sie schlief
12. ich fand

3   Present subjunctive II of the exceptions

● Pattern drills: Use the following patterns to practice the subjunctive II forms of the exceptions.

1. Wenn ich mehr Zeit **hätte** . . . .
Wenn du mehr Zeit _____ . . . .
Wenn er mehr Zeit   _____ . . . .
Wenn wir mehr Zeit _____ . . . .
Wenn ihr mehr Zeit _____ . . . .
Wenn sie mehr Zeit _____ . . . .
2. Wenn ich es tun **könnte** . . . .   (**tun**: to do)
Wenn du es tun _____ . . . .
Wenn er es tun   _____ . . . .

Wenn wir es tun _____ . . . .
Wenn ihr es tun _____ . . . .
Wenn sie es tun _____ . . . .
3. Wenn ich krank **würde** . . . .
Wenn du krank _____ . . . .
Wenn er krank   _____ . . . .
Wenn wir krank _____ . . . .
Wenn ihr krank _____ . . . .
Wenn sie krank _____ . . . .

● Put the following past tense indicative verbs into the present tense of subjunctive II. Umlaut the past tense forms with the exception of **wollen** and **sollen**.

1. ich wußte
2. sie konnten
3. wir wollten
4. du mußtest
5. ihr hattet

6. er wurde
7. ich durfte
8. wir wußten
9. du konntest
10. er hatte

● Put the following **wenn**-clauses into the present tense of subjunctive II.

1. Wenn ich es tun kann . . . .
2. Wenn wir mehr Zeit haben . . . .
3. Wenn ich die Telefonnummer weiß . . . .
4. Wenn sie es tun müssen . . . .
5. Wenn du es finden kannst . . . .
6. Wenn er einen Wagen hat . . . .

7. Wenn sie es wissen . . . .
8. Wenn sie mitkommen will . . . .
9. Wenn wir mit ihm sprechen dürfen . . . .
10. Wenn er hier sein soll . . . .
11. Wenn ich das Geld habe . . . .

● Synthetic exercises: Use the following elements to form clauses in the present tense of subjunctive II.

1. Wenn / er / haben / Wagen . . . .
2. Wenn / ich / können / tun / es . . . .
3. Wenn / du / können / finden / es . . . .
4. Wenn / wir / dürfen / sprechen / mit ihm . . . .
5. Wenn / ich / haben / das Geld . . . .
6. Wenn / sie (*they*) / wissen / es . . . .
7. Wenn / sie (*they*) / müssen / tun / es . . . .

8. Wenn / wir / haben / mehr Zeit . . . .
9. Wenn / sie (*she*) wollen / mitkommen . . . .
10. Wenn / er / sollen / sein / hier . . . .
11. Wenn / ich / wissen / Telefonnummer . . . .

● Express in German.

1. If I had the money . . . .
2. If you could find it . . . .

3. If she wanted to come . . . .
4. If they had to do it . . . .

5. If we had more time . . . .
6. If I knew the telephone number . . . .
7. If I could do it . . . .
8. If he were supposed to be here . . . .

9. If we might (got to) speak with him . . . .
10. If they knew it . . . .
11. If I had a car . . . .

3 Subjunctive II present revisited

Look at the following examples:

English	German
If he *went* home	Wenn er nach Hause **ginge** . . . .
If *he'd go* home . . . . (If he *would go* home . . . .)	Wenn er nach Hause **gehen würde** . . . .

As you see, both English and German have alternate forms for the present tense of subjunctive II:

(a) a *one-word* form (*went* / **ginge**) which is derived from the past tense of the indicative, and

(b) a *two-word* form (*would go* / **würde . . . gehen**) consisting of:

> ENGLISH   *would* + *infinitive*
> GERMAN   a conjugated form of **würde** + *infinitive*

All of the one-word forms can be found in written German. Spoken German, on the other hand, replaces many of the one-word forms with the **würde** + *infinitive* construction.

(a) The *one-word* form is used with:

> weak verbs*   (for example, **brauchte**)
> **sein** and **haben**   (for example, **wäre, hätte**)
> **wissen** and *the modals*   (for example, **wüßte, könnte**)

(b) **Würde** + *infinitive* is used with all other verbs.†

DRILLS

● Synthetic exercises: Use the following elements to form clauses in the present tense of subjunctive II. Use the **würde** + *infinitive* construction in all cases.

EXAMPLE   Wenn / er / gehen / nach Hause . . . .
                 Wenn er nach Hause **gehen würde** . . . .

---

*In modern colloquial German the **würde** construction is frequently used even with weak verbs. Instructors who prefer to have their students use the **würde** construction with weak verbs should feel free to do so.

†The one-word forms of **gehen (ginge)** and **kommen (käme)** are occasionally found in spoken German, but the **würde** + *infinitive* construction is far more common.

1. Wenn / wir / kommen / später . . . .
2. Wenn / ich / fliegen / nach Frankfurt . . . .
3. Wenn / er / bleiben / länger . . . .
4. Wenn / du / gehen / früher / ins Bett . . . .
5. Wenn / er / denken / daran . . . .
6. Wenn / du / anrufen / ihn . . . .
7. Wenn / er / zurückkommen / heute . . . .
8. Wenn / sie (they) / bringen / es heute . . . .
9. Wenn / wir / fahren / mit dem Zug . . . .
10. Wenn / er / geben / es mir . . . .
11. Wenn / sie (they) / schlafen / länger . . . .

● Express in German. Use only the **würde** + *infinitive* construction. The **würde** construction must be used regardless of whether the English equivalent uses a one-word or a two-word form. The use of the **würde** construction depends solely on the German verb.

1. If he'd come back today . . . .
2. If you'd call him up . . . .
3. If we went by train . . . .
4. If I flew to Frankfurt . . . .
5. If he'd give it to me . . . .
6. If you'd go to bed earlier . . . .
7. If we came later . . . .
8. If he thought of it . . . .
9. If they brought it today . . . .
10. If he stayed longer . . . .
11. If they'd sleep longer . . . .

MIXED DRILLS: PRESENT TENSE SUBJUNCTIVE II

This drill contains strong verbs and exceptions. One-word forms should be used for **sein, haben, wissen,** and the modals. Otherwise the **würde** construction should be used.

● Put the following **wenn**-clauses into the present tense of subjunctive II.

a.
1. Wenn es leichter ist . . . .
2. Wenn er länger bleibt . . . .
3. Wenn wir mehr Zeit haben . . . .
4. Wenn du ihn anrufst . . . .
5. Wenn sie mitkommen will . . . .
6. Wenn ich es tun kann . . . .
7. Wenn sie wirklich krank ist . . . .
8. Wenn sie länger schlafen . . . .
9. Wenn sie es wissen . . . .
10. Wenn wir später kommen . . . .

b.
1. Wenn er es mir gibt . . . .
2. Wenn ich das Geld habe . . . .
3. Wenn du früher ins Bett gehst . . . .
4. Wenn er einen Wagen hat . . . .
5. Wenn ich die Telefonnummer weiß . . . .
6. Wenn er nach Frankfurt fliegt . . . .
7. Wenn du es finden kannst . . . .
8. Wenn wir mit dem Zug fahren . . . .
9. Wenn sie es tun müssen . . . .

In addition to the verbs contained in the previous drill, this exercise contains weak verbs. Weak verbs use the one-word subjunctive II forms. (See drills, pp. 426–27).

● Put the following **wenn**-clauses into the present tense of subjunctive II.

a.
1. Wenn ich es brauche . . . .
2. Wenn du ihn anrufst . . . .
3. Wenn sie klug ist . . . . (**klug:** smart)
4. Wenn wir mit dem Zug fahren . . . .
5. Wenn es nicht so viel kostet . . . .
6. Wenn du es finden kannst . . . .

7. Wenn er länger bleibt . . . .
8. Wenn wir mehr Zeit haben . . . .
9. Wenn er mehr arbeitet . . . .
10. Wenn wir später kommen . . . .

b. 1. Wenn er es braucht . . . .
2. Wenn sie wirklich krank ist . . . .
3. Wenn sie länger schlafen . . . .
4. Wenn ich die Telefonnummer weiß . . . .
5. Wenn er weniger raucht . . . .
6. Wenn sie näher wohnen . . . .
7. Wenn sie es tun müssen . . . .
8. Wenn du früher ins Bett gehst . . . .
9. Wenn sie es wissen . . . .
10. Wenn ich es mache . . . .

c. 1. Wenn er nach Frankfurt fliegt . . . .
2. Wenn ich es tun kann . . . .
3. Wenn er heute zurückkommt . . . .
4. Wenn es leichter ist . . . .
5. Wenn Sie ihn fragen . . . .
6. Wenn er es mir gibt . . . .
7. Wenn wir mit ihm sprechen dürfen . . . .
8. Wenn ich das Geld habe . . . .
9. Wenn er einen Wagen hat . . . .

● Express in German.

a. 1. If she were really sick . . . .
2. If it didn't cost so much . . . .
3. If he flew to Frankfurt . . . .
4. If I had the money . . . .
5. If he worked more . . . .
6. If you'd call him up . . . .
7. If I could do it . . . .
8. If they'd sleep longer . . . .
9. If I needed it . . . .
10. If they had to do it . . . .

b. 1. If you'd go to bed earlier . . . .
2. If it were easier . . . .

3. If he'd stay longer . . . .
4. If we had more time . . . .
5. If they knew it . . . .
6. If I did it . . . .
7. If they lived closer . . . .
8. If we went by train . . . .
9. If he had a car . . . .
10. If he'd give it to me . . . .

c. 1. If you'd ask him . . . .   (**Sie**-form)
2. If we came later . . . .

4 Past tense forms of subjunctive II

The past tense of subjunctive II is *derived from the past perfect tense of the indicative:*

Past Perfect Indicative	Past Subjunctive II
Er **war** gekommen	Wenn er gekommen wäre . . . .
(He had come.)	(If he had come . . . .)
Er **hatte** es gemacht.	Wenn er es gemacht hätte . . . .
(He had done it.)	(If he had done it . . . .)

1. Forms

The past tense of subjunctive II is composed of:

a form of **wäre** or **hätte** + a *past participle*
hätte   gemacht
wären   gekommen

2. Usage

The difference in meaning between the past perfect indicative and the past subjunctive II should be quite clear. First look at a past perfect indicative sentence:

Er war gekommen.   (He had come.)

This is a statement of fact. The person in question actually did come. Now look at a past tense subjunctive II clause:

Wenn er gekommen wäre . . . .   (If he had come . . . .)

This is a contrary-to-fact statement. The implication is that the person in question did *not* come. In other words, the past tense of subjunctive II is used to *talk* about things that did not actually happen.

DRILLS

● Verbs taking **haben**: Put the following **wenn**-clauses into the past tense of subjunctive II.

EXAMPLE   Wenn er es gemacht hat . . . .
                 Wenn er es gemacht **hätte** . . . .

1. Wenn du mehr gearbeitet hast . . . .
2. Wenn sie ihn gesehen haben . . . .
3. Wenn er ihre Telefonnummer gewußt hat . . . .
4. Wenn du ihm geantwortet hast . . . .
5. Wenn du in der Stadt gewohnt hast . . . .
6. Wenn er gekonnt hat . . . .
7. Wenn sie mehr Zeit gehabt haben . . . .
8. Wenn er ihn angerufen hat . . . .

● Verbs taking **sein**: Put the following **wenn**-clauses into the past tense of subjunctive II.

EXAMPLE   Wenn er gekommen ist . . . .
                 Wenn er gekommen **wäre** . . . .

1. Wenn er mit dem Zug gefahren ist . . . .
2. Wenn sie wirklich krank gewesen ist . . . .
3. Wenn Sie geflogen sind . . . .
4. Wenn du früher ins Bett gegangen bist . . . .
5. Wenn er heute zurückgekommen ist . . . .
6. Wenn ihr länger geblieben seid . . . .
7. Wenn er hier gewesen ist . . . .

● Mixed drills: Put the following **wenn**-clauses into the past tense of subjunctive II.

a. 1. Wenn sie mehr Zeit gehabt haben . . . .
   2. Wenn er ihn angerufen hat . . . .
   3. Wenn du früher ins Bett gegangen bist . . . .
   4. Wenn sie ihn gesehen haben . . . .
   5. Wenn du mehr gearbeitet hast . . . .
   6. Wenn er mit dem Zug gefahren ist . . . .

7. Wenn du ihm geantwortet hast . . . .
8. Wenn sie wirklich krank gewesen ist . . . .
9. Wenn sie geflogen sind . . . .
10. Wenn er gekonnt hat . . . .

b. 1. Wenn ihr länger geblieben seid . . . .

2. Wenn er heute zurückgekommen ist . . . .
3. Wenn er ihre Telefonnummer gewußt hat . . . .
4. Wenn er hier gewesen ist . . . .
5. Wenn du in der Stadt gewohnt hast . . . .

● Synthetic exercises: Use the following elements to form subjunctive II clauses in the past tense.

EXAMPLE   Wenn / er / zurückkommen / heute
Wenn er heute **zurückgekommen wäre** · · · ·

a. 1. Wenn / er / fahren / mit / Zug . . . .
2. Wenn / du / arbeiten / mehr . . . .
3. Wenn / sie (they) / haben / mehr / Zeit . . . .
4. Wenn / sie (she) / sein / wirklich / krank . . . .
5. Wenn / er / wissen / ihre Telefonnummer . . . .
6. Wenn / du / gehen / früher / in / Bett . . . .
7. Wenn / er / können . . . .

8. Wenn / er / zurückkommen / heute . . . .
9. Wenn / du / wohnen / in / Stadt . . . .
10. Wenn / sie (they) / sehen / ihn . . . .

b. 1. Wenn / ihr / bleiben / länger . . . .
2. Wenn / er / sein / hier . . . .
3. Wenn / Sie / fliegen . . . .
4. Wenn / du / antworten / ihm . . . .
5. Wenn / er / anrufen / ihn . . . .
6. Wenn / du / anziehen / dich warm . . . .

● Express in German.

a. 1. If he had been here . . . .
2. If you (du) had worked more . . . .
3. If he had called him up . . . .
4. If you (Sie) had flown . . . .
5. If he had come back today . . . .
6. If they had more time . . . .
7. If you (ihr) had stayed longer . . . .
8. If he had known her telephone number . . . .
9. If she had really been sick . . . .
10. If he had been able to . . . .

b. 1. If you (du) had gone to bed earlier . . . .
2. If I had seen him . . . .
3. If you (Sie) had lived downtown . . . .
4. If he had gone by train . . . .
5. If you (du) had dressed warmly . . . .
6. If you had answered him . . . .

MIXED DRILLS: PRESENT AND PAST SUBJUNCTIVE II

● Synthetic exercises: Use the following elements to form subjunctive II clauses in the present and past tense.

EXAMPLE   Wenn / er / kommen / heute . . . .

Wenn er heute **kommen würde** · · · ·
Wenn er heute **gekommen wäre** · · · ·

a. 1. Wenn / er / sein / hier . . . .
2. Wenn / sie (they) / haben / mehr Zeit . . . .

3. Wenn / er / fahren / mit / Zug . . . .
4. Wenn / er / wissen / ihr- / Telefonnummer . . . .

5. Wenn / Sie / fliegen . . . .
6. Wenn / er / arbeiten / mehr . . . .
7. Wenn / er / zurückkommen / heute . . . .
8. Wenn / wir / wohnen / in / Stadt . . . .
9. Wenn / du / gehen / früher / in / Bett . . . .
10. Wenn / sie (they) / sehen / ihn . . . .

b. 1. Wenn / er / können . . . .
2. Wenn / sie (she) / sein / wirklich / krank . . . .

3. Wenn / ihr / bleiben / länger . . . .
4. Wenn / er / anrufen / ihn . . . .
5. Wenn / er / glauben / es . . . .
6. Wenn / er / geben / es / mir . . . .
7. Wenn / wir / kommen / später . . . .
8. Wenn / es / sein / leichter . . . .
9. Wenn / sie (they) / schlafen / länger . . . .
10. Wenn / ich / haben / das Geld . . . .

c. 1. Wenn / es / kosten / nicht so viel . . . .

● **Express in German.**

a. 1. If she were really sick . . . .
   If she had really been sick . . . .
2. If he called him . . . .
   If he had called him . . . .
3. If they had more time . . . .
   If they had had more time . . . .
4. If you'd fly . . . .
   If you had flown . . . .
5. If it didn't cost so much . . . .
   If it hadn't cost so much . . . .
6. If you worked more . . . .
   If you had worked more . . . .
7. If he were here . . . .
   If he had been here . . . .
8. If we lived downtown . . . .
   If we had lived downtown . . . .
9. If he'd give it to me . . . .
   If he had given it to me . . . .
10. If he came back today . . . .
    If he had come back today . . . .

b. 1. If he knew her telephone number . . . .
   If he had known her telephone number . . . .

2. If we came later . . . .
   If we had come later . . . .
3. If they slept longer . . . .
   If they had slept longer . . . .
4. If it were easier . . . .
   If it had been easier . . . .
5. If I had the money . . . .
   If I had had the money . . . .
6. If they saw him . . . .
   If they had seen him . . . .
7. If he could . . . .
   If he had been able to . . . .
8. If you'd go to bed earlier . . . .
   If you had gone to bed earlier . . . .
9. If he came by train . . . .
   If he had come by train . . . .
10. If he believed it . . . .
    If he had believed it . . . .

c. 1. If we stayed longer . . . .
   If we had stayed longer . . . .

D Conditional Sentences: Dann-Clauses

As you have already seen, conditional sentences follow an "if-then" **(wenn-dann)** pattern. Up to this point you have only drilled **wenn**-clauses. Now look at the following dann -clauses ("then"-clauses):

PRESENT INDICATIVE   Wenn er das Geld hat, **(dann)** kauft er es.
                       If he has the money, (then) he'll buy it.

PRESENT SUBJUNCTIVE II	Wenn er das Geld hätte, **(dann)** würde **er es** kaufen.
	If he had the money, *he would buy it.*
PAST SUBJUNCTIVE II	Wenn er das Geld gehabt hätte, **(dann)** hätte **er es** gekauft.
	If he had had the money, *(then) he would have bought it.*

1 Present indicative

Wenn er das Geld hat, kauft er es.

▶ **Note** The verb comes first in the **dann**-clause. Only the word **dann** can come before it. But **dann** is normally omitted:

Wenn . . .   .

The inflected verbs of the two clauses are separated only by a comma. This is in keeping with the rules governing word order that you learned in Lesson 9, Level One: *If a compound sentence begins with a subordinate clause, then the conjugated verb is the first element in the main clause.*

Subordinate Clause	Main Clause
Wenn er das Geld hat,	**kauft** er es.

2 Present subjunctive II

a. Word order

Wenn er das Geld hätte, würde er es kaufen.

The conjugated verb form **(würde)** is the first element of the **dann**-clause. If an infinitive **(kaufen)** is used to complete the meaning of the clause, it must appear at the end of the sentence.

. . . , würde . . . **kaufen**

b. Usage

1. The *one-word* form is used with:

the modal auxiliaries (for example, **könnte**)

Wenn er das Geld hätte, könnte er es tun.

sein (for example, **wäre**)*

Wenn er das Geld hätte, wäre er glücklich.

---

*Modern colloquial German frequently uses **würde . . . sein** rather than **wäre** in the **dann**-clause:

Wenn er das Geld hätte, **würde** er glücklich **sein.**

2. **Würde** + *infinitive* is used with all other verbs. (In contrast to **wenn**-clause usage, even **haben, wissen,** and *weak verbs* use the **würde** construction.)

Wenn er das Geld hätte, _{würde} er es _{kaufen.}

3 Past subjunctive II

Word order

Wenn er das Geld gehabt hätte, _{hätte} er es _{gekauft.}

1. The conjugated verb form **(hätte)** is the first element in the **dann**-clause.

2. The past participle **(gekauft)** is the last element in the clause.

E Inversion in Conditional Sentences

Look at the following examples:

PRESENT INDICATIVE	Ich _{helfe} dir, wenn ich kann. (I'll help you, if I can.)
PRESENT SUBJUNCTIVE II	Ich _{würde} dir _{helfen,} wenn ich könnte. (I'd help you, if I could.)
PAST SUBJUNCTIVE II	Ich _{hätte} dir _{geholfen,} wenn ich gekonnt hätte. (I would have helped you, if I had been able to.)

A conditional sentence may begin with the **dann**-clause. When it does:

1. The word **dann** is never used.

2. The **dann**-clause uses normal (declarative) word order:

Ich **helfe** dir, ...
Ich **würde** dir **helfen,** . . . .
Ich **hätte** dir **geholfen,** . . . .

F Mixed Tenses in Conditional Sentences

When the situation requires it, both English and German can mix tenses within the same sentence. The basic logical pattern of such sentences always looks like this:
If A *had happened* in the *past,* B *would be* the case *now.*

Past Subjunctive II	Present Subjunctive II
Wenn du früher ins Bett _{gegangen wärest,} (If you *had gone* to bed earlier,	_{würdest} du jetzt nicht so müde _{sein.} you *would*n't *be* so tired now.)

DRILLS

1   Present tense subjunctive II: the **dann**-clause

● The **würde** construction (all verbs except **sein** and the modals): Supply the correct form of **würde**.

1. Wenn ich mehr Zeit hätte, _____ ich es machen.
2. Wenn ich das Geld hätte, _____ ich es kaufen.
3. Wenn er hier wäre, _____ du es wissen.
4. Wenn ich es wüßte, _____ ich es dir sagen.
5. Wenn sie wirklich krank wäre, _____ sie (she) nach Hause gehen.
6. Wenn wir mehr Geld hätten, _____ wir länger bleiben.
7. Wenn es leichter wäre, _____ sie (she) es selber machen.   (**selber**: herself)
8. Wenn er es brauchte, _____ wir es ihm geben.
9. Wenn ich ihre Telefonnummer wüßte, _____ ich sie anrufen.

(**die Telefonnummer**: telephone number)

● The one-word form (the modals and often **sein**): Supply the correct subjunctive II forms of the verbs in parentheses.

1. Wenn wir mehr Zeit hätten, _____ wir es machen.
   (können)
2. Wenn Sie früher kommen würden, _____ ich Sie abholen.
   (können)
3. Wenn wir fliegen würden, _____wir in zwei Stunden da.   (**die Stunde, –n**: hour)
   (sein)
4. Wenn er nicht hier wäre, _____ ich es allein machen.
   (müssen)

● Supply the correct form of subjunctive II.

EXAMPLE   Wenn ich Zeit hätte, _____ ich ins Kino _____ .
           (gehen)

           Wenn ich Zeit hätte, **würde** ich ins Kino **gehen**.

1. Wenn ich es wüßte, _____ ich es dir _____ .
   (sagen)
2. Wenn sie wirklich krank wäre, _____ sie nach Hause _____ .
   (gehen)
3. Wenn er es brauchte, _____ ich es ihm _____ .
   (geben)
4. Wenn wir mehr Zeit hätten, _____ wir es machen.
   (können)
5. Wenn er hier wäre, _____ du es _____ .
   (wissen)
6. Wenn wir fliegen würden, _____ wir in zwei Stunden da.
   (sein)
7. Wenn Sie früher kommen würden, _____ ich Sie abholen.
   (können)

8. Wenn ich das Geld hätte, _____ ich es _____.
   (kaufen)

9. Wenn er nicht hier wäre, _____ ich es allein machen.
   (müssen)

10. Wenn wir mehr Geld hätten, _____ wir länger _____.
    (bleiben)

11. Wenn ich ihre Telefonnummer wüßte, _____ ich sie _____.
    (an · rufen)

12. Wenn ich mehr Zeit hätte, _____ ich es _____.
    (machen)

● Synthetic exercises: Form the suggested **dann**-clause using the present tense of subjunctive II.

EXAMPLE   Wenn ich Zeit hätte, ich / gehen / Kino
           Wenn ich Zeit hätte, **würde** ich ins Kino **gehen**.

1. Wenn ich mehr Geld hätte, ich / kaufen / es
2. Wenn sie wirklich krank wäre, sie / gehen / nach Hause
3. Wenn wir fliegen würden, wir / sein / in zwei Stunden da
4. Wenn ich ihre Telefonnummer wüßte, ich / anrufen / sie
5. Wenn wir mehr Zeit hätten, wir / können / machen / es
6. Wenn ich es wüßte, ich / sagen / es dir
7. Wenn er es brauchte, wir / geben / es ihm
8. Wenn er nicht hier wäre, ich / müssen / machen / es allein
9. Wenn ich mehr Zeit hätte, ich / machen / es
10. Wenn er hier wäre, du / wissen / es
11. Wenn wir mehr Geld hätten, wir / bleiben / länger
12. Wenn Sie früher kommen würden, ich / können / abholen / Sie

● Express in German: the **dann**-clause.

1. Wenn ich ihre Telefonnummer wüßte, _____.
   (I'd call her)

2. Wenn wir mehr Geld hätten, _____.
   (we'd stay longer)

3. Wenn ich mehr Zeit hätte, _____.
   (I'd do it)

4. Wenn er es brauchte, _____.
   (we'd give it to him)

5. Wenn Sie früher kommen würden, _____.
   (I could pick you up)

6. Wenn ich es wüßte, _____.
   (I'd tell you)

7. Wenn wir fliegen würden, _____.
   (we'd be there in two hours)

8. Wenn wir mehr Zeit hätten, _____.
   (we could do it)

9. Wenn er hier wäre, _____.
   (you'd know it)

10. Wenn ich das Geld hätte, _____.
    (I'd buy it)

11. Wenn sie wirklich krank wäre, _____.
    (she'd go home)

12. Wenn er nicht hier wäre, _____.
    (I'd have to do it alone)

- Express in German.

1. If I had more time, I'd do it.
2. If he needed it, we'd give it to him.
3. If I had the money, I'd buy it.
4. If we had more money, we'd stay longer.
5. If you came earlier, I could pick you up.
6. If she were really sick, she'd go home.
7. If I knew (it), I'd tell you.

8. If he were here, you'd know it.
9. If we had more time, we could do it.
10. If I knew her telephone number, I'd call her.
11. If we flew, we'd be there in two hours.
12. If he weren't here, I'd have to do it alone.

2   Past tense subjunctive II: the **dann**-clause.

- Supply the correct form of **hätte** or **wäre**.

1. Wenn ich mehr Zeit gehabt hätte, _____ ich es gemacht.
2. Wenn er es gebraucht hätte, _____ wir es ihm gegeben.
3. Wenn ich ihre Telefonnummer gewußt hätte, _____ ich sie angerufen.
4. Wenn sie wirklich krank gewesen wäre, _____ sie (she) nach Hause gegangen.
5. Wenn ich es gewußt hätte, _____ ich es dir gesagt.
6. Wenn er hier gewesen wäre, _____ du es gewußt.
7. Wenn ich das Geld gehabt hätte, _____ ich es gekauft.
8. Wenn wir mehr Geld gehabt hätten, _____ wir länger geblieben.
9. Wenn wir geflogen wären, _____ wir in zwei Stunden da gewesen.

- Supply the correct past tense form of subjunctive II.

EXAMPLE   Wenn ich Zeit gehabt hätte, _____ ich ins Kino _____.
                                                (gehen)

Wenn ich Zeit gehabt hätte, **wäre** ich ins Kino **gegangen**.

1. Wenn ich das Geld gehabt hätte, _____ ich es _____.
                                        (kaufen)

2. Wenn er es gebraucht hätte, _____ wir es ihm _____.
                                    (geben)

3. Wenn ich ihre Telefonnummer gewußt hätte, _____ ich sie _____.
                                                (an·rufen)

4. Wenn wir mehr Geld gehabt hätten, _____ wir länger _____.
                                        (bleiben)

5. Wenn er hier gewesen wäre, _____ du es _____.
                                (wissen)

6. Wenn wir geflogen wären, _____ wir in zwei Stunden da _____.
                                (sein)

7. Wenn ich mehr Zeit gehabt hätte, _____ ich es _____.
                                        (machen)

8. Wenn ich es gewußt hätte, _____ ich es dir _____.
   (sagen)
9. Wenn sie wirklich krank gewesen wäre, _____ sie nach Hause _____.
   (gehen)

● Synthetic exercises: **Form the suggested dann**-clause using the past tense of subjunctive II.

EXAMPLE   Wenn ich Zeit gehabt hätte, ich / gehen / Kino
           Wenn ich Zeit gehabt hätte, **wäre** ich ins Kino **gegangen.**

1. Wenn ich ihre Telefonnummer gewußt hätte, ich / anrufen / sie
2. Wenn ich das Geld gehabt hätte, ich / kaufen / es
3. Wenn er es gebraucht hätte, wir / geben / es ihm
4. Wenn sie wirklich krank gewesen wäre, sie (she) / gehen / nach Hause
5. Wenn ich es gewußt hätte, ich / sagen / es dir
6. Wenn ich mehr Zeit gehabt hätte, ich / machen / es
7. Wenn wir geflogen wären, wir / sein / in zwei Stunden da
8. Wenn er hier gewesen wäre, du / wissen / es
9. Wenn wir mehr Geld gehabt hätten, wir / bleiben / länger

● Express in German: the **dann**-clause.

EXAMPLE   Wenn ich Zeit gehabt hätte, _____.
                                        (I would have gone to the movies)
           Wenn ich Zeit gehabt hätte, **wäre** ich ins Kino **gegangen.**

	(1)	(2)
would	have	gone
	wäre	**gegangen**

1. Wenn ich das Geld gehabt hätte, _____.
   (I would have bought it)
2. Wenn wir geflogen wären, _____.
   (we would have been there in two hours)
3. Wenn ich ihre Telefonnummer gewußt hätte, _____.
   (I would have called her)
4. Wenn er es gebraucht hätte, _____.
   (we would have given it to him)
5. Wenn ich mehr Zeit gehabt hätte, _____.
   (I would have done it)
6. Wenn wir mehr Geld gehabt hätten, _____.
   (we would have stayed longer)
7. Wenn sie wirklich krank gewesen wäre, _____.
   (she would have gone home)
8. Wenn ich es gewußt hätte, _____.
   (I would have told you)
9. Wenn er hier gewesen wäre, _____.
   (you would have known it)

- Express in German.

  1. If I had had more time, I would have done it.
  2. If he'd needed it, we would have given it to him.
  3. If we had had more money, we would have stayed longer.
  4. If I had known her telephone number, I would have called her.
  5. If I had known (it), I would have told you.
  6. If she had really been sick, she would have gone home.
  7. If I had had the money, I would have bought it.
  8. If he had been here, you would have known it.
  9. If we had flown, we would have been there in two hours.

3 Subjunctive II: Present and past tenses

- Synthetic exercises: Form the suggested **dann**-clause in the present **and past** tenses of subjunctive II. The tense of the **wenn**-clause will determine the tense of the **dann**-clause.

  1. Wenn ich mehr Zeit hätte, ich / machen / es
     Wenn ich mehr Zeit gehabt hätte, ich / machen / es
  2. Wenn ich ihre Telefonnummer wüßte, ich / anrufen / sie
     Wenn ich ihre Telefonnummer gewußt hätte, ich / anrufen / sie
  3. Wenn wir fliegen würden, wir / sein / in zwei Stunden da
     Wenn wir geflogen wären, wir / sein / in zwei Stunden da
  4. Wenn ich das Geld hätte, ich / kaufen / es
     Wenn ich das Geld gehabt hätte, ich / kaufen / es
  5. Wenn Sie früher kommen würden, ich / können / abholen / Sie
  6. Wenn er hier wäre, du / wissen / es
     Wenn er hier gewesen wäre, du / wissen / es
  7. Wenn wir mehr Zeit hätten, wir / können / machen / es
  8. Wenn er es brauchte, wir / geben / es / ihm
     Wenn er es gebraucht hätte, wir / geben / es / ihm
  9. Wenn sie wirklich krank wäre, sie (she) / gehen / nach Hause
     Wenn sie wirklich krank gewesen wäre, sie (she) / gehen / nach Hause
  10. Wenn ich es wüßte, ich / sagen / es / dir
      Wenn ich es gewußt hätte, ich / sagen / es / dir
  11. Wenn wir mehr Geld hätten, wir / bleiben / länger
      Wenn wir mehr Geld gehabt hätten, wir / bleiben / länger
  12. Wenn er nicht hier wäre, ich / müssen / machen / es allein

- Express in German.

  1. If I had the money, I'd buy it.
     If I had had the money, I would have bought it.
  2. If he needed it, we'd give it to him.
     If he had needed it, we would have given it to him.
  3. If I knew her telephone number, I'd call her.
     If I had known her telephone number, I would have called her.
  4. If we flew, we'd be there in two hours.
     If we had flown, we would have been there in two hours.
  5. If I knew (it), I'd tell you.
     If I had known (it), I would have told you.
  6. If we had more time, we could do it.

7. If you'd come earlier, I could pick you up.
8. If I had more time, I would do it.
   If I had had more time, I would have done it.
9. If he were here, you'd know it.
   If he had been here, you would have known it.
10. If we had more money, we'd stay longer.
    If we had had more money, we would have stayed longer.
11. If he weren't here, I'd have to do it alone.
12. If she were really sick, she'd go home.
    If she had really been sick, she would have gone home.

4   Present tense subjunctive II: the **wenn**-clause in 2nd position

● Supply the correct form of subjunctive II. Remember:

1. The one-word form is used with: weak verbs
   sein and **haben** (for example: **wäre, hätte**)
   wissen and the modals (for example: **wüßte, könnte**)

2. **Würde** + *infinitive* is used with all other verbs.

EXAMPLE   Es wäre besser, wenn Sie mit dem Zug _____ .
           (fahren)

Es wäre besser, wenn Sie mit dem Zug **fahren würden**.

Ich würde es kaufen, wenn es nicht so viel _____ .
           (kosten)

Ich würde es kaufen, wenn es nicht so viel **kostete**.

1. Es wäre viel besser, wenn wir einen Wagen _____ .
   (haben)
2. Ich würde mitkommen, wenn ich das Geld _____ .
   (haben)
3. Es wäre leichter, wenn wir in der Stadt _____ .
   (wohnen)
4. Ich würde es kaufen, wenn es nicht so viel _____ .
   (kosten)
5. Es wäre viel besser, wenn Sie später _____ .
   (kommen)
6. Er würde es machen, wenn er _____ .
   (können)
7. Ich würde es dir sagen, wenn ich es _____ .
   (wissen)
8. Es wäre leichter, wenn er Deutsch _____ .*
   (können)
9. Es wäre besser, wenn Sie mit dem Zug _____ .
   (fahren)

---

*"to know," in the sense of possessing an ability:
Er kann Deutsch. (He knows German—he can read it, write it, and so on.)

• Synthetic exercises: Form the suggested **wenn**-clause using the present tense of subjunctive II.

1. Ich würde es kaufen, wenn / es / kosten / nicht so viel
2. Es wäre leichter, wenn / wir / haben / Wagen
3. Er würde es machen, wenn / er / können
4. Ich würde mitkommen, wenn / ich / haben / Geld
5. Es wäre besser, wenn / Sie / kommen / später
6. Ich würde es dir sagen, wenn / ich / wissen / es
7. Es wäre leichter, wenn / sie (they) / können / Deutsch
8. Es wäre leichter, wenn / wir / wohnen / in / Stadt
9. Es wäre besser, wenn / Sie / fahren / mit / Zug

5 Past tense subjunctive II: The **wenn**-clause in 2nd position

• Supply the correct form of the past tense subjunctive II.

EXAMPLE Ich hätte es gekauft, wenn es nicht so viel _____.
(kosten)

Ich hätte es gekauft, wenn es nicht so viel **gekostet hätte.**

1. Es wäre leichter gewesen, wenn wir in der Stadt _____.
(wohnen)

2. Ich hätte es gekauft, wenn es nicht so viel _____.
(kosten)

3. Es wäre besser gewesen, wenn Sie mit dem Zug _____.
(fahren)

4. Ich hätte es dir gesagt, wenn ich es _____.
(wissen)

5. Es wäre besser gewesen, wenn Sie später _____.
(zurückkommen)

6. Es wäre leichter gewesen, wenn wir einen Wagen _____.
(haben)

7. Er hätte es gemacht, wenn er _____.
(können)

8. Ich wäre mitgekommen, wenn ich das Geld _____.
(haben)

9. Es wäre leichter gewesen, wenn sie (they) Deutsch _____.
(können)

• Synthetic exercises: Form the suggested **wenn**-clause using the past tense of subjunctive II.

1. Es wäre besser gewesen, wenn / Sie / kommen / später
2. Ich hätte es gekauft, wenn / es / kosten / nicht / so viel
3. Es wäre leichter gewesen, wenn / wir / haben / Wagen
4. Es wäre besser gewesen, wenn / Sie / fahren / mit / Zug
5. Ich hätte es dir gesagt, wenn / ich / wissen / es
6. Es wäre leichter gewesen, wenn / wir / wohnen / in / Stadt
7. Er hätte es gemacht, wenn / er / können
8. Ich wäre mitgekommen, wenn / ich / haben / das Geld
9. Es wäre leichter gewesen, wenn / sie (they) / können / Deutsch

6   Present and past tense subjunctive II: The wenn-clause in 2nd position

- Synthetic exercises: Form the suggested **wenn**-clause in the present and past tenses of subjunctive II. The tense of the first clause will determine the tense of the **wenn**-clause.

    1. Es wäre leichter, wenn / wir / haben / Wagen
       Es wäre leichter gewesen, wenn / wir / haben / Wagen
    2. Es wäre besser, wenn / Sie / kommen / später
       Es wäre besser gewesen, wenn / Sie / kommen / später
    3. Er würde es machen, wenn / er / können
       Er hätte es gemacht, wenn / er / können
    4. Ich würde mitkommen, wenn / ich / haben / Geld
       Ich wäre mitgekommen, wenn / ich / haben / Geld
    5. Ich würde es kaufen, wenn / es / kosten / nicht so viel
       Ich hätte es gekauft, wenn / es / kosten / nicht so viel
    6. Es wäre leichter, wenn / wir / wohnen / in / Stadt
       Es wäre leichter gewesen, wenn / wir / wohnen / in / Stadt
    7. Ich würde es dir sagen, wenn / ich / wissen / es
       Ich hätte es dir gesagt, wenn / ich / wissen / es
    8. Es wäre leichter, wenn / sie (they) / können / Deutsch
       Es wäre leichter gewesen, wenn / sie (they) können / Deutsch
    9. Es wäre besser, wenn / Sie / fahren / mit / Zug
       Es wäre besser gewesen, wenn / Sie / fahren / mit / Zug

- Express in German.

    1. I'd buy it if it didn't cost so much.
       I would have bought it if it hadn't cost so much.
    2. It would be better if you came later.
       It would have been better if you had come later.
    3. It would be easier if we lived downtown.
       It would have been easier if we had lived downtown.
    4. It would be easier if we had a car.
       It would have been easier if we had had a car.
    5. He'd do it if he could.
       He would have done it if he could have.
    6. It would be better if you went by train. (use **fahren**)
       It would have been better if you had gone by train.
    7. I'd tell you if I knew (it).
       I would have told you if I had known (it).
    8. It would be easier if they knew German. (use **können**)
       It would have been easier if they had known German.
    9. I'd come along if I had the money.
       I would have come along if I had had the money.

7   Mixed tenses in conditional sentences

- Supply the appropriate present subjunctive II form of **sein**.

    1. Wenn du später gegessen hättest, _____ du jetzt nicht so hungrig.
    2. Wenn wir geflogen wären, _____ wir schon da.

3. Er hätte es mir nicht gesagt, wenn es nicht wahr _____.
4. Wenn du früher ins Bett gegangen wärest, _____ du nicht so müde.

● Synthetic exercises (second clause): Form the second clause of each sentence using the present subjunctive II.

1. Er hätte es mir nicht gesagt, wenn / es / sein / nicht wahr
2. Wenn du früher ins Bett gegangen wärest, du / sein / nicht so müde
3. Wenn wir geflogen wären, wir / sein / schon da
4. Wenn du später gegessen hättest, du / sein / jetzt nicht so hungrig

● Synthetic exercises (first clause): Form the first clause of each sentence using the past subjunctive II.

1. Wenn / du / essen / später, wärest du jetzt nicht so hungrig.
2. Wenn / du / gehen / früher ins Bett, wärest du nicht so müde.
3. Er / sagen / es mir nicht, wenn es nicht wahr wäre.
4. Wenn / wir / fliegen, wären wir schon da.

● Synthetic exercises (both clauses): Form complete sentences using the tenses indicated.

1. Wenn / du / gehen / früher ins Bett // du / sein / nicht so müde
   (*past subjunctive II*)   (*present subjunctive II*)

2. Wenn / wir / fliegen // wir / sein / schon / da
   (*past subjunctive II*)   (*present subjunctive II*)

3. Wenn / du / später / essen // du / sein / jetzt / nicht so hungrig
   (*past subjunctive II*)   (*present subjunctive II*)

4. Er / sagen / es mir nicht // wenn / es / sein / nicht wahr
   (*past subjunctive II*)   (*present subjunctive II*)

● Express in German.

1. If we had flown, we would already be there.
2. If you had gone to bed earlier, you wouldn't be so tired.
3. He wouldn't have told it to me if it weren't true.
4. If you had eaten later, you wouldn't be so hungry now.

GRAND MIX

1   Synthetic exercises

● Form the suggested sentences. The tense of the first clause will cue the tense of the second clause, unless otherwise indicated.

a. 1. Wenn er es gebraucht hätte, wir / geben / es ihm
    2. Ich wäre gekommen, wenn / ich / haben / Geld
    3. Wenn ich das Geld hätte, ich / kaufen / es
    4. Wenn wir mehr Geld gehabt hätten, wir / bleiben / länger

5. Es wäre leichter, wenn / wir / wohnen / in / Stadt
6. Wenn er hier wäre, du / wissen / es
7. Wenn ich mehr Zeit hätte, ich / machen / es
8. Wenn sie wirklich krank gewesen wäre, sie (*she*) / gehen / nach Hause
9. Es wäre leichter, wenn / wir / haben / Wagen
10. Wenn Sie früher kommen würden, ich / können / abholen / Sie

b. 1. Wenn wir geflogen wären, wir / sein / in zwei Stunden da
2. Ich würde es kaufen, wenn / es / kosten / nicht so viel
3. Wenn ich es gewußt hätte, ich / sagen / es dir
4. Wenn du später gegessen hättest, du / sein / jetzt nicht so hungrig   (*present subjunctive II*)
5. Ich würde es dir sagen, wenn / ich / wissen / es
6. Wenn ich ihre Telefonnummer gewußt hätte, ich / anrufen / sie
7. Wenn wir mehr Zeit hätten, wir / können / machen / es
8. Wenn wir geflogen wären, wir / sein / schon da   (*present subjunctive II*)
9. Es wäre besser gewesen, wenn / Sie / fahren / mit / Zug
10. Wenn ich es wüßte, ich / sagen / es dir

c. 1. Er hätte es mir nicht gesagt, wenn / es / sein / nicht wahr   (*present subjunctive II*)
2. Es wäre leichter gewesen, wenn / sie (*she*) / können / Deutsch
3. Wenn er nicht hier wäre, ich / müssen / machen / es / allein
4. Es wäre besser gewesen, wenn / Sie / kommen / später
5. Wenn ich das Geld gehabt hätte, ich / kaufen / es
6. Er würde es machen, wenn / er / können
7. Wenn sie wirklich krank wäre, sie / gehen / nach Hause
8. Es wäre leichter gewesen, wenn / wir / wohnen / in / Stadt
9. Wenn wir mehr Geld hätten, wir / bleiben / länger
10. Es wäre leichter gewesen, wenn / wir / haben / Wagen

d. 1. Wenn er es brauchte, wir / geben / es ihm
2. Wenn ich mehr Zeit gehabt hätte, ich / machen / es
3. Es wäre besser, wenn / Sie / kommen / später
4. Wenn ich ihre Telefonnummer wüßte, ich / anrufen / sie
5. Wenn du früher ins Bett gegangen wärest, du / sein / nicht so müde   (*present subjunctive II*)
6. Ich würde mitkommen, wenn / ich / haben / das Geld
7. Wenn wir fliegen würden, wir / sein / in zwei Stunden da

2   Express in German

a. 1. If I had the money, I'd buy it.
2. If I had known her telephone number, I would have called her.
3. It would be easier if we had a car.
4. If I had had more time, I would have done it.
5. If he were here, you'd know it.
6. If we had flown, we would already be there.
7. I'd come along if I had the money.
8. If we had more time, we could do it.
9. He'd do it if he could.
10. If we had had more money, we would have stayed longer.

b. 1. It would be better if you came later.
2. If I knew (it), I'd tell you.
3. If he had needed it, we would have given it to him.

4. I'd buy it if it didn't cost so much.
5. If he weren't here, I'd have to do it alone.
6. If she had really been sick, she would have gone home.
7. I'd tell you if I knew.
8. If I knew her telephone number, I'd call her.
9. It would be easier if we lived downtown.
10. If you had eaten later, you wouldn't be so hungry now.

c. 1. If we had more money, we'd stay longer.
2. If we had flown, we would have been there in two hours.
3. It would have been easier if they had known German.
4. If you'd come earlier, I'd pick you up.
5. It would have been better if you had gone by train. (use **fahren**)
6. If you had gone to bed earlier, you wouldn't be so tired.
7. If we flew, we would be there in two hours.
8. It would have been easier if we had had a car.
9. If I had known (it), I would have told you.
10. If he needed it, we'd give it to him.

d. 1. I would have come along, if I had had the money.
2. If I had more time, I'd do it.
3. It would have been better if you had come later.
4. If I had had the money, I would have bought it.
5. If she were really sick, she'd go home.

VOCABULARY

können (kann) to know
how (*in the sense
of possessing
an ability*)
konnte, gekonnt
näher closer

selber oneself, herself,
myself (*etc.*)
die **Stunde, –n** hour
die **Telefonnummer, –n**
telephone number

tun (tut) to do
tat, getan
verdienen to earn

Lesson 9   Level THREE

A The Infinitival Clause

English and German form infinitival clauses in essentially the same way:

> Er bat mich, **ihn nach Hause zu fahren** .   (He asked me to drive him home.)
> Es ist nett, **Sie wiederzusehen** .   (It's nice to see you again.)

The only real difference is that the German *infinitive must be at the end of its clause,* and it is always immediately preceded by the preposition **zu:**

> . . . , ihn nach Hause **zu** fahren.   (. . . to drive him home.)
> . . . , Sie wieder **zu** sehen.   (. . . to see you again.)

With separable-prefix verbs **(wieder·sehen),** the **zu** comes between the prefix and the basic verb (wieder**zu**sehen).

▶ Note   Sie fing an **zu schreien.**   (She began to scream.)

When the construction consists *only* of an infinitive and the preposition **zu (zu schreien),** it is not considered to be a clause. For this reason it is *not* separated from the main clause by a comma. But as soon as another element is added, the infinitival construction becomes a full clause and must be separated from the main clause by a comma:

> Sie fing an, laut zu schreien.

DRILLS

Infinitival constructions

- Synthetic exercises: Use the following elements to construct sentences with infinitival clauses.

> EXAMPLE   Es ist zu spät // gehen / ins Kino
> Es ist zu spät, ins Kino **zu gehen** .

1. Es fängt an // werden / interessant   **(an·fangen, fängt . . . an, fing . . . an, angefangen:** to begin)
2. Er bat mich // fahren / ihn / nach Hause
3. Ich hatte keine Chance // antworten / ihm
4. Es ist gut // sein / wieder / hier
5. Es ist zu früh // gehen / ins Bett
6. Es freut mich // kennenlernen / Sie   (*I am pleased;* lit.: *it pleases me*)
7. Wir hatten keine Zeit // suchen / es
8. Es ist nett // wiedersehen / dich
9. Er hat versprochen // geben / es / mir   **(versprechen, verspricht, versprach, versprochen:** to promise)
10. Sie fängt an // werden / böse
11. Es ist sinnlos // warten / länger   **(sinnlos:** senseless; **länger:** [any] longer)

448

• Complete the infinitival clauses.

1. Es ist sinnlos, länger _____. (to wait)

2. Ich hatte keine Chance, ihm _____. (to answer)

3. Es ist zu früh, ins Bett _____. (to go)

4. Sie fängt an, böse _____. (to get, become)

5. Er bat mich, ihn nach Hause _____. (to drive)

6. Es ist gut, wieder hier _____. (to be)

7. Es freut mich, Sie _____. (to meet)

8. Er hat versprochen, es mir _____. (to give)

9. Es fängt an, interessant _____. (to get, become)

10. Wir hatten keine Zeit, es _____. (to look for)

11. Es ist nett, dich _____. (to see . . . again)

• Express the infinitival clauses in German.

1. Wir hatten keine Zeit, _____. (to look for it)

2. Es ist nett, _____. (to see you again)

3. Er hat versprochen, _____. (to give it to me)

4. Es ist sinnlos, _____. (to wait [any] longer)

5. Sie fängt an, _____. (to get mad)

6. Es freut mich, _____. (to meet you)

7. Er bat mich, _____. (to drive him home)

8. Es fängt an, _____. (to get interesting)

9. Ich hatte keine Chance, _____. (to answer him)

10. Es ist zu früh, _____. (to go to bed)

11. Es ist gut, _____. (to be here again)

• Express in German.

1. It's too early to go to bed.
2. We didn't have any time to look for it.
3. He asked me to drive him home.
4. It's beginning to get interesting.
5. Pleased to meet you.
6. It's senseless to wait (any) longer.

7. It's nice to see you again.
8. I didn't have a chance to answer him.
9. It's good to be here again.
10. She's beginning to get mad.
11. He promised to give it to me.

B um . . . zu, ohne . . . zu, statt . . . zu

The prepositions **um, ohne,** and **statt** may introduce infinitival clauses:

$$\left.\begin{array}{l}\textbf{um}\\\textbf{ohne}\\\textbf{statt}\end{array}\right\}\ldots\ \textbf{zu}\ +\ \textit{infinitive}$$

um . . . zu	Er kam, **um** mich ab **zu** holen.
	(He came [*in order*] *to* pick me up.)
ohne . . . zu	Er hat es getan, **ohne** mich **zu** fragen.
	(He did it *without* asking me.)
statt . . . zu	**Statt** hier **zu** sitzen, sollten wir etwas tun.
	(*Instead of* sitting here, we should do something.)

1. **Um . . . zu** *must* be used (instead of just **zu**) when one can sensibly use the phrase "in order to" in the equivalent English sentence.

2. **Ohne . . . zu** and **statt . . . zu** are used with *infinitives.* The English equivalents require a verb form ending with "-ing."

. . . , ohne mich **zu fragen.** (. . . , without *asking* me.)
Statt hier **zu sitzen,** . . . . (Instead of *sitting* here, ...)

DRILLS

um . . . zu, ohne . . . zu, statt . . . zu

• Supply the suggested preposition.

um . . . zu	in order to
ohne . . . zu	without . . . -ing
statt . . . zu	instead of . . . -ing

EXAMPLE   Ich fahre nach Berlin, _____ meine Eltern zu besuchen.
                                               (in order to)
          Ich fahre nach Berlin, **um** meine Eltern zu besuchen.

1. Ich bin gekommen, _____ dir zu helfen.
                              (in order to)

2. Er hat es getan, _____ mich zu fragen.
                           (without)

3. Er kam, _____ mich abzuholen.
                    (in order to)

4. _____ hier zu sitzen, sollten wir etwas tun.
       (Instead of)

5. Ich fahre nach Berlin, _____ meine Eltern zu besuchen.
                                  (in order to)   (die Eltern [*plural only*]: parents)

6. Sie stand auf und ging weg, _____ ein Wort zu sagen.   (das Wort: word)
                                      (without)

7. _____ eine Wohnung zu mieten, wollen wir ein Haus kaufen.   (mieten: to rent)
       (Instead of)

8. Er ging vorbei, _____ mich zu sehen.   (vorbei · gehen: to walk by)
                         (without)

- Supply the suggested combination of a preposition + **zu**.

EXAMPLE   Ich fahre nach Berlin, _____ meine Eltern _____ besuchen.

(in order to)

Ich fahre nach Berlin, **um** meine Eltern **zu** besuchen.

1. Er ging vorbei, _____ mich ___ sehen.

(without)

2. Er kam, _____ mich ab___ holen.

(in order to)

3. _____ eine Wohnung ___ mieten, wollen wir ein Haus kaufen.

(Instead of)

4. Sie stand auf und ging weg, _____ ein Wort ___ sagen.

(without)

5. Ich bin gekommen, _____ dir ___ helfen.

(in order to)

6. _____ hier ___ sitzen, sollten wir etwas tun.

(Instead of)

7. Ich fahre nach Berlin, _____ meine Eltern ___ besuchen.

(in order to)

8. Er hat es getan, _____ mich ___ fragen.

(without)

- Synthetic exercises: Use the following elements to construct sentences with infinitival clauses.

EXAMPLE   Er kam // um / abholen / mich

Er kam, **um** mich **abzuholen.**

1. Ich fahre nach Berlin // um / besuchen / meine Eltern
2. Er ging vorbei // ohne / sehen / mich
3. Ich bin gekommen // um / helfen / dir
4. Statt / sitzen / hier // sollten wir etwas tun.
5. Sie stand auf und ging weg // ohne / sagen / ein Wort
6. Er kam // um / abholen / mich
7. Statt / mieten / Wohnung // wollen wir ein Haus kaufen.
8. Er hat es getan // ohne / fragen / mich

- Express the following infinitival clauses in German.

1. Ich fahre nach Berlin, _____.

(to visit my parents)

2. Er hat es getan, _____.

(without asking me)

3. Er kam, _____.

(to pick me up)

4. _____, sollten wir etwas tun.

(Instead of sitting here)

5. Ich bin gekommen, _____.

(to help you)

6. Sie stand auf und ging weg, _____.
   (without saying a word)

7. _____, wollen wir ein Haus kaufen.
   (Instead of renting an apartment)

8. Er ging vorbei, _____.
   (without seeing me)

- Express in German.

1. He came to pick me up.
2. He did it without asking me.
3. I'm going to Berlin to visit my parents.
4. Instead of renting an apartment, we want to buy a house.
5. I came to help you.
6. She got up and left without saying a word.
7. Instead of sitting here, we should do something.
8. He walked by without seeing me.

C sein + zu + Infinitive

Look at the following examples:

Das **ist** schwer **zu sagen.**	(That *is* hard *to say.*)
Das Stück **ist** nicht leicht **zu verstehen.**	(The play *isn't* easy *to understand.*)

Both English and German have the same pattern, but it is far more common in German. In fact, many German sentences of this type have no exact counterpart in English.

Das **ist** nicht **zu machen.**	(That can't be done.)
Der Wagen **ist** nicht **zu reparieren.**	(The car can't be repaired.)

When the pattern doesn't work in English, one usually finds "can" + a *passive infinitive* (passive infinitive = "be" + *past participle*, such as "be done"):

ist zu machen   can be done

DRILLS

sein + zu + infinitive

- Supply **zu** + infinitive.

1. Das ist schwer _____.
   (to say)

2. So etwas ist nicht leicht _____.
   (to find)   (**so etwas:** something like that)

3. Das ist leicht _____.
   (to do)

4. Sein Wagen war nicht _____.
   ([couldn't] be repaired)

5. Der Brief war leicht _____.
   (to translate)

(übersetzen: to translate)

6. Das Stück ist schwer _____.
   (to understand)

7. Das ist nicht _____.
   (to do)

● Synthetic exercises: Construct sentences from the following elements using the correct form of
sein + **zu** + the infinitive.

EXAMPLE   Das / sein / leicht / finden
           Das **ist** leicht **zu finden**.

1. Das / sein / leicht / machen
2. Das / sein / schwer / sagen
3. Dieser Brief / sein / leicht / übersetzen
4. Sein Wagen / sein / nicht / reparieren

5. So etwas / sein / nicht leicht / finden
6. Das Stück / sein / schwer / verstehen
7. Das / sein / nicht / machen

● Express in German.

1. The letter was easy to translate.
2. That's hard to say.
3. That can't be done.
4. The play is hard to understand.

5. His car couldn't be repaired.
6. That's easy to do.
7. Something like that isn't easy to find.

D Contrastive Grammar

There are three common environments where English uses infinitival constructions
but German does not.

1. A clause introduced by a question word:

Ich weiß nicht, **wann** ich kommen sollte.   I don't know *when* to come.
               was ich machen sollte.   *what* to do.
               wohin ich gehen sollte.   *where* to go.

In these instances English has a choice between two constructions:

I don't know *what to do.*
I don't know *what I should do.*

But German has no such choice. It must use a construction similar to the second English example, a clause with a subject and a *conjugated verb:*

Ich weiß nicht, was ich machen sollte.

2. A main clause with **sagen:**

Er sagte mir, daß ich es tun sollte.   (He told me to do it.)
(He told me that I should do it.)

Here again English has a choice, and German does not. After **sagen,** German uses a full clause with a subject and a conjugated verb (most often a form of **sollen**).

3. The special case of **wollen:**

You have already seen **wollen** followed by infinitives without **zu:**

Er will essen.   (He wants to eat.)

This is normal modal usage in German. In our example, the verb **essen** is called a *dependent infinitive,* and it can be modified and complemented in various ways.

Er will hier essen.   (Hier is an adverb showing where he wants to eat.)

Er will Steak essen.   (Steak is the direct object of essen; it shows what he wants to eat.)

English has analogous constructions:

He wants to eat here.   (Here is an adverb modifying to eat.)
He wants to eat steak.   (Steak is the direct object of to eat.)

But look at this example:

He wants us to eat here.

How is "us" functioning in this sentence? It is certainly not the direct object of "to eat." (Otherwise the sentence would read, "He wants to eat us here.") Who is doing the eating? "Us is," or, more properly, "We are." By an odd English grammatical convention, "us" (a direct object!) is functioning as the *subject* of the infinitival phrase.

German can't do this. In German, the object of the verb **wollen** cannot function as the subject of an infinitival clause. In such cases German has to use a full clause with a conjugated verb.

Thus   Er will hier essen.   (He wants to eat here.)
Er will Steak essen.   (He wants to eat steak.)
but   Er will, daß wir hier essen.   (He wants us to eat here.)
(Lit.: He wants that we eat here.)

DRILLS

1 Sentence combination

• The following sentences can*not* use infinitival constructions, even though English commonly uses them in these environments. Combine these pairs of sentences, omitting items in parentheses from the compound sentences. Subordinate word order is required in all cases.

EXAMPLE   Wissen Sie (es)?
            Wohin sollten wir gehen?

            Wissen Sie, **wohin wir gehen sollten?**

1. Können Sie (es) mir sagen?
   Wie kommt man zum Bahnhof?
2. Ich weiß (es) nicht.
   Wann sollte ich kommen?
3. Wissen Sie (es)?
   Wie macht man das?
4. Wissen Sie (es)?
   Wohin sollten wir gehen?
5. Ich bin nicht sicher.
   Mit wem sollte ich sprechen?   (**wem**: whom [*dat. of* **wer**])
6. Wir wußten (es) nicht.
   Was sollten wir tun?

• Combine the following clauses with the subordinating conjunction **daß**.

1. Er sagte (es) mir.   **daß**   Ich sollte es Ihnen geben.
2. Ich sagte (es) ihm.   **daß**   Er sollte es tun.
3. Er will (es).   **daß**   Ich mache es.
4. Ich will (es).   **daß**   Du nimmst ihn mit.
5. Sie sagte (es) mir.   **daß**   Ich sollte nach Hause gehen.

2 Synthetic exercises

1. Ich weiß nicht // wann / ich / sollen / kommen
2. Er sagte mir // daß / ich / sollen / geben / es Ihnen
3. Wissen Sie // wie / man / machen / das / ?
4. Ich sagte ihm // daß / er / sollen / tun / es
5. Ich will // daß / du / mitnehmen / ihn
6. Wissen Sie // wohin / wir / sollen / gehen / ?
7. Ich bin nicht sicher // mit wem / ich / sollen / sprechen
8. Sie sagte mir // daß / ich / sollen / gehen / nach Hause
9. Können Sie mir sagen // wie / man / kommen / Bahnhof / ?
10. Er will // daß / ich / machen / es
11. Wir wußten nicht // was / wir / sollen / tun

3 Express in German: subordinate clause only

● Supply the subordinate clause suggested by the English cues. Two English equivalents are given for each subordinate clause. The first is colloquial English. The second is a "literal" translation similar to the German sentence structure.

1. Wir wußten nicht, _____.
   (what to do,
   what we should do)

2. Ich sagte ihm, _____.
   (to do it,
   that he should do it)

3. Wissen Sie, _____?
   (where to go,
   where we should go)

4. Er sagte mir, _____.
   (to give it to you,
   that I should give it to you)

5. Ich weiß nicht, _____.
   (when to come,
   when I should come)

6. Er will, _____.
   (me to do it,
   that I do it)

7. Ich bin nicht sicher, _____.
   (who to talk to,
   who I should talk to)

8. Sie sagte mir, _____.
   (to go home,
   that I should go home)

9. Wissen Sie, _____?
   (how to do it,
   how one does that)

10. Können Sie mir sagen, _____?
    (how to get to the station,
    how one gets to the station)

11. Ich will, _____.
    (you to take him along,
    "that you take him along")

4 Express in German

1. I don't know when to come.
2. We didn't know what to do.
3. I told him to do it.
4. She told me to go home.
5. I'm not sure who to talk to.
6. Can you tell me how to get to the station?
7. He told me to give it to you.
8. He wants me to do it.
9. Do you know how to do it?
10. I want you to take him along.
11. Do you know where to go?

MIXED DRILLS

1 Synthetic exercises

a. 1. Es ist nett // wiedersehen / dich
   2. Er hat es getan // ohne / fragen / mich
   3. Das / sein / leicht / machen
   4. Es ist sinnlos // warten / länger
   5. Ich weiß nicht // wann / ich / sollen / kommen
   6. Ich fahre nach Berlin // um / besuchen / meine Eltern
   7. Es ist zu früh // gehen / ins Bett
   8. Ich sagte ihm // daß / er / sollen / tun / es
   9. Der Brief / sein / leicht / übersetzen
   10. Ich hatte keine Chance // antworten / ihm

b. 1. Wir wußten nicht // was / wir / sollen / tun
   2. Ich bin gekommen // um / helfen / dir
   3. Sie sagte mir // daß / ich / sollen / gehen / nach Hause
   4. Es fängt an // werden / interessant
   5. Statt / sitzen / einfach hier // sollten wir etwas tun.
   6. Das / sein / schwer / sagen
   7. Er will // daß / ich / machen / es
   8. Er kam // um / abholen / mich
   9. Ich bin nicht sicher // mit wem / ich / sollen / sprechen
   10. Er bat mich // fahren / ihn / nach Hause

c. 1. Sein Wagen / sein / nicht / reparieren
   2. Er ging vorbei // ohne / sehen / mich
   3. Können Sie mir sagen // wie / man / kommen / Bahnhof / ?
   4. Es ist gut // sein / wieder / hier
   5. Statt / mieten / Wohnung // wollen wir ein Haus kaufen.
   6. So etwas / sein / nicht leicht / finden
   7. Sie fängt an // werden / böse
   8. Wissen Sie // wohin / wir / sollen / gehen / ?
   9. Es freut mich // kennenlernen / Sie
   10. Er hat versprochen // geben / es mir

d. 1. Wissen Sie // wie / man / machen / das / ?
   2. Sie stand auf und ging weg // ohne / sagen / Wort
   3. Wir hatten keine Zeit // suchen / es
   4. Das Stück / sein / schwer / verstehen
   5. Er sagte mir // daß / ich / sollen / geben / es Ihnen
   6. Das / sein / nicht / machen

2 Express in German

a. 1. It's too early to go to bed.
   2. That's easy to do.
   3. I came to help you.
   4. I don't know when to come.
   5. It's nice to see you again.
   6. He did it without asking me.

7. I told him to do it.
8. It's beginning to get interesting.
9. The letter was easy to translate.
10. He came to pick me up.

b. 1. He told me to give it to you.
2. It's senseless to wait any longer.
3. She got up and left without saying a word.
4. The play was hard to understand.
5. He asked me to drive him home.
6. Instead of just sitting here, we should do something.
7. We didn't know what to do.
8. His car couldn't be repaired.
9. He promised to give it to me.
10. I'm going to Berlin to visit my parents.

c. 1. She told me to go home.
2. She's beginning to get mad.
3. That's hard to say.

4. He wants me to do it.
5. Pleased to meet you.
6. Instead of renting an apartment, we want to buy a house.
7. Do you know how to do that?
8. We don't have any time to look for it.
9. Can you tell me how to get to the station?
10. He walked by without seeing me.

d. 1. I didn't have a chance to answer him.
2. Do you know where to go?
3. It's good to be here again.
4. That can't be done.
5. I'm not sure who to talk to.

VOCABULARY

an · fangen (fängt an) to begin
   fing an, angefangen
die **Eltern** (pl. only) parents
   länger (any) longer
   mieten rent
   sinnlos senseless
   so etwas something like that
   übersetzen to translate

versprechen (verspricht) to promise
   versprach, versprochen
vorbei · gehen to walk by
   ging . . . vorbei, ist vorbeigegangen
das **Wort, ⁻er** word

Reading IX

Ein Flug° nach Deutschland

der Flug, ⁼e: flight (*of planes*)

Wenn Sie nach Deutschland fliegen, buchen° Sie am besten einen Direktflug° (oder, wie viele Deutsche sagen: einen Nonstopflug°). Und passen Sie auf,° wann Ihr Flug in Deutschland ankommt. Genau wie° in einer fremden Stadt wollen Sie in einem

buchen: to book

der Direktflug, ⁼e: direct flight
der Nonstopflug, ⁼e: non stop flight
auf · passen: to watch out (for)

genau wie: just as

NICHT RAUCHEN   BITTE ANSCHNALLEN
SCHWIMMWESTE UNTER IHREM SITZ

fremden Land morgens ankommen. Sagen wir, Sie fliegen von New York nach Frankfurt. Vom Kennedy Flughafen° in New York nach dem Rhein–Main Flughafen/Frankfurt fliegen Sie ungefähr sieben Stunden. Aber Sie müssen auch mit einem Zeitunterschied° rechnen:° es ist nämlich° 5 Stunden später in Frankfurt als in New York. Also,° wenn Sie um 9 Uhr abends (21.00 Uhr) von New York abfliegen,° ist es schon 2.00 Uhr morgens in Frankfurt (mitteleuropäische Zeit° [MEZ]). Nach einem Flug von 7 Stunden kommen Sie also um 9.00 Uhr morgens (Ortszeit°) an. Sie werden höchstens° vier bis fünf Stunden schlafen können, und Sie werden vielleicht Schwierigkeiten° mit dem Zeitsprung° haben.

Im Flugzeug° wird Ihre Umgebung° schon halb deutsch: Sie sehen deutsche Zeitungen und Zeitschriften, die Stewardessen° sind meistens° deutsch und die Ansagen° werden auf deutsch und auf englisch gemacht. Auch die Schilder° sind oft auf deutsch, besonders wenn Sie Lufthansa fliegen. Statt „FASTEN SEATBELTS" steht „BITTE AN-SCHNALLEN".° Wenn Sie etwas trinken wollen, können Sie entweder° mit amerikanischem oder mit deutschem Geld zahlen.

Kurz° vor der Landung° macht der Flugkapitän° eine Ansage. Er gibt Ihnen den Wetterbericht,° die

der Flughafen, ⸚: airport

der Zeitunterschied, –e: time change   **rechnen mit:** to take into account **nämlich:** namely
also: so, thus
ab·fliegen: to depart

mitteleuropäische Zeit: Central European Time

die Ortszeit: local time   **höchstens:** at most

die Schwierigkeit, –en: difficulty **der Zeitsprung:** jet lag

das Flugzeug, –e: airplane **die Umgebung, –en:** surroundings

die Stewardeß, –essen: stewardess **meistens:** mostly, in most cases **die Ansage, –n:** announcement
das Schild, –er: sign

an·schnallen: to fasten seatbelts

entweder . . . oder: either . . . or

kurz: shortly   **die Landung, –en:** landing **der Flugkapitän, –e:** flight captain **der Wetterbericht, –e:** weather report

Fragen 1–4, pp. 463–64

Ortszeit, und sagt Ihnen, zum Beispiel, daß das Flugzeug voraussichtlich° in 20 Minuten im Rhein–Main Flughafen landen° wird. Dann hören Sie eine Ansage von der Stewardeß. Sie sagt, daß Sie nicht mehr rauchen dürfen, daß Sie sich anschnallen° sollen, und daß Sie Ihren Sitz° aufrecht° stellen sollen. Eine Minute° bevor das Flugzeug hält, sagt sie, daß Sie sitzenbleiben° sollen, bis die Maschine° völlig° zum Stillstand° gekommen ist.

Sie nehmen Ihr Handgepäck° und steigen mit den anderen Passagieren° aus. Als erstes gehen Sie durch die Paßkontrolle.° Die Paßkontrolle ist meistens nur eine Formalität,° und der Beamte° wird Ihren Paß nur kurz ansehen. Sie gehen dann zur Gepäckausgabe° und warten, bis Ihr Gepäck auf der Transportanlage° vorbeikommt. (Hoffentlich° haben Sie nur wenig Gepäck mitgebracht, denn Sie müssen es selber tragen.) Sie nehmen Ihre Koffer° und gehen zum Zoll.° Da sehen Sie zwei Ausgänge° mit den Schildern „Anmeldefreie Waren"° und „Anmeldepflichtige Waren".° In den meisten Fällen° dürfen Sie ruhig° durch den Ausgang mit dem Schild „Anmeldefreie Waren" gehen. (Sie dürfen 200 Zigaretten, einen Liter° Wein oder Whisky und ein halbes Pfund° Kaffee zollfrei° mitbringen).

voraussichtlich: according to our estimates

landen: to land

sich an·schnallen: to fasten one's seatbelt

der Sitz, –e: seat **aufrecht**: vertical

die Minute, –n: minute

sitzen·bleiben: to remain seated
  die Maschine, –n: (here) aircraft
völlig: completely **der Stillstand**: stop

das Handgepäck: hand luggage

der Passagier, –e: passenger

die Paßkontrolle: immigration, passport check

die Formalität, –en: formality
  der Beamte, –n (*adj. noun*): official

die Gepäckausgabe, –n: baggage claim area

die Transportanlage, –n: luggage carousel
  hoffentlich: it is to be hoped

der Koffer, –: suitcase

der Zoll: customs **der Ausgang, ̈–e**: exit

anmeldefreie Waren: nothing to declare

anmeldepflichtige Waren: goods to declare
  der Fall, ̈–e: case
ruhig: just, without worrying

der Liter, –: liter

das Pfund: pound **zollfrei**: duty free

Fragen 5–8, 464

Erst jetzt° sind Sie wirklich° in Deutschland und jetzt brauchen Sie „wirkliches" Geld und das heißt von nun an° Deutsche Mark. In der Ankunftshalle° ist eine Wechselstube,° wo sie amerikanische Dollars° und Reiseschecks wechseln° können. Wechselstuben sind meistens von halb acht Uhr morgens bis halb zehn Uhr abends geöffnet.° Meistens müssen Sie Ihren Reisepaß vorzeigen.° Sie sollten genug wechseln, daß Sie mindestens° DM 100 bei sich° haben. Wenn Sie mit etwas deutschem Geld ankommen wollen, ist das auch möglich. In den internationalen° Flughäfen können Sie so viele Dollars wechseln wie Sie wollen.

Vom Rhein–Main Flughafen nach Frankfurt sind es° 11 Kilometer (1 km = 0,625 Meilen°), nach Mainz sind es ungefähr 40 km und nach Wiesbaden 42. Und es ist sehr leicht, dorthinzukommen,° denn, wie in vielen internationalen Flughäfen in Europa, gibt es

erst jetzt: not until now   **wirklich**: really

von nun an: from now on
 die Ankunftshalle, –n: arrival hall
die Wechselstube, –n: foreign currency
 exchange
der Dollar, –s: dollar   **wechseln**: to exchange

geöffnet: open

vor·zeigen: to show

mindestens: at least   **bei sich**: on you

international: international

es sind: *the plural form is used with* **es**
 because **es** *refers to* **11 Kilometer** (*a plural form*)
die Meile, –n: mile

dorthin·kommen: to get there

Flug Flight		nach to	über via	planm. scheduled	verspätet delayed	Flugsteig Gate
LH	606	TEL AVIV		9 50		B50-
OA	172	ATHEN-SALONIKI		9 55		B52-
LH	322	ANKARA-MUENCHEN		10 00		A 2-
LH	516	LIMA-CARACAS		10 00		B39-
LH	400	NEW YORK		10 00		A 6-
LH	346	WARSCHAU		10 05		A 3-
LH	360	BELGRAD		10 05		A15-
LH	650	OSAKA-ANCHORAGE		10 05		A17-
SQ	072	LONDON		10 05		B45-
LH	016	STOCKHOLM		10 10		A 4-
PA	413	NEW YORK		10 10		B32-
SR	533	ZUERICH		10 10		B42-
LH	170	BARCELONA		10 15		B55-
LZ	6032	BOURGAS		10 15		C63-
LH	290	ROM		10 20		B56-
PA	686	BERLIN		10 20		B -

einen kleinen Bahnhof unter dem Flughafengebäude.° Nicht weit° von dem Zollausgang° ist ein
Fahrkartenautomat. Sie kaufen da Ihre Fahrkarte
und fahren mit der Rolltreppe zwei Stockwerke
nach unten° in den Bahnhof. Nach Frankfurt
dauert° es nur 10 Minuten, nach Mainz ungefähr
eine halbe Stunde. Dann sind Sie in einem richtigen°
Bahnhof in einer Stadt.

das Flughafengebäude, –: terminal
nicht weit: not far
der Zollausgang, ⁼e: customs exit

nach unten: down
dauern: to take (of time)
richtig: real

agen
9-16
464

FRAGEN

1. Wie fliegt man am besten?
   (Man / sollen / buchen / Direktflug)
   (Und / man / sollen / an·kommen / morgens)
2. Sie fliegen von New York ab und wollen um 9 Uhr morgens in Frankfurt ankommen. Wann
   fliegen Sie ab? Warum?
   (Man / ab·fliegen / 9.00 / abends / New York)
   (Dann / es / sein / schon / 2.00 / morgens / Frankfurt)
   (Das / sein / M. . . E. . . Z. . .)
   (Flug / dauern / 7 Stunden // und / man / an·kommen / also / 9.00 / morgens /
   Frankfurt)

3. Wie lange schläft man im Flugzeug?
(Man / können / schlafen / höchstens / 4 - 5 / Stunden)

4. Wie sieht die Umgebung im Flugzeug aus, besonders wenn Sie mit Lufthansa fliegen?
(In / Flugzeug / Umgebung / werden / halb deutsch)
(Man / sehen / deutsch / Zeitungen // Stewardessen / sein / meistens / deutsch // und / Ansagen / gemacht [passive] / deutsch / englisch)
(Man / sehen / auch / deutsch / Schilder)
(Und / man / können / zahlen / amerikanisch / oder / deutsch / Geld)

5. Was für Ansagen macht der Flugkapitän kurz vor der Landung?
(Er / geben / Wetterbericht / Ortszeit)
(Er / sagen / auch // wann / Flugzeug / landen) [2nd clause future]

6. Was für Ansagen macht die Stewardeß?
(Sie / sagen // daß / man / dürfen / rauchen / nicht mehr)
(Sie / sagen / auch // daß / man / sollen / an · schnallen [refl.] // und / daß / man / sollen / stellen / Sitz / aufrecht)

7. Was macht man gleich nach der Landung?
(Man / gehen / durch / Paßkontrolle)
(Dann / man / gehen / zu / Gepäckausgabe)
(Man / warten / bis / Gepäck / vorbei · kommen / auf / Transportanlage)
(Man / nehmen / Koffer / und / gehen / dann / zu / Zoll)

8. Was sieht man da?
(Da / man / sehen / 2 Ausgänge / mit / Schilder / „Anmeldefreie Waren" / „Anmeldepflichtige Waren")

9. Wo bekommen Sie deutsches Geld?
(In / Ankunftshalle / sein / Wechselstube)
(Da / Sie / können / wechseln / Reiseschecks / und / amerikanisch / Dollars)
(Meistens / man / müssen / vor · zeigen / Reisepaß)

10. Wieviel und was für Geld soll man bei sich haben?
(Man / sollen / haben / mindestens / DM 100)

11. Ist es möglich, deutsches Geld in den Vereinigten Staaten zu bekommen?
(Ja // in / viel- / international / Flughäfen / Sie / können / wechseln / Dollars)

12a. Wieviele Kilometer sind es vom Rhein–Main Flughafen nach Frankfurt?
(Es / sein / 11 Kilometer)
  b. Ungefähr wieviele Meilen sind das?
(Es / sein / ungefähr / . . .)

13a. Wieviele Kilometer sind es vom Rhein–Main Flughafen nach Mainz?
(Es / sein / ungefähr / 40 km)
  b. Ungefähr wieviele Meilen sind das?
(Es / sein / ungefähr / . . .)

14. Wie kommt man vom Flughafen nach Frankfurt oder Mainz?
(Es / geben / klein / Bahnhof / unter / Flughafengebäude)

15. Wo bekommt man seine Fahrkarte?
(Man / bekommen / Fahrkarte / von / Fahrkartenautomat)

16. Wie kommt man in den Bahnhof?
(Man / fahren / mit / Rolltreppe / in / Bahnhof)

Peter Bichsel:
„Der Mann mit dem Gedächtnis"°

das Gedächtnis: memory

Ich kannte einen Mann, der wußte den ganzen Fahrplan auswendig,° denn° das einzige,° was ihm Freude machte,° waren Eisenbahnen, und er verbrachte° seine Zeit auf° dem Bahnhof, schaute,° wie die Züge ankamen und wie sie wegfuhren. Er bestaunte° die Wagen,° die Kraft° der Lokomotiven,° die Größe° der Räder,° bestaunte die aufspringenden° Kondukteure° und den Bahnhofsvorstand.°

auswendig: by heart **denn:** because
 das einzige: the only thing
einem Freude machen: to make one happy
verbringen: to spend (of time) **verbrachte,**
 verbracht auf (dem Bahnhof): outside,
 by the tracks **schauen:** to look
bestaunen: to stare at with amazement
 der Wagen, –: (here) railroad car **die Kraft:**
 power **die Lokomotive, –n:** locomotive
die Größe: size **das Rad, ⁻er:** wheel
aufspringend: (here) someone jumping aboard
 der Kondukteur, –e: conductor
der Bahnhofsvorstand, ⁻e: station master

Er kannte jeden Zug, wußte, woher° er kam, wohin er ging, wann er irgendwo° ankommen wird, und welche Züge von da wieder abfahren und wann diese ankommen werden.

woher: where . . . from

irgendwo: somewhere

Er wußte die Nummern der Züge, er wußte an welchen Tagen sie fahren, ob sie einen Speisewagen haben, ob sie die Anschlüsse° abwarten° oder nicht. Er wußte, welche Züge Postwagen° führen° und wieviel eine Fahrkarte nach Frauenfeld, nach Olten, nach Niederbipp oder irgendwohin° kostete.

der Anschluß, ⁻sse: connection
 ab · warten: to wait for (connecting trains)
der Postwagen, –: postal car
 führen: (here) to carry

irgendwohin: any place

Er ging in keine Wirtschaft,° ging nicht ins Kino, nicht spazieren, er besaß° kein Fahrrad,° kein Radio,° kein Fernsehen,° las keine Zeitungen, keine Bücher, und wenn er Briefe bekommen hätte, hätte er auch diese nicht gelesen. Dazu fehlte° ihm die Zeit, denn er verbrachte seine Tage im Bahnhof, und

die Wirtschaft, –en: Gaststätte
besitzen: to own **besaß, besessen**
 das Fahrrad, ⁻er: bicycle
das Radio, –s: radio **das Fernsehen:** TV

die Zeit fehlte ihm: lit. he was lacking the time
 fehlen (+ dat.) to lack

nur wenn der Fahrplan wechselte,° im Mai und im Oktober, sah man ihn einige Wochen nicht mehr.

Dann saß er zu Hause an seinem Tisch und lernte auswendig, las den neuen Fahrplan von der ersten bis zur° letzten Seite, merkte° sich die Änderungen° und freute° sich über sie.

Es kam auch vor,° daß ihn jemand nach einer Abfahrtszeit° fragte. Dann strahlte° er übers ganze Gesicht° und wollte genau° wissen, wohin die Reise gehe,° und wer ihn fragte, verpaßte° die Abfahrtszeit bestimmt,° denn er ließ den Frager° nicht mehr los,° gab sich nicht damit zufrieden,° die Zeit zu nennen,° er nannte gleich die Nummer des Zuges, die Anzahl° der Wagen, die möglichen Anschlüsse, die Fahrzeiten;° erklärte,° daß man mit diesem Zug nach Paris fahren könne,° wo man umsteigen müsse° und wann man ankäme,° und er begriff° nicht, daß das die Leute nicht interessierte.° Wenn ihn aber jemand stehenließ° und weiter ging,° bevor er sein ganzes Wissen° erzählt hatte, wurde er böse, beschimpfte° die Leute und rief ihnen nach:° „Sie haben keine Ahnung° von Eisenbahnen!"

Er selbst bestieg° nie einen Zug. Das hätte auch keinen Sinn,° sagte er, denn er wisse° ja zum voraus,° wann der Zug ankomme.°

„Nur Leute mit schlechtem Gedächtnis fahren Eisenbahn," sagte er, „denn wenn sie ein gutes Gedächtnis hätten, so könnten sie sich doch wie ich die Abfahrts- und die Ankunftszeit merken, und sie müßten nicht fahren, um die Zeit zu erleben."°

Ich versuchte es ihm zu erklären, ich sagte: „Es gibt aber Leute, die° freuen sich über die Fahrt,° die

---

wechseln: to change

bis zur: up to the sich etwas merken: to make a mental note of something die Änderung, –en: change
sich freuen über: to be happy about

vor·kommen: to happen kam . . . vor, ist vorgekommen
die Abfahrtszeit, –en: departure time
strahlen: to beam
das Gesicht, –er: face genau: exactly

gehe: geht verpassen: to miss
bestimmt: definitely der Frager, –: person asking a question
los·lassen: to let go ließ . . . los, losgelassen
sich zufrieden geben mit: to be satisfied with gab . . . zufrieden, zufriedengegeben
nennen: to mention nannte, genannt
die Anzahl: number
die Fahrzeit, –en: travelling time
erklären: to explain
könne: kann
müsse: muß ankäme: ankommt begreifen: to understand, conceive begriff, begriffen
interessieren: to interest
stehen·lassen: to leave standing (läßt . . . stehen), ließ stehen, stehengelassen weiter·gehen: to walk on by
das Wissen: knowledge
beschimpfen: to curse at nach·rufen (+ dat.) to scream after rief . . . nach, nachgerufen
die Ahnung: idea, glimmer

besteigen: to climb onto bestieg, bestiegen

einen Sinn haben: to make sense wisse: weiß

zum voraus: im voraus ankomme: ankommt

um die Zeit zu erleben: in order to experience time

die = sie die Fahrt: trip

fahren gern Eisenbahn und schauen zum Fenster hinaus und schauen,° wo sie vorbeikommen.“°

zum Fenster hinaus·schauen: to look out the window   vorbei·kommen: to pass
kam . . . vorbei, ist vorbeigekommen

Da wurde er böse, denn er glaubte, ich wolle° ihn auslachen,° und er sagte: „Auch das steht im Fahrplan, sie kommen an Luterbach vorbei und an Deitigen, an Wangen, Niederbipp, Önsingen, Oberbuchsiten, Egerkingen und Hägendorf.“

wolle: wollte

aus·lachen: to laugh at

„Vielleicht müssen die Leute mit der Bahn° fahren, weil sie irgendwohin wollen,“ sagte ich.

die Bahn: Eisenbahn

„Auch das kann nicht wahr sein,“ sagte er, „denn fast alle kommen irgend einmal° zurück, und es gibt sogar° Leute, die° steigen jeden Morgen hier ein und kommen jeden Abend zurück—so ein schlechtes Gedächtnis haben sie.“

irgend einmal: some time or other

sogar: even   die = sie

Und er begann die Leute auf dem Bahnhof zu beschimpfen. Er rief ihnen nach: „Ihr Idioten,° ihr habt kein Gedächtnis.“ Er rief ihnen nach: „An Hägendorf werdet ihr vorbeikommen,“ und er glaubte, er verderbe ihnen damit den Spaß.°

der Idiot, −en: idiot

einem den Spaß verderben: to spoil someone's fun   verderben: to spoil (verdirbt), verdarb, verdorben   verderbe = verdirbt

Er rief: „Sie Dummkopf,° Sie sind schon gestern gefahren.“ Und als die Leute nur lachten,° begann° er sie von den Trittbrettern° zu reißen° und beschwor° sie, ja nicht mit dem Zug zu fahren.

der Dummkopf, ⁼e: fool
lachen: to laugh   beginnen: to begin begann, begonnen
das Trittbrett, −er: steps of a train reißen: to tear, yank riß, gerissen
beschwören: to plead with beschwor, beschworen

„Ich kann Ihnen alles erklären,“ schrie° er, „Sie kommen um 14 Uhr 27 an Hägendorf vorbei, ich weiß es genau, und Sie werden es sehen, sie verbrauchen° Ihr Geld für nichts, im Fahrplan steht alles.“

schreien: to yell, scream   schrie, geschrieen

verbrauchen: to use up

Bereits° versuchte er die Leute zu verprügeln.° „Wer° nicht hören will, muß fühlen,°“ rief er.

bereits: already   verprügeln: to beat up

wer: whoever   fühlen: to feel

Da blieb dem Bahnhofsvorstand nichts anderes übrig,° als dem Mann zu sagen, daß er ihm den Bahnhof verbieten° müsse,° wenn er sich nicht anständig° aufführe.° Und der Mann erschrak,° weil er ohne Bahnhof nicht leben konnte, und er sagte kein Wort mehr, saß den ganzen Tag auf der Bank,° sah die Züge ankommen und die Züge wegfahren, und nur hie und da° flüsterte° er einige Zahlen° vor sich hin,° und er schaute den Leuten nach° und konnte sie nicht begreifen.

Hier wäre die Geschichte° eigentlich° zu Ende.°

(Fortsetzung° folgt°)

Da blieb dem Bahnhofsvorstand nichts anderes übrig: There was nothing left for the station master to do **verbieten:** to forbid (*here:* the man from coming to the station) **verbot, verboten müsse:** muß **anständig:** decently, properly **sich auf·führen:** to behave, act **aufführe: aufführt** **erschrecken:** to be stunned **(erschrickt) erschrak, ist erschrocken die Bank:** bench

hie und da: now and then **flüstern:** to whisper **die Zahl, –en:** number **vor sich hin:** to himself **nach·schauen** (+ *dat.*): to look after

die Geschichte, –n: story **eigentlich:** actually **zu Ende:** finished, at an end

die Fortsetzung, –en: continuation **folgen:** to follow

INTRODUCTORY EXERCISES

Supply the correct forms of the verbs in parentheses. Do each sentence in the present tense, past tense, and present perfect tense, except where otherwise indicated.

A. 1. Der Mann _____ den ganzen Fahrplan auswendig.
       (*wissen)

    2. Eisenbahnen _____ dem Mann Freude.
       (machen)

    3. Er _____ seine Zeit auf dem Bahnhof.
       (*verbringen)

    4. Er _____ die Züge ankommen und abfahren. [*pres. and past only*]
       (*sehen)

    5. Er _____ die Wagen und die Kraft der Lokomotiven.
       (bestaunen)

    6. Er _____ jeden Zug.
       (*kennen)

    7. Er _____ woher er _____ und wohin er _____. [*pres. and past only*]
       (*wissen)   (*kommen)   (*gehen)

    8. Er _____ die Nummern der Züge und wieviel eine Fahrkarte nach
       (*wissen)

       Frauenfeld _____. [*pres. and past only*]
                  (kosten)

----

*strong or irregular verb

NOTE: since they occur so frequently and are so basic to the language, **sein, haben, werden,** and the modal auxiliaries (e.g., **können**) have not been marked with an asterisk.

B. 1. Er _____ in keine Wirtschaft und _____ keine Zeitungen.
    (*gehen)   (*lesen)

2. Wenn er Briefe _____, _____ er sie auch nicht. [subj.II, pres. and past]
    (*bekommen)   (*lesen)

3. Er _____ keine Zeit dazu.
    (haben)

4. Er _____ seine Tage im Bahnhof.
    (*verbringen)

5. Nur wenn der Fahrplan _____, _____ man ihn für eine Weile nicht mehr.
    (wechseln)   (*sehen)

6. Er _____ zu Hause und _____ den Fahrplan auswendig.
    (*sitzen)   (lernen)

7. Er _____ sich über die Änderungen.
    (freuen)

C. 1. Es _____, daß jemand ihn nach einer Abfahrtszeit _____.
    (*vor·komment)   (fragen)

2. Dann _____ er über das ganze Gesicht.
    (strahlen)

3. Er _____ alles genau wissen.
    (wollen)

4. Er _____ den Frager nicht mehr.
    (*los·lassen)

5. Der Frager _____ die Abfahrtszeit.
    (verpassen)

6. Der Mann _____, wo man umsteigen _____ und wann man _____.
    (erklären)   (müssen)   (*an·kommen)

    [pres., and past]

7. Er _____ nicht, daß die Leute nicht interessiert _____.
    (*begreifen)   (sein)

8. Wenn jemand _____, _____ er böse.
    (*weiter·gehen)   (werden)

9. Er selbst _____ nie mit einem Zug.
    (*fahren)

10. Er _____, daß es keinen Sinn _____. [pres. and past. 1st clause indicative,
    (sagen)   (haben)   second clause subj. II]

11. Er _____ im voraus, wann der Zug _____. [pres.]
    (*wissen)   (*an·kommen)

D. 1. Wenn man die Abfahrtstafel _____, _____ man nicht fahren. [subj. II,
    (*an·sehen)   (müssen)   pres., and
    past]

2. Aber die Leute _____ sich über die Fahrt.
    (freuen)

3. Sie _____ gern Eisenbahn und _____ zum Fenster.
    (*fahren)   (hinaus·schauen)

---

*strong or irregular verb

†·= separable prefix

4. Er _____, man _____ ihn auslachen. [pres. and past]
      (glauben)   (wollen)

5. Die Leute _____ mit der Bahn fahren, weil sie irgendwohin _____. [pres. and past]
      (müssen)   (wollen)

6. Fast alle Leute _____.
                  (*zurück · kommen)

7. Leute _____ jeden Morgen und _____ jeden Abend.
       (*ein · steigen)   (*zurück · kommen)

8. Sie _____ so ein schlechtes Gedächtnis.
     (haben)

E. 1. Er _____ die Leute auf dem Bahnhof.
       (beschimpfen)

    2. Er _____, er _____ ihnen den Spaß. [pres.]
       (glauben)   (*verderben)

    3. Als die Leute nur _____, _____ er sie vom Zug. [pres. and past]
                  (lachen)   (*reißen)

    4. Sie _____ den Zug nicht nehmen. [subj. II, pres., and past]
       (sollen)

    5. Er _____ ihnen alles erklären.
       (können)

    6. Sie _____ um 14 Uhr 27 an Hägendorf.
       (*vorbei · kommen)

    7. Sie _____ ihr Geld für nichts.
       (*aus · geben)

    8. Alles _____ im Fahrplan.
       (*stehen)

    9. Er _____ die Leute verprügeln.
       (wollen)

F. 1. Er _____ sich anständig benehmen.   **(benehmen**: to behave)
       (müssen)

    2. Der Mann _____ kein Wort mehr, weil er ohne Bahnhof nicht leben _____.
               (sagen)   (können)

    3. Er _____ den ganzen Tag auf der Bank.
       (*sitzen)

    4. Er _____ den Leuten und _____ sie nicht verstehen.
       (nach · schauen)   (können)

    5. Die Geschichte _____ hier zu Ende. [subj. II, pres., and past]
       (sein)

SYNTHETIC EXERCISES

Use the following elements to make complete sentences. Form the present tense, past tense, and present perfect tense, except where otherwise indicated.

A. 1. Mann / wissen / ganz / Fahrplan / auswendig
    2. Eisenbahnen / machen / Mann / Freude
    3. Er / verbringen / sein- / Zeit / auf / Bahnhof

4. Er / sehen / Züge / an·kommen / und / ab·fahren   [*pres. and past only*]
5. Er / bestaunen / Wagen / und / Kraft / Lokomotiven [*gen.*]
6. Er / kennen / jed– / Zug
7. Er / wissen // woher / er / kommen // und / wohin / er / gehen   [*pres. and past only*]
8. Er / wissen / Nummern / Züge [*gen.*] // und / wieviel / Fahrkarte / kosten / nach Frauenfeld   [*pres. and past only*]

B. 1. Er / gehen / in / kein / Wirtschaft // und / lesen / kein / Zeitungen
2. Wenn / er / bekommen / Briefe // er / lesen / sie / auch nicht   [*subj. II, pres., and past*]
3. Er / haben / kein / Zeit / dazu
4. Er / verbringen / sein– / Tage / in / Bahnhof
5. Nur / wenn / Fahrplan / wechseln // man / sehen / [*him*] / für / Weile / nicht mehr
6. Er / sitzen / Hause // und / lernen / Fahrplan / auswendig
7. Er / freuen [*refl.*] / über / Änderungen

C. 1. Es / vor·kommen // daß / jemand / fragen / [*him*] / nach / ein / Abfahrtszeit
2. Dann / er / strahlen / über / ganz / Gesicht
3. Er / wollen / wissen / alles genau
4. Er / los·lassen / Frager / nicht mehr
5. Frager / verpassen / Abfahrtszeit
6. Mann / erklären // wo / man / müssen / um·steigen // und / wann / man / an·kommen   [*pres. and past*]
7. Er / begreifen / nicht // daß / Leute / sein / nicht interessiert
8. Wenn / jemand / weiter·gehen // er / werden / böse
9. Er selbst / fahren / nie / mit / Zug
10. Er / sagen // daß / es / haben / kein / Sinn
[*pres. and past. First clause indicative, second clause subj. II*]
11. Er / wissen / in / voraus // wann / Zug / ankommen   [*pres.*]

D. 1. Wenn / man / an·sehen / Abfahrtstafel // man / müssen / fahren / nicht   [*subj. II, pres., and past*]
2. Aber / Leute / freuen [*refl.*] / über / Fahrt
3. Sie / fahren / gern / Eisenbahn / und / hinaus·schauen / zu / Fenster
4. Er / glauben // man / wollen / aus·lachen / [*him*]   [*pres. and past*]
5. Leute / müssen / fahren / mit / Bahn // weil / sie / wollen / irgendwohin   [*pres. and past*]
6. Das / können / sein / nicht wahr
7. Fast / all– / Leute / zurück·kommen
8. Leute / ein·steigen / jed– / Morgen // und / zurück·kommen / jed– / Abend
9. Sie / haben / so ein / schlecht / Gedächtnis

E. 1. Er / beschimpfen / Leute / auf / Bahnhof
2. Er / glauben // er / verderben / [*them*] / Spaß   [*pres.*]
3. Als / Leute / lachen / nur // er / reißen / sie / von / Zug   [*pres. and past*]
4. Sie / sollen / nehmen / Zug / nicht   [*subj. II, pres., and past*]
5. Er / können / erklären / [*to them*] / alles
6. Sie / vorbei·kommen / 14.27 / an Hägendorf
7. Sie / aus·geben / Geld / für nichts
8. Alles / stehen / in / Fahrplan
9. Er / wollen / verprügeln / Leute

F. 1. Er / müssen / benehmen [*refl.*] / anständig   [*pres. and past*]
2. Mann / sagen / kein Wort mehr // weil / er / können / leben / ohne Bahnhof / nicht
3. Er / sitzen / ganz / Tag / auf / Bank
4. Er / nach·schauen / Leute // und / können / verstehen / sie nicht
5. Geschichte / sein / hier / zu Ende   [*subj. II, pres., and past*]

Lesson 10   Level ONE

A Relative Pronouns and Relative Clauses

1 Introduction

A relative clause is another kind of subordinate clause. Instead of using a conjunction to join two clauses, it uses a relative pronoun.

Main Clause	Relative Clause
That's the *waiter*	*who* served us.
That's the *gun*	*that* killed him.

Who and *that* are relative pronouns; they *relate* the relative clause to the main clause by *referring to one of the elements in the main clause* (*who* refers to *waiter* and *that* refers to *gun*). *Waiter* and *gun* are called the *antecedents* of *who* and *that*.

2 Relative pronouns

a. English relative pronouns

English has two sets of relative pronouns: one for people, another for things.

	People	Things
SUBJECT	who	that (which)
OBJECT	who (whom)	that (which)
POSSESSIVE	whose	whose (of which)

If the antecedent is a *person*, the relative pronoun is "who":

the waiter, who

If the antecedent is a *thing*, the relative pronoun is "that":

the gun, that

b. German relative pronouns

As you know, German uses grammatical gender (**der** Anzug = **er**), not natural gender (the suit = *it*). And so it uses the same relative pronouns for both people and things.

1. The antecedent determines gender and number.

   If the antecedent is masculine, the pronoun must also be masculine; if the antecedent is plural, the pronoun must also be plural, and so on. For this reason, German has masculine, neuter, feminine, and plural relative pronouns.

   > Das ist **der Mann,** der gestern hier war.
   > (That's the man *who* was here yesterday.)

   > Das ist **der Bus,** der zur Uni fährt.
   > (That's the bus *that* goes to the university.)

2. The function in the clause determines case.

   The case of a relative pronoun depends on how it is used in the relative clause.

   > NOM. Das ist der Mann, der gestern hier war.
   >   **Der** is the *subject* of the relative clause.

   > ACC. Das ist der Mann, den ich meine.
   >   **Den** is the direct object of **meinen.**

c. Table of German relative pronouns

Notice how many forms of the relative pronoun are the same as the definite article.

	Masc.	*Neut.*	*Fem.*	*Pl.*
NOM.	der	das	die	die
ACC.	den	das	die	die
DAT.	dem	dem	der	**denen**
GEN.	**dessen**	**dessen**	**deren**	**deren**

▶ **Note** Pay particular attention to the *five forms in boldface;* they are *unlike* the definite article.

3 Summary

a. Word order

Relative clauses, being subordinate clauses, have subordinate word order: *The inflected verb form is at the end of the clause.*

> Das ist der Mann, der gestern hier war.

b. Gender and number

The gender and number of a relative pronoun are the same as the gender and number of the noun to which the relative pronoun refers (its antecedent).

> Das ist **der Mann,** der gestern hier war.
> Das sind **die Leute,** die gestern hier waren.

c. Case

The case of a relative pronoun depends on its *function in the relative clause*. The following examples are all in the masculine singular:

NOM.   Das ist der Mann, **der** gestern hier war.
           (who was here yesterday)

ACC.   Das ist der Mann, **den** ich meine.
           (I mean; whom I mean)
      Das ist der Mann, für **den** ich arbeite.
           (I work for; for whom I work)

DAT.   Das ist der Mann, **dem** ich es gegeben habe.
           (I gave it to; to whom I gave it)
      Das ist der Mann, nach **dem** Sie gefragt haben.
           (you were asking about; about whom you were asking)

GEN.   Das ist der Mann, **dessen** Stimme ich hörte.
           (whose voice I heard)

As the examples show, a relative pronoun can have various grammatical functions. It can be:

NOM.	A subject (nominative case):	der Mann, **der** gestern hier war
ACC.	An accusative object of a verb:	der Mann, **den** ich meine
	An accusative object of a preposition:	der Mann, **für den** ich arbeite
DAT.	A dative object of a verb:	der Mann, **dem** ich es gegeben habe
	A dative object of a preposition:	der Mann, **nach dem** Sie gefragt haben
GEN.	A possessive (genitive case):	der Mann, **dessen** Stimme ich hörte

▶ **Note**   Like other relative pronouns, **dessen** and **deren** have the same gender and number as the person(s) or thing(s) they refer to (their antecedents), *not* the gender or number of the thing(s) possessed.

der Mann, dessen Stimme

It is the antecedent (**der** Mann) that determines the gender of the relative pronoun (**dessen:** masculine).

4 Position and punctuation of relative clauses

Der Mann, **dem ich es gegeben habe**, ist nie zurückgekommen.
(The man [whom] I gave it to never came back.)

1. A German relative clause comes immediately after the antecedent in the main clause. The only exception to this is a sentence in which *only one word would follow* the relative clause. For example:

Hast du **den Wagen** gesehen, **den** er gefahren hat?
(Did you see the car that he was driving?)

(Otherwise the sentence would read:

Hast du **den Wagen, den** er gefahren hat, **gesehen?**

Here the final word of the main clause **[gesehen]** is tacked onto the end of the sentence, awkwardly.)

2. German relative clauses are always set off by commas.

3. A German relative pronoun is normally the first element of a relative clause. The only exception to this rule is when the relative pronoun is the object of a preposition:

Das ist der Mann, **für den** ich arbeite.

5 No omission of relative pronoun

It is common to omit a relative pronoun from an English sentence. However, relative pronouns may never be omitted in German:

Das ist der Mann, **den** ich meine.   (That's the man I mean [whom I mean].)
Das ist der Mann, **für den** ich arbeite.   (That's the man I work for [for whom I work].)

▶ Note   If a preposition is involved it normally appears at the end of an English relative clause:

the man I work *for*

In German, the preposition must always *precede* the relative pronoun:

der Mann, **für den** ich arbeite

In other words, the German pattern is the same as the more formal English pattern:

the man, *for whom* I work

DRILLS

1   Relative pronouns

• Supply the correct forms of the relative pronoun. This exercise drills only the nominative case.

	Masc.	*Neut.*	*Fem.*	*Pl.*
NOM.	der	das	die	die

1. der Bus, _____ zur Uni fährt   (**die Uni:** student slang for university)
   (that)
2. die Bar, _____ früher hier war   (**früher,** *here:* before)
   (that)

3. das Haus, _____ an der Ecke stand
   (that)

4. der Kellner, _____ uns bedient hat   (**der Kellner**: waiter; **bedienen**: to serve)
   (who)

5. die Leute, _____ heute abend kommen
   (who)

6. eine Straße, _____ zum Bahnhof führt   (**führen**: to lead [to], go to)
   (that)

7. die Leute, _____ nebenan wohnen   (**nebenan**: next door)
   (who)

8. das Mädchen, _____ gerade hier war
   (who)

9. die Frau, _____ neben ihm saß
   (who)

10. der Revolver, _____ ihn getötet hat   (**der Revolver**: gun; **töten**: to kill)
    (that)

● Supply the correct forms of the relative pronoun. This exercise drills only the accusative case.

	Masc.	Neut.	Fem.	Pl.
ACC.	den	das	die	die

1. die Arbeit, _____ er geschrieben hat
   (that)

2. der Wagen, _____ er gefahren hat
   (that)

3. die Marke, an _____ ich gedacht habe   (**die Marke**: brand)
   (that)

4. das letzte Mal, _____ ich ihn sah
   (that)

5. der Kerl, _____ ich meine   (**der Kerl**: guy)
   (whom)

6. eine Nacht, _____ ich nie vergessen werde
   (that)

7. die Sachen, _____ sie da haben   (**die Sache, –n**: thing)
   (that)

8. der Brief, auf _____ ich warte
   (that)

9. die Platte, _____ ich kaufen will   (**die Platte**: record)
   (that)

10. das Paket, _____ du von zu Hause gekriegt hast
    (that)
                 (**von zu Hause**: from home; **kriegen**: to get, receive)

11. Freunde, _____ wir besuchen wollen
    (whom)

12. der Wein, _____ ich kaufen wollte
    (that)

13. eine Stadt, _____ ich gern besuchen würde
    (that)

- Supply the correct forms of the relative pronoun. This exercise drills only the dative case.

	Masc.	Neut.	Fem.	Pl.
DAT.	dem	dem	der	denen

1. die Familie, bei _____ er wohnt
   (that)

2. der Mann, _____ ich es gegeben habe
   (whom)

3. Leute, mit _____ man reden kann   (reden: to talk)
   (whom)

4. der Arzt, zu _____ ich ging
   (whom)

5. die Stadt, in _____ sie wohnen
   (which)

6. der Sarg, in _____ Graf Dracula geschlafen hat   (der Graf: Count)
   (which)

7. das Mädchen, mit _____ er ausgeht
   (whom)

8. die Mädchen, mit _____ er ausgeht (pl.)
   (whom)

9. das Hotel, nach _____ Sie gefragt haben   (fragen nach: to ask about)
   (which)

- Supply the correct forms of the relative pronoun. This exercise drills only the genitive case.

	Masc.	Neut.	Fem.	Pl.
GEN.	dessen	dessen	deren	deren

1. das Mädchen, _____ Vater gerade hier war
   (whose)

2. eine Jacke, _____ Farbe mir gefällt   (die Farbe: color; gefallen: to please)
   (whose)

3. der Mann, _____ Stimme ich hörte   (die Stimme: voice)
   (whose)

4. die Leute, _____ Haus wir gekauft haben
   (whose)

5. das Lokal, _____ Gulasch so gut war   (das Gulasch: goulash)
   (whose)

6. ein Mantel, _____ Farbe mir gefällt
   (whose)

7. das Mädchen, _____ Bild er mir gezeigt hat
   (whose)

• Supply the correct forms of the relative pronoun. This exercise drills only masculine nouns.

	Masc.
NOM.	der
ACC.	den
DAT.	dem
GEN.	**dessen**

1. der Bus, _____ zur Uni fährt
   (that)
2. der Arzt, zu _____ ich ging
   (whom)
3. der Wagen, _____ er gefahren hat
   (that)
4. der Mann, _____ Stimme ich hörte
   (whose)
5. der Kerl, _____ ich meine
   (whom)
6. der Sarg, in _____ Graf Dracula geschlafen hat
   (which)
7. der Mann, für _____ ich arbeite
   (whom)
8. ein Mantel, _____ Farbe mir gefällt
   (whose)
9. der Kellner, _____ uns bedient hat
   (who)
10. der Mann, _____ ich es gegeben habe
    (to whom)
11. der Brief, auf _____ ich wartete
    (which)
12. der Revolver, _____ ihn getötet hat
    (which)
13. der Wein, _____ ich kaufen wollte
    (which)

• Supply the correct forms of the relative pronoun. This exercise drills only neuter nouns.

	Neut.
NOM.	das
ACC.	das
DAT.	dem
GEN.	**dessen**

1. das Mädchen, _____ gerade hier war
   (who)
2. das Steak, _____ ich bestellte
   (that)

3. das letzte Mal, _____ ich ihn sah
   (that)

4. das Mädchen, mit _____ er ausgeht
   (whom)

5. das Haus, _____ wir kaufen wollten
   (that)

6. das Lokal, _____ Gulasch so gut war
   (whose)

7. das Hotel, nach _____ Sie gefragt haben
   (which)

8. das Mädchen, _____ Vater gerade hier war
   (whose)

9. das Paket, _____ du von zu Hause gekriegt hast
   (that)

● Supply the correct forms of the relative pronoun. This exercise drills only feminine nouns.

	Fem.
NOM.	die
ACC.	die
DAT.	der
GEN.	deren

1. eine Stadt, _____ ich gern besuchen würde
   (that)

2. die Familie, bei _____ er wohnt
   (which)

3. die Frau, _____ neben ihm saß
   (who)

4. die Stadt, in _____ sie wohnen
   (which)

5. eine Nacht, _____ ich nie vergessen werde
   (that)

6. eine Jacke, _____ Farbe mir gefällt
   (whose)

7. die Platte, _____ ich kaufen will
   (that)

8. die Bar, _____ früher hier war
   (that)

9. die Arbeit, _____ er geschrieben hat
   (that)

10. die Straße, _____ zum Bahnhof führt
    (that)

11. die Universität, an _____ er studiert hat
    (which)

12. die Marke, an _____ ich gedacht habe
    (which)

• Supply the correct forms of the relative pronoun. This exercise drills only plural nouns.

	Pl.
NOM.	die
ACC.	die
DAT.	denen
GEN.	deren

1. die Leute, _____ heute abend kommen
   (who)
2. die Leute, _____ nebenan wohnen
   (who)
3. Freunde, _____ wir besuchen wollen
   (who)
4. Leute, mit _____ man reden kann
   (whom)
5. die Studenten, _____ wir nach Mainz schicken
   (who)
6. die Leute, _____ Haus wir gekauft haben
   (whose)
7. die Sachen, _____ sie da haben
   (that)

• Mixed drills: Supply the correct forms of the relative pronoun.

a. 1. der Revolver, _____ ihn getötet hat
      (that)
   2. die Platte, _____ ich kaufen will
      (that)
   3. die Studenten, _____ wir nach Mainz schicken
      (whom)
   4. der Wagen, _____ er gefahren hat
      (that)
   5. die Leute, _____ nebenan wohnen
      (who)
   6. die Familie, bei _____ er wohnt
      (which)
   7. der Mann, _____ Stimme ich hörte
      (whose)
   8. das Haus, _____ wir kaufen wollten
      (that)
   9. eine Stadt, _____ ich gern besuchen würde
      (that)
   10. der Arzt, zu _____ ich ging
      (whom)

b. 1. die Stadt, in _____ sie wohnen
       (which)

    2. der Mann, für _____ ich arbeite
       (whom)

    3. eine Jacke, _____ Farbe mir gefällt
       (whose)

    4. das letzte Mal, _____ ich ihn sah
       (that)

    5. der Kellner, _____ uns bedient hat
       (who)

    6. Leute, mit _____ man gut reden kann
       (whom)

    7. die Frau, _____ neben ihm saß
       (who)

    8. das Lokal, _____ Gulasch so gut war
       (whose)

    9. der Brief, auf _____ ich wartete
       (which)

    10. Freunde, _____ wir besuchen wollen
        (whom)

c. 1. das Mädchen, _____ gerade hier war
       (who)

    2. die Mädchen, mit _____ er ausgeht (pl.)
       (whom)

    3. der Bus, _____ zur Uni fährt
       (that)

    4. eine Nacht, _____ ich nie vergessen werde
       (that)

    5. ein Mantel, _____ Farbe mir gefällt
       (whose)

    6. das Mädchen, mit _____ er ausgeht
       (whom)

    7. die Sachen, _____ sie da haben
       (that)

    8. die Universität, an _____ er studiert hat
       (which)

    9. die Leute, _____ Haus wir gekauft haben
       (whose)

    10. der Wein, _____ ich kaufen wollte
        (that)

d. 1. die Bar, _____ früher hier war
       (that)

    2. das Mädchen, _____ Vater gerade hier war
       (whose)

    3. die Marke, an _____ ich gedacht habe
       (which)

    4. das Hotel, nach _____ Sie gefragt haben
       (which)

5. die Leute, _____ heute abend kommen
(who)

6. das Paket, _____ du von zu Hause bekommen hast
(that)

7. die Arbeit, _____ er geschrieben hat
(that)

8. der Kerl, _____ ich meine
(whom)

9. die Straße, _____ zum Bahnhof führt
(that)

10. der Sarg, in _____ Graf Dracula geschlafen hat
(which)

• Mixed drills—whole sentences: Supply the correct forms of the relative pronoun.

a. 1. Ist das der Kellner, _____ uns bedient hat?
(who)

2. Da ist die Platte, _____ ich kaufen will.
(that)

3. Kennst du das Mädchen, mit _____ er ausgeht?
(whom)

4. Das ist der Kerl, _____ ich meine.
(whom)

5. Die Sachen, _____ sie da haben, sind alle zu teuer.
(that)

6. Die Familie, bei _____ er wohnt, ist sehr nett.
(which)

7. Kennst du die Leute, _____ heute abend kommen?
(who)

8. Und das war das letzte Mal, _____ ich ihn sah.
(that)

9. Ist das das Lokal, _____ Gulasch so gut war?
(whose)

(das Lokal: place, in the sense of restaurant)

10. Die Mädchen, mit _____ er ausgeht, sind alle sehr hübsch.
(whom)

b. 1. Hast du den Wagen gesehen, _____ er gefahren hat?
(that)

2. Wer war die Frau, _____ neben ihm saß?
(who)

3. Das ist der Revolver, _____ ihn getötet hat.
(that)

4. Wir haben Freunde da, _____ wir besuchen wollen.
(whom)

5. Die kleine Stadt, in _____ sie wohnen, hat nur e i n* Kino.
(which)

---

*When stressed, the word **ein** means "one."

6. Da ist eine Jacke, _____ Farbe mir gefällt.
   (whose)

7. Wer war das Mädchen, _____ gerade hier war?
   (who)

8. Das war eine Nacht, _____ ich nie vergessen werde.
   (that)

9. Das sind die Leute, _____ Haus wir gekauft haben.
   (whose)

10. Der Wein, _____ ich kaufen wollte, war nicht mehr da.
    (that)

c. 1. Die Arbeit, _____ er geschrieben hat, war sehr gut.
      (that)

2. Das ist der Mann, _____ Stimme ich gehört habe.
   (whose)

3. München ist eine Stadt, _____ ich gern besuchen würde.
   (that)

4. Was war in dem Paket, _____ du von zu Hause gekriegt hast?
   (that)

5. Das ist die Universität, an _____ er studiert hat.
   (which)

6. Der Arzt, zu _____ ich ging, war wirklich sehr gut.
   (whom)

7. Das sind die Studenten, _____ wir nach Mainz schicken.
   (whom)

8. Das ist das Haus, _____ wir kaufen wollten.
   (that)

9. Wo ist die Bar, _____ früher hier war?
   (that)

10. Das ist der Mann, für _____ ich arbeite.
    (whom)

d. 1. Das Bier, _____ sie hier haben, ist gar nicht schlecht.   (**gar nicht:** not at all)
      (that)

2. Das ist die Marke, an _____ ich gedacht habe.
   (which)

3. Nein, ich meine das Mädchen, _____ Vater gerade hier war.
   (whose)

4. Wo hält der Bus, _____ zur Universität fährt?   (**halten,** *here:* to stop)
   (that)

5. Die Leute, _____ nebenan wohnen, sind ziemlich laut.
   (who)

6. Ist das das Hotel, nach _____ Sie gefragt haben?
   (which)

7. Da ist ein Mantel, _____ Farbe mir gefällt.
   (whose)

8. Gibt es eine andere Straße, _____ zum Bahnhof führt?
   (that)

9. Das sind Leute, mit _____ man reden kann.
(whom)

10. Und hier ist der Sarg, in _____ Graf Dracula geschlafen hat.
(which)

e. 1. Hier ist der Brief, auf _____ du gewartet hast.
(which)

2 Express in German: relative clause only

• Complete the following sentences by expressing the relative clauses in German. The relative clauses are in colloquial English. For this reason:

Relative pronouns are often omitted:

Das ist das Haus, _____.   Das ist das Haus, **das wir kaufen wollten.**
(we wanted to buy)

and prepositions are frequently found *at the end* (rather than the beginning) of the clause:

Das ist der Mann, _____.   Das ist der Mann, **für den ich arbeite.**
(I work *for*)

a. 1. Wer war das Mädchen, _____?
(who was just here)

2. Wir haben Freunde da, _____.
(who we want to visit)

3. Die Familie, _____, ist sehr nett.
(he lives with)

4. Das ist der Kerl, _____.
(I mean)

5. Wer war die Frau, _____?
(who was sitting next to him)

6. Kennst du das Mädchen, _____?
(he goes out with)

7. Der Wein, _____, war nicht mehr da.
(I wanted to buy)

8. Ist das das Lokal, _____?
(whose goulash was so good)

9. Die Sachen, _____, sind alle zu teuer.
(they have there)

10. Das ist der Revolver, _____.
(that killed him)

b. 1. Und das war das letzte Mal, _____.
(I saw him)

2. Das war eine Nacht, _____.
(I'll never forget)

3. Der Arzt, _____, war wirklich sehr gut.
(I went to)

4. Das sind die Leute, _____.
(whose house we bought)

5. Die kleine Stadt, _____, hat nur ein Kino.
   (they live in)

6. Hast du den Wagen gesehen, _____?
   (he was driving)

7. Hier ist ein Mantel, _____.
   (whose color I like)

8. Das ist das Haus, _____.
   (we wanted to buy)

9. Das ist die Marke, _____.
   (I was thinking of)

10. Das Bier, _____, ist gar nicht schlecht.
    (they have here)

c. 1. Ist das der Kellner, _____?
     (who served us)

   2. Da ist eine Jacke, _____.
      (whose color I like)

   3. Die Leute, _____, sind ziemlich laut.
      (who live next door)

   4. Nein, ich meine das Mädchen, _____.
      (whose father was just here)

   5. Da ist die Platte, _____.
      (I want to buy)

   6. Hier ist der Brief, _____.
      (you were waiting for)

   7. Das sind Leute, _____.
      (you can talk to)

   8. Das sind die Studenten, _____.
      (we're sending to Mainz)

   9. Ist das das Hotel, _____?
      (you were asking about)

  10. Wo ist die Bar, _____?
      (that was here before)

d. 1. Kennst du die Leute, _____?
     (who are coming this evening)

   2. Das ist der Mann, _____.
      (I work for)

   3. München ist eine Stadt, _____.
      (I'd like to visit)

   4. Was war in dem Paket, _____?
      (you got from home)

   5. Die Arbeit, _____, war seht gut.
      (he wrote)

   6. Wo hält der Bus, _____?
      (that goes to the university)

   7. Das ist der Mann, _____.
      (whose voice I heard)

   8. Gibt es eine andere Straße, _____?
      (that goes to the railroad station)

   9. Das ist die Universität, _____.
      (he studied at)

• Express in German. The relative clauses are in italics.

a. 1. Who was the girl *who was just here?*
   2. There's the record *I want to buy.*
   3. That's the guy *I mean.*
   4. The family *he lives with* is very nice.
   5. Do you know the people *who are coming this evening?*
   6. Is that the hotel *you were asking about?*
   7. Who was the woman *who was sitting next to him?*
   8. Did you see the car *he was driving?*
   9. The things *they have there* are all too expensive.
   10. That's the university *he studied at.*

b. 1. No, I mean the girl *whose father was just here.*
   2. The doctor *I went to* was really very good.
   3. That's the gun *that killed him.*
   4. And that was the last time *I saw him.*
   5. Where does the bus stop *that goes to the university?*
   6. That was a night *I'll never forget.*
   7. Those are the people *whose house we bought.*
   8. We have friends there that *we want to visit.*

9. That's a coat *whose color I like.*
10. The beer *they have here* isn't bad at all.

c. 1. Munich is a city *I'd like to visit.*
   2. That's the man *I work for.*
   3. Those are people *you can talk to.*
   4. That's the house *we wanted to buy.*
   5. Do you know the girl *he goes out with?*
   6. Where's the bar *that was here before?*
   7. There's a sports coat *whose color I like.*
   8. Is that the waiter *who served us?*
   9. Those are the students *we're sending to Mainz.*
   10. Here's the letter *you were waiting for.*

d. 1. What was in the package *you got from home?*
   2. That's the brand *I was thinking of.*
   3. The people *who live next door* are pretty loud.
   4. The wine *I wanted to buy* wasn't there anymore.
   5. The paper *he wrote* was very good.
   6. That's the man *whose voice I heard.*
   7. Is there another street *that goes to the railroad station?*

VOCABULARY

bedienen to serve
die **Farbe, –n** color
fragen nach (+ *dat.*) to ask about
früher *here:* before
führen to lead (to), go to
gar nicht not at all
gefallen (gefällt) to please
gefiel, gefallen
Das gefällt mir.: I like that.

der **Graf, –en, –en** count
das **Gulasch** goulash
halten (hält) to stop
hielt, gehalten
von zu Hause from home
der **Kellner, –** waiter
der **Kerl, –e** guy
kriegen to get, receive
das **Lokal, -e** place (*in the sense of restaurant or bar*)

die **Marke, –n** brand
nebenan next door
die **Platte, –n** record
reden to talk
der **Revolver, –** revolver
die **Sache, –n** thing
die **Stimme, –n** voice
töten to kill
die **Uni, -s** university (*student slang*)

Lesson 10   Level TWO

A Da(r)- and Wo(r)-Compounds: Review and Expansion

1 da(r)-compounds

Look at the following examples:

NOUN	Was hast du **gegen seine Freundin?**
PRONOUN	Was hast du **gegen sie?**

If the object of a preposition is a *person*, a personal pronoun may replace the noun as the object of the preposition:

> gegen **seine Freundin**
> gegen **sie**

However, if the object of a preposition is a *thing* (not a person), a personal pronoun may *not* be substituted for the noun. Instead a special construction is used:

> Was hast du **gegen seinen Plan?**
> Was hast du **dagegen?**
>
> Ich warte **auf den Zug.**
> Ich warte **darauf.**

This construction consists of **da(r)-** + the *preposition* involved.

1. If the preposition begins with a *consonant*, **da** is used: **dagegen**

2. If the preposition begins with a *vowel*, **dar** is used: **darauf**

PERSONS	THINGS
Was hast du **gegen sie?** (against *her*)	Was hast du **dagegen?** (against *it*) Ich warte **darauf.** (for *it*)
With *persons* one uses: preposition + pronoun	With *things* one uses: **da(r)** + preposition

DRILLS

1 Substitution drills: personal pronouns and **da(r)**-compounds

● Replace the noun objects of the prepositions with personal pronouns.

1. Was hältst du von seiner Schwester?
2. War sie böse auf Herrn Richter?
3. Erinnerst du dich an Karl-Heinz?
4. Ich habe zwei Stunden auf das Mädchen warten müssen. (use natural gender for the pronoun *her*)
5. Er hat nach deinem Vater gefragt.
6. Was hast du gegen seine Freundin?

● Replace the noun objects of the prepositions with **da(r)**-compounds.

1. Was hast du für deinen neuen Wagen bezahlt?
2. Er wohnt gleich neben dem Bahnhof.
3. Haben Sie an diese Möglichkeit gedacht?   (die Möglichkeit: possibility)
4. Er hat mich um Hilfe gebeten.   (die Hilfe: help)
5. Was hältst du von seinem neuen Buch?
6. Ich habe lange auf das Geld warten müssen.
7. Was hast du gegen seinen Plan?
8. Wenn ich mich nur an ihren Namen erinnern könnte.
9. Ich freue mich auf nächsten Sommer.
10. Sind Sie mit dem Resultat zufrieden?
11. Sie hat mich an die Party erinnert.

● Mixed drill: Replace the noun objects of the prepositions with personal pronouns or the appropriate **da(r)**-compounds.

1. Sie hat mich an die Party erinnert.
2. Was hast du gegen seine Freundin?
3. Sind Sie mit dem Resultat zufrieden?
4. Ich freue mich auf nächsten Sommer.
5. Er hat mich um Hilfe gebeten.
6. Was hältst du von seiner Schwester?
7. Er hat nach deinem Vater gefragt.
8. Wenn ich mich nur an ihren Namen erinnern könnte.
9. Was hast du für deinen neuen Wagen bezahlt?
10. War sie böse auf Herrn Richter?
11. Ich habe lange auf das Geld warten müssen.
12. Haben Sie an diese Möglichkeit gedacht?
13. Was hast du gegen seinen Plan?
14. Erinnerst du dich an Karl-Heinz?
15. Er wohnt gleich neben dem Bahnhof.
16. Ich habe zwei Stunden auf das Mädchen warten müssen.
17. Was hältst du von seinem neuen Buch?

- Express in German.

1. What do you have against it?
2. She reminded me of it.
3. Was she mad at him?
4. What did you pay for it?
5. Did you think of it?
6. Do you remember him?
7. I'm looking forward to it.
8. He asked me for it.
9. What do you think of her?
10. I had to wait a long time for it.
11. If I could only remember it.
12. What do you have against her?
13. What do you think of it?
14. Are you satisfied with it?
15. He asked about him.
16. I had to wait two hours for her.

2 The question word **wer**

The question word **wer** has accusative, dative, and genitive forms that are analogous to the relative pronoun **der:**

NOM.	**wer**	who
ACC.	**wen**	who (whom)
DAT.	**wem**	who (whom)
GEN.	**wessen**	whose

EXAMPLES:

NOM.	Wer ist da?	Who's there?
ACC.	Wen meinst du?	Who do you mean?
DAT.	Wem hast du es gegeben?	Who did you give it *to*?
GEN.	Wessen Buch ist das?	Whose book is that?

2 The question word **wer**

- Supply the correct form of **wer.** Use the English sentences as cues.

1. _____ kommt heute abend? *Who's coming this evening?*
2. _____ meinen Sie? *Who do you mean?*
3. _____ Idee war das? *Whose idea was that?*
4. _____ hat es getan? *Who did it?*
5. _____ hat er es gesagt? *Who did he tell it to?*
6. _____ Wagen ist das? *Whose car is that?*
7. _____ hast du da gesehen? *Who did you see there?*
8. _____ hat er es gegeben? *Who did he give it to?*
9. _____ soll ich glauben?* *Who should I believe?*
10. _____ Mappe ist das? *Whose briefcase is that?*

(**die Mappe:** briefcase)

- Synthetic exercises: Form complete sentences in the tenses indicated.

1. Wer / kommen / heute abend / ? (*present*)
2. Wem / geben / er / es / ? (*present perfect*)

---

*Glauben takes the dative when referring to people.

3. Wessen Idee / sein / das / ? (*past*)
4. Wen / meinen / du / ? (*present*)
5. Wer / tun / es / ? (*past and present perfect*)
6. Wessen Wagen / sein / das / ? (*present*)
7. Wem / sagen / er / das / ? (*present perfect*)
8. Wen / sehen / du / da / ? (*present perfect*)
9. Wessen Mappe / sein / das / ? (*present*)
10. Wem / sollen / ich / glauben / ? (*present*)

(**tun, tat, hat getan:** to do)

● Express in German.

1. Whose car is that?
2. Who do you mean?
3. Who did he give it to?
4. Who's coming this evening?
5. Who did you see there?

6. Whose idea was that?
7. Who should I believe? (use **soll**)
8. Who did it?
9. Whose briefcase is that?
10. Who did he tell it to?

B Question Words with Prepositions: Wer and Wo(r)-Compounds

German treats **wo(r)**-compounds in basically the same way as it does **da(r)**-compounds.

1 wer with persons

Look at the following examples:

> **An wen** hast du gedacht? (*Who were you thinking of?*)
> **Nach wem** hat er gefragt? (*Who was he asking about?*)

If the object of a preposition is a *person*, the appropriate forms of **wer** must be used:

> An wen . . . ? *Who . . . of?*
> Nach wem . . . ? *Who . . . about?*

2 wo(r)-compounds with things

If the object of the preposition is a thing, a **wo(r)**-compound is used:

> Woran hast du gedacht? (*What were you thinking of?*)
> Wonach hat er gefragt? (*What was he asking about?*)

The **wo(r)**-compound consists of **wo(r)** + the *preposition*.

1. If the preposition begins with a *consonant*, wo- is used: wonach

2. If the preposition begins with a *vowel*, wor- is used: woran

PERSONS	THINGS
An wen hast du gedacht? (of whom)	**Woran** hast du gedacht? (of what)
With *persons* one uses: preposition + appropriate form of **wer**	With *things* one uses: **wo(r)** + preposition

DRILLS

1 Fill-ins

- **wer** with persons: Supply the appropriate form of **wer**.

  1. Mit _____ ist sie ausgegangen?
  2. Für _____ hast du es gekauft?
  3. Nach _____ hat er gefragt?
  4. An _____ hast du gedacht?
 (**denken an** + *acc.*)

  5. Mit _____ wollen Sie sprechen?
  6. Auf _____ wartet er?
 (**warten auf** + *acc.*)

- **wo(r)**-compounds with things: Prefix the correct form of **wo(r)**- to the prepositions.

  EXAMPLE   ____auf wartest du?
                Worauf wartest du?

  1. ___an hast du gedacht?
  2. ___über haben sie gesprochen?

  3. ___nach hat er gefragt?
  4. ___auf wartest du?

- Persons: Supply the preposition and the appropriate form of **wer**. Use the English sentences as cues.

  1. _____ ist sie ausgegangen?   *Who did she go out with?*
    (With whom)

  2. _____ hast du gedacht?   *Who were you thinking of?*
    (Of whom)

  3. _____ hat er gefragt?   *Who was he asking about?*
    (About whom)

  4. _____ hast du es gekauft?   *Who did you buy it for?*
    (For whom)

  5. _____ wollen Sie sprechen?   *Who do you want to speak to (with)?*
    (With whom)

  6. _____ wartet er?   *Who is he waiting for?*
    (For whom)

- Things: Supply the appropriate **wo(r)**-compound.

  1. _____ hast du gedacht?   *What were you thinking of?*
    (Of what)

  2. _____ hat er gefragt?   *What was he asking about?*
    (About what)

3. _____ wartest du?   *What are you waiting for?*
   (For what)

4. _____ haben sie gesprochen?   *What were they talking about?*
   (About what)

● Mixed drill.

1. _____ hast du es gekauft?   *Who did you buy it for?*
   (For whom)

2. _____ haben sie gesprochen?   *What were they talking about?*
   (About what)

3. _____ hast du gedacht?   *What were you thinking of?*
   (Of what)

4. _____ wartet er?   *Who's he waiting for?*
   (For whom)

5. _____ ist sie ausgegangen?   *Who did she go out with?*
   (With whom)

6. _____ hat er gefragt?   *Who was he asking about?*
   (About whom)

7. _____ wartest du?   *What are you waiting for?*
   (For what)

8. _____ wollen Sie sprechen?   *Who do you want to talk to (with)?*
   (With whom)

9. _____ hast du gedacht?   *Who were you thinking of?*
   (Of whom)

10. _____ hat er gefragt?   *What was he asking about?*
    (About what)

2   Express in German

1. What were you thinking of?   6. Who did you buy it for?
2. Who's he waiting for?   7. Who were you thinking of?
3. Who do you want to talk to (with)?   8. What are you waiting for?
4. What were they talking about?   9. Who did she go out with?
5. What was he asking about?   10. Who was he asking about?

C Wer-, Was-, and Wo(r)-Clauses

You have already seen the question words **wer** and **was** functioning as subordinating words (Lesson 9, Level One). **Wo(r)**-compounds have the same subordinating effect on word order:

> **Worüber** haben sie gesprochen?
> Weißt du, **worüber** sie gesprochen haben?

Now you will see how similar these *question-word clauses* are to *relative clauses*. They can in fact be thought of as a special kind of relative construction.

1 wer-clauses

Look at the following examples to see just how much a **wer**-clause resembles a relative clause:

NOM.   Wissen Sie, wer das ist?
(Do you know *who* that is?)

ACC.   Ich weiß nicht, wen Sie meinen.
(I don't know *who*[m] you mean.)
Weißt du, auf wen er wartet?
(Do you know *who* he's waiting *for*? [*Lit.: for whom* he's waiting])

DAT.   Er hat vergessen, wem er es gegeben hat?
(He forgot *who*[m] he gave it *to*?)
Ich weiß nicht, mit wem er ausgegangen ist.
(I don't know *who* he went out *with*. [*Lit.: with whom* he went out])

GEN.   Ich möchte wissen, wessen Idee das war.
(I'd like to know *whose* idea that was.)

The choice between **wer** and **der** is simple. A form of **der** is used if there is an *antecedent*. A form of **wer** is used if there is *no antecedent*.

Ist das der Kellner, der uns bedient hat?
but   Weißt du, wer uns bedient hat?

Wie heißt das Mädchen, mit dem er ausgeht?
but   Ich weiß nicht, mit wem er ausgeht.

In the first of the above examples, **der Kellner** is the antecedent of **der.** But in the next sentence, **wer** has no antecedent in the main clause:

Ist das **der Kellner, der.** . . .
Ich weiß nicht, **wer.** . . .

Similarly, **das Mädchen** is the antecedent of **dem,** but the **wem** in our last example has no antecedent at all:

Wie heißt **das Mädchen,** mit **dem.** . . .
Ich weiß nicht, mit **wem.** . . .

2 was- and wo(r)-clauses

Look at the following examples

NOM.   Weißt du, was das ist?
(Do you know *what* that is?)

ACC.   Er wußte nicht, was er tat.
(He didn't know *what* he was doing.)
Ich weiß nicht, woran er gedacht hat.
(I don't know *what* he was thinking of.)

DAT.   Wissen Sie, wonach er gefragt hat?
(Do you know *what* he was asking *about*?)

As you can see, these **was-** and **wo(r)**-clauses behave just like **wer**-clauses. The only difference is that they don't refer to people.

Special uses of **was**

The relative pronoun **was** must also be used when the *antecedent* is:

1. A superlative adjective used as a noun:

   Das ist das Beste, was wir haben.   (That's *the best that* we have.)

2. A neuter pronoun indicating quantity:

alles	everything
etwas	something
nichts	nothing

   Das ist alles, was ich weiß.   (That's *all that* I know.)

3 No omission of German relative pronouns

As was pointed out in Lesson 10, Level One, *relative pronouns may never be omitted in German:*

   Das ist das Beste, was wir haben.   (That's the best we have.)

DRILLS

1 The relative pronoun **wer**

• Supply the correct forms of the pronoun and, where necessary, the preposition.

1. Haben Sie gehört, _____ heute abend kommt?
   (who)

2. Ich weiß nicht, _____ Sie meinen.
   (whom)

3. Können Sie mir sagen, _____ Wagen das ist?
   (whose)

4. Ich weiß nicht, _____ er ausgegangen ist.
   (with whom)

5. Ich bin nicht sicher, _____ er es gesagt hat.
   (to whom)

6. Wissen Sie, _____ er gedacht hat?
   (of whom)

7. Ich weiß nicht, _____ es getan hat.
   (who)

8. Er hat vergessen, _____ er es gegeben hat.
   (to whom)

9. Weißt du, _____ er wartet?
   (for whom)

10. Ich möchte wissen, _____ Idee das war.
    (whose)

11. Ich weiß nicht, _____ ich glauben soll.   (**glauben** + *dat., with people:* to believe)
    (whom)

12. Kannst du herausfinden, _____ er gefragt hat?   (**heraus·finden:** to find out)
    (about whom)

13. Nein, ich weiß nicht, _____ Mappe das ist.
    (whose)

2   The relative pronoun **was**

● Supply the correct pronouns or **wo(r)**-compounds.

1. Hast du ihn gefragt, _____ er machen will.
   (what)

2. Ich weiß nicht, _____ er gedacht hat.
   (of what)

3. Das ist das Beste, _____ wir haben.
   (that)

4. Er wußte nicht, _____ er tat.
   (what)

5. Das ist alles, _____ ich weiß.
   (that)

6. Hast du gehört, _____ sie gesprochen haben?
   (about what)

7. Das ist etwas, _____ ich nicht verstehen kann.
   (that)

8. Wissen Sie, _____ er gefragt hat?
   (about what)

9. Sie hatten nichts, _____ ich gebrauchen konnte.   ·(**gebrauchen:** to use)
   (that)

10. Das ist das Nächste, _____ wir tun müssen.   (**das Nächste:** the next thing)
    (that)

11. Weißt du, _____ das ist?
    (what)

3   Mixed drills

a. 1. Ich bin nicht sicher, _____ er es gesagt hat.
       (who [he told it] to)

    2. Das ist das Beste, _____ wir haben, mein Herr.
       (that)

    3. Ich weiß nicht, _____ Sie meinen.
       (whom)

    4. Er wußte nicht, _____ er tat.
       (what)

    5. Hast du gehört, _____ sie gesprochen haben?
       (what [they were talking] about)

    6. Können Sie mir sagen, _____ Wagen das ist?
       (whose)

7. Ich weiß nicht, _____ sie ist.
   (who)

8. Kannst du herausfinden, _____ er gefragt hat?
   (who [he was asking] about)

9. Ich weiß nicht, _____ er gedacht hat.
   (what [he was thinking] of)

10. Das ist etwas, _____ ich nicht verstehen kann.
    (that)

b. 1. Weißt du, _____ das ist?
   (what)

2. Wissen Sie, _____ er gefragt hat?
   (what [he was asking] about)

3. Sie hatten nichts, _____ ich gebrauchen konnte.
   (that)

4. Ich weiß nicht, _____ er ausgegangen ist.
   (who [he went out] with)

5. Das ist alles, _____ ich weiß.
   (that)

6. Er hat vergessen, _____ er es gegeben hat.
   (who [he gave it] to)

7. Weißt du, _____ er wartet?
   (who [he's waiting] for)

8. Hast du ihn gefragt, _____ er machen will?
   (what)

9. Ich möchte wissen, _____ Idee das war.
   (whose)

10. Ich weiß nicht, _____ ich glauben sollte.
    (whom)

c. 1. Das ist das Nächste, _____ wir tun müssen.
   (that)

2. Wissen Sie, _____ er gedacht hat?
   (who [he was thinking] of)

3. Haben Sie gehört, _____ heute abend kommt?
   (who)

4. Hat er dir gesagt, _____ er da gesehen hat?
   (whom)

5. Nein, ich weiß nicht, _____ Mappe das ist.
   (whose)

4 Relative clauses

• Complete the following sentences by expressing the relative clauses in German.

a. 1. Das ist alles, _____.
   (that I know)

2. Ich weiß nicht, _____.
   (who you mean)

3. Ich möchte wissen, _____.
(whose idea that was)

4. Das ist das Nächste, _____.
(that we have to do)

5. Weißt du, _____?
(who he's waiting for)

6. Haben Sie gehört, _____?
(who's coming this evening)

7. Ich bin nicht sicher, _____.
(who he told it to)

8. Weißt du, _____?
(what that is)

9. Hast du gehört, _____?
(what they were talking about)

10. Können Sie mir sagen, _____?
(whose car that is)

b. 1. Kannst du herausfinden, _____?
(who he was asking about)

2. Hast du ihn gefragt, _____?
(what he wants to do)

3. Ich weiß nicht, _____.
(what he was thinking of)

4. Er hat vergessen, _____.
(who he gave it to)

5. Nein, ich weiß nicht, _____.
(whose briefcase that is)

6. Wissen Sie, _____?
(what he was asking about)

7. Das ist das Beste, _____, mein Herr.
(that we have)

8. Ich weiß nicht, _____.
(who she is)

9. Das ist etwas, _____.
(that I can't understand)

10. Ich weiß nicht, _____.
(who he went out with)

c. 1. Wissen Sie, _____?
(who he was thinking of)

2. Er wußte nicht, _____.
(what he was doing)

3. Ich weiß nicht, _____.
(who I should believe)

5 Express in German

a. 1. I don't know who she is.
2. Did you hear what they were talking about?
3. He didn't know what he was doing.
4. Can you tell me whose car that is?
5. I don't know who he's waiting for.
6. That's all I know.
7. That's something I can't understand.
8. I don't know what he was thinking of.
9. He forgot who he gave it to.
10. Do you know what he was asking about?

b. 1. Have you heard who's coming this evening?
2. Do you know what that is?
3. Can you find out who he was asking about?

4. I'm not sure who I told it to.
5. That's the best we have, Sir.
6. I don't know who you mean.
7. I'd like to know whose idea that was.
8. Do you know who he was thinking of?
9. I don't know who he went out with.
10. That's the next thing we have to do.

c. 1. Did you ask him what he wants to do?
2. I don't know who I should believe.
3. No, I don't know whose briefcase that is.

MIXED DRILLS (Levels I and II)

1 Fill-ins

a. 1. Da ist die Platte, _____ ich kaufen will.
      (that)

2. Das ist der Mann, _____ ich arbeite.
      (for whom)

3. Er wußte nicht, _____ er tat.
      (what)

4. Der Arzt, _____ ich ging, war wirklich sehr gut.
      (to whom)

5. Wer war die Frau, _____ neben ihm saß?
      (who)

6. Ich weiß nicht, _____ er wartet.
      (who [he's waiting] for)

7. Kennst du die Leute, _____ heute abend kommen?
      (who)

8. Das sind die Leute, _____ Haus wir kauften.
      (whose)

9. Er hat vergessen, _____ er es gegeben hat.
      (who [he gave it] to)

10. Nein, ich weiß nicht, _____ Mappe das ist.
       (whose)

b. 1. Der Wein, _____ ich kaufen wollte, war nicht mehr da.
       (that)

2. Das ist die Marke, _____ ich gedacht habe.
       (that [I was thinking] of)

3. Ich weiß nicht, _____ ich glauben sollte.
       (who)

4. Ist das der Kellner, _____ uns bedient hat?
       (who)

5. Kennst du das Mädchen, _____ er ausgeht?
       (who [he goes out] with)

6. Das sind Leute, _____ man reden kann.
       (who [you can talk] to)

7. Das ist der Revolver, _____ ihn getötet hat.
       (that)

8. Die Sachen, _____ sie da haben, sind alle zu teuer.
       (that)

9. Das ist das Beste, _____ wir haben, mein Herr.
       (that)

10. Und das war das letzte Mal, _____ ich ihn sah.
       (that)

c. 1. Haben Sie ihn gefragt, _____ er machen will?
       (what)

2. Die Leute, _____ nebenan wohnen, sind ziemlich laut.
       (who)

3. Wo hält der Bus, _____ zur Uni fährt?
       (that)

4. Haben Sie gehört, _____ heute abend kommt?
       (who)

5. Hier ist der Brief, _____ Sie gewartet haben.
       (that [you were waiting] for)

6. Da ist eine Jacke, _____ Farbe mir gefällt.
       (whose)

7. Ich weiß nicht, _____ Sie meinen.
       (who)

8. München ist eine Stadt, _____ ich gern besuchen würde.
       (that)

9. Ist das das Hotel, _____ Sie gefragt haben?
       (that [you were asking] about)

10. Das ist alles, _____ ich weiß.
       (that)

d. 1. Da ist ein Mantel, _____ Farbe mir gefällt.
       (whose)

2. Die Familie, _____ er wohnt, ist sehr nett.
       (that [he lives] with)

3. Wissen Sie, _____ er gedacht hat?
       (who [he was thinking] of)

4. Das ist der Kerl, _____ ich meine.
       (who)

5. Das war eine Nacht, _____ ich nie vergessen werde.
   (that)

6. Ich möchte wissen, _____ Idee das war.
   (whose)

7. Das ist etwas, _____ ich nicht verstehen kann.
   (that)

8. Wo ist die Bar, _____ früher hier war?
   (that)

9. Ich bin nicht sicher, _____ ich es gegeben habe.
   (who)

10. Das ist das Nächste, _____ wir tun müssen.
    (that)

e. 1. Das ist die Universität, _____ er studiert hat.
       (that [he studied] at)

    2. Nein, ich meine das Mädchen, _____ Vater gerade hier war.
       (whose)

    3. Ich weiß nicht, _____ er ausgegangen ist.
       (who [he went out] with)

    4. Das ist das Haus, _____ wir kaufen wollten.
       (that)

    5. Ich weiß nicht, _____ er gedacht hat.
       (what [he was thinking] of)

    6. Wissen Sie, _____ er gefragt hat?
       (what [he was asking] about)

    7. Gibt es eine andere Straße, _____ zum Bahnhof führt?
       (that)

    8. Ich weiß nicht, _____ sie ist.
       (who)

    9. Das ist der Mann, _____ Stimme ich hörte.
       (whose)

    10. Haben Sie gehört, _____ sie gesprochen haben?
        (what [they were talking] about)

f. 1. Das sind die Studenten, _____ wir nach Mainz schicken.
       (who)

    2. Kannst du mir sagen, _____ Wagen das ist?
       (whose)

    3. Wer war das Mädchen, _____ gerade hier war?
       (who)

    4. Können Sie herausfinden, _____ er gefragt hat?
       (who [he was asking] about)

    5. Hast du den Wagen gesehen, _____ er gefahren hat?
       (that)

    6. Wir haben Freunde da, _____ wir besuchen wollen.
       (who)

a. 1. Is that the waiter who served us?
2. That's the man whose voice I heard.
3. I don't know who he went out with.
4. That's the man I work for.
5. That's all that I know.
6. We have friends there who we want to visit.
7. I don't know what he was thinking of.
8. The wine I wanted to buy wasn't there any more.
9. Those are people you can talk to.
10. Is that the hotel you were asking about?

b. 1. The things they have there are all too expensive.
2. Can you tell me whose car that is?
3. And that was the last time I saw him.
4. The family he lives with is very nice.
5. I don't know who you mean.
6. Is there another street that goes to the station?
7. I don't know who he's waiting for.
8. Those are the people whose house we bought.
9. I'm not sure who I gave it to.
10. He didn't know what he was doing.

c. 1. Munich is a city I'd like to visit.
2. That's the guy I mean.
3. No, I don't know whose briefcase that is.
4. There's the record I want to buy.
5. That's the best we have, Sir.
6. Did you see the car he was driving?
7. I don't know who she is.
8. That's the brand I was thinking of.

9. Did you hear what they were talking about?
10. Do you know who he was thinking of?

d. 1. There's a coat whose color I like.
2. Did you hear who's coming this evening?
3. Do you know the girl he goes out with?
4. That's the house we wanted to buy.
5. I'd like to know whose idea that was.
6. Where's the bar that was here before?
7. The doctor I went to was really very good.
8. That's the next thing we have to do.
9. Do you know what he was asking about?
10. Here's the letter you were waiting for.

e. 1. He forgot who he gave it to.
2. Do you know the people who are coming this evening?
3. Where does the bus stop that goes to the university?
4. That's something that I can't understand.
5. There's a sports coat whose color I like.
6. Did you ask him what he wants to do?

VOCABULARY

gebrauchen to use
glauben (+ *dat. with people*) to believe
heraus · finden to find out
    fand . . . heraus, herausgefunden
die **Hilfe** help

die **Mappe, –n** briefcase
die **Möglichkeit, –en** possibility
das **Nächste** (*adj. noun*) the next thing
    tun (tut) to do
    tat, getan

Lesson 10 Level THREE

A Conditional Sentences with Modal Auxiliaries

Look at the following examples:

INDICATIVE	Wenn er seinen Wagen hat, **kann** er uns nach Hause fahren. (If he has his car, he *can* drive us home.)
PRES. SUBJ. II	Wenn er seinen Wagen hätte, **könnte** er uns nach Hause fahren. (If he had his car, he *could* drive us home.)
PAST SUBJ. II	Wenn er seinen Wagen gehabt hätte, **hätte** er uns nach Hause fahren **können**. (If he had had his car, he *could have* driven us home.)

1 Present tense of subjunctive II

The **würde** construction is *not* used with modals.

> Wenn er seinen Wagen hätte, **könnte** er uns nach Hause fahren.

2 Past tense of subjunctive II

a. Double infinitive: **fahren können**

> Wenn er seinen Wagen gehabt hätte, hätte er uns nach Hause **fahren können**.

This is a double-infinitive construction. (For a complete explanation, see Lesson 7, Level Three, pp. 339–40.)

b. **hätte** before the double infinitive

Look at this new example:

> Ich hätte es ihm gesagt, wenn ich ihn **hätte finden können**.

Here you see a double-infinitive construction in a subordinate clause; in this case, a **wenn**-clause. When the auxiliary **(hätte)** is forced to the end of the clause by the subordinating conjunction **(wenn)**, it must come *before* the double infinitive. (See Lesson 9, Level One, p. 419.)

. . . wenn ich ihn hätte **finden können**

3 Contrastive grammar

Look at the following simple sentences:*

INDICATIVE	Du kannst es tun.	(You can do it.)
PRES. SUBJ. II	Du könntest es tun.	(You could do it.)
PAST SUBJ. II	Du hättest es tun können.	(You could have done it.)

As you can see, the English and German modal constructions are parallel in the indicative and in the present tense of the subjunctive. But look at how differently they form the *past tense* of the subjunctive:

Du hättest es tun können.
You *could* have *done* it.

The German modal construction is "regular"; that is to say, the past tense of subjunctive II is formed in the usual way:

PRESENT TENSE	Du **könntest** es tun.
PAST TENSE	Du **hättest** es tun **können.**

But English does something odd here. It leaves the modal alone and changes the dependent infinitive:

PRESENT TENSE	You could *do* it.
PAST TENSE	You could *have done* it.

DRILLS

1 Present tense subjunctive II

• Supply the correct form of subjunctive II.

1. Was _____ wir machen?
   (sollen)

2. Du _____ es tun.
   (können)

3. Er _____ um drei Uhr vorbeikommen.
   (sollen)

4. Dann _____ wir länger bleiben.
   (müssen)

5. Du _____ wirklich nach Hause gehen.
   (sollen)

6. Sie _____ es vergessen.
   (können)

---

*Subjunctive II can be used in simple sentences as well as in conditional sentences.

● Synthetic exercises: Form the suggested sentences using the present tense of subjunctive II.

1. Er / sollen / vorbeikommen / um drei Uhr
2. Du / können / tun / es
3. Dann / müssen / wir / bleiben / länger

4. Du / sollen / gehen / wirklich nach Hause
5. Sie (they) / können / vergessen / es
6. Was / sollen / wir / machen / ?

● Express in German.

1. You could do it.
2. He should come by at three o'clock.
3. You should really go home.

4. Then we'd have to stay longer.
5. What should we do?
6. They could forget it.

2   Past tense subjunctive II

● Supply the correct form of **hätte**.

1. Er _____ es tun können.
2. Du _____ wirklich nach Hause gehen sollen.
3. Was _____ wir machen sollen?

4. Er _____ um drei Uhr vorbeikommen sollen.
5. Dann _____ wir länger bleiben müssen.
6. Sie (they) _____ es vergessen können.

● Supply the complete modal expression.

EXAMPLE   Er _____ um drei Uhr vorbeikommen _____ .
                   (sollen)

            Er **hätte** um drei Uhr vorbeikommen **sollen.**

1. Du _____ wirklich nach Hause gehen _____ .
        (sollen)
2. Dann _____ wir länger bleiben _____ .
           (müssen)
3. Was _____ wir machen _____ ?
        (sollen)
4. Du _____ es machen _____ .
        (können)
5. Er _____ um drei Uhr vorbeikommen _____ .
        (sollen)
6. Sie (they) _____ es vergessen _____ .
              (können)

● Synthetic exercises: Form the suggested sentences using the past tense of subjunctive II.

1. Er / sollen / vorbeikommen / um drei Uhr
2. Sie (they) / können / vergessen / es
3. Du / sollen / gehen / wirklich nach Hause

4. Dann / müssen / wir / bleiben / länger
5. Du / können / tun / es
6. Was / sollen / wir / machen / ?

- Express in German (cued). The double infinitive is given as a cue at the end of each sentence.

    1. You could have done it. **(tun können)**
    2. He should have come by at three o'clock. **(vorbeikommen sollen)**
    3. You really should have gone home. **(gehen sollen)**
    4. They could have forgotten it. **(vergessen können)**
    5. What should we have done? **(machen sollen)**
    6. Then we would have had to stay longer. **(bleiben müssen)**

- Express in German.

    1. You really should have gone home.
    2. They could have forgotten it.
    3. He should have come by at three o'clock.

    4. You could have done it.
    5. What should we have done?
    6. Then we would have had to stay longer.

3　Present and past subjunctive II

- Synthetic exercises: Form the suggested sentences in the present and past tenses of subjunctive II.

    1. Er / sollen / vorbeikommen / um drei Uhr
    2. Du / können / tun / es
    3. Was / sollen / wir / machen / ?

    4. Sie / können / vergessen / es
    5. Du / sollen / gehen / wirklich nach Hause
    6. Dann / müssen / wir / bleiben / länger

- Express in German.

    1. What should we do?
       What should we have done?
    2. They could forget it.
       They could have forgotten it.
    3. He should come by at three o'clock.
       He should have come by at three o'clock.

    4. You could do it.
       You could have done it.
    5. Then we'd have to stay longer.
       Then we would have had to stay longer.
    6. You should really go home.
       You really should have gone home.

4　Present tense subjunctive II: the **dann**-clause

- Supply the correct form of subjunctive II.

    1. Wenn Sie früher kommen würden, _____ ich Sie abholen.
       (können)
    2. Wenn wir mehr Zeit hätten, _____ wir es machen.
       (können)
    3. Wenn er wirklich dagegen wäre, _____ er etwas tun.
       (sollen)
    4. Wenn er seinen Wagen hätte, _____ er uns nach Hause fahren.
       (können)
    5. Wenn es leichter wäre, _____ wir es machen.
       (können)
    6. Wenn er nicht hier wäre, _____ ich es allein machen.
       (müssen)

- Synthetic exercises: Form the suggested **dann**-clause using the present tense of subjunctive II.

> EXAMPLE Wenn es ein wenig leichter wäre, wir / können / machen / es
> Wenn es ein wenig leichter wäre, könnten wir es machen.

1. Wenn er früher kommen würde, ich / können / abholen / ihn
2. Wenn wir mehr Zeit hätten, wir / können / machen / es
3. Wenn er seinen Wagen hätte, er / können / fahren / uns nach Hause
4. Wenn er nicht hier wäre, ich / müssen / machen / es allein
5. Wenn er wirklich dagegen wäre, er / sollen / tun / etwas
6. Wenn es ein wenig leichter wäre, wir / können / machen / es

5 Past tense subjunctive II: the **dann**-clause

- Supply the correct form of the auxiliary **hätte**.

1. Wenn er wirklich dagegen gewesen wäre, _____ er etwas tun sollen.
2. Wenn wir mehr Zeit gehabt hätten, _____ wir es machen können.
3. Wenn es leichter gewesen wäre, _____ wir es machen können.
4. Wenn er früher gekommen wäre, _____ ich ihn abholen können.
5. Wenn er seinen Wagen gehabt hätte, _____ er uns nach Hause fahren können.
6. Wenn er nicht hier gewesen wäre, _____ ich es allein machen müssen.

- Supply the complete modal expression.

> EXAMPLE Wenn es ein wenig leichter gewesen wäre, _____ wir es machen _____.
> (können)
>
> Wenn es ein wenig leichter gewesen wäre, hätten wir es machen können.

1. Wenn wir mehr Zeit gehabt hätten, _____ wir es machen _____.
   (können)
2. Wenn er früher gekommen wäre, _____ ich ihn abholen _____.
   (können)
3. Wenn er nicht hier gewesen wäre, _____ ich es allein machen _____.
   (müssen)
4. Wenn es leichter gewesen wäre, _____ wir es machen _____.
   (können)
5. Wenn er seinen Wagen gehabt hätte, _____ er uns nach Hause fahren _____.
   (können)
6. Wenn er wirklich dagegen gewesen wäre, _____ er etwas tun _____.
   (sollen)

- Synthetic exercises: Form the suggested **dann**-clause using the past tense of subjunctive II.

> EXAMPLE Wenn es ein wenig leichter gewesen wäre, wir / können / machen / es
> Wenn es ein wenig leichter gewesen wäre, hätten wir es machen können.

1. Wenn er seinen Wagen gehabt hätte, er / können / fahren / uns / nach Hause
2. Wenn wir mehr Zeit gehabt hätten, wir / können / machen / es
3. Wenn es ein wenig leichter gewesen wäre, wir / können / machen / es

4. Wenn er wirklich dagegen gewesen wäre, er / sollen / tun / etwas
5. Wenn er früher gekommen wäre, ich / können / abholen / ihn
6. Wenn er nicht hier gewesen wäre, ich / müssen / machen / es allein

6   Present and past subjunctive II: the **dann**-clause

● Synthetic exercises: Form the suggested **dann**-clause in the present and past tenses of subjunctive II. The tense of the **wenn**-clause will determine the tense of the **dann**-clause.

1. Wenn es ein wenig leichter wäre, wir / können / machen / es
   Wenn es ein wenig leichter gewesen wäre, wir / können / machen / es
2. Wenn er früher kommen würde, ich / können / abholen / ihn
   Wenn er früher gekommen wäre, ich / können / abholen / ihn
3. Wenn wir mehr Zeit hätten, wir / können / machen / es
   Wenn wir mehr Zeit gehabt hätten, wir / können / machen / es
4. Wenn er nicht hier wäre, ich / müssen / machen / es / allein
   Wenn er nicht hier gewesen wäre, / ich / müssen / machen / es / allein
5. Wenn er seinen Wagen hätte, er / können / fahren / uns nach Hause
   Wenn er seinen Wagen gehabt hätte, er / können / fahren / uns nach Hause
6. Wenn er wirklich dagegen wäre, er / sollen / tun / etwas
   Wenn er wirklich dagegen gewesen wäre, er / sollen / tun / etwas

● Express in German.

1. If we had more time, we could do it.
   If we had had more time, we could have done it.
2. If he had his car, he could drive us home.
   If he had had his car, he could have driven us home.
3. If he weren't here, I'd have to do it alone.
   If he had not been here, I would have had to do it alone.
4. If he came earlier, I could pick him up.
   If he had come earlier, I could have picked him up.
5. If it were a little easier, we could do it.
   If it had been a little easier, we could have done it.
6. If he were really against it, he should do something.
   If he had really been against it, he should have done something.

7   Present tense subjunctive II: the **wenn**-clause

● Supply the correct form of subjunctive II.

1. Es wäre nett, wenn sie (*they*) kommen _____ .
   (können)

2. Er würde fragen, wenn er es wissen _____ .
   (wollen)

3. Es wäre besser, wenn Sie es früher erledigen _____ .
   (können)

4. Sie würde es uns sagen, wenn sie (*she*) mitkommen _____ .
   (wollen)

- Synthetic exercises: Form the suggested **wenn**-clause using the present tense of subjunctive II.

    1. Er würde fragen, wenn / er / wollen / wissen / es
    2. Es wäre besser, wenn / Sie / können / erledigen / es früher
    3. Es wäre nett, wenn / sie (they) / können / kommen
    4. Sie würde es uns sagen, wenn / sie (she) / wollen / mitkommen

- Express in German: the **wenn**-clause.

    1. Es wäre nett, _____.
       (if they could come)
    2. Es wäre besser, _____.
       (if you could take care of it earlier)
    3. Er würde fragen, _____.
       (if he wanted to know [it])
    4. Sie würde es uns sagen, _____.
       (if she wanted to come along)

- Express in German.

    1. He'd ask, if he wanted to know (it).
    2. It would be nice if they could come.
    3. She'd tell us if she wanted to come along.
    4. It would be better if you could take care of it earlier.

   8   Past tense subjunctive II: the **wenn**-clause

- Supply the correct form of **hätte**.

    1. Es wäre nett gewesen, wenn sie (they) _____ kommen können.
    2. Er hätte gefragt, wenn er es _____ wissen wollen.
    3. Es wäre besser gewesen, wenn Sie es früher _____ erledigen können.
    4. Sie hätte es uns gesagt, wenn sie (she) _____ mitkommen wollen.

- Combine the following pairs of sentences.

    1. Er hätte gefragt.   **wenn**   Er hätte es wissen wollen.
    2. Es wäre nett gewesen.   **wenn**   Sie hätten kommen können.
    3. Es wäre besser gewesen.   **wenn**   Sie hätten es früher erledigen können.
    4. Sie hätte es uns gesagt.   **wenn**   Sie hätte mitkommen wollen.

- Supply the complete modal expression.

    EXAMPLE   Er hätte gefragt, wenn er es _____ wissen _____.
                                          (wollen)

                   Er hätte gefragt, wenn er es **hätte** wissen **wollen.**

    1. Es wäre nett gewesen, wenn sie (they) _____ kommen _____.
                                             (können)
    2. Er hätte gefragt, wenn er es _____ wissen _____.
                                    (wollen)
    3. Es wäre besser gewesen, wenn Sie es früher _____ erledigen _____.
                                                  (können)
    4. Sie hätte es uns gesagt, wenn sie (she) _____ mitkommen _____.
                                               (wollen)

- Synthetic exercises: Form the suggested **wenn**-clause using the past tense of subjunctive II.

  EXAMPLE   Er hätte gefragt, wenn / er / wollen / wissen / es
                      Er hätte gefragt, wenn er es **hätte** wissen **wollen.**

  1. Es wäre besser gewesen, wenn / Sie / können / erledigen / es früher
  2. Sie hätte es uns gesagt, wenn / sie (*she*) / wollen / mitkommen
  3. Es wäre nett gewesen, wenn / sie (*they*) / können / kommen
  4. Er hätte gefragt, wenn / er / wollen / wissen / es

- Express in German: the **dann**-clause (cued). The double infinitive is given as a cue at the end of the **dann**-clause.

  1. Es wäre nett gewesen, _____. **(kommen können)**
                         (if they had been able to come)
  2. Er hätte gefragt, _____. **(wissen wollen)**
                (if he had wanted to know [it])
  3. Es wäre besser gewesen, _____. **(erledigen können)**
               (if you could have taken care of it earlier)
  4. Sie hätte es uns gesagt, _____. **(mitkommen wollen)**
               (if she had wanted to come along)

- Express in German.

  1. It would have been nice if they had been able to come.
  2. She would have told us if she had wanted to come along.
  3. He would have asked if he had wanted to know it.
  4. It would have been better if you could have taken care of it earlier.

9   Present and past subjunctive II: the **wenn**-clause

- Synthetic exercises: Form the suggested **wenn**-clause in the present and past tenses of subjunctive II. The tense of the first clause will determine the tense of the **wenn**-clause.

  1. Er würde fragen, wenn / er / wollen / wissen / es
     Er hätte gefragt, wenn / er / wollen / wissen / es

  2. Es wäre nett, wenn / sie (*they*) / können / kommen
     Es wäre nett gewesen, wenn / sie (*they*) / können / kommen

  3. Sie würde es uns sagen, wenn / sie (*she*) / wollen / mitkommen
     Sie hätte es uns gesagt, wenn / sie (*she*) / wollen / mitkommen

  4. Es wäre besser, wenn / Sie / können / erledigen / es früher
     Es wäre besser gewesen, wenn / Sie / können / erledigen / es früher

- Express in German: the **dann**-clause.

  1. Es wäre nett, _____.
                (if you could come)

     Es wäre nett gewesen, _____.
                       (if you could have come)

2. Er würde fragen, _____.
   (if he wanted to know [it])

   Er hätte gefragt, _____.
   (if he had wanted to know [it])

3. Es wäre besser, _____.
   (if you could take care of it earlier)

   Es wäre besser gewesen, _____.
   (if you could have taken care of it earlier)

4. Sie würde es uns sagen, _____.
   (if she wanted to come along)

   Sie hätte es uns gesagt, _____.
   (if she had wanted to come along)

- Express in German.

   1. It would be better, if you could take care of it earlier.
      It would have been better, if you could have taken care of it earlier.
   2. She'd tell us if she wanted to come along.
      She would have told us if she had wanted to come along.
   3. It would be nice if they could come along.
      It would have been nice if they could have come along.
   4. He'd ask if he wanted to know (it).
      He would have asked if he had wanted to know (it).

GRAND MIX

1 Synthetic exercises

- Form the suggested sentences. In compound sentences, the tense of the first clause will determine the tense of the second clause. The tense of simple sentences will be indicated in parentheses.

   a. 1. Wenn er seinen Wagen hätte, er / können / fahren / uns nach Hause
       2. Er würde fragen, wenn / er / wollen / wissen / es
       3. Wenn wir mehr Zeit gehabt hätten, wir / können / machen / es
       4. Was / sollen / wir / machen / ? (past subjunctive II)
       5. Wenn er früher kommen würde, ich / können / abholen / ihn
       6. Wenn es ein wenig leichter gewesen wäre, wir / können / machen / es
       7. Du / sollen / gehen / wirklich nach Hause (present subjunctive II)
       8. Wenn er seinen Wagen gehabt hätte, er / können / fahren / uns nach Hause
       9. Es wäre nett gewesen, wenn / sie / können / kommen
      10. Er / sollen / vorbeikommen / um drei Uhr (present subjunctive II)

   b. 1. Wenn er früher gekommen wäre, ich / können / abholen / ihn
       2. Sie hätte es uns gesagt, wenn / sie / wollen / mitkommen
       3. Wenn er nicht hier wäre, ich / müssen / machen / es allein
       4. Du / können / tun / es (past subjunctive II)
       5. Es wäre nett, wenn / sie / können / kommen
       6. Dann / müssen / wir / bleiben / länger (present subjunctive II)
       7. Du / sollen / gehen / wirklich nach Hause (past subjunctive II)
       8. Sie (they) / können / vergessen / es (present subjunctive II)
       9. Wenn wir mehr Zeit hätten, wir / können / machen / es
      10. Er / sollen / vorbeikommen / um drei Uhr (past subjunctive II)

c. 1. Du / können / tun / es   (*present subjunctive II*)
   2. Sie würde es uns sagen, wenn / sie / wollen / mitkommen
   3. Sie / können / vergessen / es   (*past subjunctive II*)
   4. Dann / müssen / wir / bleiben / länger   (*past subjunctive II*)
   5. Er hätte gefragt, wenn / er / wollen / wissen / es
   6. Wenn es ein wenig leichter wäre, wir / können / machen / es
   7. Wenn er nicht hier gewesen wäre, ich / müssen / machen / es allein
   8. Was / sollen / wir / machen / ?   (*present subjunctive II*)

2   Express in German

a. 1. It would be nice if they could come.
   2. If it were a little easier, we could do it.
   3. If he had had his car, he could have driven us home.
   4. He would have asked if he had wanted to know (it).
   5. What should we have done?
   6. You should really go home.
   7. If we had more time, we could do it.
   8. You could have done it.
   9. She'd tell us if she wanted to come along.
   10. If he had come earlier, I could have picked him up.

   6. If we had had more time, we could have done it.
   7. You could do it.
   8. If he had come earlier, I could have picked him up.
   9. She would have told us if she had wanted to come along.
   10. You should have really gone home.

b. 1. He should have come by at three o'clock.
   2. If he weren't here, I'd have to do it alone.
   3. If it had been a little easier, we could have done it.
   4. It would have been nice if they could have come.
   5. What should we do?

c. 1. Then we'd have to stay longer.
   2. If he were really against it, he should do something.
   3. If he had his car, he could drive us home.
   4. He'd ask if he wanted to know (it).

B Other Uses of Subjunctive II

1 Wishes

Look at the following examples:

Wenn er nur hier wäre!	(If he *were* only here!)
Wenn er nur hier gewesen wäre!	(If he *had* only *been* here!)
Wenn ich es nur finden könnte!	(If I *could* only find it!)
Wenn ich es nur hätte finden können!	(If I only *could have* found it!)

1. By their very nature, wishes are *contrary to facts* as they are now; for this reason, the subjunctive II is used in expressing wishes.

2. The structure of such sentences is very simple. To express a wish one simply adds the word **nur** (only, just) to a subjunctive II **wenn**-clause:

   Wenn er kommen würde . . . .   (If he'd come . . . .)
   Wenn er **nur** kommen würde!   (If he'd *only* come!)

3. In expressing wishes, the würde construction is used with *all verbs except:*

   sein, haben, wissen, and the *modal auxiliaries*

▶ Note 1   Like **nicht** and **wohl, nur** comes after objects but before adverbs.

▶ Note 2   The **würde** construction is even used with weak verbs in expressing wishes:

   Wenn er mir nur **antworden würde!**   (If he'd only answer me!)

DRILLS

Subjunctive II used for wishes

● Supply the correct present tense form of subjunctive II.

   EXAMPLE   Wenn er nur _____!
                              (kommen)
              Wenn er nur **kommen würde!**

1. Wenn ich nur sicher _____!
                       (sein)
2. Wenn er mir nur _____!
                    (antworten)
3. Wenn er es nur _____!
                  (wissen)
4. Wenn du mir nur _____!
                   (glauben)

5. Wenn ich es nur finden _____!
                          (können)
6. Wenn sie (they) nur hier _____!
                            (sein)
7. Wenn wir nur länger schlafen
   _____!
   (können)

● Supply the correct past tense form of subjunctive II.

   EXAMPLE   Wenn er nur _____!
                              (kommen)
              Wenn er nur **gekommen wäre!**

1. Wenn er mir nur _____!
                    (antworten)
2. Wenn sie (they) nur hier _____!
                            (sein)

3. Wenn du mir nur _____!
                   (glauben)
4. Wenn er es nur _____!
                  (wissen)

5. Wenn ich es nur _____ finden _____!
   (können)
6. Wenn er nur gestern _____!
   (kommen)
7. Wenn ich nur sicher _____!
   (sein)

8. Wenn wir nur länger _____
   (können)
   schlafen _____!

- Put the verbs into the present and past tenses of subjunctive II, unless otherwise indicated.

EXAMPLE   Wenn er nur _____!
           (kommen)

Wenn er nur **kommen würde**!
Wenn er nur **gekommen wäre**!

1. Wenn du mir nur _____!
   (glauben)
2. Wenn sie (they) nur hier _____!
   (sein)
3. Wenn er es nur _____!
   (wissen)
4. Wenn wir nur länger schlafen
   _____!
   (können)

5. Wenn er mir nur _____!
   (antworten)
6. Wenn er nur gestern _____!
   (kommen)
   (past only)
7. Wenn ich nur sicher _____!
   (sein)
8. Wenn ich es nur finden _____!
   (können)

- Synthetic exercises: Use the following elements to express wishes in both the present tense and the past tense of subjunctive II, unless otherwise indicated.

EXAMPLE   Wenn / er / kommen / nur / !

Wenn er nur **kommen würde**!
Wenn er nur **gekommen wäre**!

1. Wenn / sie (they) / sein / nur hier / !
2. Wenn / ich / wissen / es nur / !
3. Wenn / wir / können / schlafen / nur länger / !
4. Wenn / er / antworten / mir nur / !
5. Wenn / ich / sein / nur sicher / !
6. Wenn / du / glauben / mir nur / !
7. Wenn / ich / können / finden / es nur / !
8. Wenn / er / kommen / nur gestern / ! (past only)

- Express in German.

1. If I were only sure!
   If I had only been sure!
2. If I only knew (it)!
   If I had only known it!
3. If we could only sleep longer!
   If we only could have slept longer!
4. If he had only come yesterday!
5. If you would just believe me!
   If you had just believed me!

6. If he'd only answer me!
   If he had only answered me!
7. If they were only here!
   If they had only been here!
8. If I could only find it!
   If I only could have found it!

2 Forms of politeness

Look at the following examples:

Will you call him?	**Werden** Sie ihn anrufen?
Would you call him?	Würden Sie ihn anrufen?
Can you help me?	**Können** Sie mir helfen?
Could you help me?	Könnten Sie mir helfen?
Do you have time now?	**Haben** Sie jetzt Zeit?
Would you have time now?	Hätten Sie jetzt Zeit?

Using subjunctive II (instead of the indicative) takes the harshness out of a question or request. Both German and English use the subjunctive as a form of politeness.

▶ Note   In sentences of this kind, the **würde** construction is used with *all verbs except:*

sein, haben, wissen and the *modal auxiliaries*

DRILLS

• Put the following indicative sentences into subjunctive II to stress politeness.

EXAMPLE   Kann ich mitkommen?
Könnte ich mitkommen?

1. Werden Sie ihn anrufen?
2. Können Sie mir sagen, wo er wohnt?
3. Sind Sie dagegen?
4. Werden Sie das für mich erledigen?
5. Haben Sie jetzt Zeit?
6. Können wir zuschauen? (zu·schauen: to watch)
7. Werden Sie mir helfen?
8. Können Sie mich nach Hause fahren?

• Synthetic exercises: Use the following elements to form subjunctive II sentences.

1. Werden / Sie / helfen / mir / ?
2. Sein / Sie / dagegen / ?
3. Können / Sie / sagen / mir // wo / er / wohnen / ?
4. Werden / Sie / anrufen / ihn / ?
5. Können / Sie / fahren / mich nach Hause / ?
6. Haben / Sie / jetzt Zeit / ?
7. Werden / Sie / erledigen / das für mich / ?
8. Können / wir / zuschauen / ?

• Express in German.

1. Would you call him up?
2. Could you drive me home?
3. Would you have time?
4. Would you be against it?
5. Could we watch?
6. Would you help me?
7. Could you tell me where he lives?
8. Would you take care of that for me?

3 Contrary-to-fact situations with **als ob** (as if)

Look at the following examples:

Als ob ich das nicht wüßte!	(As if I didn't know that!)
Als ob ich das nicht gewußt hätte!	(As if I hadn't known that!)

Als ob constructions refer to *contrary-to-fact* situations and therefore require the use of subjunctive II. They also require *dependent word order* (that is, a conjugated verb at the end of the clause).

▶ Note As in the **wenn**-clause, one-word subjunctive II forms are used with:

weak verbs, **sein** and **haben,** **wissen** and the *modals*

Otherwise the **würde** construction is used.

DRILLS

• Supply the correct present tense subjunctive II form.

EXAMPLE Als ob wir so etwas _____!
         (tun)
         Als ob wir so etwas **tun würden**!

1. Als ob ich das nicht _____!
   (wissen)
2. Als ob wir so etwas _____!
   (tun)
3. Als ob man zu viel Geld haben _____!
   (können)
4. Es war, als ob sie (*she*) mir etwas sagen _____.
   (wollen)

(**so etwas:** anything like that)

• Supply the correct past tense subjunctive II form.

EXAMPLE Als ob wir so etwas _____!
         (tun)
         Als ob wir so etwas **getan hätten**!

1. Als ob ich das nicht _____!
   (wissen)
2. Als ob wir so etwas _____!
   (tun)
3. Es war, als ob wir es nie vorher _____.
   (sehen)
4. Als ob sie (*she*) das nicht oft genug _____!
   (sagen)

(**tun, tat, hat getan:** to do)

- Supply the correct subjunctive II form using the tense or tenses in parentheses.

EXAMPLE   Als ob wir so etwas _____! (*present and past*)
           (tun)

Als ob wir so etwas **tun würden**!
Als ob wir so etwas **getan hätten**!

1. Als ob ich das nicht _____! (*present and past*)
   (wissen)
2. Als ob sie (*she*) das nicht oft genug _____! (*past*)
   (sagen)
3. Als ob man zu viel Geld haben _____! (*present*)
   (können)
4. Als ob wir so etwas _____! (*present and past*)
   (tun)
5. Es war, als ob wir es nie vorher _____. (*past*)
   (sehen)
6. Es war, als ob sie (*she*) mir etwas sagen _____. (*present*)
   (wollen)

- Synthetic exercises: Use the following elements to form subjunctive II sentences in the tenses indicated.

1. Als ob / man / können / haben / zu viel Geld / ! (*present*)
2. Als ob / sie / sagen / das / nicht oft genug / ! (*past*)
3. Es war // als ob / sie / wollen / sagen / mir etwas (*present*)
4. Als ob / ich / wissen / das nicht / ! (*present and past*)
5. Als ob / wir / tun / so etwas / ! (*present and past*)
6. Es war // als ob / wir / sehen / es / nie vorher (*past*)

- Express in German.

1. As if we'd do anything like that!
   As if we had done anything like that!
2. As if one could have too much money!
3. It was as if she wanted to tell me something.
4. As if I didn't know that!
   As if I hadn't known that!
5. As if she hadn't said that often enough!
6. It was as if we had never seen it before.

MIXED DRILLS

1   Mixed synthetic exercises

- Form the suggested sentences using subjunctive II. Use the tense indicated in parentheses.

a. 1. Werden / Sie / anrufen / ihn / ? (*present*)
   2. Wenn / ich / sein / nur sicher / ! (*present*)
   3. Wenn / er / antworten / mir nur / ! (*past*)
   4. Als ob / man / können / haben / zu viel Geld / ! (*present*)
   5. Haben / Sie / jetzt Zeit / ? (*present*)
   6. Wenn / ich / können / finden / es nur / ! (*present*)
   7. Wenn / er / kommen / nur gestern / ! (*past*)

8. Es war / als ob / sie (she) / wollen / sagen / mir etwas. (*present*)
9. Können / Sie / sagen / mir // wo / er / wohnen / ? (*present*)
10. Wenn / ich / wissen / es nur / ! (*present*)

b. 1. Wenn / ich / können / finden / es nur / ! (*past*)
2. Können / wir / zuschauen / ? (*present*)
3. Als ob / ich / wissen / das nicht / ! (*present*)
4. Wenn / sie (they) / sein / nur hier / ! (*present*)
5. Wenn / ich / sein / nur sicher / ! (*past*)
6. Als ob / wir / tun / so etwas / ! (*present*)
7. Sein / Sie / dagegen / ? (*present*)
8. Wenn / ich / wissen / es nur / ! (*past*)
9. Es war // als ob / wir / sehen / es nie vorher (*past*)
10. Wenn / du / glauben / mir nur / ! (*present*)

c. 1. Als ob / wir / tun / so etwas / ! (*past*)
2. Wenn / er / antworten / mir / nur / ! (*present*)
3. Können / Sie / fahren / mich nach Hause / ? (*present*)
4. Wenn / wir / können / schlafen / nur länger / ! (*present*)
5. Wenn / sie (they) / sein / nur hier / ! (*past*)
6. Werden / Sie / helfen / mir / ? (*present*)
7. Als ob / ich / wissen / das nicht / ! (*past*)
8. Wenn / du / glauben / mir nur / ! (*past*)
9. Werden / Sie / erledigen / das für mich / ? (*present*)

2 Express in German

a. 1. If I were only sure!
2. If he'd only answer me!
3. Could you drive me home?
4. If he had only come yesterday!
5. As if I didn't know that!
6. If they were only here!
7. If I had only known!
8. Would you help me?
9. It was as if we had never seen it before.
10. If we could only sleep longer!

b. 1. Could we watch?
2. As if we'd do something like that!
3. If he had only answered me!

4. Would you call him up?
5. As if one could have too much money!
6. If I could only find it!
7. If they had only been here!
8. As if I hadn't known that!
9. Could you tell me where he lives?
10. If you'd just believe me!

c. 1. If I only could have found it!
2. Would you have time?
3. If I only knew!
4. If I had only been sure!
5. Would you be against it?
6. If you had just believed me!
7. Would you take care of that for me?

VOCABULARY

so etwas something like that   **zu · schauen** to watch

Reading **X**

Reisen° und Reisebüros°

das Reisen: travel   das Reisebüro, –s: travel agency

Ein deutsches Reisebüro kann vieles° für Sie machen und Ihnen wirklich helfen. Zuerst° können Sie Broschüren° und Prospekte° von Ihrem Reiseziel° bekommen. In den meisten Broschüren finden

vieles: a lot of things

zuerst: first of all

die Broschüre, –n: brochure   der Prospekt, –e: pamphlet

das Reiseziel, –e: destination

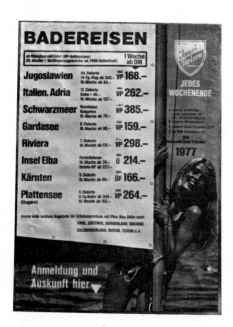

Sie einen Stadtplan oder einen Plan° der Gegend° und Hinweise° über die Sehenswürdigkeiten.° Und die Leute, die da arbeiten, können Ihnen auch Auskunft geben. Sie können sogar° eine ganze Reise° für Sie planen.° Zum Beispiel, sie können Ihre Hotelzimmer im voraus reservieren und Ihre Bahn-° und Flugkarten° für Sie besorgen.° Wenn Sie in Deutschland herumreisen,° fahren Sie normalerweise mit der Eisenbahn. Es ist billiger und fast so schnell, wie wenn man mit dem Flugzeug reist. Und ein Reisebüro kann Ihnen sogar Platzkarten° bestellen.

Sagen wir, Sie wollen ein Hotelzimmer in München bestellen. Sie sagen der Angestellten,° Sie wollen

der Plan, ⁼e: map   **die Gegend, –en**: area, region
der Hinweis, –e: tip, information
   die Sehenswürdigkeit, –en: sight, place to see

sogar: even

die Reise, –n: trip   **planen**: to plan

die Bahnkarte, –n: railroad ticket   **die Flugkarte, –n**: flight ticket   **besorgen**: to get, take care of
herum · reisen: to travel around

die Platzkarte, –n: reserved seat

die Angestellte, –n (*adj. noun*): employee (*fem.*)

fünf Tage in München bleiben, und sagen auch, wieviel Sie pro° Nacht ausgeben wollen. Unterkünfte° gibt es in allen Preislagen.° Sie können DM 85 für den *Bayerischen Hof*° oder die *Vier Jahreszeiten*° ausgeben, oder DM 25 in einem der vielen Hotels garni. (Ein Hotel garni ist ein kleines Hotel, meistens ohne Restaurant, aber mit Frühstück.) Sie sagen der Angestellten, Sie möchten ungefähr DM 30 ausgeben, und sie zeigt Ihnen eine Liste mit Zimmern in dieser Preislage. Und sie gibt Ihnen auch Broschüren von den Hotels, wenn sie welche° hat. Aber passen Sie auf!° Bevor Sie buchen,° fragen Sie, was die Vermittlungsgebühr° ist.

Sobald° die Bestätigung° da ist, bezahlen Sie dem Reisebüro den Zimmerpreis für eine Nacht und Sie bekommen einen Gutschein.° Wenn Sie in München ankommen und in Ihr Hotel gehen, geben Sie dem Mann am Empfang diesen Gutschein. Sie haben also° für Ihre erste Nacht im voraus bezahlt.

pro: per
die Unterkunft, ¨e: place to stay
  die Preislage, –n: price range

der Bayerische Hof
die Vier Jahreszeiten } names of hotels in Munich

welche: some **auf · passen:** to watch out
buchen: to book
  die Vermittlungsgebühr, –en: fee, charge

sobald (*subord. conj.*): as soon as
  die Bestätigung, –en: confirmation

der Gutschein, –e: voucher

also: thus, so

Altstadt in Mainz

Starnberger See

Wie gesagt, können Sie da auch Ihre Fahrkarte nach
München bekommen. Sie sind also reisefertig° und
haben sogar schon ein Hotelzimmer an° Ihrem
Reiseziel.

reisefertig: ready to go
an: at

ragen
1–6,
524

Wenn Sie im voraus planen möchten, können Sie
sogar zwei, drei oder mehr Reiseziele haben. Dann
können Sie für jede Stadt ein Hotelzimmer im
voraus bestellen und auch die Fahrkarten zwischen
Ihren Reisezielen vom Reisebüro kaufen. Damit
hätten Sie eine ganze Reise im voraus gebucht.
Wenn Sie in den Großstädten° bleiben, können Sie
mit dem Bus, der Straßenbahn° oder mit einem Taxi
in der Stadt herumfahren. Wenn Sie aufs Land°
wollen, mieten° Sie sich einen Leihwagen° für einen
Tag oder zwei. Einen internationalen Führerschein°

die Großstadt, ⸚e: large city
die Straßenbahn, –en: street car
aufs Land: (to go) to the country
mieten: to rent der Leihwagen, –: rental car
der Führerschein, –e: driver's license

bekommen Sie für sehr wenig Geld vom AAA (*Automobile Association of America*), Sie brauchen nicht einmal° ein Mitglied° von AAA zu sein.

nicht einmal: not even
   das Mitglied, —er: member

Man kann natürlich billiger reisen. Sie wissen schon, daß es preiswerte° Charterflüge° gibt, die viel weniger kosten als normale Flüge. In Deutschland gibt es eine ganze Reihe° von Reiseveranstaltern,° die viele verschiedene° Reisen zu billigen Preisen anbieten.° *DER* (Deutsches Reisebüro), *Touropa*, *Scharnow*, *InterTours* unter anderen° haben viele interessante Pauschalreisen,° die halb° so viel kosten, wie wenn man sie selber planen würde.

preiswert: inexpensive
   der Charterflug, ⸚e: charter flight

die Reihe, —n: number, group
   der Reiseveranstalter, —: tour organizer
verschieden: different an · bieten: to offer

unter anderen: among others
   die Pauschalreise, —n: package tour
   halb: half

Diese Reisen sind meistens so organisiert,° daß Sie tun können, was Sie wollen. Sie müssen nur mit

organisieren: to organize

Burg Pfalz am Rhein

bestimmten° Zügen fahren und in bestimmten Hotels übernachten° und es hängt von Ihnen ab,° wie
Sie Ihre Mahlzeiten° möchten. Sie können im Hotel
nur frühstücken, wenn Sie wollen. Sie können
Halbpension buchen—d.h.,° Frühstück und eine
Mahlzeit—oder Vollpension (alle drei Mahlzeiten
inbegriffen°). Also, wie Sie wollen. Sie können das
Gefühl haben, daß Sie auf einer „Tour" sind, und
andere Leute kennenlernen, oder Sie können tun,
was *Sie* wollen.

Oder, wenn Sie ganz selbständig° bleiben wollen,
und auch billig reisen wollen, kaufen Sie sich einen
Student Rail Pass. Mit so einem Paß können Sie
zwei Monate lang° für etwa $250 durch ganz West-
europa° fahren. Er gilt aber nur für° die zweite
Klasse. Wenn man nicht mehr Student ist, kann man
einen *Eurailpass* kaufen. Der ist aber für die erste
Klasse und kostet ungefähr fünfzig Prozent mehr.
Aber Vorsicht,° beide Pässe muß man in Amerika
kaufen!

Wenn Sie wirklich „frei" bleiben wollen, dann
buchen Sie nichts im voraus. Sie kommen in einer
Stadt an, gehen zur Zimmervermittlung und fragen
nach billigen Privatzimmern. Das sind Zimmer in
einem Haus oder in einer Wohnung, die Sie für nicht
zu viel Geld mieten° können. Auch gibt es Jugend-
herbergen° an vielen Orten;° wo Sie für etwa vier
Mark übernachten können. Einen Ausweis° müssen
Sie aber haben, und den° bekommen Sie von der
AYH (*American Youth Hostel Association*), Dela-
plane, VA 22025. Dieser Ausweis kostet ungefähr $12
pro Jahr, aber er spart Ihnen später viel Geld.

Wenn man als Student in Deutschland ist, entweder°
für ein Semester, oder für das ganze Jahr, kann man

Fragen 13, pp. 524–25

---

bestimmt: certain

übernachten: to stay overnight
   ab·hängen von: to depend on
die Mahlzeit, –en: meal

d.h. = das heißt: that is

inbegriffen: included

selbständig: independent

zwei Monate lang: for two months
Westeuropa: Western Europe
   gelten (gilt) für: to be valid for

Vorsicht! Watch it!

mieten: to rent
die Jugendherberge, –n: youth hostel
   der Ort, –e: place
der Ausweis, –e: (*here*): membership card

den = ihn

entweder . . . oder: either . . . or

vom Studentenreisebüro° an der Universität sehr billige Reisen bekommen. Diese Reisen werden teilweise° staatlich° unterstützt.°

das Studentenreisebüro, –s: student travel agency

teilweise: partially **staatlich**: by the state **unterstützen**: to support, subsidize

Fragen
14–18,
p. 525

Und wenn Sie nach Amerika zurückfliegen° wollen, können Sie auch zu einem Reisebüro gehen und da Ihren Rückflug° buchen.

zurück · fliegen: to fly back

der Rückflug, ⁼e: return flight

FRAGEN

1. Was kann ein deutsches Reisebüro für einen tun?   (**einen**: *acc. form of* **man**)
   (Man / können / bekommen / Broschüren / von / Reiseziel)
   (In / meist– / Broschüren / man / finden / Stadtplan)
   (Leute / in / Reisebüro / können / geben / Auskunft)
   (Sie / können / reservieren / Hotelzimmer // und / besorgen / Fahrkarten)

2. Wie reist man meistens in Deutschland?
   (Normalerweise / man / fahren / mit / Eisenbahn)
   (Es / sein / billiger / und / fast so schnell // wie wenn / man / reisen / mit / Flugzeug)

3. Wie reservieren Sie ein Hotelzimmer in einem Reisebüro?
   (Sie / fragen / Angestellt– / hinter / Theke)
   (Sie / sagen / Angestellt– // wie lange / Sie / wollen / bleiben // und / wieviel / Sie / wollen / aus · geben)
   (Angestellt– / zeigen / [*to you*] / Liste / mit / Zimmer / in / Ihr / Preislage)
   (Und / sie / geben / [*to you*] / Broschüren / von / Hotels)

4. Was ist ein Hotel garni?
   (Hotel garni / sein / klein / Hotel / ohne / Restaurant)

5. Was macht man, nachdem das Zimmer bestätigt worden ist?   (**bestätigt**: confirmed)
   (Man / bezahlen / Reisebüro / Zimmerpreis / für / 1 / Nacht)
   (Und / man / bekommen / Gutschein)

6. Was macht man mit dem Gutschein?
   (Man / geben / Empfang / in / Hotel / Gutschein)
   (erst– / Nacht / sein / schon / bezahlt)

7. Kann man eine ganze Reise im voraus buchen?
   (Ja // man / können / bestellen / Hotelzimmer / für / viel– / Städte)
   (Man / können / kaufen / auch / Fahrkarten / zwischen / Reiseziele)

8. Wie kommt man herum, wenn man angekommen ist?
   (In / Großstädte / man / können / herum · fahren / mit / Bus / oder / Straßenbahn / oder / mit / Taxi)
   (Wenn / man / wollen / aufs Land // man / mieten / Leihwagen)

9. Wie fliegt man am billigsten nach Europa?
   (Es / geben / Charterflüge // die / kosten / viel weniger als / normale / Flüge)

10. Was tun Reiseveranstalter?
    (Sie / an · bieten / verschieden / Reisen / zu / billig / Preise)

11. Wieviel kosten Pauschalreisen?
    (Pauschalreisen / kosten / halb so viel // wie wenn / man / planen / Reise / selber)

12. Wie sind diese Reisen organisiert?
(Man / müssen / fahren / mit / bestimmt / Züge)
(Und / man / müssen / übernachten / in / bestimmt / Hotels)
(Man / können / frühstücken / in / Hotel / nur // wenn / man / wollen)
(Oder / man / können / buchen / Halb- oder Vollpension)

13. Was ist Halbpension?
(Halbpension / sein / Frühstück // und / ein / Mahlzeit)

14. Was kostet ein *Student Rail Pass* und was kann man damit tun?
(*Student Rail Pass* / kosten / etwa / $250 // und / gelten / nur / für / 2. Klasse)
(Damit / man / können / fahren / durch / ganz Westeuropa)

15. Was ist ein *Eurailpass*?
(Er / sein / wie / *Student Rail Pass* // aber / er / gelten / für / 1. Klasse)
(Und / er / kosten / ungefähr / 50% / mehr)

16. Was macht man, wenn man wirklich „frei" bleiben will?
(Dann / man / buchen / nichts im voraus)
(Man / an·kommen / in / Stadt // und / gehen / zu / Zimmervermittlung)
(Da / man / fragen / nach / billig / Privatzimmer)
(Man / können / übernachten / auch / in Jugendherbergen)
(Für / Jugendherbergen / man / brauchen / Ausweis)

17. Welche Möglichkeiten gibt es für Studenten?
(Studentenreisebüro / an / Universität / an·bieten / billig / Reisen)

18. Wie kann Ihnen ein Reisebüro bei der Rückreise helfen?   (**Rückreise**: return trip)
(Reisebüro / können / buchen / Ihr / Rückflug)

Peter Bichsel:
„Der Mann mit dem Gedächtnis"

(Fortsetzung)

Aber viele Jahre später wurde im Bahnhof ein Auskunftsbüro° eröffnet.° Dort saß ein Beamter° in Uniform° hinter dem Schalter, und er wußte auf° alle Fragen über die Bahn eine Antwort. Das glaubte der Mann mit dem Gedächtnis nicht, und er ging jeden Tag ins neue Auskunftsbüro und fragte etwas sehr Kompliziertes,° um den Beamten zu prüfen.°

Er fragte: „Welche Zugnummer hat der Zug, der um 16 Uhr 24 an den Sonntagen im Sommer in Lübeck ankommt?" Der Beamte schlug ein Buch auf° und nannte° die Zahl.°

Er fragte: „Wann bin ich in Moskau, wenn ich hier mit dem Zug um 6 Uhr 59 abfahre?", und der Beamte sagte es ihm.

Da ging der Mann mit dem Gedächtnis nach Hause, verbrannte° seine Fahrpläne° und vergaß alles, was er wußte.

Am andern° Tag aber fragte er den Beamten: „Wie viele Stufen° hat die Treppe° vor dem Bahnhof?", und der Beamte sagte: „Ich weiß es nicht."

Jetzt rannte° der Mann durch den ganzen Bahnhof, machte Luftsprünge° vor Freude° und rief: „Er weiß es nicht, er weiß es nicht."

das Auskunftsbüro, –s: information office **eröffnen:** to open **der Beamte, –n** (*adj. noun*): official
die Uniform, –en: uniform **auf (für):** for

etwas Kompliziertes (*adj. noun*): something complicated **prüfen:** to test

auf · schlagen: to open (a book) **(schlägt . . . auf), schlug . . . auf, aufgeschlagen**
nennen: to name (*here:* to say, tell) **nannte, genannt die Zahl, –en:** number

verbrennen: to burn **verbrannte, verbrannt der Fahrplan, ⁼e:** time table

am andern Tag: the next day
die Stufe, –n: step **die Treppe, –n:** flight of stairs

rennen: to run **rannte, ist gerannt**
Luftsprünge machen: to jump into the air **vor Freude:** for joy

Und er ging hin° und zählte° die Stufen der Bahn-
hofstreppe° und prägte sich die Zahl in sein
Gedächtnis ein,° in dem° jetzt keine Abfahrtszeiten
mehr waren.

hin: over   zählen: to count
die Bahnhofstreppe, –n: flight of stairs
  leading into the station
sich etwas in sein Gedächtnis ein · prägen: to
  commit something to memory
  in dem: in which (*referring to* Gedächtnis)

Dann sah man ihn nie mehr im Bahnhof.

Er ging jetzt in der Stadt von Haus zu Haus und
zählte die Treppenstufen° und merkte sie sich° und
er wußte jetzt Zahlen, die in keinem Buch° der Welt°
stehen.

die Treppenstufe, –n: step in a flight of stairs
  sich etwas merken: to make a mental
  note of something
die in keinem Buch: die *refers to* Zahlen
  (. . . that [are] in no book)   die Welt: world

Als er aber die Zahl der Treppenstufen in der ganzen
Stadt kannte, kam er auf den Bahnhof, ging an den
Bahnschalter,° kaufte sich eine Fahrkarte und stieg
zum ersten Mal in seinem Leben in einen Zug, um in
eine andere Stadt zu fahren und auch dort die
Treppenstufen zu zählen, und dann weiter zu
fahren, um die Treppenstufen in der ganzen Welt zu
zählen, um etwas zu wissen, was niemand° weiß
und was kein Beamter in Büchern nachlesen° kann.

der Bahnschalter, –: ticket window

niemand: no one
nach · lesen: to look up (liest . . . nach),
  las . . . nach, nachgelesen

INTRODUCTORY EXERCISES

Supply the correct forms of the verbs in parentheses. Do each sentence in the present tense, past tense,
and present perfect tense, except where otherwise indicated.

A. 1. Ein Auskunftsbüro _____ im Bahnhof eröffnet. [*passive*]
       (werden)
    2. Ein Beamter _____ hinter dem Schalter.
       (*sitzen)
    3. Er _____ eine Antwort für alle Fragen.
       (*wissen)
    4. Der Mann _____ es nicht.
       (glauben)
    5. Er _____ jeden Tag und _____ etwas Kompliziertes.
       (*hin · gehen)   (fragen)
    6. Er _____ den Beamten prüfen.
       (wollen)

B. 1. Welcher Zug _____ um 16 Uhr 24 in Lübeck?
      (*an · kommen)

   2. Der Beamte _____ein Buch und _____die Nummer des Zuges.
        (*auf · schlagen)   (*nennen)

   3. Der Mann mit dem Gedächtnis _____nach Hause.
                                    (*gehen)

   4. Er _____ seine Fahrpläne und _____ alles.
        (*verbrennen)   (*vergessen)

   5. Später _____ er, wieviele Stufen die Treppe vor dem Bahnhof _____.
        (fragen)   (haben)

   6. Der Beamte _____ es nicht.
        (*wissen)

   7. Der Mann _____ durch den Bahnhof und _____ vor Freude.
        (*rennen)   (*springen)

                              (springen, sprang, ist gesprungen: to jump)

   8. Er _____ und _____ die Stufen der Bahnhofstreppe.
        (*gehen)   (zählen)

C. 1. Dann _____ man ihn nicht mehr im Bahnhof.
        (*sehen)

   2. Er _____ von Haus zu Haus und _____ die Treppenstufen.
        (*gehen)   (zählen)

   3. In keinem Buch der Welt _____ solche Zahlen.
                               (*stehen)

   4. Endlich _____ er die Zahl der Treppenstufen in der ganzen Stadt.
        (*kennen)

   5. Dann _____ er zum Bahnhof und _____ sich eine Fahrkarte.
        (*gehen)   (kaufen)

   6. Er _____ in einen Zug und _____ in eine andere Stadt.
        (*ein · steigen)   (*fahren)

   7. Dort _____ er die Treppenstufen.
        (zählen)

   8. Solche Zahlen _____ in keinem Buch, aber der Mann _____ sie.
        (*stehen)   (*wissen)

SYNTHETIC EXERCISES

Use the following elements to make complete sentences. Form the present tense, past tense, and present perfect tense, except where otherwise indicated.

A. 1. Auskunftsbüro / eröffnet [*passive*] / in / Bahnhof
   2. Beamter / sitzen / hinter / Schalter
   3. Er / wissen / Antwort / für / all– / Fragen
   4. Mann / glauben / es / nicht
   5. Er / hin · gehen / jed– / Tag // und / fragen / etwas Kompliziert-
   6. Er / wollen / prüfen / Beamter

B. 1. Welch– / Zug / an · kommen / 16.27 / in Lübeck / ?
    2. Beamter / auf · schlagen // Buch / und / nennen / Nummer / Zug [*gen.*]
    3. Mann / mit / Gedächtnis / gehen / Haus
    4. Er / verbrennen / sein– / Fahrpläne // und / vergessen / alles
    5. Später / er / fragen // wieviel / Stufen / haben / Treppe / vor / Bahnhof
    6. Beamter / wissen / es nicht
    7. Mann / rennen / durch / Bahnhof / und / springen / vor Freude
    8. Er / gehen / und / zählen / Stufen / Bahnhofstreppe [*gen.*]   [*pres. and past*]

C. 1. Dann / man / sehen / ihn / nicht mehr / in / Bahnhof
    2. Er / gehen / von Haus zu Haus // und / zählen / Treppenstufen
    3. In / kein / Buch / Welt [*gen.*] / stehen / solch– / Zahlen
    4. Endlich / er / kennen / Zahl / Treppenstufen [*gen.*] / in / ganz / Stadt
    5. Dann / er / gehen / zu / Bahnhof // und / kaufen / Fahrkarte
    6. Er / ein · steigen / in / ein / Zug // und / fahren / in / ander– / Stadt
    7. Dort / er / zählen / Treppenstufen
    8. Solch– / Zahlen / stehen / in / kein / Buch // aber / Mann / wissen / sie

Lesson 11

A Indirect Quotation

There are two basic ways of reporting what somebody else has said. One way is to use direct quotation:

ORIGINAL WORDS   It's too difficult.   Es ist zu schwer.
DIRECT QUOTATION   He said, "It's too difficult."   Er sagte: „Es ist zu schwer."

As you see, the speaker's *exact words* are enclosed in quotation marks. The only differences between English and German are in punctuation. Where English sets the quotation off with a comma, German uses a colon; and German lowers the first quotation mark.

    The other way—far more common—is to use indirect quotation to report another person's words. Sometimes the indirect quotation is exactly the same as the original words:

ORIGINAL WORDS   It's too difficult.
INDIRECT QUOTATION   He said that it's too difficult.

Sometimes small changes are necessary to keep the sense straight:

ORIGINAL WORDS   *My* feet hurt.
INDIRECT QUOTATION   She says *her* feet hurt.

This is the most common kind of change. If the original words are in the 1st person, they are normally changed into the 3rd person in indirect quotation. The logic of such changes is the same in both English and German.

B Formal Written German: Subjunctive I

1 Usage

Formal written German uses a special mood, subjunctive I, for indirect quotations. Look at the following examples:

DIRECT QUOTE	Herr Kurt sagte: „Es **ist** zu schwer." (Mr. Kurt said, "It's too difficult.")
INDIRECT QUOTE	Herr Kurt sagte, es **sei** zu schwer. (Mr. Kurt said it's too difficult.)

A subjunctive I form (for example, **sei**) underlines the fact that the speaker is *reporting someone else's words* or *expressing someone else's opinion*. In our example, the use of the subjunctive I form **(sei)** *stresses* that it is Mr. Kurt's opinion that is being expressed and that the person quoting Mr. Kurt takes no responsibility for that opinion. The speaker is neither agreeing or disagreeing with Mr. Kurt, but merely attributing the statement to its source. For this reason the most common place to find the subjunctive I is in newspaper articles or in radio and TV newscasts. Suppose, for example, that during an interview, a prominent German politician said:

> „Franz Josef Strauß ist ein Idiot!"   (Franz Josef Strauss is an idiot!)

How would the interviewer report it? Suppose he were to write:

> Der Minister sagte, Franz Josef Strauß **ist** ein Idiot.

The use of the indicative might be interpreted to mean that the newspaper agreed with the minister's comment. This might result in a libel suit against the paper. To play it safe, the reporter would write:

> Der Minister sagte, Franz Josef Strauß **sei** ein Idiot.

using the subjunctive I form **(sei)** to stress the fact that it is the minister's opinion and that the newspaper takes no responsibility for it.

2 Forms

a. Present tense

The present tense of subjunctive I is formed by adding the following endings to the *infinitive stem* of the verb:

-e	-en
-est	-et
-e	-en

Infinitive:

	machen		können	
ich	mach	e	könn	e
du	mach	est	könn	est
er	mach	e	könn	e
wir	mach	en	könn	en
ihr	mach	et	könn	et
Sie, sie	mach	en	könn	en

▶ Note   **Können** uses its infinitive stem, not its special singular stem **kann-**.

Verbs that have a stem-vowel shift in the indicative do *not* have this shift in subjunctive I:

	Indicative	Subjunctive I	Indicative	Subjunctive I
ich	gebe	gebe	laufe	laufe
du	**gibst**	gebest	**läufst**	laufest
er	**gibt**	gebe	**läuft**	laufe
wir	geben	geben	laufen	laufen
ihr	gebt	gebet	lauft	laufet
Sie, sie	geben	geben	laufen	laufen

Substituting subjunctive II for subjunctive I

A reporter using subjunctive I wants to make it perfectly clear that he is not using the indicative. But the examples above show that in many instances the indicative form and the subjunctive I form are exact look-alikes. In such cases, the reporter will use the corresponding subjunctive II form. For example:

	Indicative	Subjunctive I		Subjunctive II
ich	kann	könne		—
du	kannst	könnest		—
er	kann	könne		—
wir	können	**(können)**	*thus*	könnten
ihr	könnt	könnet		—
Sie, sie	können	**(können)**	*thus*	könnten

▶ Note   There is only one exception to the rule for forming subjunctive I: **sein** has its own special forms.

ich sei	wir seien
du seiest	ihr seiet
er sei	Sie, sie seien

b. Future tense

The future tense of subjunctive I is similar to the future tense of the indicative. The only difference is that the auxiliary **werden** *uses subjunctive I forms.*

> Er sagte, er werde kommen.

c. Past tense

The past tense of subjunctive I is derived from the *present perfect* tense of the indicative:

Present Perfect Indicative	**Past Subjunctive I**
Er **ist** gekommen.	Er sei gekommen.
Er **hat** es getan.	Er habe es getan.

It is composed of:

> a subjunctive I form of sein or haben + *a past participle*

▶ **Note** If the direct quotation is in any tense denoting *past time,* the indirect quotation is in the *past tense of subjunctive I:*

Past Time Indicative	**Past Subjunctive I**
„Er **war** hier."	
„Es **ist** hier *gewesen."*	Er sagte, er sei hier gewesen.
„Er **war** hier **gewesen."**	

C Conversational German: Indicative or Subjunctive II

Conversational German does not use subjunctive I. Instead it chooses between the indicative and subjunctive II for indirect quotation. The choice of mood depends on whether the speaker thinks he is reporting something that is unalterable fact or something that is still subject to change. Look at the following two quotations, both of which are in the indicative:

QUOTE
: „Es gibt eine Haltestelle vor dem Bahnhof."
: „Ich treffe dich vor dem Bahnhof."

INDIRECT QUOTATION
: Er sagte, daß es eine Haltestelle vor dem Bahnhof gibt .
: (He said that there is a bus stop in front of the station.)
: Er sagte, daß er mich vor dem Bahnhof treffen würde .
: (He said that he would meet me in front of the station.)

The fact that there is a bus stop in front of the station does not seem to be open to change. That someone is going to meet me, later, in front of the station, *does* seem less certain. The person could change his mind, and so it won't be a fact until he has actually met me.

DRILLS

1 Subjunctive I: 3rd person singular only

- Present tense: Put the following sentences into subjunctive I; if **daß** is used, put the conjugated verb at the end of the clause.

1. Er braucht mehr Zeit.
   Er sagte, daß er . . . .
2. Er kann es nicht vor Dienstag machen.
   Er sagte, er . . . .
3. Es ist nicht nötig.   (**nötig:** necessary)
   Er sagte, daß es . . . .

4. Er vergißt alles.
   Er sagte, daß er . . . .
5. Sie will es sich überlegen.
   (**sich überlegen:** to think about, think over)
   Sie sagte, sie . . . .

- Past tense: Put the following sentences into subjunctive I. Remember that subjunctive I has only *one* past tense form:

sei or habe + past participle

1. Man hat ihn nicht gefragt.
   Er sagte, man . . . .
2. Er hat den Titel vergessen.   (**der Titel:** title)
   Er sagte, daß er . . . .
3. Er war nicht da.
   Er sagte, daß er . . . .

4. Er ging nach Hause.
   Er sagte, daß er . . . .
5. Er stand um fünf Uhr auf.
   Er sagte, er . . . .
6. Er konnte es nicht finden.
   Er sagte, er . . . .

- Present and past tense: Put the following sentences into subjunctive I.

1. Er braucht mehr Zeit.
   Er sagte, daß er . . . .
2. Er hat den Titel vergessen.
   Er sagte, daß er . . . .
3. Es ist nicht nötig.
   Er sagte, daß es . . . .
4. Er war nicht da.
   Er sagte, daß er . . . .
5. Er ging nach Hause.
   Er sagte, daß er . . . .
6. Er kann es nicht vor Dienstag machen.
   Er sagte, er . . . .

7. Er stand um fünf Uhr auf.
   Er sagte, er . . . .
8. Sie will es sich überlegen.
   Sie sagte, sie . . . .
9. Man hat ihn nicht gefragt.
   Er sagte, man . . . .
10. Er konnte es nicht finden.
    Er sagte, er . . . .
11. Er vergißt alles.
    Er sagte, daß er . . . .

2 Subjunctive I: 3rd person plural only

- Present tense: Put the following sentences into subjunctive I. Remember that you have to use subjunctive II if the subjunctive I form is identical to the indicative. This will be the case with all verbs except for **seien,** which is recognizable as subjunctive I.

1. Sie haben keine Zeit.
   Sie sagten, daß sie . . . .
2. Sie wollen es nicht tun.
   Sie sagten, daß sie . . . .
3. Sie können es morgen machen.
   Sie sagten, sie . . . .

4. Sie sind zu Hause.
   Sie sagten, daß sie . . . .
5. Die Platten kosten zu viel.
   Sie sagten, daß die Platten . . . .
6. Sie brauchen mehr Geld.
   Sie sagten, daß sie . . . .

- Past tense: Put the following sentences into subjunctive I. Remember that the past tense is a compound tense: **seien** or **hätten** + *past participle*.

  1. Sie sind um sieben Uhr hier gewesen.
     Sie sagten, daß sie . . . .
  2. Sie haben es verkauft.
     Sie sagten, daß sie . . . .
  3. Sie waren zu Hause.
     Sie sagten, daß sie . . . .

  4. Sie haben es nicht finden können.
     Sie sagten, sie . . . .
  5. Sie kamen später.
     Sie sagten, daß sie . . . .

- Present and past tense: Put the following sentences into subjunctive I.

  1. Sie brauchen mehr Geld.
     Sie sagten, daß sie . . . .
  2. Sie haben es verkauft.
     Sie sagten, daß sie . . . .
  3. Sie haben keine Zeit.
     Sie sagten, daß sie . . . .
  4. Die Platten kosten zu viel.
     Sie sagten, daß die Platten . . . .
  5. Sie waren zu Hause.
     Sie sagten, daß sie . . . .
  6. Sie sind um sieben Uhr hier gewesen.
     Sie sagten, daß sie . . . .

  7. Sie wollen es nicht tun.
     Sie sagten, daß sie . . . .
  8. Sie sind zu Hause.
     Sie sagten, daß sie . . . .
  9. Sie haben es nicht finden können.
     Sie sagten, sie . . . .
  10. Sie können das morgen machen.
      Sie sagten, sie . . . .
  11. Sie kamen später.
      Sie sagten, daß sie . . . .

3 Grand mix

- Put the following sentences into subjunctive I.

  a. 1. Es ist nicht nötig.
         Er sagte, daß es . . . .
      2. Er ging nach Hause.
         Er sagte, daß er . . . .
      3. Sie haben keine Zeit.
         Sie sagten, daß sie . . . .
      4. Er hat den Titel vergessen.
         Er sagte, daß er . . . .
      5. Sie haben es nicht finden können.
         Sie sagten, sie . . . .
      6. Er braucht mehr Zeit.
         Er sagte, daß er . . . .
      7. Sie wollen es nicht tun.
         Sie sagten, daß sie . . . .
      8. Er kann es nicht vor Dienstag machen.
         Er sagte, er . . . .
      9. Die Platten kosten zu viel.
         Sie sagten, daß die Platten . . . .
      10. Er war nicht da.
          Er sagte, daß er . . . .

      3. Sie will es sich überlegen.
         Sie sagte, sie . . . .
      4. Sie brauchen mehr Geld.
         Sie sagten, daß sie . . . .
      5. Er stand um fünf Uhr auf.
         Er sagte, er . . . .
      6. Sie sind zu Hause.
         Sie sagten, daß sie . . . .
      7. Sie haben es verkauft.
         Sie sagten, daß sie . . . .
      8. Er vergißt alles.
         Er sagte, daß er . . . .
      9. Man hat ihn nicht gefragt.
         Er sagte, man . . . .
      10. Sie können das morgen machen.
          Sie sagten, sie . . . .

  b. 1. Sie sind um sieben Uhr hier gewesen.
         Sie sagten, daß sie . . . .
      2. Sie kamen später.
         Sie sagten, daß sie . . . .

  c. 1. Sie waren zu Hause.
         Sie sagten, daß sie . . . .
      2. Er konnte es nicht finden.
         Er sagte, er . . . .

4 Indirect quotations in conversational German

- Assumed facts: Keep the following sentences in the indicative, making only the necessary word order changes.

1. Er hat es nicht gelesen.
   Er sagte, daß er . . . .
2. Sie kennen die Stadt nicht sehr gut.
   Sie sagten, daß sie . . . .
3. Er hat es verkauft.
   Er sagte, daß er . . . .

4. Sie konnte nicht schlafen.
   Sie sagte, daß sie . . . .
5. Er hat es schon gemacht.
   Er sagte, daß er . . . .

- Situations open to change: Put the following sentences into subjunctive II.

1. Sie werden es machen.
   Sie sagten, daß sie . . . .
2. Er wird um zehn Uhr vorbeikommen.
   Er sagte, daß er . . . .
3. Er wird später kommen.
   Er sagte, daß er . . . .
4. Sie werden es uns geben.
   Sie sagten, daß sie . . . .

5. Sie werden mitkommen.
   Sie sagten, daß sie . . . .
6. Er wird auf mich warten.
   Er sagte, daß er . . . .
7. Sie werden uns helfen.
   Sie sagten, daß sie . . . .

D Lassen, Sehen, and Hören

Structurally, **lassen, sehen,** and **hören** behave like modal auxiliaries:

I hear him singing.	Ich **höre** ihn **singen.**
I heard him singing (sing).	Ich **hörte** ihn **singen.**
I'll hear him singing (sing).	Ich **werde** ihn **singen hören.**
I (have) heard him singing (sing).	Ich **habe** ihn **singen hören.**
I had heard him singing (sing).	Ich **hatte** ihn **singen hören.**

Like modals, these verbs form their perfect tenses with a *double-infinitive con-struction when there is a dependent infinitive involved:*

Ich habe ihn **singen hören.**
but Ich habe es **gehört.**

1 The senses: **sehen** and **hören**

In theory, any of the verbs used to indicate the senses function as **hören** does in the examples above. In practice, however, **sehen** and **hören** are the sense verbs most commonly used.

After verbs of this type, English very often uses a present participle (singing). German always uses a *dependent infinitive.*

Ich höre ihn **singen.** (I hear him singing.)

▶ **Note**   Compare the following sentences:

MODAL	I want her to sing.	Ich will, **daß sie singt.**
HÖREN, SEHEN, LASSEN	I heard him sing.	Ich hörte **ihn singen.**

An English modal (normally, "to want") can take an *object* that *also functions as the logical subject* of the dependent infinitive. In the sentence

I want her to sing.

the object of the modal "want" (in this case "her") also functions as the subject of the dependent infinitive (*she* is to sing). As you learned before (Lesson 9, Level Three, pp. 453–54), such a construction is impossible *with German modal auxiliaries.* Instead German requires a full clause containing a *subject* and a *conjugated verb form* (for example, daß **sie singt**).

But unlike the modals, **hören, sehen,** and **lassen** are like their English counterparts. In the sentence

Ich hörte **ihn** singen.   (I heard *him* sing.)

the object of **hörte (ihn)** also functions as the logical subject of the dependent infinitive (*he* was doing the singing).

▶ **Rule**   Unlike the modals, **hören, sehen,** and **lassen** can take objects that are also the logical subjects of the dependent infinitive.

Ich sah **den Wagen** vorbeifahren.   (I saw *the car* drive by.)
Ich ließ **ihn** gehen.   (I let *him* go.)

2 lassen

Lassen has two basic meanings:

1. to let or allow (permission)

Er ließ ihn gehen.   (He *let* him go.)
Er ließ mich seinen Wagen nehmen.   (He *let* me take his car.)

▶ **Note 1**   **Lassen** takes an accusative object:

Er ließ **ihn** gehen.

▶ **Note 2**   Er ließ **mich seinen Wagen** nehmen.

In this sentence, both verbs have direct objects:

mich is the object of **lassen**
and   **seinen Wagen** is the object of **nehmen**

2. to have (something done)

Er läßt den Wagen reparieren.   (He's *having* the car *repaired.*)

▶ **Note 1**   *to have something done*
                                 to have the car repaired

When English uses the word "have" in this sense, it completes the sentence with a past *participle* (have *done*, have *repaired*). German, however, only uses the *infinitive* form after **lassen:**

> Er läßt den Wagen **reparieren.**   (He's having the car *repaired*.)
> Er ließ ihn **gehen.**   (He let him go.)

In other words, it is English that has variant forms; German has only *one pattern* (**lassen** + *infinitive*).

▶ **Note 2**   The second use of **lassen** (to have something done) indicates that the subject of the sentence is not actually performing the action described but is *having or making someone else perform it.* English often does not show this distinction clearly. Instead of:

> We're *having* a house *built.*

one may say: We're *building* a house.

But to a German, this last sentence would mean that you are building the house with your own hands. If someone else is doing the work, a German says:

> Wir **lassen** uns* ein Haus **bauen.**

DRILLS

1   Fill-ins

● Fill in the blanks, using the present tense of the suggested verb.

1. Ich _____ ihn kommen.
   (see)

2. Er _____ den Wagen reparieren.
   (is having [repaired])

3. _____ Sie ihn klingeln?   (**klingeln:** to ring, such as a doorbell)
   (Do you hear)

4. Ich _____ ihn gehen.
   (am letting)

5. _____ du den Wagen vorbeifahren?
   (Do you see)

6. Ich _____ es mir schicken.
   (am having [sent])

7. Ich _____ mir die Haare schneiden.   (**mir die Haare**: my hair)†
   (am going to have)

*****uns** is merely a dative of reference, meaning "for ourselves."
†See Lesson 8, Level One, p. 365.

8. Ich _____ ihn die Tür zumachen.
   (hear)

9. Wir _____ uns ein Haus bauen.
   (having [built])

(bauen: to build)

10. Ich _____ ihn weggehen.
    (hear)

11. Er _____ uns seinen Wagen nehmen.
    (is letting)

12. Ich _____ ihn in sein Büro gehen.
    (see)

2 Tense changes

- Put the following sentences into the past and present perfect tenses, unless otherwise indicated.

1. Er läßt ihn gehen.
2. Ich höre ihn die Tür zumachen.
3. Er läßt uns seinen Wagen nehmen.
4. Ich sehe ihn kommen.
5. Ich lasse es mir schicken.
6. Hören Sie ihn klingeln?
   (present perfect only)
7. Ich lasse mir die Haare schneiden.
8. Siehst du den Wagen vorbeifahren?
   (present perfect only)
9. Er läßt den Wagen reparieren.
10. Ich höre ihn weggehen.
11. Wir lassen uns ein Haus bauen.

- Put the following sentences into the future tense, using the auxiliary **werden.**

1. Ich sehe den Wagen vorbeifahren.
2. Er läßt mich gehen.
3. Ich sehe ihn kommen.
4. Sie hören uns klingeln.
5. Ich lasse es mir schicken.
6. Wir hören ihn weggehen.
7. Er läßt uns seinen Wagen nehmen.

3 Synthetic exercises

- Form complete sentences in the tense or tenses indicated.

1. Ich / sehen / ihn / kommen *(past and present perfect)*
2. Er / lassen / ihn / gehen *(past, present perfect, and future)*
3. Ich / hören / ihn / zumachen / Tür *(past)*
4. Wir / lassen / uns / Haus / bauen *(present, past, and present perfect)*
5. Hören / Sie / ihn / klingeln / ? *(present perfect and future)*
6. Er / lassen / Wagen / reparieren *(past and present perfect)*
7. Ich / sehen / ihn / gehen / in sein Büro *(past)*
8. Ich / lassen / mir Haare / schneiden *(present)*
9. Sehen / du / Wagen / vorbeifahren / ? *(present perfect)*
10. Ich / lassen / es mir / schicken *(present, past, and present perfect)*
11. Ich / hören / ihn / weggehen *(past and future)*
12. Er / lassen / uns / nehmen / Wagen *(past)*

4   Express in German

● Use the tense or tenses indicated.

1. He let him go. (*past and present perfect*)
2. I heard him leave. (*past*)
3. He had the car repaired. (*past and present perfect*)
4. I saw him coming. (*past and present perfect*)
5. I'm going to have my hair cut. (*present*)
6. I heard him close the door. (*past*)
7. I had it sent (to me). (*past and present perfect*)
8. Did you see a car drive by? (*present perfect*)
9. He'll let us go. (*future*)
10. Did you hear him ring? (*present perfect*)
11. We're building a house (. . . having . . . built). (*present*)
12. I'll hear him leave. (*future*)
13. He let us take his car. (*past*)
14. I'm having it sent to me. (*present*)
15. I saw him go into his office. (*past*)
16. Will you hear him ring? (*future*)

E Passive with Modal Auxiliaries

Look at the following examples:

The house *has to*	be sold.	Das Haus **muß**	verkauft werden.
The house *had to*	be sold.	Das Haus **mußte**	verkauft werden.
The house *will have to*	be sold.	Das Haus **wird**	verkauft werden **müssen**.
The house *has had to*	be sold.	Das Haus **hat**	verkauft werden **müssen**.
The house *had had to*	be sold.	Das Haus **hatte**	verkauft werden **müssen**.

This construction is made up of two elements:

A Conjugated Form of the Modal + A Passive Infinitive

muß   verkauft werden

1 The passive infinitive

1. As you learned previously, the passive voice is composed of

werden + *a past participle*

The passive infinitive is composed of the same elements. One must just remember that **werden** follows the past participle:

verkauft **werden**

2. **Verkauft werden** occurs in every tense. The passive infinitive is the *unchanging* part of such a construction. Contrast:

ENGLISH *be* *sold*
GERMAN **verkauft werden**

2 Tense change

The only elements that change in the above sentences are the forms of **müssen;** *shifts in tense will affect only the modal part of the expression.* Since **verkauft werden** is a passive *infinitive,* the double infinitive construction is used in the perfect tenses:

Das Haus hat **verkauft werden** müssen.

DRILLS

1 Form drill

• Form new sentences in the present tense by adding the suggested modals to the following passive sentences.

EXAMPLE   Das wird schnell gemacht. (müssen)
Das **muß** schnell gemacht **werden.**

1. Das wird geändert. (müssen)
2. Das Zimmer wird nicht vermietet. (können)
3. Er wird heute operiert. (müssen)
4. Der Kühlschrank wird nicht repariert. (können)
5. Er wird nach Hause gebracht. (müssen)
6. Das wird schnell gemacht. (müssen)

2 Tense drills

• Put the following sentences into the past and present perfect tenses.

EXAMPLE   Das muß schnell gemacht werden.

Das **mußte** schnell gemacht werden.
Das **hat** schnell gemacht werden **müssen.**

1. Er muß heute operiert werden.
2. Das Zimmer kann nicht vermietet werden.
3. Er muß nach Hause gebracht werden.
4. Das muß geändert werden.
5. Der Kühlschrank kann nicht repariert werden.
6. Das muß schnell gemacht werden.

3 The variable factor: the form of the modal

• Complete the following sentences in the tense indicated.

EXAMPLE   Das _____ schnell gemacht werden _____. (*perfect*)
                    (had to)

Das **hat** schnell gemacht werden **müssen**.

1. Er _____ heute operiert werden _____. (*perfect*)
        (had to)
2. Das Zimmer _____ nicht vermietet werden. (*past*)
            (could)
3. Er _____ nach Hause gebracht werden _____. (*perfect*)
        (had to)
4. Das _____ schnell erledigt werden. (*present*)
        (has to)
5. Der Kühlschrank _____ nicht repariert werden _____. (*perfect*)
            (could)
6. Das _____ geändert werden. (*past*)
        (had to)

4 The constant factor: the passive infinitive

• Complete the following sentences by supplying the passive infinitive.

EXAMPLE   Das muß schnell _____.
                    (be done)

Das muß schnell **gemacht werden**.

1. Das mußte _____.
            (be changed)
2. Der Kühlschrank hat nicht _____ können.
                    (be repaired)
3. Er muß heute _____.
                (be operated on)
4. Das Zimmer konnte nicht _____.
                    (be rented)
5. Das muß schnell _____.
                (be done)
6. Er hat nach Hause _____ müssen.
                (be taken)

5 Express in German

1. The room couldn't be rented.
2. That had to be changed.
3. He had to be taken home.
4. That has to be done fast.
5. The refrigerator couldn't be repaired.
6. He has to be operated (on) today.

F Da-Compounds as Anticipatory Words

Sometimes a **da**-compound is used to anticipate an entire clause. Look at the following sentence:

> Er kann sich nicht daran erinnern, wo er es gelesen hat
> (He can't remember where he read it.)

In this sentence, the word **daran** is a cue or marker that shows that there is more to come. The first clause only tells us that he can't remember something. The second clause is more specific: it tells us exactly what he can't remember. It answers the question:

> **Woran** kann er sich nicht erinnern?

The answer to the question is:

> wo er es gelesen hat

▶ Note   This is a very idiomatic area of the language. As you can see from the following example, English and German often go very different ways:

> Ich bin **dafür, daß sie mitkommt.**
> (I'm for her coming along. *Lit.*: I'm for it that she comes along.)

DRILLS

1   Synthetic exercises

● Complete the following sentences by forming the final clause in the tense indicated.

1. Er kann sich nicht daran gewöhnen, daß / er / haben / kein / Wagen / mehr (*present*)

    (**mehr**: anymore)

2. Er kann sich nicht daran erinnern, wo / er / lesen / es (*present perfect*)
3. Ich warte noch darauf, daß / er / kommen (*present*)   (**noch**: still)
4. Sie hat mich daran erinnert, daß / es / sein / ihr Geburtstag (*past*) (**der Geburtstag**: birthday)

2   Fill-ins

● Supply the appropriate **da**-compound.

1. Er kann sich nicht _____ erinnern, wo er es gelesen hat.
2. Ich warte noch _____, daß er kommt.
3. Er kann sich nicht _____ gewöhnen, daß er keinen Wagen mehr hat.
4. Sie hat mich _____ erinnert, daß es ihr Geburtstag war.

3 Express in German (second clause)

1. Er kann sich nicht daran gewöhnen, _____.
   (that he doesn't have a car any more)
2. Ich warte noch darauf, _____.
   (that he comes)
3. Sie hat mich daran erinnert, _____.
   (that it was her birthday)
4. Er kann sich nicht daran erinnern, _____.
   (where he read it)

4 Express in German

1. She reminded me that it was her birthday.
2. He can't remember where he read it.
3. I'm still waiting for him to come.
4. He can't get used to not having a car anymore.

VOCABULARY

bauen to build
erinnern an (+ *acc.*) to remind of
   sich **erinnern an** (+ *acc.*) to remember
der **Geburtstag, –e** birthday
sich **gewöhnen an** (+ *acc.*) to get used to
   Haare: sich **die Haare** to get a haircut
      schneiden lassen
   klingeln to ring (*such as a doorbell*)

lassen (läßt) to let, allow (*permission*)
   ließ, gelassen to have (something done)
mehr anymore
noch still
nötig necessary
der **Titel, –** title
sich **überlegen** to think about, think over

Vocabulary

► **Note**   Only definitions applicable to the text are given.

The nominative singular and plural forms of nouns are given, except when they are not commonly used. Unusual genitive singular endings are also supplied.

Strong verbs and mixed verbs are indicated by color. The principal parts of these verbs are given, including the third person singular of the present tense (in parentheses) when it is irregular.

Weak verbs appear in the infinitive form only.

Verbs with separable prefixes are indicated by a bullet: **ab·holen.**

A

der **Abend, –e** evening
das **Abendessen, –** supper, dinner
abends in the evening
aber but
die **Abfahrt, –en** departure
die **Abfahrtstafel, –n** departure board
die **Abfahrtszeit, –en** departure time
ab·fliegen to depart (by plane)
flog . . . ab, ist abgeflogen
ab·geben to turn in, leave (gibt ab), gab . . . ab, abgegeben
ab·hängen von to depend on
hing . . . ab, abgehangen
ab·holen to pick up
die **Abreise** departure
ab·reisen to depart, leave
ab·schicken to send off
das **Abteil, –e** compartment
die **Abteilung, –en** department
ab·warten to wait (for something)
acht eight
acht– (*adj.*) eighth
achtzehn eighteen
achtzig eighty
addieren to add
die **Adresse, –n** address
die **Ähnlichkeit, –en** similarity

die **Ahnung, –en** idea, glimmer
allein alone
allerdings however, but, of course, to be sure
allerlei all kinds of
alles everything
allzu all too
als (*subord. conj.*) when (past time only)
als than
als ob as if, as though
also so, then, therefore; OK
alt old
der **Alte** (*adj. noun*) old man
Amerika America
der **Amerikaner, –** (*m.*) American
die **Amerikanerin, –nen** (*f.*) American
amerikanisch American
an (+ *dat. or acc.*) on, onto, at, over to (normally used with vertical surfaces)
an·bieten to offer
bot . . . an, angeboten
ander– other
ändern to change
anders different, differently
die **Änderung, –en** change
der **Anfang, –e** beginning
an·fangen to begin (fängt an), fing . . . an, angefangen

die **Anfangszeit, –en** time the performance starts
die **Angestellte** (*adj. noun*) employee (*f.*)
die **Angst, –e** fear
an·kommen to arrive (kommt . . . an), kam . . . an, ist angekommen
an·kreuzen to mark, check
die **Ankunft** arrival
die **Ankunftshalle, –n** arrival hall
die **Ankunftstafel, –n** arrival board
an·machen to turn on
das **Anmeldeformular, –e** registration form
sich **an·melden** to check in
an·nehmen to accept; to suppose (nimmt . . . an), nahm . . . an, angenommen
an·rufen to phone, call
rief . . . an, angerufen
die **Ansage, –n** announcement
der **Anschluß, -sse** connecting train, plane or bus
an·schnallen to fasten seatbelts
sich **an·schnallen** to fasten one's seatbelt
an·sehen to look at (sieht . . . an) sah . . . an angesehen

sich **etwas an·sehen** to take a look at, look over, inspect

anständig decent, proper

die **Antwort, –en** answer

antworten (+ *dat.*) to answer; (**auf** + *acc.*) to answer a question

der **Anwalt, ⸚e** lawyer

die **Anzahl** number

an·zeigen to show, indicate

an·ziehen to put on (clothing) (**zieht** . . . **an**), **zog** . . . **an**, **angezogen**

   sich **an·ziehen** to get dressed

der **Anzug, ⸚e** suit

der **Apfelsaft, ⸚e** apple juice

die **Apotheke, –n** pharmacy

appetitlich appetizing

der **April** April

die **Arbeit, –en** work; term paper

arbeiten (**an** + *dat.*) to work (on)

arm poor

der **Arm, –e** arm

der **Arme** (*adj. noun*) poor man

die **Art, –en** kind, sort

der **Artikel, –** article

der **Arzt, ⸚e** doctor

die **Atmosphäre, –n** atmosphere

Au! Ouch!

auch also, too

auf (+ *dat.* or *acc.*) on (on top of); in (in a language); (+ *acc.*) for (a period of time)

   sich **auf·führen** to behave

auf·machen to open

auf·passen to watch out, be careful

aufrecht vertical

auf·springen to jump aboard

auf·stehen to stand up, get up (**steht** . . . **auf**), **stand** . . . **auf**, **ist aufgestanden**

der **Aufzug, ⸚e** elevator

das **Auge, –n** eye

der **Augenblick, –e** moment

der **August** August

aus (+ *dat.*) from (with place names); out of

aus·füllen to fill out

der **Ausgang, ⸚e** exit

   aus·geben to spend (money) (**gibt** . . . **aus**), **gab** . . . **aus**, **ausgegeben**

ausgefüllt filled out, completed

aus·gehen to go out (**geht** . . . **aus**), **ging** . . . **aus**, **ist ausgegangen**

aus·helfen to help out (**hilft** . . . **aus**), **half** . . . **aus**, **ausgeholfen**

sich **aus·kennen** to know one's way around **kannte** . . . **aus**, **ausgekannt**

die **Auskunft, ⸚e** information

das **Auskunftsbüro, –s** information office

aus·lachen to laugh at

das **Ausland** foreign countries

ausländisch foreign

die **Auslandsabteilung, –en** foreign exchange department

die **Auslandsreise, –en** trip abroad

aus·machen to turn off

die **Ausnahme, –n** exception

   aus·sehen to look, appear (**sieht** . . . **aus**), **sah** . . . **aus**, **ausgesehen**

außen outside

außer (+ *dat.*) except (for), besides, aside from

außerdem besides that

aus·steigen to get off (a train, bus or plane) **stieg** . . . **aus**, **ist ausgestiegen**

sich (**etwas**) **aus·suchen** to pick (something) out

die **Auswahl, –en** selection

der **Ausweis, –e** membership card, I.D.

auswendig by heart

aus·ziehen to take off (clothing) (**zieht** . . . **aus**), **zog** . . . **aus**, **ausgezogen**

   sich **aus·ziehen** to get undressed

der **Automat, –en** vending machine

B

die **Bäckerei, –en** bakery

die **Backwaren** (*pl. only*) baked goods

das **Bad, ⸚er** bath

der **Bademantel, ⸚** robe

die **Bahn, –en** railroad

der **Bahnhof, ⸚e** train (railroad) station

die **Bahnhofstreppe, –n** flight of stairs leading into the station

der **Bahnhofsvorstand, ⸚e** station master

die **Bahnkarte, –n** railroad ticket

der **Bahnschalter, –** ticket window

die **Bahnverbindung, –en** train connection

bald soon

der **Ball, ⸚e** ball

die **Bank, ⸚e** bench

die **Bank, –en** bank

das **Bankkonto,** *pl.* **–konten** bank account

die **Bar, –s** bar, cocktail lounge

bauen to build

der **Baum, ⸚e** tree

Bayern Bavaria

der **Beamte** (*adj. noun*) official

beantworten to answer (a question or a letter, not a person)

bedeuten to mean

bedienen to serve

die **Bedienung** service

sich **beeilen** to hurry

begegnen (+ *dat.*) to run into

der **Beginn** beginning

beginnen to begin **begann, begonnen**

begleiten to escort

begreifen to understand, conceive of **begriff, begriffen**

behalten to keep (**behält**), **behielt, behalten**

bei (+ *dat.*) near, in the vicinity of; at (somebody's house); at, with (with business or professional establishments); with (in the sense of *on one's person*)

beide both

das **Beispiel, –e** example

   zum Beispiel for example

   z.B. = Zum Beispiel

bekannt known

der **Bekannte** (*adj. noun*) a friend, acquaintance

die **Bekleidung, –en** clothing

bekommen to get, receive (**bekommt**), **bekam, bekommen**

beliebt popular

beliebtest- most popular

benutzen to use

das **Benzin** gas

bequem comfortable

bereit ready

bereits already

beschimpfen to curse at
beschwören to plead with
  beschwor, beschworen
besetzt occupied, crowded
besitzen to own
  besaß, besessen
besonder- special
besonders especially
besorgen to get, take care of
besprechen to discuss
  (bespricht), besprach, besprochen
besser better
die **Bestätigung, -en** confirmation
bestaunen to stare at with
  amazement, gawk
besteigen to climb onto
  bestieg, bestiegen
bestellen to order
bestenfalls at best
bestimmt certain, certainly,
  definitely
etwas Bestimmtes something
  in particular
der **Besuch, -e** visit
besuchen to visit
betäubt benumbed
der **Betrag, ⸚e** amount
das **Bett, -en** bed
das **Bettlaken, -** sheet
bevor (*subord. conj.*) before
bezahlen to pay
die **Bibliothek, -en** library
biegen to turn
  bogen,
  ist gebogen
das **Bier, -e** beer
das **Bild, -er** picture
das **Billiard** billiards
billig cheap
billiger less expensive
bis (+ *acc.*) until (with time
  expressions); as far as
  (with places)
bis (*subord. conj.*) until
Bis morgen! See you tomorrow.
bis zum, bis zur up to the
ein bißchen a little (bit)
bitte please; there you are;
  you're welcome
bitte schön there you are
Bitte schön? May I help
  you?
Bitte sehr? What would you
  like?
bitten (**um** + *acc.*) to ask for
  bat, gebeten
bleiben to stay, remain
  blieb, ist geblieben

der **Bleistift, -e** pencil
blond blond
die **Blonde** (*adj. noun*) blonde
bloß just
die **Blume, -n** flower
die **Bluse, -n** blouse
böse (**auf** + *acc.*) mad (at)
die **Bratkartoffel, -n** hash brown
  potatoes
die **Bratwurst, ⸚e** bratwurst,
  fried sausage
brauchen to need, use
braun brown
brechen to break
  (bricht), brach, gebrochen
die **Brezel, -n** pretzel
der **Brief, -e** letter
die **Briefmarke, -n** stamp
das **Briefpapier** stationery
bringen to bring, take
  brachte, gebracht
die **Broschüre, -n** brochure
das **Brot, -e** bread
das **Bröthchen, -** hard roll
der **Bruder, ⸚** brother
das **Buch, ⸚er** book
buchen to book
der **Buchhändler, -** bookseller
die **Buchhandlung, -en** bookstore
buchstabieren to spell
das **Büro, -s** office
der **Bus, -se** bus
die **Bushaltestelle, -n** bus stop

C

die **Chance, -n** chance
der **Charterflug, ⸚e** charter flight
der **Chef, -s** boss
chinesisch Chinese
die **Cola, -s** Coke
die **Couch, -es** couch

D

da (*adv.*) there
da (*subord. conj.*) since, because
dabei near by
dagegen on the other hand
die **Dame, -n** lady
der **Damenrock, ⸚e** skirt
danke thanks
  danke schön thanks very
  much
danken (+ *dat.*) to thank
dann then
darauf on it
daraus out of it
Was darf's sein? What
  would you like?
das (*def. art.*) the (neuter),
  that

d.h. = das heißt that is
daß (*subord. conj.*) that
das **Datum, die Daten** date
dauern to take, last
davon of it
dazu along with it, in addition, extra
dazwischen in between
decken to cover; to set (a
  table)
dein (*poss. adj.*) your
demonstrieren to demonstrate
denken (**an** + *acc.*) to think
  of (someone)
  dachte, gedacht
denn (*coord. conj.*) because
deprimiert depressed
der (*def. art.*) the (m.), that
der (*rel. pronoun*) who, that
derselbe (m.) the same
deshalb for that reason
deswegen therefore
deutsch (*adj.*) German
(das) **Deutsch** German (language)
der **Deutsche** (*adj. noun*) German
die **Deutsche Bundesbahn** German Federal Railroad
Deutschland Germany
der **Dezember** December
dick fat
die (*def. art.*) the (f.), that
der **Dienstag** Tuesday
dieselbe (f.) the same
dies- (*demonstr. adj.*) this
diesmal this time
direkt direct
der **Direktflug, ⸚e** direct flight
der **Direktor, -en** director
doch see footnote p. 95
doch but, "come on," "aw"
  (Sei *doch* vernünftig!:
  Come on, be reasonable.)
der **Dollar, -s** dollar
der **Dom, -e** cathedral
der **Donnerstag** Thursday
das **Doppelzimmer, -** double
  room
dort there (location)
dorthin there (motion)
dorthin·kommen to get
  there
  kam . . . dorthin, ist dort-
  hingekommen
die **Dose, -n** can
das **Drehkreuz, -e** turnstile
drei three
dreißig thirty
dreizehn thirteen
dritt- third
drüben (over) there

drücken to push

du you (*fam. sing.*)

dumm dumb, stupid

der **Dummkopf, ∸e** fool

dunkel dark

durch (+ *acc.*) through

durchgehend throughout the day

durchsuchen to search

dürfen may, be permitted, to be allowed to

(**darf**), **durfte, gedurft**

der **Durst** thirst

Durst haben to be thirsty

E

die **Ecke, -n** corner

eigen of its own

eigentlich actually

der **Eilzug, ∸e** *lit.:* fast train

ein (*indef. art.*) a

einem recht sein to be all right with someone

einfach simple, simply; one way ticket

eingeschlossen included

eingezeichnet indicated

einige some

der **Einkauf, ∸e** purchase

ein · kaufen to shop

das **Einkaufen** buying, shopping

einkaufen gehen to go shopping

ging . . . einkaufen, ist . . . einkaufen gegangen

die **Einkaufssituation, -en** shopping situation

die **Einkaufstasche, -en** shopping bag, satchel for carrying groceries

der **Einkaufswagen, -** shopping cart

ein · laden to invite

(**lädt . . . ein**), **lud . . . ein, eingeladen**

ein · lösen to cash (a check)

einmal once, one time; one order of; first of all

nicht einmal not even

noch einmal again

ein · packen to wrap up

sich (**etwas**) **ein · prägen** to commit (something) to memory

die **Einrichtung, -en** institution

eins (ein-) one

einsam lonely

ein · schlafen to fall asleep, go to sleep

(**schläft . . . ein**), **schlief . . . ein, ist . . . eingeschlafen**

ein · steigen to board (a train, bus)

stieg . . . ein, ist . . . eingestiegen

ein · stellen (**in** + *acc.*) to transfer to

die **Eintrittskarte, -n** ticket (for admission)

ein · werfen to insert

(**wirft . . . ein**), **warf . . . ein, eingeworfen**

das **Einzelzimmer, -** single room

das **einzige** the only thing

das **Eis** ice cream

die **Eisenbahn, -en** railroad

die **Elektroartikel** (*pl.*) electrical supplies

das **Elektrogeschäft, -e** store for electrical supplies

elf eleven

die **Eltern** (*pl. only*) parents

der **Empfang, ∸e** reception desk; reception clerk

am Empfang at the reception desk

empfehlen to recommend

(**empfiehlt**), **empfahl, empfohlen**

das **Ende, -n** end

enden to end, stop

endlich finally

der **Endpreis, -e** all-inclusive price

England England

englisch English; rare (meat)

entlang · gehen to go through, along

ging . . . entlang, ist . . . entlanggegangen

sich **enschließen** to decide

entschloß sich, sich entschlossen

entschuldigen to excuse

sich **entschuldigen** to excuse oneself, apologize

Entschuldigung! Excuse me!

entweder . . . oder either . . . or

die **Epoche, -n** epoch, era

er he, it

das **Erdbeereis** strawberry ice cream

das **Erdgeschoß, -sse** main floor, lobby

erfahren to find out

(**erfährt**), **erfuhr, erfahren**

die **Erfrischung, -en** refreshment

erinnern (**an** + *acc.*) to remind of

sich **erinnern** (**an** + *acc.*) to remember

sich **erkälten** to catch cold

die **Erkältung, -en** cold (illness)

erkennen to recognize

erkannte, erkannt

erklären to explain

erleben to experience

erledigen to take care of (something)

eröffnen to open

erreichen to reach

erschrecken to be frightened, shocked

(**erschrickt**), **erschrak, ist erschrocken**

erst (*adv.*) only, not until

erst jetzt not until now

erst- (*adj.*) first

als erstes the first thing

erwarten to expect

die **Erzählung, -en** story

es it

essen to eat

(**ißt**), **aß, gegessen**

das **Essen, -** food

etwa about, approximately

etwa so something like this

etwas something, a little; somewhat

euer (*poss. adj.*) your (*fam. pl.*)

Europa Europe

die **EWG** European Common Market

das **Experiment, -e** experiment

F

das **Fachgeschäft, -e** specialized store

fahren to drive

(**fährt**), **fuhr, ist . . . gefahren**

der **Fahrer, -** driver

die **Fahrkarte, -en** ticket

der **Fahrkartenautomat, -en** ticket machine

der **Fahrkartenschalter, -** ticket window

der **Fahrplan, ∸e** timetable

der **Fahrpreis, -e** price of a ticket

das **Fahrrad, ∸er** bicycle

die **Fahrt, -en** trip

die **Fahrzeit, -en** travel time

fallen to fall

(**fällt**), **fiel, ist . . . gefallen**

die **Falte, -n** pleat

die **Familie, -n** family

das **Farbdia, -s** color slide

die **Farbe, -n** color

fast almost

faul lazy
der **Februar** February
der **Feiertag, –e** holiday
die **Feinkost** delicatessen food
das **Fenster, –** window
   zum Fenster
     hinaus·schauen to look
     out of the window
die **Ferien** (*pl.*) vacation
der **Fernseher, –** television set
   fertig ready
   fertig·machen to get ready
    sich fertig·machen to get
    (oneself) ready
   fertig mit finished with
   fertig·schreiben to finish
    writing
    schrieb . . . fertig, fertigge-
    schrieben
das **Feuerzeug, –e** lighter
der **Film, –e** movie
   finden to find
    fand, gefunden
die **Firma, Firmen** firm, business
der **Fisch, –e** fish
die **Flasche, –n** bottle
das **Fleisch** meat
   fliegen to fly
    flog, ist . . . geflogen
der **Flug, –̈e** flight
der **Flughafen, –̈** airport
das **Flughafengebäude, –** terminal
der **Flugkapitän, –e** flight captain
die **Flugkarte, –n** ticket
das **Flugzeug, –e** airplane
das **Fluor** fluoride
   flüstern to whisper
   folgen to follow
   folgend following
die **Form, –en** form
die **Formalität, –en** formality
die **Formel, –n** formula
   formell formal
die **Fortsetzung, –en** continuation
das **Fotogeschäft, –e**
   photography shop
die **Frage, –n** question
   eine Frage stellen to ask a
    question
   fragen (nach + *dat.*) to ask
    (about)
der **Frager, –** person asking a
   question
(das) **Frankreich** France
   französisch French
die **Frau, –en** woman; wife; Mrs.
das **Fräulein, –** young woman;
   Miss
   frei free; empty (seats)

frei·haben to have available
   (**hat . . . frei), hatte . . .**
   frei, freigehabt
frei·halten to hold (a room)
   (**hält . . . frei), hielt . . .**
   frei, freigehalten
der **Freitag** Friday
   fremd strange, foreign
der **Fremde** (*adj. noun*) stranger,
   tourist
der **Fremdenführer, –** tour guide
   fressen to eat (of animals)
   (**frißt), fraß, gefressen**
die **Freude, –n** pleasure, joy
   einem Freude machen to
    make one happy
   freuen to please
    sich freuen (auf + *acc.*) to
    look forward to
    sich freuen (über + *acc.*)
    to be happy about
der **Freund, –e** (*m.*) friend
die **Freundin, –nen** (*f.*) friend
   freundlich (zu) friendly (to)
   frisch fresh
der **Friseur, –e** barber
   früh early
der **Frühling** spring
das **Frühstück** breakfast
   frühstücken to have break-
    fast
das **Frühstückszimmer, –** break-
    fast room
   fühlen to feel
    sich fühlen to feel (e.g.,
    How do you feel?)
   führen to lead; carry
der **Führerschein, –e** driver's license
   fünf five
   fünfzehn fifteen
   fünfzig fifty
der **Fünfziger, –** 50-mark bill
das **Funktaxi, –s** radio cab
   für (+ *acc.*) for
   furchtbar frightful, frighten-
    ing
der **Fuß, –̈e** foot
   zu Fuß gehen to walk
der **fußball** soccer
die **Fußgängerzone, –n** pedestrian mall

G
der **Gang, –̈e** aisle
   gar nicht not at all
die **Garage, –n** garage
   ganz whole, all, completely
die **Gaststätte, –n** German restaurant
das **Gebäude, –** building

   geben to give
    (**gibt), gab, gegeben**
   es gibt there is, there are
das **Gebiet, –e** area, region
   geboren born
   gebrauchen to use
der **Geburtsort, –e** birthplace
der **Geburtstag, –e** birthday
das **Gedächtnis, –se** memory
der **Gedanke, –ns, –n** thought
   gefallen (+ *dat.*) to please
    (**gefällt), gefiel, gefallen**
    es gafällt mir I like it
das **Gefühl, –e** feeling
   gegen (+ *acc.*) against; into,
    up against
der **Gegensatz, –̈e** opposite
   im Gegensatz zu in con-
    trast to
   gegenüber (+ *dat.*) opposite,
    across from
   gegenüber von across from
   gehaftet guaranteed (respon-
    sible for)
   gehen
    ging, ist . . . gegangen
   gehen (auf + *acc.*) to lead to
   gehen . . . hinein to go into,
    enter
das **Geld, –er** money
der **Geldbeutel, –** wallet
der **Geldschein, –e** bill
   gelten für to be valid for
    (**gilt), galt, gegolten**
das **Gemüse, –** vegetables
der **Gemüseladen, –̈** vegetable
   shop
   genau just, exactly
   genau so . . . wie just as . . .
    as
   genießen to enjoy
    genoß, genossen
   genug enough
   geöffnet open
das **Gepäck** luggage
die **Gepäckausgabe, –n** baggage
   claim area
   gerade (*adv.*) just, right now
   geradeaus straight ahead
das **Gericht, –e** dish, meal
   gerichtet (an + *acc.*) di-
    rected to
   gern fine, gladly
   gern (lieber, am liebsten)
    like to (*prefer to, like to*
    best of all)
das **Geschäft, –e** business, store
   geschehen to happen
    (**geschieht), geschah, ist**
    geschehen
das **Geschenk, –e** gift

die **Geschichte, –en** story
geschieden divorced
haben . . . geschlossen to be closed (stores)
Hat's geschmeckt? How was it? Did it taste good?
das **Gesicht, –er** face
das **Gespräch, –e** conversation
gestern yesterday
gestern abend last night, yesterday evening
gesund healthy
das **Getränk, –e** beverage
getrennt separately
sich **gewöhnen (an** + *acc.***)** to get used to
gewöhnlich usually
gewußt past participle of *wissen*
das **Glas, ̈–er** glass
glauben (+ *acc. obj.***)** to believe (something)
glauben (+ *dat. obj.***)** to believe (someone)
gleich immediately, right away
das **Gleis, –e** track
die **Gleisnummer, –n** track number
glücklich happy
glücklicherweise fortunately
die **Glühbirne, –n** lightbulb
(das) **golf** golf
Du lieber Gott! Good God!
der **Graf, –en, –en** Count (title)
greifen to reach
griff, gegriffen
grell loud
groß (größer, größt–) big
großartig great
die **Größe, –n** size
die **Großstadt, ̈–e** large city
grün green
das **Gruppenbild, –er** group portrait
der **Gruß, ̈–e** greeting
das **Gulasch** goulash
die **Gulaschsuppe, –n** goulash soup
gut fine
gut (besser, best–) good, well (better, best)
das **Gutenbergmuseum** Museum of the History of Printing
der **Gutschein, –e** voucher

H

das **Haar, –e** hair (normally used in plural in German)
sich die Haare schneiden lassen to get a haircut

haben to have
(hat), hatte, gehabt
das **Hackfleisch** ground meat
halb half
Halt! Stop!
Halt's Maul! Shut up!
halten to hold
(hält), hielt, gehalten
halten von to think of (used in asking for an opinion)
die **Haltestelle, –n** bus stop
die **Hand, ̈–e** hand
Hände hoch! Hands up!
das **Handgepäck** hand luggage
hängen to hang (*intransitive*)
hing, ist . . . gehangen
hängen (hängte, gehängt) to hang (*transitive*)
hassen to hate
ich hätte gern I'd like
häufig frequently
der **Hauptbahnhof, ̈–e** main railroad station
der **Hauptfilm, –e** feature film
die **Hauptmahlzeit, –en** main meal
die **Hauptpost** main post office
das **Hauptziel, –e** main destination
das **Haus, ̈–er** house
nach Hause home (destination)
zu Hause home, at home (location)
die **Haushaltsartikel (***pl.***)** household goods
heiraten to marry
heiß hot
heißen to be called; to mean
hieß, geheißen
Wie heißt er? What's his name?
helfen (+ *dat.***)** to help
(hilft), half, geholfen
das **Hemd, –en** shirt
heraus·finden to find out
fand . . . heraus, herausgefunden
heraus·ziehen to withdraw, pull out
zog . . . heraus, herausgezogen
der **Herbst** autumn, fall
der **Herr, –n, –en** Mr.; gentleman
mein Herr sir
die **Herrenabteilung, –en** men's department
herum·reisen to travel around
herunter down
heute today

heute abend this evening, tonight
hie und da now and then
hier here (location)
hierher here (destination)
die **Hilfe, –n** help
hilfsbereit eager to help
das **Hilton** Hilton (hotel)
hin to (as in *where to*)
hin und zurück there and back, round trip
hinauf up
hinauf·gehen to go upstairs
ging . . . hinauf, ist . . hinaufgegangen
hinauf·steigen to rise
stieg . . . hinauf, ist . . . hinaufgestiegen
hinein·schieben to insert
schob . . . hinein, hineingeschoben
hin·gehen to go to, head for
ging . . . hin, ist . . . hingegangen
hin·legen to put down
sich **hin·legen** to lie down
hinten in the back
hinter (+ *dat.* or *acc.***)** behind, in back of
hinunter down
der **Hinweis, –e** tip, information
hinzu·zählen to add
hoch (höher, höchst–) high; up; tall
höchstens at most
hoch·tragen to carry up
(trägt . . . hoch), trug . . . hoch, hochgetragen
hoffentlich hopefully
holen to get, go get
Holland Holland
holländisch Dutch
das **Holz, ̈–er** wood
hören to hear
die **Hose, –n** pants
eine Hose (*sing.***)** a pair of pants
das **Hotel, –s** hotel
hübsch pretty
der **Hund, –e** dog
hundert hundred
hundertmal a hundred times
der **Hunger** hunger
Er hat Hunger. He's hungry.
hungrig (sein) (to be) hungry
der **Hut, ̈–e** hat

I
ich I
die **Idee, –n** idea

identifizieren to identify
identisch (mit) identical (to)
der **Idiot, –en, –en** idiot
ihr (*pers. pron.*) you (*fam. pl.*)
ihr (*poss. adj.*) her; their
Ihr (*poss. adj.*) your (*polite form*)
der **Imbißautomat, –en** snack vending machine
immer always
die **Imprägnierung, –en** waterproofing
in (+ *dat.* or *acc.*) in, into
inbegriffen included
innen inside
interessant interesting
interessieren to interest
  sich **interessieren** (**für** + *acc.*) to be interested (in)
international international
irgendeinmal sometime or other
irgendwo somewhere
irgendwohin anyplace, anywhere
Italien Italy
italienisch Italian

J
ja yes
die **Jacke, –n** sportscoat
das **Jahr, –e** year
der **Januar** January
jawohl yes (stronger than *ja*)
je . . . desto the . . . the (e.g., *the more the better*)
jeder each, every
jetzt now
die **Jugendherberge, –n** youth hostel
jugoslawisch Yugoslavian
der **Juli** July
jung young
der **Junge, –n, –n** boy
Jungens (*pl. only*) you guys (slang)
der **Juni** June

K
der **Kaffee** coffee
das **Kalbsschnitzel, –** veal cutlet
kalt cold
der **Kamin, –e** fireplace
kaputt broken
die **Karte, –n** postcard; ticket; map; menu (*Speisekarte*)
der **Karton, –s** carton, box
der **Käse, –** cheese

das **Käsebrot, –e** (open-faced) cheese sandwich
die **Kasse, –n** cashier, checkout counter; insurance plan (*Krankenkasse*)
der **Kassenbon, –s** chit, receipt
die **Kassiererin, –nen** (*f.*) checkout clerk
die **Katastrophe, –n** catastrophe
die **Katze, –n** cat
kaufen to buy
das **Kaufhaus, –̈er** department store
die **Kaufhausgruppe, –n** department store chain
kaum scarcely, hardly
kein not a, not any, no
keineswegs by no means
die **Kellertür, –en** cellar door
der **Kellner, –** waiter
die **Kellnerin, –nen** waitress
kennen to know, be acquainted with
  kannte, gekannt
kennen·lernen to meet, make (someone's) acquaintance
der **Kerl, –e** guy
die **Kerze, –n** candle
der **Kilometer, –** kilometer
das **Kind, –er** child
das **Kino, –s** the movies
der **Kinobesuch, –e** going to the movies
der **Kiosk, –e** newsstand
Klar! Sure!
die **Klasse, –n** class
Klasse! Great! Terrific!
das **Klavier, –e** piano
das **Kleid, –er** dress; (*pl.*) dresses or clothes
klein small
der **Kleine** (*adj. noun*) little man; little boy
das **Kleingeld** change
die **Kleinstadt, –̈e** small town
klingeln to ring (doorbell)
klingen to sound
  klang, geklungen
klopfen to knock
klug smart, clever
die **Kneipe, –n** bar
der **Koffer, –** suitcase
Köln Cologne
kommen to come
  kam, ist gekommen
kommen . . . wieder to come back
der **Kommentar, –e** commentary
kompliziert complicated
der **Kondukteur, –e** conductor

können can, be able to (ability); can (possibility); to know (in the sense of having an ability: Er *kann* Deutsch.)
  (**kann**), **konnte, gekonnt**
das **Konzert, –e** concert
der **Kopf, –̈e** head
die **Kopie, –n** copy
der **Korken, –** cork
der **Korridor, –e** hall, passageway
kosten to cost
die **Kostprobe, –n** sample (of something to eat or drink)
die **Kraft, –̈e** power
krank sick
das **Krankenhaus, –̈er** hospital
die **Krankenkasse, –n** health insurance plan
die **Krawatte, –n** necktie
der **Krieg, –e** war
kriegen to get, receive
kritisieren to criticize
die **Küche, –n** kitchen; food, cuisine
der **Kugelschreiber, –** ballpoint pen
der **Kühlschrank, –̈e** refrigerator
der **Kunde, –n, –n** customer
das **Kurfürstliche Schloß** residence of the Prince Elector
der **Kurs, –e** course; exchange rate
die **Kurstafel, –n** sign showing exchange rates
der **Kurswagen, –** passenger car with special destination
kurz short

L
lachen to laugh
der **Laden, –̈** store
die **Lampe, –n** lamp
das **Land, –̈er** country
  aufs Land (gehen) (to go) to the country
landen to land
das **Landesmuseum, –museen** state museum
die **Landung, –en** landing
lang (*adj.*) long
lange (*adv.*) long, for a long time
so lange that long
der **Lange** (*adj. noun*) tall man
länger longer, any longer
langsam slow(ly)
längst a long time ago, long since

langweilig boring
der **Lärm** noise
  lassen to let, allow; to have (something done)
  (läßt), ließ, gelassen
der **Lastwagen, -** truck
  laufen to run
  (läuft), lief, ist gelaufen
  laut loud
  leben to live, be alive
das **Leben, -** life
das **Lebensmittel, -** grocery item
die **Lebensmittelabteilung, -en** grocery department
  lebhaft busy
der **Lederstiefel, -** leather boot
  legen to lay
  leicht easy, easily; light
  leider unfortunately
der **Leihwagen, -** rental car
  leise softly
das **Leitungswasser, -** tap water
  lernen to learn; to study
  lesen to read
  (liest), las, gelesen
  letzt- last
die **Leuchttafel, -n** illuminated sign
die **Leute** (*pl. only*) people
das **Licht, -er** light
  lieb- dear
  lieben to love
der **Liebling, -e** darling
  liefern to deliver
  leigen to lie; to be located
  lag, gelegen
  liegen . . . zentral to be centrally located
die **Linie, -n** line; number (bus or streetcar)
  links left, to the left
die **Liste, -n** list
der **Liter, -** liter
der **Lodenmantel, ∺** loden coat
  sich **lohnen** to be worthwhile
das **Lokal, -e** place (restaurant or bar)
die **Lokomotive, -n** locomotive
  los loose
  Was ist mit ihm los? What's wrong with him?
  los·gehen to start
  ging . . . los, ist losgegangen
  los·lassen to let go
  (läßt . . . los), ließ . . . los, losgelassen
  los·werden to get rid of
  (wird . . . los), wurde . . . los, ist . . . losgeworden

  los·ziehen to start, set out
  zog . . . los, ist . . . losgezogen
die **Luftpost** air mail
  Luftsprünge machen to jump up in the air

M

  machen to make; to do; to cost; to take (a trip)
  es sich einfach machen to make it easy for oneself
  es sich schwer machen to make it difficult for oneself
  es macht nichts it doesn't matter
das **Mädchen, -** girl
die **Mahlzeit, -en** meal
der **Mai** May
  Mailand Milan (Italy)
  mal just (as in *Just imagine that!*)
das **(-te) Mal** the (-th) time
  zum ersten Mal for the first time
  man (*pron.*) one
  manchmal sometimes
der **Mann, ∺er** man; husband
der **Mantel, ∺** coat, overcoat
die **Mappe, -n** briefcase
die **Mark, -** mark (currency)
die **Marke, -n** brand
der **März** March
die **Maschine, -n** machine
das **Medikament, -e** medication, drug
  mehr more
  mehrere several
  mehrmals several times
die **Meile, -n** mile
  mein my
  meinen to mean; to have an opinion about
  meist- most
  meistens mostly
  eine Menge a lot (of something)
die **Mensa** student dining hall
  Mensch! Man!
  merken to notice
  sich **(etwas) merken** to make a (mental) note of (something)
die **Metzgerei, -en** butcher shop
die **Miete, -n** rent
  mieten to rent
die **Milch** milk
  mindestens at least
der **Minister, -** minister (political)
die **Minute, -n** minute

  mit (+ *dat.*) with; by (train, bus, plane, etc.)
  mit·bringen to bring along
  brachte . . . mit, mitgebracht
das **Mitglied, -er** member
  mit·kommen to come along
  kam . . . mit, ist . . . mitgekommen
  mit·nehmen to take along
  (nimmt . . . mit), nahm . . . mit, mitgenommen
der **Mittag** noon
das **Mittagessen, -** lunch
  mittags around noon
die **Mittagskarte, -n** lunch menu
die **Mitte, -n** middle
  mittel medium
  mittelalterlich medieval
  mitteleuropäisch Central European
die **Mitternacht** midnight
der **Mittwoch** Wednesday
die **Möbel** (*pl. only*) furniture
  Ich möchte I'd like to
  modern modern
  mögen to like (liking, fondness)
  (mag), mochte, gemocht
die **Möglichkeit, -en** possibility
der **Moment, -e** moment
  im Moment at the moment
  Moment! Moment mal! Just a moment!
der **Monat, -e** month
der **Montag** Monday
  morgen tomorrow
der **Morgen, -** morning
  morgens in the morning
der **Motor, -en** motor
  müde tired
  München Munich
die **Münze, -n** coin
  müssen to have to, must
  (muß), mußte, gemußt
die **Mutter, ∺** mother

N

  na well (*Well, what do you expect?*)
  nach (+ *dat.*) to (destination with place names); after (time expressions)
  nach unten down
  nach Hause home (destination)
  nachdem (*subord. conj.*) after
  nach·lesen to look (something) up

(liest . . . nach), las . . .
nach, nachgelesen

der **Nachmittag, -e** afternoon

nachmittags in the afternoon

nach · rufen (+ *dat.*) to call after

rief . . . nach, nachgerufen

nach · schauen (+ *dat.*) to look after

nach · schlagen to look (something) up

(schlägt . . . nach), schlug . . . nach, nachgeschlagen

nach · sehen to take a look, look up

(sieht . . . nach), sah . . . nach, nachgesehen

nächst- next

die **Nacht, ⁼e** night

nachts at night

die **Nähe** vicinity

näher closer

der **Nahverkehr** local trains (*lit.:* local traffic)

der **Nahverkehrszug, ⁼e** local train

der **Name, -ns, -n** name

Auf welchen Namen? In what name?

nämlich namely, in fact

die **Nationalität, -en** nationality

natürlich of course

neben (+ *dat.* or *acc.*) beside, next to, alongside of

nebenan next to it

nehmen to take

(nimmt), nahm, genommen

nein no

nennen to call

nannte, genannt

nett nice

der **Netzplan, ⁼e** map of rail or bus lines

neu new

neun nine

neunzehn nineteen

neunzig ninety

nicht not

nicht so . . . wie not as . . . as

nichts nothing

nie never

nie wieder never again

niemand no one

noch still

noch nicht not yet

der **Nonstopflug, ⁼e** nonstop flight

normalerweise normally

nötig necessary

der **November** November

null zero

die **Nummer, -n** number

nun now

nur only

O

ob (*subord. conj.*) if, whether

der **Ober, -** waiter, headwaiter

Herr Ober! Waiter!

oder or

oft often

ohne (+ *acc.*) without

ohne . . . zu (+ *inf.*) without . . . -ing

der **Oktober** October

der **Onkel, -** uncle

operieren to operate (on)

die **Ordnung, -en** order

in Ordnung OK

Geht in Ordnung. That's fine.

organisieren to organize

sich **orientieren über** to acquaint oneself with, get to know

die **Orientierungstafel, -n** directory (store or office)

der **Ort, -e** place

die **Ortszeit** local time

P

ein paar a few

packen to pack

die **Packung, -en** box, package

das **Paket, -e** package

die **Paketannahme, -n** package counter

die **Panik** panic

die **Papiertüte, -n** paper bag

der **Park, -s** park

der **Partner, -** partner

die **Party, Parties** party

der **Paß, ⁼sse** short for *Reisepaß*: passport

der **Passagier, -e** passenger

passen to fit

die **Paßkontrolle, -n** immigration, passport check

die **Paßnummer, -n** passport number

der **Patient, -en, -en** patient

die **Pauschalreise, -en** package tour

die **Pause, -n** pause, intermission, break

eine Pause machen to take a break

die **Person, -en** person

der **Pfadfinder, -** boy scout

der **Pfennig, -e** penny, 1/100th of a mark

Pfui! Yuch!

das **Pfund, -e** pound

das **Plakat, -e** poster

der **Plan, ⁼e** plan

planen to plan

der **Plastikbeutel, -** sturdy plastic bag

die **Platte, -n** record

der **Plattenspieler, -** record player

der **Platz, ⁼e** place, seat; space; square (city)

die **Platzkarte, -n** reserved seat

pleite broke

plötzlich suddenly

die **Politik** politics

der **Politiker, -** politician

die **Polizei** (*sing. only*) police, fuzz

die **Pommes frites** French fries

die **Post** mail; post office

die **Postkarte, -n** postcard

der **Postwagen, -** mail car

die **Praxis, die Praxen** doctor's or lawyer's office

der **Preis, -e** price

die **Preislage, -n** price range

die **Preisliste, -n** price list

die **Preistafel, -n** sign showing prices

preiswert reasonable

die **Presse** press

Prima! Great!

privat private

das **Problem, -e** problem

der **Professor, -en** professor

das **Programm, -e** program

der **Prospekt, -e** pamphlet

das **Prozent, -e** percent

prüfen to test

der **Pullover, -** sweater, pullover

putzen to brush, clean

Q

die **Quittung, -en** receipt

R

das **Rad, ⁼er** wheel

das **Radio, -s** radio

im Radio on the radio

rasieren to shave (someone)

sich **rasieren** to shave (oneself)

das **Rathaus, ⁼er** city hall

rauchen to smoke

räumen to clear, empty

rechnen mit to take into account

die **Rechnung, –en** bill
recht · haben to be right
einem recht · sein to be all right with someone
rechts right, to the right
reden to talk, discuss
das **Regal, –e** shelf, rack
der **Regenmantel, ⸚** raincoat
reich rich; varied
die **Reihe, –n** number, group, variety; row
reinigen to clean
die **chemische Reinigung, –en** dry cleaning
die **Reise, –n** trip
das **Reisebüro, –s** travel agency
reisefertig ready to go
reisen to travel
das **Reisen** travel
der **Reisepaß, ⸚sse** passport
der **Reisescheck, –s** traveler's check
der **Reiseveranstalter, –** tour organizer
das **Reiseziel, –e** destination
reißen to tear, yank
riß, gerissen
rennen to run
rannte, ist gerannt
reparieren to repair
reservieren to reserve
das **Restaurant, –s** restaurant
das **Resultat, –e** result
der **Revolver, –** gun
rezeptfrei nonprescription (drug)
rezeptpflichtig prescription (drug)
der **Rheindampfer, –** Rhine river steamer
die **Rheingoldhalle** convention center in Mainz
richtig correct, right; real
das **Ringbuchpapier** paper for ring binders
der **Rock, ⸚e** skirt
rollen to roll
die **Rolltreppe, –n** escalator
der **Roman, –e** novel
rot red
der **Rückflug, ⸚e** return flight
rufen to call
rief, gerufen
die **Ruhe** quiet, peace
in Ruhe in peace, alone
der **Ruhetag, –e** day off
ruhig just, without any worry; quiet
das **Rumpsteak, –s** rumpsteak

S

die **Sache, –n** thing
sagen to say, tell
der **Sakko, –s** jacket
der **Salat, –e** salad
der **Samstag** Saturday
der **Sarg, ⸚e** coffin
saufen to drink (in the sense of to booze)
(säuft), soff, gesoffen
die **Schachtel, –n** pack, box
der **Schalter, –** window (e.g., ticket or bank teller's window)
die **Schande** disgrace
schauen to look
der **Scheck, –s** check
schenken to give (a present)
schicken to send
schieben to shove
schob, geschoben
die **Schiebetür, –en** sliding door
schießen to shoot
schoß, geschossen
das **Schiff, –e** ship
das **Schild, –er** sign
das **Schinkenbrot, –e** (open-faced) ham sandwich
schlafen to sleep
(schläft), schlief, geschlafen
die **Schlange, –n** line (of people)
schlecht bad
schleppen to drag
schließen to close
schloß, geschlossen
das **Schließfach, ⸚er** locker
der **Schlitz, –e** slot
der **Schlüssel, –** key
schmecken to taste; to taste good
der **Schnaps, ⸚e** schnapps
schneiden to cut
schnitt, geschnitten
sich schneiden to cut oneself
schnell quick(ly), fast
der **Schnellzug, ⸚e** express train
das **Schnitzel, –** schnitzel, cutlet
schon already
schön pretty, beautiful; fine
der **Schoß, ⸚e** lap
schrecklich terrible, horrible
schreiben (über + acc.) to write (about)
schrieb, geschrieben
die **Schreibmaschine, –n** typewriter
der **Schreibtisch, –e** desk
die **Schreibwaren** (pl. only) writing supplies

das **Schreibwarengeschäft, –e** stationery store
schreien to yell, scream
schrie, geschrieen
der **Schuh, –e** shoe
das **Schuhgeschäft, –e** shoe store
die **Schuppen** (pl.) dandruff
schwach weak
die **Schwäche, –n** weakness
schwarz black
die **Schweiz** Switzerland
die **Schwellenangst, ⸚e** fear of entering a place
schwer hard, difficult; heavy
die **Schwester, –n** sister; nurse
die **Schwierigkeit, –en** difficulty
sechs six
sechzehn sixteen
sechzig sixty
sehen to see
(sieht), sah, gesehen
sehen . . . an to look at
die **Sehenswürdigkeit, –en** sight, place of interest
sehr very
sein to be
(ist), war, ist gewesen
sein (poss. adj.) his; its
seit (+ dat.) for (a period of past time); since (with a point in time)
seitdem (subord. conj.) since, ever since
die **Seite, –n** side; page
die **Sekretärin, –nen** secretary
selber herself, myself, oneself, etc.
selbständig independent
die **Selbstbedienung** self service
selbstverständlich of course
selten seldom
das **Semester, –** semester
der **Senf** mustard
der **September** September
servieren to serve
der **Sessel, –** easy chair
setzen to put, set
sich setzen to sit down
das **Shampoo, –s** shampoo
sicher certain(ly), sure
die **Sicherung, –en** fuse
sie (pers. pron.) she; they
Sie (pers. pron.) you (sing. and pl.)
sieben seven
siebt– seventh
siebzehn seventeen
siebzig seventy
singen to sing
sang, gesungen

der **Sinn** sense, meaning
    einen Sinn haben to make
      sense
    sinnlos senseless
der **Sitz, –e** seat
    sitzen to sit
      saß, gesessen
    sitzen · bleiben to remain
      seated
      blieb . . . sitzen, ist . . . sit-
      zengeblieben
der **Sitzplatz, ⁻e** seat
    ski · laufen to ski
      (läuft . . . ski), lief . . . ski,
      ist skigelaufen
    skilaufen · gehen to go skiing
    so so, that way
    so etwas something like that
    so . . . wie as . . . as
    sobald (*subord. conj.*) as
      soon as
das **Sofa, –s** sofa
    sofort immediately
    sogar even; in fact
    sogenannt so-called
    sollen to be supposed to
      (obligation); to be said
      to, supposed to (supposi-
      tion); shall (suggestion)
      sollte, gesollt
der **Sommer** summer
das **Sonderangebot, –e** special,
    sale-priced item
der **Sonntag** Sunday
    sonntags on Sunday
    sonst otherwise
die **Sorte, –n** kind
    sowieso anyway
das **Spanisch** Spanish (language)
    sparen to save (money)
der **Spaß, ⁻e** joke, fun
    **einem den Spaß verder-
      ben** to spoil someone's
      fun
    spät late
    später later
    erst später not until later
    spazieren · gehen to go for a
      walk
      ging . . . spazieren, ist . . .
      spazierengegangen
die **Speisekarte, –n** menu
der **Speisewagen, –** dining car
die **Spezialabteilung, –en** special
    department
die **Spezialität, –en** specialty
    speziell special
der **Spiegel, –** mirror
das **Spiegelei, –er** fried egg
    spielen to play

das **Sporthemd, –en** sports shirt
    sprechen to speak
      (spricht), sprach, gespro-
      chen
    sprechen (mit + *dat.*) to
      talk to
    sprechen (über + *acc.*) to
      talk about
der **Sprudel, –** soda water
    staatlich state
die **Stadt, ⁻e** city, town
der **Stadtplan, ⁻e** map of the
    city
der **Stadtteil, –e** part of town
das **Stadttheater, –** civic theater
das **Stadtzentrum, –zentren** cen-
    ter of town
    stark strong, powerful
    statt (+ *gen.*) instead of
    statt . . . zu (+ *inf.*) instead
      of . . . -ing
das **Steak, –s** steak
    stecken to put; to be (but
      not be easily visible)
    stehen to stand
      stand, gestanden
    stehen . . . auf to get up
    stehen · bleiben to stop
      blieb . . . stehen, ist . . .
      stehengeblieben
    stehen · lassen to leave
      standing, leave as is
      (läßt . . . stehen), ließ . . .
      stehen, stehengelassen
der **Stehimbiß, –sse** stand-up
    snack bar
    stehlen to steal
      (stiehlt), stahl, gestohlen
    steif stiff, formal
    steigen to climb
      stieg, ist gestiegen
    stellen to put
die **Stellung, –en** job
die **Stewardeß, –essen** stewardess
der **Stift, –e** pen; pencil
    still still, quiet
der **Stillstand** stop
die **Stimme, –n** voice
der **Stock, ⁻e** floor
das **Stockwerk, –e** floor, story
    strahlen to beam
die **Straße, –n** street
die **Straßenbahn, –en** streetcar
der **Straßenverkauf** street vend-
    ing
die **Strecke, –n** distance
das **Streichholz, ⁻er** match
das **Stück, –e** play; piece
die **Stückwäsche** things to be
    laundered

der **Student, –en, –en** student
das **Studentenreisebüro, –s** stu-
    dent travel agency
    studieren (an + *dat.*) to
      study (at)
die **Stufe, –n** step
der **Stuhl, ⁻e** chair
die **Stunde, –n** hour
    suchen to look for
der **Supermarkt, ⁻e** supermarket
die **Suppe, –n** soup

T

die **Tabakwaren** (*pl. only*) to-
    bacco products
die **Tafel, –n** blackboard
der **Tag, –e** day
    tagelang for days
die **Tagesspezialität, –en** daily
    special
    tagsüber days, during the day
die **Tante, –n** aunt
    tanzen to dance
die **Tasche, –n** pocket
die **Taschenbuchausgabe, –n** pa-
    perback edition
das **Taschentuch, ⁻er** handker-
    chief
die **Tasse, –n** cup
die **Taste, –n** button, key
    tausend thousand
das **Taxi, –s** (*also pl.* **Taxen**) taxi
die **Taxizentrale, –n** taxi dis-
    patcher
das **Telefon, –e** telephone
das **Telefongespräch, –e** phone
    call, telephone conversa-
    tion
    telefonieren to make a
      phone call
die **Telefonnummer, –n** tele-
    phone number
das **Telegramm, –e** telegram
der **Teller, –** plate
das **Tennis** tennis
der **Termin, –e** appointment
    teuer expensive
das **Theater, –** theater
die **Theke, –n** counter, bar
die **Tinte, –n** ink
der **Tisch, –e** table
der **Titel, –** title
die **Toilettenartikel** (*pl. only*) toi-
    letries
    tot dead
der **Tote** (*adj. noun*) dead man
    töten to kill
der **Tourist, –en** tourist
    tragen to carry
      (trägt), trug, getragen

die **Transportanlage, –n** luggage carousel

das **Transportband, –er** conveyor belt

treffen to meet, run into (**trifft**), **traf, getroffen**

der **Trenchmantel, –** trench coat

die **Treppe, –n** flight of stairs

die **Treppenstufe, –n** step in a flight of stairs

trinken to drink **trank, getrunken**

trinken . . . aus to empty one's glass

das **Trinkgeld, –er** tip

das **Trittbrett, –er** steps (of a train)

trotz (+ *gen.*) in spite of

Tschüß! See you! Bye! (informal)

die **Tube, –n** tube

tun to do **tat, getan**

der **Tunnel, –s** tunnel

die **Tür, –en** door

typisch typical(ly)

U

üben to practice

über (+ *dat.* or *acc.*) over, above; via, by way of; across

überall everywhere

überfahren to run over (someone or something) (**überfährt**), **überfuhr, überfahren**

der **Übergang, –e** passage

das **Übergewicht** excess baggage

sich **überlegen** to think about, think over

übernachten to stay the night

die **Überraschung, –en** surprise

übersetzen to translate

die **Übung, –en** exercise

die **Uhr, –en** clock **zwei Uhr** two o'clock

die **Uhrzeit, –en** time of day

um (+ *acc.*) around; at (in time expressions)

um . . . zu (+ *inf.*) in order to

die **Umgebung, –en** surrounding

der **Umschlag, –e** envelope

um·steigen to change (trains or buses) **stieg . . . um, ist . . . umgestiegen**

und and

ungefähr about, approximately

die **Uniform, –en** uniform

die **Universität, –en** university die **Uni** slang form for *Universität*

die **Unkosten** (*pl. only*) expenses

unser (*poss. adj.*) our

unten below, down; downstairs

unter (+ *dat.* or *acc.*) under, among

unter anderen among others

das **Untergeschoß, –sse** lower level

die **Unterkunft, –e** place to stay

der **Unterschied, –e** difference

unterschreiben to sign **unterschrieb, unterschrieben**

unterstützen to support, subsidize

unterwegs on the way

die **USA** (*pl.*) the USA

V

der **Vater, –** father

sich **verändern** to change (e.g., *He's changed.*)

verbieten to forbid **verbot, verboten**

die **Verbindung, –en** (train or bus) connection

verbrauchen to use up

verbrennen to burn **verbrannte, verbrannt**

verbringen to spend (time) **verbrachte, verbracht**

verderben to spoil (**verdirbt**), **verdarb, verdorben**

verdienen to earn

die **Vereinigten Staaten** (*pl.*) the United States

vergessen to forget (**vergißt**), **vergaß, vergessen**

verhaftet (*adj.*) arrested, under arrest

verkaufen to sell

der **Verkäufer, –** salesman, vendor

die **Verkäuferin, –nen** saleswoman, vendor

die **Verlängerungsschnur, –e** extension cord

verlassen to leave (**verläßt**), **verließ, verlassen**

verloren lost

vermieten to rent

die **Vermittlungsgebühr, –en** fee, service charge

vernünftig reasonable

verpassen to miss (a train or plane)

verprügeln to beat, beat up

verrückt crazy

verschieden different

verschiedenes several different things

versprechen to promise (**verspricht**), **versprach, versprochen**

verstehen to understand **verstand, verstanden**

versuchen to try

der **Verwandte** (*adj. noun*) relative

Verzeihung! Excuse me!

viel much **viel mehr** much more, many more

viele many, a lot of

vieles a lot of things

vielleicht perhaps, maybe

vier four

das **Viertel, –** quarter **viertel nach** quarter after (in time expressions) **viertel vor** quarter to (in time expressions)

vierzehn fourteen

vierzig forty

der **Volkswagen, –** Volkswagen

voll full

völlig completely

von (+ *dat.*) from, by, of

vor (+ *dat.* or *acc.*) in front of; before, ago (time expressions)

vor sich hin to oneself

im voraus in advance

voraussichtlich according to estimates

vorbei·gehen (**an** + *dat.*) to walk by (someone or something) **ging . . . vorbei, ist . . . vorbeigegangen**

vorbei·kommen to come by, drop by **kam . . . vorbei, ist . . . vorbeigekommen**

vor·bereiten to prepare **bereitete . . . vor, vorbereitet**

vor·haben to plan, intend (**hat . . . vor**), **hatte . . . vor, vorgehabt**

vorher before

vor·kommen to happen **kam . . . vor, ist . . . vorgekommen**

die **Vorlesung, –en** lecture

vormittags before noon
der **Vorname, -ns, -n** first name
vorne up front
vornehm elegant, high class
Vorsicht! Careful! Watch out!
vorsichtig careful
vor·stellen to introduce
  sich **vor·stellen** to introduce (oneself)
  sich (etwas) **vor·stellen** to imagine (something), picture to (oneself)
die **Vorstellung, -en** showing
vor·zeigen to show, present

W

der **Wagen, -** car; railroad car
wählen to choose
wahr true
während (+ *gen.*) during
wahrscheinlich probably
die **Wand, ⸚e** wall
wann when (question word)
die **Ware, -n** merchandise
  anmeldefreie Waren duty-free goods, nothing to declare
  anmeldepflichtige Waren dutiable goods, goods to declare
warm warm
warten (**auf** + *acc.*) to wait (for)
warum why
was what (question word); that (relative pron.)
'was colloquial form of *etwas*
was für what kind of
was noch what else (in questions)
waschen to wash (**wäscht**), **wusch, gewaschen**
  sich **waschen** to wash (oneself)
die **Wäscherei, -en** laundry
das **Waschmittel, -** laundry supplies
das **Wasser, -** water
das **Wechselgeld** change
der **Wechselkurs, -e** rate of exchange
wechseln to cash (a check); to change
die **Wechselstube, -n** foreign currency exchange
weg away; gone
der **Weg, -e** way, road
wegen (+ *gen.*) because of, due to, on account of

weg·gehen to go away
  ging . . . weg, ist . . . weggegangen
weg·laufen to run away
  (**läuft . . . weg**), **lief . . . weg, ist . . . weggelaufen**
weil (*subord. conj.*) because
die **Weile, -n** while
der **Wein, -e** wine
das **Weingebiet, -e** wine-growing area
die **Weinkarte, -n** wine list
die **Weinstube, -n** establishment specializing in wine
weit far
weiter farther
  und so weiter and so on
  usw. = und so weiter
weiter·gehen to walk on by
  ging . . . weiter, ist . . . weitergegangen
welcher which (question word)
wen who(m) (*acc. of* **wer**)
sich wenden zu to turn to [**wenden** also has weak (regular) forms] **wandte, gewandt**
wenig little
  ein wenig a little, a bit; somewhat
wenige few
die **Welt, -en** world
wenn (*subord, conj.*) if (in *if . . . then* situations); when (with pres. or future only)
wer who (question word)
der **Werbefilm, -e** film commercial
die **Werbung, -en** advertising
werden to become (**wird**), **wurde, ist geworden**
werfen to throw (**wirft**), **warf, geworfen**
das **Wertzeichen, -** officialese for postage stamp
die **Weste, -n** cardigan
Westeuropa Western Europe
das **Wetter** weather
der **Wetterbericht, -e** weather report
wichtig important
wie how (question word); as, like, such as
Auf Wiederhören! Good-bye! (telephone only)
wieder·sehen to see again (**sieht . . . wieder**), **sah . . . wieder, wiedergesehen**
Auf Wiedersehen! good-bye!

Wien Vienna
das **Wienerschnitzel, -** wiener-schnitzel
wieviel how much (question word)
wild wild
der **Winter** winter
wir we
wirklich really
die **Wirtschaft, -en** inn
wissen to know (**weiß**), **wußte, gewußt**)
das **Wissen** knowledge
wo where (question word)
die **Woche, -n** week
das **Wochenende, -n** weekend
die **Wochenendeinkäufe** (*pl. only*) weekend shopping
woher where from
wohin where to
wohl probably
wohnen to live, reside
die **Wohnung, -en** apartment
das **Wohnzimmer, -** living room
wollen to want to (volition); to claim to, to consider oneself [to be] (assertion, opinion) (**will**), **wollte, gewollt**
das **Wort, ⸚er** word
wundern to surprise
  sich **wundern** to be surprised
der **Wunsch, ⸚e** wish
die **Wurst, ⸚e** sausage
das **Würstchen, -** sausage
wußte past tense of *wissen*

Z

die **Zahl, -en** number
zahlen to pay
der **Zahn, ⸚e** tooth
zehn ten
zehnmal ten times
das **Zeichen, -** sign
zeigen to show, point at
die **Zeit, -en** time
  Höchste Zeit! High time! It's about time!
die **Zeitschrift, -en** magazine
der **Zeitsprung, ⸚e** jet lag
die **Zeitung, -en** newspaper
der **Zeitungskiosk, -e** newsstand
der **Zeitunterschied, -e** time difference
ziehen to pull **zog, gezogen**
das **Ziel, -e** destination
der **Zielbahnhof, ⸚e** station to which a railroad car is going

ziemlich rather, fairly

die **Zigarette, –n** cigarette

die **Zigarre, –n** cigar

das **Zimmer, –** room

der **Zimmernachweis, –e** list of available rooms

der **Zimmerpreis, –e** price of a room

die **Zimmervermittlung, –en** room agency

der **Zoll** customs; duty

der **Zollausgang, ⁓e** customs exit

zollfrei duty free

zu (*adv.*) too

zu (*prep. + dat.*) to; at; for

zuerst first, first of all

zufrieden mit satisfied with

sich **zufrieden · geben mit** to be satisfied with (gibt . . . zufrieden), gab . . . zufrieden, zufrieden-gegeben

der **Zug, ⁓e** train

zugleich at the same time

zu · hören (*dat. obj.*) to listen

auf einen **zu · kommen** to come towards a person kam . . . zu, ist . . . zuge-kommen

zu · machen to close

zurück back

zurück · bringen to bring back, take back brachte . . . zurück, zurückgebracht

zurück · fliegen to fly back flog . . . zurück, ist . . . zurückgeflogen

zurück · kommen to come back kam . . . zurück, ist . . . zurückgekommen

zurück · stellen to put back

zusammen together

zusammen · bleiben to stay together blieb . . . zusammen, ist . . . zusammengeblieben

zu · schauen to watch

der **Zuschlag, ⁓e** surcharge, extra charge

die **Zuschlagskarte, –n** sur-charge ticket

zu · sein to be closed (ist . . . zu), war . . . zu, ist . . . zugewesen

zuverlässig reliable

zwanzig twenty

der **Zwanzigmarkschein, –e** twenty mark bill

zwei two

zweimal twice, two times; two orders of

zweit– second

zwischen (+ *dat.* or *acc.*) between

zwo = zwei two

Index

559

H
I
J